BIG BOOK OF
IPSEC RFCS

BIG BOOK OF IPSEC RFCS

Compiled by
Pete Loshin

Morgan Kaufmann

An Imprint of ACADEMIC PRESS
A Harcourt Science and Technology Company
San Diego   San Francisco   New York   Boston
London   Sydney   Tokyo

ACADEMIC PRESS

A Harcourt Science and Technology Company

525 B Street, Suite 1900, San Diego, CA 92101-4495 USA

http://www.academicpress.com

Academic Press

24-28 Oval Road, London NW1 7DX United Kingdom

http://www.hbuk.co.uk/ap/

Morgan Kaufmann Publishers

340 Pine Street, Sixth Floor, San Francisco, CA 94104-3205

http://www.mkp.com

Library of Congress Catalog Number: 99-64629

International Standard Book Number: 0-12-455839-9

Printed in the United States of America

99 00 01 02 03 VHG 9 8 7 6 5 4 3 2 1

This book is dedicated to the members of the Internet Engineering Task Force.

Table of Contents

Foreword

Back in the distant mists of time, when the earth was still cooling and the dangers of computer networking were starting to attract public attention (was it really as long ago as 1992?), a group of people decided that it might be nice to formally add security to the Internet Protocol. What would eventually become the IPSEC Working Group (standardizing the IPsec suite of specifications) met for the first time late that year at the IETF meeting in Washington DC. After the inevitable charter discussions, the inevitable establishment of a new mailing list (the existing one is never acceptable for some reason), and the inevitable agreement upon an aggressive (read "optimistic", "starry-eyed") schedule for producing the documents, the work began in earnest.

There was little dispute that this whole project was a very good idea. IPv4 was widely deployed and all indications were that deployment of IPv6 would make the v4 deployment look like a small laboratory experiment. Security breaches were making headlines and the transition to v6 afforded a golden opportunity to install, on a world-wide basis, a fundamental infrastructure to provide part of the solution. Finally, the cryptographic building blocks — algorithms such as DES and 3-DES, RSA, and DH — had reached a sufficiently high comfort level with most experts that it made sense (with the appropriate caveats) to start using them for security at this scale. No one suffered from the illusion that IPsec would provide all the security ever required for communications (it was well recognized that there is often a legitimate and pressing need for application-layer security as well), but a good architecture for network-layer security was seen by many as a practical way to solve real problems for the real world.

The proposal was made for the new Working Group to standardize specifications in two areas: a security protocol for protecting transmitted data packets in the network layer; and an application-layer key management protocol for creating, sharing, and renewing the necessary cryptographic keys. Steve Crocker (then IETF Security Area Director), in a note posted to the IPSEC mailing list on November 25, 1992, made the following observation:

> *I have two concerns. My lesser concern is that without some form of usable key management, only ad hoc use of the network authentication/ encryption protocol will exist. My greater concern is that work on the key management will get bogged down and never emerge.*

This last sentence very nearly turned out to be prophetic. By mid-1996 no agreement had yet been reached on a key management protocol and (to make matters even more complicated) new ones were still being proposed. The group was mired in a number of deadlocked political battles and the chance of any kind of satisfactory resolution seemed distressingly small. However, hope springs eternal in the IETF breast — this book is solid testimony to the fact that the primary IPsec specifications eventually did reach a reasonable level of agreement and that all the pain and struggle in their formation can now happily be relegated to one or two sentences in a preface.

The IPSEC Working Group, in some sense, represents the best and the worst of the IETF process. It is an environment in which "rough consensus and running code" can still outweigh the opinion of an Ivy-league Ph.D. or endorsement from an industry giant, which is cause for optimism. On the other hand, the opportunity for a group of sharp minds and sharper words to slow, de-rail, and almost halt progress entirely is very great, which can be a cause for concern. Perhaps the old IETF protocol implementation maxim (see, for example, p.23 of RFC 791, or p.13 or RFC 793) could usefully be applied to Working Group mailing lists: "Be conservative in what you send, and liberal in what you accept from others."

This book is a collection of Request-for-Comments (RFCs), both standards-track and informational specifications, that together define IPsec. Although every one of these RFCs is available on-line through the usual IETF public repositories, it may well be argued that their collection here is valuable for several reasons, of which two, to my mind, are primary. Firstly, the aggregation of related, relevant information is much more important than any of the individual pieces of data. Anyone familiar with traffic analysis or database security will tell you that an aggregation gives a more complete picture, allows inferences to be drawn, and enables critical relationships to be seen which would otherwise go unnoticed. The collection in this book will be of immense value both to implementers of IPsec and to those who wish to study its properties and architecture.

Secondly, the formal printing, binding, and widespread distribution of a suite of *proposed standards* can do wonders for the public perception of their maturity, stability, and completeness. One very good example of this was the

1993 publication of a bound copy of the Public-Key Cryptography Standards (PKCS) #1 - #10. Then, as now, such publication may be an important factor in the industry adoption and implementation of a set of protocols which has, in reality, reached a relatively early stage in the formal standardization process.

IPsec is an important suite of specifications and plays a critical role in the whole communications security picture. I am confident that this book will contribute in a significant way to its overall deployment and success.

Carlisle Adams
1999

Preface

This easily could have been a 2000-page book. Publishers love really big fat books because they can charge a lot of money for them. I probably could have convinced some publisher that what the world really needs is a book that reproduces all the most important Internet Protocol security specifications — and then explains everything in each of them.

I've got two big problems with this approach to big books: First, I don't have the stamina to write a 2000-page book, even if 500 pages or so have already been written. And second, there's no way I could make those documents more readable than they already are. What am I going to say about the overall organization of the IP Security Architecture that hasn't been explained in RFC 2401, "Security Architecture for the Internet Protocol"? Can I add anything to documents explaining how the cryptographic algorithms work, especially when those documents, like RFC 1320, "The MD4 Message-Digest Algorithm," or RFC 2144, "The CAST-128 Encryption Algorithm," are written by the same people who created the algorithms (Ronald Rivest and Carlisle Adams, respectively)?

An RFC goes through many revisions and passes under the scrutiny of many highly intelligent, technically savvy readers. Spelling errors are rare, and (particularly for standards-track documents that have gone through the RFC editing process two or more times) the prose is usually clear and to the point. What you have in your hand includes some of the best examples of technical writing available.

Few of the documents included in this collection can stand entirely on its own: each refers to the others. That was one of the criteria used to select them. But collected together like this, they become a unified whole.

Introduction

The Internet Protocol Security Architecture (IPsec) is the product of years of work by many dedicated individuals. IPsec presents the blueprint for doing security on the Internet at the IP layer. Applications like virtual private networks (VPNs) depend on IPsec; any IP application can avail itself of the IPsec services to add security and data integrity functions.

Containing, as it does, the contents of the most important and most current specifications for IPsec, this book is *the* definitive guide to the IPsec protocols and specifications. But all the RFCs are available for free, online. Why would anyone buy this book? For several reasons, listed in order of increasing importance:

- You may be able to read these specifications online, but if you want to read them while away from your computer, you must print them out. If you want to take notes, you must print them out. If you want to share them with coworkers, you must print them out. There is no denying the appeal of the printed page when working with complicated technical documents.
- This is a comprehensive collection of IPsec RFCs. All the RFCs — and only IPsec RFCs — are here. You can flip from one specification to another, bookmark the important parts, and flip from one highlight to another instantly — much faster than is possible with a browser.
- Each RFC, as written, stands alone. Each defines some terms, but some use terms defined in predecessor documents. Putting them together, and in context, makes them that much more valuable.
- Nowhere is this material collected together; nowhere has it ever been formally indexed in print. A high-quality index means that you no longer must search through dozens of different documents looking for the answer to a question — all answers are included in a single book, and you can search for a term in all the relevant documents in a single procedure.

What Is in This Book

IPsec consists of several sets of protocols and specifications; each is documented in an RFC. This book collects the most important RFCs defining IPsec. These documents define most aspects of the IP Security Architecture, and everything to do with that architecture. The frontmatter of this volume is intentionally brief; there is no need to provide an overview to the volume when one of the included RFCs provides the most authoritative overview possible. It is not necessary to provide a road map to the documents, as this is provided in RFC 2411, "IP Security Document Roadmap." Even a glossary is unnecessary, as each RFC includes its own definitions.

We have included only the original text of the RFCs, as they would appear on your computer screen or printed out on paper, using a monospace font so that all ASCII character drawings are rendered correctly. On each page, the original headers and footers appear, and the only numbering you'll find in the book is that assigned to the original RFCs. Those who are accustomed to working with RFCs sometimes find reformatted versions to be jarring—the original format is familiarly and reassuringly authoritative.

We have created an index to the RFCs. Index entries identify the RFC number and the page number within that RFC. This makes it possible for you to cite an RFC and a page number that can be used by anyone with access to the RFC itself, even if they do so online.

We spent considerable effort on deciding how to order the RFCs for this book. Should we put them in a logical narrative order, so that the volume can be read as an introduction to IPsec? This approach was tempting, but after more consideration, was discarded. Doing it that way would have retained most of the numerical RFC ordering—but not all. The result would have been a book that appeared to contain the RFCs in numerical order, but with some RFCs stuck in the "wrong" order.

Far better, we decided, to keep the numerical ordering. You can still start at the beginning, with RFC 2401, "Security Architecture for the Internet Protocol," but that RFC just happens to be in the middle of the volume. Ultimately, this is a reference volume, and reference volumes must retain a logical and simple ordering. If you want to read the RFCs in narrative order, try starting with RFC 2401 through 2412; the rest of the RFCs can be read as background or supplements.

The RFCs

There are 23 RFCs included in this volume. These are the documents that define IPsec. Some define it explicitly, such as RFC 2401, which specifies a comprehensive vision for IPsec. Others define it as supporting documents, such as RFC 2144, "The CAST-128 Encryption Algorithm," which describes one of the encryption algorithms that can be used with IPsec protocols. Here are very brief descriptions of each RFC (you'll find somewhat more detailed abstracts at the start of almost all RFCs).

RFC 1320, The MD4 Message-Digest Algorithm
This informational RFC describes the MD4 message-digest algorithm devised by Ronald Rivest. It is used to generate 128-bit "fingerprints" when the algorithm is given any length of data as input.

RFC 1321, The MD5 Message-Digest Algorithm
This informational RFC describes the MD5 message-digest algorithm devised by Ronald Rivest. It is used to generate 128-bit "fingerprints" when the algorithm is given any length of data as input.

RFC 1828, IP Authentication Using Keyed MD5
This RFC documents a proposed Internet standard for using the MD5 message digest with a secret key with the IPsec Authentication Header (AH) to insure that the contents of the IP datagram have not been modified in transit. See also RFC 2402.

RFC 1829, The ESP DES-CBC Transform
This RFC documents a proposed Internet standard for using the Cipher Block Chaining (CBC) mode of the US Data Encryption Standard (DES) encryption algorithm with the Encapsulating Security Payload (ESP) protocol to encrypt the contents of an IP datagram. See also RFC 2406.

RFC 2040, The RC5, RC5-CBC, RC5-CBC-Pad, and RC5-CTS Algorithms
This RFC is an informational document describing four versions of the RC5 encryption algorithm. The RFC's goal is to describe the algorithms in sufficient detail to allow interoperable implementations.

RFC 2085, HMAC-MD5 IP Authentication with Replay Prevention
This RFC documents a proposed Internet standard for using keyed MD5 (RFC 1828 and RFC 1321) with a hashed message authentication code (RFC 2104) for creating authentication data (RFC 2402).

RFC 2104, HMAC: Keyed-Hashing for Message Authentication
This informational RFC describes a method for generating a message authentication code (MAC) based on cryptographic hash functions (HMAC).

RFC 2144, The CAST-128 Encryption Algorithm
This informational RFC describes the CAST-128 encryption algorithm, for consideration as a candidate for strong encryption of Internet data.

RFC 2202, Test Cases for HMAC-MD5 and HMAC-SHA-1
This informational RFC provides two sets of test cases for HMAC, one for the MD5 message digest algorithm, the other for the National Institute of Standards and Technology (NIST) Secure Hash Algorithm (SHA). These test cases can be used for conformance testing.

RFC 2268, A Description of the RC2(r) Encryption Algorithm
This informational RFC describes the RC2 encryption algorithm.

RFC 2401, Security Architecture for the Internet Protocol
This RFC describes a proposed Internet standard for the base architecture for IPsec compliant systems, to provide security (encryption and authentication) for IPv4 and IPv6 packets, applied at the IP level. It defines a framework for security work, and references other specifications for actual security protocols (such as Authentication Header, RFC 2402, and Encapsulating Security Payload, RFC 2406), key management (such as the Internet Security Association and Key Management Protocol, RFC 2408 and the Internet Key Exchange, RFC 2409), and algorithms for encryption and authentication (such as MD4, MD5, CAST-128, RC2, RC5, DES, and so on).

RFC 2402, IP Authentication Header
This RFC describes a proposed Internet standard for providing data origin authentication for IP packets.

RFC 2403, The Use of HMAC-MD5-96 within ESP and AH
This RFC describes a proposed Internet standard for using MD5 (RFC 1321) with HMAC (RFC 2104) for a keyed authentication mechanism within the Authentication Header (RFC 2402) and the Encapsulating Security Payload (RFC 2406). When used together, HMAC and MD5 act as a keyed authentication mechanism.

RFC 2404, The Use of HMAC-SHA-1-96 within ESP and AH
This RFC describes a proposed Internet standard for using SHA-1 (Secure Hash Standard) with HMAC (RFC 2104) for a keyed authentication mechanism within the Authentication Header (RFC 2402) and the Encapsulating Security Payload (RFC 2406). When used together, HMAC and SHA-1 act as a keyed authentication mechanism.

RFC 2405, The ESP DES-CBC Cipher Algorithm With Explicit IV
This RFC documents a proposed Internet standard for using the DES-CBC cipher algorithm (RFC 1829) as applied to the Encapsulating Security Payload protocol (RFC 2406) for data encryption.

RFC 2406, IP Encapsulating Security Payload (ESP)
This RFC documents a proposed Internet standard for using encryption, message digest, and authentication algorithms to protect IPv4 and IPv6 datagrams.

RFC 2407, The Internet IP Security Domain of Interpretation for ISAKMP
This RFC documents a proposed Internet standard. IPsec uses an entity called a security association for the purpose of connecting an IP node with an identifier and with security information for that identifier. ISAKMP (RFC 2408) defines a framework for managing security associations. This document defines a Domain of Interpretation (DOI) that is used to negotiate security associations.

RFC 2408, Internet Security Association and Key Management Protocol (ISAKMP)
This RFC documents a proposed Internet standard for the Internet Security Association and Key Management Protocol (ISAKMP). ISAKMP "defines the procedures for authenticating a communicating peer, creation and management of Security Associations, key generation techniques, and threat of mitigation (e.g., denial of service and replay attacks)."

RFC 2409, The Internet Key Exchange (IKE)
This RFC documents a proposed Internet standard for exchanging authenticated keying material to be used with ISAKMP (RFC 2408).

RFC 2410, The NULL Encryption Algorithm and Its Use with IPsec
This RFC documents a proposed Internet standard for an "encryption" algorithm, the NULL algorithm, which actually does not do any encryption. When used for encrypting with the Encapsulating Security Payload (RFC 2406), the NULL algorithm makes it possible to do authentication only within ESP.

RFC 2411, IP Security Document Roadmap
This informational RFC documents the relationships among IPsec RFCs, as well as providing a guideline for development of collateral specifications.

RFC 2412, The OAKLEY Key Determination Protocol
This informational RFC documents the OAKLEY protocol. OAKLEY defines a mechanism by which two authenticated entities can agree on secret (and secure) keying material. OAKLEY uses the Diffie-Hellman key exchange algorithm.

RFC 2451, The ESP CBC-Mode Cipher Algorithms
This RFC documents a proposed Internet standard for using any type of Cipher Block Chaining (CBC) encryption algorithm with the Encapsulating Security Payload (RFC 2406) protocol.

RFC 2631, Diffie-Hellman Key Agreement Method

This RFC describes a standard for a variation on the Diffie-Hellman algorithm used by two parties to agree on a shared secret for use as keying material for cryptographic functions. This function is vital for public key encryption over open channels.

Getting RFCs Online

We could waste several pages with pointers to different web sites and mailing lists where you can find out more about RFCs in general and IPsec in particular. Let's just say, you can find plenty of online resources (including up to date pointers to all those online resources) at this web site:

http://www.Internet-Standard.com

Another good starting point is the IETF home page at:

http://www.ietf.org

For More Information

We intend this volume to be a tool for network implementers and deployers. Please let me know if you find it useful—and please let me know if you know a way to make it even more useful. For more information about Internet standards in general, or about this and other books about Internet standards, try the Internet-Standard.com web site. If you have a comment to make, a question to ask, an error to report, or anything else you'd like to tell me, send it to me at:

pete@loshin.com

Hearing from readers of material I've edited or written is usually the best part of my day; I'd love to hear what you think!

Network Working Group   R. Rivest
Request for Comments: 1320   MIT Laboratory for Computer Science
Obsoletes: RFC 1186   and RSA Data Security, Inc.
                                                        April 1992

The MD4 Message-Digest Algorithm

Status of thie Memo

Acknowlegements

We would like to thank Don Coppersmith, Burt Kaliski, Ralph Merkle,
and Noam Nisan for numerous helpful comments and suggestions.

Table of Contents

1. Executive Summary

   This document describes the MD4 message-digest algorithm [1]. The
   algorithm takes as input a message of arbitrary length and produces
   as output a 128-bit "fingerprint" or "message digest" of the input.
   It is conjectured that it is computationally infeasible to produce
   two messages having the same message digest, or to produce any
   message having a given prespecified target message digest. The MD4
   algorithm is intended for digital signature applications, where a
   large file must be "compressed" in a secure manner before being
   encrypted with a private (secret) key under a public-key cryptosystem
   such as RSA.

   The MD4 algorithm is designed to be quite fast on 32-bit machines. In
   addition, the MD4 algorithm does not require any large substitution
   tables; the algorithm can be coded quite compactly.

The MD4 algorithm is being placed in the public domain for review and possible adoption as a standard.

This document replaces the October 1990 RFC 1186 [2]. The main difference is that the reference implementation of MD4 in the appendix is more portable.

For OSI-based applications, MD4's object identifier is

md4 OBJECT IDENTIFIER ::=
    {iso(1) member-body(2) US(840) rsadsi(113549) digestAlgorithm(2) 4}

In the X.509 type AlgorithmIdentifier [3], the parameters for MD4 should have type NULL.

2. Terminology and Notation

In this document a "word" is a 32-bit quantity and a "byte" is an eight-bit quantity. A sequence of bits can be interpreted in a natural manner as a sequence of bytes, where each consecutive group of eight bits is interpreted as a byte with the high-order (most significant) bit of each byte listed first. Similarly, a sequence of bytes can be interpreted as a sequence of 32-bit words, where each consecutive group of four bytes is interpreted as a word with the low-order (least significant) byte given first.

Let x_i denote "x sub i". If the subscript is an expression, we surround it in braces, as in x_{i+1}. Similarly, we use ^ for superscripts (exponentiation), so that x^i denotes x to the i-th power.

Let the symbol "+" denote addition of words (i.e., modulo-2^{32} addition). Let X <<< s denote the 32-bit value obtained by circularly shifting (rotating) X left by s bit positions. Let not(X) denote the bit-wise complement of X, and let X v Y denote the bit-wise OR of X and Y. Let X xor Y denote the bit-wise XOR of X and Y, and let XY denote the bit-wise AND of X and Y.

3. MD4 Algorithm Description

We begin by supposing that we have a b-bit message as input, and that we wish to find its message digest. Here b is an arbitrary nonnegative integer; b may be zero, it need not be a multiple of eight, and it may be arbitrarily large. We imagine the bits of the message written down as follows:

$$m_0 \ m_1 \ ... \ m_{b-1}$$

The following five steps are performed to compute the message digest
of the message.

3.1 Step 1. Append Padding Bits

The message is "padded" (extended) so that its length (in bits) is
congruent to 448, modulo 512. That is, the message is extended so
that it is just 64 bits shy of being a multiple of 512 bits long.
Padding is always performed, even if the length of the message is
already congruent to 448, modulo 512.

Padding is performed as follows: a single "1" bit is appended to the
message, and then "0" bits are appended so that the length in bits of
the padded message becomes congruent to 448, modulo 512. In all, at
least one bit and at most 512 bits are appended.

3.2 Step 2. Append Length

A 64-bit representation of b (the length of the message before the
padding bits were added) is appended to the result of the previous
step. In the unlikely event that b is greater than 2^64, then only
the low-order 64 bits of b are used. (These bits are appended as two
32-bit words and appended low-order word first in accordance with the
previous conventions.)

At this point the resulting message (after padding with bits and with
b) has a length that is an exact multiple of 512 bits. Equivalently,
this message has a length that is an exact multiple of 16 (32-bit)
words. Let M[0 ... N-1] denote the words of the resulting message,
where N is a multiple of 16.

3.3 Step 3. Initialize MD Buffer

A four-word buffer (A,B,C,D) is used to compute the message digest.
Here each of A, B, C, D is a 32-bit register. These registers are
initialized to the following values in hexadecimal, low-order bytes
first):

        word A: 01 23 45 67
        word B: 89 ab cd ef
        word C: fe dc ba 98
        word D: 76 54 32 10

3.4 Step 4. Process Message in 16-Word Blocks

   We first define three auxiliary functions that each take as input
   three 32-bit words and produce as output one 32-bit word.

         F(X,Y,Z) = XY v not(X) Z
         G(X,Y,Z) = XY v XZ v YZ
         H(X,Y,Z) = X xor Y xor Z

   In each bit position F acts as a conditional: if X then Y else Z.
   The function F could have been defined using + instead of v since XY
   and not(X)Z will never have "1" bits in the same bit position.)   In
   each bit position G acts as a majority function: if at least two of
   X, Y, Z are on, then G has a "1" bit in that bit position, else G has
   a "0" bit. It is interesting to note that if the bits of X, Y, and Z
   are independent and unbiased, the each bit of f(X,Y,Z) will be
   independent and unbiased, and similarly each bit of g(X,Y,Z) will be
   independent and unbiased. The function H is the bit-wise XOR or
   parity" function; it has properties similar to those of F and G.

   Do the following:

      Process each 16-word block. */
      For i = 0 to N/16-1 do

         /* Copy block i into X. */
         For j = 0 to 15 do
           Set X[j] to M[i*16+j].
         end /* of loop on j */

         /* Save A as AA, B as BB, C as CC, and D as DD. */
         AA = A
         BB = B
         CC = C
         DD = D

         /* Round 1. */
         /* Let [abcd k s] denote the operation
             a = (a + F(b,c,d) + X[k]) <<< s. */
         /* Do the following 16 operations. */
         [ABCD 0 3] [DABC 1 7] [CDAB 2 11] [BCDA 3 19]
         [ABCD 4 3] [DABC 5 7] [CDAB 6 11] [BCDA 7 19]
         [ABCD 8 3] [DABC 9 7] [CDAB 10 11] [BCDA 11 19]
         [ABCD 12 3] [DABC 13 7] [CDAB 14 11] [BCDA 15 19]

         /* Round 2. */
         /* Let [abcd k s] denote the operation
             a = (a + G(b,c,d) + X[k] + 5A827999) <<< s. */

```
    /* Do the following 16 operations. */
    [ABCD  0  3]  [DABC  4  5]  [CDAB  8  9]  [BCDA 12 13]
    [ABCD  1  3]  [DABC  5  5]  [CDAB  9  9]  [BCDA 13 13]
    [ABCD  2  3]  [DABC  6  5]  [CDAB 10  9]  [BCDA 14 13]
    [ABCD  3  3]  [DABC  7  5]  [CDAB 11  9]  [BCDA 15 13]

    /* Round 3. */
    /* Let [abcd k s] denote the operation
         a = (a + H(b,c,d) + X[k] + 6ED9EBA1) <<< s. */
    /* Do the following 16 operations. */
    [ABCD  0  3]  [DABC  8  9]  [CDAB  4 11]  [BCDA 12 15]
    [ABCD  2  3]  [DABC 10  9]  [CDAB  6 11]  [BCDA 14 15]
    [ABCD  1  3]  [DABC  9  9]  [CDAB  5 11]  [BCDA 13 15]
    [ABCD  3  3]  [DABC 11  9]  [CDAB  7 11]  [BCDA 15 15]

    /* Then perform the following additions. (That is, increment each
       of the four registers by the value it had before this block
       was started.) */
    A = A + AA
    B = B + BB
    C = C + CC
    D = D + DD

  end /* of loop on i */
```

Note. The value 5A..99 is a hexadecimal 32-bit constant, written with
the high-order digit first. This constant represents the square root
of 2. The octal value of this constant is 013240474631.

The value 6E..A1 is a hexadecimal 32-bit constant, written with the
high-order digit first. This constant represents the square root of
3. The octal value of this constant is 015666365641.

See Knuth, The Art of Programming, Volume 2 (Seminumerical
Algorithms), Second Edition (1981), Addison-Wesley. Table 2, page
660.

3.5 Step 5. Output

The message digest produced as output is A, B, C, D. That is, we
begin with the low-order byte of A, and end with the high-order byte
of D.

This completes the description of MD4. A reference implementation in
C is given in the appendix.

4. Summary

The MD4 message-digest algorithm is simple to implement, and provides
a "fingerprint" or message digest of a message of arbitrary length.
It is conjectured that the difficulty of coming up with two messages
having the same message digest is on the order of 2^{64} operations,
and that the difficulty of coming up with any message having a given
message digest is on the order of 2^{128} operations. The MD4 algorithm
has been carefully scrutinized for weaknesses. It is, however, a
relatively new algorithm and further security analysis is of course
justified, as is the case with any new proposal of this sort.

References

   [1] Rivest, R., "The MD4 message digest algorithm", in A.J. Menezes
       and S.A. Vanstone, editors, Advances in Cryptology - CRYPTO '90
       Proceedings, pages 303-311, Springer-Verlag, 1991.

   [2] Rivest, R., "The MD4 Message Digest Algorithm", RFC 1186, MIT,
       October 1990.

   [3] CCITT Recommendation X.509 (1988), "The Directory -
       Authentication Framework".

   [4] Rivest, R., "The MD5 Message-Digest Algorithm", RFC 1321, MIT and
       RSA Data Security, Inc, April 1992.

APPENDIX A - Reference Implementation

This appendix contains the following files:

        global.h — global header file

        md4.h — header file for MD4

        md4c.c — source code for MD4

        mddriver.c — test driver for MD2, MD4 and MD5

The driver compiles for MD5 by default but can compile for MD2 or MD4
if the symbol MD is defined on the C compiler command line as 2 or 4.

The implementation is portable and should work on many different
plaforms. However, it is not difficult to optimize the implementation
on particular platforms, an exercise left to the reader. For example,
on "little-endian" platforms where the lowest-addressed byte in a 32-
bit word is the least significant and there are no alignment
restrictions, the call to Decode in MD4Transform can be replaced with

a typecast.

A.1 global.h

```
/* GLOBAL.H - RSAREF types and constants
 */

/* PROTOTYPES should be set to one if and only if the compiler supports
     function argument prototyping.
   The following makes PROTOTYPES default to 0 if it has not already
     been defined with C compiler flags.
 */
#ifndef PROTOTYPES
#define PROTOTYPES 0
#endif

/* POINTER defines a generic pointer type */
typedef unsigned char *POINTER;

/* UINT2 defines a two byte word */
typedef unsigned short int UINT2;

/* UINT4 defines a four byte word */
typedef unsigned long int UINT4;

/* PROTO_LIST is defined depending on how PROTOTYPES is defined above.
   If using PROTOTYPES, then PROTO_LIST returns the list, otherwise it
     returns an empty list.
 */

#if PROTOTYPES
#define PROTO_LIST(list) list
#else
#define PROTO_LIST(list) ()
#endif
```

A.2 md4.h

```
/* MD4.H - header file for MD4C.C
 */

/* Copyright (C) 1991-2, RSA Data Security, Inc. Created 1991. All
   rights reserved.

   License to copy and use this software is granted provided that it
   is identified as the "RSA Data Security, Inc. MD4 Message-Digest
   Algorithm" in all material mentioning or referencing this software
   or this function.
```

```
 */

/* MD4 context. */
typedef struct {
  UINT4 state[4];                                   /* state (ABCD) */
  UINT4 count[2];          /* number of bits, modulo 2^64 (lsb first) */
  unsigned char buffer[64];                         /* input buffer */
} MD4_CTX;

void MD4Init PROTO_LIST ((MD4_CTX *));
void MD4Update PROTO_LIST
  ((MD4_CTX *, unsigned char *, unsigned int));
void MD4Final PROTO_LIST ((unsigned char [16], MD4_CTX *));
```

A.3 md4c.c

```
/* MD4C.C - RSA Data Security, Inc., MD4 message-digest algorithm
 */

/* Copyright (C) 1990-2, RSA Data Security, Inc. All rights reserved.
```

These notices must be retained in any copies of any part of this
documentation and/or software.
```
 */

#include "global.h"
#include "md4.h"

/* Constants for MD4Transform routine.
 */
#define S11 3
#define S12 7
#define S13 11
#define S14 19
#define S21 3
#define S22 5
#define S23 9
#define S24 13
#define S31 3
#define S32 9
#define S33 11
#define S34 15

static void MD4Transform PROTO_LIST ((UINT4 [4], unsigned char [64]));
static void Encode PROTO_LIST
  ((unsigned char *, UINT4 *, unsigned int));
static void Decode PROTO_LIST
  ((UINT4 *, unsigned char *, unsigned int));
static void MD4_memcpy PROTO_LIST ((POINTER, POINTER, unsigned int));
static void MD4_memset PROTO_LIST ((POINTER, int, unsigned int));

static unsigned char PADDING[64] = {
  0x80, 0, 0, 0, 0, 0, 0, 0, 0, 0, 0, 0, 0, 0, 0, 0, 0, 0, 0, 0, 0, 0,
  0, 0, 0, 0, 0, 0, 0, 0, 0, 0, 0, 0, 0, 0, 0, 0, 0, 0, 0, 0, 0, 0, 0,
  0, 0, 0, 0, 0, 0, 0, 0, 0, 0, 0, 0, 0, 0, 0, 0, 0, 0, 0
};

/* F, G and H are basic MD4 functions.
 */
#define F(x, y, z) (((x) & (y)) | ((~x) & (z)))
#define G(x, y, z) (((x) & (y)) | ((x) & (z)) | ((y) & (z)))
#define H(x, y, z) ((x) ^ (y) ^ (z))

/* ROTATE_LEFT rotates x left n bits.
 */
#define ROTATE_LEFT(x, n) (((x) << (n)) | ((x) >> (32-(n))))

/* FF, GG and HH are transformations for rounds 1, 2 and 3 */
/* Rotation is separate from addition to prevent recomputation */
```

```
#define FF(a, b, c, d, x, s) { \
    (a) += F ((b), (c), (d)) + (x); \
    (a) = ROTATE_LEFT ((a), (s)); \
  }
#define GG(a, b, c, d, x, s) { \
    (a) += G ((b), (c), (d)) + (x) + (UINT4)0x5a827999; \
    (a) = ROTATE_LEFT ((a), (s)); \
  }
#define HH(a, b, c, d, x, s) { \
    (a) += H ((b), (c), (d)) + (x) + (UINT4)0x6ed9eba1; \
    (a) = ROTATE_LEFT ((a), (s)); \
  }

/* MD4 initialization. Begins an MD4 operation, writing a new context.
 */
void MD4Init (context)
MD4_CTX *context;                                       /* context */
{
  context->count[0] = context->count[1] = 0;

  /* Load magic initialization constants.
   */
  context->state[0] = 0x67452301;
  context->state[1] = 0xefcdab89;
  context->state[2] = 0x98badcfe;
  context->state[3] = 0x10325476;
}

/* MD4 block update operation. Continues an MD4 message-digest
     operation, processing another message block, and updating the
     context.
 */
void MD4Update (context, input, inputLen)
MD4_CTX *context;                                       /* context */
unsigned char *input;                                /* input block */
unsigned int inputLen;                      /* length of input block */
{
  unsigned int i, index, partLen;

  /* Compute number of bytes mod 64 */
  index = (unsigned int)((context->count[0] >> 3) & 0x3F);
  /* Update number of bits */
  if ((context->count[0] += ((UINT4)inputLen << 3))
      < ((UINT4)inputLen << 3))
    context->count[1]++;
  context->count[1] += ((UINT4)inputLen >> 29);

  partLen = 64 - index;
```

```
  /* Transform as many times as possible.
   */
  if (inputLen >= partLen) {
    MD4_memcpy
      ((POINTER)&context->buffer[index], (POINTER)input, partLen);
    MD4Transform (context->state, context->buffer);

    for (i = partLen; i + 63 < inputLen; i += 64)
      MD4Transform (context->state, &input[i]);

    index = 0;
  }
  else
    i = 0;

  /* Buffer remaining input */
  MD4_memcpy
    ((POINTER)&context->buffer[index], (POINTER)&input[i],
     inputLen-i);
}

/* MD4 finalization. Ends an MD4 message-digest operation, writing the
     the message digest and zeroizing the context.
 */
void MD4Final (digest, context)
unsigned char digest[16];                          /* message digest */
MD4_CTX *context;                                  /* context */
{
  unsigned char bits[8];
  unsigned int index, padLen;

  /* Save number of bits */
  Encode (bits, context->count, 8);

  /* Pad out to 56 mod 64.
   */
  index = (unsigned int)((context->count[0] >> 3) & 0x3f);
  padLen = (index < 56) ? (56 - index) : (120 - index);
  MD4Update (context, PADDING, padLen);

  /* Append length (before padding) */
  MD4Update (context, bits, 8);
  /* Store state in digest */
  Encode (digest, context->state, 16);

  /* Zeroize sensitive information.
   */
  MD4_memset ((POINTER)context, 0, sizeof (*context));
```

```
}

/* MD4 basic transformation. Transforms state based on block.
 */
static void MD4Transform (state, block)
UINT4 state[4];
unsigned char block[64];
{
  UINT4 a = state[0], b = state[1], c = state[2], d = state[3], x[16];

  Decode (x, block, 64);

  /* Round 1 */
  FF (a, b, c, d, x[ 0], S11); /* 1 */
  FF (d, a, b, c, x[ 1], S12); /* 2 */
  FF (c, d, a, b, x[ 2], S13); /* 3 */
  FF (b, c, d, a, x[ 3], S14); /* 4 */
  FF (a, b, c, d, x[ 4], S11); /* 5 */
  FF (d, a, b, c, x[ 5], S12); /* 6 */
  FF (c, d, a, b, x[ 6], S13); /* 7 */
  FF (b, c, d, a, x[ 7], S14); /* 8 */
  FF (a, b, c, d, x[ 8], S11); /* 9 */
  FF (d, a, b, c, x[ 9], S12); /* 10 */
  FF (c, d, a, b, x[10], S13); /* 11 */
  FF (b, c, d, a, x[11], S14); /* 12 */
  FF (a, b, c, d, x[12], S11); /* 13 */
  FF (d, a, b, c, x[13], S12); /* 14 */
  FF (c, d, a, b, x[14], S13); /* 15 */
  FF (b, c, d, a, x[15], S14); /* 16 */

  /* Round 2 */
  GG (a, b, c, d, x[ 0], S21); /* 17 */
  GG (d, a, b, c, x[ 4], S22); /* 18 */
  GG (c, d, a, b, x[ 8], S23); /* 19 */
  GG (b, c, d, a, x[12], S24); /* 20 */
  GG (a, b, c, d, x[ 1], S21); /* 21 */
  GG (d, a, b, c, x[ 5], S22); /* 22 */
  GG (c, d, a, b, x[ 9], S23); /* 23 */
  GG (b, c, d, a, x[13], S24); /* 24 */
  GG (a, b, c, d, x[ 2], S21); /* 25 */
  GG (d, a, b, c, x[ 6], S22); /* 26 */
  GG (c, d, a, b, x[10], S23); /* 27 */
  GG (b, c, d, a, x[14], S24); /* 28 */
  GG (a, b, c, d, x[ 3], S21); /* 29 */
  GG (d, a, b, c, x[ 7], S22); /* 30 */
  GG (c, d, a, b, x[11], S23); /* 31 */
  GG (b, c, d, a, x[15], S24); /* 32 */
```

```
  /* Round 3 */
  HH (a, b, c, d, x[ 0], S31); /* 33 */
  HH (d, a, b, c, x[ 8], S32); /* 34 */
  HH (c, d, a, b, x[ 4], S33); /* 35 */
  HH (b, c, d, a, x[12], S34); /* 36 */
  HH (a, b, c, d, x[ 2], S31); /* 37 */
  HH (d, a, b, c, x[10], S32); /* 38 */
  HH (c, d, a, b, x[ 6], S33); /* 39 */
  HH (b, c, d, a, x[14], S34); /* 40 */
  HH (a, b, c, d, x[ 1], S31); /* 41 */
  HH (d, a, b, c, x[ 9], S32); /* 42 */
  HH (c, d, a, b, x[ 5], S33); /* 43 */
  HH (b, c, d, a, x[13], S34); /* 44 */
  HH (a, b, c, d, x[ 3], S31); /* 45 */
  HH (d, a, b, c, x[11], S32); /* 46 */
  HH (c, d, a, b, x[ 7], S33); /* 47 */
  HH (b, c, d, a, x[15], S34); /* 48 */

  state[0] += a;
  state[1] += b;
  state[2] += c;
  state[3] += d;

  /* Zeroize sensitive information.
   */
  MD4_memset ((POINTER)x, 0, sizeof (x));
}

/* Encodes input (UINT4) into output (unsigned char). Assumes len is
     a multiple of 4.
 */
static void Encode (output, input, len)
unsigned char *output;
UINT4 *input;
unsigned int len;
{
  unsigned int i, j;

  for (i = 0, j = 0; j < len; i++, j += 4) {
    output[j] = (unsigned char)(input[i] & 0xff);
    output[j+1] = (unsigned char)((input[i] >> 8) & 0xff);
    output[j+2] = (unsigned char)((input[i] >> 16) & 0xff);
    output[j+3] = (unsigned char)((input[i] >> 24) & 0xff);
  }
}

/* Decodes input (unsigned char) into output (UINT4). Assumes len is
     a multiple of 4.
```

```
 */
static void Decode (output, input, len)

UINT4 *output;
unsigned char *input;
unsigned int len;
{
  unsigned int i, j;

  for (i = 0, j = 0; j < len; i++, j += 4)
    output[i] = ((UINT4)input[j]) | (((UINT4)input[j+1]) << 8) |
      (((UINT4)input[j+2]) << 16) | (((UINT4)input[j+3]) << 24);
}

/* Note: Replace "for loop" with standard memcpy if possible.
 */
static void MD4_memcpy (output, input, len)
POINTER output;
POINTER input;
unsigned int len;
{
  unsigned int i;

  for (i = 0; i < len; i++)
    output[i] = input[i];
}

/* Note: Replace "for loop" with standard memset if possible.
 */
static void MD4_memset (output, value, len)
POINTER output;
int value;
unsigned int len;
{
  unsigned int i;

  for (i = 0; i < len; i++)
    ((char *)output)[i] = (char)value;
}

A.4 mddriver.c

/* MDDRIVER.C - test driver for MD2, MD4 and MD5
 */

/* Copyright (C) 1990-2, RSA Data Security, Inc. Created 1990. All
   rights reserved.
```

```
     */

/* The following makes MD default to MD5 if it has not already been
     defined with C compiler flags.
 */
#ifndef MD
#define MD MD5
#endif

#include <stdio.h>
#include <time.h>
#include <string.h>
#include "global.h"
#if MD == 2
#include "md2.h"
#endif
#if MD == 4
#include "md4.h"
#endif
#if MD == 5
#include "md5.h"
#endif

/* Length of test block, number of test blocks.
 */
#define TEST_BLOCK_LEN 1000
#define TEST_BLOCK_COUNT 1000

static void MDString PROTO_LIST ((char *));
static void MDTimeTrial PROTO_LIST ((void));
static void MDTestSuite PROTO_LIST ((void));
static void MDFile PROTO_LIST ((char *));
static void MDFilter PROTO_LIST ((void));
static void MDPrint PROTO_LIST ((unsigned char [16]));

#if MD == 2
#define MD_CTX MD2_CTX
#define MDInit MD2Init
#define MDUpdate MD2Update
#define MDFinal MD2Final
```

```
#endif
#if MD == 4
#define MD_CTX MD4_CTX
#define MDInit MD4Init
#define MDUpdate MD4Update
#define MDFinal MD4Final
#endif
#if MD == 5
#define MD_CTX MD5_CTX
#define MDInit MD5Init
#define MDUpdate MD5Update
#define MDFinal MD5Final
#endif

/* Main driver.

   Arguments (may be any combination):
     -sstring - digests string
     -t       - runs time trial
     -x       - runs test script
     filename - digests file
     (none)   - digests standard input
 */
int main (argc, argv)
int argc;
char *argv[];
{
  int i;

  if (argc > 1)
    for (i = 1; i < argc; i++)
      if (argv[i][0] == '-' && argv[i][1] == 's')
        MDString (argv[i] + 2);
      else if (strcmp (argv[i], "-t") == 0)
        MDTimeTrial ();
      else if (strcmp (argv[i], "-x") == 0)
        MDTestSuite ();
      else
        MDFile (argv[i]);
  else
    MDFilter ();

  return (0);
}

/* Digests a string and prints the result.
 */
static void MDString (string)
```

```
char *string;
{
  MD_CTX context;
  unsigned char digest[16];
  unsigned int len = strlen (string);

  MDInit (&context);
  MDUpdate (&context, string, len);
  MDFinal (digest, &context);

  printf ("MD%d (\"%s\") = ", MD, string);
  MDPrint (digest);
  printf ("\n");
}

/* Measures the time to digest TEST_BLOCK_COUNT TEST_BLOCK_LEN-byte
     blocks.
 */
static void MDTimeTrial ()
{
  MD_CTX context;
  time_t endTime, startTime;
  unsigned char block[TEST_BLOCK_LEN], digest[16];
  unsigned int i;

  printf
    ("MD%d time trial. Digesting %d %d-byte blocks ...", MD,
     TEST_BLOCK_LEN, TEST_BLOCK_COUNT);

  /* Initialize block */
  for (i = 0; i < TEST_BLOCK_LEN; i++)
    block[i] = (unsigned char)(i & 0xff);

  /* Start timer */
  time (&startTime);

  /* Digest blocks */
  MDInit (&context);
  for (i = 0; i < TEST_BLOCK_COUNT; i++)
    MDUpdate (&context, block, TEST_BLOCK_LEN);
  MDFinal (digest, &context);

  /* Stop timer */
  time (&endTime);

  printf (" done\n");
  printf ("Digest = ");
  MDPrint (digest);
```

```
  printf ("\nTime = %ld seconds\n", (long)(endTime-startTime));
  printf
    ("Speed = %ld bytes/second\n",
      (long)TEST_BLOCK_LEN * (long)TEST_BLOCK_COUNT/(endTime-startTime));
}

/* Digests a reference suite of strings and prints the results.
 */
static void MDTestSuite ()
{
  printf ("MD%d test suite:\n", MD);

  MDString ("");
  MDString ("a");
  MDString ("abc");
  MDString ("message digest");
  MDString ("abcdefghijklmnopqrstuvwxyz");
  MDString
    ("ABCDEFGHIJKLMNOPQRSTUVWXYZabcdefghijklmnopqrstuvwxyz0123456789");
  MDString

    ("12345678901234567890123456789012345678901234567890\
1234567890123456789012345678901234567890");
}

/* Digests a file and prints the result.
 */
static void MDFile (filename)
char *filename;
{
  FILE *file;
  MD_CTX context;
  int len;
  unsigned char buffer[1024], digest[16];

  if ((file = fopen (filename, "rb")) == NULL)
    printf ("%s can't be opened\n", filename);

  else {
    MDInit (&context);
    while (len = fread (buffer, 1, 1024, file))
      MDUpdate (&context, buffer, len);
    MDFinal (digest, &context);

    fclose (file);

    printf ("MD%d (%s) = ", MD, filename);
    MDPrint (digest);
```

```
    printf ("\n");
  }
}

/* Digests the standard input and prints the result.
 */
static void MDFilter ()
{
  MD_CTX context;
  int len;
  unsigned char buffer[16], digest[16];

  MDInit (&context);
  while (len = fread (buffer, 1, 16, stdin))
    MDUpdate (&context, buffer, len);
  MDFinal (digest, &context);

  MDPrint (digest);
  printf ("\n");
}

/* Prints a message digest in hexadecimal.
 */
static void MDPrint (digest)
unsigned char digest[16];

{
  unsigned int i;

  for (i = 0; i < 16; i++)
    printf ("%02x", digest[i]);
}
```

A.5 Test suite

   The MD4 test suite (driver option "-x") should print the following
   results:

```
MD4 test suite:
MD4 ("") = 31d6cfe0d16ae931b73c59d7e0c089c0
MD4 ("a") = bde52cb31de33e46245e05fbdbd6fb24
MD4 ("abc") = a448017aaf21d8525fc10ae87aa6729d
MD4 ("message digest") = d9130a8164549fe818874806e1c7014b
MD4 ("abcdefghijklmnopqrstuvwxyz") = d79e1c308aa5bbcdeea8ed63df412da9
MD4 ("ABCDEFGHIJKLMNOPQRSTUVWXYZabcdefghijklmnopqrstuvwxyz0123456789") =
043f8582f241db351ce627e153e7f0e4
MD4 ("12345678901234567890123456789012345678901234567890123456
78901234567890") = e33b4ddc9c38f2199c3e7b164fcc0536
```

Security Considerations

   The level of security discussed in this memo is considered to be
   sufficient for implementing moderate security hybrid digital-
   signature schemes based on MD4 and a public-key cryptosystem. We do
   not know of any reason that MD4 would not be sufficient for
   implementing very high security digital-signature schemes, but
   because MD4 was designed to be exceptionally fast, it is "at the
   edge" in terms of risking successful cryptanalytic attack. After
   further critical review, it may be appropriate to consider MD4 for
   very high security applications. For very high security applications
   before the completion of that review, the MD5 algorithm [4] is
   recommended.

Author's Address

   Ronald L. Rivest
   Massachusetts Institute of Technology
   Laboratory for Computer Science
   NE43-324
   545 Technology Square
   Cambridge, MA   02139-1986

   Phone: (617) 253-5880
   EMail: rivest@theory.lcs.mit.edu

The MD5 Message-Digest Algorithm

Status of this Memo

   This memo provides information for the Internet community. It does
   not specify an Internet standard. Distribution of this memo is
   unlimited.

Acknowlegements

   We would like to thank Don Coppersmith, Burt Kaliski, Ralph Merkle,
   David Chaum, and Noam Nisan for numerous helpful comments and
   suggestions.

Table of Contents

1. Executive Summary

   This document describes the MD5 message-digest algorithm. The
   algorithm takes as input a message of arbitrary length and produces
   as output a 128-bit "fingerprint" or "message digest" of the input.
   It is conjectured that it is computationally infeasible to produce
   two messages having the same message digest, or to produce any
   message having a given prespecified target message digest. The MD5
   algorithm is intended for digital signature applications, where a
   large file must be "compressed" in a secure manner before being
   encrypted with a private (secret) key under a public-key cryptosystem
   such as RSA.

The MD5 algorithm is designed to be quite fast on 32-bit machines. In addition, the MD5 algorithm does not require any large substitution tables; the algorithm can be coded quite compactly.

The MD5 algorithm is an extension of the MD4 message-digest algorithm 1,2]. MD5 is slightly slower than MD4, but is more "conservative" in design. MD5 was designed because it was felt that MD4 was perhaps being adopted for use more quickly than justified by the existing critical review; because MD4 was designed to be exceptionally fast, it is "at the edge" in terms of risking successful cryptanalytic attack. MD5 backs off a bit, giving up a little in speed for a much greater likelihood of ultimate security. It incorporates some suggestions made by various reviewers, and contains additional optimizations. The MD5 algorithm is being placed in the public domain for review and possible adoption as a standard.

For OSI-based applications, MD5's object identifier is

md5 OBJECT IDENTIFIER ::=
  iso(1) member-body(2) US(840) rsadsi(113549) digestAlgorithm(2) 5}

In the X.509 type AlgorithmIdentifier [3], the parameters for MD5 should have type NULL.

2. Terminology and Notation

In this document a "word" is a 32-bit quantity and a "byte" is an eight-bit quantity. A sequence of bits can be interpreted in a natural manner as a sequence of bytes, where each consecutive group of eight bits is interpreted as a byte with the high-order (most significant) bit of each byte listed first. Similarly, a sequence of bytes can be interpreted as a sequence of 32-bit words, where each consecutive group of four bytes is interpreted as a word with the low-order (least significant) byte given first.

Let x_i denote "x sub i". If the subscript is an expression, we surround it in braces, as in x_{i+1}. Similarly, we use ^ for superscripts (exponentiation), so that x^i denotes x to the i-th power.

Let the symbol "+" denote addition of words (i.e., modulo-2^{32} addition). Let X <<< s denote the 32-bit value obtained by circularly shifting (rotating) X left by s bit positions. Let not(X) denote the bit-wise complement of X, and let X v Y denote the bit-wise OR of X and Y. Let X xor Y denote the bit-wise XOR of X and Y, and let XY denote the bit-wise AND of X and Y.

3. MD5 Algorithm Description

We begin by supposing that we have a b-bit message as input, and that we wish to find its message digest. Here b is an arbitrary nonnegative integer; b may be zero, it need not be a multiple of eight, and it may be arbitrarily large. We imagine the bits of the message written down as follows:

        m_0 m_1 ... m_{b-1}

The following five steps are performed to compute the message digest of the message.

3.1 Step 1. Append Padding Bits

The message is "padded" (extended) so that its length (in bits) is congruent to 448, modulo 512. That is, the message is extended so that it is just 64 bits shy of being a multiple of 512 bits long. Padding is always performed, even if the length of the message is already congruent to 448, modulo 512.

Padding is performed as follows: a single "1" bit is appended to the message, and then "0" bits are appended so that the length in bits of the padded message becomes congruent to 448, modulo 512. In all, at least one bit and at most 512 bits are appended.

3.2 Step 2. Append Length

A 64-bit representation of b (the length of the message before the padding bits were added) is appended to the result of the previous step. In the unlikely event that b is greater than 2^64, then only the low-order 64 bits of b are used. (These bits are appended as two 32-bit words and appended low-order word first in accordance with the previous conventions.)

At this point the resulting message (after padding with bits and with b) has a length that is an exact multiple of 512 bits. Equivalently, this message has a length that is an exact multiple of 16 (32-bit) words. Let M[0 ... N-1] denote the words of the resulting message, where N is a multiple of 16.

3.3 Step 3. Initialize MD Buffer

A four-word buffer (A,B,C,D) is used to compute the message digest. Here each of A, B, C, D is a 32-bit register. These registers are initialized to the following values in hexadecimal, low-order bytes first):

```
           word A: 01 23 45 67
           word B: 89 ab cd ef
           word C: fe dc ba 98
           word D: 76 54 32 10
```

3.4 Step 4. Process Message in 16-Word Blocks

    We first define four auxiliary functions that each take as input
    three 32-bit words and produce as output one 32-bit word.

```
           F(X,Y,Z) = XY v not(X) Z
           G(X,Y,Z) = XZ v Y not(Z)
           H(X,Y,Z) = X xor Y xor Z
           I(X,Y,Z) = Y xor (X v not(Z))
```

    In each bit position F acts as a conditional: if X then Y else Z.
    The function F could have been defined using + instead of v since XY
    and not(X)Z will never have 1's in the same bit position.) It is
    interesting to note that if the bits of X, Y, and Z are independent
    and unbiased, the each bit of F(X,Y,Z) will be independent and
    unbiased.

    The functions G, H, and I are similar to the function F, in that they
    act in "bitwise parallel" to produce their output from the bits of X,
    Y, and Z, in such a manner that if the corresponding bits of X, Y,
    and Z are independent and unbiased, then each bit of G(X,Y,Z),
    H(X,Y,Z), and I(X,Y,Z) will be independent and unbiased. Note that
    the function H is the bit-wise "xor" or "parity" function of its
    inputs.

    This step uses a 64-element table T[1 ... 64] constructed from the
    sine function. Let T[i] denote the i-th element of the table, which
    is equal to the integer part of 4294967296 times abs(sin(i)), where i
    is in radians. The elements of the table are given in the appendix.

    Do the following:

    /* Process each 16-word block. */
    For i = 0 to N/16-1 do

      /* Copy block i into X. */
      For j = 0 to 15 do
        Set X[j] to M[i*16+j].
      end /* of loop on j */

      /* Save A as AA, B as BB, C as CC, and D as DD. */
      AA = A
      BB = B
```
```

```
        CC = C
        DD = D

        /* Round 1. */
        /* Let [abcd k s i] denote the operation
            a = b + ((a + F(b,c,d) + X[k] + T[i]) <<< s). */
        /* Do the following 16 operations. */
        [ABCD  0  7  1]  [DABC  1 12  2]  [CDAB  2 17  3]  [BCDA  3 22   4]
        [ABCD  4  7  5]  [DABC  5 12  6]  [CDAB  6 17  7]  [BCDA  7 22   8]
        [ABCD  8  7  9]  [DABC  9 12 10]  [CDAB 10 17 11]  [BCDA 11 22  12]
        [ABCD 12  7 13]  [DABC 13 12 14]  [CDAB 14 17 15]  [BCDA 15 22  16]

        /* Round 2. */
        /* Let [abcd k s i] denote the operation
            a = b + ((a + G(b,c,d) + X[k] + T[i]) <<< s). */
        /* Do the following 16 operations. */
        [ABCD  1  5 17]  [DABC  6  9 18]  [CDAB 11 14 19]  [BCDA  0 20 20]
        [ABCD  5  5 21]  [DABC 10  9 22]  [CDAB 15 14 23]  [BCDA  4 20 24]
        [ABCD  9  5 25]  [DABC 14  9 26]  [CDAB  3 14 27]  [BCDA  8 20 28]
        [ABCD 13  5 29]  [DABC  2  9 30]  [CDAB  7 14 31]  [BCDA 12 20 32]

        /* Round 3. */
        /* Let [abcd k s t] denote the operation
            a = b + ((a + H(b,c,d) + X[k] + T[i]) <<< s). */
        /* Do the following 16 operations. */
        [ABCD  5  4 33]  [DABC  8 11 34]  [CDAB 11 16 35]  [BCDA 14 23 36]
        [ABCD  1  4 37]  [DABC  4 11 38]  [CDAB  7 16 39]  [BCDA 10 23 40]
        [ABCD 13  4 41]  [DABC  0 11 42]  [CDAB  3 16 43]  [BCDA  6 23 44]
        [ABCD  9  4 45]  [DABC 12 11 46]  [CDAB 15 16 47]  [BCDA  2 23 48]

        /* Round 4. */
        /* Let [abcd k s t] denote the operation
            a = b + ((a + I(b,c,d) + X[k] + T[i]) <<< s). */
        /* Do the following 16 operations. */
        [ABCD  0  6 49]  [DABC  7 10 50]  [CDAB 14 15 51]  [BCDA  5 21 52]
        [ABCD 12  6 53]  [DABC  3 10 54]  [CDAB 10 15 55]  [BCDA  1 21 56]
        [ABCD  8  6 57]  [DABC 15 10 58]  [CDAB  6 15 59]  [BCDA 13 21 60]
        [ABCD  4  6 61]  [DABC 11 10 62]  [CDAB  2 15 63]  [BCDA  9 21 64]

        /* Then perform the following additions. (That is increment each
           of the four registers by the value it had before this block
           was started.) */
        A = A + AA
        B = B + BB
        C = C + CC
        D = D + DD

     end /* of loop on i */
```

3.5 Step 5. Output

The message digest produced as output is A, B, C, D. That is, we begin with the low-order byte of A, and end with the high-order byte of D.

This completes the description of MD5. A reference implementation in C is given in the appendix.

4. Summary

The MD5 message-digest algorithm is simple to implement, and provides a "fingerprint" or message digest of a message of arbitrary length. It is conjectured that the difficulty of coming up with two messages having the same message digest is on the order of 2^{64} operations, and that the difficulty of coming up with any message having a given message digest is on the order of 2^{128} operations. The MD5 algorithm has been carefully scrutinized for weaknesses. It is, however, a relatively new algorithm and further security analysis is of course justified, as is the case with any new proposal of this sort.

5. Differences Between MD4 and MD5

The following are the differences between MD4 and MD5:

1. A fourth round has been added.

2. Each step now has a unique additive constant.

3. The function g in round 2 was changed from (XY v XZ v YZ) to (XZ v Y not(Z)) to make g less symmetric.

4. Each step now adds in the result of the previous step. This promotes a faster "avalanche effect".

5. The order in which input words are accessed in rounds 2 and 3 is changed, to make these patterns less like each other.

6. The shift amounts in each round have been approximately optimized, to yield a faster "avalanche effect." The shifts in different rounds are distinct.

References

    [1] Rivest, R., "The MD4 Message Digest Algorithm", RFC 1320, MIT and
        RSA Data Security, Inc., April 1992.

    [2] Rivest, R., "The MD4 message digest algorithm", in A.J. Menezes
        and S.A. Vanstone, editors, Advances in Cryptology - CRYPTO '90
        Proceedings, pages 303-311, Springer-Verlag, 1991.

    [3] CCITT Recommendation X.509 (1988), "The Directory -
        Authentication Framework."

APPENDIX A - Reference Implementation

    This appendix contains the following files taken from RSAREF: A
    Cryptographic Toolkit for Privacy-Enhanced Mail:

    global.h — global header file

    md5.h — header file for MD5

    md5c.c — source code for MD5

    For more information on RSAREF, send email to <rsaref@rsa.com>.

    The appendix also includes the following file:

    mddriver.c — test driver for MD2, MD4 and MD5

    The driver compiles for MD5 by default but can compile for MD2 or MD4
    if the symbol MD is defined on the C compiler command line as 2 or 4.

    The implementation is portable and should work on many different
    plaforms. However, it is not difficult to optimize the implementation
    on particular platforms, an exercise left to the reader. For example,
    on "little-endian" platforms where the lowest-addressed byte in a 32-
    bit word is the least significant and there are no alignment
    restrictions, the call to Decode in MD5Transform can be replaced with
    a typecast.

A.1 global.h

```
/* GLOBAL.H - RSAREF types and constants
 */

/* PROTOTYPES should be set to one if and only if the compiler supports
   function argument prototyping.
The following makes PROTOTYPES default to 0 if it has not already
```

```
  been defined with C compiler flags.
 */
#ifndef PROTOTYPES
#define PROTOTYPES 0
#endif

/* POINTER defines a generic pointer type */
typedef unsigned char *POINTER;

/* UINT2 defines a two byte word */
typedef unsigned short int UINT2;

/* UINT4 defines a four byte word */
typedef unsigned long int UINT4;

/* PROTO_LIST is defined depending on how PROTOTYPES is defined above.
If using PROTOTYPES, then PROTO_LIST returns the list, otherwise it
  returns an empty list.
 */
#if PROTOTYPES
#define PROTO_LIST(list) list
#else
#define PROTO_LIST(list) ()
#endif
```

A.2 md5.h

```
/* MD5.H - header file for MD5C.C
 */
```

These notices must be retained in any copies of any part of this
documentation and/or software.
 */

```
/* MD5 context. */
typedef struct {
  UINT4 state[4];                                    /* state (ABCD) */
  UINT4 count[2];         /* number of bits, modulo 2^64 (lsb first) */
  unsigned char buffer[64];                          /* input buffer */
} MD5_CTX;

void MD5Init PROTO_LIST ((MD5_CTX *));
void MD5Update PROTO_LIST
  ((MD5_CTX *, unsigned char *, unsigned int));
void MD5Final PROTO_LIST ((unsigned char [16], MD5_CTX *));
```

A.3 md5c.c

```
/* MD5C.C - RSA Data Security, Inc., MD5 message-digest algorithm
 */
```

```
#include "global.h"
#include "md5.h"

/* Constants for MD5Transform routine.
 */
```

```
#define S11 7
#define S12 12
#define S13 17
#define S14 22
#define S21 5
#define S22 9
#define S23 14
#define S24 20
#define S31 4
#define S32 11
#define S33 16
#define S34 23
#define S41 6
#define S42 10
#define S43 15
#define S44 21

static void MD5Transform PROTO_LIST ((UINT4 [4], unsigned char [64]));
static void Encode PROTO_LIST
  ((unsigned char *, UINT4 *, unsigned int));
static void Decode PROTO_LIST
  ((UINT4 *, unsigned char *, unsigned int));
static void MD5_memcpy PROTO_LIST ((POINTER, POINTER, unsigned int));
static void MD5_memset PROTO_LIST ((POINTER, int, unsigned int));

static unsigned char PADDING[64] = {
  0x80, 0, 0, 0, 0, 0, 0, 0, 0, 0, 0, 0, 0, 0, 0, 0, 0, 0, 0, 0, 0, 0,
  0, 0, 0, 0, 0, 0, 0, 0, 0, 0, 0, 0, 0, 0, 0, 0, 0, 0, 0, 0, 0, 0, 0,
  0, 0, 0, 0, 0, 0, 0, 0, 0, 0, 0, 0, 0, 0, 0, 0, 0, 0, 0
};

/* F, G, H and I are basic MD5 functions.
 */
#define F(x, y, z) (((x) & (y)) | ((~x) & (z)))
#define G(x, y, z) (((x) & (z)) | ((y) & (~z)))
#define H(x, y, z) ((x) ^ (y) ^ (z))
#define I(x, y, z) ((y) ^ ((x) | (~z)))

/* ROTATE_LEFT rotates x left n bits.
 */
#define ROTATE_LEFT(x, n) (((x) << (n)) | ((x) >> (32-(n))))

/* FF, GG, HH, and II transformations for rounds 1, 2, 3, and 4.
Rotation is separate from addition to prevent recomputation.
 */
#define FF(a, b, c, d, x, s, ac) { \
  (a) += F ((b), (c), (d)) + (x) + (UINT4)(ac); \
  (a) = ROTATE_LEFT ((a), (s)); \
```

```
(a) += (b); \
  }
#define GG(a, b, c, d, x, s, ac) { \
 (a) += G ((b), (c), (d)) + (x) + (UINT4)(ac); \
 (a) = ROTATE_LEFT ((a), (s)); \
 (a) += (b); \
  }
#define HH(a, b, c, d, x, s, ac) { \
 (a) += H ((b), (c), (d)) + (x) + (UINT4)(ac); \
 (a) = ROTATE_LEFT ((a), (s)); \
 (a) += (b); \
  }
#define II(a, b, c, d, x, s, ac) { \
 (a) += I ((b), (c), (d)) + (x) + (UINT4)(ac); \
 (a) = ROTATE_LEFT ((a), (s)); \
 (a) += (b); \
  }

/* MD5 initialization. Begins an MD5 operation, writing a new context.
 */
void MD5Init (context)
MD5_CTX *context;                                        /* context */
{
  context->count[0] = context->count[1] = 0;
  /* Load magic initialization constants.
*/
  context->state[0] = 0x67452301;
  context->state[1] = 0xefcdab89;
  context->state[2] = 0x98badcfe;
  context->state[3] = 0x10325476;
}

/* MD5 block update operation. Continues an MD5 message-digest
  operation, processing another message block, and updating the
  context.
 */
void MD5Update (context, input, inputLen)
MD5_CTX *context;                                        /* context */
unsigned char *input;                                /* input block */
unsigned int inputLen;                     /* length of input block */
{
  unsigned int i, index, partLen;

  /* Compute number of bytes mod 64 */
  index = (unsigned int)((context->count[0] >> 3) & 0x3F);

  /* Update number of bits */
  if ((context->count[0] += ((UINT4)inputLen << 3))
```

```
   < ((UINT4)inputLen << 3))
 context->count[1]++;
  context->count[1] += ((UINT4)inputLen >> 29);

  partLen = 64 - index;

  /* Transform as many times as possible.
*/
  if (inputLen >= partLen) {
 MD5_memcpy
   ((POINTER)&context->buffer[index], (POINTER)input, partLen);
 MD5Transform (context->state, context->buffer);

 for (i = partLen; i + 63 < inputLen; i += 64)
   MD5Transform (context->state, &input[i]);

 index = 0;
  }
  else
 i = 0;

  /* Buffer remaining input */
  MD5_memcpy
 ((POINTER)&context->buffer[index], (POINTER)&input[i],
  inputLen-i);
}

/* MD5 finalization. Ends an MD5 message-digest operation, writing the
  the message digest and zeroizing the context.
 */
void MD5Final (digest, context)
unsigned char digest[16];                          /* message digest */
MD5_CTX *context;                                  /* context */
{
  unsigned char bits[8];
  unsigned int index, padLen;

  /* Save number of bits */
  Encode (bits, context->count, 8);

  /* Pad out to 56 mod 64.
*/
  index = (unsigned int)((context->count[0] >> 3) & 0x3f);
  padLen = (index < 56) ? (56 - index) : (120 - index);
  MD5Update (context, PADDING, padLen);

  /* Append length (before padding) */
  MD5Update (context, bits, 8);
```

```
  /* Store state in digest */
  Encode (digest, context->state, 16);

  /* Zeroize sensitive information.
*/
  MD5_memset ((POINTER)context, 0, sizeof (*context));
}

/* MD5 basic transformation. Transforms state based on block.
 */
static void MD5Transform (state, block)
UINT4 state[4];
unsigned char block[64];
{
  UINT4 a = state[0], b = state[1], c = state[2], d = state[3], x[16];

  Decode (x, block, 64);

  /* Round 1 */
  FF (a, b, c, d, x[ 0], S11, 0xd76aa478); /* 1 */
  FF (d, a, b, c, x[ 1], S12, 0xe8c7b756); /* 2 */
  FF (c, d, a, b, x[ 2], S13, 0x242070db); /* 3 */
  FF (b, c, d, a, x[ 3], S14, 0xc1bdceee); /* 4 */
  FF (a, b, c, d, x[ 4], S11, 0xf57c0faf); /* 5 */
  FF (d, a, b, c, x[ 5], S12, 0x4787c62a); /* 6 */
  FF (c, d, a, b, x[ 6], S13, 0xa8304613); /* 7 */
  FF (b, c, d, a, x[ 7], S14, 0xfd469501); /* 8 */
  FF (a, b, c, d, x[ 8], S11, 0x698098d8); /* 9 */
  FF (d, a, b, c, x[ 9], S12, 0x8b44f7af); /* 10 */
  FF (c, d, a, b, x[10], S13, 0xffff5bb1); /* 11 */
  FF (b, c, d, a, x[11], S14, 0x895cd7be); /* 12 */
  FF (a, b, c, d, x[12], S11, 0x6b901122); /* 13 */
  FF (d, a, b, c, x[13], S12, 0xfd987193); /* 14 */
  FF (c, d, a, b, x[14], S13, 0xa679438e); /* 15 */
  FF (b, c, d, a, x[15], S14, 0x49b40821); /* 16 */

 /* Round 2 */
  GG (a, b, c, d, x[ 1], S21, 0xf61e2562); /* 17 */
  GG (d, a, b, c, x[ 6], S22, 0xc040b340); /* 18 */
  GG (c, d, a, b, x[11], S23, 0x265e5a51); /* 19 */
  GG (b, c, d, a, x[ 0], S24, 0xe9b6c7aa); /* 20 */
  GG (a, b, c, d, x[ 5], S21, 0xd62f105d); /* 21 */
  GG (d, a, b, c, x[10], S22,  0x2441453); /* 22 */
  GG (c, d, a, b, x[15], S23, 0xd8a1e681); /* 23 */
  GG (b, c, d, a, x[ 4], S24, 0xe7d3fbc8); /* 24 */
  GG (a, b, c, d, x[ 9], S21, 0x21e1cde6); /* 25 */
  GG (d, a, b, c, x[14], S22, 0xc33707d6); /* 26 */
  GG (c, d, a, b, x[ 3], S23, 0xf4d50d87); /* 27 */
```

```
GG (b, c, d, a, x[ 8], S24, 0x455a14ed); /* 28 */
GG (a, b, c, d, x[13], S21, 0xa9e3e905); /* 29 */
GG (d, a, b, c, x[ 2], S22, 0xfcefa3f8); /* 30 */
GG (c, d, a, b, x[ 7], S23, 0x676f02d9); /* 31 */
GG (b, c, d, a, x[12], S24, 0x8d2a4c8a); /* 32 */

/* Round 3 */
HH (a, b, c, d, x[ 5], S31, 0xfffa3942); /* 33 */
HH (d, a, b, c, x[ 8], S32, 0x8771f681); /* 34 */
HH (c, d, a, b, x[11], S33, 0x6d9d6122); /* 35 */
HH (b, c, d, a, x[14], S34, 0xfde5380c); /* 36 */
HH (a, b, c, d, x[ 1], S31, 0xa4beea44); /* 37 */
HH (d, a, b, c, x[ 4], S32, 0x4bdecfa9); /* 38 */
HH (c, d, a, b, x[ 7], S33, 0xf6bb4b60); /* 39 */
HH (b, c, d, a, x[10], S34, 0xbebfbc70); /* 40 */
HH (a, b, c, d, x[13], S31, 0x289b7ec6); /* 41 */
HH (d, a, b, c, x[ 0], S32, 0xeaa127fa); /* 42 */
HH (c, d, a, b, x[ 3], S33, 0xd4ef3085); /* 43 */
HH (b, c, d, a, x[ 6], S34,  0x4881d05); /* 44 */
HH (a, b, c, d, x[ 9], S31, 0xd9d4d039); /* 45 */
HH (d, a, b, c, x[12], S32, 0xe6db99e5); /* 46 */
HH (c, d, a, b, x[15], S33, 0x1fa27cf8); /* 47 */
HH (b, c, d, a, x[ 2], S34, 0xc4ac5665); /* 48 */

/* Round 4 */
II (a, b, c, d, x[ 0], S41, 0xf4292244); /* 49 */
II (d, a, b, c, x[ 7], S42, 0x432aff97); /* 50 */
II (c, d, a, b, x[14], S43, 0xab9423a7); /* 51 */
II (b, c, d, a, x[ 5], S44, 0xfc93a039); /* 52 */
II (a, b, c, d, x[12], S41, 0x655b59c3); /* 53 */
II (d, a, b, c, x[ 3], S42, 0x8f0ccc92); /* 54 */
II (c, d, a, b, x[10], S43, 0xffeff47d); /* 55 */
II (b, c, d, a, x[ 1], S44, 0x85845dd1); /* 56 */
II (a, b, c, d, x[ 8], S41, 0x6fa87e4f); /* 57 */
II (d, a, b, c, x[15], S42, 0xfe2ce6e0); /* 58 */
II (c, d, a, b, x[ 6], S43, 0xa3014314); /* 59 */
II (b, c, d, a, x[13], S44, 0x4e0811a1); /* 60 */
II (a, b, c, d, x[ 4], S41, 0xf7537e82); /* 61 */
II (d, a, b, c, x[11], S42, 0xbd3af235); /* 62 */
II (c, d, a, b, x[ 2], S43, 0x2ad7d2bb); /* 63 */
II (b, c, d, a, x[ 9], S44, 0xeb86d391); /* 64 */

state[0] += a;
state[1] += b;
state[2] += c;
state[3] += d;

/* Zeroize sensitive information.
```

```
*/
  MD5_memset ((POINTER)x, 0, sizeof (x));
}

/* Encodes input (UINT4) into output (unsigned char). Assumes len is
  a multiple of 4.
 */
static void Encode (output, input, len)
unsigned char *output;
UINT4 *input;
unsigned int len;
{
  unsigned int i, j;

  for (i = 0, j = 0; j < len; i++, j += 4) {
 output[j] = (unsigned char)(input[i] & 0xff);
 output[j+1] = (unsigned char)((input[i] >> 8) & 0xff);
 output[j+2] = (unsigned char)((input[i] >> 16) & 0xff);
 output[j+3] = (unsigned char)((input[i] >> 24) & 0xff);
  }
}

/* Decodes input (unsigned char) into output (UINT4). Assumes len is
  a multiple of 4.
 */
static void Decode (output, input, len)
UINT4 *output;
unsigned char *input;
unsigned int len;
{
  unsigned int i, j;

  for (i = 0, j = 0; j < len; i++, j += 4)
 output[i] = ((UINT4)input[j]) | (((UINT4)input[j+1]) << 8) |
   (((UINT4)input[j+2]) << 16) | (((UINT4)input[j+3]) << 24);
}

/* Note: Replace "for loop" with standard memcpy if possible.
 */

static void MD5_memcpy (output, input, len)
POINTER output;
POINTER input;
unsigned int len;
{
  unsigned int i;

  for (i = 0; i < len; i++)
```

```
 output[i] = input[i];
}

/* Note: Replace "for loop" with standard memset if possible.
 */
static void MD5_memset (output, value, len)
POINTER output;
int value;
unsigned int len;
{
  unsigned int i;

  for (i = 0; i < len; i++)
 ((char *)output)[i] = (char)value;
}
```

A.4 mddriver.c

```
/* MDDRIVER.C - test driver for MD2, MD4 and MD5
 */

/* Copyright (C) 1990-2, RSA Data Security, Inc. Created 1990. All
rights reserved.

RSA Data Security, Inc. makes no representations concerning either
the merchantability of this software or the suitability of this
software for any particular purpose. It is provided "as is"
without express or implied warranty of any kind.

These notices must be retained in any copies of any part of this
documentation and/or software.
 */

/* The following makes MD default to MD5 if it has not already been
  defined with C compiler flags.
 */
#ifndef MD
#define MD MD5
#endif

#include <stdio.h>
#include <time.h>
#include <string.h>
#include "global.h"
#if MD == 2
#include "md2.h"
#endif
#if MD == 4
```

```
#include "md4.h"
#endif
#if MD == 5
#include "md5.h"
#endif

/* Length of test block, number of test blocks.
 */
#define TEST_BLOCK_LEN 1000
#define TEST_BLOCK_COUNT 1000

static void MDString PROTO_LIST ((char *));
static void MDTimeTrial PROTO_LIST ((void));
static void MDTestSuite PROTO_LIST ((void));
static void MDFile PROTO_LIST ((char *));
static void MDFilter PROTO_LIST ((void));
static void MDPrint PROTO_LIST ((unsigned char [16]));

#if MD == 2
#define MD_CTX MD2_CTX
#define MDInit MD2Init
#define MDUpdate MD2Update
#define MDFinal MD2Final
#endif
#if MD == 4
#define MD_CTX MD4_CTX
#define MDInit MD4Init
#define MDUpdate MD4Update
#define MDFinal MD4Final
#endif
#if MD -- 5
#define MD_CTX MD5_CTX
#define MDInit MD5Init
#define MDUpdate MD5Update
#define MDFinal MD5Final
#endif

/* Main driver.

Arguments (may be any combination):
  -sstring - digests string
  -t       - runs time trial
  -x       - runs test script
  filename - digests file
  (none)   - digests standard input
 */
int main (argc, argv)
int argc;
```

```
char *argv[];
{
  int i;

  if (argc > 1)
 for (i = 1; i < argc; i++)
   if (argv[i][0] == '-' && argv[i][1] == 's')
     MDString (argv[i] + 2);
   else if (strcmp (argv[i], "-t") == 0)
     MDTimeTrial ();
   else if (strcmp (argv[i], "-x") == 0)
     MDTestSuite ();
   else
     MDFile (argv[i]);
  else
 MDFilter ();

  return (0);
}

/* Digests a string and prints the result.
 */
static void MDString (string)
char *string;
{
  MD_CTX context;
  unsigned char digest[16];
  unsigned int len = strlen (string);

  MDInit (&context);
  MDUpdate (&context, string, len);
  MDFinal (digest, &context);

  printf ("MD%d (\"%s\") = ", MD, string);
  MDPrint (digest);
  printf ("\n");
}

/* Measures the time to digest TEST_BLOCK_COUNT TEST_BLOCK_LEN-byte
  blocks.
 */
static void MDTimeTrial ()
{
  MD_CTX context;
  time_t endTime, startTime;
  unsigned char block[TEST_BLOCK_LEN], digest[16];
  unsigned int i;
```

```
  printf
("MD%d time trial. Digesting %d %d-byte blocks ...", MD,
 TEST_BLOCK_LEN, TEST_BLOCK_COUNT);

  /* Initialize block */
  for (i = 0; i < TEST_BLOCK_LEN; i++)
block[i] = (unsigned char)(i & 0xff);

  /* Start timer */
  time (&startTime);

  /* Digest blocks */
  MDInit (&context);
  for (i = 0; i < TEST_BLOCK_COUNT; i++)
MDUpdate (&context, block, TEST_BLOCK_LEN);
  MDFinal (digest, &context);

  /* Stop timer */
  time (&endTime);

  printf (" done\n");
  printf ("Digest = ");
  MDPrint (digest);
  printf ("\nTime = %ld seconds\n", (long)(endTime-startTime));
  printf
("Speed = %ld bytes/second\n",
  (long)TEST_BLOCK_LEN * (long)TEST_BLOCK_COUNT/(endTime-startTime));
}

/* Digests a reference suite of strings and prints the results.
 */
static void MDTestSuite ()
{
  printf ("MD%d test suite:\n", MD);

  MDString ("");
  MDString ("a");
  MDString ("abc");
  MDString ("message digest");
  MDString ("abcdefghijklmnopqrstuvwxyz");
  MDString
("ABCDEFGHIJKLMNOPQRSTUVWXYZabcdefghijklmnopqrstuvwxyz0123456789");
  MDString
("12345678901234567890123456789012345678901234567890\
12345678901234567890123456789012345678901234567890");
}

/* Digests a file and prints the result.
```

```
 */
static void MDFile (filename)
char *filename;
{
  FILE *file;
  MD_CTX context;
  int len;
  unsigned char buffer[1024], digest[16];

  if ((file = fopen (filename, "rb")) == NULL)
printf ("%s can't be opened\n", filename);

  else {
MDInit (&context);
while (len = fread (buffer, 1, 1024, file))
  MDUpdate (&context, buffer, len);
MDFinal (digest, &context);

  fclose (file);

 printf ("MD%d (%s) = ", MD, filename);
 MDPrint (digest);
 printf ("\n");
  }
}

/* Digests the standard input and prints the result.
 */
static void MDFilter ()
{
  MD_CTX context;
  int len;
  unsigned char buffer[16], digest[16];

  MDInit (&context);
  while (len = fread (buffer, 1, 16, stdin))
 MDUpdate (&context, buffer, len);
  MDFinal (digest, &context);

  MDPrint (digest);
  printf ("\n");
}

/* Prints a message digest in hexadecimal.
 */
static void MDPrint (digest)
unsigned char digest[16];
{
```

```
  unsigned int i;

  for (i = 0; i < 16; i++)
 printf ("%02x", digest[i]);
}
```

A.5 Test suite

   The MD5 test suite (driver option "-x") should print the following
   results:

```
MD5 test suite:
MD5 ("") = d41d8cd98f00b204e9800998ecf8427e
MD5 ("a") = 0cc175b9c0f1b6a831c399e269772661
MD5 ("abc") = 900150983cd24fb0d6963f7d28e17f72
MD5 ("message digest") = f96b697d7cb7938d525a2f31aaf161d0
MD5 ("abcdefghijklmnopqrstuvwxyz") = c3fcd3d76192e4007dfb496cca67e13b
MD5 ("ABCDEFGHIJKLMNOPQRSTUVWXYZabcdefghijklmnopqrstuvwxyz0123456789") =
d174ab98d277d9f5a5611c2c9f419d9f
MD5 ("12345678901234567890123456789012345678901234567890123456
78901234567890") = 57edf4a22be3c955ac49da2e2107b67a
```

Security Considerations

   The level of security discussed in this memo is considered to be
   sufficient for implementing very high security hybrid digital-
   signature schemes based on MD5 and a public-key cryptosystem.

Author's Address

   Ronald L. Rivest
   Massachusetts Institute of Technology
   Laboratory for Computer Science
   NE43-324
   545 Technology Square
   Cambridge, MA   02139-1986

   Phone: (617) 253-5880
   EMail: rivest@theory.lcs.mit.edu

Network Working Group   P. Metzger
Request for Comments: 1828   Piermont
Category: Standards Track   W. Simpson
                                                          Daydreamer
                                                         August 1995

IP Authentication using Keyed MD5

Status of this Memo

   This document specifies an Internet standards track protocol for the
   Internet community, and requests discussion and suggestions for
   improvements. Please refer to the current edition of the "Internet
   Official Protocol Standards" (STD 1) for the standardization state
   and status of this protocol. Distribution of this memo is unlimited.

Abstract

   This document describes the use of keyed MD5 with the IP
   Authentication Header.

Table of Contents

1. Introduction

    The Authentication Header (AH) [RFC-1826] provides integrity and
    authentication for IP datagrams. This specification describes the AH
    use of keys with Message Digest 5 (MD5) [RFC-1321].

    All implementations that claim conformance or compliance with the
    Authentication Header specification MUST implement this keyed MD5
    mechanism.

    This document assumes that the reader is familiar with the related
    document "Security Architecture for the Internet Protocol" [RFC-
    1825], which defines the overall security plan for IP, and provides
    important background for this specification.

1.1. Keys

    The secret authentication key shared between the communicating
    parties SHOULD be a cryptographically strong random number, not a
    guessable string of any sort.

    The shared key is not constrained by this transform to any particular
    size. Lengths of up to 128 bits MUST be supported by the
    implementation, although any particular key may be shorter. Longer
    keys are encouraged.

1.2. Data Size

    MD5's 128-bit output is naturally 64-bit aligned. Typically, there
    is no further padding of the Authentication Data field.

1.3. Performance

    MD5 software speeds are adequate for commonly deployed LAN and WAN
    links, but reportedly are too slow for newer link technologies [RFC-
    1810].

    Nota Bene:
        Suggestions are sought on alternative authentication algorithms
        that have significantly faster throughput, are not patent-
        encumbered, and still retain adequate cryptographic strength.

2. Calculation

   The 128-bit digest is calculated as described in [RFC-1321]. The
   specification of MD5 includes a portable 'C' programming language
   description of the MD5 algorithm.

   The form of the authenticated message is

          key, keyfill, datagram, key, MD5fill

   First, the variable length secret authentication key is filled to the
   next 512-bit boundary, using the same pad with length technique
   defined for MD5.

   Then, the filled key is concatenated with (immediately followed by)
   the invariant fields of the entire IP datagram (variant fields are
   zeroed), concatenated with (immediately followed by) the original
   variable length key again.

   A trailing pad with length to the next 512-bit boundary for the
   entire message is added by MD5 itself. The 128-bit MD5 digest is
   calculated, and the result is inserted into the Authentication Data
   field.

   Discussion:
      When the implementation adds the keys and padding in place before
      and after the IP datagram, care must be taken that the keys and/or
      padding are not sent over the link by the link driver.

Security Considerations

   Users need to understand that the quality of the security provided by
   this specification depends completely on the strength of the MD5 hash
   function, the correctness of that algorithm's implementation, the
   security of the key management mechanism and its implementation, the
   strength of the key [CN94], and upon the correctness of the
   implementations in all of the participating nodes.

   At the time of writing of this document, it is known to be possible
   to produce collisions in the compression function of MD5 [dBB93].
   There is not yet a known method to exploit these collisions to attack
   MD5 in practice, but this fact is disturbing to some authors
   [Schneier94].

   It has also recently been determined [vOW94] that it is possible to
   build a machine for $10 Million that could find two chosen text

variants with a common MD5 hash value. However, it is unclear
whether this attack is applicable to a keyed MD5 transform.

This attack requires approximately 24 days. The same form of attack
is useful on any iterated n-bit hash function, and the time is
entirely due to the 128-bit length of the MD5 hash.

Although there is no substantial weakness for most IP security
applications, it should be recognized that current technology is
catching up to the 128-bit hash length used by MD5. Applications
requiring extremely high levels of security may wish to move in the
near future to algorithms with longer hash lengths.

Acknowledgements

This document was reviewed by the IP Security Working Group of the
Internet Engineering Task Force (IETF). Comments should be submitted
to the ipsec@ans.net mailing list.

Some of the text of this specification was derived from work by
Randall Atkinson for the SIP, SIPP, and IPv6 Working Groups.

The basic concept and use of MD5 is derived in large part from the
work done for SNMPv2 [RFC-1446].

Steve Bellovin, Phil Karn, Charles Lynn, Dave Mihelcic, Hilarie
Orman, Jeffrey Schiller, Joe Touch, and David Wagner provided useful
critiques of earlier versions of this draft.

References

    [CN94]   Carroll, J.M., and Nudiati, S., "On Weak Keys and Weak Data:
               Foiling the Two Nemeses", Cryptologia, Vol. 18 No. 23 pp.
               253-280, July 1994.

    [dBB93]   den Boer, B., and Bosselaers, A., "Collisions for the
               Compression function of MD5", Advances in Cryptology —
               Eurocrypt '93 Proceedings, Berlin: Springer-Verlag 1994

    [KR95]   Kaliski, B., and Robshaw, M., "Message authentication with
               MD5", CryptoBytes (RSA Labs Technical Newsletter), vol.1
               no.1, Spring 1995.

[RFC-1321]
        Rivest, R., "The MD5 Message-Digest Algorithm", RFC 1321,
        MIT and RSA Data Security, Inc., April 1992.

[RFC-1446]
        Galvin, J., and K. McCloghrie, "Security Protocols for
        Version 2 of the Simple Network Management Protocol
        (SNMPv2)", RFC 1446, TIS, Hughes LAN Systems, April
        1993.

[RFC-1700]
        Reynolds, J., and J. Postel, "Assigned Numbers", STD 2,
        RFC 1700, USC/Information Sciences Institute, October 1994.

[RFC-1800]
        Postel, J., "Internet Official Protocol Standards", STD 1,
        RFC 1800, USC/Information Sciences Institute, July 1995.

[RFC-1810]
        Touch, J., "Report on MD5 Performance", RFC 1810,
        USC/Information Sciences Institute, June 1995.

[RFC-1825]
        Atkinson, R., "Security Architecture for the Internet
        Protocol", RFC 1825, NRL, August 1995.

[RFC-1826]
        Atkinson, R., "IP Authentication Header", RFC 1826, NRL
        August 1995.

[Schneier94]
        Schneier, B., "Applied Cryptography", John Wiley & Sons, New
        York, NY, 1994. ISBN 0-471-59756-2

[vOW94] van Oorschot, P. C., and Wiener, M. J., "Parallel Collision
        Search with Applications to Hash Functions and Discrete
        Logarithms", Proceedings of the 2nd ACM Conf. Computer and
        Communications Security, Fairfax, VA, November 1994.

Author's Address

    Questions about this memo can also be directed to:

        Perry Metzger
        Piermont Information Systems Inc.
        160 Cabrini Blvd., Suite #2
        New York, NY 10033

        perry@piermont.com

        William Allen Simpson
        Daydreamer
        Computer Systems Consulting Services
        1384 Fontaine
        Madison Heights, Michigan 48071

        Bill.Simpson@um.cc.umich.edu
            bsimpson@MorningStar.com

Network Working Group   P. Karn
Request for Comments: 1829   Qualcomm
Category: Standards Track   P. Metzger
                                                                  Piermont
                                                                W. Simpson
                                                                Daydreamer
                                                               August 1995

The ESP DES-CBC Transform

Status of this Memo

   This document specifies an Internet standards track protocol for the
   Internet community, and requests discussion and suggestions for
   improvements. Please refer to the current edition of the "Internet
   Official Protocol Standards" (STD 1) for the standardization state
   and status of this protocol. Distribution of this memo is unlimited.

Abstract

   This document describes the DES-CBC security transform for the IP
   Encapsulating Security Payload (ESP).

Table of Contents

RFC 1829

1. Introduction

    The Encapsulating Security Payload (ESP) [RFC-1827] provides
    confidentiality for IP datagrams by encrypting the payload data to be
    protected. This specification describes the ESP use of the Cipher
    Block Chaining (CBC) mode of the US Data Encryption Standard (DES)
    algorithm [FIPS-46, FIPS-46-1, FIPS-74, FIPS-81].

    All implementations that claim conformance or compliance with the
    Encapsulating Security Payload specification MUST implement this
    DES-CBC transform.

    This document assumes that the reader is familiar with the related
    document "Security Architecture for the Internet Protocol"
    [RFC-1825], which defines the overall security plan for IP, and
    provides important background for this specification.

1.1. Keys

    The secret DES key shared between the communicating parties is eight
    octets in length. This key consists of a 56-bit quantity used by the
    DES algorithm. The 56-bit key is stored as a 64-bit (eight octet)
    quantity, with the least significant bit of each octet used as a
    parity bit.

1.2. Initialization Vector

    This mode of DES requires an Initialization Vector (IV) that is eight
    octets in length.

    Each datagram contains its own IV. Including the IV in each datagram
    ensures that decryption of each received datagram can be performed,
    even when other datagrams are dropped, or datagrams are re-ordered in
    transit.

    The method for selection of IV values is implementation dependent.

    Notes:
        A common acceptable technique is simply a counter, beginning with
        a randomly chosen value. While this provides an easy method for
        preventing repetition, and is sufficiently robust for practical
        use, cryptanalysis may use the rare serendipitous occurrence when
        a corresponding bit position in the first DES block increments in
        exactly the same fashion.

Other implementations exhibit unpredictability, usually through a
pseudo-random number generator. Care should be taken that the
periodicity of the number generator is long enough to prevent
repetition during the lifetime of the session key.

1.3. Data Size

The DES algorithm operates on blocks of eight octets. This often
requires padding after the end of the unencrypted payload data.

Both input and output result in the same number of octets, which
facilitates in-place encryption and decryption.

On receipt, if the length of the data to be decrypted is not an
integral multiple of eight octets, then an error is indicated, as
described in [RFC-1825].

1.4. Performance

At the time of writing, at least one hardware implementation can
encrypt or decrypt at about 1 Gbps [Schneier94, p. 231].

2. Payload Format

```
+-+-+-+-+-+-+-+-+-+-+-+-+-+-+-+-+-+-+-+-+-+-+-+-+-+-+-+-+-+-+-+-+
|                 Security Parameters Index (SPI)               |
+-+-+-+-+-+-+-+-+-+-+-+-+-+-+-+-+-+-+-+-+-+-+-+-+-+-+-+-+-+-+-+-+
|                                                              |
~                   Initialization Vector (IV)                 ~
|                                                              |
+-+-+-+-+-+-+-+-+-+-+-+-+-+-+-+-+-+-+-+-+-+-+-+-+-+-+-+-+-+-+-+-+
|                                                              |
~                       Payload Data                           ~
|                                                              |
+-+-+-+-+-+-+-+-+-+-+-+-+-+-+-+-+-+-+-+-+-+-+-+-+-+-+-+-+-+-+-+-+
        ... Padding          | Pad Length  | Payload Type  |
+-+-+-+-+-+-+-+-+-+-+-+-+-+-+-+-+-+-+-+-+-+-+-+-+-+-+-+-+-+-+-+-+
```

Security Parameters Index (SPI)

   A 32-bit value identifying the Security Parameters for this
   datagram. The value MUST NOT be zero.

Initialization Vector (IV)

   The size of this field is variable, although it is constant for
   all DES-CBC datagrams of the same SPI and IP Destination. Octets
   are sent in network order (most significant octet first)
   [RFC-1700].

   The size MUST be a multiple of 32-bits. Sizes of 32 and 64 bits
   are required to be supported. The use of other sizes is beyond
   the scope of this specification. The size is expected to be
   indicated by the key management mechanism.

   When the size is 32-bits, a 64-bit IV is formed from the 32-bit
   value followed by (concatenated with) the bit-wise complement of
   the 32-bit value. This field size is most common, as it aligns
   the Payload Data for both 32-bit and 64-bit processing.

   All conformant implementations MUST also correctly process a
   64-bit field size. This provides strict compatibility with
   existing hardware implementations.

      It is the intent that the value not repeat during the lifetime
      of the encryption session key. Even when a full 64-bit IV is
      used, the session key SHOULD be changed at least as frequently
      as 2**32 datagrams.

Payload Data

   The size of this field is variable.

   Prior to encryption and after decryption, this field begins with
   the IP Protocol/Payload header specified in the Payload Type
   field. Note that in the case of IP-in-IP encapsulation (Payload
   Type 4), this will be another IP header.

Padding

   The size of this field is variable.

   Prior to encryption, it is filled with unspecified implementation
   dependent (preferably random) values, to align the Pad Length and
   Payload Type fields at an eight octet boundary.

   After decryption, it MUST be ignored.

Pad Length

   This field indicates the size of the Padding field. It does not
   include the Pad Length and Payload Type fields. The value
   typically ranges from 0 to 7, but may be up to 255 to permit
   hiding of the actual data length.

   This field is opaque. That is, the value is set prior to
   encryption, and is examined only after decryption.

Payload Type

   This field indicates the contents of the Payload Data field, using
   the IP Protocol/Payload value. Up-to-date values of the IP
   Protocol/Payload are specified in the most recent "Assigned
   Numbers" [RFC-1700].

   This field is opaque. That is, the value is set prior to
   encryption, and is examined only after decryption.

      For example, when encrypting an entire IP datagram (Tunnel-
      Mode), this field will contain the value 4, which indicates
      IP-in-IP encapsulation.

3. Algorithm

    In DES-CBC, the base DES encryption function is applied to the XOR of
    each plaintext block with the previous ciphertext block to yield the
    ciphertext for the current block. This provides for
    re-synchronization when datagrams are lost.

    For more explanation and implementation information for DES, see
    [Schneier94].

3.1. Encryption

    Append zero or more octets of (preferably random) padding to the
    plaintext, to make its modulo 8 length equal to 6. For example, if
    the plaintext length is 41, 5 octets of padding are added.

    Append a Pad Length octet containing the number of padding octets
    just added.

    Append a Payload Type octet containing the IP Protocol/Payload value
    which identifies the protocol header that begins the payload.

    Provide an Initialization Vector (IV) of the size indicated by the
    SPI.

    Encrypt the payload with DES in CBC mode, producing a ciphertext of
    the same length.

    Octets are mapped to DES blocks in network order (most significant
    octet first) [RFC-1700]. Octet 0 (modulo 8) of the payload
    corresponds to bits 1-8 of the 64-bit DES input block, while octet 7
    (modulo 8) corresponds to bits 57-64 of the DES input block.

    Construct an appropriate IP datagram for the target Destination, with
    the indicated SPI, IV, and payload.

    The Total/Payload Length in the encapsulating IP Header reflects the
    length of the encrypted data, plus the SPI, IV, padding, Pad Length,
    and Payload Type octets.

3.2. Decryption

    First, the SPI field is removed and examined. This is used as an
    index into the local Security Parameter table to find the negotiated

parameters and decryption key.

The negotiated form of the IV determines the size of the IV field.
These octets are removed, and an appropriate 64-bit IV value is
constructed.

The encrypted part of the payload is decrypted using DES in the CBC
mode.

The Payload Type is removed and examined. If it is unrecognized, the
payload is discarded with an appropriate ICMP message.

The Pad Length is removed and examined. The specified number of pad
octets are removed from the end of the decrypted payload, and the IP
Total/Payload Length is adjusted accordingly.

The IP Header(s) and the remaining portion of the decrypted payload
are passed to the protocol receive routine specified by the Payload
Type field.

Security Considerations

Users need to understand that the quality of the security provided by
this specification depends completely on the strength of the DES
algorithm, the correctness of that algorithm's implementation, the
security of the key management mechanism and its implementation, the
strength of the key [CN94], and upon the correctness of the
implementations in all of the participating nodes.

Among other considerations, applications may wish to take care not to
select weak keys, although the odds of picking one at random are low
[Schneier94, p 233].

The cut and paste attack described by [Bell95] exploits the nature of
all Cipher Block Chaining algorithms. When a block is damaged in
transmission, on decryption both it and the following block will be
garbled by the decryption process, but all subsequent blocks will be
decrypted correctly. If an attacker has legitimate access to the
same key, this feature can be used to insert or replay previously
encrypted data of other users of the same engine, revealing the
plaintext. The usual (ICMP, TCP, UDP) transport checksum can detect
this attack, but on its own is not considered cryptographically
strong. In this situation, user or connection oriented integrity
checking is needed [RFC-1826].

At the time of writing of this document, [BS93] demonstrated a

differential cryptanalysis based chosen-plaintext attack requiring
2^47 plaintext-ciphertext pairs, and [Matsui94] demonstrated a linear
cryptanalysis based known-plaintext attack requiring only 2^43
plaintext-ciphertext pairs. Although these attacks are not
considered practical, they must be taken into account.

More disturbingly, [Weiner94] has shown the design of a DES cracking
machine costing $1 Million that can crack one key every 3.5 hours.
This is an extremely practical attack.

One or two blocks of known plaintext suffice to recover a DES key.
Because IP datagrams typically begin with a block of known and/or
guessable header text, frequent key changes will not protect against
this attack.

It is suggested that DES is not a good encryption algorithm for the
protection of even moderate value information in the face of such
equipment. Triple DES is probably a better choice for such purposes.

However, despite these potential risks, the level of privacy provided
by use of ESP DES-CBC in the Internet environment is far greater than
sending the datagram as cleartext.

Acknowledgements

This document was reviewed by the IP Security Working Group of the
Internet Engineering Task Force (IETF). Comments should be submitted
to the ipsec@ans.net mailing list.

Some of the text of this specification was derived from work by
Randall Atkinson for the SIP, SIPP, and IPv6 Working Groups.

The use of DES for confidentiality is closely modeled on the work
done for SNMPv2 [RFC-1446].

Steve Bellovin, Steve Deering, Karl Fox, Charles Lynn, Craig Metz,
Dave Mihelcic and Jeffrey Schiller provided useful critiques of
earlier versions of this draft.

References

   [Bell95] Bellovin, S., "An Issue With DES-CBC When Used Without
             Strong Integrity", Proceedings of the 32nd IETF, Danvers,
             MA, April 1995.

   [BS93]   Biham, E., and Shamir, A., "Differential Cryptanalysis of
             the Data Encryption Standard", Berlin: Springer-Verlag,
             1993.

   [CN94]   Carroll, J.M., and Nudiati, S., "On Weak Keys and Weak Data:
             Foiling the Two Nemeses", Cryptologia, Vol. 18 No. 23 pp.
             253-280, July 1994.

   [FIPS-46]
             US National Bureau of Standards, "Data Encryption Standard",
             Federal Information Processing Standard (FIPS) Publication
             46, January 1977.

   [FIPS-46-1]
             US National Bureau of Standards, "Data Encryption Standard",
             Federal Information Processing Standard (FIPS) Publication
             46-1, January 1988.

   [FIPS-74]
             US National Bureau of Standards, "Guidelines for
             Implementing and Using the Data Encryption Standard",
             Federal Information Processing Standard (FIPS) Publication
             74, April 1981.

   [FIPS-81]
             US National Bureau of Standards, "DES Modes of Operation"
             Federal Information Processing Standard (FIPS) Publication
             81, December 1980.

   [Matsui94]
             Matsui, M., "Linear Cryptanalysis method dor DES Cipher,"
             Advances in Cryptology — Eurocrypt '93 Proceedings, Berlin:
             Springer-Verlag, 1994.

   [RFC-1446]
             Galvin, J., and McCloghrie, K., "Security Protocols for
             Version 2 of the Simple Network Management Protocol
             (SNMPv2)", RFC-1446, DDN Network Information Center, April
             1993.

   [RFC-1700]
             Reynolds, J., and Postel, J., "Assigned Numbers", STD 2,

          RFC-1700, USC/Information Sciences Institute, October 1994.

[RFC-1800]
          Postel, J., "Internet Official Protocol Standards", STD 1,
          RFC-1800, USC/Information Sciences Institute, July 1995.

[RFC-1825]
          Atkinson, R., "Security Architecture for the Internet
          Protocol", RFC-1825, Naval Research Laboratory, July 1995.

[RFC-1826]
          Atkinson, R., "IP Authentication Header", RFC-1826, Naval
          Research Laboratory, July 1995.

[RFC-1827]
          Atkinson, R., "IP Encapsulating Security Protocol (ESP)",
          RFC-1827, Naval Research Laboratory, July 1995.

[Schneier94]
          Schneier, B., "Applied Cryptography", John Wiley & Sons, New
          York, NY, 1994. ISBN 0-471-59756-2

[Weiner94]
          Wiener, M.J., "Efficient DES Key Search", School of Computer
          Science, Carleton University, Ottawa, Canada, TR-244, May
          1994. Presented at the Rump Session of Crypto '93.

Author's Address

   Questions about this memo can also be directed to:

      Phil Karn
      Qualcomm, Inc.
      6455 Lusk Blvd.
      San Diego, California 92121-2779

      karn@unix.ka9q.ampr.org

      Perry Metzger
      Piermont Information Systems Inc.
      160 Cabrini Blvd., Suite #2
      New York, NY 10033

      perry@piermont.com

      William Allen Simpson
      Daydreamer
      Computer Systems Consulting Services
      1384 Fontaine
      Madison Heights, Michigan 48071

      Bill.Simpson@um.cc.umich.edu
          bsimpson@MorningStar.com

Network Working Group   R. Baldwin
Request for Comments: 2040   RSA Data Security, Inc.
Category: Informational   R. Rivest
                          MIT Laboratory for Computer Science
                                  and RSA Data Security, Inc.
                                                   October 1996

The RC5, RC5-CBC, RC5-CBC-Pad, and RC5-CTS Algorithms

Status of this Memo

Acknowledgments

   We would like to thank Steve Dusse, Victor Chang, Tim Mathews, Brett
   Howard, and Burt Kaliski for helpful suggestions.

Table of Contents

1. Executive Summary

   This document defines four ciphers with enough detail to ensure
   interoperability between different implementations. The first cipher
   is the raw RC5 block cipher. The RC5 cipher takes a fixed size input
   block and produces a fixed sized output block using a transformation
   that depends on a key. The second cipher, RC5-CBC, is the Cipher
   Block Chaining (CBC) mode for RC5. It can process messages whose
   length is a multiple of the RC5 block size. The third cipher, RC5-
   CBC-Pad, handles plaintext of any length, though the ciphertext will
   be longer than the plaintext by at most the size of a single RC5

block. The RC5-CTS cipher is the Cipher Text Stealing mode of RC5,
which handles plaintext of any length and the ciphertext length
matches the plaintext length.

The RC5 cipher was invented by Professor Ronald L. Rivest of the
Massachusetts Institute of Technology in 1994. It is a very fast and
simple algorithm that is parameterized by the block size, the number
of rounds, and key length. These parameters can be adjusted to meet
different goals for security, performance, and exportability.

RSA Data Security Incorporated has filed a patent application on the
RC5 cipher and for trademark protection for RC5, RC5-CBC, RC5-CBC-
Pad, RC5-CTS and assorted variations.

2. Overview

This memo is a restatement of existing published material. The
description of RC5 follows the notation and order of explanation
found in the original RC5 paper by Professor Rivest [2]. The CBC
mode appears in reference works such as the one by Bruce Schneier
[6]. The CBC-Pad mode is the same as in the Public Key Cryptography
Standard (PKCS) number five [5]. Sample C code [8] is included for
clarity only and is equivalent to the English language descriptions.

The ciphers will be explained in a bottom up object-oriented fashion.
First, RC5 keys will be presented along with the key expansion
algorithm. Second, the RC5 block cipher is explained, and finally,
the RC5-CBC and RC5-CBC-Pad ciphers are specified. For brevity, only
the encryption process is described. Decryption is achieved by
inverting the steps of encryption.

The object-oriented description found here should make it easier to
implement interoperable systems, though it is not as terse as the
functional descriptions found in the references. There are two
classes of objects, keys and cipher algorithms. Both classes share
operations that create and destroy these objects in a manner that
ensures that secret information is not returned to the memory
manager.

Keys also have a "set" operation that copies a secret key into the
object. The "set" operation for the cipher objects defines the
number of rounds, and the initialization vector.

There are four operations for the cipher objects described in this
memo. There is binding a key to a cipher object, setting a new
initialization vector for a cipher object without changing the key,
encrypting part of a message (this would be performed multiple times
for long messages), and processing the last part of a message which

may add padding or check the length of the message.

In summary, the cipher will be explained in terms of these operations:

RC5_Key_Create   - Create a key object.

RC5_Key_Destroy   - Destroy a key object.

RC5_Key_Set   - Bind a user key to a key object.

RC5_CBC_Create   - Create a cipher object.

RC5_CBC_Destroy   - Destroy a cipher object.

RC5_CBC_Encrypt_Init   - Bind a key object to a cipher object.

RC5_CBC_SetIV   - Set a new IV without changing the key.

RC5_CBC_Encrypt_Update   - Process part of a message.

RC5_CBC_Encrypt_Final   - Process the end of a message.

3. Terminology and Notation

The term "word" refers to a string of bits of a particular length that can be operated on as either an unsigned integer or as a bit vector. For example a "word" might be 32 or 64 bits long depending on the desired block size for the RC5 cipher. A 32 bit word will produce a 64 bit block size. For best performance the RC5 word size should match the register size of the CPU. The term "byte" refers to eight bits.

The following variables will be used throughout this memo with these meanings:

W This is the word size for RC5 measured in bits. It is half the block size. The word sizes covered by this memo are 32 and 64.

WW This is the word size for RC5 measured in bytes.

B This is the block size for RC5 measured in bits. It is twice the word size. When RC5 is used as a 64 bit block cipher, B is 64 and W is 32. $0 < B < 257$. In the sample code, B, is used as a variable instead of a cipher system parameter, but this usage should be obvious from context.

BB This is the block size for RC5 measured in bytes. BB = B / 8.

b   This is the byte length of the secret key. 0 <= b < 256.

K   This is the secret key which is treated as a sequence of b
    bytes indexed by: K[0], ..., K[b-1].

R   This is the number of rounds of the inner RC5 transform.
    0 <= R < 256.

T   This is the number of words in the expanded key table. It is
    always 2*(R + 1). 1 < T < 513.

S   This is the expanded key table which is treated as a sequence
    of words indexed by: S[0], ..., S[T-1].

N   This is the byte length of the plaintext message.

P   This is the plaintext message which is treated as a sequence of
    N bytes indexed by: P[0], ..., P[N-1].

C   This is the ciphertext output which is treated as a sequence of
    bytes indexed by: C[0], C[1], ...

I   This is the initialization vector for the CBC mode which is
    treated as a sequence of bytes indexed by: I[0], ..., I[BB-1].

4. Description of RC5 Keys

   Like most block ciphers, RC5 expands a small user key into a table of
   internal keys. The byte length of the user key is one of the
   parameters of the cipher, so the RC5 user key object must be able to
   hold variable length keys. A possible structure for this in C is:

   ```
   /* Definition of RC5 user key object. */
   typedef struct rc5UserKey
   {
     int          keyLength; /* In Bytes. */
     unsigned char   *keyBytes;
   } rc5UserKey;
   ```

   The basic operations on a key are to create, destroy and set. To
   avoid exposing key material to other parts of an application, the
   destroy operation zeros the memory allocated for the key before
   releasing it to the memory manager. A general key object may support
   other operations such as generating a new random key and deriving a
   key from key-agreement information.

4.1 Creating an RC5 Key

  To create a key, the memory for the key object must be allocated and
  initialized. The C code below assumes that a function called
  "malloc" will return a block of uninitialized memory from the heap,
  or zero indicating an error.

```
/* Allocate and initialize an RC5 user key.
 * Return 0 if problems.
 */
rc5UserKey *RC5_Key_Create ()
{
  rc5UserKey *pKey;

  pKey = (rc5UserKey *) malloc (sizeof(*pKey));
  if (pKey != ((rc5UserKey *) 0))
  {
      pKey->keyLength = 0;
      pKey->keyBytes = (unsigned char *) 0;
  }
  return (pKey);
}
```

4.2 Destroying an RC5 Key

  To destroy a key, the memory must be zeroed and released to the
  memory manager. The C code below assumes that a function called
  "free" will return a block of memory to the heap.

```
/* Zero and free an RC5 user key.
 */
void RC5_Key_Destroy (pKey)
  rc5UserKey       *pKey;
{
  unsigned char    *to;
  int           count;

  if (pKey == ((rc5UserKey *) 0))
      return;
  if (pKey->keyBytes == ((unsigned char *) 0))
      return;
  to = pKey->keyBytes;
  for (count = 0 ; count < pKey->keyLength ; count++)
      *to++ = (unsigned char) 0;
  free (pKey->keyBytes);
  pKey->keyBytes = (unsigned char *) 0;
  pKey->keyLength = 0;
  free (pKey);
```

```
     }
```

4.3 Setting an RC5 Key

   Setting the key object makes a copy of the secret key into a block of
   memory allocated from the heap.

```
   /* Set the value of an RC5 user key.
    * Copy the key bytes so the caller can zero and
    * free the original.
    * Return zero if problems
    */
   int RC5_Key_Set (pKey, keyLength, keyBytes)
     rc5UserKey   *pKey;
     int          keyLength;
     unsigned char  *keyBytes;
   {
     unsigned char   *keyBytesCopy;
     unsigned char   *from, *to;
     int          count;

     keyBytesCopy = (unsigned char *) malloc (keyLength);
     if (keyBytesCopy == ((unsigned char *) 0))
         return (0);
     from = keyBytes;
     to = keyBytesCopy;
     for (count = 0 ; count < keyLength ; count++)
         *to++ = *from++;
     pKey->keyLength = count;
     pKey->keyBytes = keyBytesCopy;
     return (1);
   }
```

5. Description of RC5 Key Expansion

   This section describes the key expansion algorithm. To be specific,
   the sample code assumes that the block size is 64 bits. Several
   programming parameters depend on the block size.

```
   /* Definitions for RC5 as a 64 bit block cipher. */
   /* The "unsigned int" will be 32 bits on all but */
   /* the oldest compilers, which will make it 16 bits. */
   /* On a DEC Alpha "unsigned long" is 64 bits, not 32. */
   #define RC5_WORD     unsigned int
   #define W            (32)
   #define WW           (W / 8)
   #define ROT_MASK     (W - 1)
   #define BB           ((2 * W) / 8) /* Bytes per block */
```

```
/* Define macros used in multiple procedures. */
/* These macros assumes ">>" is an unsigned operation, */
/* and that x and s are of type RC5_WORD. */
#define SHL(x,s)     ((RC5_WORD)((x)<<((s)&ROT_MASK)))
#define SHR(x,s,w)   ((RC5_WORD)((x)>>((w)-((s)&ROT_MASK))))
#define ROTL(x,s,w)  ((RC5_WORD)(SHL((x),(s))|SHR((x),(s),(w))))
```

5.1 Definition of initialization constants

Two constants, Pw and Qw, are defined for any word size W by the
expressions:

$$Pw = Odd((e-2)*2**W)$$

$$Qw = Odd((phi-1)*2**W)$$

where e is the base of the natural logarithm (2.71828 ...), and phi
is the golden ratio (1.61803 ...), and 2**W is 2 raised to the power
of W, and Odd(x) is equal to x if x is odd, or equal to x plus one if
x is even. For W equal to 16, 32, and 64, the Pw and Qw constants
are the following hexadecimal values:

```
#define P16   0xb7e1
#define Q16   0x9e37
#define P32   0xb7e15163
#define Q32   0x9e3779b9
#define P64   0xb7e151628aed2a6b
#define Q64   0x9e3779b97f4a7c15
#if W == 16
#define Pw    P16 /* Select 16 bit word size */
#define Qw    Q16
#endif
#if W == 32
#define Pw    P32 /* Select 32 bit word size */
#define Qw    Q32
#endif
#if W == 64
#define Pw    P64 /* Select 64 bit word size */
#define Qw    Q64
#endif
```

5.2 Interface definition

The key expansion routine converts the b-byte secret key, K, into an
expanded key, S, which is a sequence of $T = 2*(R+1)$ words. The
expansion algorithm uses two constants that are derived from the
constants, e, and phi. These are used to initialize S, which is then
modified using K. A C code procedure header for this routine could
be:

```
/* Expand an RC5 user key.
 */
void RC5_Key_Expand (b, K, R, S)
  int      b; /* Byte length of secret key */
  char       *K; /* Secret key */
  int      R; /* Number of rounds */
  RC5_WORD *S;    /* Expanded key buffer, 2*(R+1) words */
{
```

5.3 Convert secret key from bytes to words

This step converts the b-byte key into a sequence of words stored in
the array L. On a little-endian processor this is accomplished by
zeroing the L array and copying in the b bytes of K. The following C
code will achieve this effect on all processors:

```
int i, j, k, LL, t, T;
RC5_WORD    L[256/WW];  /* Based on max key size */
RC5_WORD    A, B;

/* LL is number of elements used in L. */
LL = (b + WW - 1) / WW;
for (i = 0 ; i < LL ; i++)  {
    L[i] = 0;
}
for (i = 0 ; i < b ; i++)  {
    t = (K[i] & 0xFF) << (8*(i%4)); /* 0, 8, 16, 24*/
    L[i/WW] = L[i/WW] + t;
}
```

5.4 Initialize the expanded key table

This step fills in the S table with a fixed (key independent)
pseudo-random pattern using an arithmetic progression based on Pw and
Qw modulo $2**W$. The element S[i] equals $i*Qw + Pw$ modulo $2**W$. This
table could be precomputed and copied as needed or computed on the
fly. In C code it can be computed by:

```
    T = 2*(R+1);
    S[0] = Pw;
    for (i = 1 ; i < T ; i++)  {
        S[i] = S[i-1] + Qw;
    }
```

5.5 Mix in the secret key

This step mixes the secret key, K, into the expanded key, S. First
the number of iterations of the mixing function, k, is set to three
times the maximum of the number of initialized elements of L, called
LL, and the number of elements in S, called T. Each iteration is
similar to an interation of the encryption inner loop in that two
variables A and B are updated by the first and second halves of the
iteration.

Initially A and B are zero as are the indexes into the S array, i,
and the L array, j. In the first half of the iteration, a partial
result is computed by summing S[i], A and B. The new value for A is
this partial result rotated left three bits. The A value is then
placed into S[i]. The second half of the iteration computes a second
partial result that is the sum of L[j], A and B. The second partial
result is then rotated left by A+B bit positions and set to be the
new value for B. The new B value is then placed into L[j]. At the
end of the iteration, i and j are incremented modulo the size of
their respective arrays. In C code:

```
    i = j = 0;
    A = B = 0;
    if (LL > T)
        k = 3 * LL; /* Secret key len > expanded key. */
    else
        k = 3 * T;  /* Secret key len < expanded key. */
    for ( ; k > 0 ; k--)  {
        A = ROTL(S[i] + A + B, 3, W);
        S[i] = A;
        B = ROTL(L[j] + A + B, A + B, W);
        L[j] = B;
        i = (i + 1) % T;
        j = (j + 1) % LL;
    }
    return;
} /* End of RC5_Key_Expand */
```

6. Description of RC5 Block Cipher

   This section describes the RC5 block cipher by explaining the steps
   required to perform an encryption of a single input block. The
   decryption process is the reverse of these steps so it will not be
   explained. The RC5 cipher is parameterized by a version number, V, a
   round count, R, and a word size in bits, W. This description
   corresponds to original version of RC5 (V = 16 decimal) and covers
   any positive value for R and the values 16, 32, and 64 for W.

   The inputs to this process are the expanded key table, S, the number
   of rounds, R, the input buffer pointer, in, and the output buffer
   pointer, out. A possible C code procedure header for this would be:

```
void RC5_Block_Encrypt (S, R, in, out)
   RC5_WORD    *S;
   int  R;
   char    *in;
   char    *out;
{
```

6.1 Loading A and B values

   This step converts input bytes into two unsigned integers called A
   and B. When RC5 is used as a 64 bit block cipher A and B are 32 bit
   values. The first input byte becomes the least significant byte of
   A, the fourth input byte becomes the most significant byte of A, the
   fifth input byte becomes the least significant byte of B and the last
   input byte becomes the most significant byte of B. This conversion
   can be very efficient for little-endian processors such as the Intel
   family. In C code this could be expressed as:

```
   int  i;
   RC5_WORD    A, B;

   A  =  in[0] & 0xFF;
   A +=  (in[1] & 0xFF) << 8;
   A +=  (in[2] & 0xFF) << 16;
   A +=  (in[3] & 0xFF) << 24;
   B  =  in[4] & 0xFF;
   B +=  (in[5] & 0xFF) << 8;
   B +=  (in[6] & 0xFF) << 16;
   B +=  (in[7] & 0xFF) << 24;
```

6.2 Iterating the round function

   This step mixes the expanded key with the input to perform the
   fundamental encryption operation. The first two words of the
   expanded key are added to A and B respectively, and then the round
   function is repeated R times.

   The first half of the round function computes a new value for A based
   on the values of A, B, and the next unused word in the expanded key
   table. Specifically, A is XOR'ed with B and then this first partial
   result is rotated to the left by an amount specified by B to form the
   second partial result. The rotation is performed on a W bit boundary
   (i.e., 32 bit rotation for the version of RC5 that has a 64 bit block
   size). The actual rotation amount only depends on the least
   significant log base-2 of W bits of B. The next unused word of the
   expanded key table is then added to the second partial result and
   this becomes the new value for A.

   The second half of the round function is identical except the roles
   of A and B are switched. Specifically, B is exclusive or'ed with A
   and then this first partial result is rotated to the left by an
   amount specified by A to form the second partial result. The next
   unused word of the expanded key table is then added to the second
   partial result and this becomes the new value for B.

   One way to express this in C code is:

```
 A = A + S[0];
 B = B + S[1];
 for (i = 1 ; i <= R ; i++) {
     A = A ^ B;
     A = ROTL(A, B, W) + S[2*i];
     B = B ^ A;
     B = ROTL(B, A, W) + S[(2*i)+1];
 }
```

6.3 Storing the A and B values

   The final step is to convert A and B back into a sequence of bytes.
   This is the inverse of the load operation. An expression of this in
   C code could be:

```
 out[0] = (A >>  0) & 0xFF;
 out[1] = (A >>  8) & 0xFF;
 out[2] = (A >> 16) & 0xFF;
 out[3] = (A >> 24) & 0xFF;
 out[4] = (B >>  0) & 0xFF;
 out[5] = (B >>  8) & 0xFF;
```

```
        out[6] = (B >> 16) & 0xFF;
        out[7] = (B >> 24) & 0xFF;
        return;
    } /* End of RC5_Block_Encrypt */
```

7. Description of RC5-CBC and RC5-CBC-Pad

   This section describes the CBC and CBC-Pad modes of the RC5 cipher.
   This description is based on the RC5 key objects and RC5 block cipher
   described earlier.

7.1 Creating cipher objects

   The cipher object needs to keep track of the padding mode, the number
   of rounds, the expanded key, the initialization vector, the CBC
   chaining block, and an input buffer. A possible structure definition
   for this in C code would be:

```
/* Definition of the RC5 CBC algorithm object.
 */
typedef struct rc5CBCAlg
{
    int           Pad;    /* 1 = RC5-CBC-Pad, 0 = RC5-CBC. */
    int           R;      /* Number of rounds. */
    RC5_WORD      *S;      /* Expanded key. */
    unsigned char I[BB];  /* Initialization vector. */
    unsigned char chainBlock[BB];
    unsigned char inputBlock[BB];
    int           inputBlockIndex; /* Next inputBlock byte. */
} rc5CBCAlg;
```

   To create a cipher algorithm object, the parameters must be checked
   and then space allocated for the expanded key table. The expanded
   key is initialized using the method described earlier. Finally, the
   state variables (padding mode, number of rounds, and the input
   buffer) are set to their initial values. In C this could be
   accomplished by:

```
/* Allocate and initialize the RC5 CBC algorithm object.
 * Return 0 if problems.
 */
rc5CBCAlg *RC5_CBC_Create (Pad, R, Version, bb, I)
    int     Pad;        /* 1 = RC5-CBC-Pad, 0 = RC5-CBC. */
    int     R;          /* Number of rounds. */
    int     Version;    /* RC5 version number. */
    int     bb;         /* Bytes per RC5 block == IV len. */
    char    *I;         /* CBC IV, bb bytes long. */
{
```

```
    rc5CBCAlg     *pAlg;
    int           index;

    if ((Version != RC5_FIRST_VERSION) ||
        (bb != BB) ||    (R < 0) || (255 < R))
        return ((rc5CBCAlg *) 0);
    pAlg = (rc5CBCAlg *) malloc (sizeof(*pAlg));
    if (pAlg == ((rc5CBCAlg *) 0))
        return ((rc5CBCAlg *) 0);
    pAlg->S = (RC5_WORD *) malloc (BB * (R + 1));
    if (pAlg->S == ((RC5_WORD *) 0))      {
        free (pAlg);
        return ((rc5CBCAlg *) 0);
    }
    pAlg->Pad = Pad;
    pAlg->R = R;
    pAlg->inputBlockIndex = 0;
    for (index = 0 ; index < BB ; index++)
        pAlg->I[index] = I[index];
    return (pAlg);
}
```

7.2 Destroying cipher objects

   Destroying the cipher object is the inverse of creating it with care
   being take to zero memory before returning it to the memory manager.
   In C this could be accomplished by:

```
   /* Zero and free an RC5 algorithm object.
    */
   void RC5_CBC_Destroy (pAlg)
     rc5CBCAlg    *pAlg;
   {
     RC5_WORD    *to;
     int        count;

     if (pAlg == ((rc5CBCAlg *) 0))
         return;
     if (pAlg->S == ((RC5_WORD *) 0))
         return;
     to = pAlg->S;
     for (count = 0 ; count < (1 + pAlg->R) ; count++)
     {
         *to++ = 0;  /* Two expanded key words per round. */
         *to++ = 0;
     }
     free (pAlg->S);
     for (count = 0 ; count < BB ; count++)
```

```
    {
        pAlg->I[count] = (unsigned char) 0;
        pAlg->inputBlock[count] = (unsigned char) 0;
        pAlg->chainBlock[count] = (unsigned char) 0;
    }
    pAlg->Pad = 0;
    pAlg->R = 0;
    pAlg->inputBlockIndex = 0;
    free (pAlg);
}
```

7.3 Setting the IV for cipher objects

   For CBC cipher objects, the state of the algorithm depends on the
   expanded key, the CBC chain block, and any internally buffered input.
   Often the same key is used with many messages that each have a unique
   initialization vector. To avoid the overhead of creating a new
   cipher object, it makes more sense to provide an operation that
   allows the caller to change the initialization vector for an existing
   cipher object. In C this could be accomplished by the following
   code:

```
/* Setup a new initialization vector for a CBC operation
 * and reset the CBC object.
 * This can be called after Final without needing to
 * call Init or Create again.
 * Return zero if problems.
 */
int RC5_CBC_SetIV (pAlg, I)
  rc5CBCAlg   *pAlg;
  char        *I;     /* CBC Initialization vector, BB bytes. */
{
  int      index;

  pAlg->inputBlockIndex = 0;
  for (index = 0 ; index < BB ; index++)
  {
      pAlg->I[index] = pAlg->chainBlock[index] = I[index];
      pAlg->inputBlock[index] = (unsigned char) 0;
  }
  return (1);
}
```

7.4 Binding a key to a cipher object

   The operation that binds a key to a cipher object performs the key
   expansion. Key expansion could be an operation on keys, but that
   would not work correctly for ciphers that modify the expanded key as

they operate. After expanding the key, this operation must
initialize the CBC chain block from the initialization vector and
prepare the input buffer to receive the first character. In C this
could be done by:

```
/* Initialize the encryption object with the given key.
 * After this routine, the caller frees the key object.
 * The IV for this CBC object can be changed by calling
 * the SetIV routine.  The only way to change the key is
 * to destroy the CBC object and create a new one.
 * Return zero if problems.
 */
int RC5_CBC_Encrypt_Init (pAlg, pKey)
  rc5CBCAlg        *pAlg;
  rc5UserKey  *pKey;
{
  if ((pAlg == ((rc5CBCAlg *) 0)) ||
      (pKey == ((rc5UserKey *) 0)))
      return (0);
  RC5_Key_Expand (Key->keyLength, pKey->keyBytes,
                  pAlg->R, pAlg->S);
  return (RC5_CBC_SetIV(pAlg, pAlg->I));
}
```

7.5 Processing part of a message

The encryption process described here uses the Init-Update-Final
paradigm. The update operation can be performed on a sequence of
message parts in order to incrementally produce the ciphertext.
After the last part is processed, the Final operation is called to
pick up any plaintext bytes or padding that are buffered inside the
cipher object. An appropriate procedure header for this operation
would be:

```
/* Encrypt a buffer of plaintext.
 * The plaintext and ciphertext buffers can be the same.
 * The byte len of the ciphertext is put in *pCipherLen.
 * Call this multiple times passing successive
 * parts of a large message.
 * After the last part has been passed to Update,
 * call Final.
 * Return zero if problems like output buffer too small.
 */
int RC5_CBC_Encrypt_Update (pAlg, N, P,
                            pCipherLen, maxCipherLen, C)
  rc5CBCAlg   *pAlg;       /* Cipher algorithm object. */
  int         N;          /* Byte length of P. */
  char        *P;          /* Plaintext buffer. */
```

```
    int        *pCipherLen;/* Gets byte len of C. */
    int         maxCipherLen;  /* Size of C. */
    char       *C;             /* Ciphertext buffer. */
{
```

7.5.1   Output buffer size check.

The first step of plaintext processing is to make sure that the
output buffer is big enough hold the ciphertext. The ciphertext will
be produced in multiples of the block size and depends on the number
of plaintext characters passed to this operation plus any characters
that are in the cipher object's internal buffer. In C code this
would be:

```
    int        plainIndex, cipherIndex, j;

    /* Check size of the output buffer. */
    if (maxCipherLen < (((pAlg->inputBlockIndex+N)/BB)*BB))
    {
        *pCipherLen = 0;
        return (0);
    }
```

7.5.2   Divide plaintext into blocks

The next step is to add characters to the internal buffer until a
full block has been constructed. When that happens, the buffer
pointers are reset and the input buffer is exclusive-or'ed (XORed)
with the CBC chaining block. The byte order of the chaining block is
the same as the input block. For example, the ninth input byte is
XOR'ed with the first ciphertext byte. The result is then passed to
the RC5 block cipher which was described earlier. To reduce data
movement and byte alignment problems, the output of RC5 can be
directly written into the CBC chaining block. Finally, this output
is copied to the ciphertext buffer provided by the user. Before
returning, the actual size of the ciphertext is passed back to the
caller. In C, this step can be performed by:

```
    plainIndex = cipherIndex = 0;
    while (plainIndex < N)
    {
        if (pAlg->inputBlockIndex < BB)
        {
            pAlg->inputBlock[pAlg->inputBlockIndex]
                 = P[plainIndex];
            pAlg->inputBlockIndex++;
            plainIndex++;
        }
```

```
        if (pAlg->inputBlockIndex == BB)
        {   /* Have a complete input block, process it. */
            pAlg->inputBlockIndex = 0;
            for (j = 0 ; j < BB ; j++)
            {   /* XOR in the chain block. */
                pAlg->inputBlock[j] = pAlg->inputBlock[j]
                                ^ pAlg->chainBlock[j];
            }
            RC5_Block_Encrypt(pAlg->S, pAlg->R
                            pAlg->inputBlock,
                            pAlg->chainBlock);
            for (j = 0 ; j < BB ; j++)
            {   /* Output the ciphertext. */
                C[cipherIndex] = pAlg->chainBlock[j];
                cipherIndex++;
            }
        }
    }
    *pCipherLen = cipherIndex;
    return (1);
} /* End of RC5_CBC_Encrypt_Update */
```

7.6 Final block processing

   This step handles the last block of plaintext. For RC5-CBC, this
   step just performs error checking to ensure that the plaintext length
   was indeed a multiple of the block length. For RC5-CBC-Pad, padding
   bytes are added to the plaintext. The pad bytes are all the same and
   are set to a byte that represents the number of bytes of padding.
   For example if there are eight bytes of padding, the bytes will all
   have the hexadecimal value 0x08. There will be between one and BB
   padding bytes, inclusive. In C code this would be:

```
   /* Produce the final block of ciphertext including any
    * padding, and then reset the algorithm object.
    * Return zero if problems.
    */
   int RC5_CBC_Encrypt_Final (pAlg, pCipherLen, maxCipherLen, C)
     rc5CBCAlg   *pAlg;
     int         *pCipherLen;    /* Gets byte len of C. */
     int          maxCipherLen;  /* Len of C buffer. */
     char        *C;             /* Ciphertext buffer. */
   {
     int     cipherIndex, j;
     int     padLength;

     /* For non-pad mode error if input bytes buffered. */
     *pCipherLen = 0;
```

```
    if ((pAlg->Pad == 0) && (pAlg->inputBlockIndex != 0))
        return (0);

    if (pAlg->Pad == 0)
        return (1);
    if (maxCipherLen < BB)
        return (0);

    padLength = BB - pAlg->inputBlockIndex;
    for (j = 0 ; j < padLength ; j++)
    {
        pAlg->inputBlock[pAlg->inputBlockIndex]
                = (unsigned char) padLength;
        pAlg->inputBlockIndex++;
    }
    for (j = 0 ; j < BB ; j++)
    {   /* XOR the chain block into the plaintext block. */
        pAlg->inputBlock[j] = pAlg->inputBlock[j]
                              ^ pAlg->chainBlock[j];
    }
    RC5_Block_Encrypt(pAlg->S, pAlg->R,
                      pAlg->inputBlock, pAlg->chainBlock);
    cipherIndex = 0;
    for (j = 0 ; j < BB ; j++)
    {   /* Output the ciphertext. */
        C[cipherIndex] = pAlg->chainBlock[j];
        cipherIndex++;
    }
    *pCipherLen = cipherIndex;

    /* Reset the CBC algorithm object. */
    return (RC5_CBC_SetIV(pAlg, pAlg->I));
} /* End of RC5_CBC_Encrypt_Final */
```

8. Description of RC5-CTS

    The Cipher Text Stealing (CTS) mode for block ciphers is described by
    Schneier on pages 195 and 196 of [6]. This mode handles any length
    of plaintext and produces ciphertext whose length matches the
    plaintext length. The CTS mode behaves like the CBC mode for all but
    the last two blocks of the plaintext. The following steps describe
    how to handle the last two portions of the plaintext, called Pn-1 and
    Pn, where the length of Pn-1 equals the block size, BB, and the
    length of the last block, Pn, is Ln bytes. Notice that Ln ranges
    from 1 to BB, inclusive, so Pn could in fact be a complete block.

1. Exclusive-or Pn-1 with the previous ciphertext
   block, Cn-2, to create Xn-1.

2. Encrypt Xn-1 to create En-1.

3. Select the first Ln bytes of En-1 to create Cn.

4. Pad Pn with zeros at the end to create P of length BB.

5. Exclusive-or En-1 with P to create to create Dn.

6. Encrypt Dn to create Cn-1

7. The last two parts of the ciphertext are Cn-1 and
   Cn respectively.

To implement CTS encryption, the RC5-CTS object must hold on to
(buffer) at most 2*BB bytes of plaintext and process them specially
when the RC5_CTS_Encrypt_Final routine is called.

The following steps describe how to decrypt Cn-1 and Cn.

1. Decrypt Cn-1 to create Dn.

2. Pad Cn with zeros at the end to create C of length BB.

3. Exclusive-or Dn with C to create Xn.

4. Select the first Ln bytes of Xn to create Pn.

5. Append the tail (BB minus Ln) bytes of Xn to Cn
   to create En.

6. Decrypt En to create Pn-1.

7. The last two parts of the plaintext are Pn-1 and
   Pn respectively.

9. Test Program and Vectors

   To help confirm the correctness of an implementation, this section
   gives a test program and results from a set of test vectors.

9.1 Test Program

   The following test program written in C reads test vectors from its
   input stream and writes results on its output stream. The following
   subsections give a set of test vectors for inputs and the resulting

outputs.

```c
#include <stdio.h>

#define BLOCK_LENGTH     (8 /* bytes */)
#define MAX_KEY_LENGTH   (64 /* bytes */)
#define MAX_PLAIN_LENGTH (128 /* bytes */)
#define MAX_CIPHER_LENGTH(MAX_PLAIN_LENGTH + BLOCK_LENGTH)
#define MAX_ROUNDS       (20)
#define MAX_S_LENGTH     (2 * (MAX_ROUNDS + 1))

typedef struct test_vector
{
  int padding_mode;
  int rounds;
  char    keytext[2*MAX_KEY_LENGTH+1];
  int key_length;
  char    key[MAX_KEY_LENGTH];
  char    ivtext[2*BLOCK_LENGTH+1];
  int iv_length;
  char    iv[BLOCK_LENGTH];
  char    plaintext[2*MAX_PLAIN_LENGTH+1];
  int plain_length;
  char    plain[MAX_PLAIN_LENGTH];
  char    ciphertext[2*MAX_CIPHER_LENGTH+1];
  int cipher_length;
  char    cipher[MAX_CIPHER_LENGTH];
  RC5_WORD    S[MAX_S_LENGTH];
} test_vector;

void show_banner()
{
  (void) printf("RC5 CBC Tester.\n");
  (void) printf("Each input line should contain the following\n");
  (void) printf("test parameters separated by a single space:\n");
  (void) printf("- Padding mode flag.  Use 1 for RC5_CBC_Pad, else
0.\n");
  (void) printf("- Number of rounds for RC5.\n");
  (void) printf("- Key bytes in hexadecimal.  Two characters per
byte like '01'.\n");
  (void) printf("- IV bytes in hexadecimal.  Must be 16 hex
characters.\n");
  (void) printf("- Plaintext bytes in hexadecimal.\n");
  (void) printf("An end of file or format error terminates the
tester.\n");
  (void) printf("\n");
}
```

```
/* Convert a buffer from ascii hex to bytes.
 * Set pTo_length to the byte length of the result.
 * Return 1 if everything went OK.
 */
int hex_to_bytes (from, to, pTo_length)
  char    *from, *to;
  int     *pTo_length;
{
  char    *pHex;  /* Ptr to next hex character. */
  char    *pByte;    /* Ptr to next resulting byte. */
  int  byte_length = 0;
  int  value;

  pByte = to;
  for (pHex = from ; *pHex != 0 ; pHex += 2)  {
      if (1 != sscanf(pHex, "%02x", &value))
          return (0);
      *pByte++ = ((char)(value & 0xFF));
      byte_length++;
  }
  *pTo_length = byte_length;
  return (1);
}

/* Convert a buffer from bytes to ascii hex.
 * Return 1 if everything went OK.
 */
int bytes_to_hex (from, from_length, to)
  char    *from, *to;
  int from_length;
{
  char    *pHex;  /* Ptr to next hex character. */
  char    *pByte;    /* Ptr to next resulting byte. */
  int  value;

  pHex = to;
  for (pByte = from ; from_length > 0 ; from_length--)  {
      value = *pByte++ & 0xFF;
      (void) sprintf(pHex, "%02x", value);
      pHex += 2;
  }
  return (1);
}

/* Return 1 if get a valid test vector. */
int get_test_vector(ptv)
  test_vector *ptv;
{
```

```
   if (1 != scanf("%d", &ptv->padding_mode))
      return (0);
   if (1 != scanf("%d", &ptv->rounds))
      return (0);
   if ((ptv->rounds < 0) || (MAX_ROUNDS < ptv->rounds))
      return (0);
   if (1 != scanf("%s", &ptv->keytext))
      return (0);
   if (1 != hex_to_bytes(ptv->keytext, ptv->key,
                      &ptv->key_length))
      return (0);
   if (1 != scanf("%s", &ptv->ivtext))
      return (0);
   if (1 != hex_to_bytes(ptv->ivtext, ptv->iv,
                      &ptv->iv_length))
      return (0);
   if (BLOCK_LENGTH != ptv->iv_length)
      return (0);
   if (1 != scanf("%s", &ptv->plaintext))
      return (0);
   if (1 != hex_to_bytes(ptv->plaintext, ptv->plain,
                      &ptv->plain_length))
      return (0);
   return (1);
}

void run_test (ptv)
   test_vector *ptv;
{
   rc5UserKey  *pKey;
   rc5CBCAlg      *pAlg;
   int           numBytesOut;

   pKey = RC5_Key_Create ();
   RC5_Key_Set (pKey, ptv->key_length, ptv->key);

   pAlg = RC5_CBC_Create (ptv->padding_mode,
                 ptv->rounds,
                 RC5_FIRST_VERSION,
                 BB,
                 ptv->iv);
   (void) RC5_CBC_Encrypt_Init (pAlg, pKey);
   ptv->cipher_length = 0;
   (void) RC5_CBC_Encrypt_Update (pAlg,
                 ptv->plain_length, ptv->plain,
                 &(numBytesOut),
                 MAX_CIPHER_LENGTH - ptv->cipher_length,
                 &(ptv->cipher[ptv->cipher_length]));
```

```
    ptv->cipher_length += numBytesOut;
    (void) RC5_CBC_Encrypt_Final (pAlg,
                  &(numBytesOut),
                  MAX_CIPHER_LENGTH - ptv->cipher_length,
                  &(ptv->cipher[ptv->cipher_length]));
    ptv->cipher_length += numBytesOut;
    bytes_to_hex (ptv->cipher, ptv->cipher_length,
                ptv->ciphertext);
    RC5_Key_Destroy (pKey);
    RC5_CBC_Destroy (pAlg);
}

void show_results (ptv)
    test_vector *ptv;
{
    if (ptv->padding_mode)
        printf ("RC5_CBC_Pad ");
    else
        printf ("RC5_CBC     ");
    printf ("R = %2d ", ptv->rounds);
    printf ("Key = %s ", ptv->keytext);
    printf ("IV = %s ", ptv->ivtext);
    printf ("P = %s ", ptv->plaintext);
    printf ("C = %s", ptv->ciphertext);
    printf ("\n");
}

int main(argc, argv)
    int argc;
    char *argv[];
{
    test_vector tv;
    test_vector *ptv = &tv;

    show_banner();
    while (get_test_vector(ptv))  {
        run_test(ptv);
        show_results(ptv);
    }
    return (0);
}
```

9.2 Test vectors

The following text is an input file to the test program presented in
the previous subsection. The output is given in the next subsection.

```
0 00 00                  0000000000000000 0000000000000000
0 00 00                  0000000000000000 ffffffffffffffff
0 00 00                  0000000000000001 0000000000000000
0 00 00                  0000000000000000 0000000000000001
0 00 00                  0102030405060708 1020304050607080
0 01 11                  0000000000000000 0000000000000000
0 02 00                  0000000000000000 0000000000000000
0 02 00000000            0000000000000000 0000000000000000
0 08 00                  0000000000000000 0000000000000000
0 08 00                  0102030405060708 1020304050607080
0 12 00                  0102030405060708 1020304050607080
0 16 00                  0102030405060708 1020304050607080
0 08 01020304            0000000000000000 ffffffffffffffff
0 12 01020304            0000000000000000 ffffffffffffffff
0 16 01020304            0000000000000000 ffffffffffffffff
0 12 0102030405060708    0000000000000000 ffffffffffffffff
0 08 0102030405060708    0102030405060708 1020304050607080
0 12 0102030405060708    0102030405060708 1020304050607080
0 16 0102030405060708    0102030405060708 1020304050607080
0 08 01020304050607081020304050607080
                         0102030405060708 1020304050607080
0 12 01020304050607081020304050607080
                         0102030405060708 1020304050607080
0 16 01020304050607081020304050607080
                         0102030405060708 1020304050607080

0 12 0102030405          0000000000000000 ffffffffffffffff
0 08 0102030405          0000000000000000 ffffffffffffffff
0 08 0102030405          7875dbf6738c6478 0808080808080808
1 08 0102030405          0000000000000000 ffffffffffffffff

0 08 0102030405          0000000000000000 0000000000000000
0 08 0102030405          7cb3f1df34f94811 1122334455667701

1 08 0102030405          0000000000000000
ffffffffffffffff7875dbf6738c647811223344556677
```

9.3 Test results

   The following text is the output produced by the test program run on
   the inputs given in the previous subsection.

   RC5 CBC Tester.
   Each input line should contain the following
   test parameters separated by a single space:
   - Padding mode flag. Use 1 for RC5_CBC_Pad, else 0.
   - Number of rounds for RC5.
   - Key bytes in hexadecimal. Two characters per byte
     like '01'.
   - IV bytes in hexadecimal. Must be 16 hex characters.
   - Plaintext bytes in hexadecimal.
   An end of file or format error terminates the tester.

   RC5_CBC   R =   0 Key = 00 IV = 0000000000000000
    P = 0000000000000000 C = 7a7bba4d79111d1e
   RC5_CBC   R =   0 Key = 00 IV = 0000000000000000
    P = ffffffffffffffff C = 797bba4d78111d1e
   RC5_CBC   R =   0 Key = 00 IV = 0000000000000001
    P = 0000000000000000 C = 7a7bba4d79111d1f
   RC5_CBC   R =   0 Key = 00 IV = 0000000000000000
    P = 0000000000000001 C = 7a7bba4d79111d1f
   RC5_CBC   R =   0 Key = 00 IV = 0102030405060708
    P = 1020304050607080 C = 8b9ded91ce7794a6
   RC5_CBC   R =   1 Key = 11 IV = 0000000000000000
    P = 0000000000000000 C = 2f759fe7ad86a378
   RC5_CBC   R =   2 Key = 00 IV = 0000000000000000
    P = 0000000000000000 C = dca2694bf40e0788
   RC5_CBC   R =   2 Key = 00000000 IV = 0000000000000000
    P = 0000000000000000 C = dca2694bf40e0788
   RC5_CBC   R =   8 Key = 00 IV = 0000000000000000
    P = 0000000000000000 C = dcfe098577eca5ff
   RC5_CBC   R =   8 Key = 00 IV = 0102030405060708
    P = 1020304050607080 C = 9646fb77638f9ca8
   RC5_CBC   R = 12 Key = 00 IV = 0102030405060708
    P = 1020304050607080 C = b2b3209db6594da4
   RC5_CBC   R = 16 Key = 00 IV = 0102030405060708
    P = 1020304050607080 C = 545f7f32a5fc3836
   RC5_CBC   R =   8 Key = 01020304 IV = 0000000000000000
    P = ffffffffffffffff C = 8285e7c1b5bc7402
   RC5_CBC   R = 12 Key = 01020304 IV = 0000000000000000
    P = ffffffffffffffff C = fc586f92f7080934
   RC5_CBC   R = 16 Key = 01020304 IV = 0000000000000000
    P = ffffffffffffffff C = cf270ef9717ff7c4
   RC5_CBC   R = 12 Key = 0102030405060708 IV = 0000000000000000
    P = ffffffffffffffff C = e493f1c1bb4d6e8c

```
RC5_CBC     R =   8 Key = 0102030405060708 IV = 0102030405060708
 P = 1020304050607080 C = 5c4c041e0f217ac3
RC5_CBC     R = 12 Key = 0102030405060708 IV = 0102030405060708
 P = 1020304050607080 C = 921f12485373b4f7
RC5_CBC     R = 16 Key = 0102030405060708 IV = 0102030405060708
 P = 1020304050607080 C = 5ba0ca6bbe7f5fad
RC5_CBC     R =   8 Key = 01020304050607081020304050607080
 IV = 0102030405060708
 P = 1020304050607080 C = c533771cd0110e63
RC5_CBC     R = 12 Key = 01020304050607081020304050607080
 IV = 0102030405060708
 P = 1020304050607080 C = 294ddb46b3278d60
RC5_CBC     R = 16 Key = 01020304050607081020304050607080
 IV = 0102030405060708
 P = 1020304050607080 C = dad6bda9dfe8f7e8
RC5_CBC     R = 12 Key = 0102030405 IV = 0000000000000000
 P = ffffffffffffffff C = 97e0787837ed317f
RC5_CBC     R =   8 Key = 0102030405 IV = 0000000000000000
 P = ffffffffffffffff C = 7875dbf6738c6478
RC5_CBC     R =   8 Key = 0102030405 IV = 7875dbf6738c6478
 P = 0808080808080808 C = 8f34c3c681c99695
RC5_CBC_Pad R =   8 Key = 0102030405 IV = 0000000000000000
 P = ffffffffffffffff C = 7875dbf6738c64788f34c3c681c99695
RC5_CBC     R =   8 Key = 0102030405 IV = 0000000000000000
 P = 0000000000000000 C = 7cb3f1df34f94811
RC5_CBC     R =   8 Key = 0102030405 IV = 7cb3f1df34f94811
 P = 1122334455667701 C = 7fd1a023a5bba217
RC5_CBC_Pad R =   8 Key = 0102030405 IV = 0000000000000000
 P = ffffffffffffffff7875dbf6738c647811223344556677
 C = 7875dbf6738c64787cb3f1df34f948117fd1a023a5bba217
```

10. Security Considerations

The RC5 cipher is relatively new so critical reviews are still being
performed. However, the cipher's simple structure makes it easy to
analyze and hopefully easier to assess its strength. Reviews so far
are very promising.

Early results [1] suggest that for RC5 with a 64 bit block size (32
bit word size), 12 rounds will suffice to resist linear and
differential cyptanalysis. The 128 bit block version has not been
studied as much as the 64 bit version, but it appears that 16 rounds
would be an appropriate minimum. Block sizes less than 64 bits are
academically interesting but should not be used for cryptographic
security. Greater security can be achieved by increasing the number
of rounds at the cost of decreasing the throughput of the cipher.

The length of the secret key helps determine the cipher's resistance
to brute force key searching attacks. A key length of 128 bits
should give adequate protection against brute force key searching by
a well funded opponent for a couple decades [7]. For RC5 with 12
rounds, the key setup time and data encryption time are the same for
all key lengths less than 832 bits, so there is no performance reason
for choosing short keys. For larger keys, the key expansion step
will run slower because the user key table, L, will be longer than
the expanded key table, S. However, the encryption time will be
unchanged since it is only a function of the number of rounds.

To comply with export regulations it may be necessary to choose keys
that only have 40 unknown bits. A poor way to do this would be to
choose a simple 5 byte key. This should be avoided because it would
be easy for an opponent to pre-compute key searching information.
Another common mechanism is to pick a 128 bit key and publish the
first 88 bits. This method reveals a large number of the entries in
the user key table, L, and the question of whether RC5 key expansion
provides adequate security in this situation has not been studied,
though it may be fine. A conservative way to conform to a 40 bit
limitation is to pick a seed value of 128 bits, publish 88 bits of
this seed, run the entire seed through a hash function like MD5 [4],
and use the 128 bit output of the hash function as the RC5 key.

In the case of 40 unknown key bits with 88 known key bits (i.e., 88
salt bits) there should still be 12 or more rounds for the 64 bit
block version of RC5, otherwise the value of adding salt bits to the
key is likely to be lost.

The lifetime of the key also influences security. For high security
applications, the key to any 64 bit block cipher should be changed
after encrypting 2^{32} blocks (2^{64} blocks for a 128 bit block
cipher). This helps to guard against linear and differential
cryptanalysis. For the case of 64 bit blocks, this rule would
recommend changing the key after 2^{40} (i.e. 10^{12}) bytes are
encrypted. See Schneier [6] page 183 for further discussion.

11. ASN.1 Identifiers

   For applications that use ASN.1 descriptions, it is necessary to
   define the algorithm identifier for these ciphers along with their
   parameter block formats. The ASN.1 definition of an algorithm
   identifier already exists and is listed below for reference.

   AlgorithmIdentifier ::= SEQUENCE {
     algorithm   OBJECT IDENTIFIER,
     parameters   ANY DEFINED BY algorithm OPTIONAL
   }

   The values for the algorithm field are:

   RC5_CBC OBJECT IDENTIFIER ::=
      { iso (1) member-body (2) US (840) rsadsi (113549)
        encryptionAlgorithm (3) RC5CBC (8) }

   RC5_CBC_Pad OBJECT IDENTIFIER ::=
   { iso (1) member-body (2) US (840) rsadsi (113549)
     encryptionAlgorithm (3) RC5CBCPAD (9) }

   The structure of the parameters field for these algorithms is given
   below. NOTE: if the iv field is not included, then the
   initialization vector defaults to a block of zeros whose size depends
   on the blockSizeInBits field.

   RC5_CBC_Parameters ::= SEQUENCE {
     version   INTEGER (v1_0(16)),
     rounds   INTEGER (8..127),
     blockSizeInBits   INTEGER (64, 128),
     iv   OCTET STRING OPTIONAL
   }

References

   [1] Kaliski, Burton S., and Yinqun Lisa Yin, "On Differential and
   Linear Cryptanalysis of the RC5 Encryption Algorithm", In Advances
   in Cryptology - Crypto '95, pages 171-184, Springer-Verlag, New
   York, 1995.

   [2] Rivest, Ronald L., "The RC5 Encryption Algorithm", In
   Proceedings of the Second International Workshop on Fast Software
   Encryption, pages 86-96, Leuven Belgium, December 1994.

   [3] Rivest, Ronald L., "RC5 Encryption Algorithm", In Dr. Dobbs
   Journal, number 226, pages 146-148, January 1995.

    [4] Rivest, Ronald L., "The MD5 Message-Digest Algorithm", RFC
    1321.

    [5] RSA Laboratories, "Public Key Cryptography Standards (PKCS)",
    RSA Data Security Inc. See ftp.rsa.com.

    [6] Schneier, Bruce, "Applied Cryptography", Second Edition, John
    Wiley and Sons, New York, 1996. Errata: on page 195, line 13, the
    reference number should be [402].

    [7] Business Software Alliance, Matt Blaze et al., "Minimum Key
    Length for Symmetric Ciphers to Provide Adequate Commercial
    Security", http://www.bsa.org/bsa/cryptologists.html.

    [8] RSA Data Security Inc., "RC5 Reference Code in C", See the web
    site: www.rsa.com, for availability. Not available with the first
    draft of this document.

Authors' Addresses

    Robert W. Baldwin
    RSA Data Security, Inc.
    100 Marine Parkway
    Redwood City, CA 94065

    Phone: (415) 595-8782
    Fax: (415) 595-1873
    EMail: baldwin@rsa.com, or baldwin@lcs.mit.edu

    Ronald L. Rivest
    Massachusetts Institute of Technology
    Laboratory for Computer Science
    NE43-324
    545 Technology Square
    Cambridge, MA 02139-1986

    Phone: (617) 253-5880
    EMail: rivest@theory.lcs.mit.edu

Network Working Group   M. Oehler
Request for Comments: 2085   NSA
Category: Standards Track   R. Glenn
                                                                   NIST
                                                          February 1997

                HMAC-MD5 IP Authentication with Replay Prevention

Status of This Memo

   This document specifies an Internet standards track protocol for the
   Internet community, and requests discussion and suggestions for
   improvements. Please refer to the current edition of the "Internet
   Official Protocol Standards" (STD 1) for the standardization state
   and status of this protocol. Distribution of this memo is unlimited.

Abstract

   This document describes a keyed-MD5 transform to be used in
   conjunction with the IP Authentication Header [RFC-1826]. The
   particular transform is based on [HMAC-MD5]. An option is also
   specified to guard against replay attacks.

Table of Contents

1. Introduction

   The Authentication Header (AH) [RFC-1826] provides integrity and
   authentication for IP datagrams. The transform specified in this
   document uses a keyed-MD5 mechanism [HMAC-MD5]. The mechanism uses
   the (key-less) MD5 hash function [RFC-1321] which produces a message
   digest. When combined with an AH Key, authentication data is
   produced. This value is placed in the Authentication Data field of
   the AH [RFC-1826]. This value is also the basis for the data
   integrity service offered by the AH protocol.

To provide protection against replay attacks, a Replay Prevention
field is included as a transform option. This field is used to help
prevent attacks in which a message is stored and re-used later,
replacing or repeating the original. The Security Parameters Index
(SPI) [RFC-1825] is used to determine whether this option is included
in the AH.

Familiarity with the following documents is assumed: "Security
Architecture for the Internet Protocol" [RFC-1825], "IP
Authentication Header" [RFC-1826], and "HMAC-MD5: Keyed-MD5 for
Message Authentication" [HMAC-MD5].

All implementations that claim conformance or compliance with the IP
Authentication Header specification [RFC-1826] MUST implement this
HMAC-MD5 transform.

1.1 Terminology

In this document, the words that are used to define the
significance of each particular requirement are usually capitalized.
These words are:

- MUST

This word or the adjective "REQUIRED" means that the item is an
absolute requirement of the specification.

- SHOULD

This word or the adjective "RECOMMENDED" means that there might
exist valid reasons in particular circumstances to ignore this item,
but the full implications should be understood and the case carefully
weighed before taking a different course.

1.2 Keys

The "AH Key" is used as a shared secret between two communicating
parties. The Key is not a "cryptographic key" as used in a
traditional sense. Instead, the AH key (shared secret) is hashed with
the transmitted data and thus, assures that an intervening party
cannot duplicate the authentication data.

Even though an AH key is not a cryptographic key, the rudimentary
concerns of cryptographic keys still apply. Consider that the
algorithm and most of the data used to produce the output is known.
The strength of the transform lies in the singular mapping of the key
(which needs to be strong) and the IP datagram (which is known) to
the authentication data. Thus, implementations should, and as

frequently as possible, change the AH key. Keys need to be chosen at random, or generated using a cryptographically strong pseudo-random generator seeded with a random seed. [HMAC-MD5]

All conforming and compliant implementations MUST support a key length of 128 bits or less. Implementations SHOULD support longer key lengths as well. It is advised that the key length be chosen to be the length of the hash output, which is 128 bits for MD5. For other key lengths the following concerns MUST be considered.

A key length of zero is prohibited and implementations MUST prevent key lengths of zero from being used with this transform, since no effective authentication could be provided by a zero-length key. Keys having a length less than 128 bits are strongly discouraged as it would decrease the security strength of the function. Keys longer than 128 bits are acceptable, but the extra length may not significantly increase the function strength. A longer key may be advisable if the randomness of the key is suspect. MD5 operates on 64-byte blocks. Keys longer than 64-bytes are first hashed using MD5. The resulting hash is then used to calculate the authentication data.

1.3 Data Size

MD5 produces a 128-bit value which is used as the authentication data. It is naturally 64 bit aligned and thus, does not need any padding for machines with native double words.

2. Packet Format

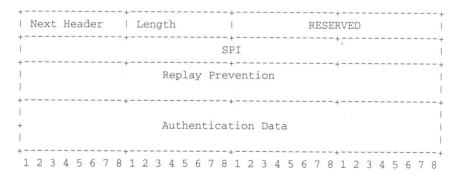

```
+---------------+---------------+---------------+---------------+
| Next Header   | Length        |               RESERVED        |
+---------------+---------------+---------------+---------------+
|                               SPI                             |
+---------------+---------------+---------------+---------------+
|                                                               |
|                        Replay Prevention                      |
|                                                               |
+---------------+---------------+---------------+---------------+
|                                                               |
+                       Authentication Data                     |
|                                                               |
+---------------+---------------+---------------+---------------+
 1 2 3 4 5 6 7 8 1 2 3 4 5 6 7 8 1 2 3 4 5 6 7 8 1 2 3 4 5 6 7 8
```

The Next Header, RESERVED, and SPI fields are specified in [RFC-1826]. The Length field is the length of the Replay Prevention field and the Authentication Data in 32-bit words.

2.1 Replay Prevention

The Replay Prevention field is a 64-bit value used to guarantee that
each packet exchanged between two parties is different. Each IPsec
Security Association specifies whether Replay Prevention is used for
that Security Association. If Replay Prevention is NOT in use, then
the Authentication Data field will directly follow the SPI field.

The 64-bit field is an up counter starting at a value of 1.

The secret shared key must not be used for a period of time that
allows the counter to wrap, that is, to transmit more than 2^{64}
packets using a single key.

Upon receipt, the replay value is assured to be increasing. The
implementation may accept out of order packets. The number of packets
to accept out of order is an implementation detail. If an "out of
order window" is supported, the implementation shall ensure that any
and all packets accepted out of order are guaranteed not to have
arrived before. That is, the implementation will accept any packet at
most once.

When the destination address is a multicast address, replay
protection is in use, and more than one sender is sharing the same
IPsec Security Association to that multicast destination address,
then Replay Protection SHOULD NOT be enabled. When replay protection
is desired for a multicast session having multiple senders to the
same multicast destination address, each sender SHOULD have its own
IPsec Security Association.

[ESP-DES-MD5] provides example code that implements a 32 packet
replay window and a test routine to show how it works.

2.2 Authentication Data Calculation

The authentication data is the output of the authentication algorithm
(MD5). This value is calculated over the entire IP datagram. Fields
within the datagram that are variant during transit and the
authentication data field itself, must contain all zeros prior to the
computation [RFC-1826]. The Replay Prevention field if present, is
included in the calculation.

The definition and reference implementation of MD5 appears in [RFC-
1321]. Let 'text' denote the data to which HMAC-MD5 is to be applied
and K be the message authentication secret key shared by the parties.
If K is longer than 64-bytes it MUST first be hashed using MD5. In
this case, K is the resulting hash.

We define two fixed and different strings ipad and opad as follows
(the 'i' and 'o' are mnemonics for inner and outer):

        ipad = the byte 0x36 repeated 64 times
        opad = the byte 0x5C repeated 64 times.
To compute HMAC-MD5 over the data `text' we perform
        MD5(K XOR opad, MD5(K XOR ipad, text))
Namely,
   (1) append zeros to the end of K to create a 64 byte string
       (e.g., if K is of length 16 bytes it will be appended with 48
       zero bytes 0x00)
   (2) XOR (bitwise exclusive-OR) the 64 byte string computed in step
       (1) with ipad
   (3) append the data stream 'text' to the 64 byte string resulting
       from step (2)
   (4) apply MD5 to the stream generated in step (3)
   (5) XOR (bitwise exclusive-OR) the 64 byte string computed in
       step (1) with opad
   (6) append the MD5 result from step (4) to the 64 byte string
       resulting from step (5)
   (7) apply MD5 to the stream generated in step (6) and output
       the result

   This computation is described in more detail, along with example
   code and performance improvements, in [HMAC-MD5]. Implementers
   should consult [HMAC-MD5] for more information on this technique
   for keying a cryptographic hash function.

3. Security Considerations

   The security provided by this transform is based on the strength of
   MD5, the correctness of the algorithm's implementation, the security
   of the key management mechanism and its implementation, the strength
   of the associated secret key, and upon the correctness of the
   implementations in all of the participating systems. [HMAC-MD5]
   contains a detailed discussion on the strengths and weaknesses of
   MD5.

Acknowledgments

   This document is largely based on text written by Hugo Krawczyk. The
   format used was derived from work by William Simpson and Perry
   Metzger. The text on replay prevention is derived directly from work
   by Jim Hughes.

References

[RFC-1825]   Atkinson, R., "Security Architecture for the Internet
              Protocol", RFC 1852, Naval Research Laboratory,
              July 1995.
[RFC-1826]   Atkinson, R., "IP Authentication Header",
              RFC 1826, August 1995.
[RFC-1828]   Metzger, P., and W. Simpson, "IP Authentication using
              Keyed MD5", RFC 1828, August 1995.
[RFC-1321]   Rivest, R., "The MD5 Message-Digest Algorithm",
              RFC 1321, April 1992.
[HMAC-MD5]   Krawczyk, H., Bellare, M., and R. Canetti,
              "HMAC: Keyed-Hashing for Message Authentication",
              RFC 2104, February 1997.
[ESP-DES-MD5] Hughes, J., "Combined DES-CBC, MD5, and Replay
              Prevention Security Transform", Work in Progress.

Authors' Addresses

    Michael J. Oehler
    National Security Agency
    Atn: R23, INFOSEC Research and Development
    9800 Savage Road
    Fort Meade, MD 20755

    EMail: mjo@tycho.ncsc.mil

    Robert Glenn
    NIST
    Building 820, Room 455
    Gaithersburg, MD 20899

    EMail: rob.glenn@nist.gov

Network Working Group   H. Krawczyk
Request for Comments: 2104   IBM
Category: Informational   M. Bellare
                                                                  UCSD
                                                            R. Canetti
                                                                   IBM
                                                         February 1997

HMAC: Keyed-Hashing for Message Authentication

Status of This Memo

Abstract

   This document describes HMAC, a mechanism for message authentication
   using cryptographic hash functions. HMAC can be used with any
   iterative cryptographic hash function, e.g., MD5, SHA-1, in
   combination with a secret shared key. The cryptographic strength of
   HMAC depends on the properties of the underlying hash function.

1. Introduction

   Providing a way to check the integrity of information transmitted
   over or stored in an unreliable medium is a prime necessity in the
   world of open computing and communications. Mechanisms that provide
   such integrity check based on a secret key are usually called
   "message authentication codes" (MAC). Typically, message
   authentication codes are used between two parties that share a secret
   key in order to validate information transmitted between these
   parties. In this document we present such a MAC mechanism based on
   cryptographic hash functions. This mechanism, called HMAC, is based
   on work by the authors [BCK1] where the construction is presented and
   cryptographically analyzed. We refer to that work for the details on
   the rationale and security analysis of HMAC, and its comparison to
   other keyed-hash methods.

HMAC can be used in combination with any iterated cryptographic hash
function. MD5 and SHA-1 are examples of such hash functions. HMAC
also uses a secret key for calculation and verification of the
message authentication values. The main goals behind this
construction are

* To use, without modifications, available hash functions.
  In particular, hash functions that perform well in software,
  and for which code is freely and widely available.

* To preserve the original performance of the hash function without
  incurring a significant degradation.

* To use and handle keys in a simple way.

* To have a well understood cryptographic analysis of the strength of
  the authentication mechanism based on reasonable assumptions on the
  underlying hash function.

* To allow for easy replaceability of the underlying hash function in
  case that faster or more secure hash functions are found or
  required.

This document specifies HMAC using a generic cryptographic hash
function (denoted by H). Specific instantiations of HMAC need to
define a particular hash function. Current candidates for such hash
functions include SHA-1 [SHA], MD5 [MD5], RIPEMD-128/160 [RIPEMD].
These different realizations of HMAC will be denoted by HMAC-SHA1,
HMAC-MD5, HMAC-RIPEMD, etc.

Note: To the date of writing of this document MD5 and SHA-1 are the
most widely used cryptographic hash functions. MD5 has been recently
shown to be vulnerable to collision search attacks [Dobb]. This
attack and other currently known weaknesses of MD5 do not compromise
the use of MD5 within HMAC as specified in this document (see
[Dobb]); however, SHA-1 appears to be a cryptographically stronger
function. To this date, MD5 can be considered for use in HMAC for
applications where the superior performance of MD5 is critical.   In
any case, implementers and users need to be aware of possible
cryptanalytic developments regarding any of these cryptographic hash
functions, and the eventual need to replace the underlying hash
function. (See section 6 for more information on the security of
HMAC.)

2. Definition of HMAC

   The definition of HMAC requires a cryptographic hash function, which
   we denote by H, and a secret key K. We assume H to be a cryptographic
   hash function where data is hashed by iterating a basic compression
   function on blocks of data.   We denote by B the byte-length of such
   blocks (B=64 for all the above mentioned examples of hash functions),
   and by L the byte-length of hash outputs (L=16 for MD5, L=20 for
   SHA-1).   The authentication key K can be of any length up to B, the
   block length of the hash function. Applications that use keys longer
   than B bytes will first hash the key using H and then use the
   resultant L byte string as the actual key to HMAC. In any case the
   minimal recommended length for K is L bytes (as the hash output
   length). See section 3 for more information on keys.

   We define two fixed and different strings ipad and opad as follows
   (the 'i' and 'o' are mnemonics for inner and outer):

                    ipad = the byte 0x36 repeated B times
                    opad = the byte 0x5C repeated B times.

   To compute HMAC over the data `text' we perform

                    H(K XOR opad, H(K XOR ipad, text))

   Namely,

       (1) append zeros to the end of K to create a B byte string
           (e.g., if K is of length 20 bytes and B=64, then K will be
            appended with 44 zero bytes 0x00)
       (2) XOR (bitwise exclusive-OR) the B byte string computed in step
           (1) with ipad
       (3) append the stream of data 'text' to the B byte string resulting
           from step (2)
       (4) apply H to the stream generated in step (3)
       (5) XOR (bitwise exclusive-OR) the B byte string computed in
           step (1) with opad
       (6) append the H result from step (4) to the B byte string
           resulting from step (5)
       (7) apply H to the stream generated in step (6) and output
           the result

   For illustration purposes, sample code based on MD5 is provided as an
   appendix.

3. Keys

   The key for HMAC can be of any length (keys longer than B bytes are
   first hashed using H). However, less than L bytes is strongly
   discouraged as it would decrease the security strength of the
   function. Keys longer than L bytes are acceptable but the extra
   length would not significantly increase the function strength. (A
   longer key may be advisable if the randomness of the key is
   considered weak.)

   Keys need to be chosen at random (or using a cryptographically strong
   pseudo-random generator seeded with a random seed), and periodically
   refreshed. (Current attacks do not indicate a specific recommended
   frequency for key changes as these attacks are practically
   infeasible. However, periodic key refreshment is a fundamental
   security practice that helps against potential weaknesses of the
   function and keys, and limits the damage of an exposed key.)

4. Implementation Note

   HMAC is defined in such a way that the underlying hash function H can
   be used with no modification to its code. In particular, it uses the
   function H with the pre-defined initial value IV (a fixed value
   specified by each iterative hash function to initialize its
   compression function). However, if desired, a performance
   improvement can be achieved at the cost of (possibly) modifying the
   code of H to support variable IVs.

   The idea is that the intermediate results of the compression function
   on the B-byte blocks (K XOR ipad) and (K XOR opad) can be precomputed
   only once at the time of generation of the key K, or before its first
   use. These intermediate results are stored and then used to
   initialize the IV of H each time that a message needs to be
   authenticated. This method saves, for each authenticated message,
   the application of the compression function of H on two B-byte blocks
   (i.e., on (K XOR ipad) and (K XOR opad)). Such a savings may be
   significant when authenticating short streams of data. We stress
   that the stored intermediate values need to be treated and protected
   the same as secret keys.

   Choosing to implement HMAC in the above way is a decision of the
   local implementation and has no effect on inter-operability.

5. Truncated output

   A well-known practice with message authentication codes is to
   truncate the output of the MAC and output only part of the bits
   (e.g., [MM, ANSI]). Preneel and van Oorschot [PV] show some
   analytical advantages of truncating the output of hash-based MAC
   functions. The results in this area are not absolute as for the
   overall security advantages of truncation. It has advantages (less
   information on the hash result available to an attacker) and
   disadvantages (less bits to predict for the attacker). Applications
   of HMAC can choose to truncate the output of HMAC by outputting the t
   leftmost bits of the HMAC computation for some parameter t (namely,
   the computation is carried in the normal way as defined in section 2
   above but the end result is truncated to t bits). We recommend that
   the output length t be not less than half the length of the hash
   output (to match the birthday attack bound) and not less than 80 bits
   (a suitable lower bound on the number of bits that need to be
   predicted by an attacker). We propose denoting a realization of HMAC
   that uses a hash function H with t bits of output as HMAC-H-t. For
   example, HMAC-SHA1-80 denotes HMAC computed using the SHA-1 function
   and with the output truncated to 80 bits. (If the parameter t is not
   specified, e.g. HMAC-MD5, then it is assumed that all the bits of the
   hash are output.)

6. Security

   The security of the message authentication mechanism presented here
   depends on cryptographic properties of the hash function H: the
   resistance to collision finding (limited to the case where the
   initial value is secret and random, and where the output of the
   function is not explicitly available to the attacker), and the
   message authentication property of the compression function of H when
   applied to single blocks (in HMAC these blocks are partially unknown
   to an attacker as they contain the result of the inner H computation
   and, in particular, cannot be fully chosen by the attacker).

   These properties, and actually stronger ones, are commonly assumed
   for hash functions of the kind used with HMAC. In particular, a hash
   function for which the above properties do not hold would become
   unsuitable for most (probably, all) cryptographic applications,
   including alternative message authentication schemes based on such
   functions. (For a complete analysis and rationale of the HMAC
   function the reader is referred to [BCK1].)

Given the limited confidence gained so far as for the cryptographic
strength of candidate hash functions, it is important to observe the
following two properties of the HMAC construction and its secure use
for message authentication:

1. The construction is independent of the details of the particular
hash function H in use and then the latter can be replaced by any
other secure (iterative) cryptographic hash function.

2. Message authentication, as opposed to encryption, has a
"transient" effect. A published breaking of a message authentication
scheme would lead to the replacement of that scheme, but would have
no adversarial effect on information authenticated in the past. This
is in sharp contrast with encryption, where information encrypted
today may suffer from exposure in the future if, and when, the
encryption algorithm is broken.

The strongest attack known against HMAC is based on the frequency of
collisions for the hash function H ("birthday attack") [PV,BCK2], and
is totally impractical for minimally reasonable hash functions.

As an example, if we consider a hash function like MD5 where the
output length equals L=16 bytes (128 bits) the attacker needs to
acquire the correct message authentication tags computed (with the
same secret key K!) on about 2**64 known plaintexts. This would
require the processing of at least 2**64 blocks under H, an
impossible task in any realistic scenario (for a block length of 64
bytes this would take 250,000 years in a continuous 1Gbps link, and
without changing the secret key K during all this time). This attack
could become realistic only if serious flaws in the collision
behavior of the function H are discovered (e.g. collisions found
after 2**30 messages). Such a discovery would determine the immediate
replacement of the function H (the effects of such failure would be
far more severe for the traditional uses of H in the context of
digital signatures, public key certificates, etc.).

Note: this attack needs to be strongly contrasted with regular
collision attacks on cryptographic hash functions where no secret key
is involved and where 2**64 off-line parallelizable (!) operations
suffice to find collisions. The latter attack is approaching
feasibility [VW] while the birthday attack on HMAC is totally
impractical. (In the above examples, if one uses a hash function
with, say, 160 bit of output then 2**64 should be replaced by 2**80.)

A correct implementation of the above construction, the choice of
random (or cryptographically pseudorandom) keys, a secure key
exchange mechanism, frequent key refreshments, and good secrecy
protection of keys are all essential ingredients for the security of
the integrity verification mechanism provided by HMAC.

Appendix -- Sample Code

    For the sake of illustration we provide the following sample code for
    the implementation of HMAC-MD5 as well as some corresponding test
    vectors (the code is based on MD5 code as described in [MD5]).

```
/*
** Function: hmac_md5
*/

void
hmac_md5(text, text_len, key, key_len, digest)
unsigned char*  text;                  /* pointer to data stream */
int             text_len;              /* length of data stream */
unsigned char*  key;                   /* pointer to authentication key */
int             key_len;               /* length of authentication key */
caddr_t         digest;                /* caller digest to be filled in */

{
        MD5_CTX context;
        unsigned char k_ipad[65];     /* inner padding -
                                       * key XORd with ipad
                                       */
        unsigned char k_opad[65];     /* outer padding -
                                       * key XORd with opad
                                       */
        unsigned char tk[16];
        int i;
        /* if key is longer than 64 bytes reset it to key=MD5(key) */
        if (key_len > 64) {

                MD5_CTX         tctx;

                MD5Init(&tctx);
                MD5Update(&tctx, key, key_len);
                MD5Final(tk, &tctx);

                key = tk;
                key_len = 16;
        }

        /*
         * the HMAC_MD5 transform looks like:
         *
         * MD5(K XOR opad, MD5(K XOR ipad, text))
         *
         * where K is an n byte key
         * ipad is the byte 0x36 repeated 64 times
```

```
       * opad is the byte 0x5c repeated 64 times
       * and text is the data being protected
       */

      /* start out by storing key in pads */
      bzero( k_ipad, sizeof k_ipad);
      bzero( k_opad, sizeof k_opad);
      bcopy( key, k_ipad, key_len);
      bcopy( key, k_opad, key_len);

      /* XOR key with ipad and opad values */
      for (i=0; i<64; i++) {
              k_ipad[i] ^= 0x36;
              k_opad[i] ^= 0x5c;
      }
      /*
       * perform inner MD5
       */
      MD5Init(&context);                    /* init context for 1st
                                             * pass */
      MD5Update(&context, k_ipad, 64)       /* start with inner pad */
      MD5Update(&context, text, text_len);  /* then text of datagram */
      MD5Final(digest, &context);           /* finish up 1st pass */
      /*
       * perform outer MD5
       */
      MD5Init(&context);                    /* init context for 2nd
                                             * pass */
      MD5Update(&context, k_opad, 64);      /* start with outer pad */
      MD5Update(&context, digest, 16);      /* then results of 1st
                                             * hash */
      MD5Final(digest, &context);           /* finish up 2nd pass */
}
```

Test Vectors (Trailing '\0' of a character string not included in test):

```
  key =         0x0b0b0b0b0b0b0b0b0b0b0b0b0b0b0b0b
  key_len =     16 bytes
  data =        "Hi There"
  data_len =    8  bytes
  digest =      0x9294727a3638bb1c13f48ef8158bfc9d

  key =         "Jefe"
  data =        "what do ya want for nothing?"
  data_len =    28 bytes
  digest =      0x750c783e6ab0b503eaa86e310a5db738

  key =         0xAAAAAAAAAAAAAAAAAAAAAAAAAAAAAAAA
```

```
key_len            16 bytes
data =             0xDDDDDDDDDDDDDDDDDDDD...
                   ..DDDDDDDDDDDDDDDDDDDD...
                   ..DDDDDDDDDDDDDDDDDDDD...
                   ..DDDDDDDDDDDDDDDDDDDD...
                   ..DDDDDDDDDDDDDDDDDDDD
data_len =         50 bytes
digest =           0x56be34521d144c88dbb8c733f0e8b3f6
```

Acknowledgments

   Pau-Chen Cheng, Jeff Kraemer, and Michael Oehler, have provided
   useful comments on early drafts, and ran the first interoperability
   tests of this specification. Jeff and Pau-Chen kindly provided the
   sample code and test vectors that appear in the appendix. Burt
   Kaliski, Bart Preneel, Matt Robshaw, Adi Shamir, and Paul van
   Oorschot have provided useful comments and suggestions during the
   investigation of the HMAC construction.

References

   [ANSI]   ANSI X9.9, "American National Standard for Financial
            Institution Message Authentication (Wholesale)," American
            Bankers Association, 1981.   Revised 1986.

   [Atk]   Atkinson, R., "IP Authentication Header", RFC 1826, August
            1995.

   [BCK1]   M. Bellare, R. Canetti, and H. Krawczyk,
            "Keyed Hash Functions and Message Authentication",
            Proceedings of Crypto'96, LNCS 1109, pp. 1-15.
            (http://www.research.ibm.com/security/keyed-md5.html)

   [BCK2]   M. Bellare, R. Canetti, and H. Krawczyk,
            "Pseudorandom Functions Revisited: The Cascade Construction",
            Proceedings of FOCS'96.

   [Dobb]   H. Dobbertin, "The Status of MD5 After a Recent Attack",
            RSA Labs' CryptoBytes, Vol. 2 No. 2, Summer 1996.
            http://www.rsa.com/rsalabs/pubs/cryptobytes.html

   [PV]   B. Preneel and P. van Oorschot, "Building fast MACs from hash
            functions", Advances in Cryptology — CRYPTO'95 Proceedings,
            Lecture Notes in Computer Science, Springer-Verlag Vol.963,
            1995, pp. 1-14.

   [MD5]   Rivest, R., "The MD5 Message-Digest Algorithm",
            RFC 1321, April 1992.

```
```

[MM]   Meyer, S. and Matyas, S.M., Cryptography, New York Wiley, 1982.

[RIPEMD] H. Dobbertin, A. Bosselaers, and B. Preneel, "RIPEMD-160: A strengthened version of RIPEMD", Fast Software Encryption, LNCS Vol 1039, pp. 71-82. ftp://ftp.esat.kuleuven.ac.be/pub/COSIC/bosselae/ripemd/.

[SHA]   NIST, FIPS PUB 180-1: Secure Hash Standard, April 1995.

[Tsu]   G. Tsudik, "Message authentication with one-way hash functions", In Proceedings of Infocom'92, May 1992. (Also in "Access Control and Policy Enforcement in Internetworks", Ph.D. Dissertation, Computer Science Department, University of Southern California, April 1991.)

[VW]   P. van Oorschot and M. Wiener, "Parallel Collision Search with Applications to Hash Functions and Discrete Logarithms", Proceedings of the 2nd ACM Conf. Computer and Communications Security, Fairfax, VA, November 1994.

Authors' Addresses

Hugo Krawczyk
IBM T.J. Watson Research Center
P.O.Box 704
Yorktown Heights, NY 10598

EMail: hugo@watson.ibm.com

Mihir Bellare
Dept of Computer Science and Engineering
Mail Code 0114
University of California at San Diego
9500 Gilman Drive
La Jolla, CA 92093

EMail: mihir@cs.ucsd.edu

Ran Canetti
IBM T.J. Watson Research Center
P.O.Box 704
Yorktown Heights, NY 10598

EMail: canetti@watson.ibm.com

11

RFC 2104

Network Working Group   C. Adams
Request for Comments: 2144   Entrust Technologies
Category: Informational   May 1997

The CAST-128 Encryption Algorithm

Status of this Memo

Abstract

   There is a need in the Internet community for an unencumbered
   encryption algorithm with a range of key sizes that can provide
   security for a variety of cryptographic applications and protocols.

   This document describes an existing algorithm that can be used to
   satisfy this requirement. Included are a description of the cipher
   and the key scheduling algorithm (Section 2), the s-boxes (Appendix
   A), and a set of test vectors (Appendix B).

TABLE OF CONTENTS

1. Introduction

   This document describes the CAST-128 encryption algorithm, a DES-like
   Substitution-Permutation Network (SPN) cryptosystem which appears to
   have good resistance to differential cryptanalysis, linear
   cryptanalysis, and related-key cryptanalysis. This cipher also
   possesses a number of other desirable cryptographic properties,
   including avalanche, Strict Avalanche Criterion (SAC), Bit
   Independence Criterion (BIC), no complementation property, and an
   absence of weak and semi-weak keys. It thus appears to be a good

candidate for general-purpose use throughout the Internet community
wherever a cryptographically-strong, freely-available encryption
algorithm is required.

Adams [Adams] discusses the CAST design procedure in some detail;
analyses can also be obtained on-line (see, for example, [Web1] or
[Web2]).

2. Description of Algorithm

CAST-128 belongs to the class of encryption algorithms known as
Feistel ciphers; overall operation is thus similar to the Data
Encryption Standard (DES). The full encryption algorithm is given in
the following four steps.

INPUT: plaintext m1...m64; key K = k1...k128.
OUTPUT: ciphertext c1...c64.

1. (key schedule) Compute 16 pairs of subkeys {Kmi, Kri} from K
   (see Sections 2.1 and 2.4).
2. (L0,R0) <— (m1...m64). (Split the plaintext into left and
   right 32-bit halves L0 = m1...m32 and R0 = m33...m64.)
3. (16 rounds) for i from 1 to 16, compute Li and Ri as follows:
   Li = Ri-1;
   Ri = Li-1 ^ f(Ri-1,Kmi,Kri), where f is defined in Section 2.2
     (f is of Type 1, Type 2, or Type 3, depending on i).
4. c1...c64 <— (R16,L16). (Exchange final blocks L16, R16 and
   concatenate to form the ciphertext.)

Decryption is identical to the encryption algorithm given above,
except that the rounds (and therefore the subkey pairs) are used in
reverse order to compute (L0,R0) from (R16,L16).

See Appendix B for test vectors which can be used to verify
correctness of an implementation of this algorithm.

2.1. Pairs of Round Keys

CAST-128 uses a pair of subkeys per round: a 32-bit quantity Km is
used as a "masking" key and a 5-bit quantity Kr is used as a
"rotation" key.

2.2. Non-Identical Rounds

Three different round functions are used in CAST-128. The rounds are
as follows (where "D" is the data input to the f function and "Ia" -
"Id" are the most significant byte through least significant byte of
I, respectively). Note that "+" and "-" are addition and subtraction
modulo 2**32, "^" is bitwise XOR, and "<<<" is the circular left-
shift operation.

```
    Type 1:  I = ((Kmi + D) <<< Kri)
             f = ((S1[Ia] ^ S2[Ib]) - S3[Ic]) + S4[Id]

    Type 2:  I = ((Kmi ^ D) <<< Kri)
             f = ((S1[Ia] - S2[Ib]) + S3[Ic]) ^ S4[Id]

    Type 3:  I = ((Kmi - D) <<< Kri)
             f = ((S1[Ia] + S2[Ib]) ^ S3[Ic]) - S4[Id]
```

Rounds 1, 4, 7, 10, 13, and 16 use f function Type 1.
Rounds 2, 5, 8, 11, and 14 use f function Type 2.
Rounds 3, 6, 9, 12, and 15 use f function Type 3.

2.3. Substitution Boxes

CAST-128 uses eight substitution boxes: s-boxes S1, S2, S3, and S4
are round function s-boxes; S5, S6, S7, and S8 are key schedule s-
boxes. Although 8 s-boxes require a total of 8 KBytes of storage,
note that only 4 KBytes are required during actual encryption /
decryption since subkey generation is typically done prior to any
data input.

See Appendix A for the contents of s-boxes S1 - S8.

2.4. Key Schedule

Let the 128-bit key be x0x1x2x3x4x5x6x7x8x9xAxBxCxDxExF, where x0
represents the most significant byte and xF represents the least
significant byte.

Let z0..zF be intermediate (temporary) bytes.
Let Si[] represent s-box i and let "^" represent XOR addition.

The subkeys are formed from the key x0x1x2x3x4x5x6x7x8x9xAxBxCxDxExF
as follows.

```
z0z1z2z3 = x0x1x2x3 ^ S5[xD] ^ S6[xF] ^ S7[xC] ^ S8[xE] ^ S7[x8]
z4z5z6z7 = x8x9xAxB ^ S5[z0] ^ S6[z2] ^ S7[z1] ^ S8[z3] ^ S8[xA]
z8z9zAzB = xCxDxExF ^ S5[z7] ^ S6[z6] ^ S7[z5] ^ S8[z4] ^ S5[x9]
zCzDzEzF = x4x5x6x7 ^ S5[zA] ^ S6[z9] ^ S7[zB] ^ S8[z8] ^ S6[xB]
K1  = S5[z8] ^ S6[z9] ^ S7[z7] ^ S8[z6] ^ S5[z2]
K2  = S5[zA] ^ S6[zB] ^ S7[z5] ^ S8[z4] ^ S6[z6]
K3  = S5[zC] ^ S6[zD] ^ S7[z3] ^ S8[z2] ^ S7[z9]
K4  = S5[zE] ^ S6[zF] ^ S7[z1] ^ S8[z0] ^ S8[zC]
x0x1x2x3 = z8z9zAzB ^ S5[z5] ^ S6[z7] ^ S7[z4] ^ S8[z6] ^ S7[z0]
x4x5x6x7 = z0z1z2z3 ^ S5[x0] ^ S6[x2] ^ S7[x1] ^ S8[x3] ^ S8[z2]
x8x9xAxB = z4z5z6z7 ^ S5[x7] ^ S6[x6] ^ S7[x5] ^ S8[x4] ^ S5[z1]
xCxDxExF = zCzDzEzF ^ S5[xA] ^ S6[x9] ^ S7[xB] ^ S8[x8] ^ S6[z3]
K5  = S5[x3] ^ S6[x2] ^ S7[xC] ^ S8[xD] ^ S5[x8]
K6  = S5[x1] ^ S6[x0] ^ S7[xE] ^ S8[xF] ^ S6[xD]
K7  = S5[x7] ^ S6[x6] ^ S7[x8] ^ S8[x9] ^ S7[x3]
K8  = S5[x5] ^ S6[x4] ^ S7[xA] ^ S8[xB] ^ S8[x7]
z0z1z2z3 = x0x1x2x3 ^ S5[xD] ^ S6[xF] ^ S7[xC] ^ S8[xE] ^ S7[x8]
z4z5z6z7 = x8x9xAxB ^ S5[z0] ^ S6[z2] ^ S7[z1] ^ S8[z3] ^ S8[xA]
z8z9zAzB = xCxDxExF ^ S5[z7] ^ S6[z6] ^ S7[z5] ^ S8[z4] ^ S5[x9]
zCzDzEzF = x4x5x6x7 ^ S5[zA] ^ S6[z9] ^ S7[zB] ^ S8[z8] ^ S6[xB]
K9  = S5[z3] ^ S6[z2] ^ S7[zC] ^ S8[zD] ^ S5[z9]
K10 = S5[z1] ^ S6[z0] ^ S7[zE] ^ S8[zF] ^ S6[zC]
K11 = S5[z7] ^ S6[z6] ^ S7[z8] ^ S8[z9] ^ S7[z2]
K12 = S5[z5] ^ S6[z4] ^ S7[zA] ^ S8[zB] ^ S8[z6]
x0x1x2x3 = z8z9zAzB ^ S5[z5] ^ S6[z7] ^ S7[z4] ^ S8[z6] ^ S7[z0]
x4x5x6x7 = z0z1z2z3 ^ S5[x0] ^ S6[x2] ^ S7[x1] ^ S8[x3] ^ S8[z2]
x8x9xAxB = z4z5z6z7 ^ S5[x7] ^ S6[x6] ^ S7[x5] ^ S8[x4] ^ S5[z1]
xCxDxExF = zCzDzEzF ^ S5[xA] ^ S6[x9] ^ S7[xB] ^ S8[x8] ^ S6[z3]
K13 = S5[x8] ^ S6[x9] ^ S7[x7] ^ S8[x6] ^ S5[x3]
K14 = S5[xA] ^ S6[xB] ^ S7[x5] ^ S8[x4] ^ S6[x7]
K15 = S5[xC] ^ S6[xD] ^ S7[x3] ^ S8[x2] ^ S7[x8]
K16 = S5[xE] ^ S6[xF] ^ S7[x1] ^ S8[x0] ^ S8[xD]
```

[The remaining half is identical to what is given above, carrying on from the last created x0..xF to generate keys K17 - K32.]

```
z0z1z2z3 = x0x1x2x3 ^ S5[xD] ^ S6[xF] ^ S7[xC] ^ S8[xE] ^ S7[x8]
z4z5z6z7 = x8x9xAxB ^ S5[z0] ^ S6[z2] ^ S7[z1] ^ S8[z3] ^ S8[xA]
z8z9zAzB = xCxDxExF ^ S5[z7] ^ S6[z6] ^ S7[z5] ^ S8[z4] ^ S5[x9]
zCzDzEzF = x4x5x6x7 ^ S5[zA] ^ S6[z9] ^ S7[zB] ^ S8[z8] ^ S6[xB]
K17 = S5[z8] ^ S6[z9] ^ S7[z7] ^ S8[z6] ^ S5[z2]
K18 = S5[zA] ^ S6[zB] ^ S7[z5] ^ S8[z4] ^ S6[z6]
K19 = S5[zC] ^ S6[zD] ^ S7[z3] ^ S8[z2] ^ S7[z9]
K20 = S5[zE] ^ S6[zF] ^ S7[z1] ^ S8[z0] ^ S8[zC]
x0x1x2x3 = z8z9zAzB ^ S5[z5] ^ S6[z7] ^ S7[z4] ^ S8[z6] ^ S7[z0]
x4x5x6x7 = z0z1z2z3 ^ S5[x0] ^ S6[x2] ^ S7[x1] ^ S8[x3] ^ S8[z2]
x8x9xAxB = z4z5z6z7 ^ S5[x7] ^ S6[x6] ^ S7[x5] ^ S8[x4] ^ S5[z1]
xCxDxExF = zCzDzEzF ^ S5[xA] ^ S6[x9] ^ S7[xB] ^ S8[x8] ^ S6[z3]
K21 = S5[x3] ^ S6[x2] ^ S7[xC] ^ S8[xD] ^ S5[x8]
K22 = S5[x1] ^ S6[x0] ^ S7[xE] ^ S8[xF] ^ S6[xD]
K23 = S5[x7] ^ S6[x6] ^ S7[x8] ^ S8[x9] ^ S7[x3]
K24 = S5[x5] ^ S6[x4] ^ S7[xA] ^ S8[xB] ^ S8[x7]
z0z1z2z3 = x0x1x2x3 ^ S5[xD] ^ S6[xF] ^ S7[xC] ^ S8[xE] ^ S7[x8]
z4z5z6z7 = x8x9xAxB ^ S5[z0] ^ S6[z2] ^ S7[z1] ^ S8[z3] ^ S8[xA]
z8z9zAzB = xCxDxExF ^ S5[z7] ^ S6[z6] ^ S7[z5] ^ S8[z4] ^ S5[x9]
zCzDzEzF = x4x5x6x7 ^ S5[zA] ^ S6[z9] ^ S7[zB] ^ S8[z8] ^ S6[xB]
K25 = S5[z3] ^ S6[z2] ^ S7[zC] ^ S8[zD] ^ S5[z9]
K26 = S5[z1] ^ S6[z0] ^ S7[zE] ^ S8[zF] ^ S6[zC]
K27 = S5[z7] ^ S6[z6] ^ S7[z8] ^ S8[z9] ^ S7[z2]
K28 = S5[z5] ^ S6[z4] ^ S7[zA] ^ S8[zB] ^ S8[z6]
x0x1x2x3 = z8z9zAzB ^ S5[z5] ^ S6[z7] ^ S7[z4] ^ S8[z6] ^ S7[z0]
x4x5x6x7 = z0z1z2z3 ^ S5[x0] ^ S6[x2] ^ S7[x1] ^ S8[x3] ^ S8[z2]
x8x9xAxB = z4z5z6z7 ^ S5[x7] ^ S6[x6] ^ S7[x5] ^ S8[x4] ^ S5[z1]
xCxDxExF = zCzDzEzF ^ S5[xA] ^ S6[x9] ^ S7[xB] ^ S8[x8] ^ S6[z3]
K29 = S5[x8] ^ S6[x9] ^ S7[x7] ^ S8[x6] ^ S5[x3]
K30 = S5[xA] ^ S6[xB] ^ S7[x5] ^ S8[x4] ^ S6[x7]
K31 = S5[xC] ^ S6[xD] ^ S7[x3] ^ S8[x2] ^ S7[x8]
K32 = S5[xE] ^ S6[xF] ^ S7[x1] ^ S8[x0] ^ S8[xD]
```

2.4.1. Masking Subkeys And Rotate Subkeys

Let Km1, ..., Km16 be 32-bit masking subkeys (one per round).
Let Kr1,   , Kr16 be 32-bit rotate subkeys (one per round); only the least significant 5 bits are used in each round.

```
for (i=1; i<=16; i++)  { Kmi = Ki;   Kri = K16+i; }
```

2.5. Variable Keysize

The CAST-128 encryption algorithm has been designed to allow a key
size that can vary from 40 bits to 128 bits, in 8-bit increments
(that is, the allowable key sizes are 40, 48, 56, 64, ..., 112, 120,
and 128 bits. For variable keysize operation, the specification is
as follows:

1) For key sizes up to and including 80 bits (i.e., 40, 48, 56, 64,
   72, and 80 bits), the algorithm is exactly as specified but uses
   12 rounds instead of 16;

2) For key sizes greater than 80 bits, the algorithm uses the full 16
   rounds;

3) For key sizes less than 128 bits, the key is padded with zero
   bytes (in the rightmost, or least significant, positions) out to
   128 bits (since the CAST-128 key schedule assumes an input key of
   128 bits).

Note that although CAST-128 can support all 12 key sizes listed
above, 40 bits, 64 bits, 80 bits, and 128 bits are the sizes that
find utility in typical environments. Therefore, it will likely be
sufficient for most implementations to support some subset of only
these four sizes.

In order to avoid confusion when variable keysize operation is used,
the name CAST-128 is to be considered synonymous with the name CAST5;
this allows a keysize to be appended without ambiguity. Thus, for
example, CAST-128 with a 40-bit key is to be referred to as CAST5-40;
where a 128-bit key is explicitly intended, the name CAST5-128 should
be used.

2.6. CAST5 Object Identifiers

For those who may be using CAST in algorithm negotiation within a
protocol, or in any other context which may require the use of OBJECT
IDENTIFIERs, the following OIDs have been defined.

algorithms OBJECT IDENTIFIER ::=
   { iso(1) memberBody(2) usa(840) nt(113533) nsn(7) algorithms(66) }

```
cast5CBC OBJECT IDENTIFIER ::= { algorithms cast5CBC(10) }

    Parameters ::= SEQUENCE {
        iv          OCTET STRING DEFAULT 0,    — Initialization vector
        keyLength   INTEGER                    — Key length, in bits
    }
```

Note: The iv is optional and defaults to all-zero. On the encoding end, if an all-zero iv is used, then it should absent from the Parameters. On the decoding end, an absent iv should be interpreted as meaning all-zeros.

This is encryption and decryption in CBC mode using the CAST-128 symmetric block cipher algorithm.

```
cast5MAC OBJECT IDENTIFIER ::= { algorithms cast5MAC(11) }

    Parameters ::= SEQUENCE {
        macLength   INTEGER,       — MAC length, in bits
        keyLength   INTEGER        — Key length, in bits
    }
```

This is message authentication using the CAST-128 symmetric block cipher algorithm.

```
pbeWithMD5AndCast5CBC OBJECT IDENTIFIER ::=
    { algorithms pbeWithMD5AndCAST5-CBC(12) }

    Parameters ::= SEQUENCE {
        salt            OCTET STRING,
        iterationCount  INTEGER,       — Total number of hash iterations
        keyLength       INTEGER        — Key length, in bits
    }
```

Note: The IV is derived from the hashing procedure and therefore need not be included in Parameters.

This is password-based encryption and decryption in CBC mode using MD5 and the CAST-128 symmetric block cipher . See PKCS #5 (which uses the DES cipher) for details of the PBE computation.

2.7. Discussion

   CAST-128 is a 12- or 16-round Feistel cipher that has a blocksize of
   64 bits and a keysize of up to 128 bits; it uses rotation to provide
   intrinsic immunity to linear and differential attacks; it uses a
   mixture of XOR, addition and subtraction (modulo 2**32) in the round
   function; and it uses three variations of the round function itself
   throughout the cipher. Finally, the 8x32 s-boxes used in the round
   function each have a minimum nonlinearity of 74 and a maximum entry
   of 2 in the difference distribution table.

   This cipher appears to have cryptographic strength in accordance with
   its keysize (128 bits) and has very good encryption / decryption
   performance: 3.3 MBytes/sec on a 150 MHz Pentium processor.

3. Intellectual Property Considerations

   The CAST-128 cipher described in this document is available worldwide
   on a royalty-free basis for commercial and non-commercial uses.

4. Security Considerations

   This entire memo is about security since it describes an algorithm
   which is specifically intended for cryptographic purposes.

5. References

   [Adams] Adams, C., "Constructing Symmetric Ciphers using the CAST
   Design Procedure", Designs, Codes, and Cryptography (to appear).

   [Web1] "Constructing Symmetric Ciphers using the CAST Design
   Procedure" (identical to [Adams] but available on-line) and "CAST
   Design Procedure Addendum", http://www.entrust.com/library.htm.

   [Web2] "CAST Encryption Algorithm Related Publications",
   http://adonis.ee.queensu.ca:8000/cast/cast.html.

6. Author's Address

   Carlisle Adams
   Entrust Technologies
   750 Heron Road,
   Ottawa, Canada, K1V 1A7

   E-mail: cadams@entrust.com
   Phone: +1.613.763.9008

Appendix A. S-Boxes

S-Box S1

```
30fb40d4 9fa0ff0b 6beccd2f 3f258c7a 1e213f2f 9c004dd3 6003e540 cf9fc949
bfd4af27 88bbbdb5 e2034090 98d09675 6e63a0e0 15c361d2 c2e7661d 22d4ff8e
28683b6f c07fd059 ff2379c8 775f50e2 43c340d3 df2f8656 887ca41a a2d2bd2d
a1c9e0d6 346c4819 61b76d87 22540f2f 2abe32e1 aa54166b 22568e3a a2d341d0
66db40c8 a784392f 004dff2f 2db9d2de 97943fac 4a97c1d8 527644b7 b5f437a7
b82cbaef d751d159 6ff7f0ed 5a097a1f 827b68d0 90ecf52e 22b0c054 bc8e5935
4b6d2f7f 50bb64a2 d2664910 bee5812d b7332290 e93b159f b48ee411 4bff345d
fd45c240 ad31973f c4f6d02e 55fc8165 d5b1caad a1ac2dae a2d4b76d c19b0c50
882240f2 0c6e4f38 a4e4bfd7 4f5ba272 564c1d2f c59c5319 b949e354 b04669fe
b1b6ab8a c71358dd 6385c545 110f935d 57538ad5 6a390493 e63d37e0 2a54f6b3
3a787d5f 6276a0b5 19a6fcdf 7a42206a 29f9d4d5 f61b1891 bb72275e aa508167
38901091 c6b505eb 84c7cb8c 2ad75a0f 874a1427 a2d1936b 2ad286af aa56d291
d7894360 425c750d 93b39e26 187184c9 6c00b32d 73e2bb14 a0bebc3c 54623779
64459eab 3f328b82 7718cf82 59a2cea6 04ee002e 89fe78e6 3fab0950 325ff6c2
81383f05 6963c5c8 76cb5ad6 d49974c9 ca180dcf 380782d5 c7fa5cf6 8ac31511
35e79e13 47da91d0 f40f9086 a7e2419e 31366241 051ef495 aa573b04 4a805d8d
548300d0 00322a3c bf64cddf ba57a68e 75c6372b 50afd341 a7c13275 915a0bf5
6b54bfab 2b0b1426 ab4cc9d7 449ccd82 f7fbf265 ab85c5f3 1b55db94 aad4e324
cfa4bd3f 2deaa3e2 9e204d02 c8bd25ac eadf55b3 d5bd9e98 e31231b2 2ad5ad6c
954329de adbe4528 d8710f69 aa51c90f aa786bf6 22513f1e aa51a79b 2ad344cc
7b5a41f0 d37cfbad 1b069505 41ece491 b4c332e6 032268d4 c9600acc ce387e6d
bf6bb16c 6a70fb78 0d03d9c9 d4df39de e01063da 4736f464 5ad328d8 b347cc96
75bb0fc3 98511bfb 4ffbcc35 b58bcf6a e11f0abc bfc5fe4a a70aec10 ac39570a
3f04442f 6188b153 e0397a2e 5727cb79 9ceb418f 1cacd68d 2ad37c96 0175cb9d
c69dff09 c75b65f0 d9db40d8 ec0e7779 4744ead4 b11c3274 dd24cb9e 7e1c54bd
f01144f9 d2240eb1 9675b3fd a3ac3755 d47c27af 51c85f4d 56907596 a5bb15e6
580304f0 ca042cf1 011a37ea 8dbfaadb 35ba3e4a 3526ffa0 c37b4d09 bc306ed9
98a52666 5648f725 ff5e569d 0ced63d0 7c63b2cf 700b45e1 d5ea50f1 85a92872
af1fbda7 d4234870 a7870bf3 2d3b4d79 42e04198 0cd0ede7 26470db8 f881814c
474d6ad7 7c0c5e5c d1231959 381b7298 f5d2f4db ab838653 6e2f1e23 83719c9e
bd91e046 9a56456e dc39200c 20c8c571 962bda1c e1e696ff b141ab08 7cca89b9
1a69e783 02cc4843 a2f7c579 429ef47d 427b169c 5ac9f049 dd8f0f00 5c8165bf
```

S-Box S2

```
1f201094 ef0ba75b 69e3cf7e 393f4380 fe61cf7a eec5207a 55889c94 72fc0651
ada7ef79 4e1d7235 d55a63ce de0436ba 99c430ef 5f0c0794 18dcdb7d a1d6eff3
a0b52f7b 59e83605 ee15b094 e9ffd909 dc440086 ef944459 ba83ccb3 e0c3cdfb
d1da4181 3b092ab1 f997f1c1 a5e6cf7b 01420ddb e4e7ef5b 25a1ff41 e180f806
1fc41080 179bee7a d37ac6a9 fe5830a4 98de8b7f 77e83f4e 79929269 24fa9f7b
e113c85b acc40083 d7503525 f7ea615f 62143154 0d554b63 5d681121 c866c359
3d63cf73 cee234c0 d4d87e87 5c672b21 071f6181 39f7627f 361e3084 e4eb573b
602f64a4 d63acd9c 1bbc4635 9e81032d 2701f50c 99847ab4 a0e3df79 ba6cf38c
10843094 2537a95e f46f6ffe a1ff3b1f 208cfb6a 8f458c74 d9e0a227 4ec73a34
fc884f69 3e4de8df ef0e0088 3559648d 8a45388c 1d804366 721d9bfd a58684bb
e8256333 844e8212 128d8098 fed33fb4 ce280ae1 27e19ba5 d5a6c252 e49754bd
```

```
c5d655dd  eb667064  77840b4d  a1b6a801  84db26a9  e0b56714  21f043b7  e5d05860
54f03084  066ff472  a31aa153  dadc4755  b5625dbf  68561be6  83ca6b94  2d6ed23b
eccf01db  a6d3d0ba  b6803d5c  af77a709  33b4a34c  397bc8d6  5ee22b95  5f0e5304
81ed6f61  20e74364  b45e1378  de18639b  881ca122  b96726d1  8049a7e8  22b7da7b
5e552d25  5272d237  79d2951c  c60d894c  488cb402  1ba4fe5b  a4b09f6b  1ca815cf
a20c3005  8871df63  b9de2fcb  0cc6c9e9  0beeff53  e3214517  b4542835  9f63293c
ee41e729  6e1d2d7c  50045286  1e6685f3  f33401c6  30a22c95  31a70850  60930f13
73f98417  a1269859  ec645c44  52c877a9  cdff33a6  a02b1741  7cbad9a2  2180036f
50d99c08  cb3f4861  c26bd765  64a3f6ab  80342676  25a75e7b  e4e6d1fc  20c710e6
cdf0b680  17844d3b  31eef84d  7e0824e4  2ccb49eb  846a3bae  8ff77888  ee5d60f6
7af75673  2fdd5cdb  a11631c1  30f66f43  b3faec54  157fd7fa  ef8579cc  d152de58
db2ffd5e  8f32ce19  306af97a  02f03ef8  99319ad5  c242fa0f  a7e3ebb0  c68e4906
b8da230c  80823028  dcdef3c8  d35fb171  088a1bc8  bec0c560  61a3c9e8  bca8f54d
c72feffa  22822e99  82c570b4  d8d94e89  8b1c34bc  301e16e6  273be979  b0ffeaa6
61d9b8c6  00b24869  b7ffce3f  08dc283b  43daf65a  f7e19798  7619b72f  8f1c9ba4
dc8637a0  16a7d3b1  9fc393b7  a7136eeb  c6bcc63e  1a513742  ef6828bc  520365d6
2d6a77ab  3527ed4b  821fd216  095c6e2e  db92f2fb  5eea29cb  145892f5  91584f7f
5483697b  2667a8cc  85196048  8c4bacea  833860d4  0d23e0f9  6c387e8a  0ae6d249
b284600c  d835731d  dcb1c647  ac4c56ea  3ebd81b3  230eabb0  6438bc87  f0b5b1fa
8f5ea2b3  fc184642  0a036b7a  4fb089bd  649da589  a345415e  5c038323  3e5d3bb9
43d79572  7e6dd07c  06dfdf1e  6c6cc4ef  7160a539  73bfbe70  83877605  4523ecf1
```

S-Box S3
```
8defc240  25fa5d9f  eb903dbf  e810c907  47607fff  369fe44b  8c1fc644  aececa90
beb1f9bf  eefbcaea  e8cf1950  51df07ae  920e8806  f0ad0548  e13c8d83  927010d5
11107d9f  07647db9  b2e3e4d4  3d4f285e  b9afa820  fade82e0  a067268b  8272792e
553fb2c0  489ae22b  d4ef9794  125e3fbc  21fffcee  825b1bfd  9255c5ed  1257a240
4e1a8302  bae07fff  528246e7  8e57140e  3373f7bf  8c9f8188  a6fc4ee8  c982b5a5
a8c01db7  579fc264  67094f31  f2bd3f5f  40fff7c1  1fb78dfc  8e6bd2c1  437be59b
99b03dbf  b5dbc64b  638dc0e6  55819d99  a197c81c  4a012d6e  c5884a28  ccc36f71
b843c213  6c0743f1  8309893c  0feddd5f  2f7fe850  d7c07f7e  02507fbf  5afb9a04
a747d2d0  1651192e  af70bf3e  58c31380  5f98302e  727cc3c4  0a0fb402  0f7fef82
8c96fdad  5d2c2aae  8ee99a49  50da88b8  8427f4a0  1eac5790  796fb449  8252dc15
efbd7d9b  a672597d  ada840d8  45f54504  fa5d7403  e83ec305  4f91751a  925669c2
23efe941  a903f12e  60270df2  0276e4b6  94fd6574  927985b2  8276dbcb  02778176
f8af918d  4e48f79e  8f616ddf  e29d840e  842f7d83  340ce5c8  96bbb682  93b4b148
ef303cab  984faf28  779faf9b  92dc560d  224d1e20  8437aa88  7d29dc96  2756d3dc
8b907cee  b51fd240  e7c07ce3  e566b4a1  c3e9615e  3cf8209d  6094d1e3  cd9ca341
5c76460e  00ea983b  d4d67881  fd47572c  f76cedd9  bda8229c  127dadaa  438a074e
1f97c090  081bdb8a  93a07ebe  b938ca15  97b03cff  3dc2c0f8  8d1ab2ec  64380e51
68cc7bfb  d90f2788  12490181  5de5ffd4  dd7ef86a  76a2e214  b9a40368  925d958f
4b39fffa  ba39aee9  a4ffd30b  faf7933b  6d498623  193cbcfa  27627545  825cf47a
61bd8ba0  d11e42d1  cead04f4  127ea392  10428db7  8272a972  9270c4a8  127de50b
285ba1c8  3c62f44f  35c0eaa5  e805d231  428929fb  b4fcdf82  4fb66a53  0e7dc15b
1f081fab  108618ae  fcfd086d  f9ff2889  694bcc11  236a5cae  12deca4d  2c3f8cc5
d2d02dfe  f8ef5896  e4cf52da  95155b67  494a488c  b9b6a80c  5c8f82bc  89d36b45
3a609437  ec00c9a9  44715253  0a874b49  d773bc40  7c34671c  02717ef6  4feb5536
a2d02fff  d2bf60c4  d43f03c0  50b4ef6d  07478cd1  006e1888  a2e53f55  b9e6d4bc
```

```
a2048016 97573833 d7207d67 de0f8f3d 72f87b33 abcc4f33 7688c55d 7b00a6b0
947b0001 570075d2 f9bb88f8 8942019e 4264a5ff 856302e0 72dbd92b ee971b69
6ea22fde 5f08ae2b af7a616d e5c98767 cf1febd2 61efc8c2 f1ac2571 cc8239c2
67214cb8 b1e583d1 b7dc3e62 7f10bdce f90a5c38 0ff0443d 606e6dc6 60543a49
5727c148 2be98a1d 8ab41738 20e1be24 af96da0f 68458425 99833be5 600d457d
282f9350 8334b362 d91d1120 2b6d8da0 642b1e31 9c305a00 52bce688 1b03588a
f7baefd5 4142ed9c a4315c11 83323ec5 dfef4636 a133c501 e9d3531c ee353783
```

S-Box S4
```
9db30420 1fb6e9de a7be7bef d273a298 4a4f7bdb 64ad8c57 85510443 fa020ed1
7e287aff e60fb663 095f35a1 79ebf120 fd059d43 6497b7b1 f3641f63 241e4adf
28147f5f 4fa2b8cd c9430040 0cc32220 fdd30b30 c0a5374f 1d2d00d9 24147b15
ee4d111a 0fca5167 71ff904c 2d195ffe 1a05645f 0c13fefe 081b08ca 05170121
80530100 e83e5efe ac9af4f8 7fe72701 d2b8ee5f 06df4261 bb9e9b8a 7293ea25
ce84ffdf f5718801 3dd64b04 a26f263b 7ed48400 547eebe6 446d4ca0 6cf3d6f5
2649abdf aea0c7f5 36338cc1 503f7e93 d3772061 11b638e1 72500e03 f80eb2bb
abe0502e ec8d77de 57971e81 e14f6746 c9335400 6920318f 081dbb99 ffc304a5
4d351805 7f3d5ce3 a6c866c6 5d5bcca9 daec6fea 9f926f91 9f46222f 3991467d
a5bf6d8e 1143c44f 43958302 d0214eeb 022083b8 3fb6180c 18f8931e 281658e6
26486e3e 8bd78a70 7477e4c1 b506e07c f32d0a25 79098b02 e4eabb81 28123b23
69dead38 1574ca16 df871b62 211c40b7 a51a9ef9 0014377b 041e8ac8 09114003
bd59e4d2 e3d156d5 4fe876d5 2f91a340 557be8de 00eae4a7 0ce5c2ec 4db4bba6
e756bdff dd3369ac ec17b035 06572327 99afc8b0 56c8c391 6b65811c 5e146119
6e85cb75 be07c002 c2325577 893ff4ec 5bbfc92d d0ec3b25 b7801ab7 8d6d3b24
20c763ef c366a5fc 9c382880 0ace3205 aac9548a eca1d7c7 041afa32 1d16625a
6701902c 9b757a54 31d477f7 9126b031 36cc6fdb c70b8b46 d9e66a48 56e55a79
026a4ceb 52437eff 2f8f76b4 0df980a5 8674cde3 edda04eb 17a9be04 2c18f4df
b7747f9d ab2af7b4 efc34d20 2e096b7c 1741a254 e5b6a035 213d42f6 2c1c7c26
61c2f50f 6552daf9 d2c231f8 25130f69 d8167fa2 0418f2c8 001a96a6 0d1526ab
63315c21 5e0a72ec 49bafefd 187908d9 8d0dbd86 311170a7 3e9b640c cc3e10d7
d5cad3b6 0caec388 f73001e1 6c728aff 71eae2a1 1f9af36e cfcbd12f c1de8417
ac07be6b cb44a1d8 8b9b0f56 013988c3 b1c52fca b4be31cd d8782806 12a3a4e2
6f7de532 58fd7eb6 d01ee900 24adffc2 f4990fc5 9711aac5 001d7b95 82e5e7d2
109873f6 00613096 c32d9521 ada121ff 29908415 7fbb977f af9eb3db 29c9ed2a
5ce2a465 a730f32c d0aa3fe8 8a5cc091 d49e2ce7 0ce454a9 d60acd86 015f1919
77079103 dea03af6 78a8565e dee356df 21f05cbe 8b75e387 b3c50651 b8a5c3ef
d8eeb6d2 e523be77 c2154529 2f69efdf afe67afb f470c4b2 f3e0eb5b d6cc9876
39e4460c 1fda8538 1987832f ca007367 a99144f8 296b2998 492fc295 9266beab
b5676e69 9bd3ddda df7e052f db25701c 1b5e51ee f65324e6 6afce36c 0316cc04
8644213e b7dc59d0 7965291f ccd6fd43 41823979 932bcdf6 b657c34d 4edfd282
7ae5290c 3cb9536b 851e20fe 9833557e 13ecf0b0 d3ffb372 3f85c5c1 0aef7ed2
```

S-Box S5
```
7ec90c04 2c6e74b9 9b0e66df a6337911 b86a7fff 1dd358f5 44dd9d44 1731167f
08fbf1fa e7f511cc d2051b00 735aba00 2ab722d8 386381cb acf6243a 69befd7a
e6a2e77f f0c720cd c4494816 ccf5c180 38851640 15b0a848 e68b18cb 4caadeff
5f480a01 0412b2aa 259814fc 41d0efe2 4e40b48d 248eb6fb 8dba1cfe 41a99b02
1a550a04 ba8f65cb 7251f4e7 95a51725 c106ecd7 97a5980a c539b9aa 4d79fe6a
```

```
f2f3f763 68af8040 ed0c9e56 11b4958b e1eb5a88 8709e6b0 d7e07156 4e29fea7
6366e52d 02d1c000 c4ac8e05 9377f571 0c05372a 578535f2 2261be02 d642a0c9
df13a280 74b55bd2 682199c0 d421e5ec 53fb3ce8 c8adedb3 28a87fc9 3d959981
5c1ff900 fe38d399 0c4eff0b 062407ea aa2f4fb1 4fb96976 90c79505 b0a8a774
ef55a1ff e59ca2c2 a6b62d27 e66a4263 df65001f 0ec50966 dfdd55bc 29de0655
911e739a 17af8975 32c7911c 89f89468 0d01e980 524755f4 03b63cc9 0cc844b2
bcf3f0aa 87ac36e9 e53a7426 01b3d82b 1a9e7449 64ee2d7e cddbb1da 01c94910
b868bf80 0d26f3fd 9342ede7 04a5c284 636737b6 50f5b616 f24766e3 8eca36c1
136e05db fef18391 fb887a37 d6e7f7d4 c7fb7dc9 3063fcdf b6f589de ec2941da
26e46695 b7566419 f654efc5 d08d58b7 48925401 c1bacb7f e5ff550f b6083049
5bb5d0e8 87d72e5a ab6a6ee1 223a66ce c62bf3cd 9e0885f9 68cb3e47 086c010f
a21de820 d18b69de f3f65777 fa02c3f6 407edac3 cbb3d550 1793084d b0d70eba
0ab378d5 d951fb0c ded7da56 4124bbe4 94ca0b56 0f5755d1 e0e1e56e 6184b5be
580a249f 94f74bc0 e327888e 9f7b5561 c3dc0280 05687715 646c6bd7 44904db3
66b4f0a3 c0f1648a 697ed5af 49e92ff6 309e374f 2cb6356a 85808573 4991f840
76f0ae02 083be84d 28421c9a 44489406 736e4cb8 c1092910 8bc95fc6 7d869cf4
134f616f 2e77118d b31b2be1 aa90b472 3ca5d717 7d161bba 9cad9010 af462ba2
9fe459d2 45d34559 d9f2da13 dbc65487 f3e4f94e 176d486f 097c13ea 631da5c7
445f7382 175683f4 cdc66a97 70be0288 b3cdcf72 6e5dd2f3 20936079 459b80a5
be60e2db a9c23101 eba5315c 224e42f2 1c5c1572 f6721b2c 1ad2fff3 8c25404e
324ed72f 4067b7fd 0523138e 5ca3bc78 dc0fd66e 75922283 784d6b17 58ebb16e
44094f85 3f481d87 fcfeae7b 77b5ff76 8c2302bf aaf47556 5f46b02a 2b092801
3d38f5f7 0ca81f36 52af4a8a 66d5e7c0 df3b0874 95055110 1b5ad7a8 f61ed5ad
6cf6e479 20758184 d0cefa65 88f7be58 4a046826 0ff6f8f3 a09c7f70 5346aba0
5ce96c28 e176eda3 6bac307f 376829d2 85360fa9 17e3fe2a 24b79767 f5a96b20
d6cd2595 68ff1ebf 7555442c f19f06be f9e0659a eeb9491d 34010718 bb30cab8
e822fe15 88570983 750e6249 da627e55 5e76ffa8 b1534546 6d47de08 efe9e7d4


S-Box S6
f6fa8f9d 2cac6ce1 4ca34867 e2337f7c 95db08e7 016843b4 eced5cbc 325553ac
bf9f0960 dfa1e2ed 83f0579d 63ed86b9 1ab6a6b8 de5ebe39 f38ff732 8989b138
33f14961 c01937bd f506c6da e4625e7e a308ea99 4e23e33c 79cbd7cc 48a14367
a3149619 fec94bd5 a114174a eaa01866 a084db2d 09a8486f a888614a 2900af98
01665991 e1992863 c8f30c60 2e78ef3c d0d51932 cf0fec14 f7ca07d2 d0a82072
fd41197e 9305a6b0 e86be3da 74bed3cd 372da53c 4c7f4448 dab5d440 6dba0ec3
083919a7 9fbaeed9 49dbcfb0 4e670c53 5c3d9c01 64bdb941 2c0e636a ba7dd9cd
ea6f7388 e70bc762 35f29adb 5c4cdd8d f0d48d8c b88153e2 08a19866 1ae2eac8
284caf89 aa928223 9334be53 3b3a21bf 16434be3 9aea3906 efe8c36e f890cdd9
80226dae c340a4a3 df7e9c09 a694a807 5b7c5ecc 221db3a6 9a69a02f 68818a54
ceb2296f 53c0843a fe893655 25bfe68a b4628abc cf222ebf 25ac6f48 a9a99387
53bddb65 e76ffbe7 e967fd78 0ba93563 8e342bc1 e8a11be9 4980740d c8087dfc
8de4bf99 a11101a0 7fd37975 da5a26c0 e81f994f 9528cd89 fd339fed b87834bf
5f04456d 22258698 c9c4c83b 2dc156be 4f628daa 57f55ec5 e2220abe d2916ebf
4ec75b95 24f2c3c0 42d15d99 cd0d7fa0 7b6e27ff a8dc8af0 7345c106 f41e232f
35162386 e6ea8926 3333b094 157ec6f2 372b74af 692573e4 e9a9d848 f3160289
3a62ef1d a787e238 f3a5f676 74364853 20951063 4576698d b6fad407 592af950
36f73523 4cfb6e87 7da4cec0 6c152daa cb0396a8 c50dfe5d fcd707ab 0921c42f
89dff0bb 5fe2be78 448f4f33 754613c9 2b05d08d 48b9d585 dc049441 c8098f9b
```

```
7dede786 c39a3373 42410005 6a091751 0ef3c8a6 890072d6 28207682 a9a9f7be
bf32679d d45b5b75 b353fd00 cbb0e358 830f220a 1f8fb214 d372cf08 cc3c4a13
8cf63166 061c87be 88c98f88 6062e397 47cf8e7a b6c85283 3cc2acfb 3fc06976
4e8f0252 64d8314d da3870e3 1e665459 c10908f0 513021a5 6c5b68b7 822f8aa0
3007cd3e 74719eef dc872681 073340d4 7e432fd9 0c5ec241 8809286c f592d891
08a930f6 957ef305 b7fbffbd c266e96f 6fe4ac98 b173ecc0 bc60b42a 953498da
fba1ae12 2d4bd736 0f25faab a4f3fceb e2969123 257f0c3d 9348af49 361400bc
e8816f4a 3814f200 a3f94043 9c7a54c2 bc704f57 da41e7f9 c25ad33a 54f4a084
b17f5505 59357cbe edbd15c8 7f97c5ab ba5ac7b5 b6f6deaf 3a479c3a 5302da25
653d7e6a 54268d49 51a477ea 5017d55b d7d25d88 44136c76 0404a8c8 b8e5a121
b81a928a 60ed5869 97c55b96 eaec991b 29935913 01fdb7f1 088e8dfa 9ab6f6f5
3b4cbf9f 4a5de3ab e6051d35 a0e1d855 d36b4cf1 f544edeb b0e93524 bebb8fbd
a2d762cf 49c92f54 38b5f331 7128a454 48392905 a65b1db8 851c97bd d675cf2f
```

S-Box S7
```
85e04019 332bf567 662dbfff cfc65693 2a8d7f6f ab9bc912 de6008a1 2028da1f
0227bce7 4d642916 18fac300 50f18b82 2cb2cb11 b232e75c 4b3695f2 b28707de
a05fbcf6 cd4181e9 e150210c e24ef1bd b168c381 fde4e789 5c79b0d8 1e8bfd43
4d495001 38be4341 913cee1d 92a79c3f 089766be baeeadf4 1286becf b6eacb19
2660c200 7565bde4 64241f7a 8248dca9 c3b3ad66 28136086 0bd8dfa8 356d1cf2
107789be b3b2e9ce 0502aa8f 0bc0351e 166bf52a eb12ff82 e3486911 d34d7516
4e7b3aff 5f43671b 9cf6e037 4981ac83 334266ce 8c9341b7 d0d854c0 cb3a6c88
47bc2829 4725ba37 a66ad22b 7ad61f1e 0c5cbafa 4437f107 b6e79962 42d2d816
0a961288 e1a5c06e 13749e67 72fc081a b1d139f7 f9583745 cf19df58 bec3f756
c06eba30 07211b24 45c28829 c95e317f bc8ec511 38bc46e9 c6e6fa14 bae8584a
ad4ebc46 468f508b 7829435f f124183b 821dba9f aff60ff4 ea2c4e6d 16e39264
92544a8b 009b4fc3 aba68ced 9ac96f78 06a5b79a b2856e6e 1aec3ca9 be838688
0e0804e9 55f1be56 e7e5363b b3a1f25d f7debb85 61fe033c 16746233 3c034c28
da6d0c74 79aac56c 3ce4e1ad 51f0c802 98f8f35a 1626a49f eed82b29 1d382fe3
0c4fb99a bb325778 3ec6d97b 6e77a6a9 cb658b5c d45230c7 2bd1408b 60c03eb7
b9068d78 a33754f4 f430c87d c8a71302 b96d8c32 ebd4e7be be8b9d2d 7979fb06
e7225308 8b75cf77 11ef8da4 e083c858 8d6b786f 5a6317a6 fa5cf7a0 5dda0033
f28ebfb0 f5b9c310 a0eac280 08b9767a a3d9d2b0 79d34217 021a718d 9ac6336a
2711fd60 438050e3 069908a8 3d7fedc4 826d2bef 4eeb8476 488dcf25 36c9d566
28e74e41 c2610aca 3d49a9cf bae3b9df b65f8de6 92aeaf64 3ac7d5e6 9ea80509
f22b017d a4173f70 dd1e16c3 15e0d7f9 50b1b887 2b9f4fd5 625aba82 6a017962
2ec01b9c 15488aa9 d716e740 40055a2c 93d29a22 e32dbf9a 058745b9 3453dc1e
d699296e 496cff6f 1c9f4986 dfe2ed07 b87242d1 19de7eae 053e561a 15ad6f8c
66626c1c 7154c24c ea082b2a 93eb2939 17dcb0f0 58d4f2ae 9ea294fb 52cf564c
9883fe66 2ec40581 763953c3 01d6692e d3a0c108 a1e7160e e4f2dfa6 693ed285
74904698 4c2b0edd 4f757656 5d393378 a132234f 3d321c5d c3f5e194 4b269301
c79f022f 3c997e7e 5e4f9504 3ffafbbd 76f7ad0e 296693f4 3d1fce6f c61e45be
d3b5ab34 f72bf9b7 1b0434c0 4e72b567 5592a33d b5229301 cfd2a87f 60aeb767
1814386b 30bcc33d 38a0c07d fd1606f2 c363519b 589dd390 5479f8e6 1cb8d647
97fd61a9 ea7759f4 2d57539d 569a58cf e84e63ad 462e1b78 6580f87e f3817914
91da55f4 40a230f3 d1988f35 b6e318d2 3ffa50bc 3d40f021 c3c0bdae 4958c24c
518f36b2 84b1d370 0fedce83 878ddada f2a279c7 94e01be8 90716f4b 954b8aa3
```

S-Box S8
```
e216300d bbddfffc a7ebdabd 35648095 7789f8b7 e6c1121b 0e241600 052ce8b5
11a9cfb0 e5952f11 ece7990a 9386d174 2a42931c 76e38111 b12def3a 37ddddfc
de9adeb1 0a0cc32c be197029 84a00940 bb243a0f b4d137cf b44e79f0 049eedfd
0b15a15d 480d3168 8bbbde5a 669ded42 c7ece831 3f8f95e7 72df191b 7580330d
94074251 5c7dcdfa abbe6d63 aa402164 b301d40a 02e7d1ca 53571dae 7a3182a2
12a8ddec fdaa335d 176f43e8 71fb46d4 38129022 ce949ad4 b84769ad 965bd862
82f3d055 66fb9767 15b80b4e 1d5b47a0 4cfde06f c28ec4b8 57e8726e 647a78fc
99865d44 608bd593 6c200e03 39dc5ff6 5d0b00a3 ae63aff2 7e8bd632 70108c0c
bbd35049 2998df04 980cf42a 9b6df491 9e7edd53 06918548 58cb7e07 3b74ef2e
522fffb1 d24708cc 1c7e27cd a4eb215b 3cf1d2e2 19b47a38 424f7618 35856039
9d17dee7 27eb35e6 c9aff67b 36baf5b8 09c467cd c18910b1 e11dbf7b 06cd1af8
7170c608 2d5e3354 d4de495a 64c6d006 bcc0c62c 3dd00db3 708f8f34 77d51b42
264f620f 24b8d2bf 15c1b79e 46a52564 f8d7e54e 3e378160 7895cda5 859c15a5
e6459788 c37bc75f db07ba0c 0676a3ab 7f229b1e 31842e7b 24259fd7 f8bef472
835ffcb8 6df4c1f2 96f5b195 fd0af0fc b0fe134c e2506d3d 4f9b12ea f215f225
a223736f 9fb4c428 25d04979 34c713f8 c4618187 ea7a6e98 7cd16efc 1436876c
f1544107 bedeee14 56e9af27 a04aa441 3cf7c899 92ecbae6 dd67016d 151682eb
a842eedf fdba60b4 f1907b75 20e3030f 24d8c29e e139673b efa63fb8 71873054
b6f2cf3b 9f326442 cb15a4cc b01a4504 f1e47d8d 844a1be5 bae7dfdc 42cbda70
cd7dae0a 57e85b7a d53f5af6 20cf4d8c cea4d428 79d130a4 3486ebfb 33d3cddc
77853b53 37effcb5 c5068778 e580b3e6 4e68b8f4 c5c8b37e 0d809ea2 398feb7c
132a4f94 43b7950e 2fee7d1c 223613bd dd06caa2 37df932b c4248289 acf3ebc3
5715f6b7 ef3478dd f267616f c148cbe4 9052815e 5e410fab b48a2465 2eda7fa4
e87b40e4 e98ea084 5889e9e1 efd390fc dd07d35b db485694 38d7e5b2 57720101
730edebc 5b643113 94917e4f 503c2fba 646f1282 7523d24a e0779695 f9c17a8f
7a5b2121 d187b896 29263a4d ba510cdf 81f47c9f ad1163ed ea7b5965 1a00726e
11403092 00da6d77 4a0cdd61 ad1f4603 605bdfb0 9eedc364 22ebe6a8 cee7d28a
a0e736a0 5564a6b9 10853209 c7eb8f37 2de705ca 8951570f df09822b bd691a6c
aa12e4f2 87451c0f e0f6a27a 3ada4819 4cf1764f 0d771c2b 67cdb156 350d8384
5938fa0f 42399ef3 36997b07 0e84093d 4aa93e61 8360d87b 1fa98b0c 1149382c
e97625a5 0614d1b7 0e25244b 0c768347 589e8d82 0d2059d1 a466bb1e f8da0a82
04f19130 ba6e4ec0 99265164 1ee7230d 50b2ad80 eaee6801 8db2a283 ea8bf59e
```

Appendix B. Test Vectors

   This appendix provides test vectors for the CAST-128 cipher described
   this document.

B.1. Single Plaintext-Key-Ciphertext Sets

   In order to ensure that the algorithm is implemented correctly, the
   following test vectors can be used for verification (values given in
   hexadecimal notation).

```
   128-bit key        = 01 23 45 67 12 34 56 78 23 45 67 89 34 56 78 9A
           plaintext  = 01 23 45 67 89 AB CD EF
           ciphertext = 23 8B 4F E5 84 7E 44 B2

   80-bit  key        = 01 23 45 67 12 34 56 78 23 45
                      = 01 23 45 67 12 34 56 78 23 45 00 00 00 00 00 00
           plaintext  = 01 23 45 67 89 AB CD EF
           ciphertext = EB 6A 71 1A 2C 02 27 1B

   40-bit  key        = 01 23 45 67 12
                      = 01 23 45 67 12 00 00 00 00 00 00 00 00 00 00 00
           plaintext  = 01 23 45 67 89 AB CD EF
           ciphertext = 7A C8 16 D1 6E 9B 30 2E
```

B.2. Full Maintenance Test

   A maintenance test for CAST-128 has been defined to verify the
   correctness of implementations. It is defined in pseudo-code as
   follows, where a and b are 128-bit vectors, aL and aR are the
   leftmost and rightmost halves of a, bL and bR are the leftmost and
   rightmost halves of b, and encrypt(d,k) is the encryption in ECB mode
   of block d under key k.

```
   Initial a = 01 23 45 67 12 34 56 78 23 45 67 89 34 56 78 9A (hex)
   Initial b = 01 23 45 67 12 34 56 78 23 45 67 89 34 56 78 9A (hex)

   do 1,000,000 times
   {
       aL = encrypt(aL,b)
       aR = encrypt(aR,b)
       bL = encrypt(bL,a)
       bR = encrypt(bR,a)
   }
```

Verify a == EE A9 D0 A2 49 FD 3B A6 B3 43 6F B8 9D 6D CA 92 (hex)
Verify b == B2 C9 5E B0 0C 31 AD 71 80 AC 05 B8 E8 3D 69 6E (hex)

Network Working Group   P. Cheng
Request for Comments: 2202   IBM
Category: Informational   R. Glenn
                                                            NIST
                                                  September 1997

Test Cases for HMAC-MD5 and HMAC-SHA-1

Status of This Memo

Abstract

   This document provides two sets of test cases for HMAC-MD5 and HMAC-
   SHA-1, respectively. HMAC-MD5 and HMAC-SHA-1 are two constructs of
   the HMAC [HMAC] message authentication function using the MD5 [MD5]
   hash function and the SHA-1 [SHA] hash function. Both constructs are
   used by IPSEC [OG,CG] and other protocols to authenticate messages.
   The test cases and results provided in this document are meant to be
   used as a conformance test for HMAC-MD5 and HMAC-SHA-1
   implementations.

1. Introduction

   The general method for constructing a HMAC message authentication
   function using a particular hash function is described in section 2
   of [HMAC]. We will not repeat the description here. Section 5 of
   [HMAC] also discusses truncating the output of HMAC; the rule is that
   we should keep the more significant bits (the bits in the left,
   assuming a network byte order (big-endian)).

   In sections 2 and 3 we provide test cases for HMAC-MD5 and HMAC-SHA-
   1, respectively. Each case includes the key, the data, and the
   result. The values of keys and data are either hexadecimal numbers
   (prefixed by "0x") or ASCII character strings in double quotes. If a
   value is an ASCII character string, then the HMAC computation for the
   corresponding test case DOES NOT include the trailing null character
   ('\0') in the string.

The C source code of the functions used to generate HMAC-SHA-1
results is listed in the Appendix. Note that these functions are
meant to be simple and easy to understand; they are not optimized in
any way. The C source code for computing HMAC-MD5 can be found in
[MD5]; or you can do a simple modification to HMAC-SHA-1 code to get
HMAC-MD5 code, as explained in the Appendix.

The test cases in this document are cross-verified by three
independent implementations, one from NIST and two from IBM Research.
One IBM implementation uses optimized code that is very different
from the code in the Appendix. An implemenation that concurs with the
results provided in this document should be interoperable with other
similar implemenations. We do not claim that such an implementation
is absolutely correct with respect to the HMAC definition in [HMAC].

2. Test Cases for HMAC-MD5

```
test_case =       1
key =             0x0b0b0b0b0b0b0b0b0b0b0b0b0b0b0b0b
key_len =         16
data =            "Hi There"
data_len =        8
digest =          0x9294727a3638bb1c13f48ef8158bfc9d

test_case =       2
key =             "Jefe"
key_len =         4
data =            "what do ya want for nothing?"
data_len =        28
digest =          0x750c783e6ab0b503eaa86e310a5db738

test_case =       3
key =             0xaaaaaaaaaaaaaaaaaaaaaaaaaaaaaaaa
key_len           16
data =            0xdd repeated 50 times
data_len =        50
digest =          0x56be34521d144c88dbb8c733f0e8b3f6

test_case =       4
key =             0x0102030405060708090a0b0c0d0e0f10111213141516171819
key_len =         25
data =            0xcd repeated 50 times
data_len =        50
digest =          0x697eaf0aca3a3aea3a75164746ffaa79
```

```
test_case  =      5
key        =      0x0c0c0c0c0c0c0c0c0c0c0c0c0c0c0c0c
key_len    =      16
data       =      "Test With Truncation"
data_len   =      20
digest     =      0x56461ef2342edc00f9bab995690efd4c
digest-96         0x56461ef2342edc00f9bab995

test_case  =      6
key        =      0xaa repeated 80 times
key_len    =      80
data       =      "Test Using Larger Than Block-Size Key - Hash Key First"
data_len   =      54
digest     =      0x6b1ab7fe4bd7bf8f0b62e6ce61b9d0cd

test_case  =      7
key        =      0xaa repeated 80 times
key_len    =      80
data       =      "Test Using Larger Than Block-Size Key and Larger
                  Than One Block-Size Data"
data_len   =      73
digest     =      0x6f630fad67cda0ee1fb1f562db3aa53e
```

3. Test Cases for HMAC-SHA-1

```
test_case  =      1
key        =      0x0b0b0b0b0b0b0b0b0b0b0b0b0b0b0b0b0b0b0b0b
key_len    =      20
data       =      "Hi There"
data_len   =      8
digest     =      0xb617318655057264e28bc0b6fb378c8ef146be00

test_case  =      2
key        =      "Jefe"
key_len    =      4
data       =      "what do ya want for nothing?"
data_len   =      28
digest     =      0xeffcdf6ae5eb2fa2d27416d5f184df9c259a7c79

test_case  =      3
key        =      0xaaaaaaaaaaaaaaaaaaaaaaaaaaaaaaaaaaaaaaaa
key_len    =      20
data       =      0xdd repeated 50 times
data_len   =      50
digest     =      0x125d7342b9ac11cd91a39af48aa17b4f63f175d3
```

```
test_case =     4
key =           0x0102030405060708090a0b0c0d0e0f10111213141516171819
key_len =       25
data =          0xcd repeated 50 times
data_len =      50
digest =        0x4c9007f4026250c6bc8414f9bf50c86c2d7235dane 7
test_case =     5
key =           0x0c0c0c0c0c0c0c0c0c0c0c0c0c0c0c0c0c0c0c0c
key_len =       20
data =          "Test With Truncation"
data_len =      20
digest =        0x4c1a03424b55e07fe7f27be1d58bb9324a9a5a04
digest-96 =     0x4c1a03424b55e07fe7f27be1

test_case =     6
key =           0xaa repeated 80 times
key_len =       80
data =          "Test Using Larger Than Block-Size Key - Hash Key First"
data_len =      54
digest =        0xaa4ae5e15272d00e95705637ce8a3b55ed402112

test_case =     7
key =           0xaa repeated 80 times
key_len =       80
data =          "Test Using Larger Than Block-Size Key and Larger
                Than One Block-Size Data"
data_len =      73
digest =        0xe8e99d0f45237d786d6bbaa7965c7808bbff1a91
data_len =      20
digest =        0x4c1a03424b55e07fe7f27be1d58bb9324a9a5a04
digest-96 =     0x4c1a03424b55e07fe7f27be1

test_case =     6
key =           0xaa repeated 80 times
key_len =       80
data =          "Test Using Larger Than Block-Size Key - Hash Key
First"
data_len =      54
digest =        0xaa4ae5e15272d00e95705637ce8a3b55ed402112

test_case =     7
key =           0xaa repeated 80 times
key_len =       80
data =          "Test Using Larger Than Block-Size Key and Larger
                Than One Block-Size Data"
data_len =      73
digest =        0xe8e99d0f45237d786d6bbaa7965c7808bbff1a91
```

4. Security Considerations

   This docuemnt raises no security issues. Discussion on the strength
   of the HMAC construction can be found in [HMAC].

References

   [HMAC]   Krawczyk, H., Bellare, M., and R. Canetti,
              "HMAC: Keyed-Hashing for Message Authentication",
              RFC 2104, February 1997.

   [MD5]   Rivest, R., "The MD5 Message-Digest Algorithm",
              RFC 1321, April 1992.

   [SHA]   NIST, FIPS PUB 180-1: Secure Hash Standard, April 1995.

   [OG]   Oehler, M., and R. Glenn,
              "HMAC-MD5 IP Authentication with Replay Prevention",
              RFC 2085, February 1997.

   [CG]   Chang, S., and R. Glenn,
              "HMAC-SHA IP Authentication with Replay Prevention",
              Work in Progress.

Authors' Addresses

   Pau-Chen Cheng
   IBM T.J. Watson Research Center
   P.O.Box 704
   Yorktown Heights, NY 10598

   EMail: pau@watson.ibm.com

   Robert Glenn
   NIST
   Building 820, Room 455
   Gaithersburg, MD 20899

   EMail: rob.glenn@nist.gov

Appendix

   This appendix contains the C reference code which implements HMAC-
   SHA-1 using an existing SHA-1 library. It assumes that the SHA-1
   library has similar API's as those of the MD5 code described in RFC
   1321. The code for HMAC-MD5 is similar, just replace the strings
   "SHA" and "sha" with "MD5" and "md5". HMAC-MD5 code is also listed in
   RFC 2104.

```c
#ifndef SHA_DIGESTSIZE
#define SHA_DIGESTSIZE  20
#endif

#ifndef SHA_BLOCKSIZE
#define SHA_BLOCKSIZE   64
#endif

#ifndef MD5_DIGESTSIZE
#define MD5_DIGESTSIZE  16
#endif

#ifndef MD5_BLOCKSIZE
#define MD5_BLOCKSIZE   64
#endif

/* Function to print the digest */
void
pr_sha(FILE* fp, char* s, int t)
{
        int     i ;

        fprintf(fp, "0x") ;
        for (i = 0 ; i < t ; i++)
                fprintf(fp, "%02x", s[i]) ;
        fprintf(fp, "0) ;
}

void truncate
(
 char*  d1,    /* data to be truncated */
 char*  d2,    /* truncated data */
 int    len    /* length in bytes to keep */
)
{
        int     i ;
        for (i = 0 ; i < len ; i++) d2[i] = d1[i];
}
```

```
/* Function to compute the digest */
void
hmac_sha
(
 char*    k,      /* secret key */
 int      lk,     /* length of the key in bytes */
 char*    d,      /* data */
 int      ld,     /* length of data in bytes */
 char*    out,    /* output buffer, at least "t" bytes */
 int      t
)
{
        SHA_CTX ictx, octx ;
        char    isha[SHA_DIGESTSIZE], osha[SHA_DIGESTSIZE] ;
        char    key[SHA_DIGESTSIZE] ;
        char    buf[SHA_BLOCKSIZE] ;
        int     i ;

        if (lk > SHA_BLOCKSIZE) {

                SHA_CTX         tctx ;

                SHAInit(&tctx) ;
                SHAUpdate(&tctx, k, lk) ;
                SHAFinal(key, &tctx) ;

                k = key ;
                lk = SHA_DIGESTSIZE ;
        }

        /**** Inner Digest ****/

        SHAInit(&ictx) ;

        /* Pad the key for inner digest */
        for (i = 0 ; i < lk ; ++i) buf[i] = k[i] ^ 0x36 ;
        for (i = lk ; i < SHA_BLOCKSIZE ; ++i) buf[i] = 0x36 ;

        SHAUpdate(&ictx, buf, SHA_BLOCKSIZE) ;
        SHAUpdate(&ictx, d, ld) ;

        SHAFinal(isha, &ictx) ;

        /**** Outter Digest ****/

        SHAInit(&octx) ;

        /* Pad the key for outter digest */
```

```
        for (i = 0 ; i < lk ; ++i) buf[i] = k[i] ^ 0x5C ;
        for (i = lk ; i < SHA_BLOCKSIZE ; ++i) buf[i] = 0x5C ;

        SHAUpdate(&octx, buf, SHA_BLOCKSIZE) ;
        SHAUpdate(&octx, isha, SHA_DIGESTSIZE) ;

        SHAFinal(osha, &octx) ;

        /* truncate and print the results */
        t = t > SHA_DIGESTSIZE ? SHA_DIGESTSIZE : t ;
        truncate(osha, out, t) ;
        pr_sha(stdout, out, t) ;

    }
```

Network Working Group   R. Rivest
Request for Comments: 2268   MIT Laboratory for Computer Science
Category: Informational   and RSA Data Security, Inc.
                                                           March 1998

                A Description of the RC2(r) Encryption Algorithm

Status of this Memo

    This memo provides information for the Internet community. It does
    not specify an Internet standard of any kind. Distribution of this
    memo is unlimited.

Copyright Notice

1. Introduction

    This memo is an RSA Laboratories Technical Note. It is meant for
    informational use by the Internet community.

    This memo describes a conventional (secret-key) block encryption
    algorithm, called RC2, which may be considered as a proposal for a
    DES replacement. The input and output block sizes are 64 bits each.
    The key size is variable, from one byte up to 128 bytes, although the
    current implementation uses eight bytes.

    The algorithm is designed to be easy to implement on 16-bit
    microprocessors. On an IBM AT, the encryption runs about twice as
    fast as DES (assuming that key expansion has been done).

1.1 Algorithm description

    We use the term "word" to denote a 16-bit quantity. The symbol + will
    denote twos-complement addition. The symbol & will denote the bitwise
    "and" operation. The term XOR will denote the bitwise "exclusive-or"
    operation. The symbol ~ will denote bitwise complement. The symbol ^
    will denote the exponentiation operation. The term MOD will denote
    the modulo operation.

    There are three separate algorithms involved:

      Key expansion. This takes a (variable-length) input key and
      produces an expanded key consisting of 64 words K[0],...,K[63].

Encryption. This takes a 64-bit input quantity stored in words
R[0], ..., R[3] and encrypts it "in place" (the result is left in
R[0], ..., R[3]).

Decryption. The inverse operation to encryption.

2. Key expansion

Since we will be dealing with eight-bit byte operations as well as
16-bit word operations, we will use two alternative notations

for referring to the key buffer:

   For word operations, we will refer to the positions of the
        buffer as K[0], ..., K[63]; each K[i] is a 16-bit word.

   For byte operations, we will refer to the key buffer as
        L[0], ..., L[127]; each L[i] is an eight-bit byte.

These are alternative views of the same data buffer. At all times it
will be true that

$$K[i] = L[2*i] + 256*L[2*i+1].$$

(Note that the low-order byte of each K word is given before the
high-order byte.)

We will assume that exactly T bytes of key are supplied, for some T
in the range $1 <= T <= 128$. (Our current implementation uses T = 8.)
However, regardless of T, the algorithm has a maximum effective key
length in bits, denoted T1. That is, the search space is $2^{(8*T)}$, or
2^{T1}, whichever is smaller.

The purpose of the key-expansion algorithm is to modify the key
buffer so that each bit of the expanded key depends in a complicated
way on every bit of the supplied input key.

The key expansion algorithm begins by placing the supplied T-byte key
into bytes L[0], ..., L[T-1] of the key buffer.

The key expansion algorithm then computes the effective key length in
bytes T8 and a mask TM based on the effective key length in bits T1.
It uses the following operations:

T8 = (T1+7)/8;
TM = 255 MOD $2^{(8 + T1 - 8*T8)}$;

Thus TM has its $8 - (8*T8 - T1)$ least significant bits set.

For example, with an effective key length of 64 bits, T1 = 64, T8 = 8 and TM = 0xff. With an effective key length of 63 bits, T1 = 63, T8 = 8 and TM = 0x7f.

Here PITABLE[0], ..., PITABLE[255] is an array of "random" bytes based on the digits of PI = 3.14159... . More precisely, the array PITABLE is a random permutation of the values 0, ..., 255. Here is the PITABLE in hexadecimal notation:

```
     0  1  2  3  4  5  6  7  8  9  a  b  c  d  e  f
00: d9 78 f9 c4 19 dd b5 ed 28 e9 fd 79 4a a0 d8 9d
10: c6 7e 37 83 2b 76 53 8e 62 4c 64 88 44 8b fb a2
20: 17 9a 59 f5 87 b3 4f 13 61 45 6d 8d 09 81 7d 32
30: bd 8f 40 eb 86 b7 7b 0b f0 95 21 22 5c 6b 4e 82
40: 54 d6 65 93 ce 60 b2 1c 73 56 c0 14 a7 8c f1 dc
50: 12 75 ca 1f 3b be e4 d1 42 3d d4 30 a3 3c b6 26
60: 6f bf 0e da 46 69 07 57 27 f2 1d 9b bc 94 43 03
70: f8 11 c7 f6 90 ef 3e e7 06 c3 d5 2f c8 66 1e d7
80: 08 e8 ea de 80 52 ee f7 84 aa 72 ac 35 4d 6a 2a
90: 96 1a d2 71 5a 15 49 74 4b 9f d0 5e 04 18 a4 ec
a0: c2 e0 41 6e 0f 51 cb cc 24 91 af 50 a1 f4 70 39
b0: 99 7c 3a 85 23 b8 b4 7a fc 02 36 5b 25 55 97 31
c0: 2d 5d fa 98 e3 8a 92 ae 05 df 29 10 67 6c ba c9
d0: d3 00 e6 cf e1 9e a8 2c 63 16 01 3f 58 e2 89 a9
e0: 0d 38 34 1b ab 33 ff b0 bb 48 0c 5f b9 b1 cd 2e
f0: c5 f3 db 47 e5 a5 9c 77 0a a6 20 68 fe 7f c1 ad
```

The key expansion operation consists of the following two loops and intermediate step:

for i = T, T+1, ..., 127 do
  L[i] = PITABLE[L[i-1] + L[i-T]];

L[128-T8] = PITABLE[L[128-T8] & TM];

for i = 127-T8, ..., 0 do
  L[i] = PITABLE[L[i+1] XOR L[i+T8]];

(In the first loop, the addition of L[i-1] and L[i-T] is performed modulo 256.)

The "effective key" consists of the values L[128-T8],..., L[127]. The intermediate step's bitwise "and" operation reduces the search space for L[128-T8] so that the effective number of key bits is T1. The expanded key depends only on the effective key bits, regardless

of the supplied key K. Since the expanded key is not itself modified
during encryption or decryption, as a pragmatic matter one can expand
the key just once when encrypting or decrypting a large block of
data.

3. Encryption algorithm

   The encryption operation is defined in terms of primitive "mix" and
   "mash" operations.

   Here the expression "x rol k" denotes the 16-bit word x rotated left
   by k bits, with the bits shifted out the top end entering the bottom
   end.

3.1 Mix up R[i]

   The primitive "Mix up R[i]" operation is defined as follows, where
   s[0] is 1, s[1] is 2, s[2] is 3, and s[3] is 5, and where the indices
   of the array R are always to be considered "modulo 4," so that R[i-1]
   refers to R[3] if i is 0 (these values are

   "wrapped around" so that R always has a subscript in the range 0 to 3
   inclusive):

   R[i] = R[i] + K[j] + (R[i-1] & R[i-2]) + ((~R[i-1]) & R[i-3]);
   j = j + 1;
   R[i] = R[i] rol s[i];

   In words: The next key word K[j] is added to R[i], and j is advanced.
   Then R[i-1] is used to create a "composite" word which is added to
   R[i]. The composite word is identical with R[i-2] in those positions
   where R[i-1] is one, and identical to R[i-3] in those positions where
   R[i-1] is zero. Then R[i] is rotated left by s[i] bits (bits rotated
   out the left end of R[i] are brought back in at the right). Here j is
   a "global" variable so that K[j] is always the first key word in the
   expanded key which has not yet been used in a "mix" operation.

3.2 Mixing round

   A "mixing round" consists of the following operations:

   Mix up R[0]
   Mix up R[1]
   Mix up R[2]
   Mix up R[3]

3.3 Mash R[i]

The primitive "Mash R[i]" operation is defined as follows (using the previous conventions regarding subscripts for R):

R[i] = R[i] + K[R[i-1] & 63];

In words: R[i] is "mashed" by adding to it one of the words of the expanded key. The key word to be used is determined by looking at the low-order six bits of R[i-1], and using that as an index into the key array K.

3.4 Mashing round

A "mashing round" consists of:

Mash R[0]
Mash R[1]
Mash R[2]
Mash R[3]

3.5 Encryption operation

The entire encryption operation can now be described as follows. Here j is a global integer variable which is affected by the mixing operations.

    1. Initialize words R[0], ..., R[3] to contain the
       64-bit input value.

    2. Expand the key, so that words K[0], ..., K[63] become
       defined.

    3. Initialize j to zero.

    4. Perform five mixing rounds.

    5. Perform one mashing round.

    6. Perform six mixing rounds.

    7. Perform one mashing round.

    8. Perform five mixing rounds.

Note that each mixing round uses four key words, and that there are 16 mixing rounds altogether, so that each key word is used exactly

once in a mixing round. The mashing rounds will refer to up to eight
of the key words in a data-dependent manner. (There may be
repetitions, and the actual set of words referred to will vary from
encryption to encryption.)

4. Decryption algorithm

The decryption operation is defined in terms of primitive operations
that undo the "mix" and "mash" operations of the encryption
algorithm. They are named "r-mix" and "r-mash" (r- denotes the
reverse operation).

Here the expression "x ror k" denotes the 16-bit word x rotated right
by k bits, with the bits shifted out the bottom end entering the top
end.

4.1 R-Mix up R[i]

The primitive "R-Mix up R[i]" operation is defined as follows, where
s[0] is 1, s[1] is 2, s[2] is 3, and s[3] is 5, and where the indices
of the array R are always to be considered "modulo 4," so that R[i-1]
refers to R[3] if i is 0 (these values are "wrapped around" so that R
always has a subscript in the range 0 to 3 inclusive):

```
R[i] = R[i] ror s[i];
R[i] = R[i] - K[j] - (R[i-1] & R[i-2]) - ((~R[i-1]) & R[i-3]);
j = j - 1;
```

In words: R[i] is rotated right by s[i] bits (bits rotated out the
right end of R[i] are brought back in at the left). Here j is a
"global" variable so that K[j] is always the key word with greatest
index in the expanded key which has not yet been used in a "r-mix"
operation. The key word K[j] is subtracted from R[i], and j is
decremented. R[i-1] is used to create a "composite" word which is
subtracted from R[i]. The composite word is identical with R[i-2] in
those positions where R[i-1] is one, and identical to R[i-3] in those
positions where R[i-1] is zero.

4.2 R-Mixing round

An "r-mixing round" consists of the following operations:

```
R-Mix up R[3]
R-Mix up R[2]
R-Mix up R[1]
R-Mix up R[0]
```

4.3 R-Mash R[i]

The primitive "R-Mash R[i]" operation is defined as follows (using
the previous conventions regarding subscripts for R):

R[i] = R[i] - K[R[i-1] & 63];

In words: R[i] is "r-mashed" by subtracting from it one of the words
of the expanded key. The key word to be used is determined by looking
at the low-order six bits of R[i-1], and using that as an index into
the key array K.

4.4 R-Mashing round

An "r-mashing round" consists of:

R-Mash R[3]
R-Mash R[2]
R-Mash R[1]
R-Mash R[0]

4.5 Decryption operation

The entire decryption operation can now be described as follows.
Here j is a global integer variable which is affected by the mixing
operations.

   1. Initialize words R[0], ..., R[3] to contain the 64-bit
      ciphertext value.

   2. Expand the key, so that words K[0], ..., K[63] become
      defined.

   3. Initialize j to 63.

   4. Perform five r-mixing rounds.

   5. Perform one r-mashing round.

   6. Perform six r-mixing rounds.

   7. Perform one r-mashing round.

   8. Perform five r-mixing rounds.

5. Test vectors

Test vectors for encryption with RC2 are provided below.

All quantities are given in hexadecimal notation.

```
Key length (bytes) = 8
Effective key length (bits) = 63
Key = 00000000 00000000
Plaintext = 00000000 00000000
Ciphertext = ebb773f9 93278eff

Key length (bytes) = 8
Effective key length (bits) = 64
Key = ffffffff ffffffff
Plaintext = ffffffff ffffffff
Ciphertext = 278b27e4 2e2f0d49

Key length (bytes) = 8
Effective key length (bits) = 64
Key = 30000000 00000000
Plaintext = 10000000 00000001
Ciphertext = 30649edf 9be7d2c2

Key length (bytes) = 1
Effective key length (bits) = 64
Key = 88
Plaintext = 00000000 00000000
Ciphertext = 61a8a244 adacccf0

Key length (bytes) = 7
Effective key length (bits) = 64
Key = 88bca90e 90875a
Plaintext = 00000000 00000000
Ciphertext = 6ccf4308 974c267f

Key length (bytes) = 16
Effective key length (bits) = 64
Key = 88bca90e 90875a7f 0f79c384 627bafb2
Plaintext = 00000000 00000000
Ciphertext = 1a807d27 2bbe5db1

Key length (bytes) = 16
Effective key length (bits) = 128
Key = 88bca90e 90875a7f 0f79c384 627bafb2
Plaintext = 00000000 00000000
Ciphertext = 2269552a b0f85ca6

Key length (bytes) = 33
Effective key length (bits) = 129
Key = 88bca90e 90875a7f 0f79c384 627bafb2 16f80a6f 85920584
      c42fceb0 be255daf 1e
```

```
Plaintext = 00000000 00000000
Ciphertext = 5b78d3a4 3dfff1f1
```

6. RC2 Algorithm Object Identifier

The Object Identifier for RC2 in cipher block chaining mode is

```
rc2CBC OBJECT IDENTIFIER
  ::= {iso(1) member-body(2) US(840) rsadsi(113549)
       encryptionAlgorithm(3) 2}
```

RC2-CBC takes parameters

```
RC2-CBCParameter ::= CHOICE {
  iv IV,
  params SEQUENCE {
    version RC2Version,
    iv IV
  }
}
```

where

```
IV ::= OCTET STRING — 8 octets
RC2Version ::= INTEGER — 1-1024
```

RC2 in CBC mode has two parameters: an 8-byte initialization vector
(IV) and a version number in the range 1-1024 which specifies in a
roundabout manner the number of effective key bits to be used for the
RC2 encryption/decryption.

The correspondence between effective key bits and version number is
as follows:

1. If the number EKB of effective key bits is in the range 1-255,
   then the version number is given by Table[EKB], where the 256-byte
   translation table Table[] is specified below. Table[] specifies a
   permutation on the numbers 0-255; note that it is not the same
   table that appears in the key expansion phase of RC2.

2. If the number EKB of effective key bits is in the range
   256-1024, then the version number is simply EKB.

   The default number of effective key bits for RC2 is 32. If RC2-CBC
   is being performed with 32 effective key bits, the parameters
   should be supplied as a simple IV, rather than as a SEQUENCE
   containing a version and an IV.

```
          0  1  2  3  4  5  6  7  8  9  a  b  c  d  e  f

  00: bd 56 ea f2 a2 f1 ac 2a b0 93 d1 9c 1b 33 fd d0
  10: 30 04 b6 dc 7d df 32 4b f7 cb 45 9b 31 bb 21 5a
  20: 41 9f e1 d9 4a 4d 9e da a0 68 2c c3 27 5f 80 36
  30: 3e ee fb 95 1a fe ce a8 34 a9 13 f0 a6 3f d8 0c
  40: 78 24 af 23 52 c1 67 17 f5 66 90 e7 e8 07 b8 60
  50: 48 e6 1e 53 f3 92 a4 72 8c 08 15 6e 86 00 84 fa
  60: f4 7f 8a 42 19 f6 db cd 14 8d 50 12 ba 3c 06 4e
  70: ec b3 35 11 a1 88 8e 2b 94 99 b7 71 74 d3 e4 bf
  80: 3a de 96 0e bc 0a ed 77 fc 37 6b 03 79 89 62 c6
  90: d7 c0 d2 7c 6a 8b 22 a3 5b 05 5d 02 75 d5 61 e3
  a0: 18 8f 55 51 ad 1f 0b 5e 85 e5 c2 57 63 ca 3d 6c
  b0: b4 c5 cc 70 b2 91 59 0d 47 20 c8 4f 58 e0 01 e2
  c0: 16 38 c4 6f 3b 0f 65 46 be 7e 2d 7b 82 f9 40 b5
  d0: 1d 73 f8 eb 26 c7 87 97 25 54 b1 28 aa 98 9d a5
  e0: 64 6d 7a d4 10 81 44 ef 49 d6 ae 2e dd 76 5c 2f
  f0: a7 1c c9 09 69 9a 83 cf 29 39 b9 e9 4c ff 43 ab
```

A. Intellectual Property Notice

RC2 is a registered trademark of RSA Data Security, Inc. RSA's
copyrighted RC2 software is available under license from RSA Data
Security, Inc.

B. Author's Address

Ron Rivest
RSA Laboratories
100 Marine Parkway, #500
Redwood City, CA 94065 USA

Phone: (650) 595-7703
EMail: rsa-labs@rsa.com

C. Full Copyright Statement

Network Working Group   S. Kent
Request for Comments: 2401   BBN Corp
Obsoletes: 1825   R. Atkinson
Category: Standards Track   @Home Network
                                                         November 1998

             Security Architecture for the Internet Protocol

Status of this Memo

Copyright Notice

Table of Contents

1. Introduction

1.1 Summary of Contents of Document

   This memo specifies the base architecture for IPsec compliant
   systems. The goal of the architecture is to provide various security
   services for traffic at the IP layer, in both the IPv4 and IPv6
   environments. This document describes the goals of such systems,
   their components and how they fit together with each other and into
   the IP environment. It also describes the security services offered
   by the IPsec protocols, and how these services can be employed in the
   IP environment. This document does not address all aspects of IPsec
   architecture. Subsequent documents will address additional
   architectural details of a more advanced nature, e.g., use of IPsec
   in NAT environments and more complete support for IP multicast. The
   following fundamental components of the IPsec security architecture
   are discussed in terms of their underlying, required functionality.
   Additional RFCs (see Section 1.3 for pointers to other documents)
   define the protocols in (a), (c), and (d).

        a. Security Protocols -- Authentication Header (AH) and
           Encapsulating Security Payload (ESP)
        b. Security Associations -- what they are and how they work,
           how they are managed, associated processing
        c. Key Management -- manual and automatic (The Internet Key
           Exchange (IKE))
        d. Algorithms for authentication and encryption

   This document is not an overall Security Architecture for the
   Internet; it addresses security only at the IP layer, provided
   through the use of a combination of cryptographic and protocol
   security mechanisms.

   The keywords MUST, MUST NOT, REQUIRED, SHALL, SHALL NOT, SHOULD,
   SHOULD NOT, RECOMMENDED, MAY, and OPTIONAL, when they appear in this
   document, are to be interpreted as described in RFC 2119 [Bra97].

1.2 Audience

   The target audience for this document includes implementers of this
   IP security technology and others interested in gaining a general
   background understanding of this system. In particular, prospective
   users of this technology (end users or system administrators) are
   part of the target audience. A glossary is provided as an appendix

to help fill in gaps in background/vocabulary. This document assumes
that the reader is familiar with the Internet Protocol, related
networking technology, and general security terms and concepts.

1.3 Related Documents

   As mentioned above, other documents provide detailed definitions of
   some of the components of IPsec and of their inter-relationship.
   They include RFCs on the following topics:

      a. "IP Security Document Roadmap" [TDG97] -- a document
         providing guidelines for specifications describing encryption
         and authentication algorithms used in this system.
      b. security protocols -- RFCs describing the Authentication
         Header (AH) [KA98a] and Encapsulating Security Payload (ESP)
         [KA98b] protocols.
      c. algorithms for authentication and encryption -- a separate
         RFC for each algorithm.
      d. automatic key management -- RFCs on "The Internet Key
         Exchange (IKE)" [HC98], "Internet Security Association and
         Key Management Protocol (ISAKMP)" [MSST97],"The OAKLEY Key
         Determination Protocol" [Orm97], and "The Internet IP
         Security Domain of Interpretation for ISAKMP" [Pip98].

2. Design Objectives

2.1 Goals/Objectives/Requirements/Problem Description

   IPsec is designed to provide interoperable, high quality,
   cryptographically-based security for IPv4 and IPv6. The set of
   security services offered includes access control, connectionless
   integrity, data origin authentication, protection against replays (a
   form of partial sequence integrity), confidentiality (encryption),
   and limited traffic flow confidentiality. These services are
   provided at the IP layer, offering protection for IP and/or upper
   layer protocols.

   These objectives are met through the use of two traffic security
   protocols, the Authentication Header (AH) and the Encapsulating
   Security Payload (ESP), and through the use of cryptographic key
   management procedures and protocols. The set of IPsec protocols
   employed in any context, and the ways in which they are employed,
   will be determined by the security and system requirements of users,
   applications, and/or sites/organizations.

   When these mechanisms are correctly implemented and deployed, they
   ought not to adversely affect users, hosts, and other Internet
   components that do not employ these security mechanisms for

protection of their traffic. These mechanisms also are designed to
be algorithm-independent. This modularity permits selection of
different sets of algorithms without affecting the other parts of the
implementation. For example, different user communities may select
different sets of algorithms (creating cliques) if required.

A standard set of default algorithms is specified to facilitate
interoperability in the global Internet. The use of these
algorithms, in conjunction with IPsec traffic protection and key
management protocols, is intended to permit system and application
developers to deploy high quality, Internet layer, cryptographic
security technology.

2.2 Caveats and Assumptions

The suite of IPsec protocols and associated default algorithms are
designed to provide high quality security for Internet traffic.
However, the security offered by use of these protocols ultimately
depends on the quality of the their implementation, which is outside
the scope of this set of standards. Moreover, the security of a
computer system or network is a function of many factors, including
personnel, physical, procedural, compromising emanations, and
computer security practices. Thus IPsec is only one part of an
overall system security architecture.

Finally, the security afforded by the use of IPsec is critically
dependent on many aspects of the operating environment in which the
IPsec implementation executes. For example, defects in OS security,
poor quality of random number sources, sloppy system management
protocols and practices, etc. can all degrade the security provided
by IPsec. As above, none of these environmental attributes are
within the scope of this or other IPsec standards.

3. System Overview

This section provides a high level description of how IPsec works,
the components of the system, and how they fit together to provide
the security services noted above. The goal of this description is
to enable the reader to "picture" the overall process/system, see how
it fits into the IP environment, and to provide context for later
sections of this document, which describe each of the components in
more detail.

An IPsec implementation operates in a host or a security gateway
environment, affording protection to IP traffic. The protection
offered is based on requirements defined by a Security Policy
Database (SPD) established and maintained by a user or system
administrator, or by an application operating within constraints

established by either of the above. In general, packets are selected
for one of three processing modes based on IP and transport layer
header information (Selectors, Section 4.4.2) matched against entries
in the database (SPD). Each packet is either afforded IPsec security
services, discarded, or allowed to bypass IPsec, based on the
applicable database policies identified by the Selectors.

3.1 What IPsec Does

   IPsec provides security services at the IP layer by enabling a system
   to select required security protocols, determine the algorithm(s) to
   use for the service(s), and put in place any cryptographic keys
   required to provide the requested services. IPsec can be used to
   protect one or more "paths" between a pair of hosts, between a pair
   of security gateways, or between a security gateway and a host. (The
   term "security gateway" is used throughout the IPsec documents to
   refer to an intermediate system that implements IPsec protocols. For
   example, a router or a firewall implementing IPsec is a security
   gateway.)

   The set of security services that IPsec can provide includes access
   control, connectionless integrity, data origin authentication,
   rejection of replayed packets (a form of partial sequence integrity),
   confidentiality (encryption), and limited traffic flow
   confidentiality. Because these services are provided at the IP
   layer, they can be used by any higher layer protocol, e.g., TCP, UDP,
   ICMP, BGP, etc.

   The IPsec DOI also supports negotiation of IP compression [SMPT98],
   motivated in part by the observation that when encryption is employed
   within IPsec, it prevents effective compression by lower protocol
   layers.

3.2 How IPsec Works

   IPsec uses two protocols to provide traffic security --
   Authentication Header (AH) and Encapsulating Security Payload (ESP).
   Both protocols are described in more detail in their respective RFCs
   [KA98a, KA98b].

        o The IP Authentication Header (AH) [KA98a] provides
          connectionless integrity, data origin authentication, and an
          optional anti-replay service.
        o The Encapsulating Security Payload (ESP) protocol [KA98b] may
          provide confidentiality (encryption), and limited traffic flow
          confidentiality. It also may provide connectionless

integrity, data origin authentication, and an anti-replay
service. (One or the other set of these security services
must be applied whenever ESP is invoked.)
o Both AH and ESP are vehicles for access control, based on the
   distribution of cryptographic keys and the management of
   traffic flows relative to these security protocols.

These protocols may be applied alone or in combination with each
other to provide a desired set of security services in IPv4 and IPv6.
Each protocol supports two modes of use: transport mode and tunnel
mode. In transport mode the protocols provide protection primarily
for upper layer protocols; in tunnel mode, the protocols are applied
to tunneled IP packets. The differences between the two modes are
discussed in Section 4.

IPsec allows the user (or system administrator) to control the
granularity at which a security service is offered. For example, one
can create a single encrypted tunnel to carry all the traffic between
two security gateways or a separate encrypted tunnel can be created
for each TCP connection between each pair of hosts communicating
across these gateways. IPsec management must incorporate facilities
for specifying:

   o which security services to use and in what combinations
   o the granularity at which a given security protection should be
      applied
   o the algorithms used to effect cryptographic-based security

Because these security services use shared secret values
(cryptographic keys), IPsec relies on a separate set of mechanisms
for putting these keys in place. (The keys are used for
authentication/integrity and encryption services.) This document
requires support for both manual and automatic distribution of keys.
It specifies a specific public-key based approach (IKE -- [MSST97,
Orm97, HC98]) for automatic key management, but other automated key
distribution techniques MAY be used. For example, KDC-based systems
such as Kerberos and other public-key systems such as SKIP could be
employed.

3.3 Where IPsec May Be Implemented

There are several ways in which IPsec may be implemented in a host or
in conjunction with a router or firewall (to create a security
gateway). Several common examples are provided below:

   a. Integration of IPsec into the native IP implementation. This
      requires access to the IP source code and is applicable to
      both hosts and security gateways.

   b. "Bump-in-the-stack" (BITS) implementations, where IPsec is
      implemented "underneath" an existing implementation of an IP
      protocol stack, between the native IP and the local network
      drivers. Source code access for the IP stack is not required
      in this context, making this implementation approach
      appropriate for use with legacy systems. This approach, when
      it is adopted, is usually employed in hosts.

   c. The use of an outboard crypto processor is a common design
      feature of network security systems used by the military, and
      of some commercial systems as well. It is sometimes referred
      to as a "Bump-in-the-wire" (BITW) implementation. Such
      implementations may be designed to serve either a host or a
      gateway (or both). Usually the BITW device is IP
      addressable. When supporting a single host, it may be quite
      analogous to a BITS implementation, but in supporting a
      router or firewall, it must operate like a security gateway.

4. Security Associations

   This section defines Security Association management requirements for
   all IPv6 implementations and for those IPv4 implementations that
   implement AH, ESP, or both. The concept of a "Security Association"
   (SA) is fundamental to IPsec. Both AH and ESP make use of SAs and a
   major function of IKE is the establishment and maintenance of
   Security Associations. All implementations of AH or ESP MUST support
   the concept of a Security Association as described below. The
   remainder of this section describes various aspects of Security
   Association management, defining required characteristics for SA
   policy management, traffic processing, and SA management techniques.

4.1 Definition and Scope

   A Security Association (SA) is a simplex "connection" that affords
   security services to the traffic carried by it. Security services
   are afforded to an SA by the use of AH, or ESP, but not both. If
   both AH and ESP protection is applied to a traffic stream, then two
   (or more) SAs are created to afford protection to the traffic stream.
   To secure typical, bi-directional communication between two hosts, or
   between two security gateways, two Security Associations (one in each
   direction) are required.

   A security association is uniquely identified by a triple consisting
   of a Security Parameter Index (SPI), an IP Destination Address, and a
   security protocol (AH or ESP) identifier. In principle, the
   Destination Address may be a unicast address, an IP broadcast
   address, or a multicast group address. However, IPsec SA management
   mechanisms currently are defined only for unicast SAs. Hence, in the

discussions that follow, SAs will be described in the context of point-to-point communication, even though the concept is applicable in the point-to-multipoint case as well.

As noted above, two types of SAs are defined: transport mode and tunnel mode. A transport mode SA is a security association between two hosts. In IPv4, a transport mode security protocol header appears immediately after the IP header and any options, and before any higher layer protocols (e.g., TCP or UDP). In IPv6, the security protocol header appears after the base IP header and extensions, but may appear before or after destination options, and before higher layer protocols. In the case of ESP, a transport mode SA provides security services only for these higher layer protocols, not for the IP header or any extension headers preceding the ESP header. In the case of AH, the protection is also extended to selected portions of the IP header, selected portions of extension headers, and selected options (contained in the IPv4 header, IPv6 Hop-by-Hop extension header, or IPv6 Destination extension headers). For more details on the coverage afforded by AH, see the AH specification [KA98a].

A tunnel mode SA is essentially an SA applied to an IP tunnel. Whenever either end of a security association is a security gateway, the SA MUST be tunnel mode. Thus an SA between two security gateways is always a tunnel mode SA, as is an SA between a host and a security gateway. Note that for the case where traffic is destined for a security gateway, e.g., SNMP commands, the security gateway is acting as a host and transport mode is allowed. But in that case, the security gateway is not acting as a gateway, i.e., not transiting traffic. Two hosts MAY establish a tunnel mode SA between themselves. The requirement for any (transit traffic) SA involving a security gateway to be a tunnel SA arises due to the need to avoid potential problems with regard to fragmentation and reassembly of IPsec packets, and in circumstances where multiple paths (e.g., via different security gateways) exist to the same destination behind the security gateways.

For a tunnel mode SA, there is an "outer" IP header that specifies the IPsec processing destination, plus an "inner" IP header that specifies the (apparently) ultimate destination for the packet. The security protocol header appears after the outer IP header, and before the inner IP header. If AH is employed in tunnel mode, portions of the outer IP header are afforded protection (as above), as well as all of the tunneled IP packet (i.e., all of the inner IP header is protected, as well as higher layer protocols). If ESP is employed, the protection is afforded only to the tunneled packet, not to the outer header.

In summary,
> a) A host MUST support both transport and tunnel mode.
> b) A security gateway is required to support only tunnel
> mode. If it supports transport mode, that should be used
> only when the security gateway is acting as a host, e.g.,
> for network management.

4.2 Security Association Functionality

The set of security services offered by an SA depends on the security
protocol selected, the SA mode, the endpoints of the SA, and on the
election of optional services within the protocol. For example, AH
provides data origin authentication and connectionless integrity for
IP datagrams (hereafter referred to as just "authentication"). The
"precision" of the authentication service is a function of the
granularity of the security association with which AH is employed, as
discussed in Section 4.4.2, "Selectors".

AH also offers an anti-replay (partial sequence integrity) service at
the discretion of the receiver, to help counter denial of service
attacks. AH is an appropriate protocol to employ when
confidentiality is not required (or is not permitted, e.g , due to
government restrictions on use of encryption). AH also provides
authentication for selected portions of the IP header, which may be
necessary in some contexts. For example, if the integrity of an IPv4
option or IPv6 extension header must be protected en route between
sender and receiver, AH can provide this service (except for the
non-predictable but mutable parts of the IP header.)

ESP optionally provides confidentiality for traffic. (The strength
of the confidentiality service depends in part, on the encryption
algorithm employed.) ESP also may optionally provide authentication
(as defined above). If authentication is negotiated for an ESP SA,
the receiver also may elect to enforce an anti-replay service with
the same features as the AH anti-replay service. The scope of the
authentication offered by ESP is narrower than for AH, i.e., the IP
header(s) "outside" the ESP header is(are) not protected. If only
the upper layer protocols need to be authenticated, then ESP
authentication is an appropriate choice and is more space efficient
than use of AH encapsulating ESP. Note that although both
confidentiality and authentication are optional, they cannot both be
omitted. At least one of them MUST be selected.

If confidentiality service is selected, then an ESP (tunnel mode) SA
between two security gateways can offer partial traffic flow
confidentiality. The use of tunnel mode allows the inner IP headers
to be encrypted, concealing the identities of the (ultimate) traffic
source and destination. Moreover, ESP payload padding also can be

invoked to hide the size of the packets, further concealing the
external characteristics of the traffic. Similar traffic flow
confidentiality services may be offered when a mobile user is
assigned a dynamic IP address in a dialup context, and establishes a
(tunnel mode) ESP SA to a corporate firewall (acting as a security
gateway). Note that fine granularity SAs generally are more
vulnerable to traffic analysis than coarse granularity ones which are
carrying traffic from many subscribers.

4.3 Combining Security Associations

The IP datagrams transmitted over an individual SA are afforded
protection by exactly one security protocol, either AH or ESP, but
not both. Sometimes a security policy may call for a combination of
services for a particular traffic flow that is not achievable with a
single SA. In such instances it will be necessary to employ multiple
SAs to implement the required security policy. The term "security
association bundle" or "SA bundle" is applied to a sequence of SAs
through which traffic must be processed to satisfy a security policy.
The order of the sequence is defined by the policy. (Note that the
SAs that comprise a bundle may terminate at different endpoints. For
example, one SA may extend between a mobile host and a security
gateway and a second, nested SA may extend to a host behind the
gateway.)

Security associations may be combined into bundles in two ways:
transport adjacency and iterated tunneling.

        o Transport adjacency refers to applying more than one
          security protocol to the same IP datagram, without invoking
          tunneling. This approach to combining AH and ESP allows
          for only one level of combination; further nesting yields
          no added benefit (assuming use of adequately strong
          algorithms in each protocol) since the processing is
          performed at one IPsec instance at the (ultimate)
          destination.

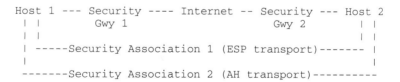

```
Host 1 --- Security ---- Internet -- Security --- Host 2
  | |         Gwy 1                      Gwy 2        | |
  | |                                                 | |
  | -----Security Association 1 (ESP transport)------- |
  |                                                     |
  -------Security Association 2 (AH transport)----------
```

        o Iterated tunneling refers to the application of multiple
          layers of security protocols effected through IP tunneling.
          This approach allows for multiple levels of nesting, since
          each tunnel can originate or terminate at a different IPsec

site along the path. No special treatment is expected for
ISAKMP traffic at intermediate security gateways other than
what can be specified through appropriate SPD entries (See
Case 3 in Section 4.5)

There are 3 basic cases of iterated tunneling -- support is
required only for cases 2 and 3.:

1. both endpoints for the SAs are the same -- The inner and
   outer tunnels could each be either AH or ESP, though it
   is unlikely that Host 1 would specify both to be the
   same, i.e., AH inside of AH or ESP inside of ESP.

```
Host 1 --- Security ---- Internet -- Security --- Host 2
 | |         Gwy 1                     Gwy 2        | |
 | |                                               | |
 | -------Security Association 1 (tunnel)---------- | |
 |                                                  |
 ---------Security Association 2 (tunnel)-------------
```

2. one endpoint of the SAs is the same -- The inner and
   uter tunnels could each be either AH or ESP.

```
Host 1 --- Security ---- Internet -- Security --- Host 2
 | |         Gwy 1                     Gwy 2         |
 | |                                   |            |
 | ----Security Association 1 (tunnel)----          |
 |                                                  |
 ---------Security Association 2 (tunnel)------------
```

3. neither endpoint is the same -- The inner and outer
   tunnels could each be either AH or ESP.

```
Host 1 --- Security ---- Internet -- Security --- Host 2
 |           Gwy 1                     Gwy 2         |
 |             |                         |          |
 |             --Security Assoc 1 (tunnel)-         |
 |                                                  |
 -----------Security Association 2 (tunnel)----------
```

These two approaches also can be combined, e.g., an SA bundle could
be constructed from one tunnel mode SA and one or two transport mode
SAs, applied in sequence. (See Section 4.5 "Basic Combinations of
Security Associations.") Note that nested tunnels can also occur
where neither the source nor the destination endpoints of any of the
tunnels are the same. In that case, there would be no host or
security gateway with a bundle corresponding to the nested tunnels.

For transport mode SAs, only one ordering of security protocols seems
appropriate. AH is applied to both the upper layer protocols and
(parts of) the IP header. Thus if AH is used in a transport mode, in
conjunction with ESP, AH SHOULD appear as the first header after IP,
prior to the appearance of ESP. In that context, AH is applied to
the ciphertext output of ESP. In contrast, for tunnel mode SAs, one
can imagine uses for various orderings of AH and ESP. The required
set of SA bundle types that MUST be supported by a compliant IPsec
implementation is described in Section 4.5.

4.4 Security Association Databases

Many of the details associated with processing IP traffic in an IPsec
implementation are largely a local matter, not subject to
standardization. However, some external aspects of the processing
must be standardized, to ensure interoperability and to provide a
minimum management capability that is essential for productive use of
IPsec. This section describes a general model for processing IP
traffic relative to security associations, in support of these
interoperability and functionality goals. The model described below
is nominal; compliant implementations need not match details of this
model as presented, but the external behavior of such implementations
must be mappable to the externally observable characteristics of this
model.

There are two nominal databases in this model: the Security Policy
Database and the Security Association Database. The former specifies
the policies that determine the disposition of all IP traffic inbound
or outbound from a host, security gateway, or BITS or BITW IPsec
implementation. The latter database contains parameters that are
associated with each (active) security association. This section
also defines the concept of a Selector, a set of IP and upper layer
protocol field values that is used by the Security Policy Database to
map traffic to a policy, i.e., an SA (or SA bundle).

Each interface for which IPsec is enabled requires nominally separate
inbound vs. outbound databases (SAD and SPD), because of the
directionality of many of the fields that are used as selectors.
Typically there is just one such interface, for a host or security
gateway (SG). Note that an SG would always have at least 2
interfaces, but the "internal" one to the corporate net, usually
would not have IPsec enabled and so only one pair of SADs and one
pair of SPDs would be needed. On the other hand, if a host had
multiple interfaces or an SG had multiple external interfaces, it
might be necessary to have separate SAD and SPD pairs for each
interface.

13

RFC 2401

4.4.1 The Security Policy Database (SPD)

Ultimately, a security association is a management construct used to
enforce a security policy in the IPsec environment. Thus an
essential element of SA processing is an underlying Security Policy
Database (SPD) that specifies what services are to be offered to IP
datagrams and in what fashion. The form of the database and its
interface are outside the scope of this specification. However, this
section does specify certain minimum management functionality that
must be provided, to allow a user or system administrator to control
how IPsec is applied to traffic transmitted or received by a host or
transiting a security gateway.

The SPD must be consulted during the processing of all traffic
(INBOUND and OUTBOUND), including non-IPsec traffic. In order to
support this, the SPD requires distinct entries for inbound and
outbound traffic. One can think of this as separate SPDs (inbound
vs. outbound). In addition, a nominally separate SPD must be
provided for each IPsec-enabled interface.

An SPD must discriminate among traffic that is afforded IPsec
protection and traffic that is allowed to bypass IPsec. This applies
to the IPsec protection to be applied by a sender and to the IPsec
protection that must be present at the receiver. For any outbound or
inbound datagram, three processing choices are possible: discard,
bypass IPsec, or apply IPsec. The first choice refers to traffic
that is not allowed to exit the host, traverse the security gateway,
or be delivered to an application at all. The second choice refers
to traffic that is allowed to pass without additional IPsec
protection. The third choice refers to traffic that is afforded
IPsec protection, and for such traffic the SPD must specify the
security services to be provided, protocols to be employed,
algorithms to be used, etc.

For every IPsec implementation, there MUST be an administrative
interface that allows a user or system administrator to manage the
SPD. Specifically, every inbound or outbound packet is subject to
processing by IPsec and the SPD must specify what action will be
taken in each case. Thus the administrative interface must allow the
user (or system administrator) to specify the security processing to
be applied to any packet entering or exiting the system, on a packet
by packet basis. (In a host IPsec implementation making use of a
socket interface, the SPD may not need to be consulted on a per
packet basis, but the effect is still the same.) The management
interface for the SPD MUST allow creation of entries consistent with
the selectors defined in Section 4.4.2, and MUST support (total)
ordering of these entries. It is expected that through the use of
wildcards in various selector fields, and because all packets on a

single UDP or TCP connection will tend to match a single SPD entry,
this requirement will not impose an unreasonably detailed level of
SPD specification. The selectors are analogous to what are found in
a stateless firewall or filtering router and which are currently
manageable this way.

In host systems, applications MAY be allowed to select what security
processing is to be applied to the traffic they generate and consume.
(Means of signalling such requests to the IPsec implementation are
outside the scope of this standard.) However, the system
administrator MUST be able to specify whether or not a user or
application can override (default) system policies. Note that
application specified policies may satisfy system requirements, so
that the system may not need to do additional IPsec processing beyond
that needed to meet an application's requirements. The form of the
management interface is not specified by this document and may differ
for hosts vs. security gateways, and within hosts the interface may
differ for socket-based vs. BITS implementations. However, this
document does specify a standard set of SPD elements that all IPsec
implementations MUST support.

The SPD contains an ordered list of policy entries. Each policy
entry is keyed by one or more selectors that define the set of IP
traffic encompassed by this policy entry. (The required selector
types are defined in Section 4.4.2.) These define the granularity of
policies or SAs. Each entry includes an indication of whether
traffic matching this policy will be bypassed, discarded, or subject
to IPsec processing. If IPsec processing is to be applied, the entry
includes an SA (or SA bundle) specification, listing the IPsec
protocols, modes, and algorithms to be employed, including any
nesting requirements. For example, an entry may call for all
matching traffic to be protected by ESP in transport mode using
3DES-CBC with an explicit IV, nested inside of AH in tunnel mode
using HMAC/SHA-1. For each selector, the policy entry specifies how
to derive the corresponding values for a new Security Association
Database (SAD, see Section 4.4.3) entry from those in the SPD and the
packet (Note that at present, ranges are only supported for IP
addresses; but wildcarding can be expressed for all selectors):

> a. use the value in the packet itself -- This will limit use
>   of the SA to those packets which have this packet's value
>   for the selector even if the selector for the policy entry
>   has a range of allowed values or a wildcard for this
>   selector.
> b. use the value associated with the policy entry -- If this
>   were to be just a single value, then there would be no
>   difference between (b) and (a). However, if the allowed
>   values for the selector are a range (for IP addresses) or

wildcard, then in the case of a range,(b) would enable use
of the SA by any packet with a selector value within the
range not just by packets with the selector value of the
packet that triggered the creation of the SA. In the case
of a wildcard, (b) would allow use of the SA by packets
with any value for this selector.

For example, suppose there is an SPD entry where the allowed value
for source address is any of a range of hosts (192.168.2.1 to
192.168.2.10). And suppose that a packet is to be sent that has a
source address of 192.168.2.3. The value to be used for the SA could
be any of the sample values below depending on what the policy entry
for this selector says is the source of the selector value:

```
         source for the  example of
         value to be     new SAD
         used in the SA  selector value
         --------------- -------------
         a. packet       192.168.2.3 (one host)
         b. SPD entry    192.168.2.1 to 192.168.2.10 (range of hosts)
```

Note that if the SPD entry had an allowed value of wildcard for the
source address, then the SAD selector value could be wildcard (any
host). Case (a) can be used to prohibit sharing, even among packets
that match the same SPD entry.

As described below in Section 4.4.3, selectors may include "wildcard"
entries and hence the selectors for two entries may overlap. (This
is analogous to the overlap that arises with ACLs or filter entries
in routers or packet filtering firewalls.) Thus, to ensure
consistent, predictable processing, SPD entries MUST be ordered and
the SPD MUST always be searched in the same order, so that the first
matching entry is consistently selected. (This requirement is
necessary as the effect of processing traffic against SPD entries
must be deterministic, but there is no way to canonicalize SPD
entries given the use of wildcards for some selectors.) More detail
on matching of packets against SPD entries is provided in Section 5.

Note that if ESP is specified, either (but not both) authentication
or encryption can be omitted. So it MUST be possible to configure
the SPD value for the authentication or encryption algorithms to be
"NULL". However, at least one of these services MUST be selected,
i.e., it MUST NOT be possible to configure both of them as "NULL".

The SPD can be used to map traffic to specific SAs or SA bundles.
Thus it can function both as the reference database for security
policy and as the map to existing SAs (or SA bundles). (To
accommodate the bypass and discard policies cited above, the SPD also

MUST provide a means of mapping traffic to these functions, even
though they are not, per se, IPsec processing.) The way in which the
SPD operates is different for inbound vs. outbound traffic and it
also may differ for host vs. security gateway, BITS, and BITW
implementations. Sections 5.1 and 5.2 describe the use of the SPD
for outbound and inbound processing, respectively.

Because a security policy may require that more than one SA be
applied to a specified set of traffic, in a specific order, the
policy entry in the SPD must preserve these ordering requirements,
when present. Thus, it must be possible for an IPsec implementation
to determine that an outbound or inbound packet must be processed
thorough a sequence of SAs. Conceptually, for outbound processing,
one might imagine links (to the SAD) from an SPD entry for which
there are active SAs, and each entry would consist of either a single
SA or an ordered list of SAs that comprise an SA bundle. When a
packet is matched against an SPD entry and there is an existing SA or
SA bundle that can be used to carry the traffic, the processing of
the packet is controlled by the SA or SA bundle entry on the list.
For an inbound IPsec packet for which multiple IPsec SAs are to be
applied, the lookup based on destination address, IPsec protocol, and
SPI should identify a single SA.

The SPD is used to control the flow of ALL traffic through an IPsec
system, including security and key management traffic (e.g., ISAKMP)
from/to entities behind a security gateway. This means that ISAKMP
traffic must be explicitly accounted for in the SPD, else it will be
discarded. Note that a security gateway could prohibit traversal of
encrypted packets in various ways, e.g., having a DISCARD entry in
the SPD for ESP packets or providing proxy key exchange. In the
latter case, the traffic would be internally routed to the key
management module in the security gateway.

4.4.2 Selectors

An SA (or SA bundle) may be fine-grained or coarse-grained, depending
on the selectors used to define the set of traffic for the SA. For
example, all traffic between two hosts may be carried via a single
SA, and afforded a uniform set of security services. Alternatively,
traffic between a pair of hosts might be spread over multiple SAs,
depending on the applications being used (as defined by the Next
Protocol and Port fields), with different security services offered
by different SAs. Similarly, all traffic between a pair of security
gateways could be carried on a single SA, or one SA could be assigned
for each communicating host pair. The following selector parameters
MUST be supported for SA management to facilitate control of SA
granularity. Note that in the case of receipt of a packet with an
ESP header, e.g., at an encapsulating security gateway or BITW

implementation, the transport layer protocol, source/destination
ports, and Name (if present) may be "OPAQUE", i.e., inaccessible
because of encryption or fragmentation. Note also that both Source
and Destination addresses should either be IPv4 or IPv6.

- Destination IP Address (IPv4 or IPv6): this may be a single IP
  address (unicast, anycast, broadcast (IPv4 only), or multicast
  group), a range of addresses (high and low values (inclusive),
  address + mask, or a wildcard address. The last three are used
  to support more than one destination system sharing the same SA
  (e.g., behind a security gateway). Note that this selector is
  conceptually different from the "Destination IP Address" field
  in the <Destination IP Address, IPsec Protocol, SPI> tuple used
  to uniquely identify an SA. When a tunneled packet arrives at
  the tunnel endpoint, its SPI/Destination address/Protocol are
  used to look up the SA for this packet in the SAD. This
  destination address comes from the encapsulating IP header.
  Once the packet has been processed according to the tunnel SA
  and has come out of the tunnel, its selectors are "looked up" in
  the Inbound SPD. The Inbound SPD has a selector called
  destination address. This IP destination address is the one in
  the inner (encapsulated) IP header. In the case of a
  transport'd packet, there will be only one IP header and this
  ambiguity does not exist. [REQUIRED for all implementations]

- Source IP Address(es) (IPv4 or IPv6): this may be a single IP
  address (unicast, anycast, broadcast (IPv4 only), or multicast
  group), range of addresses (high and low values inclusive),
  address + mask, or a wildcard address. The last three are used
  to support more than one source system sharing the same SA
  (e.g., behind a security gateway or in a multihomed host).
  [REQUIRED for all implementations]

- Name: There are 2 cases (Note that these name forms are
  supported in the IPsec DOI.)
        1. User ID
            a. a fully qualified user name string (DNS), e.g.,
               mozart@foo.bar.com
            b. X.500 distinguished name, e.g., C = US, SP = MA,
               O = GTE Internetworking, CN = Stephen T. Kent.
        2. System name (host, security gateway, etc.)
            a. a fully qualified DNS name, e.g., foo.bar.com
            b. X.500 distinguished name
            c. X.500 general name

NOTE: One of the possible values of this selector is "OPAQUE".

[REQUIRED for the following cases. Note that support for name
forms other than addresses is not required for manually keyed
SAs.

    o User ID
      - native host implementations
      - BITW and BITS implementations acting as HOSTS
        with only one user
      - security gateway implementations for INBOUND
        processing.
    o System names -- all implementations]

- Data sensitivity level: (IPSO/CIPSO labels)
  [REQUIRED for all systems providing information flow security as
  per Section 8, OPTIONAL for all other systems.]

- Transport Layer Protocol: Obtained from the IPv4 "Protocol" or
  the IPv6 "Next Header" fields. This may be an individual
  protocol number. These packet fields may not contain the
  Transport Protocol due to the presence of IP extension headers,
  e.g., a Routing Header, AH, ESP, Fragmentation Header,
  Destination Options, Hop-by-hop options, etc. Note that the
  Transport Protocol may not be available in the case of receipt
  of a packet with an ESP header, thus a value of "OPAQUE" SHOULD
  be supported.
  [REQUIRED for all implementations]

  NOTE: To locate the transport protocol, a system has to chain
  through the packet headers checking the "Protocol" or "Next
  Header" field until it encounters either one it recognizes as a
  transport protocol, or until it reaches one that isn't on its
  list of extension headers, or until it encounters an ESP header
  that renders the transport protocol opaque.

- Source and Destination (e.g., TCP/UDP) Ports: These may be
  individual UDP or TCP port values or a wildcard port. (The use
  of the Next Protocol field and the Source and/or Destination
  Port fields (in conjunction with the Source and/or Destination
  Address fields), as an SA selector is sometimes referred to as
  "session-oriented keying."). Note that the source and
  destination ports may not be available in the case of receipt of
  a packet with an ESP header, thus a value of "OPAQUE" SHOULD be
  supported.

  The following table summarizes the relationship between the
  "Next Header" value in the packet and SPD and the derived Port
  Selector value for the SPD and SAD.

Next Hdr in Packet	Transport Layer Protocol in SPD	Derived Port Selector Field Value in SPD and SAD
ESP	ESP or ANY	ANY (i.e., don't look at it)
-don't care-	ANY	ANY (i.e., don't look at it)
specific value fragment	specific value	NOT ANY (i.e., drop packet)
specific value not fragment	specific value	actual port selector field

If the packet has been fragmented, then the port information may
not be available in the current fragment. If so, discard the
fragment. An ICMP PMTU should be sent for the first fragment,
which will have the port information. [MAY be supported]

The IPsec implementation context determines how selectors are used.
For example, a host implementation integrated into the stack may make
use of a socket interface. When a new connection is established the
SPD can be consulted and an SA (or SA bundle) bound to the socket.
Thus traffic sent via that socket need not result in additional
lookups to the SPD/SAD. In contrast, a BITS, BITW, or security
gateway implementation needs to look at each packet and perform an
SPD/SAD lookup based on the selectors. The allowable values for the
selector fields differ between the traffic flow, the security
association, and the security policy.

The following table summarizes the kinds of entries that one needs to
be able to express in the SPD and SAD. It shows how they relate to
the fields in data traffic being subjected to IPsec screening.
(Note: the "wild" or "wildcard" entry for src and dst addresses
includes a mask, range, etc.)

Field	Traffic Value	SAD Entry	SPD Entry
src addr	single IP addr	single,range,wild	single,range,wildcard
dst addr	single IP addr	single,range,wild	single,range,wildcard
xpt protocol*	xpt protocol	single,wildcard	single,wildcard
src port*	single src port	single,wildcard	single,wildcard
dst port*	single dst port	single,wildcard	single,wildcard
user id*	single user id	single,wildcard	single,wildcard
sec. labels	single value	single,wildcard	single,wildcard

* The SAD and SPD entries for these fields could be "OPAQUE"
  because the traffic value is encrypted.

NOTE: In principle, one could have selectors and/or selector values
in the SPD which cannot be negotiated for an SA or SA bundle.
Examples might include selector values used to select traffic for

discarding or enumerated lists which cause a separate SA to be
created for each item on the list. For now, this is left for future
versions of this document and the list of required selectors and
selector values is the same for the SPD and the SAD. However, it is
acceptable to have an administrative interface that supports use of
selector values which cannot be negotiated provided that it does not
mislead the user into believing it is creating an SA with these
selector values. For example, the interface may allow the user to
specify an enumerated list of values but would result in the creation
of a separate policy and SA for each item on the list. A vendor
might support such an interface to make it easier for its customers
to specify clear and concise policy specifications.

4.4.3 Security Association Database (SAD)

In each IPsec implementation there is a nominal Security Association
Database, in which each entry defines the parameters associated with
one SA. Each SA has an entry in the SAD. For outbound processing,
entries are pointed to by entries in the SPD. Note that if an SPD
entry does not currently point to an SA that is appropriate for the
packet, the implementation creates an appropriate SA (or SA Bundle)
and links the SPD entry to the SAD entry (see Section 5.1.1). For
inbound processing, each entry in the SAD is indexed by a destination
IP address, IPsec protocol type, and SPI. The following parameters
are associated with each entry in the SAD. This description does not
purport to be a MIB, but only a specification of the minimal data
items required to support an SA in an IPsec implementation.

For inbound processing: The following packet fields are used to look
up the SA in the SAD:

        o Outer Header's Destination IP address: the IPv4 or IPv6
          Destination address.
          [REQUIRED for all implementations]
        o IPsec Protocol: AH or ESP, used as an index for SA lookup
          in this database. Specifies the IPsec protocol to be
          applied to the traffic on this SA.
          [REQUIRED for all implementations]
        o SPI: the 32-bit value used to distinguish among different
          SAs terminating at the same destination and using the same
          IPsec protocol.
          [REQUIRED for all implementations]

For each of the selectors defined in Section 4.4.2, the SA entry in
the SAD MUST contain the value or values which were negotiated at the
time the SA was created. For the sender, these values are used to
decide whether a given SA is appropriate for use with an outbound
packet. This is part of checking to see if there is an existing SA

that can be used. For the receiver, these values are used to check
that the selector values in an inbound packet match those for the SA
(and thus indirectly those for the matching policy). For the
receiver, this is part of verifying that the SA was appropriate for
this packet. (See Section 6 for rules for ICMP messages.) These
fields can have the form of specific values, ranges, wildcards, or
"OPAQUE" as described in section 4.4.2, "Selectors". Note that for
an ESP SA, the encryption algorithm or the authentication algorithm
could be "NULL". However they MUST not both be "NULL".

The following SAD fields are used in doing IPsec processing:

        o Sequence Number Counter: a 32-bit value used to generate the
          Sequence Number field in AH or ESP headers.
          [REQUIRED for all implementations, but used only for outbound
          traffic.]
        o Sequence Counter Overflow: a flag indicating whether overflow
          of the Sequence Number Counter should generate an auditable
          event and prevent transmission of additional packets on the
          SA.
          [REQUIRED for all implementations, but used only for outbound
          traffic.]
        o Anti-Replay Window: a 32-bit counter and a bit-map (or
          equivalent) used to determine whether an inbound AH or ESP
          packet is a replay.
          [REQUIRED for all implementations but used only for inbound
          traffic. NOTE: If anti-replay has been disabled by the
          receiver, e.g., in the case of a manually keyed SA, then the
          Anti-Replay Window is not used.]
        o AH Authentication algorithm, keys, etc.
          [REQUIRED for AH implementations]
        o ESP Encryption algorithm, keys, IV mode, IV, etc.
          [REQUIRED for ESP implementations]
        o ESP authentication algorithm, keys, etc. If the
          authentication service is not selected, this field will be
          null.
          [REQUIRED for ESP implementations]
        o Lifetime of this Security Association: a time interval after
          which an SA must be replaced with a new SA (and new SPI) or
          terminated, plus an indication of which of these actions
          should occur. This may be expressed as a time or byte count,
          or a simultaneous use of both, the first lifetime to expire
          taking precedence. A compliant implementation MUST support
          both types of lifetimes, and must support a simultaneous use
          of both. If time is employed, and if IKE employs X.509
          certificates for SA establishment, the SA lifetime must be
          constrained by the validity intervals of the certificates,
          and the NextIssueDate of the CRLs used in the IKE exchange

for the SA. Both initiator and responder are responsible for
constraining SA lifetime in this fashion.
[REQUIRED for all implementations]

NOTE: The details of how to handle the refreshing of keys
when SAs expire is a local matter. However, one reasonable
approach is:
   (a) If byte count is used, then the implementation
       SHOULD count the number of bytes to which the IPsec
       algorithm is applied. For ESP, this is the encryption
       algorithm (including Null encryption) and for AH,
       this is the authentication algorithm. This includes
       pad bytes, etc. Note that implementations SHOULD be
       able to handle having the counters at the ends of an
       SA get out of synch, e.g., because of packet loss or
       because the implementations at each end of the SA
       aren't doing things the same way.
   (b) There SHOULD be two kinds of lifetime -- a soft
       lifetime which warns the implementation to initiate
       action such as setting up a replacement SA and a
       hard lifetime when the current SA ends.
   (c) If the entire packet does not get delivered during
       the SAs lifetime, the packet SHOULD be discarded.

 o IPsec protocol mode: tunnel, transport or wildcard.
   Indicates which mode of AH or ESP is applied to traffic on
   this SA. Note that if this field is "wildcard" at the
   sending end of the SA, then the application has to specify
   the mode to the IPsec implementation. This use of wildcard
   allows the same SA to be used for either tunnel or transport
   mode traffic on a per packet basis, e.g., by different
   sockets. The receiver does not need to know the mode in
   order to properly process the packet's IPsec headers.

   [REQUIRED as follows, unless implicitly defined by context:
              - host implementations must support all modes
              - gateway implementations must support tunnel mode]

NOTE: The use of wildcard for the protocol mode of an inbound
SA may add complexity to the situation in the receiver (host
only). Since the packets on such an SA could be delivered in
either tunnel or transport mode, the security of an incoming
packet could depend in part on which mode had been used to
deliver it. If, as a result, an application cared about the
SA mode of a given packet, then the application would need a
mechanism to obtain this mode information.

       o Path MTU: any observed path MTU and aging variables. See
         Section 6.1.2.4
         [REQUIRED for all implementations but used only for outbound
         traffic]

4.5 Basic Combinations of Security Associations

This section describes four examples of combinations of security
associations that MUST be supported by compliant IPsec hosts or
security gateways. Additional combinations of AH and/or ESP in
tunnel and/or transport modes MAY be supported at the discretion of
the implementor. Compliant implementations MUST be capable of
generating these four combinations and on receipt, of processing
them, but SHOULD be able to receive and process any combination. The
diagrams and text below describe the basic cases. The legend for the
diagrams is:

```
==== = one or more security associations (AH or ESP, transport
       or tunnel)
---- = connectivity (or if so labelled, administrative boundary)
Hx   = host x
SGx  = security gateway x
X*   = X supports IPsec
```

NOTE: The security associations below can be either AH or ESP. The
mode (tunnel vs transport) is determined by the nature of the
endpoints. For host-to-host SAs, the mode can be either transport or
tunnel.

Case 1. The case of providing end-to-end security between 2 hosts
      across the Internet (or an Intranet).

```
         =======================================
         |                                     |
         H1* ------ (Inter/Intranet) ------ H2*
```

Note that either transport or tunnel mode can be selected by the
hosts. So the headers in a packet between H1 and H2 could look
like any of the following:

```
        Transport                  Tunnel
        -----------------          ---------------------
        1. [IP1][AH][upper]        4. [IP2][AH][IP1][upper]
        2. [IP1][ESP][upper]       5. [IP2][ESP][IP1][upper]
        3. [IP1][AH][ESP][upper]
```

Note that there is no requirement to support general nesting,
but in transport mode, both AH and ESP can be applied to the
packet. In this event, the SA establishment procedure MUST
ensure that first ESP, then AH are applied to the packet.

Case 2. This case illustrates simple virtual private networks
         support.

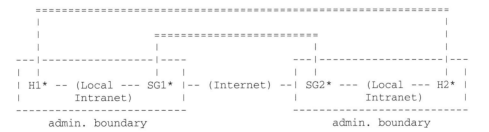

Only tunnel mode is required here. So the headers in a packet
between SG1 and SG2 could look like either of the following:

```
                 Tunnel
         --------------------
         4. [IP2][AH][IP1][upper]
         5. [IP2][ESP][IP1][upper]
```

Case 3. This case combines cases 1 and 2, adding end-to-end security
         between the sending and receiving hosts. It imposes no new
         requirements on the hosts or security gateways, other than a
         requirement for a security gateway to be configurable to pass
         IPsec traffic (including ISAKMP traffic) for hosts behind it.

```
     ================================================================
     |                                                              |
     |          =========================                           |
     |          |                       |                           |
  ---|----------------|----            ---|------------------|---
  |  |                |   |            |  |                  |  |
  | H1* -- (Local --- SG1* |-- (Internet) --| SG2* --- (Local --- H2* |
  |         Intranet)      |            |          Intranet)      |
  ------------------------                ------------------------
     admin. boundary                        admin. boundary
```

Case 4. This covers the situation where a remote host (H1) uses the
         Internet to reach an organization's firewall (SG2) and to then
         gain access to some server or other machine (H2). The remote
         host could be a mobile host (H1) dialing up to a local PPP/ARA
         server (not shown) on the Internet and then crossing the
         Internet to the home organization's firewall (SG2), etc. The

details of support for this case, (how H1 locates SG2, authenticates it, and verifies its authorization to represent H2) are discussed in Section 4.6.3, "Locating a Security Gateway".

```
=========================================================
|                                                       |
|=============================                          |
 ||                          |                          |
 ||                       ---|----------------------|---
 ||                       |  |                      |  |
H1* ------ (Internet) -----| SG2* ---- (Local ----- H2* |
     ^                     |          Intranet)        |
     |                     ----------------------------
could be dialup            admin. boundary (optional)
to PPP/ARA server
```

Only tunnel mode is required between H1 and SG2. So the choices for the SA between H1 and SG2 would be one of the ones in case 2. The choices for the SA between H1 and H2 would be one of the ones in case 1.

Note that in this case, the sender MUST apply the transport header before the tunnel header. Therefore the management interface to the IPsec implementation MUST support configuration of the SPD and SAD to ensure this ordering of IPsec header application.

As noted above, support for additional combinations of AH and ESP is optional. Use of other, optional combinations may adversely affect interoperability.

4.6 SA and Key Management

IPsec mandates support for both manual and automated SA and cryptographic key management. The IPsec protocols, AH and ESP, are largely independent of the associated SA management techniques, although the techniques involved do affect some of the security services offered by the protocols. For example, the optional anti-replay services available for AH and ESP require automated SA management. Moreover, the granularity of key distribution employed with IPsec determines the granularity of authentication provided. (See also a discussion of this issue in Section 4.7.) In general, data origin authentication in AH and ESP is limited by the extent to which secrets used with the authentication algorithm (or with a key management protocol that creates such secrets) are shared among multiple possible sources.

The following text describes the minimum requirements for both types
of SA management.

4.6.1 Manual Techniques

The simplest form of management is manual management, in which a
person manually configures each system with keying material and
security association management data relevant to secure communication
with other systems. Manual techniques are practical in small, static
environments but they do not scale well. For example, a company
could create a Virtual Private Network (VPN) using IPsec in security
gateways at several sites. If the number of sites is small, and
since all the sites come under the purview of a single administrative
domain, this is likely to be a feasible context for manual management
techniques. In this case, the security gateway might selectively
protect traffic to and from other sites within the organization using
a manually configured key, while not protecting traffic for other
destinations. It also might be appropriate when only selected
communications need to be secured. A similar argument might apply to
use of IPsec entirely within an organization for a small number of
hosts and/or gateways. Manual management techniques often employ
statically configured, symmetric keys, though other options also
exist.

4.6.2 Automated SA and Key Management

Widespread deployment and use of IPsec requires an Internet-standard,
scalable, automated, SA management protocol. Such support is
required to facilitate use of the anti-replay features of AH and ESP,
and to accommodate on-demand creation of SAs, e.g., for user- and
session-oriented keying. (Note that the notion of "rekeying" an SA
actually implies creation of a new SA with a new SPI, a process that
generally implies use of an automated SA/key management protocol.)

The default automated key management protocol selected for use with
IPsec is IKE [MSST97, Orm97, HC98] under the IPsec domain of
interpretation [Pip98]. Other automated SA management protocols MAY
be employed.

When an automated SA/key management protocol is employed, the output
from this protocol may be used to generate multiple keys, e.g., for a
single ESP SA. This may arise because:

        o the encryption algorithm uses multiple keys (e.g., triple DES)
        o the authentication algorithm uses multiple keys
        o both encryption and authentication algorithms are employed

The Key Management System may provide a separate string of bits for
each key or it may generate one string of bits from which all of them
are extracted. If a single string of bits is provided, care needs to
be taken to ensure that the parts of the system that map the string
of bits to the required keys do so in the same fashion at both ends
of the SA. To ensure that the IPsec implementations at each end of
the SA use the same bits for the same keys, and irrespective of which
part of the system divides the string of bits into individual keys,
the encryption key(s) MUST be taken from the first (left-most, high-
order) bits and the authentication key(s) MUST be taken from the
remaining bits. The number of bits for each key is defined in the
relevant algorithm specification RFC. In the case of multiple
encryption keys or multiple authentication keys, the specification
for the algorithm must specify the order in which they are to be
selected from a single string of bits provided to the algorithm.

4.6.3 Locating a Security Gateway

This section discusses issues relating to how a host learns about the
existence of relevant security gateways and once a host has contacted
these security gateways, how it knows that these are the correct
security gateways. The details of where the required information is
stored is a local matter.

Consider a situation in which a remote host (H1) is using the
Internet to gain access to a server or other machine (H2) and there
is a security gateway (SG2), e.g., a firewall, through which H1's
traffic must pass. An example of this situation would be a mobile
host (Road Warrior) crossing the Internet to the home organization's
firewall (SG2). (See Case 4 in the section 4.5 Basic Combinations of
Security Associations.) This situation raises several issues:

     1. How does H1 know/learn about the existence of the security
        gateway SG2?
     2. How does it authenticate SG2, and once it has authenticated
        SG2, how does it confirm that SG2 has been authorized to
        represent H2?
     3. How does SG2 authenticate H1 and verify that H1 is authorized
        to contact H2?
     4. How does H1 know/learn about backup gateways which provide
        alternate paths to H2?

To address these problems, a host or security gateway MUST have an
administrative interface that allows the user/administrator to
configure the address of a security gateway for any sets of
destination addresses that require its use. This includes the ability
to configure:

　　　　o the requisite information for locating and authenticating the
　　　　　security gateway and verifying its authorization to represent
　　　　　the destination host.
　　　　o the requisite information for locating and authenticating any
　　　　　backup gateways and verifying their authorization to represent
　　　　　the destination host.

　　It is assumed that the SPD is also configured with policy information
　　that covers any other IPsec requirements for the path to the security
　　gateway and the destination host.

　　This document does not address the issue of how to automate the
　　discovery/verification of security gateways.

4.7 Security Associations and Multicast

　　The receiver-orientation of the Security Association implies that, in
　　the case of unicast traffic, the destination system will normally
　　select the SPI value. By having the destination select the SPI
　　value, there is no potential for manually configured Security
　　Associations to conflict with automatically configured (e.g., via a
　　key management protocol) Security Associations or for Security
　　Associations from multiple sources to conflict with each other. For
　　multicast traffic, there are multiple destination systems per
　　multicast group. So some system or person will need to coordinate
　　among all multicast groups to select an SPI or SPIs on behalf of each
　　multicast group and then communicate the group's IPsec information to
　　all of the legitimate members of that multicast group via mechanisms
　　not defined here.

　　Multiple senders to a multicast group SHOULD use a single Security
　　Association (and hence Security Parameter Index) for all traffic to
　　that group when a symmetric key encryption or authentication
　　algorithm is employed. In such circumstances, the receiver knows only
　　that the message came from a system possessing the key for that
　　multicast group. In such circumstances, a receiver generally will
　　not be able to authenticate which system sent the multicast traffic.
　　Specifications for other, more general multicast cases are deferred
　　to later IPsec documents.

　　At the time this specification was published, automated protocols for
　　multicast key distribution were not considered adequately mature for
　　standardization. For multicast groups having relatively few members,
　　manual key distribution or multiple use of existing unicast key
　　distribution algorithms such as modified Diffie-Hellman appears
　　feasible. For very large groups, new scalable techniques will be
　　needed. An example of current work in this area is the Group Key
　　Management Protocol (GKMP) [HM97].

5. IP Traffic Processing

   As mentioned in Section 4.4.1 "The Security Policy Database (SPD)",
   the SPD must be consulted during the processing of all traffic
   (INBOUND and OUTBOUND), including non-IPsec traffic. If no policy is
   found in the SPD that matches the packet (for either inbound or
   outbound traffic), the packet MUST be discarded.

   NOTE: All of the cryptographic algorithms used in IPsec expect their
   input in canonical network byte order (see Appendix in RFC 791) and
   generate their output in canonical network byte order. IP packets
   are also transmitted in network byte order.

5.1 Outbound IP Traffic Processing

5.1.1 Selecting and Using an SA or SA Bundle

   In a security gateway or BITW implementation (and in many BITS
   implementations), each outbound packet is compared against the SPD to
   determine what processing is required for the packet. If the packet
   is to be discarded, this is an auditable event. If the traffic is
   allowed to bypass IPsec processing, the packet continues through
   "normal" processing for the environment in which the IPsec processing
   is taking place. If IPsec processing is required, the packet is
   either mapped to an existing SA (or SA bundle), or a new SA (or SA
   bundle) is created for the packet. Since a packet's selectors might
   match multiple policies or multiple extant SAs and since the SPD is
   ordered, but the SAD is not, IPsec MUST:

            1. Match the packet's selector fields against the outbound
               policies in the SPD to locate the first appropriate
               policy, which will point to zero or more SA bundles in the
               SAD.

            2. Match the packet's selector fields against those in the SA
               bundles found in (1) to locate the first SA bundle that
               matches. If no SAs were found or none match, create an
               appropriate SA bundle and link the SPD entry to the SAD
               entry. If no key management entity is found, drop the
               packet.

            3. Use the SA bundle found/created in (2) to do the required
               IPsec processing, e.g., authenticate and encrypt.

   In a host IPsec implementation based on sockets, the SPD will be
   consulted whenever a new socket is created, to determine what, if
   any, IPsec processing will be applied to the traffic that will flow
   on that socket.

NOTE: A compliant implementation MUST not allow instantiation of an
ESP SA that employs both a NULL encryption and a NULL authentication
algorithm.   An attempt to negotiate such an SA is an auditable event.

5.1.2 Header Construction for Tunnel Mode

This section describes the handling of the inner and outer IP
headers, extension headers, and options for AH and ESP tunnels.   This
includes how to construct the encapsulating (outer) IP header, how to
handle fields in the inner IP header, and what other actions should
be taken.   The general idea is modeled after the one used in RFC
2003, "IP Encapsulation with IP":

> o The outer IP header Source Address and Destination Address
>   identify the "endpoints" of the tunnel (the encapsulator and
>   decapsulator).   The inner IP header Source Address and
>   Destination Addresses identify the original sender and
>   recipient of the datagram, (from the perspective of this
>   tunnel), respectively.   (see footnote 3 after the table in
>   5.1.2.1 for more details on the encapsulating source IP
>   address.)
> o The inner IP header is not changed except to decrement the TTL
>   as noted below, and remains unchanged during its delivery to
>   the tunnel exit point.
> o No change to IP options or extension headers in the inner
>   header occurs during delivery of the encapsulated datagram
>   through the tunnel.
> o If need be, other protocol headers such as the IP
>   Authentication header may be inserted between the outer IP
>   header and the inner IP header.

The tables in the following sub-sections show the handling for the
different header/option fields (constructed = the value in the outer
field is constructed independently of the value in the inner).

5.1.2.1 IPv4 -- Header Construction for Tunnel Mode

```
                          <-- How Outer Hdr Relates to Inner Hdr -->
                          Outer Hdr at               Inner Hdr at
      IPv4                Encapsulator               Decapsulator
        Header fields:    --------------------       -----------
          version         4 (1)                      no change
          header length   constructed                no change
          TOS             copied from inner hdr (5)  no change
          total length    constructed                no change
          ID              constructed                no change
          flags (DF,MF)   constructed, DF (4)        no change
          fragmt offset   constructed                no change
```

```
         TTL                 constructed (2)           decrement (2)
         protocol            AH, ESP, routing hdr      no change
         checksum            constructed               constructed (2)
         src address         constructed (3)           no change
         dest address        constructed (3)           no change
     Options                 never copied              no change
```

   1. The IP version in the encapsulating header can be different
      from the value in the inner header.

   2. The TTL in the inner header is decremented by the
      encapsulator prior to forwarding and by the decapsulator if
      it forwards the packet. (The checksum changes when the TTL
      changes.)

      Note: The decrementing of the TTL is one of the usual actions
      that takes place when forwarding a packet. Packets
      originating from the same node as the encapsulator do not
      have their TTL's decremented, as the sending node is
      originating the packet rather than forwarding it.

   3. src and dest addresses depend on the SA, which is used to
      determine the dest address which in turn determines which src
      address (net interface) is used to forward the packet.

      NOTE: In principle, the encapsulating IP source address can
      be any of the encapsulator's interface addresses or even an
      address different from any of the encapsulator's IP
      addresses, (e.g., if it's acting as a NAT box) so long as the
      address is reachable through the encapsulator from the
      environment into which the packet is sent. This does not
      cause a problem because IPsec does not currently have any
      INBOUND processing requirement that involves the Source
      Address of the encapsulating IP header. So while the
      receiving tunnel endpoint looks at the Destination Address in
      the encapsulating IP header, it only looks at the Source
      Address in the inner (encapsulated) IP header.

   4. configuration determines whether to copy from the inner
      header (IPv4 only), clear or set the DF.

   5. If Inner Hdr is IPv4 (Protocol = 4), copy the TOS.   If Inner
      Hdr is IPv6 (Protocol = 41), map the Class to TOS.

5.1.2.2 IPv6 -- Header Construction for Tunnel Mode

   See previous section 5.1.2 for notes 1-5 indicated by (footnote
   number).

```
                      <-- How Outer Hdr  Relates Inner Hdr --->
                      Outer Hdr at              Inner Hdr at
    IPv6              Encapsulator              Decapsulator
    Header fields:    --------------------      -----------
      version         6 (1)                     no change
      class           copied or configured (6)  no change
      flow id         copied or configured      no change
      len             constructed               no change
      next header     AH,ESP,routing hdr        no change
      hop limit       constructed (2)           decrement (2)
      src address     constructed (3)           no change
      dest address    constructed (3)           no change
    Extension headers never copied              no change
```

    6. If Inner Hdr is IPv6 (Next Header = 41), copy the Class. If
       Inner Hdr is IPv4 (Next Header = 4), map the TOS to Class.

5.2 Processing Inbound IP Traffic

Prior to performing AH or ESP processing, any IP fragments are
reassembled. Each inbound IP datagram to which IPsec processing will
be applied is identified by the appearance of the AH or ESP values in
the IP Next Protocol field (or of AH or ESP as an extension header in
the IPv6 context).

Note: Appendix C contains sample code for a bitmask check for a 32
packet window that can be used for implementing anti-replay service.

5.2.1 Selecting and Using an SA or SA Bundle

Mapping the IP datagram to the appropriate SA is simplified because
of the presence of the SPI in the AH or ESP header. Note that the
selector checks are made on the inner headers not the outer (tunnel)
headers. The steps followed are:

        1. Use the packet's destination address (outer IP header),
           IPsec protocol, and SPI to look up the SA in the SAD. If
           the SA lookup fails, drop the packet and log/report the
           error.

        2. Use the SA found in (1) to do the IPsec processing, e.g.,
           authenticate and decrypt. This step includes matching the
           packet's (Inner Header if tunneled) selectors to the
           selectors in the SA. Local policy determines the
           specificity of the SA selectors (single value, list,
           range, wildcard). In general, a packet's source address
           MUST match the SA selector value. However, an ICMP packet
           received on a tunnel mode SA may have a source address

other than that bound to the SA and thus such packets
should be permitted as exceptions to this check. For an
ICMP packet, the selectors from the enclosed problem
packet (the source and destination addresses and ports
should be swapped) should be checked against the selectors
for the SA. Note that some or all of these selectors may
be inaccessible because of limitations on how many bits of
the problem packet the ICMP packet is allowed to carry or
due to encryption. See Section 6.

Do (1) and (2) for every IPsec header until a Transport
Protocol Header or an IP header that is NOT for this
system is encountered. Keep track of what SAs have been
used and their order of application.

3. Find an incoming policy in the SPD that matches the
   packet. This could be done, for example, by use of
   backpointers from the SAs to the SPD or by matching the
   packet's selectors (Inner Header if tunneled) against
   those of the policy entries in the SPD.

4. Check whether the required IPsec processing has been
   applied, i.e., verify that the SA's found in (1) and (2)
   match the kind and order of SAs required by the policy
   found in (3).

   NOTE: The correct "matching" policy will not necessarily
   be the first inbound policy found. If the check in (4)
   fails, steps (3) and (4) are repeated until all policy
   entries have been checked or until the check succeeds.

At the end of these steps, pass the resulting packet to the Transport
Layer or forward the packet. Note that any IPsec headers processed
in these steps may have been removed, but that this information,
i.e., what SAs were used and the order of their application, may be
needed for subsequent IPsec or firewall processing.

Note that in the case of a security gateway, if forwarding causes a
packet to exit via an IPsec-enabled interface, then additional IPsec
processing may be applied.

5.2.2 Handling of AH and ESP tunnels

The handling of the inner and outer IP headers, extension headers,
and options for AH and ESP tunnels should be performed as described
in the tables in Section 5.1.

6. ICMP Processing (relevant to IPsec)

   The focus of this section is on the handling of ICMP error messages.
   Other ICMP traffic, e.g., Echo/Reply, should be treated like other
   traffic and can be protected on an end-to-end basis using SAs in the
   usual fashion.

   An ICMP error message protected by AH or ESP and generated by a
   router SHOULD be processed and forwarded in a tunnel mode SA. Local
   policy determines whether or not it is subjected to source address
   checks by the router at the destination end of the tunnel. Note that
   if the router at the originating end of the tunnel is forwarding an
   ICMP error message from another router, the source address check
   would fail. An ICMP message protected by AH or ESP and generated by
   a router MUST NOT be forwarded on a transport mode SA (unless the SA
   has been established to the router acting as a host, e.g., a Telnet
   connection used to manage a router). An ICMP message generated by a
   host SHOULD be checked against the source IP address selectors bound
   to the SA in which the message arrives. Note that even if the source
   of an ICMP error message is authenticated, the returned IP header
   could be invalid. Accordingly, the selector values in the IP header
   SHOULD also be checked to be sure that they are consistent with the
   selectors for the SA over which the ICMP message was received.

   The table in Appendix D characterize ICMP messages as being either
   host generated, router generated, both, unknown/unassigned. ICMP
   messages falling into the last two categories should be handled as
   determined by the receiver's policy.

   An ICMP message not protected by AH or ESP is unauthenticated and its
   processing and/or forwarding may result in denial of service. This
   suggests that, in general, it would be desirable to ignore such
   messages. However, it is expected that many routers (vs. security
   gateways) will not implement IPsec for transit traffic and thus
   strict adherence to this rule would cause many ICMP messages to be
   discarded. The result is that some critical IP functions would be
   lost, e.g., redirection and PMTU processing. Thus it MUST be
   possible to configure an IPsec implementation to accept or reject
   (router) ICMP traffic as per local security policy.

   The remainder of this section addresses how PMTU processing MUST be
   performed at hosts and security gateways. It addresses processing of
   both authenticated and unauthenticated ICMP PMTU messages. However,
   as noted above, unauthenticated ICMP messages MAY be discarded based
   on local policy.

6.1 PMTU/DF Processing

6.1.1 DF Bit

   In cases where a system (host or gateway) adds an encapsulating
   header (ESP tunnel or AH tunnel), it MUST support the option of
   copying the DF bit from the original packet to the encapsulating
   header (and processing ICMP PMTU messages). This means that it MUST
   be possible to configure the system's treatment of the DF bit (set,
   clear, copy from encapsulated header) for each interface. (See
   Appendix B for rationale.)

6.1.2 Path MTU Discovery (PMTU)

   This section discusses IPsec handling for Path MTU Discovery
   messages. ICMP PMTU is used here to refer to an ICMP message for:

          IPv4 (RFC 792):
                 - Type = 3 (Destination Unreachable)
                 - Code = 4 (Fragmentation needed and DF set)
                 - Next-Hop MTU in the low-order 16 bits of the second
                   word of the ICMP header (labelled "unused" in RFC
                   792), with high-order 16 bits set to zero

          IPv6 (RFC 1885):
                 - Type = 2 (Packet Too Big)
                 - Code = 0 (Fragmentation needed)
                 - Next-Hop MTU in the 32 bit MTU field of the ICMP6
                   message

6.1.2.1 Propagation of PMTU

   The amount of information returned with the ICMP PMTU message (IPv4
   or IPv6) is limited and this affects what selectors are available for
   use in further propagating the PMTU information. (See Appendix B for
   more detailed discussion of this topic.)

   o PMTU message with 64 bits of IPsec header -- If the ICMP PMTU
     message contains only 64 bits of the IPsec header (minimum for
     IPv4), then a security gateway MUST support the following options
     on a per SPI/SA basis:

          a. if the originating host can be determined (or the possible
             sources narrowed down to a manageable number), send the PM
             information to all the possible originating hosts.
          b. if the originating host cannot be determined, store the PMTU
             with the SA and wait until the next packet(s) arrive from the
             originating host for the relevant security association. If

the packet(s) are bigger than the PMTU, drop the packet(s),
and compose ICMP PMTU message(s) with the new packet(s) and
the updated PMTU, and send the ICMP message(s) about the
problem to the originating host. Retain the PMTU information
for any message that might arrive subsequently (see Section
6.1.2.4, "PMTU Aging").

o PMTU message with >64 bits of IPsec header -- If the ICMP message
  contains more information from the original packet then there may
  be enough non-opaque information to immediately determine to which
  host to propagate the ICMP/PMTU message and to provide that system
  with the 5 fields (source address, destination address, source
  port, destination port, transport protocol) needed to determine
  where to store/update the PMTU. Under such circumstances, a
  security gateway MUST generate an ICMP PMTU message immediately
  upon receipt of an ICMP PMTU from further down the path.

o Distributing the PMTU to the Transport Layer -- The host mechanism
  for getting the updated PMTU to the transport layer is unchanged,
  as specified in RFC 1191 (Path MTU Discovery).

6.1.2.2 Calculation of PMTU

The calculation of PMTU from an ICMP PMTU MUST take into account the
addition of any IPsec header - AH transport, ESP transport, AH/ESP
transport, ESP tunnel, AH tunnel. (See Appendix B for discussion of
implementation issues.)

Note: In some situations the addition of IPsec headers could result
in an effective PMTU (as seen by the host or application) that is
unacceptably small. To avoid this problem, the implementation may
establish a threshold below which it will not report a reduced PMTU.
In such cases, the implementation would apply IPsec and then fragment
the resulting packet according to the PMTU. This would result in a
more efficient use of the available bandwidth.

6.1.2.3 Granularity of PMTU Processing

In hosts, the granularity with which ICMP PMTU processing can be done
differs depending on the implementation situation. Looking at a
host, there are 3 situations that are of interest with respect to
PMTU issues (See Appendix B for additional details on this topic.):

    a. Integration of IPsec into the native IP implementation
    b. Bump-in-the-stack implementations, where IPsec is implemented
       "underneath" an existing implementation of a TCP/IP protocol
       stack, between the native IP and the local network drivers

   c. No IPsec implementation -- This case is included because it
      is relevant in cases where a security gateway is sending PMTU
      information back to a host.

Only in case (a) can the PMTU data be maintained at the same
granularity as communication associations. In (b) and (c), the IP
layer will only be able to maintain PMTU data at the granularity of
source and destination IP addresses (and optionally TOS), as
described in RFC 1191. This is an important difference, because more
than one communication association may map to the same source and
destination IP addresses, and each communication association may have
a different amount of IPsec header overhead (e.g., due to use of
different transforms or different algorithms).

Implementation of the calculation of PMTU and support for PMTUs at
the granularity of individual communication associations is a local
matter. However, a socket-based implementation of IPsec in a host
SHOULD maintain the information on a per socket basis. Bump in the
stack systems MUST pass an ICMP PMTU to the host IP implementation,
after adjusting it for any IPsec header overhead added by these
systems. The calculation of the overhead SHOULD be determined by
analysis of the SPI and any other selector information present in a
returned ICMP PMTU message.

6.1.2.4 PMTU Aging

In all systems (host or gateway) implementing IPsec and maintaining
PMTU information, the PMTU associated with a security association
(transport or tunnel) MUST be "aged" and some mechanism put in place
for updating the PMTU in a timely manner, especially for discovering
if the PMTU is smaller than it needs to be. A given PMTU has to
remain in place long enough for a packet to get from the source end
of the security association to the system at the other end of the
security association and propagate back an ICMP error message if the
current PMTU is too big. Note that if there are nested tunnels,
multiple packets and round trip times might be required to get an
ICMP message back to an encapsulator or originating host.

Systems SHOULD use the approach described in the Path MTU Discovery
document (RFC 1191, Section 6.3), which suggests periodically
resetting the PMTU to the first-hop data-link MTU and then letting
the normal PMTU Discovery processes update the PMTU as necessary.
The period SHOULD be configurable.

7. Auditing

   Not all systems that implement IPsec will implement auditing. For
   the most part, the granularity of auditing is a local matter.
   However, several auditable events are identified in the AH and ESP
   specifications and for each of these events a minimum set of
   information that SHOULD be included in an audit log is defined.
   Additional information also MAY be included in the audit log for each
   of these events, and additional events, not explicitly called out in
   this specification, also MAY result in audit log entries. There is
   no requirement for the receiver to transmit any message to the
   purported transmitter in response to the detection of an auditable
   event, because of the potential to induce denial of service via such
   action.

8. Use in Systems Supporting Information Flow Security

   Information of various sensitivity levels may be carried over a
   single network. Information labels (e.g., Unclassified, Company
   Proprietary, Secret) [DoD85, DoD87] are often employed to distinguish
   such information. The use of labels facilitates segregation of
   information, in support of information flow security models, e.g.,
   the Bell-LaPadula model [BL73]. Such models, and corresponding
   supporting technology, are designed to prevent the unauthorized flow
   of sensitive information, even in the face of Trojan Horse attacks.
   Conventional, discretionary access control (DAC) mechanisms, e.g.,
   based on access control lists, generally are not sufficient to
   support such policies, and thus facilities such as the SPD do not
   suffice in such environments.

   In the military context, technology that supports such models is
   often referred to as multi-level security (MLS). Computers and
   networks often are designated "multi-level secure" if they support
   the separation of labelled data in conjunction with information flow
   security policies. Although such technology is more broadly
   applicable than just military applications, this document uses the
   acronym "MLS" to designate the technology, consistent with much
   extant literature.

   IPsec mechanisms can easily support MLS networking. MLS networking
   requires the use of strong Mandatory Access Controls (MAC), which
   unprivileged users or unprivileged processes are incapable of
   controlling or violating. This section pertains only to the use of
   these IP security mechanisms in MLS (information flow security
   policy) environments. Nothing in this section applies to systems not
   claiming to provide MLS.

As used in this section, "sensitivity information" might include
implementation-defined hierarchic levels, categories, and/or
releasability information.

AH can be used to provide strong authentication in support of
mandatory access control decisions in MLS environments. If explicit
IP sensitivity information (e.g., IPSO [Ken91]) is used and
confidentiality is not considered necessary within the particular
operational environment, AH can be used to authenticate the binding
between sensitivity labels in the IP header and the IP payload
(including user data). This is a significant improvement over
labeled IPv4 networks where the sensitivity information is trusted
even though there is no authentication or cryptographic binding of
the information to the IP header and user data. IPv4 networks might
or might not use explicit labelling. IPv6 will normally use implicit
sensitivity information that is part of the IPsec Security
Association but not transmitted with each packet instead of using
explicit sensitivity information. All explicit IP sensitivity
information MUST be authenticated using either ESP, AH, or both.

Encryption is useful and can be desirable even when all of the hosts
are within a protected environment, for example, behind a firewall or
disjoint from any external connectivity. ESP can be used, in
conjunction with appropriate key management and encryption
algorithms, in support of both DAC and MAC. (The choice of
encryption and authentication algorithms, and the assurance level of
an IPsec implementation will determine the environments in which an
implementation may be deemed sufficient to satisfy MLS requirements.)
Key management can make use of sensitivity information to provide
MAC. IPsec implementations on systems claiming to provide MLS SHOULD
be capable of using IPsec to provide MAC for IP-based communications.

8.1 Relationship Between Security Associations and Data Sensitivity

Both the Encapsulating Security Payload and the Authentication Header
can be combined with appropriate Security Association policies to
provide multi-level secure networking. In this case each SA (or SA
bundle) is normally used for only a single instance of sensitivity
information. For example, "PROPRIETARY - Internet Engineering" must
be associated with a different SA (or SA bundle) from "PROPRIETARY -
Finance".

8.2 Sensitivity Consistency Checking

An MLS implementation (both host and router) MAY associate
sensitivity information, or a range of sensitivity information with
an interface, or a configured IP address with its associated prefix
(the latter is sometimes referred to as a logical interface, or an

interface alias). If such properties exist, an implementation SHOULD compare the sensitivity information associated with the packet against the sensitivity information associated with the interface or address/prefix from which the packet arrived, or through which the packet will depart. This check will either verify that the sensitivities match, or that the packet's sensitivity falls within the range of the interface or address/prefix.

The checking SHOULD be done on both inbound and outbound processing.

8.3 Additional MLS Attributes for Security Association Databases

Section 4.4 discussed two Security Association databases (the Security Policy Database (SPD) and the Security Association Database (SAD)) and the associated policy selectors and SA attributes. MLS networking introduces an additional selector/attribute:

          - Sensitivity information.

The Sensitivity information aids in selecting the appropriate algorithms and key strength, so that the traffic gets a level of protection appropriate to its importance or sensitivity as described in section 8.1. The exact syntax of the sensitivity information is implementation defined.

8.4 Additional Inbound Processing Steps for MLS Networking

After an inbound packet has passed through IPsec processing, an MLS implementation SHOULD first check the packet's sensitivity (as defined by the SA (or SA bundle) used for the packet) with the interface or address/prefix as described in section 8.2 before delivering the datagram to an upper-layer protocol or forwarding it.

The MLS system MUST retain the binding between the data received in an IPsec protected packet and the sensitivity information in the SA or SAs used for processing, so appropriate policy decisions can be made when delivering the datagram to an application or forwarding engine. The means for maintaining this binding are implementation specific.

8.5 Additional Outbound Processing Steps for MLS Networking

An MLS implementation of IPsec MUST perform two additional checks besides the normal steps detailed in section 5.1.1. When consulting the SPD or the SAD to find an outbound security association, the MLS implementation MUST use the sensitivity of the data to select an appropriate outbound SA or SA bundle. The second check comes before forwarding the packet out to its destination, and is the sensitivity consistency checking described in section 8.2.

8.6 Additional MLS Processing for Security Gateways

An MLS security gateway MUST follow the previously mentioned inbound and outbound processing rules as well as perform some additional processing specific to the intermediate protection of packets in an MLS environment.

A security gateway MAY act as an outbound proxy, creating SAs for MLS systems that originate packets forwarded by the gateway. These MLS systems may explicitly label the packets to be forwarded, or the whole originating network may have sensitivity characteristics associated with it. The security gateway MUST create and use appropriate SAs for AH, ESP, or both, to protect such traffic it forwards.

Similarly such a gateway SHOULD accept and process inbound AH and/or ESP packets and forward appropriately, using explicit packet labeling, or relying on the sensitivity characteristics of the destination network.

9. Performance Issues

The use of IPsec imposes computational performance costs on the hosts or security gateways that implement these protocols. These costs are associated with the memory needed for IPsec code and data structures, and the computation of integrity check values, encryption and decryption, and added per-packet handling. The per-packet computational costs will be manifested by increased latency and, possibly, reduced throughout. Use of SA/key management protocols, especially ones that employ public key cryptography, also adds computational performance costs to use of IPsec. These per-association computational costs will be manifested in terms of increased latency in association establishment. For many hosts, it is anticipated that software-based cryptography will not appreciably reduce throughput, but hardware may be required for security gateways (since they represent aggregation points), and for some hosts.

The use of IPsec also imposes bandwidth utilization costs on transmission, switching, and routing components of the Internet infrastructure, components not implementing IPsec. This is due to the increase in the packet size resulting from the addition of AH and/or ESP headers, AH and ESP tunneling (which adds a second IP header), and the increased packet traffic associated with key management protocols. It is anticipated that, in most instances,

this increased bandwidth demand will not noticeably affect the
Internet infrastructure. However, in some instances, the effects may
be significant, e.g., transmission of ESP encrypted traffic over a
dialup link that otherwise would have compressed the traffic.

Note: The initial SA establishment overhead will be felt in the first
packet. This delay could impact the transport layer and application.
For example, it could cause TCP to retransmit the SYN before the
ISAKMP exchange is done. The effect of the delay would be different
on UDP than TCP because TCP shouldn't transmit anything other than
the SYN until the connection is set up whereas UDP will go ahead and
transmit data beyond the first packet.

Note: As discussed earlier, compression can still be employed at
layers above IP. There is an IETF working group (IP Payload
Compression Protocol (ippcp)) working on "protocol specifications
that make it possible to perform lossless compression on individual
payloads before the payload is processed by a protocol that encrypts
it. These specifications will allow for compression operations to be
performed prior to the encryption of a payload by IPsec protocols."

10. Conformance Requirements

All IPv4 systems that claim to implement IPsec MUST comply with all
requirements of the Security Architecture document. All IPv6 systems
MUST comply with all requirements of the Security Architecture
document.

11. Security Considerations

The focus of this document is security; hence security considerations
permeate this specification.

12. Differences from RFC 1825

This architecture document differs substantially from RFC 1825 in
detail and in organization, but the fundamental notions are
unchanged. This document provides considerable additional detail in
terms of compliance specifications. It introduces the SPD and SAD,
and the notion of SA selectors. It is aligned with the new versions
of AH and ESP, which also differ from their predecessors. Specific
requirements for supported combinations of AH and ESP are newly
added, as are details of PMTU management.

Acknowledgements

Many of the concepts embodied in this specification were derived from
or influenced by the US Government's SP3 security protocol, ISO/IEC's
NLSP, the proposed swIPe security protocol [SDNS, ISO, IB93, IBK93],
and the work done for SNMP Security and SNMPv2 Security.

For over 3 years (although it sometimes seems *much* longer), this
document has evolved through multiple versions and iterations.
During this time, many people have contributed significant ideas and
energy to the process and the documents themselves. The authors
would like to thank Karen Seo for providing extensive help in the
review, editing, background research, and coordination for this
version of the specification. The authors would also like to thank
the members of the IPsec and IPng working groups, with special
mention of the efforts of (in alphabetic order): Steve Bellovin,
Steve Deering, James Hughes, Phil Karn, Frank Kastenholz, Perry
Metzger, David Mihelcic, Hilarie Orman, Norman Shulman, William
Simpson, Harry Varnis, and Nina Yuan.

Appendix A -- Glossary

   This section provides definitions for several key terms that are
   employed in this document. Other documents provide additional
   definitions and background information relevant to this technology,
   e.g., [VK83, HA94]. Included in this glossary are generic security
   service and security mechanism terms, plus IPsec-specific terms.

      Access Control
         Access control is a security service that prevents unauthorized
         use of a resource, including the prevention of use of a resource
         in an unauthorized manner. In the IPsec context, the resource
         to which access is being controlled is often:
                 o for a host, computing cycles or data
                 o for a security gateway, a network behind the gateway
         or
                 bandwidth on that network.

      Anti-replay
         [See "Integrity" below]

      Authentication
         This term is used informally to refer to the combination of two
         nominally distinct security services, data origin authentication
         and connectionless integrity. See the definitions below for
         each of these services.

      Availability
         Availability, when viewed as a security service, addresses the
         security concerns engendered by attacks against networks that
         deny or degrade service. For example, in the IPsec context, the
         use of anti-replay mechanisms in AH and ESP support
         availability.

      Confidentiality
         Confidentiality is the security service that protects data from
         unauthorized disclosure. The primary confidentiality concern in
         most instances is unauthorized disclosure of application level
         data, but disclosure of the external characteristics of
         communication also can be a concern in some circumstances.
         Traffic flow confidentiality is the service that addresses this
         latter concern by concealing source and destination addresses,
         message length, or frequency of communication. In the IPsec
         context, using ESP in tunnel mode, especially at a security
         gateway, can provide some level of traffic flow confidentiality.
         (See also traffic analysis, below.)

Encryption
   Encryption is a security mechanism used to transform data from
   an intelligible form (plaintext) into an unintelligible form
   (ciphertext), to provide confidentiality. The inverse
   transformation process is designated "decryption". Oftimes the
   term "encryption" is used to generically refer to both
   processes.

Data Origin Authentication
   Data origin authentication is a security service that verifies
   the identity of the claimed source of data. This service is
   usually bundled with connectionless integrity service.

Integrity
   Integrity is a security service that ensures that modifications
   to data are detectable. Integrity comes in various flavors to
   match application requirements. IPsec supports two forms of
   integrity: connectionless and a form of partial sequence
   integrity. Connectionless integrity is a service that detects
   modification of an individual IP datagram, without regard to the
   ordering of the datagram in a stream of traffic. The form of
   partial sequence integrity offered in IPsec is referred to as
   anti-replay integrity, and it detects arrival of duplicate IP
   datagrams (within a constrained window). This is in contrast to
   connection-oriented integrity, which imposes more stringent
   sequencing requirements on traffic, e.g., to be able to detect
   lost or re-ordered messages. Although authentication and
   integrity services often are cited separately, in practice they
   are intimately connected and almost always offered in tandem.

Security Association (SA)
   A simplex (uni-directional) logical connection, created for
   security purposes. All traffic traversing an SA is provided the
   same security processing. In IPsec, an SA is an internet layer
   abstraction implemented through the use of AH or ESP.

Security Gateway
   A security gateway is an intermediate system that acts as the
   communications interface between two networks. The set of hosts
   (and networks) on the external side of the security gateway is
   viewed as untrusted (or less trusted), while the networks and
   hosts and on the internal side are viewed as trusted (or more
   trusted). The internal subnets and hosts served by a security
   gateway are presumed to be trusted by virtue of sharing a
   common, local, security administration. (See "Trusted
   Subnetwork" below.) In the IPsec context, a security gateway is
   a point at which AH and/or ESP is implemented in order to serve

a set of internal hosts, providing security services for these
hosts when they communicate with external hosts also employing
IPsec (either directly or via another security gateway).

SPI
    Acronym for "Security Parameters Index". The combination of a
    destination address, a security protocol, and an SPI uniquely
    identifies a security association (SA, see above). The SPI is
    carried in AH and ESP protocols to enable the receiving system
    to select the SA under which a received packet will be
    processed. An SPI has only local significance, as defined by
    the creator of the SA (usually the receiver of the packet
    carrying the SPI); thus an SPI is generally viewed as an opaque
    bit string. However, the creator of an SA may choose to
    interpret the bits in an SPI to facilitate local processing.

Traffic Analysis
    The analysis of network traffic flow for the purpose of deducing
    information that is useful to an adversary. Examples of such
    information are frequency of transmission, the identities of the
    conversing parties, sizes of packets, flow identifiers, etc.
    [Sch94]

Trusted Subnetwork
    A subnetwork containing hosts and routers that trust each other
    not to engage in active or passive attacks. There also is an
    assumption that the underlying communications channel (e.g., a
    LAN or CAN) isn't being attacked by other means.

Appendix B -- Analysis/Discussion of PMTU/DF/Fragmentation Issues

B.1 DF bit

In cases where a system (host or gateway) adds an encapsulating
header (e.g., ESP tunnel), should/must the DF bit in the original
packet be copied to the encapsulating header?

Fragmenting seems correct for some situations, e.g., it might be
appropriate to fragment packets over a network with a very small MTU,
e.g., a packet radio network, or a cellular phone hop to mobile node,
rather than propagate back a very small PMTU for use over the rest of
the path. In other situations, it might be appropriate to set the DF
bit in order to get feedback from later routers about PMTU
constraints which require fragmentation. The existence of both of
these situations argues for enabling a system to decide whether or
not to fragment over a particular network "link", i.e., for requiring
an implementation to be able to copy the DF bit (and to process ICMP
PMTU messages), but making it an option to be selected on a per
interface basis. In other words, an administrator should be able to
configure the router's treatment of the DF bit (set, clear, copy from
encapsulated header) for each interface.

Note: If a bump-in-the-stack implementation of IPsec attempts to
apply different IPsec algorithms based on source/destination ports,
it will be difficult to apply Path MTU adjustments.

B.2 Fragmentation

If required, IP fragmentation occurs after IPsec processing within an
IPsec implementation. Thus, transport mode AH or ESP is applied only
to whole IP datagrams (not to IP fragments). An IP packet to which
AH or ESP has been applied may itself be fragmented by routers en
route, and such fragments MUST be reassembled prior to IPsec
processing at a receiver. In tunnel mode, AH or ESP is applied to an
IP packet, the payload of which may be a fragmented IP packet. For
example, a security gateway, "bump-in-the-stack" (BITS), or "bump-
in-the-wire" (BITW) IPsec implementation may apply tunnel mode AH to
such fragments. Note that BITS or BITW implementations are examples
of where a host IPsec implementation might receive fragments to which
tunnel mode is to be applied. However, if transport mode is to be
applied, then these implementations MUST reassemble the fragments
prior to applying IPsec.

NOTE: IPsec always has to figure out what the encapsulating IP header fields are. This is independent of where you insert IPsec and is intrinsic to the definition of IPsec. Therefore any IPsec implementation that is not integrated into an IP implementation must include code to construct the necessary IP headers (e.g., IP2):

        o AH-tunnel -> IP2-AH-IP1-Transport-Data
        o ESP-tunnel -> IP2-ESP_hdr-IP1-Transport-Data-ESP_trailer

    ****

Overall, the fragmentation/reassembly approach described above works for all cases examined.

Implementation approach	AH Xport IPv4 IPv6	AH Tunnel IPv4 IPv6	ESP Xport IPv4 IPv6	ESP Tunnel IPv4 IPv6
Hosts (integr w/ IP stack)	Y Y	Y Y	Y Y	Y Y
Hosts (betw/ IP and drivers)	Y Y	Y Y	Y Y	Y Y
S. Gwy (integr w/ IP stack)		Y Y		Y Y
Outboard crypto processor *				

    * If the crypto processor system has its own IP address, then it
       is covered by the security gateway case. This box receives
       the packet from the host and performs IPsec processing. It
       has to be able to handle the same AH, ESP, and related
       IPv4/IPv6 tunnel processing that a security gateway would have
       to handle. If it doesn't have it's own address, then it is
       similar to the bump-in-the stack implementation between IP and
       the network drivers.

The following analysis assumes that:

    1. There is only one IPsec module in a given system's stack.
       There isn't an IPsec module A (adding ESP/encryption and
       thus) hiding the transport protocol, SRC port, and DEST port
       from IPsec module B.
    2. There are several places where IPsec could be implemented (as
       shown in the table above).
        a. Hosts with integration of IPsec into the native IP
           implementation. Implementer has access to the source
           for the stack.
        b. Hosts with bump-in-the-stack implementations, where
           IPsec is implemented between IP and the local network
           drivers. Source access for stack is not available;
           but there are well-defined interfaces that allows the
           IPsec code to be incorporated into the system.

                c. Security gateways and outboard crypto processors with
                   integration of IPsec into the stack.
         3. Not all of the above approaches are feasible in all hosts.
            But it was assumed that for each approach, there are some
            hosts for whom the approach is feasible.

   For each of the above 3 categories, there are IPv4 and IPv6, AH
   transport and tunnel modes, and ESP transport and tunnel modes -- for
   a total of 24 cases (3 x 2 x 4).

   Some header fields and interface fields are listed here for ease of
   reference -- they're not in the header order, but instead listed to
   allow comparison between the columns. (* = not covered by AH
   authentication. ESP authentication doesn't cover any headers that
   precede it.)

```
                                         IP/Transport Interface
         IPv4                IPv6        (RFC 1122 -- Sec 3.4)
         ----                ----        ---------------------
         Version = 4         Version = 6
         Header Len
         *TOS                Class,Flow Lbl  TOS
         Packet Len          Payload Len     Len
         ID                                  ID (optional)
         *Flags                              DF
         *Offset
         *TTL                *Hop Limit      TTL
         Protocol            Next Header
         *Checksum
         Src Address         Src Address     Src Address
         Dst Address         Dst Address     Dst Address
         Options?            Options?        Opt
```

         ? = AH covers Option-Type and Option-Length, but
             might not cover Option-Data.

   The results for each of the 20 cases is shown below ("works" = will
   work if system fragments after outbound IPsec processing, reassembles
   before inbound IPsec processing). Notes indicate implementation
   issues.

   a. Hosts (integrated into IP stack)
         o AH-transport --> (IP1-AH-Transport-Data)
                 - IPv4 -- works
                 - IPv6 -- works
         o AH-tunnel --> (IP2-AH-IP1-Transport-Data)
                 - IPv4 -- works
                 - IPv6 -- works

```
          o ESP-transport --> (IP1-ESP_hdr-Transport-Data-ESP_trailer)
                    - IPv4 -- works
                    - IPv6 -- works
          o ESP-tunnel -->  (IP2-ESP_hdr-IP1-Transport-Data-ESP_trailer)
                    - IPv4 -- works
                    - IPv6 -- works
```

   b. Hosts (Bump-in-the-stack) -- put IPsec between IP layer and
      network drivers. In this case, the IPsec module would have to do
      something like one of the following for fragmentation and
      reassembly.
            - do the fragmentation/reassembly work itself and
              send/receive the packet directly to/from the network
              layer. In AH or ESP transport mode, this is fine. In AH
              or ESP tunnel mode where the tunnel end is at the ultimate
              destination, this is fine. But in AH or ESP tunnel modes
              where the tunnel end is different from the ultimate
              destination and where the source host is multi-homed, this
              approach could result in sub-optimal routing because the
              IPsec module may be unable to obtain the information
              needed (LAN interface and next-hop gateway) to direct the
              packet to the appropriate network interface. This is not
              a problem if the interface and next-hop gateway are the
              same for the ultimate destination and for the tunnel end.
              But if they are different, then IPsec would need to know
              the LAN interface and the next-hop gateway for the tunnel
              end. (Note: The tunnel end (security gateway) is highly
              likely to be on the regular path to the ultimate
              destination. But there could also be more than one path
              to the destination, e.g., the host could be at an
              organization with 2 firewalls. And the path being used
              could involve the less commonly chosen firewall.) OR
            - pass the IPsec'd packet back to the IP layer where an
              extra IP header would end up being pre-pended and the
              IPsec module would have to check and let IPsec'd fragments
              go by.
                                    OR
            - pass the packet contents to the IP layer in a form such
              that the IP layer recreates an appropriate IP header

   At the network layer, the IPsec module will have access to the
   following selectors from the packet -- SRC address, DST address,
   Next Protocol, and if there's a transport layer header --> SRC
   port and DST port. One cannot assume IPsec has access to the
   Name. It is assumed that the available selector information is
   sufficient to figure out the relevant Security Policy entry and
   Security Association(s).

```
        o AH-transport  --> (IP1-AH-Transport-Data)
                - IPv4 -- works
                - IPv6 -- works
        o AH-tunnel --> (IP2-AH-IP1-Transport-Data)
                - IPv4 -- works
                - IPv6 -- works
        o ESP-transport --> (IP1-ESP_hdr-Transport-Data-ESP_trailer)
                - IPv4 -- works
                - IPv6 -- works
        o ESP-tunnel -->  (IP2-ESP_hdr-IP1-Transport-Data-ESP_trailer)
                - IPv4 -- works
                - IPv6 -- works
```

   c. Security gateways -- integrate IPsec into the IP stack

      NOTE: The IPsec module will have access to the following
      selectors from the packet -- SRC address, DST address, Next
      Protocol, and if there's a transport layer header --> SRC port
      and DST port. It won't have access to the User ID (only Hosts
      have access to User ID information.) Unlike some Bump-in-the-
      stack implementations, security gateways may be able to look up
      the Source Address in the DNS to provide a System Name, e.g., in
      situations involving use of dynamically assigned IP addresses in
      conjunction with dynamically updated DNS entries. It also won't
      have access to the transport layer information if there is an ESP
      header, or if it's not the first fragment of a fragmented
      message. It is assumed that the available selector information
      is sufficient to figure out the relevant Security Policy entry
      and Security Association(s).

```
        o AH-tunnel --> (IP2-AH-IP1-Transport-Data)
                - IPv4 -- works
                - IPv6 -- works
        o ESP-tunnel -->  (IP2-ESP_hdr-IP1-Transport-Data-ESP_trailer)
                - IPv4 -- works
                - IPv6 -- works
```

   ****

B.3 Path MTU Discovery

   As mentioned earlier, "ICMP PMTU" refers to an ICMP message used for
   Path MTU Discovery.

   The legend for the diagrams below in B.3.1 and B.3.3 (but not B.3.2)
   is:

      ==== = security association (AH or ESP, transport or tunnel)

```
            ---- = connectivity (or if so labelled, administrative boundary)
            .... = ICMP message (hereafter referred to as ICMP PMTU) for

                   IPv4:
                   - Type = 3 (Destination Unreachable)
                   - Code = 4 (Fragmentation needed and DF set)
                   - Next-Hop MTU in the low-order 16 bits of the second
                     word of the ICMP header (labelled unused in RFC 792),
                     with high-order 16 bits set to zero

                   IPv6 (RFC 1885):
                   - Type = 2 (Packet Too Big)
                   - Code = 0 (Fragmentation needed and DF set)
                   - Next-Hop MTU in the 32 bit MTU field of the ICMP6

        Hx   = host x
        Rx   = router x
        SGx  = security gateway x
        X*   = X supports IPsec
```

B.3.1 Identifying the Originating Host(s)

The amount of information returned with the ICMP message is limited
and this affects what selectors are available to identify security
associations, originating hosts, etc. for use in further propagating
the PMTU information.

In brief... An ICMP message must contain the following information
from the "offending" packet:
        - IPv4 (RFC 792) -- IP header plus a minimum of 64 bits

Accordingly, in the IPv4 context, an ICMP PMTU may identify only the
first (outermost) security association. This is because the ICMP
PMTU may contain only 64 bits of the "offending" packet beyond the IP
header, which would capture only the first SPI from AH or ESP. In
the IPv6 context, an ICMP PMTU will probably provide all the SPIs and
the selectors in the IP header, but maybe not the SRC/DST ports (in
the transport header) or the encapsulated (TCP, UDP, etc.) protocol.
Moreover, if ESP is used, the transport ports and protocol selectors
may be encrypted.

Looking at the diagram below of a security gateway tunnel (as
mentioned elsewhere, security gateways do not use transport mode)...

```
    H1    ===================             H3
      \   |                    |          /
  H0 -- SG1* ---- R1 ---- SG2* ---- R2 -- H5
    /   ^            |               \
   H2   |........|                   H4
```

Suppose that the security policy for SG1 is to use a single SA to SG2
for all the traffic between hosts H0, H1, and H2 and hosts H3, H4,
and H5. And suppose H0 sends a data packet to H5 which causes R1 to
send an ICMP PMTU message to SG1. If the PMTU message has only the
SPI, SG1 will be able to look up the SA and find the list of possible
hosts (H0, H1, H2, wildcard); but SG1 will have no way to figure out
that H0 sent the traffic that triggered the ICMP PMTU message.

```
     original          after IPsec      ICMP
     packet            processing       packet
     --------          -----------      ------
                                        IP-3 header (S = R1, D = SG1)
                                        ICMP header (includes PMTU)
                       IP-2 header      IP-2 header (S = SG1, D = SG2)
                       ESP header       minimum of 64 bits of ESP hdr (*)
     IP-1 header       IP-1 header
     TCP header        TCP header
     TCP data          TCP data
                       ESP trailer
```

    (*) The 64 bits will include enough of the ESP (or AH) header to
        include the SPI.
            - ESP -- SPI (32 bits), Seq number (32 bits)
            - AH -- Next header (8 bits), Payload Len (8 bits),
              Reserved (16 bits), SPI (32 bits)

This limitation on the amount of information returned with an ICMP
message creates a problem in identifying the originating hosts for
the packet (so as to know where to further propagate the ICMP PMTU
information). If the ICMP message contains only 64 bits of the IPsec
header (minimum for IPv4), then the IPsec selectors (e.g., Source and
Destination addresses, Next Protocol, Source and Destination ports,
etc.) will have been lost. But the ICMP error message will still
provide SG1 with the SPI, the PMTU information and the source and
destination gateways for the relevant security association.

The destination security gateway and SPI uniquely define a security
association which in turn defines a set of possible originating
hosts. At this point, SG1 could:

   a. send the PMTU information to all the possible originating hosts.
      This would not work well if the host list is a wild card or if
      many/most of the hosts weren't sending to SG1; but it might work
      if the SPI/destination/etc mapped to just one or a small number of
      hosts.
   b. store the PMTU with the SPI/etc and wait until the next packet(s)
      arrive from the originating host(s) for the relevant security
      association. If it/they are bigger than the PMTU, drop the
      packet(s), and compose ICMP PMTU message(s) with the new packet(s)
      and the updated PMTU, and send the originating host(s) the ICMP
      message(s) about the problem. This involves a delay in notifying
      the originating host(s), but avoids the problems of (a).

   Since only the latter approach is feasible in all instances, a
   security gateway MUST provide such support, as an option. However,
   if the ICMP message contains more information from the original
   packet, then there may be enough information to immediately determine
   to which host to propagate the ICMP/PMTU message and to provide that
   system with the 5 fields (source address, destination address, source
   port, destination port, and transport protocol) needed to determine
   where to store/update the PMTU. Under such circumstances, a security
   gateway MUST generate an ICMP PMTU message immediately upon receipt
   of an ICMP PMTU from further down the path. NOTE: The Next Protocol
   field may not be contained in the ICMP message and the use of ESP
   encryption may hide the selector fields that have been encrypted.

B.3.2 Calculation of PMTU

   The calculation of PMTU from an ICMP PMTU has to take into account
   the addition of any IPsec header by H1 -- AH and/or ESP transport, or
   ESP or AH tunnel. Within a single host, multiple applications may
   share an SPI and nesting of security associations may occur. (See
   Section 4.5 Basic Combinations of Security Associations for
   description of the combinations that MUST be supported). The diagram
   below illustrates an example of security associations between a pair
   of hosts (as viewed from the perspective of one of the hosts.) (ESPx
   or AHx = transport mode)

            Socket 1 ------------------------|
                                             |
            Socket 2 (ESPx/SPI-A) ---------- AHx (SPI-B) -- Internet

   In order to figure out the PMTU for each socket that maps to SPI-B,
   it will be necessary to have backpointers from SPI-B to each of the 2
   paths that lead to it -- Socket 1 and Socket 2/SPI-A.

B.3.3 Granularity of Maintaining PMTU Data

In hosts, the granularity with which PMTU ICMP processing can be done
differs depending on the implementation situation. Looking at a
host, there are three situations that are of interest with respect to
PMTU issues:

a. Integration of IPsec into the native IP implementation
b. Bump-in-the-stack implementations, where IPsec is implemented
   "underneath" an existing implementation of a TCP/IP protocol
   stack, between the native IP and the local network drivers
c. No IPsec implementation - This case is included because it is
   relevant in cases where a security gateway is sending PMTU
   information back to a host.

Only in case (a) can the PMTU data be maintained at the same
granularity as communication associations. In the other cases, the
IP layer will maintain PMTU data at the granularity of Source and
Destination IP addresses (and optionally TOS/Class), as described in
RFC 1191. This is an important difference, because more than one
communication association may map to the same source and destination
IP addresses, and each communication association may have a different
amount of IPsec header overhead (e.g., due to use of different
transforms or different algorithms). The examples below illustrate
this.

In cases (a) and (b)... Suppose you have the following situation.
H1 is sending to H2 and the packet to be sent from R1 to R2 exceeds
the PMTU of the network hop between them.

```
          ====================================
          |                                  |
          H1* --- R1 ----- R2 ---- R3 ---- H2*
           ^        |
           |.......|
```

If R1 is configured to not fragment subscriber traffic, then R1 sends
an ICMP PMTU message with the appropriate PMTU to H1. H1's
processing would vary with the nature of the implementation. In case
(a) (native IP), the security services are bound to sockets or the
equivalent. Here the IP/IPsec implementation in H1 can store/update
the PMTU for the associated socket. In case (b), the IP layer in H1
can store/update the PMTU but only at the granularity of Source and
Destination addresses and possibly TOS/Class, as noted above. So the
result may be sub-optimal, since the PMTU for a given
SRC/DST/TOS/Class will be the subtraction of the largest amount of
IPsec header used for any communication association between a given
source and destination.

In case (c), there has to be a security gateway to have any IPsec
processing. So suppose you have the following situation. H1 is
sending to H2 and the packet to be sent from SG1 to R exceeds the
PMTU of the network hop between them.

```
                    =================
                    |               |
            H1 ---- SG1* --- R --- SG2* ---- H2
             ^             |
             |.......|
```

As described above for case (b), the IP layer in H1 can store/update
the PMTU but only at the granularity of Source and Destination
addresses, and possibly TOS/Class. So the result may be sub-optimal,
since the PMTU for a given SRC/DST/TOS/Class will be the subtraction
of the largest amount of IPsec header used for any communication
association between a given source and destination.

B.3.4 Per Socket Maintenance of PMTU Data

Implementation of the calculation of PMTU (Section B.3.2) and support
for PMTUs at the granularity of individual "communication
associations" (Section B.3.3) is a local matter. However, a socket-
based implementation of IPsec in a host SHOULD maintain the
information on a per socket basis. Bump in the stack systems MUST
pass an ICMP PMTU to the host IP implementation, after adjusting it
for any IPsec header overhead added by these systems. The
determination of the overhead SHOULD be determined by analysis of the
SPI and any other selector information present in a returned ICMP
PMTU message.

B.3.5 Delivery of PMTU Data to the Transport Layer

The host mechanism for getting the updated PMTU to the transport
layer is unchanged, as specified in RFC 1191 (Path MTU Discovery).

B.3.6 Aging of PMTU Data

This topic is covered in Section 6.1.2.4.

Appendix C -- Sequence Space Window Code Example

   This appendix contains a routine that implements a bitmask check for
   a 32 packet window. It was provided by James Hughes
   (jim_hughes@stortek.com) and Harry Varnis (hgv@anubis.network.com)
   and is intended as an implementation example. Note that this code
   both checks for a replay and updates the window. Thus the algorithm,
   as shown, should only be called AFTER the packet has been
   authenticated. Implementers might wish to consider splitting the
   code to do the check for replays before computing the ICV. If the
   packet is not a replay, the code would then compute the ICV, (discard
   any bad packets), and if the packet is OK, update the window.

```
#include <stdio.h>
#include <stdlib.h>
typedef unsigned long u_long;

enum {
    ReplayWindowSize = 32
};

u_long bitmap = 0;                    /* session state - must be 32 bits */
u_long lastSeq = 0;                        /* session state */

/* Returns 0 if packet disallowed, 1 if packet permitted */
int ChkReplayWindow(u_long seq);

int ChkReplayWindow(u_long seq) {
    u_long diff;

    if (seq == 0) return 0;              /* first == 0 or wrapped */
    if (seq > lastSeq) {                 /* new larger sequence number */
        diff = seq - lastSeq;
        if (diff < ReplayWindowSize) {  /* In window */
            bitmap <<= diff;
            bitmap |= 1;                 /* set bit for this packet */
        } else bitmap = 1;               /* This packet has a "way larger" */
        lastSeq = seq;
        return 1;                        /* larger is good */
    }
    diff = lastSeq - seq;
    if (diff >= ReplayWindowSize) return 0; /* too old or wrapped */
    if (bitmap & ((u_long)1 << diff)) return 0; /* already seen */
    bitmap |= ((u_long)1 << diff);            /* mark as seen */
    return 1;                        /* out of order but good */
}

char string_buffer[512];
```

```
#define STRING_BUFFER_SIZE sizeof(string_buffer)

int main() {
    int result;
    u_long last, current, bits;

    printf("Input initial state (bits in hex, last msgnum):\n");
    if (!fgets(string_buffer, STRING_BUFFER_SIZE, stdin)) exit(0);
    sscanf(string_buffer, "%lx %lu", &bits, &last);
    if (last != 0)
    bits |= 1;
    bitmap = bits;
    lastSeq = last;
    printf("bits:%08lx last:%lu\n", bitmap, lastSeq);
    printf("Input value to test (current):\n");

    while (1) {
        if (!fgets(string_buffer, STRING_BUFFER_SIZE, stdin)) break;
        sscanf(string_buffer, "%lu", &current);
        result = ChkReplayWindow(current);
        printf("%-3s", result ? "OK" : "BAD");
        printf(" bits:%08lx last:%lu\n", bitmap, lastSeq);
    }
    return 0;
}
```

Appendix D -- Categorization of ICMP messages

The tables below characterize ICMP messages as being either host
generated, router generated, both, unassigned/unknown. The first set
are IPv4. The second set are IPv6.

IPv4

```
Type    Name/Codes                                          Reference
====================================================================
HOST GENERATED:
   3       Destination Unreachable
           2   Protocol Unreachable                         [RFC792]
           3   Port Unreachable                             [RFC792]
           8   Source Host Isolated                         [RFC792]
           14  Host Precedence Violation                    [RFC1812]
  10       Router Selection                                 [RFC1256]
```

```
Type    Name/Codes                                          Reference
====================================================================
ROUTER GENERATED:
   3       Destination Unreachable
           0   Net Unreachable                              [RFC792]
           4   Fragmentation Needed, Don't Fragment was Set [RFC792]
           5   Source Route Failed                          [RFC792]
           6   Destination Network Unknown                  [RFC792]
           7   Destination Host Unknown                     [RFC792]
           9   Comm. w/Dest. Net. is Administratively Prohibited [RFC792]
           11  Destination Network Unreachable for Type of Service[RFC792]
   5       Redirect
           0   Redirect Datagram for the Network (or subnet) [RFC792]
           2   Redirect Datagram for the Type of Service & Network[RFC792]
   9       Router Advertisement                             [RFC1256]
  18       Address Mask Reply                               [RFC950]
```

IPv4

```
Type    Name/Codes                                              Reference
=========================================================================
BOTH ROUTER AND HOST GENERATED:
   0    Echo Reply                                              [RFC792]
   3    Destination Unreachable
        1  Host Unreachable                                     [RFC792]
        10 Comm. w/Dest. Host is Administratively Prohibited    [RFC792]
        12 Destination Host Unreachable for Type of Service     [RFC792]
        13 Communication Administratively Prohibited            [RFC1812]
        15 Precedence cutoff in effect                          [RFC1812]
   4    Source Quench                                           [RFC792]
   5    Redirect
        1  Redirect Datagram for the Host                       [RFC792]
        3  Redirect Datagram for the Type of Service and Host   [RFC792]
   6    Alternate Host Address                                  [JBP]
   8    Echo                                                    [RFC792]
  11    Time Exceeded                                           [RFC792]
  12    Parameter Problem                            [RFC792,RFC1108]
  13    Timestamp                                               [RFC792]
  14    Timestamp Reply                                         [RFC792]
  15    Information Request                                     [RFC792]
  16    Information Reply                                       [RFC792]
  17    Address Mask Request                                    [RFC950]
  30    Traceroute                                              [RFC1393]
  31    Datagram Conversion Error                               [RFC1475]
  32    Mobile Host Redirect                                    [Johnson]
  39    SKIP                                                    [Markson]
  40    Photuris                                                [Simpson]


Type    Name/Codes                                              Reference
=========================================================================
UNASSIGNED TYPE OR UNKNOWN GENERATOR:
   1    Unassigned                                              [JBP]
   2    Unassigned                                              [JBP]
   7    Unassigned                                              [JBP]
  19    Reserved (for Security)                                 [Solo]
  20-29 Reserved (for Robustness Experiment)                    [ZSu]
  33    IPv6 Where-Are-You                                      [Simpson]
  34    IPv6 I-Am-Here                                          [Simpson]
  35    Mobile Registration Request                             [Simpson]
  36    Mobile Registration Reply                               [Simpson]
  37    Domain Name Request                                     [Simpson]
  38    Domain Name Reply                                       [Simpson]
  41-255 Reserved                                               [JBP]
```

                              IPv6

```
Type     Name/Codes                                        Reference
========================================================================
HOST GENERATED:
  1      Destination Unreachable                           [RFC 1885]
         4  Port Unreachable

Type     Name/Codes                                        Reference
========================================================================
ROUTER GENERATED:
  1      Destination Unreachable                           [RFC1885]
         0  No Route to Destination
         1  Comm. w/Destination is Administratively Prohibited
         2  Not a Neighbor
         3  Address Unreachable
  2      Packet Too Big                                    [RFC1885]
         0
  3      Time Exceeded                                     [RFC1885]
         0  Hop Limit Exceeded in Transit
         1  Fragment reassembly time exceeded


Type     Name/Codes                                        Reference
========================================================================
BOTH ROUTER AND HOST GENERATED:
  4      Parameter Problem                                 [RFC1885]
         0  Erroneous Header Field Encountered
         1  Unrecognized Next Header Type Encountered
         2  Unrecognized IPv6 Option Encountered
```

References

[BL73]   Bell, D.E. & LaPadula, L.J., "Secure Computer Systems:
            Mathematical Foundations and Model", Technical Report M74-
            244, The MITRE Corporation, Bedford, MA, May 1973.

[Bra97]   Bradner, S., "Key words for use in RFCs to Indicate
            Requirement Level", BCP 14, RFC 2119, March 1997.

[DoD85]   US National Computer Security Center, "Department of
            Defense Trusted Computer System Evaluation Criteria", DoD
            5200.28-STD, US Department of Defense, Ft. Meade, MD.,
            December 1985.

[DoD87]   US National Computer Security Center, "Trusted Network
            Interpretation of the Trusted Computer System Evaluation
            Criteria", NCSC-TG-005, Version 1, US Department of
            Defense, Ft. Meade, MD., 31 July 1987.

[HA94]   Haller, N., and R. Atkinson, "On Internet Authentication",
            RFC 1704, October 1994.

[HC98]   Harkins, D., and D. Carrel, "The Internet Key Exchange
            (IKE)", RFC 2409, November 1998.

[HM97]   Harney, H., and C. Muckenhirn, "Group Key Management
            Protocol (GKMP) Architecture", RFC 2094, July 1997.

[ISO]   ISO/IEC JTC1/SC6, Network Layer Security Protocol, ISO-IEC
            DIS 11577, International Standards Organisation, Geneva,
            Switzerland, 29 November 1992.

[IB93]   John Ioannidis and Matt Blaze, "Architecture and
            Implementation of Network-layer Security Under Unix",
            Proceedings of USENIX Security Symposium, Santa Clara, CA,
            October 1993.

[IBK93]   John Ioannidis, Matt Blaze, & Phil Karn, "swIPe: Network-
            Layer Security for IP", presentation at the Spring 1993
            IETF Meeting, Columbus, Ohio

[KA98a]   Kent, S., and R. Atkinson, "IP Authentication Header", RFC
            2402, November 1998.

[KA98b]   Kent, S., and R. Atkinson, "IP Encapsulating Security
            Payload (ESP)", RFC 2406, November 1998.

[Ken91]   Kent, S., "US DoD Security Options for the Internet
           Protocol", RFC 1108, November 1991.

[MSST97]   Maughan, D., Schertler, M., Schneider, M., and J. Turner,
           "Internet Security Association and Key Management Protocol
           (ISAKMP)", RFC 2408, November 1998.

[Orm97]   Orman, H., "The OAKLEY Key Determination Protocol", RFC
           2412, November 1998.

[Pip98]   Piper, D., "The Internet IP Security Domain of
           Interpretation for ISAKMP", RFC 2407, November 1998.

[Sch94]   Bruce Schneier, Applied Cryptography, Section 8.6, John
           Wiley & Sons, New York, NY, 1994.

[SDNS]   SDNS Secure Data Network System, Security Protocol 3, SP3,
           Document SDN.301, Revision 1.5, 15 May 1989, published in
           NIST Publication NIST-IR-90-4250, February 1990.

[SMPT98]   Shacham, A., Monsour, R., Pereira, R., and M. Thomas, "IP
           Payload Compression Protocol (IPComp)", RFC 2393, August
           1998.

[TDG97]   Thayer, R., Doraswamy, N., and R. Glenn, "IP Security
           Document Roadmap", RFC 2411, November 1998.

[VK83]   V.L. Voydock & S.T. Kent, "Security Mechanisms in High-
           level Networks", ACM Computing Surveys, Vol. 15, No. 2,
           June 1983.

Disclaimer

    The views and specification expressed in this document are those of
    the authors and are not necessarily those of their employers. The
    authors and their employers specifically disclaim responsibility for
    any problems arising from correct or incorrect implementation or use
    of this design.

Author Information

   Stephen Kent
   BBN Corporation
   70 Fawcett Street
   Cambridge, MA 02140
   USA

   Phone: +1 (617) 873-3988
   EMail: kent@bbn.com

   Randall Atkinson
   @Home Network
   425 Broadway
   Redwood City, CA 94063
   USA

   Phone: +1 (415) 569-5000
   EMail: rja@corp.home.net

RFC 2401

66

Network Working Group   S. Kent
Request for Comments: 2402   BBN Corp
Obsoletes: 1826   R. Atkinson
Category: Standards Track   @Home Network
                                                         November 1998

                        IP Authentication Header

Table of Contents

1. Introduction

    The IP Authentication Header (AH) is used to provide connectionless
    integrity and data origin authentication for IP datagrams (hereafter
    referred to as just "authentication"), and to provide protection
    against replays. This latter, optional service may be selected, by
    the receiver, when a Security Association is established. (Although
    the default calls for the sender to increment the Sequence Number
    used for anti-replay, the service is effective only if the receiver
    checks the Sequence Number.) AH provides authentication for as much
    of the IP header as possible, as well as for upper level protocol
    data. However, some IP header fields may change in transit and the
    value of these fields, when the packet arrives at the receiver, may
    not be predictable by the sender. The values of such fields cannot
    be protected by AH. Thus the protection provided to the IP header by
    AH is somewhat piecemeal.

    AH may be applied alone, in combination with the IP Encapsulating
    Security Payload (ESP) [KA97b], or in a nested fashion through the
    use of tunnel mode (see "Security Architecture for the Internet
    Protocol" [KA97a], hereafter referred to as the Security Architecture
    document). Security services can be provided between a pair of
    communicating hosts, between a pair of communicating security
    gateways, or between a security gateway and a host. ESP may be used
    to provide the same security services, and it also provides a
    confidentiality (encryption) service. The primary difference between
    the authentication provided by ESP and AH is the extent of the
    coverage. Specifically, ESP does not protect any IP header fields

unless those fields are encapsulated by ESP (tunnel mode). For more
details on how to use AH and ESP in various network environments, see
the Security Architecture document [KA97a].

It is assumed that the reader is familiar with the terms and concepts
described in the Security Architecture document. In particular, the
reader should be familiar with the definitions of security services
offered by AH and ESP, the concept of Security Associations, the ways
in which AH can be used in conjunction with ESP, and the different
key management options available for AH and ESP. (With regard to the
last topic, the current key management options required for both AH
and ESP are manual keying and automated keying via IKE [HC98].)

The keywords MUST, MUST NOT, REQUIRED, SHALL, SHALL NOT, SHOULD,
SHOULD NOT, RECOMMENDED, MAY, and OPTIONAL, when they appear in this
document, are to be interpreted as described in RFC 2119 [Bra97].

2. Authentication Header Format

The protocol header (IPv4, IPv6, or Extension) immediately preceding
the AH header will contain the value 51 in its Protocol (IPv4) or
Next Header (IPv6, Extension) field [STD-2].

```
 0                   1                   2                   3
 0 1 2 3 4 5 6 7 8 9 0 1 2 3 4 5 6 7 8 9 0 1 2 3 4 5 6 7 8 9 0 1
+-+-+-+-+-+-+-+-+-+-+-+-+-+-+-+-+-+-+-+-+-+-+-+-+-+-+-+-+-+-+-+-+
| Next Header   |  Payload Len  |          RESERVED             |
+-+-+-+-+-+-+-+-+-+-+-+-+-+-+-+-+-+-+-+-+-+-+-+-+-+-+-+-+-+-+-+-+
|                 Security Parameters Index (SPI)               |
+-+-+-+-+-+-+-+-+-+-+-+-+-+-+-+-+-+-+-+-+-+-+-+-+-+-+-+-+-+-+-+-+
|                    Sequence Number Field                      |
+-+-+-+-+-+-+-+-+-+-+-+-+-+-+-+-+-+-+-+-+-+-+-+-+-+-+-+-+-+-+-+-+
|                                                               |
+                Authentication Data (variable)                 |
|                                                               |
+-+-+-+-+-+-+-+-+-+-+-+-+-+-+-+-+-+-+-+-+-+-+-+-+-+-+-+-+-+-+-+-+
```

The following subsections define the fields that comprise the AH
format. All the fields described here are mandatory, i.e., they are
always present in the AH format and are included in the Integrity
Check Value (ICV) computation (see Sections 2.6 and 3.3.3).

2.1 Next Header

The Next Header is an 8-bit field that identifies the type of the
next payload after the Authentication Header. The value of this
field is chosen from the set of IP Protocol Numbers defined in the
most recent "Assigned Numbers" [STD-2] RFC from the Internet Assigned
Numbers Authority (IANA).

2.2 Payload Length

This 8-bit field specifies the length of AH in 32-bit words (4-byte
units), minus "2". (All IPv6 extension headers, as per RFC 1883,
encode the "Hdr Ext Len" field by first subtracting 1 (64-bit word)
from the header length (measured in 64-bit words). AH is an IPv6
extension header. However, since its length is measured in 32-bit
words, the "Payload Length" is calculated by subtracting 2 (32 bit
words).) In the "standard" case of a 96-bit authentication value
plus the 3 32-bit word fixed portion, this length field will be "4".
A "null" authentication algorithm may be used only for debugging
purposes. Its use would result in a "1" value for this field for
IPv4 or a "2" for IPv6, as there would be no corresponding
Authentication Data field (see Section 3.3.3.2.1 on "Authentication
Data Padding").

2.3 Reserved

This 16-bit field is reserved for future use. It MUST be set to
"zero." (Note that the value is included in the Authentication Data
calculation, but is otherwise ignored by the recipient.)

2.4 Security Parameters Index (SPI)

The SPI is an arbitrary 32-bit value that, in combination with the
destination IP address and security protocol (AH), uniquely
identifies the Security Association for this datagram. The set of
SPI values in the range 1 through 255 are reserved by the Internet
Assigned Numbers Authority (IANA) for future use; a reserved SPI
value will not normally be assigned by IANA unless the use of the
assigned SPI value is specified in an RFC. It is ordinarily selected
by the destination system upon establishment of an SA (see the
Security Architecture document for more details).

The SPI value of zero (0) is reserved for local, implementation-
specific use and MUST NOT be sent on the wire. For example, a key
management implementation MAY use the zero SPI value to mean "No
Security Association Exists" during the period when the IPsec
implementation has requested that its key management entity establish
a new SA, but the SA has not yet been established.

2.5 Sequence Number

   This unsigned 32-bit field contains a monotonically increasing
   counter value (sequence number). It is mandatory and is always
   present even if the receiver does not elect to enable the anti-replay
   service for a specific SA. Processing of the Sequence Number field
   is at the discretion of the receiver, i.e., the sender MUST always
   transmit this field, but the receiver need not act upon it (see the
   discussion of Sequence Number Verification in the "Inbound Packet
   Processing" section below).

   The sender's counter and the receiver's counter are initialized to 0
   when an SA is established. (The first packet sent using a given SA
   will have a Sequence Number of 1; see Section 3.3.2 for more details
   on how the Sequence Number is generated.) If anti-replay is enabled
   (the default), the transmitted Sequence Number must never be allowed
   to cycle. Thus, the sender's counter and the receiver's counter MUST
   be reset (by establishing a new SA and thus a new key) prior to the
   transmission of the 2^32nd packet on an SA.

2.6 Authentication Data

   This is a variable-length field that contains the Integrity Check
   Value (ICV) for this packet. The field must be an integral multiple
   of 32 bits in length. The details of the ICV computation are
   described in Section 3.3.2 below. This field may include explicit
   padding. This padding is included to ensure that the length of the
   AH header is an integral multiple of 32 bits (IPv4) or 64 bits
   (IPv6). All implementations MUST support such padding. Details of
   how to compute the required padding length are provided below. The
   authentication algorithm specification MUST specify the length of the
   ICV and the comparison rules and processing steps for validation.

3. Authentication Header Processing

3.1 Authentication Header Location

   Like ESP, AH may be employed in two ways: transport mode or tunnel
   mode. The former mode is applicable only to host implementations and
   provides protection for upper layer protocols, in addition to
   selected IP header fields. (In this mode, note that for "bump-in-
   the-stack" or "bump-in-the-wire" implementations, as defined in the
   Security Architecture document, inbound and outbound IP fragments may
   require an IPsec implementation to perform extra IP
   reassembly/fragmentation in order to both conform to this
   specification and provide transparent IPsec support. Special care is
   required to perform such operations within these implementations when
   multiple interfaces are in use.)

In transport mode, AH is inserted after the IP header and before an
upper layer protocol, e.g., TCP, UDP, ICMP, etc. or before any other
IPsec headers that have already been inserted. In the context of
IPv4, this calls for placing AH after the IP header (and any options
that it contains), but before the upper layer protocol. (Note that
the term "transport" mode should not be misconstrued as restricting
its use to TCP and UDP. For example, an ICMP message MAY be sent
using either "transport" mode or "tunnel" mode.) The following
diagram illustrates AH transport mode positioning for a typical IPv4
packet, on a "before and after" basis.

```
                 BEFORE APPLYING AH
              ---------------------------
    IPv4   |orig IP hdr  |     |      |
           |(any options)| TCP | Data |
              ---------------------------

                 AFTER APPLYING AH
              ---------------------------------
    IPv4   |orig IP hdr  |    |     |      |
           |(any options)| AH | TCP | Data |
              ---------------------------------
           |<------- authenticated ------->|
                except for mutable fields
```

In the IPv6 context, AH is viewed as an end-to-end payload, and thus
should appear after hop-by-hop, routing, and fragmentation extension
headers. The destination options extension header(s) could appear
either before or after the AH header depending on the semantics
desired. The following diagram illustrates AH transport mode
positioning for a typical IPv6 packet.

```
                   BEFORE APPLYING AH
              ---------------------------------------
    IPv6   |             | ext hdrs  |     |      |
           | orig IP hdr |if present | TCP | Data |
              ---------------------------------------

                   AFTER APPLYING AH
              ------------------------------------------------------------
    IPv6   |             |hop-by-hop, dest*, |    | dest |     |      |
           |orig IP hdr  |routing, fragment. | AH | opt* | TCP | Data |
              ------------------------------------------------------------
           |<---- authenticated except for mutable fields ----------->|

              * = if present, could be before AH, after AH, or both
```

RFC 2402

6

ESP and AH headers can be combined in a variety of modes. The IPsec
Architecture document describes the combinations of security
associations that must be supported.

Tunnel mode AH may be employed in either hosts or security gateways
(or in so-called "bump-in-the-stack" or "bump-in-the-wire"
implementations, as defined in the Security Architecture document).
When AH is implemented in a security gateway (to protect transit
traffic), tunnel mode must be used. In tunnel mode, the "inner" IP
header carries the ultimate source and destination addresses, while
an "outer" IP header may contain distinct IP addresses, e.g.,
addresses of security gateways. In tunnel mode, AH protects the
entire inner IP packet, including the entire inner IP header. The
position of AH in tunnel mode, relative to the outer IP header, is
the same as for AH in transport mode. The following diagram
illustrates AH tunnel mode positioning for typical IPv4 and IPv6
packets.

```
          ------------------------------------------------
   IPv4   | new IP hdr* |    | orig IP hdr* |    |      |
          |(any options)| AH | (any options) |TCP | Data |
          ------------------------------------------------
          |<- authenticated except for mutable fields -->|
          |            in the new IP hdr                  |


          ------------------------------------------------------------
   IPv6   |             | ext hdrs*|    |              | ext hdrs*|   |   |
          |new IP hdr*|if present| AH |orig IP hdr*|if present|TCP|Data|
          ------------------------------------------------------------
          |<-- authenticated except for mutable fields in new IP hdr ->|
```

           * = construction of outer IP hdr/extensions and modification
               of inner IP hdr/extensions is discussed below.

3.2 Authentication Algorithms

The authentication algorithm employed for the ICV computation is
specified by the SA. For point-to-point communication, suitable
authentication algorithms include keyed Message Authentication Codes
(MACs) based on symmetric encryption algorithms (e.g., DES) or on
one-way hash functions (e.g., MD5 or SHA-1). For multicast
communication, one-way hash algorithms combined with asymmetric
signature algorithms are appropriate, though performance and space
considerations currently preclude use of such algorithms. The
mandatory-to-implement authentication algorithms are described in
Section 5 "Conformance Requirements". Other algorithms MAY be
supported.

3.3 Outbound Packet Processing

In transport mode, the sender inserts the AH header after the IP
header and before an upper layer protocol header, as described above.
In tunnel mode, the outer and inner IP header/extensions can be
inter-related in a variety of ways. The construction of the outer IP
header/extensions during the encapsulation process is described in
the Security Architecture document.

If there is more than one IPsec header/extension required, the order
of the application of the security headers MUST be defined by
security policy. For simplicity of processing, each IPsec header
SHOULD ignore the existence (i.e., not zero the contents or try to
predict the contents) of IPsec headers to be applied later. (While a
native IP or bump-in-the-stack implementation could predict the
contents of later IPsec headers that it applies itself, it won't be
possible for it to predict any IPsec headers added by a bump-in-the-
wire implementation between the host and the network.)

3.3.1 Security Association Lookup

AH is applied to an outbound packet only after an IPsec
implementation determines that the packet is associated with an SA
that calls for AH processing. The process of determining what, if
any, IPsec processing is applied to outbound traffic is described in
the Security Architecture document.

3.3.2 Sequence Number Generation

The sender's counter is initialized to 0 when an SA is established.
The sender increments the Sequence Number for this SA and inserts the
new value into the Sequence Number Field. Thus the first packet sent
using a given SA will have a Sequence Number of 1.

If anti-replay is enabled (the default), the sender checks to ensure
that the counter has not cycled before inserting the new value in the
Sequence Number field. In other words, the sender MUST NOT send a
packet on an SA if doing so would cause the Sequence Number to cycle.
An attempt to transmit a packet that would result in Sequence Number
overflow is an auditable event. (Note that this approach to Sequence
Number management does not require use of modular arithmetic.)

The sender assumes anti-replay is enabled as a default, unless
otherwise notified by the receiver (see 3.4.3). Thus, if the counter
has cycled, the sender will set up a new SA and key (unless the SA
was configured with manual key management).

If anti-replay is disabled, the sender does not need to monitor or
reset the counter, e.g., in the case of manual key management (see
Section 5.) However, the sender still increments the counter and when
it reaches the maximum value, the counter rolls over back to zero.

3.3.3 Integrity Check Value Calculation

The AH ICV is computed over:
- o IP header fields that are either immutable in transit or
  that are predictable in value upon arrival at the endpoint
  for the AH SA
- o the AH header (Next Header, Payload Len, Reserved, SPI,
  Sequence Number, and the Authentication Data (which is set
  to zero for this computation), and explicit padding bytes
  (if any))
- o the upper level protocol data, which is assumed to be
  immutable in transit

3.3.3.1 Handling Mutable Fields

If a field may be modified during transit, the value of the field is
set to zero for purposes of the ICV computation. If a field is
mutable, but its value at the (IPsec) receiver is predictable, then
that value is inserted into the field for purposes of the ICV
calculation. The Authentication Data field is also set to zero in
preparation for this computation. Note that by replacing each
field's value with zero, rather than omitting the field, alignment is
preserved for the ICV calculation. Also, the zero-fill approach
ensures that the length of the fields that are so handled cannot be
changed during transit, even though their contents are not explicitly
covered by the ICV.

As a new extension header or IPv4 option is created, it will be
defined in its own RFC and SHOULD include (in the Security
Considerations section) directions for how it should be handled when
calculating the AH ICV. If the IP (v4 or v6) implementation
encounters an extension header that it does not recognize, it will
discard the packet and send an ICMP message. IPsec will never see
the packet. If the IPsec implementation encounters an IPv4 option
that it does not recognize, it should zero the whole option, using
the second byte of the option as the length. IPv6 options (in
Destination extension headers or Hop by Hop extension header) contain
a flag indicating mutability, which determines appropriate processing
for such options.

3.3.3.1.1 ICV Computation for IPv4

3.3.3.1.1.1 Base Header Fields

The IPv4 base header fields are classified as follows:

Immutable
          Version
          Internet Header Length
          Total Length
          Identification
          Protocol (This should be the value for AH.)
          Source Address
          Destination Address (without loose or strict source routing)

Mutable but predictable
          Destination Address (with loose or strict source routing)

Mutable (zeroed prior to ICV calculation)
          Type of Service (TOS)
          Flags
          Fragment Offset
          Time to Live (TTL)
          Header Checksum

     TOS -- This field is excluded because some routers are known to
            change the value of this field, even though the IP
            specification does not consider TOS to be a mutable header
            field.

     Flags -- This field is excluded since an intermediate router might
            set the DF bit, even if the source did not select it.

     Fragment Offset -- Since AH is applied only to non-fragmented IP
            packets, the Offset Field must always be zero, and thus it
            is excluded (even though it is predictable).

     TTL -- This is changed en-route as a normal course of processing
            by routers, and thus its value at the receiver is not
            predictable by the sender.

     Header Checksum -- This will change if any of these other fields
            changes, and thus its value upon reception cannot be
            predicted by the sender.

3.3.3.1.1.2 Options

   For IPv4 (unlike IPv6), there is no mechanism for tagging options as
   mutable in transit. Hence the IPv4 options are explicitly listed in
   Appendix A and classified as immutable, mutable but predictable, or
   mutable. For IPv4, the entire option is viewed as a unit; so even
   though the type and length fields within most options are immutable
   in transit, if an option is classified as mutable, the entire option
   is zeroed for ICV computation purposes.

3.3.3.1.2 ICV Computation for IPv6

3.3.3.1.2.1 Base Header Fields

   The IPv6 base header fields are classified as follows:

   Immutable
           Version
           Payload Length
           Next Header (This should be the value for AH.)
           Source Address
           Destination Address (without Routing Extension Header)

   Mutable but predictable
           Destination Address (with Routing Extension Header)

   Mutable (zeroed prior to ICV calculation)
           Class
           Flow Label
           Hop Limit

3.3.3.1.2.2 Extension Headers Containing Options

   IPv6 options in the Hop-by-Hop and Destination Extension Headers
   contain a bit that indicates whether the option might change
   (unpredictably) during transit. For any option for which contents
   may change en-route, the entire "Option Data" field must be treated
   as zero-valued octets when computing or verifying the ICV. The
   Option Type and Opt Data Len are included in the ICV calculation.
   All options for which the bit indicates immutability are included in
   the ICV calculation. See the IPv6 specification [DH95] for more
   information.

3.3.3.1.2.3 Extension Headers Not Containing Options

   The IPv6 extension headers that do not contain options are explicitly
   listed in Appendix A and classified as immutable, mutable but
   predictable, or mutable.

3.3.3.2 Padding

3.3.3.2.1 Authentication Data Padding

   As mentioned in section 2.6, the Authentication Data field explicitly
   includes padding to ensure that the AH header is a multiple of 32
   bits (IPv4) or 64 bits (IPv6). If padding is required, its length is
   determined by two factors:

                 - the length of the ICV
                 - the IP protocol version (v4 or v6)

   For example, if the output of the selected algorithm is 96-bits, no
   padding is required for either IPv4 or for IPv6. However, if a
   different length ICV is generated, due to use of a different
   algorithm, then padding may be required depending on the length and
   IP protocol version. The content of the padding field is arbitrarily
   selected by the sender. (The padding is arbitrary, but need not be
   random to achieve security.) These padding bytes are included in the
   Authentication Data calculation, counted as part of the Payload
   Length, and transmitted at the end of the Authentication Data field
   to enable the receiver to perform the ICV calculation.

3.3.3.2.2 Implicit Packet Padding

   For some authentication algorithms, the byte string over which the
   ICV computation is performed must be a multiple of a blocksize
   specified by the algorithm. If the IP packet length (including AH)
   does not match the blocksize requirements for the algorithm, implicit
   padding MUST be appended to the end of the packet, prior to ICV
   computation. The padding octets MUST have a value of zero. The
   blocksize (and hence the length of the padding) is specified by the
   algorithm specification. This padding is not transmitted with the
   packet. Note that MD5 and SHA-1 are viewed as having a 1-byte
   blocksize because of their internal padding conventions.

3.3.4 Fragmentation

   If required, IP fragmentation occurs after AH processing within an
   IPsec implementation. Thus, transport mode AH is applied only to
   whole IP datagrams (not to IP fragments). An IP packet to which AH
   has been applied may itself be fragmented by routers en route, and
   such fragments must be reassembled prior to AH processing at a
   receiver. In tunnel mode, AH is applied to an IP packet, the payload
   of which may be a fragmented IP packet. For example, a security
   gateway or a "bump-in-the-stack" or "bump-in-the-wire" IPsec
   implementation (see the Security Architecture document for details)
   may apply tunnel mode AH to such fragments.

3.4 Inbound Packet Processing

   If there is more than one IPsec header/extension present, the
   processing for each one ignores (does not zero, does not use) any
   IPsec headers applied subsequent to the header being processed.

3.4.1 Reassembly

   If required, reassembly is performed prior to AH processing. If a
   packet offered to AH for processing appears to be an IP fragment,
   i.e., the OFFSET field is non-zero or the MORE FRAGMENTS flag is set,
   the receiver MUST discard the packet; this is an auditable event. The
   audit log entry for this event SHOULD include the SPI value,
   date/time, Source Address, Destination Address, and (in IPv6) the
   Flow ID.

   NOTE: For packet reassembly, the current IPv4 spec does NOT require
   either the zero'ing of the OFFSET field or the clearing of the MORE
   FRAGMENTS flag. In order for a reassembled packet to be processed by
   IPsec (as opposed to discarded as an apparent fragment), the IP code
   must do these two things after it reassembles a packet.

3.4.2 Security Association Lookup

   Upon receipt of a packet containing an IP Authentication Header, the
   receiver determines the appropriate (unidirectional) SA, based on the
   destination IP address, security protocol (AH), and the SPI. (This
   process is described in more detail in the Security Architecture
   document.) The SA indicates whether the Sequence Number field will
   be checked, specifies the algorithm(s) employed for ICV computation,
   and indicates the key(s) required to validate the ICV.

   If no valid Security Association exists for this session (e.g., the
   receiver has no key), the receiver MUST discard the packet; this is
   an auditable event. The audit log entry for this event SHOULD
   include the SPI value, date/time, Source Address, Destination
   Address, and (in IPv6) the Flow ID.

3.4.3 Sequence Number Verification

   All AH implementations MUST support the anti-replay service, though
   its use may be enabled or disabled by the receiver on a per-SA basis.
   (Note that there are no provisions for managing transmitted Sequence
   Number values among multiple senders directing traffic to a single SA
   (irrespective of whether the destination address is unicast,
   broadcast, or multicast). Thus the anti-replay service SHOULD NOT be
   used in a multi-sender environment that employs a single SA.)

If the receiver does not enable anti-replay for an SA, no inbound
checks are performed on the Sequence Number. However, from the
perspective of the sender, the default is to assume that anti-replay
is enabled at the receiver. To avoid having the sender do
unnecessary sequence number monitoring and SA setup (see section
3.3.2), if an SA establishment protocol such as IKE is employed, the
receiver SHOULD notify the sender, during SA establishment, if the
receiver will not provide anti-replay protection.

If the receiver has enabled the anti-replay service for this SA, the
receiver packet counter for the SA MUST be initialized to zero when
the SA is established. For each received packet, the receiver MUST
verify that the packet contains a Sequence Number that does not
duplicate the Sequence Number of any other packets received during
the life of this SA. This SHOULD be the first AH check applied to a
packet after it has been matched to an SA, to speed rejection of
duplicate packets.

Duplicates are rejected through the use of a sliding receive window.
(How the window is implemented is a local matter, but the following
text describes the functionality that the implementation must
exhibit.) A MINIMUM window size of 32 MUST be supported; but a
window size of 64 is preferred and SHOULD be employed as the default.
Another window size (larger than the MINIMUM) MAY be chosen by the
receiver. (The receiver does NOT notify the sender of the window
size.)

The "right" edge of the window represents the highest, validated
Sequence Number value received on this SA. Packets that contain
Sequence Numbers lower than the "left" edge of the window are
rejected. Packets falling within the window are checked against a
list of received packets within the window. An efficient means for
performing this check, based on the use of a bit mask, is described
in the Security Architecture document.

If the received packet falls within the window and is new, or if the
packet is to the right of the window, then the receiver proceeds to
ICV verification. If the ICV validation fails, the receiver MUST
discard the received IP datagram as invalid; this is an auditable
event. The audit log entry for this event SHOULD include the SPI
value, date/time, Source Address, Destination Address, the Sequence
Number, and (in IPv6) the Flow ID. The receive window is updated
only if the ICV verification succeeds.

DISCUSSION:

> Note that if the packet is either inside the window and new, or is
> outside the window on the "right" side, the receiver MUST
> authenticate the packet before updating the Sequence Number window
> data.

3.4.4 Integrity Check Value Verification

The receiver computes the ICV over the appropriate fields of the
packet, using the specified authentication algorithm, and verifies
that it is the same as the ICV included in the Authentication Data
field of the packet. Details of the computation are provided below.

If the computed and received ICV's match, then the datagram is valid,
and it is accepted. If the test fails, then the receiver MUST
discard the received IP datagram as invalid; this is an auditable
event. The audit log entry SHOULD include the SPI value, date/time
received, Source Address, Destination Address, and (in IPv6) the Flow
ID.

DISCUSSION:

> Begin by saving the ICV value and replacing it (but not any
> Authentication Data padding) with zero. Zero all other fields
> that may have been modified during transit. (See section 3.3.3.1
> for a discussion of which fields are zeroed before performing the
> ICV calculation.) Check the overall length of the packet, and if
> it requires implicit padding based on the requirements of the
> authentication algorithm, append zero-filled bytes to the end of
> the packet as required. Perform the ICV computation and compare
> the result with the saved value, using the comparison rules
> defined by the algorithm specification. (For example, if a
> digital signature and one-way hash are used for the ICV
> computation, the matching process is more complex.)

4. Auditing

Not all systems that implement AH will implement auditing. However,
if AH is incorporated into a system that supports auditing, then the
AH implementation MUST also support auditing and MUST allow a system
administrator to enable or disable auditing for AH. For the most
part, the granularity of auditing is a local matter. However,
several auditable events are identified in this specification and for
each of these events a minimum set of information that SHOULD be
included in an audit log is defined. Additional information also MAY
be included in the audit log for each of these events, and additional
events, not explicitly called out in this specification, also MAY

result in audit log entries. There is no requirement for the
receiver to transmit any message to the purported sender in response
to the detection of an auditable event, because of the potential to
induce denial of service via such action.

5.   Conformance Requirements

Implementations that claim conformance or compliance with this
specification MUST fully implement the AH syntax and processing
described here and MUST comply with all requirements of the Security
Architecture document. If the key used to compute an ICV is manually
distributed, correct provision of the anti-replay service would
require correct maintenance of the counter state at the sender, until
the key is replaced, and there likely would be no automated recovery
provision if counter overflow were imminent. Thus a compliant
implementation SHOULD NOT provide this service in conjunction with
SAs that are manually keyed. A compliant AH implementation MUST
support the following mandatory-to-implement algorithms:

                - HMAC with MD5 [MG97a]
                - HMAC with SHA-1 [MG97b]

6.   Security Considerations

Security is central to the design of this protocol, and these
security considerations permeate the specification. Additional
security-relevant aspects of using the IPsec protocol are discussed
in the Security Architecture document.

7.   Differences from RFC 1826

This specification of AH differs from RFC 1826 [ATK95] in several
important respects, but the fundamental features of AH remain intact.
One goal of the revision of RFC 1826 was to provide a complete
framework for AH, with ancillary RFCs required only for algorithm
specification. For example, the anti-replay service is now an
integral, mandatory part of AH, not a feature of a transform defined
in another RFC. Carriage of a sequence number to support this
service is now required at all times. The default algorithms
required for interoperability have been changed to HMAC with MD5 or
SHA-1 (vs. keyed MD5), for security reasons. The list of IPv4 header
fields excluded from the ICV computation has been expanded to include
the OFFSET and FLAGS fields.

Another motivation for revision was to provide additional detail and
clarification of subtle points. This specification provides
rationale for exclusion of selected IPv4 header fields from AH
coverage and provides examples on positioning of AH in both the IPv4

and v6 contexts. Auditing requirements have been clarified in this
version of the specification. Tunnel mode AH was mentioned only in
passing in RFC 1826, but now is a mandatory feature of AH.
Discussion of interactions with key management and with security
labels have been moved to the Security Architecture document.

Acknowledgements

   For over 3 years, this document has evolved through multiple versions
   and iterations. During this time, many people have contributed
   significant ideas and energy to the process and the documents
   themselves. The authors would like to thank Karen Seo for providing
   extensive help in the review, editing, background research, and
   coordination for this version of the specification. The authors
   would also like to thank the members of the IPsec and IPng working
   groups, with special mention of the efforts of (in alphabetic order):
   Steve Bellovin, Steve Deering, Francis Dupont, Phil Karn, Frank
   Kastenholz, Perry Metzger, David Mihelcic, Hilarie Orman, Norman
   Shulman, William Simpson, and Nina Yuan.

Appendix A — Mutability of IP Options/Extension Headers

A1. IPv4 Options

This table shows how the IPv4 options are classified with regard to
"mutability". Where two references are provided, the second one
supercedes the first. This table is based in part on information
provided in RFC1700, "ASSIGNED NUMBERS", (October 1994).

```
          Opt.
Copy Class  #  Name                    Reference
---- -----  ---  ----------------------  ---------
IMMUTABLE -- included in ICV calculation
   0    0    0   End of Options List     [RFC791]
   0    0    1   No Operation            [RFC791]
   1    0    2   Security                [RFC1108(historic but in use)]
   1    0    5   Extended Security       [RFC1108(historic but in use)]
   1    0    6   Commercial Security     [expired I-D, now US MIL STD]
   1    0   20   Router Alert            [RFC2113]
   1    0   21   Sender Directed Multi-  [RFC1770]
                 Destination Delivery
MUTABLE -- zeroed
   1    0    3   Loose Source Route      [RFC791]
   0    2    4   Time Stamp              [RFC791]
   0    0    7   Record Route            [RFC791]
   1    0    9   Strict Source Route     [RFC791]
   0    2   18   Traceroute              [RFC1393]

EXPERIMENTAL, SUPERCEDED -- zeroed
   1    0    8   Stream ID               [RFC791, RFC1122 (Host Req)]
   0    0   11   MTU Probe               [RFC1063, RFC1191 (PMTU)]
   0    0   12   MTU Reply               [RFC1063, RFC1191 (PMTU)]
   1    0   17   Extended Internet Proto [RFC1385, RFC1883 (IPv6)]
   0    0   10   Experimental Measurement [ZSu]
   1    2   13   Experimental Flow Control [Finn]
   1    0   14   Experimental Access Ctl [Estrin]
   0    0   15   ???                     [VerSteeg]
   1    0   16   IMI Traffic Descriptor  [Lee]
   1    0   19   Address Extension       [Ullmann IPv7]
```

NOTE: Use of the Router Alert option is potentially incompatible with
use of IPsec. Although the option is immutable, its use implies that
each router along a packet's path will "process" the packet and
consequently might change the packet. This would happen on a hop by
hop basis as the packet goes from router to router. Prior to being
processed by the application to which the option contents are
directed, e.g., RSVP/IGMP, the packet should encounter AH processing.

However, AH processing would require that each router along the path
is a member of a multicast-SA defined by the SPI. This might pose
problems for packets that are not strictly source routed, and it
requires multicast support techniques not currently available.

NOTE: Addition or removal of any security labels (BSO, ESO, CIPSO) by
systems along a packet's path conflicts with the classification of
these IP Options as immutable and is incompatible with the use of
IPsec.

NOTE: End of Options List options SHOULD be repeated as necessary to
ensure that the IP header ends on a 4 byte boundary in order to
ensure that there are no unspecified bytes which could be used for a
covert channel.

A2. IPv6 Extension Headers

This table shows how the IPv6 Extension Headers are classified with
regard to "mutability".

```
Option/Extension Name                   Reference
-------------------------------         ---------
MUTABLE BUT PREDICTABLE -- included in ICV calculation
   Routing (Type 0)                     [RFC1883]

BIT INDICATES IF OPTION IS MUTABLE (CHANGES UNPREDICTABLY DURING TRANSIT)
   Hop by Hop options                   [RFC1883]
   Destination options                  [RFC1883]

NOT APPLICABLE
   Fragmentation                        [RFC1883]
```

     Options -- IPv6 options in the Hop-by-Hop and Destination
             Extension Headers contain a bit that indicates whether the
             option might change (unpredictably) during transit. For
             any option for which contents may change en-route, the
             entire "Option Data" field must be treated as zero-valued
             octets when computing or verifying the ICV. The Option
             Type and Opt Data Len are included in the ICV calculation.
             All options for which the bit indicates immutability are
             included in the ICV calculation. See the IPv6
             specification [DH95] for more information.

     Routing (Type 0) -- The IPv6 Routing Header "Type 0" will
             rearrange the address fields within the packet during
             transit from source to destination. However, the contents
             of the packet as it will appear at the receiver are known
             to the sender and to all intermediate hops. Hence, the

IPv6 Routing Header "Type 0" is included in the
Authentication Data calculation as mutable but predictable.
The sender must order the field so that it appears as it
will at the receiver, prior to performing the ICV
computation.

Fragmentation -- Fragmentation occurs after outbound IPsec
processing (section 3.3) and reassembly occurs before
inbound IPsec processing (section 3.4). So the
Fragmentation Extension Header, if it exists, is not seen
by IPsec.

Note that on the receive side, the IP implementation could
leave a Fragmentation Extension Header in place when it
does re-assembly. If this happens, then when AH receives
the packet, before doing ICV processing, AH MUST "remove"
(or skip over) this header and change the previous header's
"Next Header" field to be the "Next Header" field in the
Fragmentation Extension Header.

Note that on the send side, the IP implementation could
give the IPsec code a packet with a Fragmentation Extension
Header with Offset of 0 (first fragment) and a More
Fragments Flag of 0 (last fragment). If this happens, then
before doing ICV processing, AH MUST first "remove" (or
skip over) this header and change the previous header's
"Next Header" field to be the "Next Header" field in the
Fragmentation Extension Header.

References

[ATK95]   Atkinson, R., "The IP Authentication Header", RFC 1826,
           August 1995.

[Bra97]   Bradner, S., "Key words for use in RFCs to Indicate
           Requirement Level", BCP 14, RFC 2119, March 1997.

[DH95]   Deering, S., and B. Hinden, "Internet Protocol version 6
           (IPv6) Specification", RFC 1883, December 1995.

[HC98]   Harkins, D., and D. Carrel, "The Internet Key Exchange
           (IKE)", RFC 2409, November 1998.

[KA97a]   Kent, S., and R. Atkinson, "Security Architecture for the
           Internet Protocol", RFC 2401, November 1998.

[KA97b]   Kent, S., and R. Atkinson, "IP Encapsulating Security
           Payload (ESP)", RFC 2406, November 1998.

[MG97a]   Madson, C., and R. Glenn, "The Use of HMAC-MD5-96 within
          ESP and AH", RFC 2403, November 1998.

[MG97b]   Madson, C., and R. Glenn, "The Use of HMAC-SHA-1-96 within
          ESP and AH", RFC 2404, November 1998.

[STD-2]   Reynolds, J., and J. Postel, "Assigned Numbers", STD 2, RFC
          1700, October 1994. See also:
          http://www.iana.org/numbers.html

Disclaimer

   The views and specification here are those of the authors and are not
   necessarily those of their employers. The authors and their
   employers specifically disclaim responsibility for any problems
   arising from correct or incorrect implementation or use of this
   specification.

Author Information

   Stephen Kent
   BBN Corporation
   70 Fawcett Street
   Cambridge, MA   02140
   USA

   Phone: +1 (617) 873-3988
   EMail: kent@bbn.com

   Randall Atkinson
   @Home Network
   425 Broadway,
   Redwood City, CA   94063
   USA

   Phone: +1 (415) 569-5000
   EMail: rja@corp.home.net

Network Working Group   C. Madson
Request for Comments: 2403   Cisco Systems Inc.
Category: Standards Track   R. Glenn
                                                                 NIST
                                                        November 1998

The Use of HMAC-MD5-96 within ESP and AH

Status of this Memo

Copyright Notice

Abstract

   This memo describes the use of the HMAC algorithm [RFC-2104] in
   conjunction with the MD5 algorithm [RFC-1321] as an authentication
   mechanism within the revised IPSEC Encapsulating Security Payload
   [ESP] and the revised IPSEC Authentication Header [AH]. HMAC with MD5
   provides data origin authentication and integrity protection.

   Further information on the other components necessary for ESP and AH
   implementations is provided by [Thayer97a].

1. Introduction

   This memo specifies the use of MD5 [RFC-1321] combined with HMAC
   [RFC-2104] as a keyed authentication mechanism within the context of
   the Encapsulating Security Payload and the Authentication Header.
   The goal of HMAC-MD5-96 is to ensure that the packet is authentic and
   cannot be modified in transit.

   HMAC is a secret key authentication algorithm. Data integrity and
   data origin authentication as provided by HMAC are dependent upon the
   scope of the distribution of the secret key. If only the source and
   destination know the HMAC key, this provides both data origin
   authentication and data integrity for packets sent between the two
   parties; if the HMAC is correct, this proves that it must have been
   added by the source.

In this memo, HMAC-MD5-96 is used within the context of ESP and AH.
For further information on how the various pieces of ESP - including
the confidentiality mechanism — fit together to provide security
services, refer to [ESP] and [Thayer97a]. For further information on
AH, refer to [AH] and [Thayer97a].

The key words "MUST", "MUST NOT", "REQUIRED", "SHALL", "SHALL NOT",
"SHOULD", "SHOULD NOT", "RECOMMENDED", "MAY", and "OPTIONAL" in this
document are to be interpreted as described in [RFC-2119].

2. Algorithm and Mode

[RFC-1321] describes the underlying MD5 algorithm, while [RFC-2104]
describes the HMAC algorithm. The HMAC algorithm provides a framework
for inserting various hashing algorithms such as MD5.

HMAC-MD5-96 operates on 64-byte blocks of data. Padding requirements
are specified in [RFC-1321] and are part of the MD5 algorithm. If
MD5 is built according to [RFC-1321], there is no need to add any
additional padding as far as HMAC-MD5-96 is concerned. With regard
to "implicit packet padding" as defined in [AH], no implicit packet
padding is required.

HMAC-MD5-96 produces a 128-bit authenticator value. This 128-bit
value can be truncated as described in RFC 2104. For use with either
ESP or AH, a truncated value using the first 96 bits MUST be
supported. Upon sending, the truncated value is stored within the
authenticator field. Upon receipt, the entire 128-bit value is
computed and the first 96 bits are compared to the value stored in
the authenticator field. No other authenticator value lengths are
supported by HMAC-MD5-96.

The length of 96 bits was selected because it is the default
authenticator length as specified in [AH] and meets the security
requirements described in [RFC-2104].

2.1 Performance

[Bellare96a] states that "(HMAC) performance is essentially that of
the underlying hash function". [RFC-1810] provides some performance
analysis and recommendations of the use of MD5 with Internet
protocols. As of this writing no performance analysis has been done
of HMAC or HMAC combined with MD5.

[RFC-2104] outlines an implementation modification which can improve
per-packet performance without affecting interoperability.

3. Keying Material

   HMAC-MD5-96 is a secret key algorithm. While no fixed key length is
   specified in [RFC-2104], for use with either ESP or AH a fixed key
   length of 128-bits MUST be supported. Key lengths other than 128-
   bits MUST NOT be supported (i.e. only 128-bit keys are to be used by
   HMAC-MD5-96). A key length of 128-bits was chosen based on the
   recommendations in [RFC-2104] (i.e. key lengths less than the
   authenticator length decrease security strength and keys longer than
   the authenticator length do not significantly increase security
   strength).

   [RFC-2104] discusses requirements for key material, which includes a
   discussion on requirements for strong randomness. A strong pseudo-
   random function MUST be used to generate the required 128-bit key.

   At the time of this writing there are no specified weak keys for use
   with HMAC. This does not mean to imply that weak keys do not exist.
   If, at some point, a set of weak keys for HMAC are identified, the
   use of these weak keys must be rejected followed by a request for
   replacement keys or a newly negotiated Security Association.

   [ARCH] describes the general mechanism for obtaining keying material
   when multiple keys are required for a single SA (e.g. when an ESP SA
   requires a key for confidentiality and a key for authentication).

   In order to provide data origin authentication, the key distribution
   mechanism must ensure that unique keys are allocated and that they
   are distributed only to the parties participating in the
   communication.

   [RFC-2104] makes the following recommendation with regard to
   rekeying. Current attacks do not indicate a specific recommended
   frequency for key changes as these attacks are practically
   infeasible. However, periodic key refreshment is a fundamental
   security practice that helps against potential weaknesses of the
   function and keys, reduces the information avaliable to a
   cryptanalyst, and limits the damage of an exposed key.

4. Interaction with the ESP Cipher Mechanism

   As of this writing, there are no known issues which preclude the use
   of the HMAC-MD5-96 algorithm with any specific cipher algorithm.

5. Security Considerations

   The security provided by HMAC-MD5-96 is based upon the strength of
   HMAC, and to a lesser degree, the strength of MD5. [RFC-2104] claims
   that HMAC does not depend upon the property of strong collision
   resistance, which is important to consider when evaluating the use of
   MD5, an algorithm which has, under recent scrutiny, been shown to be
   much less collision-resistant than was first thought. At the time of
   this writing there are no practical cryptographic attacks against
   HMAC-MD5-96.

   [RFC-2104] states that for "minimally reasonable hash functions" the
   "birthday attack", the strongest attack know against HMAC, is
   impractical. For a 64-byte block hash such as HMAC-MD5-96, an attack
   involving the successful processing of 2**64 blocks would be
   infeasible unless it were discovered that the underlying hash had
   collisions after processing 2**30 blocks. A hash with such weak
   collision-resistance characteristics would generally be considered to
   be unusable.

   It is also important to consider that while MD5 was never developed
   to be used as a keyed hash algorithm, HMAC had that criteria from the
   onset. While the use of MD5 in the context of data security is
   undergoing reevaluation, the combined HMAC with MD5 algorithm has
   held up to cryptographic scrutiny.

   [RFC-2104] also discusses the potential additional security which is
   provided by the truncation of the resulting hash. Specifications
   which include HMAC are strongly encouraged to perform this hash
   truncation.

   As [RFC-2104] provides a framework for incorporating various hash
   algorithms with HMAC, it is possible to replace MD5 with other
   algorithms such as SHA-1. [RFC-2104] contains a detailed discussion
   on the strengths and weaknesses of HMAC algorithms.

   As is true with any cryptographic algorithm, part of its strength
   lies in the correctness of the algorithm implementation, the security
   of the key management mechanism and its implementation, the strength
   of the associated secret key, and upon the correctness of the
   implementation in all of the participating systems. [RFC-2202]
   contains test vectors and example code to assist in verifying the
   correctness of HMAC-MD5-96 code.

6. Acknowledgments

   This document is derived in part from previous works by Jim Hughes,
   those people that worked with Jim on the combined DES/CBC+HMAC-MD5
   ESP transforms, the ANX bakeoff participants, and the members of the
   IPsec working group.

   We would also like to thank Hugo Krawczyk for his comments and
   recommendations regarding some of the cryptographic specific text in
   this document.

7. References

   [RFC-1321]   Rivest, R., "MD5 Digest Algorithm", RFC 1321, April
                 1992.

   [RFC-2104]   Krawczyk, H., Bellare, M., and R. Canetti, "HMAC:
                 Keyed-Hashing for Message Authentication", RFC 2104,
                 February 1997.

   [RFC-1810]   Touch, J., "Report on MD5 Performance", RFC 1810, June
                 1995.

   [Bellare96a] Bellare, M., Canetti, R., and H. Krawczyk, "Keying Hash
                 Functions for Message Authentication", Advances in
                 Cryptography, Crypto96 Proceeding, June 1996.

   [ARCH]   Kent, S., and R. Atkinson, "Security Architecture for
                 the Internet Protocol", RFC 2401, November 1998.

   [ESP]   Kent, S., and R. Atkinson, "IP Encapsulating Security
                 Payload", RFC 2406, November 1998.

   [AH]   Kent, S., and R. Atkinson, "IP Authentication Header",
                 RFC 2402, November 1998.

   [Thayer97a]   Thayer, R., Doraswamy, N., and R. Glenn, "IP Security
                 Document Roadmap", RFC 2411, November 1998.

   [RFC-2202]   Cheng, P., and R. Glenn, "Test Cases for HMAC-MD5 and
                 HMAC-SHA-1", RFC 2202, March 1997.

   [RFC-2119]   Bradner, S., "Key words for use in RFCs to Indicate
                 Requirement Levels", BCP 14, RFC 2119, March 1997.

8. Editors' Address

   Cheryl Madson
   Cisco Systems, Inc.

   EMail: cmadson@cisco.com

   Rob Glenn
   NIST

   EMail: <rob.glenn@nist.gov>

 The IPsec working group can be contacted through the chairs:

   Robert Moskowitz
   ICSA

   EMail: rgm@icsa.net

   Ted T'so
   Massachusetts Institute of Technology

   EMail: tytso@mit.edu

9. Full Copyright Statement

   Copyright (C) The Internet Society (1998). All Rights Reserved.

Network Working Group   C. Madson
Request for Comments: 2404   Cisco Systems Inc.
Category: Standards Track   R. Glenn
                                                                NIST
                                                       November 1998

The Use of HMAC-SHA-1-96 within ESP and AH

Status of this Memo

   This document specifies an Internet standards track protocol for the
   Internet community, and requests discussion and suggestions for
   improvements. Please refer to the current edition of the "Internet
   Official Protocol Standards" (STD 1) for the standardization state
   and status of this protocol. Distribution of this memo is unlimited.

Abstract

   This memo describes the use of the HMAC algorithm [RFC-2104] in
   conjunction with the SHA-1 algorithm [FIPS-180-1] as an
   authentication mechanism within the revised IPSEC Encapsulating
   Security Payload [ESP] and the revised IPSEC Authentication Header
   [AH]. HMAC with SHA-1 provides data origin authentication and
   integrity protection.

   Further information on the other components necessary for ESP and AH
   implementations is provided by [Thayer97a].

1. Introduction

   This memo specifies the use of SHA-1 [FIPS-180-1] combined with HMAC
   [RFC-2104] as a keyed authentication mechanism within the context of
   the Encapsulating Security Payload and the Authentication Header.
   The goal of HMAC-SHA-1-96 is to ensure that the packet is authentic
   and cannot be modified in transit.

   HMAC is a secret key authentication algorithm. Data integrity and
   data origin authentication as provided by HMAC are dependent upon the
   scope of the distribution of the secret key. If only the source and
   destination know the HMAC key, this provides both data origin

authentication and data integrity for packets sent between the two
parties; if the HMAC is correct, this proves that it must have been
added by the source.

In this memo, HMAC-SHA-1-96 is used within the context of ESP and AH.
For further information on how the various pieces of ESP - including
the confidentiality mechanism -- fit together to provide security
services, refer to [ESP] and [Thayer97a]. For further information on
AH, refer to [AH] and [Thayer97a].

The key words "MUST", "MUST NOT", "REQUIRED", "SHALL", "SHALL NOT",
"SHOULD", "SHOULD NOT", "RECOMMENDED", "MAY", and "OPTIONAL" in this
document are to be interpreted as described in [RFC 2119].

2. Algorithm and Mode

[FIPS-180-1] describes the underlying SHA-1 algorithm, while [RFC-
2104] describes the HMAC algorithm. The HMAC algorithm provides a
framework for inserting various hashing algorithms such as SHA-1.

HMAC-SHA-1-96 operates on 64-byte blocks of data. Padding
requirements are specified in [FIPS-180-1] and are part of the SHA-1
algorithm. If you build SHA-1 according to [FIPS-180-1] you do not
need to add any additional padding as far as HMAC-SHA-1-96 is
concerned. With regard to "implicit packet padding" as defined in
[AH] no implicit packet padding is required.

HMAC-SHA-1-96 produces a 160-bit authenticator value. This 160-bit
value can be truncated as described in RFC2104. For use with either
ESP or AH, a truncated value using the first 96 bits MUST be
supported. Upon sending, the truncated value is stored within the
authenticator field. Upon receipt, the entire 160-bit value is
computed and the first 96 bits are compared to the value stored in
the authenticator field. No other authenticator value lengths are
supported by HMAC-SHA-1-96.

The length of 96 bits was selected because it is the default
authenticator length as specified in [AH] and meets the security
requirements described in [RFC-2104].

2.1 Performance

[Bellare96a] states that "(HMAC) performance is essentially that of
the underlying hash function". As of this writing no detailed
performance analysis has been done of SHA-1, HMAC or HMAC combined
with SHA-1.

[RFC-2104] outlines an implementation modification which can improve per-packet performance without affecting interoperability.

3. Keying Material

HMAC-SHA-1-96 is a secret key algorithm. While no fixed key length is specified in [RFC-2104], for use with either ESP or AH a fixed key length of 160-bits MUST be supported. Key lengths other than 160-bits MUST NOT be supported (i.e. only 160-bit keys are to be used by HMAC-SHA-1-96). A key length of 160-bits was chosen based on the recommendations in [RFC-2104] (i.e. key lengths less than the authenticator length decrease security strength and keys longer than the authenticator length do not significantly increase security strength).

[RFC-2104] discusses requirements for key material, which includes a discussion on requirements for strong randomness. A strong pseudo-random function MUST be used to generate the required 160-bit key.

At the time of this writing there are no specified weak keys for use with HMAC. This does not mean to imply that weak keys do not exist. If, at some point, a set of weak keys for HMAC are identified, the use of these weak keys must be rejected followed by a request for replacement keys or a newly negotiated Security Association.

[ARCH] describes the general mechanism for obtaining keying material when multiple keys are required for a single SA (e.g. when an ESP SA requires a key for confidentiality and a key for authentication).

In order to provide data origin authentication, the key distribution mechanism must ensure that unique keys are allocated and that they are distributed only to the parties participating in the communication.

[RFC-2104] makes the following recommendation with regard to rekeying. Current attacks do not indicate a specific recommended frequency for key changes as these attacks are practically infeasible. However, periodic key refreshment is a fundamental security practice that helps against potential weaknesses of the function and keys, reduces the information avaliable to a cryptanalyst, and limits the damage of an exposed key.

4. Interaction with the ESP Cipher Mechanism

As of this writing, there are no known issues which preclude the use of the HMAC-SHA-1-96 algorithm with any specific cipher algorithm.

5. Security Considerations

   The security provided by HMAC-SHA-1-96 is based upon the strength of
   HMAC, and to a lesser degree, the strength of SHA-1. At the time of
   this writing there are no practical cryptographic attacks against
   HMAC-SHA-1-96.

   [RFC-2104] states that for "minimally reasonable hash functions" the
   "birthday attack" is impractical. For a 64-byte block hash such as
   HMAC-SHA-1-96, an attack involving the successful processing of $2**80$
   blocks would be infeasible unless it were discovered that the
   underlying hash had collisions after processing $2**30$ blocks. A hash
   with such weak collision-resistance characteristics would generally
   be considered to be unusable.

   It is also important to consider that while SHA-1 was never developed
   to be used as a keyed hash algorithm, HMAC had that criteria from the
   onset.

   [RFC-2104] also discusses the potential additional security which is
   provided by the truncation of the resulting hash. Specifications
   which include HMAC are strongly encouraged to perform this hash
   truncation.

   As [RFC-2104] provides a framework for incorporating various hash
   algorithms with HMAC, it is possible to replace SHA-1 with other
   algorithms such as MD5. [RFC-2104] contains a detailed discussion on
   the strengths and weaknesses of HMAC algorithms.

   As is true with any cryptographic algorithm, part of its strength
   lies in the correctness of the algorithm implementation, the security
   of the key management mechanism and its implementation, the strength
   of the associated secret key, and upon the correctness of the
   implementation in all of the participating systems. [RFC-2202]
   contains test vectors and example code to assist in verifying the
   correctness of HMAC-SHA-1-96 code.

6. Acknowledgments

   This document is derived in part from previous works by Jim Hughes,
   those people that worked with Jim on the combined DES/CBC+HMAC-MD5
   ESP transforms, the ANX bakeoff participants, and the members of the
   IPsec working group.

   We would also like to thank Hugo Krawczyk for his comments and
   recommendations regarding some of the cryptographic specific text in
   this document.

7. References

[FIPS-180-1] NIST, FIPS PUB 180-1: Secure Hash Standard,
             April 1995.
             http://csrc.nist.gov/fips/fip180-1.txt (ascii)
             http://csrc.nist.gov/fips/fip180-1.ps (postscript)

[RFC-2104]   Krawczyk, H., Bellare, M. and R. Canetti, "HMAC: Keyed-
             Hashing for Message Authentication", RFC 2104, February
             1997.

[Bellare96a] Bellare, M., Canetti, R., and H. Krawczyk, "Keying Hash
             Functions for Message Authentication", Advances in
             Cryptography, Crypto96 Proceeding, June 1996.

[ARCH]   Kent, S., and R. Atkinson, "Security Architecture for
             the Internet Protocol", RFC 2401, November 1998.

[ESP]   Kent, S., and R. Atkinson, "IP Encapsulating Security
             Payload", RFC 2406, November 1998.

[AH]   Kent, S., and R. Atkinson, "IP Authentication Header",
             RFC 2402, November 1998.

[Thayer97a] Thayer, R., Doraswamy, N., and R. Glenn, "IP Security
             Document Roadmap", RFC 2411, November 1998.

[RFC-2202]   Cheng, P., and R. Glenn, "Test Cases for HMAC-MD5 and
             HMAC-SHA-1", RFC 2202, March 1997.

[RFC-2119]   Bradner, S., "Key words for use in RFCs to Indicate
             Requirement Levels", BCP 14, RFC 2119, March 1997.

8. Editors' Address

Cheryl Madson
Cisco Systems, Inc.

EMail: cmadson@cisco.com

Rob Glenn
NIST

EMail: rob.glenn@nist.gov

The IPsec working group can be contacted through the chairs:

   Robert Moskowitz
   ICSA

   EMail: rgm@icsa.net

   Ted T'so
   Massachusetts Institute of Technology

   EMail: tytso@mit.edu

9. Full Copyright Statement

    Copyright (C) The Internet Society (1998). All Rights Reserved.

    This document and translations of it may be copied and furnished to
    others, and derivative works that comment on or otherwise explain it
    or assist in its implementation may be prepared, copied, published
    and distributed, in whole or in part, without restriction of any
    kind, provided that the above copyright notice and this paragraph are
    included on all such copies and derivative works. However, this
    document itself may not be modified in any way, such as by removing
    the copyright notice or references to the Internet Society or other
    Internet organizations, except as needed for the purpose of
    developing Internet standards in which case the procedures for
    copyrights defined in the Internet Standards process must be
    followed, or as required to translate it into languages other than
    English.

    The limited permissions granted above are perpetual and will not be
    revoked by the Internet Society or its successors or assigns.

    This document and the information contained herein is provided on an
    "AS IS" basis and THE INTERNET SOCIETY AND THE INTERNET ENGINEERING
    TASK FORCE DISCLAIMS ALL WARRANTIES, EXPRESS OR IMPLIED, INCLUDING
    BUT NOT LIMITED TO ANY WARRANTY THAT THE USE OF THE INFORMATION
    HEREIN WILL NOT INFRINGE ANY RIGHTS OR ANY IMPLIED WARRANTIES OF
    MERCHANTABILITY OR FITNESS FOR A PARTICULAR PURPOSE.

Network Working Group   C. Madson
Request for Comments: 2405   Cisco Systems, Inc.
Category: Standards Track   N. Doraswamy
                                                  Bay Networks, Inc.
                                                     November 1998

The ESP DES-CBC Cipher Algorithm
With Explicit IV

Status of this Memo

Copyright Notice

Abstract

   This document describes the use of the DES Cipher algorithm in Cipher
   Block Chaining Mode, with an explicit IV, as a confidentiality
   mechanism within the context of the IPSec Encapsulating Security
   Payload (ESP).

1. Introduction

   This document describes the use of the DES Cipher algorithm in Cipher
   Block Chaining Mode as a confidentiality mechanism within the context
   of the Encapsulating Security Payload.

   DES is a symmetric block cipher algorithm. The algorithm is described
   in [FIPS-46-2][FIPS-74][FIPS-81]. [Schneier96] provides a general
   description of Cipher Block Chaining Mode, a mode which is applicable
   to several encryption algorithms.

   As specified in this memo, DES-CBC is not an authentication
   mechanism. [Although DES-MAC, described in [Schneier96] amongst other
   places, does provide authentication, DES-MAC is not discussed here.]

   For further information on how the various pieces of ESP fit together
   to provide security services, refer to [ESP] and [road].

The key words "MUST", "MUST NOT", "REQUIRED", "SHALL", "SHALL NOT",
"SHOULD", "SHOULD NOT", "RECOMMENDED", "MAY", and "OPTIONAL" in this
document are to be interpreted as described in [RFC-2119].

2. Algorithm and Mode

DES-CBC is a symmetric secret-key block algorithm. It has a block
size of 64 bits.

[FIPS-46-2][FIPS-74] and [FIPS-81] describe the DES algorithm, while
[Schneier96] provides a good description of CBC mode.

2.1 Performance

Phil Karn has tuned DES-CBC software to achieve 10.45 Mbps with a 90
MHz Pentium, scaling to 15.9 Mbps with a 133 MHz Pentium. Other DES
speed estimates may be found in [Schneier96].

3. ESP Payload

DES-CBC requires an explicit Initialization Vector (IV) of 8 octets
(64 bits). This IV immediately precedes the protected (encrypted)
payload. The IV MUST be a random value.

Including the IV in each datagram ensures that decryption of each
received datagram can be performed, even when some datagrams are
dropped, or datagrams are re-ordered in transit.

Implementation note:

   Common practice is to use random data for the first IV and the
   last 8 octets of encrypted data from an encryption process as the
   IV for the next encryption process; this logically extends the CBC
   across the packets. It also has the advantage of limiting the
   leakage of information from the random number genrator. No matter
   which mechnism is used, the receiver MUST NOT assume any meaning
   for this value, other than that it is an IV.

   To avoid ECB encryption of very similar plaintext blocks in
   different packets, implementations MUST NOT use a counter or other
   low-Hamming distance source for IVs.

The payload field, as defined in [ESP], is broken down according to
the following diagram:

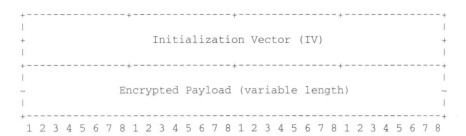

```
+---------------+---------------+---------------+---------------+
|                                                               |
+                    Initialization Vector (IV)                 +
|                                                               |
+---------------+---------------+---------------+---------------+
|                                                               |
~              Encrypted Payload (variable length)              ~
|                                                               |
+---------------------------------------------------------------+
  1 2 3 4 5 6 7 8 1 2 3 4 5 6 7 8 1 2 3 4 5 6 7 8 1 2 3 4 5 6 7 8
```

3.1 Block Size and Padding

   The DES-CBC algorithm described in this document MUST use a block
   size of 8 octets (64 bits).

   When padding is required, it MUST be done according to the
   conventions specified in [ESP].

4. Key Material

   DES-CBC is a symmetric secret key algorithm. The key size is 64-bits.
   [It is commonly known as a 56-bit key as the key has 56 significant
   bits; the least significant bit in every byte is the parity bit.]

   [arch] describes the general mechanism to derive keying material for
   the ESP transform. The derivation of the key from some amount of
   keying material does not differ between the manually- and
   automatically-keyed security associations.

   This mechanism MUST derive a 64-bit key value for use by this cipher.
   The mechanism will derive raw key values, the derivation process
   itself is not responsible for handling parity or weak key checks.

   Weak key checks SHOULD be performed. If such a key is found, the key
   SHOULD be rejected and a new SA requested.

   Implementation note:

      If an implementation chooses to do weak key checking, it should
      recognize that the known weak keys [FIPS74] have been adjusted for
      parity. Otherwise the handling of parity is a local issue.

   A strong pseudo-random function MUST be used to generate the required
   key. For a discussion on this topic, reference [RFC1750].

4.1 Weak Keys

    DES has 16 known weak keys, including so-called semi-weak keys. The
    list of weak keys can be found in [FIPS74].

4.2 Key Lifetime

    [Blaze96] discusses the costs and key recovery time for brute force
    attacks. It presents various combinations of total cost/time to
    recover a key/cost per key recovered for 40-bit and 56-bit DES keys,
    based on late 1995 estimates.

    While a brute force search of a 56-bit DES keyspace can be considered
    infeasable for the so-called casual hacker, who is simply using spare
    CPU cycles or other low-cost resources, it is within reach of someone
    willing to spend a bit more money.

    For example, for a cost of $300,000, a 56-bit DES key can be
    recovered in an average of 19 days using off-the-shelf technology and
    in only 3 hours using a custom developed chip.

    It should be noted that there are other attacks which can recover the
    key faster, that brute force attacks are considered the "worst case",
    although the easiest to implement.

    [Wiener94] also discusses a $1M machine which can break a DES key in
    3.5 hours (1993 estimates), using a known-plaintext attack. As
    discussed in the Security Considerations section, a known plaintext
    attack is reasonably likely.

    It should also be noted that over time, the total and average search
    costs as well as the average key recovery time will continue to drop.

    While the above does not provide specific recommendations for key
    lifetime, it does reinforce the point that for a given application
    the desired key lifetime is dependent upon the perceived threat (an
    educated guess as to the amount of resources available to the
    attacker) relative to the worth of the data to be protected.

    While there are no recommendations for volume-based lifetimes made
    here, it shoud be noted that given sufficient volume there is an
    increased probabilty that known plaintext can be accumulated.

5. Interaction with Authentication Algorithms

    As of this writing, there are no known issues which preclude the use
    of the DES-CBC algorithm with any specific authentication algorithm.

6. Security Considerations

[Much of this section was originally written by William Allen Simpson and Perry Metzger.]

Users need to understand that the quality of the security provided by this specification depends completely on the strength of the DES algorithm, the correctness of that algorithm's implementation, the security of the Security Association management mechanism and its implementation, the strength of the key [CN94], and upon the correctness of the implementations in all of the participating nodes.

[Bell95] and [Bell96] describe a cut and paste splicing attack which applies to all Cipher Block Chaining algorithms. This attack can be addressed with the use of an authentication mechanism.

The use of the cipher mechanism without any corresponding authentication mechanism is strongly discouraged. This cipher can be used in an ESP transform that also includes authentication; it can also be used in an ESP transform that doesn't include authentication provided there is an companion AH header. Refer to [ESP], [AH], [arch], and [road] for more details.

When the default ESP padding is used, the padding bytes have a predictable value. They provide a small measure of tamper detection on their own block and the previous block in CBC mode. This makes it somewhat harder to perform splicing attacks, and avoids a possible covert channel. This small amount of known plaintext does not create any problems for modern ciphers.

At the time of writing of this document, [BS93] demonstrated a differential cryptanalysis based chosen-plaintext attack requiring 2^{47} plaintext-ciphertext pairs, where the size of a pair is the size of a DES block (64 bits). [Matsui94] demonstrated a linear cryptanalysis based known-plaintext attack requiring only 2^{43} plaintext-ciphertext pairs. Although these attacks are not considered practical, they must be taken into account.

More disturbingly, [Wiener94] has shown the design of a DES cracking machine costing $1 Million that can crack one key every 3.5 hours. This is an extremely practical attack.

One or two blocks of known plaintext suffice to recover a DES key. Because IP datagrams typically begin with a block of known and/or guessable header text, frequent key changes will not protect against this attack.

It is suggested that DES is not a good encryption algorithm for the protection of even moderate value information in the face of such equipment. Triple DES is probably a better choice for such purposes.

However, despite these potential risks, the level of privacy provided by use of ESP DES-CBC in the Internet environment is far greater than sending the datagram as cleartext.

The case for using random values for IVs has been refined with the following summary provided by Steve Bellovin. Refer to [Bel97] for further information.

"The problem arises if you use a counter as an IV, or some other source with a low Hamming distance between successive IVs, for encryption in CBC mode. In CBC mode, the "effective plaintext" for an encryption is the XOR of the actual plaintext and the ciphertext of the preceeding block. Normally, that's a random value, which means that the effective plaintext is quite random. That's good, because many blocks of actual plaintext don't change very much from packet to packet, either.

For the first block of plaintext, though, the IV takes the place of the previous block of ciphertext. If the IV doesn't differ much from the previous IV, and the actual plaintext block doesn't differ much from the previous packet's, then the effective plaintext won't differ much, either. This means that you have pairs of ciphertext blocks combined with plaintext blocks that differ in just a few bit positions. This can be a wedge for assorted cryptanalytic attacks."

The discussion on IVs has been updated to require that an implementation not use a low-Hamming distance source for IVs.

7. References

[Bel195]   Bellovin, S., "An Issue With DES-CBC When Used Without Strong Integrity", Presentation at the 32nd Internet Engineering Task Force, Danvers Massachusetts, April 1995.

[Bel196]   Bellovin, S., "Problem Areas for the IP Security Protocols", Proceedings of the Sixth Usenix Security Symposium, July 1996.

[Bell97]   Bellovin, S., "Probable Plaintext Cryptanalysis of the
                IP Security Protocols", Proceedings of the Symposium on
                Network and Distributed System Security, San Diego, CA,
                pp. 155-160, February 1997 (also
                http://www.research.att.com/~smb/papers/probtxt.{ps,
                pdf}).

[BS93]   Biham, E., and A. Shamir, "Differential Cryptanalysis of
                the Data Encryption Standard", Berlin: Springer-Verlag,
                1993.

[Blaze96]   Blaze, M., Diffie, W., Rivest, R., Schneier, B.,
                Shimomura, T., Thompson, E., and M. Wiener, "Minimal Key
                Lengths for Symmetric Ciphers to Provide Adequate
                Commercial Security", currently available at
                http://www.bsa.org/policy/encryption/cryptographers.html.

[CN94]   Carroll, J.M., and S. Nudiati, "On Weak Keys and Weak
                Data: Foiling the Two Nemeses", Cryptologia, Vol. 18
                No. 23 pp. 253-280, July 1994.

[FIPS-46-2]   US National Bureau of Standards, "Data Encryption
                Standard", Federal Information Processing Standard
                (FIPS) Publication 46-2, December 1993,
                http://www.itl.nist.gov/div897/pubs/fip46-2.htm
                (supercedes FIPS-46-1).

[FIPS-74]   US National Bureau of Standards, "Guidelines for
                Implementing and Using the Data Encryption Standard",
                Federal Information Processing Standard (FIPS)
                Publication 74, April 1981,
                http://www.itl.nist.gov/div897/pubs/fip74.htm.

[FIPS-81]   US National Bureau of Standards, "DES Modes of
                Operation", Federal Information Processing Standard
                (FIPS) Publication 81, December 1980,
                http://www.itl.nist.gov/div897/pubs/fip81.htm.

[Matsui94]   Matsui, M., "Linear Cryptanalysis method for DES
                Cipher", Advances in Cryptology — Eurocrypt '93
                Proceedings, Berlin: Springer-Verlag, 1994.

[RFC-1750]   Eastlake, D., Crocker, S., and J. Schiller, "Randomness
                Recommendations for Security", RFC 1750, December 1994.

[RFC-2119]   Bradner, S., "Key words for use in RFCs to Indicate
                Requirement Levels", BCP 14, RFC 2119, March 1997.

7

RFC 2405

[Schneier96] Schneier, B., "Applied Cryptography Second Edition",
             John Wiley & Sons, New York, NY, 1996. ISBN 0-471-
             12845-7.

[Wiener94]   Wiener, M.J., "Efficient DES Key Search", School of
             Computer Science, Carleton University, Ottawa, Canada,
             TR-244, May 1994. Presented at the Rump Session of
             Crypto '93. [Reprinted in "Practical Cryptography for
             Data Internetworks", W.Stallings, editor, IEEE Computer
             Society Press, pp.31-79 (1996). Currently available at
             ftp://ripem.msu.edu/pub/crypt/docs/des-key-search.ps.]

[ESP]   Kent, S., and R. Atkinson, "IP Encapsulating Security
             Payload (ESP)", RFC 2406, November 1998.

[AH]   Kent, S., and R. Atkinson, "IP Authentication Header
             (AH)", RFC 2402, November 1998.

[arch]   Kent, S., and R. Atkinson, "Security Architecture for
             the Internet Protocol", RFC 2401, November 1998.

[road]   Thayer, R., Doraswamy, N., and R. Glenn, "IP Security
             Document Roadmap", RFC 2411, November 1998.

8. Acknowledgments

Much of the information provided here originated with various ESP-DES
documents authored by Perry Metzger and William Allen Simpson,
especially the Security Considerations section.

This document is also derived in part from previous works by Jim
Hughes, those people that worked with Jim on the combined DES-
CBC+HMAC-MD5 ESP transforms, the ANX bakeoff participants, and the
members of the IPsec working group.

Thanks to Rob Glenn for assisting with the nroff formatting.

The IPSec working group can be contacted via the IPSec working
group's mailing list (ipsec@tis.com) or through its chairs:

    Robert Moskowitz
    International Computer Security Association

    EMail: rgm@icsa.net

    Theodore Y. Ts'o
    Massachusetts Institute of Technology

    EMail: tytso@MIT.EDU

9. Editors' Addresses

    Cheryl Madson
    Cisco Systems, Inc.

    EMail: cmadson@cisco.com

    Naganand Doraswamy
    Bay Networks, Inc.

    EMail: naganand@baynetworks.com

10. Full Copyright Statement

RFC 2405

10

Network Working Group   S. Kent
Request for Comments: 2406   BBN Corp
Obsoletes: 1827   R. Atkinson
Category: Standards Track   @Home Network
                                                  November 1998

IP Encapsulating Security Payload (ESP)

Status of this Memo

Copyright Notice

Table of Contents

1. Introduction

    The Encapsulating Security Payload (ESP) header is designed to
    provide a mix of security services in IPv4 and IPv6. ESP may be
    applied alone, in combination with the IP Authentication Header (AH)
    [KA97b], or in a nested fashion, e.g., through the use of tunnel mode
    (see "Security Architecture for the Internet Protocol" [KA97a],
    hereafter referred to as the Security Architecture document).
    Security services can be provided between a pair of communicating
    hosts, between a pair of communicating security gateways, or between
    a security gateway and a host. For more details on how to use ESP
    and AH in various network environments, see the Security Architecture
    document [KA97a].

    The ESP header is inserted after the IP header and before the upper
    layer protocol header (transport mode) or before an encapsulated IP
    header (tunnel mode). These modes are described in more detail
    below.

    ESP is used to provide confidentiality, data origin authentication,
    connectionless integrity, an anti-replay service (a form of partial
    sequence integrity), and limited traffic flow confidentiality. The
    set of services provided depends on options selected at the time of
    Security Association establishment and on the placement of the
    implementation. Confidentiality may be selected independent of all
    other services. However, use of confidentiality without
    integrity/authentication (either in ESP or separately in AH) may
    subject traffic to certain forms of active attacks that could
    undermine the confidentiality service (see [Bel96]). Data origin
    authentication and connectionless integrity are joint services
    (hereafter referred to jointly as "authentication) and are offered as
    an option in conjunction with (optional) confidentiality. The anti-
    replay service may be selected only if data origin authentication is
    selected, and its election is solely at the discretion of the
    receiver. (Although the default calls for the sender to increment
    the Sequence Number used for anti-replay, the service is effective
    only if the receiver checks the Sequence Number.) Traffic flow

confidentiality requires selection of tunnel mode, and is most
effective if implemented at a security gateway, where traffic
aggregation may be able to mask true source-destination patterns.
Note that although both confidentiality and authentication are
optional, at least one of them MUST be selected.

It is assumed that the reader is familiar with the terms and concepts
described in the Security Architecture document. In particular, the
reader should be familiar with the definitions of security services
offered by ESP and AH, the concept of Security Associations, the ways
in which ESP can be used in conjunction with the Authentication
Header (AH), and the different key management options available for
ESP and AH. (With regard to the last topic, the current key
management options required for both AH and ESP are manual keying and
automated keying via IKE [HC98].)

The keywords MUST, MUST NOT, REQUIRED, SHALL, SHALL NOT, SHOULD,
SHOULD NOT, RECOMMENDED, MAY, and OPTIONAL, when they appear in this
document, are to be interpreted as described in RFC 2119 [Bra97].

2. Encapsulating Security Payload Packet Format

   The protocol header (IPv4, IPv6, or Extension) immediately preceding
   the ESP header will contain the value 50 in its Protocol (IPv4) or
   Next Header (IPv6, Extension) field [STD-2].

```
 0                   1                   2                   3
 0 1 2 3 4 5 6 7 8 9 0 1 2 3 4 5 6 7 8 9 0 1 2 3 4 5 6 7 8 9 0 1
+-+-+-+-+-+-+-+-+-+-+-+-+-+-+-+-+-+-+-+-+-+-+-+-+-+-+-+-+-+-+-+-+  ----
|               Security Parameters Index (SPI)                 | ^Auth.
+-+-+-+-+-+-+-+-+-+-+-+-+-+-+-+-+-+-+-+-+-+-+-+-+-+-+-+-+-+-+-+-+ |Cov-
|                      Sequence Number                          | |erage
+-+-+-+-+-+-+-+-+-+-+-+-+-+-+-+-+-+-+-+-+-+-+-+-+-+-+-+-+-+-+-+-+ | ----
|                    Payload Data* (variable)                   | |   ^
~                                                               ~ |   |
|                                                               | |Conf.
+               +-+-+-+-+-+-+-+-+-+-+-+-+-+-+-+-+-+-+-+-+-+-+-+-+ |Cov-
|               |     Padding (0-255 bytes)                     | |erage*
+-+-+-+-+-+-+-+-+               +-+-+-+-+-+-+-+-+-+-+-+-+-+-+-+-+ |   |
|                               |  Pad Length   | Next Header   | v   v
+-+-+-+-+-+-+-+-+-+-+-+-+-+-+-+-+-+-+-+-+-+-+-+-+-+-+-+-+-+-+-+-+ ------
|                 Authentication Data (variable)               |
~                                                               ~
|                                                               |
+-+-+-+-+-+-+-+-+-+-+-+-+-+-+-+-+-+-+-+-+-+-+-+-+-+-+-+-+-+-+-+-+
```

        * If included in the Payload field, cryptographic
          synchronization data, e.g., an Initialization Vector (IV, see

Section 2.3), usually is not encrypted per se, although it
often is referred to as being part of the ciphertext.

The following subsections define the fields in the header format.
"Optional" means that the field is omitted if the option is not
selected, i.e., it is present in neither the packet as transmitted
nor as formatted for computation of an Integrity Check Value (ICV,
see Section 2.7). Whether or not an option is selected is defined as
part of Security Association (SA) establishment. Thus the format of
ESP packets for a given SA is fixed, for the duration of the SA. In
contrast, "mandatory" fields are always present in the ESP packet
format, for all SAs.

2.1 Security Parameters Index

The SPI is an arbitrary 32-bit value that, in combination with the
destination IP address and security protocol (ESP), uniquely
identifies the Security Association for this datagram. The set of
SPI values in the range 1 through 255 are reserved by the Internet
Assigned Numbers Authority (IANA) for future use; a reserved SPI
value will not normally be assigned by IANA unless the use of the
assigned SPI value is specified in an RFC. It is ordinarily selected
by the destination system upon establishment of an SA (see the
Security Architecture document for more details). The SPI field is
mandatory.

The SPI value of zero (0) is reserved for local, implementation-
specific use and MUST NOT be sent on the wire. For example, a key
management implementation MAY use the zero SPI value to mean "No
Security Association Exists" during the period when the IPsec
implementation has requested that its key management entity establish
a new SA, but the SA has not yet been established.

2.2 Sequence Number

This unsigned 32-bit field contains a monotonically increasing
counter value (sequence number). It is mandatory and is always
present even if the receiver does not elect to enable the anti-replay
service for a specific SA. Processing of the Sequence Number field
is at the discretion of the receiver, i.e., the sender MUST always
transmit this field, but the receiver need not act upon it (see the
discussion of Sequence Number Verification in the "Inbound Packet
Processing" section below).

The sender's counter and the receiver's counter are initialized to 0
when an SA is established. (The first packet sent using a given SA
will have a Sequence Number of 1; see Section 3.3.3 for more details
on how the Sequence Number is generated.) If anti-replay is enabled

(the default), the transmitted Sequence Number must never be allowed
to cycle. Thus, the sender's counter and the receiver's counter MUST
be reset (by establishing a new SA and thus a new key) prior to the
transmission of the 2^32nd packet on an SA.

2.3 Payload Data

Payload Data is a variable-length field containing data described by
the Next Header field. The Payload Data field is mandatory and is an
integral number of bytes in length. If the algorithm used to encrypt
the payload requires cryptographic synchronization data, e.g., an
Initialization Vector (IV), then this data MAY be carried explicitly
in the Payload field. Any encryption algorithm that requires such
explicit, per-packet synchronization data MUST indicate the length,
any structure for such data, and the location of this data as part of
an RFC specifying how the algorithm is used with ESP. If such
synchronization data is implicit, the algorithm for deriving the data
MUST be part of the RFC.

Note that with regard to ensuring the alignment of the (real)
ciphertext in the presence of an IV:

          o For some IV-based modes of operation, the receiver treats
            the IV as the start of the ciphertext, feeding it into the
            algorithm directly. In these modes, alignment of the start
            of the (real) ciphertext is not an issue at the receiver.
          o In some cases, the receiver reads the IV in separately from
            the ciphertext. In these cases, the algorithm
            specification MUST address how alignment of the (real)
            ciphertext is to be achieved.

2.4 Padding (for Encryption)

Several factors require or motivate use of the Padding field.

          o If an encryption algorithm is employed that requires the
            plaintext to be a multiple of some number of bytes, e.g.,
            the block size of a block cipher, the Padding field is used
            to fill the plaintext (consisting of the Payload Data, Pad
            Length and Next Header fields, as well as the Padding) to
            the size required by the algorithm.

          o Padding also may be required, irrespective of encryption
            algorithm requirements, to ensure that the resulting
            ciphertext terminates on a 4-byte boundary. Specifically,

the Pad Length and Next Header fields must be right aligned
within a 4-byte word, as illustrated in the ESP packet
format figure above, to ensure that the Authentication Data
field (if present) is aligned on a 4-byte boundary.

o Padding beyond that required for the algorithm or alignment
  reasons cited above, may be used to conceal the actual
  length of the payload, in support of (partial) traffic flow
  confidentiality. However, inclusion of such additional
  padding has adverse bandwidth implications and thus its use
  should be undertaken with care.

The sender MAY add 0-255 bytes of padding. Inclusion of the Padding
field in an ESP packet is optional, but all implementations MUST
support generation and consumption of padding.

a. For the purpose of ensuring that the bits to be encrypted
   are a multiple of the algorithm's blocksize (first bullet
   above), the padding computation applies to the Payload
   Data exclusive of the IV, the Pad Length, and Next Header
   fields.

b. For the purposes of ensuring that the Authentication Data
   is aligned on a 4-byte boundary (second bullet above), the
   padding computation applies to the Payload Data inclusive
   of the IV, the Pad Length, and Next Header fields.

If Padding bytes are needed but the encryption algorithm does not
specify the padding contents, then the following default processing
MUST be used. The Padding bytes are initialized with a series of
(unsigned, 1-byte) integer values. The first padding byte appended
to the plaintext is numbered 1, with subsequent padding bytes making
up a monotonically increasing sequence: 1, 2, 3, ... When this
padding scheme is employed, the receiver SHOULD inspect the Padding
field. (This scheme was selected because of its relative simplicity,
ease of implementation in hardware, and because it offers limited
protection against certain forms of "cut and paste" attacks in the
absence of other integrity measures, if the receiver checks the
padding values upon decryption.)

Any encryption algorithm that requires Padding other than the default
described above, MUST define the Padding contents (e.g., zeros or
random data) and any required receiver processing of these Padding
bytes in an RFC specifying how the algorithm is used with ESP. In
such circumstances, the content of the Padding field will be
determined by the encryption algorithm and mode selected and defined
in the corresponding algorithm RFC. The relevant algorithm RFC MAY
specify that a receiver MUST inspect the Padding field or that a

receiver MUST inform senders of how the receiver will handle the
Padding field.

2.5 Pad Length

The Pad Length field indicates the number of pad bytes immediately
preceding it. The range of valid values is 0-255, where a value of
zero indicates that no Padding bytes are present. The Pad Length
field is mandatory.

2.6 Next Header

The Next Header is an 8-bit field that identifies the type of data
contained in the Payload Data field, e.g., an extension header in
IPv6 or an upper layer protocol identifier. The value of this field
is chosen from the set of IP Protocol Numbers defined in the most
recent "Assigned Numbers" [STD-2] RFC from the Internet Assigned
Numbers Authority (IANA). The Next Header field is mandatory.

2.7 Authentication Data

The Authentication Data is a variable-length field containing an
Integrity Check Value (ICV) computed over the ESP packet minus the
Authentication Data. The length of the field is specified by the
authentication function selected. The Authentication Data field is
optional, and is included only if the authentication service has been
selected for the SA in question. The authentication algorithm
specification MUST specify the length of the ICV and the comparison
rules and processing steps for validation.

3. Encapsulating Security Protocol Processing

3.1 ESP Header Location

Like AH, ESP may be employed in two ways: transport mode or tunnel
mode. The former mode is applicable only to host implementations and
provides protection for upper layer protocols, but not the IP header.
(In this mode, note that for "bump-in-the-stack" or "bump-in-the-
wire" implementations, as defined in the Security Architecture
document, inbound and outbound IP fragments may require an IPsec
implementation to perform extra IP reassembly/fragmentation in order
to both conform to this specification and provide transparent IPsec
support. Special care is required to perform such operations within
these implementations when multiple interfaces are in use.)

In transport mode, ESP is inserted after the IP header and before an
upper layer protocol, e.g., TCP, UDP, ICMP, etc. or before any other
IPsec headers that have already been inserted. In the context of

IPv4, this translates to placing ESP after the IP header (and any
options that it contains), but before the upper layer protocol.
(Note that the term "transport" mode should not be misconstrued as
restricting its use to TCP and UDP. For example, an ICMP message MAY
be sent using either "transport" mode or "tunnel" mode.)   The
following diagram illustrates ESP transport mode positioning for a
typical IPv4 packet, on a "before and after" basis. (The "ESP
trailer" encompasses any Padding, plus the Pad Length, and Next
Header fields.)

```
                    BEFORE APPLYING ESP
               ----------------------------
       IPv4   |orig IP hdr  |     |      |
             |(any options)| TCP | Data |
               ----------------------------


                    AFTER APPLYING ESP
               -------------------------------------------------
       IPv4   |orig IP hdr  | ESP |     |      |   ESP   | ESP|
             |(any options)| Hdr | TCP | Data | Trailer |Auth|
               -------------------------------------------------
                            |<----- encrypted ---->|
                        |<------ authenticated ----->|
```

In the IPv6 context, ESP is viewed as an end-to-end payload, and thus
should appear after hop-by-hop, routing, and fragmentation extension
headers. The destination options extension header(s) could appear
either before or after the ESP header depending on the semantics
desired. However, since ESP protects only fields after the ESP
header, it generally may be desirable to place the destination
options header(s) after the ESP header. The following diagram
illustrates ESP transport mode positioning for a typical IPv6 packet.

```
                    BEFORE APPLYING ESP
               ---------------------------------------
       IPv6   |            | ext hdrs |     |      |
             | orig IP hdr |if present| TCP | Data |
               ---------------------------------------
```

```
                    AFTER APPLYING ESP
          ---------------------------------------------------------
   IPv6   | orig |hop-by-hop,dest*,|  |dest|   |   | ESP  | ESP|
          |IP hdr|routing,fragment.|ESP|opt*|TCP|Data|Trailer|Auth|
          ---------------------------------------------------------
                                    |<---- encrypted ---->|
                                    |<---- authenticated ---->|
```

        * = if present, could be before ESP, after ESP, or both

ESP and AH headers can be combined in a variety of modes. The IPsec
Architecture document describes the combinations of security
associations that must be supported.

Tunnel mode ESP may be employed in either hosts or security gateways.
When ESP is implemented in a security gateway (to protect subscriber
transit traffic), tunnel mode must be used. In tunnel mode, the
"inner" IP header carries the ultimate source and destination
addresses, while an "outer" IP header may contain distinct IP
addresses, e.g., addresses of security gateways. In tunnel mode, ESP
protects the entire inner IP packet, including the entire inner IP
header. The position of ESP in tunnel mode, relative to the outer IP
header, is the same as for ESP in transport mode. The following
diagram illustrates ESP tunnel mode positioning for typical IPv4 and
IPv6 packets.

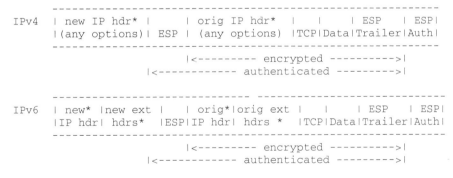

```
          ---------------------------------------------------------
   IPv4   | new IP hdr* |    | orig IP hdr* |  |   | ESP  | ESP|
          |(any options)| ESP | (any options) |TCP|Data|Trailer|Auth|
          ---------------------------------------------------------
                         |<--------- encrypted ---------->|
                         |<------------ authenticated --------->|


          ---------------------------------------------------------
   IPv6   | new* |new ext |   | orig*|orig ext |   |   | ESP  | ESP|
          |IP hdr| hdrs* |ESP|IP hdr| hdrs * |TCP|Data|Trailer|Auth|
          ---------------------------------------------------------
                         |<--------- encrypted ---------->|
                         |<------------ authenticated --------->|
```

        * = if present, construction of outer IP hdr/extensions
            and modification of inner IP hdr/extensions is
            discussed below.

3.2 Algorithms

The mandatory-to-implement algorithms are described in Section 5,
"Conformance Requirements". Other algorithms MAY be supported. Note
that although both confidentiality and authentication are optional,
at least one of these services MUST be selected hence both algorithms
MUST NOT be simultaneously NULL.

3.2.1 Encryption Algorithms

The encryption algorithm employed is specified by the SA. ESP is
designed for use with symmetric encryption algorithms. Because IP
packets may arrive out of order, each packet must carry any data
required to allow the receiver to establish cryptographic
synchronization for decryption. This data may be carried explicitly
in the payload field, e.g., as an IV (as described above), or the
data may be derived from the packet header. Since ESP makes
provision for padding of the plaintext, encryption algorithms
employed with ESP may exhibit either block or stream mode
characteristics. Note that since encryption (confidentiality) is
optional, this algorithm may be "NULL".

3.2.2 Authentication Algorithms

The authentication algorithm employed for the ICV computation is
specified by the SA. For point-to-point communication, suitable
authentication algorithms include keyed Message Authentication Codes
(MACs) based on symmetric encryption algorithms (e.g., DES) or on
one-way hash functions (e.g., MD5 or SHA-1). For multicast
communication, one-way hash algorithms combined with asymmetric
signature algorithms are appropriate, though performance and space
considerations currently preclude use of such algorithms. Note that
since authentication is optional, this algorithm may be "NULL".

3.3 Outbound Packet Processing

In transport mode, the sender encapsulates the upper layer protocol
information in the ESP header/trailer, and retains the specified IP
header (and any IP extension headers in the IPv6 context). In tunnel
mode, the outer and inner IP header/extensions can be inter-related
in a variety of ways. The construction of the outer IP
header/extensions during the encapsulation process is described in
the Security Architecture document. If there is more than one IPsec
header/extension required by security policy, the order of the
application of the security headers MUST be defined by security
policy.

RFC 2406

10

3.3.1 Security Association Lookup

ESP is applied to an outbound packet only after an IPsec
implementation determines that the packet is associated with an SA
that calls for ESP processing. The process of determining what, if
any, IPsec processing is applied to outbound traffic is described in
the Security Architecture document.

3.3.2 Packet Encryption

In this section, we speak in terms of encryption always being applied
because of the formatting implications. This is done with the
understanding that "no confidentiality" is offered by using the NULL
encryption algorithm. Accordingly, the sender:

1. encapsulates (into the ESP Payload field):
      - for transport mode -- just the original upper layer
        protocol information.
      - for tunnel mode -- the entire original IP datagram.
2. adds any necessary padding.
3. encrypts the result (Payload Data, Padding, Pad Length, and
   Next Header) using the key, encryption algorithm, algorithm
   mode indicated by the SA and cryptographic synchronization
   data (if any).
      - If explicit cryptographic synchronization data, e.g.,
        an IV, is indicated, it is input to the encryption
        algorithm per the algorithm specification and placed
        in the Payload field.
      - If implicit cryptographic synchronication data, e.g.,
        an IV, is indicated, it is constructed and input to
        the encryption algorithm as per the algorithm
        specification.

The exact steps for constructing the outer IP header depend on the
mode (transport or tunnel) and are described in the Security
Architecture document.

If authentication is selected, encryption is performed first, before
the authentication, and the encryption does not encompass the
Authentication Data field. This order of processing facilitates
rapid detection and rejection of replayed or bogus packets by the
receiver, prior to decrypting the packet, hence potentially reducing
the impact of denial of service attacks. It also allows for the
possibility of parallel processing of packets at the receiver, i.e.,
decryption can take place in parallel with authentication. Note that
since the Authentication Data is not protected by encryption, a keyed
authentication algorithm must be employed to compute the ICV.

3.3.3 Sequence Number Generation

The sender's counter is initialized to 0 when an SA is established. The sender increments the Sequence Number for this SA and inserts the new value into the Sequence Number field. Thus the first packet sent using a given SA will have a Sequence Number of 1.

If anti-replay is enabled (the default), the sender checks to ensure that the counter has not cycled before inserting the new value in the Sequence Number field. In other words, the sender MUST NOT send a packet on an SA if doing so would cause the Sequence Number to cycle. An attempt to transmit a packet that would result in Sequence Number overflow is an auditable event. (Note that this approach to Sequence Number management does not require use of modular arithmetic.)

The sender assumes anti-replay is enabled as a default, unless otherwise notified by the receiver (see 3.4.3). Thus, if the counter has cycled, the sender will set up a new SA and key (unless the SA was configured with manual key management).

If anti-replay is disabled, the sender does not need to monitor or reset the counter, e.g., in the case of manual key management (see Section 5). However, the sender still increments the counter and when it reaches the maximum value, the counter rolls over back to zero.

3.3.4 Integrity Check Value Calculation

If authentication is selected for the SA, the sender computes the ICV over the ESP packet minus the Authentication Data. Thus the SPI, Sequence Number, Payload Data, Padding (if present), Pad Length, and Next Header are all encompassed by the ICV computation. Note that the last 4 fields will be in ciphertext form, since encryption is performed prior to authentication.

For some authentication algorithms, the byte string over which the ICV computation is performed must be a multiple of a blocksize specified by the algorithm. If the length of this byte string does not match the blocksize requirements for the algorithm, implicit padding MUST be appended to the end of the ESP packet, (after the Next Header field) prior to ICV computation. The padding octets MUST have a value of zero. The blocksize (and hence the length of the padding) is specified by the algorithm specification. This padding is not transmitted with the packet. Note that MD5 and SHA-1 are viewed as having a 1-byte blocksize because of their internal padding conventions.

3.3.5 Fragmentation

   If necessary, fragmentation is performed after ESP processing within
   an IPsec implementation. Thus, transport mode ESP is applied only to
   whole IP datagrams (not to IP fragments). An IP packet to which ESP
   has been applied may itself be fragmented by routers en route, and
   such fragments must be reassembled prior to ESP processing at a
   receiver. In tunnel mode, ESP is applied to an IP packet, the
   payload of which may be a fragmented IP packet. For example, a
   security gateway or a "bump-in-the-stack" or "bump-in-the-wire" IPsec
   implementation (as defined in the Security Architecture document) may
   apply tunnel mode ESP to such fragments.

   NOTE: For transport mode -- As mentioned at the beginning of Section
   3.1, bump-in-the-stack and bump-in-the-wire implementations may have
   to first reassemble a packet fragmented by the local IP layer, then
   apply IPsec, and then fragment the resulting packet.

   NOTE: For IPv6 -- For bump-in-the-stack and bump-in-the-wire
   implementations, it will be necessary to walk through all the
   extension headers to determine if there is a fragmentation header and
   hence that the packet needs reassembling prior to IPsec processing.

3.4 Inbound Packet Processing

3.4.1 Reassembly

   If required, reassembly is performed prior to ESP processing. If a
   packet offered to ESP for processing appears to be an IP fragment,
   i.e., the OFFSET field is non-zero or the MORE FRAGMENTS flag is set,
   the receiver MUST discard the packet; this is an auditable event. The
   audit log entry for this event SHOULD include the SPI value,
   date/time received, Source Address, Destination Address, Sequence
   Number, and (in IPv6) the Flow ID.

   NOTE: For packet reassembly, the current IPv4 spec does NOT require
   either the zero'ing of the OFFSET field or the clearing of the MORE
   FRAGMENTS flag. In order for a reassembled packet to be processed by
   IPsec (as opposed to discarded as an apparent fragment), the IP code
   must do these two things after it reassembles a packet.

3.4.2 Security Association Lookup

   Upon receipt of a (reassembled) packet containing an ESP Header, the
   receiver determines the appropriate (unidirectional) SA, based on the
   destination IP address, security protocol (ESP), and the SPI. (This
   process is described in more detail in the Security Architecture
   document.) The SA indicates whether the Sequence Number field will

be checked, whether the Authentication Data field should be present, and it will specify the algorithms and keys to be employed for decryption and ICV computations (if applicable).

If no valid Security Association exists for this session (for example, the receiver has no key), the receiver MUST discard the packet; this is an auditable event. The audit log entry for this event SHOULD include the SPI value, date/time received, Source Address, Destination Address, Sequence Number, and (in IPv6) the cleartext Flow ID.

3.4.3 Sequence Number Verification

All ESP implementations MUST support the anti-replay service, though its use may be enabled or disabled by the receiver on a per-SA basis. This service MUST NOT be enabled unless the authentication service also is enabled for the SA, since otherwise the Sequence Number field has not been integrity protected. (Note that there are no provisions for managing transmitted Sequence Number values among multiple senders directing traffic to a single SA (irrespective of whether the destination address is unicast, broadcast, or multicast). Thus the anti-replay service SHOULD NOT be used in a multi-sender environment that employs a single SA.)

If the receiver does not enable anti-replay for an SA, no inbound checks are performed on the Sequence Number. However, from the perspective of the sender, the default is to assume that anti-replay is enabled at the receiver. To avoid having the sender do unnecessary sequence number monitoring and SA setup (see section 3.3.3), if an SA establishment protocol such as IKE is employed, the receiver SHOULD notify the sender, during SA establishment, if the receiver will not provide anti-replay protection.

If the receiver has enabled the anti-replay service for this SA, the receive packet counter for the SA MUST be initialized to zero when the SA is established. For each received packet, the receiver MUST verify that the packet contains a Sequence Number that does not duplicate the Sequence Number of any other packets received during the life of this SA. This SHOULD be the first ESP check applied to a packet after it has been matched to an SA, to speed rejection of duplicate packets.

Duplicates are rejected through the use of a sliding receive window. (How the window is implemented is a local matter, but the following text describes the functionality that the implementation must exhibit.) A MINIMUM window size of 32 MUST be supported; but a window size of 64 is preferred and SHOULD be employed as the default.

Another window size (larger than the MINIMUM) MAY be chosen by the receiver. (The receiver does NOT notify the sender of the window size.)

The "right" edge of the window represents the highest, validated Sequence Number value received on this SA. Packets that contain Sequence Numbers lower than the "left" edge of the window are rejected. Packets falling within the window are checked against a list of received packets within the window. An efficient means for performing this check, based on the use of a bit mask, is described in the Security Architecture document.

If the received packet falls within the window and is new, or if the packet is to the right of the window, then the receiver proceeds to ICV verification. If the ICV validation fails, the receiver MUST discard the received IP datagram as invalid; this is an auditable event. The audit log entry for this event SHOULD include the SPI value, date/time received, Source Address, Destination Address, the Sequence Number, and (in IPv6) the Flow ID. The receive window is updated only if the ICV verification succeeds.

DISCUSSION:

   Note that if the packet is either inside the window and new, or is outside the window on the "right" side, the receiver MUST authenticate the packet before updating the Sequence Number window data.

3.4.4 Integrity Check Value Verification

   If authentication has been selected, the receiver computes the ICV over the ESP packet minus the Authentication Data using the specified authentication algorithm and verifies that it is the same as the ICV included in the Authentication Data field of the packet. Details of the computation are provided below.

   If the computed and received ICV's match, then the datagram is valid, and it is accepted. If the test fails, then the receiver MUST discard the received IP datagram as invalid; this is an auditable event. The log data SHOULD include the SPI value, date/time received, Source Address, Destination Address, the Sequence Number, and (in IPv6) the cleartext Flow ID.

DISCUSSION:

   Begin by removing and saving the ICV value (Authentication Data field). Next check the overall length of the ESP packet minus the Authentication Data. If implicit padding is required, based on

the blocksize of the authentication algorithm, append zero-filled
bytes to the end of the ESP packet directly after the Next Header
field. Perform the ICV computation and compare the result with
the saved value, using the comparison rules defined by the
algorithm specification. (For example, if a digital signature and
one-way hash are used for the ICV computation, the matching
process is more complex.)

3.4.5 Packet Decryption

As in section 3.3.2, "Packet Encryption", we speak here in terms of
encryption always being applied because of the formatting
implications. This is done with the understanding that "no
confidentiality" is offered by using the NULL encryption algorithm.
Accordingly, the receiver:

  1. decrypts the ESP Payload Data, Padding, Pad Length, and Next
     Header using the key, encryption algorithm, algorithm mode,
     and cryptographic synchronization data (if any), indicated by
     the SA.
        - If explicit cryptographic synchronization data, e.g.,
          an IV, is indicated, it is taken from the Payload
          field and input to the decryption algorithm as per the
          algorithm specification.
        - If implicit cryptographic synchronization data, e.g.,
          an IV, is indicated, a local version of the IV is
          constructed and input to the decryption algorithm as
          per the algorithm specification.
  2. processes any padding as specified in the encryption
     algorithm specification. If the default padding scheme (see
     Section 2.4) has been employed, the receiver SHOULD inspect
     the Padding field before removing the padding prior to
     passing the decrypted data to the next layer.
  3. reconstructs the original IP datagram from:
        - for transport mode -- original IP header plus the
          original upper layer protocol information in the ESP
          Payload field
        - for tunnel mode -- tunnel IP header + the entire IP
          datagram in the ESP Payload field.

The exact steps for reconstructing the original datagram depend on
the mode (transport or tunnel) and are described in the Security
Architecture document. At a minimum, in an IPv6 context, the
receiver SHOULD ensure that the decrypted data is 8-byte aligned, to
facilitate processing by the protocol identified in the Next Header
field.

If authentication has been selected, verification and decryption MAY be performed serially or in parallel. If performed serially, then ICV verification SHOULD be performed first. If performed in parallel, verification MUST be completed before the decrypted packet is passed on for further processing. This order of processing facilitates rapid detection and rejection of replayed or bogus packets by the receiver, prior to decrypting the packet, hence potentially reducing the impact of denial of service attacks. Note:

If the receiver performs decryption in parallel with authentication, care must be taken to avoid possible race conditions with regard to packet access and reconstruction of the decrypted packet.

Note that there are several ways in which the decryption can "fail":

a. The selected SA may not be correct -- The SA may be mis-selected due to tampering with the SPI, destination address, or IPsec protocol type fields. Such errors, if they map the packet to another extant SA, will be indistinguishable from a corrupted packet, (case c). Tampering with the SPI can be detected by use of authentication. However, an SA mismatch might still occur due to tampering with the IP Destination Address or the IPsec protocol type field.

b. The pad length or pad values could be erroneous -- Bad pad lengths or pad values can be detected irrespective of the use of authentication.

c. The encrypted ESP packet could be corrupted -- This can be detected if authentication is selected for the SA.,

In case (a) or (c), the erroneous result of the decryption operation (an invalid IP datagram or transport-layer frame) will not necessarily be detected by IPsec, and is the responsibility of later protocol processing.

4. Auditing

Not all systems that implement ESP will implement auditing. However, if ESP is incorporated into a system that supports auditing, then the ESP implementation MUST also support auditing and MUST allow a system administrator to enable or disable auditing for ESP. For the most part, the granularity of auditing is a local matter. However, several auditable events are identified in this specification and for each of these events a minimum set of information that SHOULD be included in an audit log is defined. Additional information also MAY be included in the audit log for each of these events, and additional

events, not explicitly called out in this specification, also MAY
result in audit log entries. There is no requirement for the
receiver to transmit any message to the purported sender in response
to the detection of an auditable event, because of the potential to
induce denial of service via such action.

5. Conformance Requirements

Implementations that claim conformance or compliance with this
specification MUST implement the ESP syntax and processing described
here and MUST comply with all requirements of the Security
Architecture document. If the key used to compute an ICV is manually
distributed, correct provision of the anti-replay service would
require correct maintenance of the counter state at the sender, until
the key is replaced, and there likely would be no automated recovery
provision if counter overflow were imminent. Thus a compliant
implementation SHOULD NOT provide this service in conjunction with
SAs that are manually keyed. A compliant ESP implementation MUST
support the following mandatory-to-implement algorithms:

        - DES in CBC mode [MD97]
        - HMAC with MD5 [MG97a]
        - HMAC with SHA-1 [MG97b]
        - NULL Authentication algorithm
        - NULL Encryption algorithm

Since ESP encryption and authentication are optional, support for the
2 "NULL" algorithms is required to maintain consistency with the way
these services are negotiated. NOTE that while authentication and
encryption can each be "NULL", they MUST NOT both be "NULL".

6. Security Considerations

Security is central to the design of this protocol, and thus security
considerations permeate the specification. Additional security-
relevant aspects of using the IPsec protocol are discussed in the
Security Architecture document.

7. Differences from RFC 1827

This document differs from RFC 1827 [ATK95] in several significant
ways. The major difference is that, this document attempts to
specify a complete framework and context for ESP, whereas RFC 1827
provided a "shell" that was completed through the definition of
transforms. The combinatorial growth of transforms motivated the
reformulation of the ESP specification as a more complete document,
with options for security services that may be offered in the context
of ESP. Thus, fields previously defined in transform documents are

now part of this base ESP specification. For example, the fields
necessary to support authentication (and anti-replay) are now defined
here, even though the provision of this service is an option. The
fields used to support padding for encryption, and for next protocol
identification, are now defined here as well. Packet processing
consistent with the definition of these fields also is included in
the document.

Acknowledgements

Many of the concepts embodied in this specification were derived from
or influenced by the US Government's SP3 security protocol, ISO/IEC's
NLSP, or from the proposed swIPe security protocol. [SDNS89, ISO92,
IB93].

For over 3 years, this document has evolved through multiple versions
and iterations. During this time, many people have contributed
significant ideas and energy to the process and the documents
themselves. The authors would like to thank Karen Seo for providing
extensive help in the review, editing, background research, and
coordination for this version of the specification. The authors
would also like to thank the members of the IPsec and IPng working
groups, with special mention of the efforts of (in alphabetic order):
Steve Bellovin, Steve Deering, Phil Karn, Perry Metzger, David
Mihelcic, Hilarie Orman, Norman Shulman, William Simpson and Nina
Yuan.

References

   [ATK95]   Atkinson, R., "IP Encapsulating Security Payload (ESP)",
             RFC 1827, August 1995.

   [Bel96]   Steven M. Bellovin, "Problem Areas for the IP Security
             Protocols", Proceedings of the Sixth Usenix Unix Security
             Symposium, July, 1996.

   [Bra97]   Bradner, S., "Key words for use in RFCs to Indicate
             Requirement Level", BCP 14, RFC 2119, March 1997.

   [HC98]   Harkins, D., and D. Carrel, "The Internet Key Exchange
             (IKE)", RFC 2409, November 1998.

   [IB93]   John Ioannidis & Matt Blaze, "Architecture and
             Implementation of Network-layer Security Under Unix",
             Proceedings of the USENIX Security Symposium, Santa Clara,
             CA, October 1993.

[ISO92]   ISO/IEC JTC1/SC6, Network Layer Security Protocol, ISO-IEC
           DIS 11577, International Standards Organisation, Geneva,
           Switzerland, 29 November 1992.

[KA97a]   Kent, S., and R. Atkinson, "Security Architecture for the
           Internet Protocol", RFC 2401, November 1998.

[KA97b]   Kent, S., and R. Atkinson, "IP Authentication Header", RFC
           2402, November 1998.

[MD97]   Madson, C., and N. Doraswamy, "The ESP DES-CBC Cipher
           Algorithm With Explicit IV", RFC 2405, November 1998.

[MG97a]   Madson, C., and R. Glenn, "The Use of HMAC-MD5-96 within
           ESP and AH", RFC 2403, November 1998.

[MG97b]   Madson, C., and R. Glenn, "The Use of HMAC-SHA-1-96 within
           ESP and AH", RFC 2404, November 1998.

[STD-2]   Reynolds, J., and J. Postel, "Assigned Numbers", STD 2, RFC
           1700, October 1994. See also:
           http://www.iana.org/numbers.html

[SDNS89]   SDNS Secure Data Network System, Security Protocol 3, SP3,
           Document SDN.301, Revision 1.5, 15 May 1989, as published
           in NIST Publication NIST-IR-90-4250, February 1990.

Disclaimer

   The views and specification here are those of the authors and are not
   necessarily those of their employers. The authors and their
   employers specifically disclaim responsibility for any problems
   arising from correct or incorrect implementation or use of this
   specification.

Author Information

Stephen Kent
BBN Corporation
70 Fawcett Street
Cambridge, MA 02140
USA

Phone: +1 (617) 873-3988
EMail: kent@bbn.com

Randall Atkinson
@Home Network
425 Broadway,
Redwood City, CA 94063
USA

Phone: +1 (415) 569-5000
EMail: rja@corp.home.net

Full Copyright Statement

Network Working Group   D. Piper
Request for Comments: 2407   Network Alchemy
Category: Standards Track   November 1998

        The Internet IP Security Domain of Interpretation for ISAKMP

Status of this Memo

Copyright Notice

IESG Note

   Section 4.4.4.2 states, "All implememtations within the IPSEC DOI
   MUST support ESP_DES...". Recent work in the area of cryptanalysis
   suggests that DES may not be sufficiently strong for many
   applications. Therefore, it is very likely that the IETF will
   deprecate the use of ESP_DES as a mandatory cipher suite in the near
   future. It will remain as an optional use protocol. Although the
   IPsec working group and the IETF in general have not settled on an
   alternative algorithm (taking into account concerns of security and
   performance), implementers may want to heed the recommendations of
   section 4.4.4.3 on the use of ESP_3DES.

1. Abstract

   The Internet Security Association and Key Management Protocol
   (ISAKMP) defines a framework for security association management and
   cryptographic key establishment for the Internet. This framework
   consists of defined exchanges, payloads, and processing guidelines
   that occur within a given Domain of Interpretation (DOI). This
   document defines the Internet IP Security DOI (IPSEC DOI), which
   instantiates ISAKMP for use with IP when IP uses ISAKMP to negotiate
   security associations.

   For a list of changes since the previous version of the IPSEC DOI,
   please see Section 7.

2. Introduction

Within ISAKMP, a Domain of Interpretation is used to group related
protocols using ISAKMP to negotiate security associations. Security
protocols sharing a DOI choose security protocol and cryptographic
transforms from a common namespace and share key exchange protocol
identifiers. They also share a common interpretation of DOI-specific
payload data content, including the Security Association and
Identification payloads.

Overall, ISAKMP places the following requirements on a DOI
definition:

    o define the naming scheme for DOI-specific protocol identifiers
    o define the interpretation for the Situation field
    o define the set of applicable security policies
    o define the syntax for DOI-specific SA Attributes (Phase II)
    o define the syntax for DOI-specific payload contents
    o define additional Key Exchange types, if needed
    o define additional Notification Message types, if needed

The remainder of this document details the instantiation of these
requirements for using the IP Security (IPSEC) protocols to provide
authentication, integrity, and/or confidentiality for IP packets sent
between cooperating host systems and/or firewalls.

For a description of the overall IPSEC architecture, see [ARCH],
[AH], and [ESP].

3. Terms and Definitions

The keywords MUST, MUST NOT, REQUIRED, SHALL, SHALL NOT, SHOULD,
SHOULD NOT, RECOMMENDED, MAY, and OPTIONAL, when they appear in this
document, are to be interpreted as described in [RFC 2119].

4.1 IPSEC Naming Scheme

Within ISAKMP, all DOI's must be registered with the IANA in the
"Assigned Numbers" RFC [STD-2]. The IANA Assigned Number for the
Internet IP Security DOI (IPSEC DOI) is one (1). Within the IPSEC
DOI, all well-known identifiers MUST be registered with the IANA
under the IPSEC DOI. Unless otherwise noted, all tables within this
document refer to IANA Assigned Numbers for the IPSEC DOI. See
Section 6 for further information relating to the IANA registry for
the IPSEC DOI.

All multi-octet binary values are stored in network byte order.

4.2 IPSEC Situation Definition

   Within ISAKMP, the Situation provides information that can be used by
   the responder to make a policy determination about how to process the
   incoming Security Association request. For the IPSEC DOI, the
   Situation field is a four (4) octet bitmask with the following
   values.

              Situation   Value
              ---------   -----
              SIT_IDENTITY_ONLY   0x01
              SIT_SECRECY   0x02
              SIT_INTEGRITY   0x04

4.2.1 SIT_IDENTITY_ONLY

   The SIT_IDENTITY_ONLY type specifies that the security association
   will be identified by source identity information present in an
   associated Identification Payload. See Section 4.6.2 for a complete
   description of the various Identification types. All IPSEC DOI
   implementations MUST support SIT_IDENTITY_ONLY by including an
   Identification Payload in at least one of the Phase I Oakley
   exchanges ([IKE], Section 5) and MUST abort any association setup
   that does not include an Identification Payload.

   If an initiator supports neither SIT_SECRECY nor SIT_INTEGRITY, the
   situation consists only of the 4 octet situation bitmap and does not
   include the Labeled Domain Identifier field (Figure 1, Section 4.6.1)
   or any subsequent label information. Conversely, if the initiator
   supports either SIT_SECRECY or SIT_INTEGRITY, the Labeled Domain
   Identifier MUST be included in the situation payload.

4.2.2 SIT_SECRECY

   The SIT_SECRECY type specifies that the security association is being
   negotiated in an environment that requires labeled secrecy. If
   SIT_SECRECY is present in the Situation bitmap, the Situation field
   will be followed by variable-length data that includes a sensitivity
   level and compartment bitmask. See Section 4.6.1 for a complete
   description of the Security Association Payload format.

   If an initiator does not support SIT_SECRECY, SIT_SECRECY MUST NOT be
   set in the Situation bitmap and no secrecy level or category bitmaps
   shall be included.

   If a responder does not support SIT_SECRECY, a SITUATION-NOT-
   SUPPORTED Notification Payload SHOULD be returned and the security
   association setup MUST be aborted.

4.2.3 SIT_INTEGRITY

   The SIT_INTEGRITY type specifies that the security association is
   being negotiated in an environment that requires labeled integrity.
   If SIT_INTEGRITY is present in the Situation bitmap, the Situation
   field will be followed by variable-length data that includes an
   integrity level and compartment bitmask. If SIT_SECRECY is also in
   use for the association, the integrity information immediately
   follows the variable-length secrecy level and categories. See
   section 4.6.1 for a complete description of the Security Association
   Payload format.

   If an initiator does not support SIT_INTEGRITY, SIT_INTEGRITY MUST
   NOT be set in the Situation bitmap and no integrity level or category
   bitmaps shall be included.

   If a responder does not support SIT_INTEGRITY, a SITUATION-NOT-
   SUPPORTED Notification Payload SHOULD be returned and the security
   association setup MUST be aborted.

4.3 IPSEC Security Policy Requirements

   The IPSEC DOI does not impose specific security policy requirements
   on any implementation. Host system policy issues are outside of the
   scope of this document.

   However, the following sections touch on some of the issues that must
   be considered when designing an IPSEC DOI host implementation. This
   section should be considered only informational in nature.

4.3.1 Key Management Issues

   It is expected that many systems choosing to implement ISAKMP will
   strive to provide a protected domain of execution for a combined IKE
   key management daemon. On protected-mode multiuser operating
   systems, this key management daemon will likely exist as a separate
   privileged process.

   In such an environment, a formalized API to introduce keying material
   into the TCP/IP kernel may be desirable. The IP Security
   architecture does not place any requirements for structure or flow
   between a host TCP/IP kernel and its key management provider.

4.3.2 Static Keying Issues

Host systems that implement static keys, either for use directly by
IPSEC, or for authentication purposes (see [IKE] Section 5.4), should
take steps to protect the static keying material when it is not
residing in a protected memory domain or actively in use by the
TCP/IP kernel.

For example, on a laptop, one might choose to store the static keys
in a configuration store that is, itself, encrypted under a private
password.

Depending on the operating system and utility software installed, it
may not be possible to protect the static keys once they've been
loaded into the TCP/IP kernel, however they should not be trivially
recoverable on initial system startup without having to satisfy some
additional form of authentication.

4.3.3 Host Policy Issues

It is not realistic to assume that the transition to IPSEC will occur
overnight. Host systems must be prepared to implement flexible
policy lists that describe which systems they desire to speak
securely with and which systems they require speak securely to them.
Some notion of proxy firewall addresses may also be required.

A minimal approach is probably a static list of IP addresses, network
masks, and a security required flag or flags.

A more flexible implementation might consist of a list of wildcard
DNS names (e.g. '*.foo.bar'), an in/out bitmask, and an optional
firewall address. The wildcard DNS name would be used to match
incoming or outgoing IP addresses, the in/out bitmask would be used
to determine whether or not security was to be applied and in which
direction, and the optional firewall address would be used to
indicate whether or not tunnel mode would be needed to talk to the
target system though an intermediate firewall.

4.3.4 Certificate Management

Host systems implementing a certificate-based authentication scheme
will need a mechanism for obtaining and managing a database of
certificates.

Secure DNS is to be one certificate distribution mechanism, however
the pervasive availability of secure DNS zones, in the short term, is
doubtful for many reasons. What's far more likely is that hosts will

need an ability to import certificates that they acquire through
secure, out-of-band mechanisms, as well as an ability to export their
own certificates for use by other systems.

However, manual certificate management should not be done so as to
preclude the ability to introduce dynamic certificate discovery
mechanisms and/or protocols as they become available.

4.4 IPSEC Assigned Numbers

The following sections list the Assigned Numbers for the IPSEC DOI:
Situation Identifiers, Protocol Identifiers, Transform Identifiers,
AH, ESP, and IPCOMP Transform Identifiers, Security Association
Attribute Type Values, Labeled Domain Identifiers, ID Payload Type
Values, and Notify Message Type Values.

4.4.1 IPSEC Security Protocol Identifier

The ISAKMP proposal syntax was specifically designed to allow for the
simultaneous negotiation of multiple Phase II security protocol
suites within a single negotiation. As a result, the protocol suites
listed below form the set of protocols that can be negotiated at the
same time. It is a host policy decision as to what protocol suites
might be negotiated together.

The following table lists the values for the Security Protocol
Identifiers referenced in an ISAKMP Proposal Payload for the IPSEC
DOI.

Protocol ID	Value
RESERVED	0
PROTO_ISAKMP	1
PROTO_IPSEC_AH	2
PROTO_IPSEC_ESP	3
PROTO_IPCOMP	4

4.4.1.1 PROTO_ISAKMP

The PROTO_ISAKMP type specifies message protection required during
Phase I of the ISAKMP protocol. The specific protection mechanism
used for the IPSEC DOI is described in [IKE]. All implementations
within the IPSEC DOI MUST support PROTO_ISAKMP.

NB: ISAKMP reserves the value one (1) across all DOI definitions.

4.4.1.2 PROTO_IPSEC_AH

   The PROTO_IPSEC_AH type specifies IP packet authentication. The
   default AH transform provides data origin authentication, integrity
   protection, and replay detection. For export control considerations,
   confidentiality MUST NOT be provided by any PROTO_IPSEC_AH transform.

4.4.1.3 PROTO_IPSEC_ESP

   The PROTO_IPSEC_ESP type specifies IP packet confidentiality.
   Authentication, if required, must be provided as part of the ESP
   transform. The default ESP transform includes data origin
   authentication, integrity protection, replay detection, and
   confidentiality.

4.4.1.4 PROTO_IPCOMP

   The PROTO_IPCOMP type specifies IP payload compression as defined in
   [IPCOMP].

4.4.2 IPSEC ISAKMP Transform Identifiers

   As part of an ISAKMP Phase I negotiation, the initiator's choice of
   Key Exchange offerings is made using some host system policy
   description. The actual selection of Key Exchange mechanism is made
   using the standard ISAKMP Proposal Payload. The following table
   lists the defined ISAKMP Phase I Transform Identifiers for the
   Proposal Payload for the IPSEC DOI.

       Transform   Value
       ---------   -----
       RESERVED   0
       KEY_IKE   1

   Within the ISAKMP and IPSEC DOI framework it is possible to define
   key establishment protocols other than IKE (Oakley). Previous
   versions of this document defined types both for manual keying and
   for schemes based on use of a generic Key Distribution Center (KDC).
   These identifiers have been removed from the current document.

   The IPSEC DOI can still be extended later to include values for
   additional non-Oakley key establishment protocols for ISAKMP and
   IPSEC, such as Kerberos [RFC-1510] or the Group Key Management
   Protocol (GKMP) [RFC-2093].

4.4.2.1 KEY_IKE

    The KEY_IKE type specifies the hybrid ISAKMP/Oakley Diffie-Hellman
    key exchange (IKE) as defined in the [IKE] document. All
    implementations within the IPSEC DOI MUST support KEY_IKE.

4.4.3 IPSEC AH Transform Identifiers

    The Authentication Header Protocol (AH) defines one mandatory and
    several optional transforms used to provide authentication,
    integrity, and replay detection. The following table lists the
    defined AH Transform Identifiers for the ISAKMP Proposal Payload for
    the IPSEC DOI.

    Note: the Authentication Algorithm attribute MUST be specified to
    identify the appropriate AH protection suite. For example, AH_MD5
    can best be thought of as a generic AH transform using MD5. To
    request the HMAC construction with AH, one specifies the AH_MD5
    transform ID along with the Authentication Algorithm attribute set to
    HMAC-MD5. This is shown using the "Auth(HMAC-MD5)" notation in the
    following sections.

              Transform ID   Value
              ------------   -----
              RESERVED   0-1
              AH_MD5   2
              AH_SHA   3
              AH_DES   4

    Note: all mandatory-to-implement algorithms are listed as "MUST"
    implement (e.g. AH_MD5) in the following sections. All other
    algorithms are optional and MAY be implemented in any particular
    implementation.

4.4.3.1 AH_MD5

    The AH_MD5 type specifies a generic AH transform using MD5. The
    actual protection suite is determined in concert with an associated
    SA attribute list. A generic MD5 transform is currently undefined.

    All implementations within the IPSEC DOI MUST support AH_MD5 along
    with the Auth(HMAC-MD5) attribute. This suite is defined as the
    HMAC-MD5-96 transform described in [HMACMD5].

    The AH_MD5 type along with the Auth(KPDK) attribute specifies the AH
    transform (Key/Pad/Data/Key) described in RFC-1826.

Use of AH_MD5 with any other Authentication Algorithm attribute value
is currently undefined.

4.4.3.2 AH_SHA

The AH_SHA type specifies a generic AH transform using SHA-1. The
actual protection suite is determined in concert with an associated
SA attribute list. A generic SHA transform is currently undefined.

All implementations within the IPSEC DOI MUST support AH_SHA along
with the Auth(HMAC-SHA) attribute. This suite is defined as the
HMAC-SHA-1-96 transform described in [HMACSHA].

Use of AH_SHA with any other Authentication Algorithm attribute value
is currently undefined.

4.4.3.3 AH_DES

The AH_DES type specifies a generic AH transform using DES. The
actual protection suite is determined in concert with an associated
SA attribute list. A generic DES transform is currently undefined.

The IPSEC DOI defines AH_DES along with the Auth(DES-MAC) attribute
to be a DES-MAC transform. Implementations are not required to
support this mode.

Use of AH_DES with any other Authentication Algorithm attribute value
is currently undefined.

4.4.4 IPSEC ESP Transform Identifiers

The Encapsulating Security Payload (ESP) defines one mandatory and
many optional transforms used to provide data confidentiality. The
following table lists the defined ESP Transform Identifiers for the
ISAKMP Proposal Payload for the IPSEC DOI.

Note: when authentication, integrity protection, and replay detection
are required, the Authentication Algorithm attribute MUST be
specified to identify the appropriate ESP protection suite. For
example, to request HMAC-MD5 authentication with 3DES, one specifies
the ESP_3DES transform ID with the Authentication Algorithm attribute
set to HMAC-MD5. For additional processing requirements, see Section
4.5 (Authentication Algorithm).

```
Transform ID                          Value
------------                          -----
RESERVED                              0
ESP_DES_IV64                          1
ESP_DES                               2
ESP_3DES                              3
ESP_RC5                               4
ESP_IDEA                              5
ESP_CAST                              6
ESP_BLOWFISH                          7
ESP_3IDEA                             8
ESP_DES_IV32                          9
ESP_RC4                               10
ESP_NULL                              11
```

Note: all mandatory-to-implement algorithms are listed as "MUST"
implement (e.g. ESP_DES) in the following sections. All other
algorithms are optional and MAY be implemented in any particular
implementation.

4.4.4.1 ESP_DES_IV64

The ESP_DES_IV64 type specifies the DES-CBC transform defined in
RFC-1827 and RFC-1829 using a 64-bit IV.

4.4.4.2 ESP_DES

The ESP_DES type specifies a generic DES transform using DES-CBC.
The actual protection suite is determined in concert with an
associated SA attribute list. A generic transform is currently
undefined.

All implementations within the IPSEC DOI MUST support ESP_DES along
with the Auth(HMAC-MD5) attribute. This suite is defined as the
[DES] transform, with authentication and integrity provided by HMAC
MD5 [HMACMD5].

4.4.4.3 ESP_3DES

The ESP_3DES type specifies a generic triple-DES transform. The
actual protection suite is determined in concert with an associated
SA attribute list. The generic transform is currently undefined.

All implementations within the IPSEC DOI are strongly encouraged to
support ESP_3DES along with the Auth(HMAC-MD5) attribute. This suite
is defined as the [ESPCBC] transform, with authentication and
integrity provided by HMAC MD5 [HMACMD5].

4.4.4.4 ESP_RC5

   The ESP_RC5 type specifies the RC5 transform defined in [ESPCBC].

4.4.4.5 ESP_IDEA

   The ESP_IDEA type specifies the IDEA transform defined in [ESPCBC].

4.4.4.6 ESP_CAST

   The ESP_CAST type specifies the CAST transform defined in [ESPCBC].

4.4.4.7 ESP_BLOWFISH

   The ESP_BLOWFISH type specifies the BLOWFISH transform defined in
   [ESPCBC].

4.4.4.8 ESP_3IDEA

   The ESP_3IDEA type is reserved for triple-IDEA.

4.4.4.9 ESP_DES_IV32

   The ESP_DES_IV32 type specifies the DES-CBC transform defined in
   RFC-1827 and RFC-1829 using a 32-bit IV.

4.4.4.10 ESP_RC4

   The ESP_RC4 type is reserved for RC4.

4.4.4.11 ESP_NULL

   The ESP_NULL type specifies no confidentiality is to be provided by
   ESP. ESP_NULL is used when ESP is being used to tunnel packets which
   require only authentication, integrity protection, and replay
   detection.

   All implementations within the IPSEC DOI MUST support ESP_NULL. The
   ESP NULL transform is defined in [ESPNULL]. See the Authentication
   Algorithm attribute description in Section 4.5 for additional
   requirements relating to the use of ESP_NULL.

4.4.5 IPSEC IPCOMP Transform Identifiers

   The IP Compression (IPCOMP) transforms define optional compression
   algorithms that can be negotiated to provide for IP payload
   compression ([IPCOMP]). The following table lists the defined IPCOMP
   Transform Identifiers for the ISAKMP Proposal Payload within the

IPSEC DOI.

    Transform ID   Value
    -----------   -----
    RESERVED   0
    IPCOMP_OUI   1
    IPCOMP_DEFLATE   2
    IPCOMP_LZS   3

4.4.5.1 IPCOMP_OUI

    The IPCOMP_OUI type specifies a proprietary compression transform.
    The IPCOMP_OUI type must be accompanied by an attribute which further
    identifies the specific vendor algorithm.

4.4.5.2 IPCOMP_DEFLATE

    The IPCOMP_DEFLATE type specifies the use of the "zlib" deflate
    algorithm as specified in [DEFLATE].

4.4.5.3 IPCOMP_LZS

    The IPCOMP_LZS type specifies the use of the Stac Electronics LZS
    algorithm as specified in [LZS].

4.5 IPSEC Security Association Attributes

    The following SA attribute definitions are used in Phase II of an IKE
    negotiation. Attribute types can be either Basic (B) or Variable-
    Length (V). Encoding of these attributes is defined in the base
    ISAKMP specification.

    Attributes described as basic MUST NOT be encoded as variable.
    Variable length attributes MAY be encoded as basic attributes if
    their value can fit into two octets. See [IKE] for further
    information on attribute encoding in the IPSEC DOI. All restrictions
    listed in [IKE] also apply to the IPSEC DOI.

Attribute Types

```
        class                   value           type
----------------------------------------------------
SA Life Type                      1               B
SA Life Duration                  2               V
Group Description                 3               B
Encapsulation Mode                4               B
Authentication Algorithm          5               B
Key Length                        6               B
Key Rounds                        7               B
Compress Dictionary Size          8               B
Compress Private Algorithm        9               V
```

Class Values

  SA Life Type
  SA Duration

    Specifies the time-to-live for the overall security
    association. When the SA expires, all keys negotiated under
    the association (AH or ESP) must be renegotiated. The life
    type values are:

    ```
    RESERVED                   0
    seconds                    1
    kilobytes                  2
    ```

    Values 3-61439 are reserved to IANA. Values 61440-65535 are
    for private use. For a given Life Type, the value of the
    Life Duration attribute defines the actual length of the
    component lifetime -- either a number of seconds, or a number
    of Kbytes that can be protected.

    If unspecified, the default value shall be assumed to be
    28800 seconds (8 hours).

    An SA Life Duration attribute MUST always follow an SA Life
    Type which describes the units of duration.

    See Section 4.5.4 for additional information relating to
    lifetime notification.

  Group Description

    Specifies the Oakley Group to be used in a PFS QM
    negotiation. For a list of supported values, see Appendix A
    of [IKE].

Encapsulation Mode
    RESERVED   0
    Tunnel   1
    Transport   2

    Values 3-61439 are reserved to IANA. Values 61440-65535 are
    for private use.

    If unspecified, the default value shall be assumed to be
    unspecified (host-dependent).

Authentication Algorithm
    RESERVED   0
    HMAC-MD5   1
    HMAC-SHA   2
    DES-MAC   3
    KPDK   4

    Values 5-61439 are reserved to IANA. Values 61440-65535 are
    for private use.

    There is no default value for Auth Algorithm, as it must be
    specified to correctly identify the applicable AH or ESP
    transform, except in the following case.

    When negotiating ESP without authentication, the Auth
    Algorithm attribute MUST NOT be included in the proposal.

    When negotiating ESP without confidentiality, the Auth
    Algorithm attribute MUST be included in the proposal and the
    ESP transform ID must be ESP_NULL.

Key Length
    RESERVED   0

    There is no default value for Key Length, as it must be
    specified for transforms using ciphers with variable key
    lengths. For fixed length ciphers, the Key Length attribute
    MUST NOT be sent.

Key Rounds
    RESERVED   0

    There is no default value for Key Rounds, as it must be
    specified for transforms using ciphers with varying numbers
    of rounds.

Compression Dictionary Size
  RESERVED   0

    Specifies the log2 maximum size of the dictionary.

    There is no default value for dictionary size.

Compression Private Algorithm

    Specifies a private vendor compression algorithm. The first
    three (3) octets must be an IEEE assigned company_id (OUI).
    The next octet may be a vendor specific compression subtype,
    followed by zero or more octets of vendor data.

4.5.1 Required Attribute Support

  To ensure basic interoperability, all implementations MUST be
  prepared to negotiate all of the following attributes.

        SA Life Type
        SA Duration
        Auth Algorithm

4.5.2 Attribute Parsing Requirement (Lifetime)

  To allow for flexible semantics, the IPSEC DOI requires that a
  conforming ISAKMP implementation MUST correctly parse an attribute
  list that contains multiple instances of the same attribute class, so
  long as the different attribute entries do not conflict with one
  another. Currently, the only attributes which requires this
  treatment are Life Type and Duration.

  To see why this is important, the following example shows the binary
  encoding of a four entry attribute list that specifies an SA Lifetime
  of either 100MB or 24 hours. (See Section 3.3 of [ISAKMP] for a
  complete description of the attribute encoding format.)

    Attribute #1:
      0x80010001 (AF = 1, type = SA Life Type, value = seconds)

    Attribute #2:
      0x00020004 (AF = 0, type = SA Duration, length = 4 bytes)
      0x00015180 (value = 0x15180 = 86400 seconds = 24 hours)

    Attribute #3:
      0x80010002 (AF = 1, type = SA Life Type, value = KB)

```
Attribute #4:
  0x00020004  (AF = 0, type = SA Duration, length = 4 bytes)
  0x000186A0  (value = 0x186A0 = 100000KB = 100MB)
```

If conflicting attributes are detected, an ATTRIBUTES-NOT-SUPPORTED Notification Payload SHOULD be returned and the security association setup MUST be aborted.

4.5.3 Attribute Negotiation

If an implementation receives a defined IPSEC DOI attribute (or attribute value) which it does not support, an ATTRIBUTES-NOT-SUPPORT SHOULD be sent and the security association setup MUST be aborted, unless the attribute value is in the reserved range.

If an implementation receives an attribute value in the reserved range, an implementation MAY chose to continue based on local policy.

4.5.4 Lifetime Notification

When an initiator offers an SA lifetime greater than what the responder desires based on their local policy, the responder has three choices: 1) fail the negotiation entirely; 2) complete the negotiation but use a shorter lifetime than what was offered; 3) complete the negotiation and send an advisory notification to the initiator indicating the responder's true lifetime. The choice of what the responder actually does is implementation specific and/or based on local policy.

To ensure interoperability in the latter case, the IPSEC DOI requires the following only when the responder wishes to notify the initiator: if the initiator offers an SA lifetime longer than the responder is willing to accept, the responder SHOULD include an ISAKMP Notification Payload in the exchange that includes the responder's IPSEC SA payload. Section 4.6.3.1 defines the payload layout for the RESPONDER-LIFETIME Notification Message type which MUST be used for this purpose.

4.6 IPSEC Payload Content

The following sections describe those ISAKMP payloads whose data representations are dependent on the applicable DOI.

4.6.1 Security Association Payload

The following diagram illustrates the content of the Security Association Payload for the IPSEC DOI. See Section 4.2 for a description of the Situation bitmap.

```
 0 1 2 3 4 5 6 7 8 9 0 1 2 3 4 5 6 7 8 9 0 1 2 3 4 5 6 7 8 9 0 1
+-+-+-+-+-+-+-+-+-+-+-+-+-+-+-+-+-+-+-+-+-+-+-+-+-+-+-+-+-+-+-+-+
! Next Payload !   RESERVED    !        Payload Length          !
+-+-+-+-+-+-+-+-+-+-+-+-+-+-+-+-+-+-+-+-+-+-+-+-+-+-+-+-+-+-+-+-+
!                 Domain of Interpretation (IPSEC)              |
+-+-+-+-+-+-+-+-+-+-+-+-+-+-+-+-+-+-+-+-+-+-+-+-+-+-+-+-+-+-+-+-+
!                      Situation (bitmap)                       !
+-+-+-+-+-+-+-+-+-+-+-+-+-+-+-+-+-+-+-+-+-+-+-+-+-+-+-+-+-+-+-+-+
!                   Labeled Domain Identifier                   !
+-+-+-+-+-+-+-+-+-+-+-+-+-+-+-+-+-+-+-+-+-+-+-+-+-+-+-+-+-+-+-+-+
!  Secrecy Length (in octets)  !          RESERVED              !
+-+-+-+-+-+-+-+-+-+-+-+-+-+-+-+-+-+-+-+-+-+-+-+-+-+-+-+-+-+-+-+-+
~                        Secrecy Level                          ~
+-+-+-+-+-+-+-+-+-+-+-+-+-+-+-+-+-+-+-+-+-+-+-+-+-+-+-+-+-+-+-+-+
! Secrecy Cat. Length (in bits) !         RESERVED              !
+-+-+-+-+-+-+-+-+-+-+-+-+-+-+-+-+-+-+-+-+-+-+-+-+-+-+-+-+-+-+-+-+
~                    Secrecy Category Bitmap                     ~
+-+-+-+-+-+-+-+-+-+-+-+-+-+-+-+-+-+-+-+-+-+-+-+-+-+-+-+-+-+-+-+-+
! Integrity Length (in octets)  !         RESERVED              !
+-+-+-+-+-+-+-+-+-+-+-+-+-+-+-+-+-+-+-+-+-+-+-+-+-+-+-+-+-+-+-+-+
~                        Integrity Level                        ~
+-+-+-+-+-+-+-+-+-+-+-+-+-+-+-+-+-+-+-+-+-+-+-+-+-+-+-+-+-+-+-+-+
! Integ. Cat. Length (in bits)  !         RESERVED              !
+-+-+-+-+-+-+-+-+-+-+-+-+-+-+-+-+-+-+-+-+-+-+-+-+-+-+-+-+-+-+-+-+
~                   Integrity Category Bitmap                    ~
+-+-+-+-+-+-+-+-+-+-+-+-+-+-+-+-+-+-+-+-+-+-+-+-+-+-+-+-+-+-+-+-+
```

Figure 1: Security Association Payload Format

The Security Association Payload is defined as follows:

   o Next Payload (1 octet) - Identifier for the payload type of
      the next payload in the message. If the current payload is the
      last in the message, this field will be zero (0).

   o RESERVED (1 octet) - Unused, must be zero (0).

   o Payload Length (2 octets) - Length, in octets, of the current
      payload, including the generic header.

   o Domain of Interpretation (4 octets) - Specifies the IPSEC DOI,
      which has been assigned the value one (1).

   o Situation (4 octets) - Bitmask used to interpret the remainder
      of the Security Association Payload. See Section 4.2 for a
      complete list of values.

o Labeled Domain Identifier (4 octets) - IANA Assigned Number used
   to interpret the Secrecy and Integrity information.

o Secrecy Length (2 octets) - Specifies the length, in octets, of
   the secrecy level identifier, excluding pad bits.

o RESERVED (2 octets) - Unused, must be zero (0).

o Secrecy Level (variable length) - Specifies the mandatory
   secrecy level required. The secrecy level MUST be padded with
   zero (0) to align on the next 32-bit boundary.

o Secrecy Category Length (2 octets) - Specifies the length, in
   bits, of the secrecy category (compartment) bitmap, excluding
   pad bits.

o RESERVED (2 octets) - Unused, must be zero (0).

o Secrecy Category Bitmap (variable length) - A bitmap used to
   designate secrecy categories (compartments) that are required.
   The bitmap MUST be padded with zero (0) to align on the next
   32-bit boundary.

o Integrity Length (2 octets) - Specifies the length, in octets,
   of the integrity level identifier, excluding pad bits.

o RESERVED (2 octets) - Unused, must be zero (0).

o Integrity Level (variable length) - Specifies the mandatory
   integrity level required. The integrity level MUST be padded
   with zero (0) to align on the next 32-bit boundary.

o Integrity Category Length (2 octets) - Specifies the length, in
   bits, of the integrity category (compartment) bitmap, excluding
   pad bits.

o RESERVED (2 octets) - Unused, must be zero (0).

o Integrity Category Bitmap (variable length) - A bitmap used to
   designate integrity categories (compartments) that are required.
   The bitmap MUST be padded with zero (0) to align on the next
   32-bit boundary.

4.6.1.1 IPSEC Labeled Domain Identifiers

The following table lists the assigned values for the Labeled Domain
Identifier field contained in the Situation field of the Security
Association Payload.

```
Domain                          Value
-------                         -----
RESERVED                        0
```

4.6.2 Identification Payload Content

   The Identification Payload is used to identify the initiator of the
   Security Association. The identity of the initiator SHOULD be used
   by the responder to determine the correct host system security policy
   requirement for the association. For example, a host might choose to
   require authentication and integrity without confidentiality (AH)
   from a certain set of IP addresses and full authentication with
   confidentiality (ESP) from another range of IP addresses. The
   Identification Payload provides information that can be used by the
   responder to make this decision.

   During Phase I negotiations, the ID port and protocol fields MUST be
   set to zero or to UDP port 500. If an implementation receives any
   other values, this MUST be treated as an error and the security
   association setup MUST be aborted. This event SHOULD be auditable.

   The following diagram illustrates the content of the Identification
   Payload.

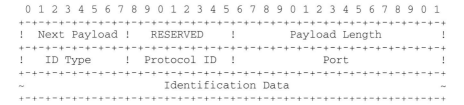

```
  0 1 2 3 4 5 6 7 8 9 0 1 2 3 4 5 6 7 8 9 0 1 2 3 4 5 6 7 8 9 0 1
 +-+-+-+-+-+-+-+-+-+-+-+-+-+-+-+-+-+-+-+-+-+-+-+-+-+-+-+-+-+-+-+-+
 ! Next Payload !   RESERVED    !        Payload Length          !
 +-+-+-+-+-+-+-+-+-+-+-+-+-+-+-+-+-+-+-+-+-+-+-+-+-+-+-+-+-+-+-+-+
 !   ID Type    !  Protocol ID  !             Port               !
 +-+-+-+-+-+-+-+-+-+-+-+-+-+-+-+-+-+-+-+-+-+-+-+-+-+-+-+-+-+-+-+-+
 ~                     Identification Data                       ~
 +-+-+-+-+-+-+-+-+-+-+-+-+-+-+-+-+-+-+-+-+-+-+-+-+-+-+-+-+-+-+-+-+
```

                  Figure 2: Identification Payload Format

   The Identification Payload fields are defined as follows:

     o Next Payload (1 octet) - Identifier for the payload type of
        the next payload in the message. If the current payload is the
        last in the message, this field will be zero (0).

     o RESERVED (1 octet) - Unused, must be zero (0).

     o Payload Length (2 octets) - Length, in octets, of the
        identification data, including the generic header.

     o Identification Type (1 octet) - Value describing the identity
        information found in the Identification Data field.

    o Protocol ID (1 octet) - Value specifying an associated IP
       protocol ID (e.g. UDP/TCP). A value of zero means that the
       Protocol ID field should be ignored.

    o Port (2 octets) - Value specifying an associated port. A value
       of zero means that the Port field should be ignored.

    o Identification Data (variable length) - Value, as indicated by
       the Identification Type.

4.6.2.1 Identification Type Values

The following table lists the assigned values for the Identification
Type field found in the Identification Payload.

```
ID Type                         Value
-------                         -----
RESERVED                          0
ID_IPV4_ADDR                      1
ID_FQDN                           2
ID_USER_FQDN                      3
ID_IPV4_ADDR_SUBNET               4
ID_IPV6_ADDR                      5
ID_IPV6_ADDR_SUBNET               6
ID_IPV4_ADDR_RANGE                7
ID_IPV6_ADDR_RANGE                8
ID_DER_ASN1_DN                    9
ID_DER_ASN1_GN                   10
ID_KEY_ID                        11
```

For types where the ID entity is variable length, the size of the ID
entity is computed from size in the ID payload header.

When an IKE exchange is authenticated using certificates (of any
format), any ID's used for input to local policy decisions SHOULD be
contained in the certificate used in the authentication of the
exchange.

4.6.2.2 ID_IPV4_ADDR

The ID_IPV4_ADDR type specifies a single four (4) octet IPv4 address.

4.6.2.3 ID_FQDN

The ID_FQDN type specifies a fully-qualified domain name string. An
example of a ID_FQDN is, "foo.bar.com". The string should not
contain any terminators.

4.6.2.4 ID_USER_FQDN

The ID_USER_FQDN type specifies a fully-qualified username string, An example of a ID_USER_FQDN is, "piper@foo.bar.com". The string should not contain any terminators.

4.6.2.5 ID_IPV4_ADDR_SUBNET

The ID_IPV4_ADDR_SUBNET type specifies a range of IPv4 addresses, represented by two four (4) octet values. The first value is an IPv4 address. The second is an IPv4 network mask. Note that ones (1s) in the network mask indicate that the corresponding bit in the address is fixed, while zeros (0s) indicate a "wildcard" bit.

4.6.2.6 ID_IPV6_ADDR

The ID_IPV6_ADDR type specifies a single sixteen (16) octet IPv6 address.

4.6.2.7 ID_IPV6_ADDR_SUBNET

The ID_IPV6_ADDR_SUBNET type specifies a range of IPv6 addresses, represented by two sixteen (16) octet values. The first value is an IPv6 address. The second is an IPv6 network mask. Note that ones (1s) in the network mask indicate that the corresponding bit in the address is fixed, while zeros (0s) indicate a "wildcard" bit.

4.6.2.8 ID_IPV4_ADDR_RANGE

The ID_IPV4_ADDR_RANGE type specifies a range of IPv4 addresses, represented by two four (4) octet values. The first value is the beginning IPv4 address (inclusive) and the second value is the ending IPv4 address (inclusive). All addresses falling between the two specified addresses are considered to be within the list.

4.6.2.9 ID_IPV6_ADDR_RANGE

The ID_IPV6_ADDR_RANGE type specifies a range of IPv6 addresses, represented by two sixteen (16) octet values. The first value is the beginning IPv6 address (inclusive) and the second value is the ending IPv6 address (inclusive). All addresses falling between the two specified addresses are considered to be within the list.

4.6.2.10 ID_DER_ASN1_DN

The ID_DER_ASN1_DN type specifies the binary DER encoding of an ASN.1 X.500 Distinguished Name [X.501] of the principal whose certificates are being exchanged to establish the SA.

4.6.2.11 ID_DER_ASN1_GN

   The ID_DER_ASN1_GN type specifies the binary DER encoding of an ASN.1
   X.500 GeneralName [X.509] of the principal whose certificates are
   being exchanged to establish the SA.

4.6.2.12 ID_KEY_ID

   The ID_KEY_ID type specifies an opaque byte stream which may be used
   to pass vendor-specific information necessary to identify which pre-
   shared key should be used to authenticate Aggressive mode
   negotiations.

4.6.3 IPSEC Notify Message Types

   ISAKMP defines two blocks of Notify Message codes, one for errors and
   one for status messages. ISAKMP also allocates a portion of each
   block for private use within a DOI. The IPSEC DOI defines the
   following private message types for its own use.

```
        Notify Messages - Error Types       Value
        -----------------------------       -----
        RESERVED                            8192

        Notify Messages - Status Types      Value
        -----------------------------       -----
        RESPONDER-LIFETIME                  24576
        REPLAY-STATUS                       24577
        INITIAL-CONTACT                     24578
```

   Notification Status Messages MUST be sent under the protection of an
   ISAKMP SA: either as a payload in the last Main Mode exchange; in a
   separate Informational Exchange after Main Mode or Aggressive Mode
   processing is complete; or as a payload in any Quick Mode exchange.
   These messages MUST NOT be sent in Aggressive Mode exchange, since
   Aggressive Mode does not provide the necessary protection to bind the
   Notify Status Message to the exchange.

   Nota Bene: a Notify payload is fully protected only in Quick Mode,
   where the entire payload is included in the HASH(n) digest. In Main
   Mode, while the notify payload is encrypted, it is not currently
   included in the HASH(n) digests. As a result, an active substitution
   attack on the Main Mode ciphertext could cause the notify status
   message type to be corrupted. (This is true, in general, for the
   last message of any Main Mode exchange.) While the risk is small, a
   corrupt notify message might cause the receiver to abort the entire
   negotiation thinking that the sender encountered a fatal error.

Implementation Note: the ISAKMP protocol does not guarantee delivery of Notification Status messages when sent in an ISAKMP Informational Exchange. To ensure receipt of any particular message, the sender SHOULD include a Notification Payload in a defined Main Mode or Quick Mode exchange which is protected by a retransmission timer.

4.6.3.1 RESPONDER-LIFETIME

The RESPONDER-LIFETIME status message may be used to communicate the IPSEC SA lifetime chosen by the responder.

When present, the Notification Payload MUST have the following format:

  o Payload Length - set to length of payload + size of data (var)
  o DOI - set to IPSEC DOI (1)
  o Protocol ID - set to selected Protocol ID from chosen SA
  o SPI Size - set to either sixteen (16) (two eight-octet ISAKMP
     cookies) or four (4) (one IPSEC SPI)
  o Notify Message Type - set to RESPONDER-LIFETIME (Section 4.6.3)
  o SPI - set to the two ISAKMP cookies or to the sender's inbound
     IPSEC SPI
  o Notification Data - contains an ISAKMP attribute list with the
     responder's actual SA lifetime(s)

Implementation Note: saying that the Notification Data field contains an attribute list is equivalent to saying that the Notification Data field has zero length and the Notification Payload has an associated attribute list.

4.6.3.2 REPLAY-STATUS

The REPLAY-STATUS status message may be used for positive confirmation of the responder's election on whether or not he is to perform anti-replay detection.

When present, the Notification Payload MUST have the following format:

  o Payload Length - set to length of payload + size of data (4)
  o DOI - set to IPSEC DOI (1)
  o Protocol ID - set to selected Protocol ID from chosen SA
  o SPI Size - set to either sixteen (16) (two eight-octet ISAKMP
     cookies) or four (4) (one IPSEC SPI)
  o Notify Message Type - set to REPLAY-STATUS
  o SPI - set to the two ISAKMP cookies or to the sender's inbound
     IPSEC SPI
  o Notification Data - a 4 octet value:

```
                0 = replay detection disabled
                1 = replay detection enabled
```

4.6.3.3 INITIAL-CONTACT

The INITIAL-CONTACT status message may be used when one side wishes
to inform the other that this is the first SA being established with
the remote system. The receiver of this Notification Message might
then elect to delete any existing SA's it has for the sending system
under the assumption that the sending system has rebooted and no
longer has access to the original SA's and their associated keying
material. When used, the content of the Notification Data field
SHOULD be null (i.e. the Payload Length should be set to the fixed
length of Notification Payload).

When present, the Notification Payload MUST have the following
format:

    o Payload Length - set to length of payload + size of data (0)
    o DOI - set to IPSEC DOI (1)
    o Protocol ID - set to selected Protocol ID from chosen SA
    o SPI Size - set to sixteen (16) (two eight-octet ISAKMP cookies)
    o Notify Message Type - set to INITIAL-CONTACT
    o SPI - set to the two ISAKMP cookies
    o Notification Data - <not included>

4.7 IPSEC Key Exchange Requirements

The IPSEC DOI introduces no additional Key Exchange types.

5. Security Considerations

This entire memo pertains to the Internet Key Exchange protocol
([IKE]), which combines ISAKMP ([ISAKMP]) and Oakley ([OAKLEY]) to
provide for the derivation of cryptographic keying material in a
secure and authenticated manner. Specific discussion of the various
security protocols and transforms identified in this document can be
found in the associated base documents and in the cipher references.

6. IANA Considerations

This document contains many "magic" numbers to be maintained by the
IANA. This section explains the criteria to be used by the IANA to
assign additional numbers in each of these lists. All values not
explicitly defined in previous sections are reserved to IANA.

6.1 IPSEC Situation Definition

The Situation Definition is a 32-bit bitmask which represents the environment under which the IPSEC SA proposal and negotiation is carried out. Requests for assignments of new situations must be accompanied by an RFC which describes the interpretation for the associated bit.

If the RFC is not on the standards-track (i.e., it is an informational or experimental RFC), it must be explicitly reviewed and approved by the IESG before the RFC is published and the transform identifier is assigned.

The upper two bits are reserved for private use amongst cooperating systems.

6.2 IPSEC Security Protocol Identifiers

The Security Protocol Identifier is an 8-bit value which identifies a security protocol suite being negotiated. Requests for assignments of new security protocol identifiers must be accompanied by an RFC which describes the requested security protocol. [AH] and [ESP] are examples of security protocol documents.

If the RFC is not on the standards-track (i.e., it is an informational or experimental RFC), it must be explicitly reviewed and approved by the IESG before the RFC is published and the transform identifier is assigned.

The values 249-255 are reserved for private use amongst cooperating systems.

6.3 IPSEC ISAKMP Transform Identifiers

The IPSEC ISAKMP Transform Identifier is an 8-bit value which identifies a key exchange protocol to be used for the negotiation. Requests for assignments of new ISAKMP transform identifiers must be accompanied by an RFC which describes the requested key exchange protocol. [IKE] is an example of one such document.

If the RFC is not on the standards-track (i.e., it is an informational or experimental RFC), it must be explicitly reviewed and approved by the IESG before the RFC is published and the transform identifier is assigned.

The values 249-255 are reserved for private use amongst cooperating systems.

6.4 IPSEC AH Transform Identifiers

The IPSEC AH Transform Identifier is an 8-bit value which identifies
a particular algorithm to be used to provide integrity protection for
AH. Requests for assignments of new AH transform identifiers must be
accompanied by an RFC which describes how to use the algorithm within
the AH framework ([AH]).

If the RFC is not on the standards-track (i.e., it is an
informational or experimental RFC), it must be explicitly reviewed
and approved by the IESG before the RFC is published and the
transform identifier is assigned.

The values 249-255 are reserved for private use amongst cooperating
systems.

6.5 IPSEC ESP Transform Identifiers

The IPSEC ESP Transform Identifier is an 8-bit value which identifies
a particular algorithm to be used to provide secrecy protection for
ESP. Requests for assignments of new ESP transform identifiers must
be accompanied by an RFC which describes how to use the algorithm
within the ESP framework ([ESP]).

If the RFC is not on the standards-track (i.e., it is an
informational or experimental RFC), it must be explicitly reviewed
and approved by the IESG before the RFC is published and the
transform identifier is assigned.

The values 249-255 are reserved for private use amongst cooperating
systems.

6.6 IPSEC IPCOMP Transform Identifiers

The IPSEC IPCOMP Transform Identifier is an 8-bit value which
identifier a particular algorithm to be used to provide IP-level
compression before ESP. Requests for assignments of new IPCOMP
transform identifiers must be accompanied by an RFC which describes
how to use the algorithm within the IPCOMP framework ([IPCOMP]). In
addition, the requested algorithm must be published and in the public
domain.

If the RFC is not on the standards-track (i.e., it is an
informational or experimental RFC), it must be explicitly reviewed
and approved by the IESG before the RFC is published and the
transform identifier is assigned.

The values 1-47 are reserved for algorithms for which an RFC has been approved for publication. The values 48-63 are reserved for private use amongst cooperating systems. The values 64-255 are reserved for future expansion.

6.7 IPSEC Security Association Attributes

The IPSEC Security Association Attribute consists of a 16-bit type and its associated value. IPSEC SA attributes are used to pass miscellaneous values between ISAKMP peers. Requests for assignments of new IPSEC SA attributes must be accompanied by an Internet Draft which describes the attribute encoding (Basic/Variable-Length) and its legal values. Section 4.5 of this document provides an example of such a description.

The values 32001-32767 are reserved for private use amongst cooperating systems.

6.8 IPSEC Labeled Domain Identifiers

The IPSEC Labeled Domain Identifier is a 32-bit value which identifies a namespace in which the Secrecy and Integrity levels and categories values are said to exist. Requests for assignments of new IPSEC Labeled Domain Identifiers should be granted on demand. No accompanying documentation is required, though Internet Drafts are encouraged when appropriate.

The values 0x80000000-0xffffffff are reserved for private use amongst cooperating systems.

6.9 IPSEC Identification Type

The IPSEC Identification Type is an 8-bit value which is used as a discriminant for interpretation of the variable-length Identification Payload. Requests for assignments of new IPSEC Identification Types must be accompanied by an RFC which describes how to use the identification type within IPSEC.

If the RFC is not on the standards-track (i.e., it is an informational or experimental RFC), it must be explicitly reviewed and approved by the IESG before the RFC is published and the transform identifier is assigned.

The values 249-255 are reserved for private use amongst cooperating systems.

6.10 IPSEC Notify Message Types

The IPSEC Notify Message Type is a 16-bit value taken from the range of values reserved by ISAKMP for each DOI. There is one range for error messages (8192-16383) and a different range for status messages (24576-32767). Requests for assignments of new Notify Message Types must be accompanied by an Internet Draft which describes how to use the identification type within IPSEC.

The values 16001-16383 and the values 32001-32767 are reserved for private use amongst cooperating systems.

7. Change Log

7.1 Changes from V9

    o add explicit reference to [IPCOMP], [DEFLATE], and [LZS]
    o allow RESPONDER-LIFETIME and REPLAY-STATUS to be directed
       at an IPSEC SPI in addition to the ISAKMP "SPI"
    o added padding exclusion to Secrecy and Integrity Length text
    o added forward reference to Section 4.5 in Section 4.4.4
    o update document references

7.2 Changes from V8

    o update IPCOMP identifier range to better reflect IPCOMP draft
    o update IANA considerations per Jeff/Ted's suggested text
    o eliminate references to DES-MAC ID ([DESMAC])
    o correct bug in Notify section; ISAKMP Notify values are 16-bits

7.3 Changes from V7

    o corrected name of IPCOMP (IP Payload Compression)
    o corrected references to [ESPCBC]
    o added missing Secrecy Level and Integrity Level to Figure 1
    o removed ID references to PF_KEY and ARCFOUR
    o updated Basic/Variable text to align with [IKE]
    o updated document references and add intro pointer to [ARCH]
    o updated Notification requirements; remove aggressive reference
    o added clarification about protection for Notify payloads
    o restored RESERVED to ESP transform ID namespace; moved ESP_NULL
    o added requirement for ESP_NULL support and [ESPNULL] reference
    o added clarification on Auth Alg use with AH/ESP
    o added restriction against using conflicting AH/Auth combinations

7.4 Changes from V6

The following changes were made relative to the IPSEC DOI V6:

- o added IANA Considerations section
- o moved most IANA numbers to IANA Considerations section
- o added prohibition on sending (V) encoding for (B) attributes
- o added prohibition on sending Key Length attribute for fixed
     length ciphers (e.g. DES)
- o replaced references to ISAKMP/Oakley with IKE
- o renamed ESP_ARCFOUR to ESP_RC4
- o updated Security Considerations section
- o updated document references

7.5 Changes from V5

   The following changes were made relative to the IPSEC DOI V5:

- o changed SPI size in Lifetime Notification text
- o changed REPLAY-ENABLED to REPLAY-STATUS
- o moved RESPONDER-LIFETIME payload definition from Section 4.5.4
     to Section 4.6.3.1
- o added explicit payload layout for 4.6.3.3
- o added Implementation Note to Section 4.6.3 introduction
- o changed AH_SHA text to require SHA-1 in addition to MD5
- o updated document references

7.6 Changes from V4

   The following changes were made relative to the IPSEC DOI V4:

- o moved compatibility AH KPDK authentication method from AH
     transform ID to Authentication Algorithm identifier
- o added REPLAY-ENABLED notification message type per Architecture
- o added INITIAL-CONTACT notification message type per list
- o added text to ensure protection for Notify Status messages
- o added Lifetime qualification to attribute parsing section
- o added clarification that Lifetime notification is optional
- o removed private Group Description list (now points at [IKE])
- o replaced Terminology with pointer to RFC-2119
- o updated HMAC MD5 and SHA-1 ID references
- o updated Section 1 (Abstract)
- o updated Section 4.4 (IPSEC Assigned Numbers)
- o added restriction for ID port/protocol values for Phase I

7.7 Changes from V3 to V4

   The following changes were made relative to the IPSEC DOI V3, that
   was posted to the IPSEC mailing list prior to the Munich IETF:

- o added ESP transform identifiers for NULL and ARCFOUR

   o renamed HMAC Algorithm to Auth Algorithm to accommodate
      DES-MAC and optional authentication/integrity for ESP
   o added AH and ESP DES-MAC algorithm identifiers
   o removed KEY_MANUAL and KEY_KDC identifier definitions
   o added lifetime duration MUST follow lifetype attribute to
      SA Life Type and SA Life Duration attribute definition
   o added lifetime notification and IPSEC DOI message type table
   o added optional authentication and confidentiality
      restrictions to MAC Algorithm attribute definition
   o corrected attribute parsing example (used obsolete attribute)
   o corrected several Internet Draft document references
   o added ID_KEY_ID per ipsec list discussion (18-Mar-97)
   o removed Group Description default for PFS QM ([IKE] MUST)

Acknowledgments

   This document is derived, in part, from previous works by Douglas
   Maughan, Mark Schertler, Mark Schneider, Jeff Turner, Dan Harkins,
   and Dave Carrel. Matt Thomas, Roy Pereira, Greg Carter, and Ran
   Atkinson also contributed suggestions and, in many cases, text.

References

   [AH]   Kent, S., and R. Atkinson, "IP Authentication Header", RFC
             2402, November 1998.

   [ARCH]   Kent, S., and R. Atkinson, "Security Architecture for the
             Internet Protocol", RFC 2401, November 1998.

   [DEFLATE] Pereira, R., "IP Payload Compression Using DEFLATE", RFC
             2394, August 1998.

   [ESP]   Kent, S., and R. Atkinson, "IP Encapsulating Security
             Payload (ESP)", RFC 2406, November 1998.

   [ESPCBC] Pereira, R., and R. Adams, "The ESP CBC-Mode Cipher
             Algorithms", RFC 2451, November 1998.

   [ESPNULL] Glenn, R., and S. Kent, "The NULL Encryption Algorithm and
             Its Use With IPsec", RFC 2410, November 1998.

   [DES]   Madson, C., and N. Doraswamy, "The ESP DES-CBC Cipher
             Algorithm With Explicit IV", RFC 2405, November 1998.

   [HMACMD5] Madson, C., and R. Glenn, "The Use of HMAC-MD5 within ESP
             and AH", RFC 2403, November 1998.

    [HMACSHA] Madson, C., and R. Glenn, "The Use of HMAC-SHA-1-96 within
               ESP and AH", RFC 2404, November 1998.

    [IKE]   Harkins, D., and D. Carrel, D., "The Internet Key Exchange
               (IKE)", RFC 2409, November 1998.

    [IPCOMP]   Shacham, A., Monsour, R., Pereira, R., and M. Thomas, "IP
               Payload Compression Protocol (IPComp)", RFC 2393, August
               1998.

    [ISAKMP]   Maughan, D., Schertler, M., Schneider, M., and J. Turner,
               "Internet Security Association and Key Management Protocol
               (ISAKMP)", RFC 2408, November 1998.

    [LZS]   Friend, R., and R. Monsour, "IP Payload Compression Using
               LZS", RFC 2395, August 1998.

    [OAKLEY]   Orman, H., "The OAKLEY Key Determination Protocol", RFC
               2412, November 1998.

    [X.501]   ISO/IEC 9594-2, "Information Technology - Open Systems
               Interconnection - The Directory: Models", CCITT/ITU
               Recommendation X.501, 1993.

    [X.509]   ISO/IEC 9594-8, "Information Technology - Open Systems
               Interconnection - The Directory: Authentication
               Framework", CCITT/ITU Recommendation X.509, 1993.

Author's Address

   Derrell Piper
   Network Alchemy
   1521.5 Pacific Ave
   Santa Cruz, California, 95060
   United States of America

   Phone: +1 408 460-3822
   EMail: ddp@network-alchemy.com

Full Copyright Statement

   Copyright (C) The Internet Society (1998). All Rights Reserved.

Network Working Group   D. Maughan
Request for Comments: 2408   National Security Agency
Category: Standards Track   M. Schertler
                                                 Securify, Inc.
                                                 M. Schneider
                                         National Security Agency
                                                    J. Turner
                                         RABA Technologies, Inc.
                                                November 1998

Internet Security Association and Key Management Protocol (ISAKMP)

Status of this Memo

Copyright Notice

Abstract

This memo describes a protocol utilizing security concepts necessary
for establishing Security Associations (SA) and cryptographic keys in
an Internet environment. A Security Association protocol that
negotiates, establishes, modifies and deletes Security Associations
and their attributes is required for an evolving Internet, where
there will be numerous security mechanisms and several options for
each security mechanism. The key management protocol must be robust
in order to handle public key generation for the Internet community
at large and private key requirements for those private networks with
that requirement. The Internet Security Association and Key
Management Protocol (ISAKMP) defines the procedures for
authenticating a communicating peer, creation and management of
Security Associations, key generation techniques, and threat
mitigation (e.g. denial of service and replay attacks). All of
these are necessary to establish and maintain secure communications
(via IP Security Service or any other security protocol) in an
Internet environment.

RFC 2408

Table of Contents

List of Figures

1 Introduction

This document describes an Internet Security Association and Key
Management Protocol (ISAKMP). ISAKMP combines the security concepts
of authentication, key management, and security associations to
establish the required security for government, commercial, and
private communications on the Internet.

The Internet Security Association and Key Management Protocol
(ISAKMP) defines procedures and packet formats to establish,
negotiate, modify and delete Security Associations (SA). SAs contain
all the information required for execution of various network
security services, such as the IP layer services (such as header
authentication and payload encapsulation), transport or application
layer services, or self-protection of negotiation traffic. ISAKMP
defines payloads for exchanging key generation and authentication
data. These formats provide a consistent framework for transferring
key and authentication data which is independent of the key
generation technique, encryption algorithm and authentication
mechanism.

ISAKMP is distinct from key exchange protocols in order to cleanly
separate the details of security association management (and key
management) from the details of key exchange. There may be many
different key exchange protocols, each with different security
properties. However, a common framework is required for agreeing to
the format of SA attributes, and for negotiating, modifying, and
deleting SAs. ISAKMP serves as this common framework.

Separating the functionality into three parts adds complexity to the
security analysis of a complete ISAKMP implementation. However, the
separation is critical for interoperability between systems with
differing security requirements, and should also simplify the
analysis of further evolution of a ISAKMP server.

ISAKMP is intended to support the negotiation of SAs for security
protocols at all layers of the network stack (e.g., IPSEC, TLS, TLSP,
OSPF, etc.). By centralizing the management of the security
associations, ISAKMP reduces the amount of duplicated functionality
within each security protocol. ISAKMP can also reduce connection
setup time, by negotiating a whole stack of services at once.

The remainder of section 1 establishes the motivation for security
negotiation and outlines the major components of ISAKMP, i.e.
Security Associations and Management, Authentication, Public Key
Cryptography, and Miscellaneous items. Section 2 presents the
terminology and concepts associated with ISAKMP. Section 3 describes
the different ISAKMP payload formats. Section 4 describes how the
payloads of ISAKMP are composed together as exchange types to
establish security associations and perform key exchanges in an
authenticated manner. Additionally, security association
modification, deletion, and error notification are discussed.
Section 5 describes the processing of each payload within the context
of ISAKMP exchanges, including error handling and associated actions.
The appendices provide the attribute values necessary for ISAKMP and
requirement for defining a new Domain of Interpretation (DOI) within
ISAKMP.

1.1 Requirements Terminology

The keywords MUST, MUST NOT, REQUIRED, SHALL, SHALL NOT, SHOULD,
SHOULD NOT, RECOMMENDED, MAY, and OPTIONAL, when they appear in this
document, are to be interpreted as described in [RFC-2119].

1.2 The Need for Negotiation

ISAKMP extends the assertion in [DOW92] that authentication and key
exchanges must be combined for better security to include security
association exchanges. The security services required for

communications depends on the individual network configurations and
environments. Organizations are setting up Virtual Private Networks
(VPN), also known as Intranets, that will require one set of security
functions for communications within the VPN and possibly many
different security functions for communications outside the VPN to
support geographically separate organizational components, customers,
suppliers, sub-contractors (with their own VPNs), government, and
others. Departments within large organizations may require a number
of security associations to separate and protect data (e.g.
personnel data, company proprietary data, medical) on internal
networks and other security associations to communicate within the
same department. Nomadic users wanting to "phone home" represent
another set of security requirements. These requirements must be
tempered with bandwidth challenges. Smaller groups of people may
meet their security requirements by setting up "Webs of Trust".
ISAKMP exchanges provide these assorted networking communities the
ability to present peers with the security functionality that the
user supports in an authenticated and protected manner for agreement
upon a common set of security attributes, i.e. an interoperable
security association.

1.3 What can be Negotiated?

Security associations must support different encryption algorithms,
authentication mechanisms, and key establishment algorithms for other
security protocols, as well as IP Security. Security associations
must also support host-oriented certificates for lower layer
protocols and user- oriented certificates for higher level protocols.
Algorithm and mechanism independence is required in applications such
as e-mail, remote login, and file transfer, as well as in session
oriented protocols, routing protocols, and link layer protocols.
ISAKMP provides a common security association and key establishment
protocol for this wide range of security protocols, applications,
security requirements, and network environments.

ISAKMP is not bound to any specific cryptographic algorithm, key
generation technique, or security mechanism. This flexibility is
beneficial for a number of reasons. First, it supports the dynamic
communications environment described above. Second, the independence
from specific security mechanisms and algorithms provides a forward
migration path to better mechanisms and algorithms. When improved
security mechanisms are developed or new attacks against current
encryption algorithms, authentication mechanisms and key exchanges
are discovered, ISAKMP will allow the updating of the algorithms and
mechanisms without having to develop a completely new KMP or patch
the current one.

ISAKMP has basic requirements for its authentication and key exchange components. These requirements guard against denial of service, replay / reflection, man-in-the-middle, and connection hijacking attacks. This is important because these are the types of attacks that are targeted against protocols. Complete Security Association (SA) support, which provides mechanism and algorithm independence, and protection from protocol threats are the strengths of ISAKMP.

1.4 Security Associations and Management

A Security Association (SA) is a relationship between two or more entities that describes how the entities will utilize security services to communicate securely. This relationship is represented by a set of information that can be considered a contract between the entities. The information must be agreed upon and shared between all the entities. Sometimes the information alone is referred to as an SA, but this is just a physical instantiation of the existing relationship. The existence of this relationship, represented by the information, is what provides the agreed upon security information needed by entities to securely interoperate. All entities must adhere to the SA for secure communications to be possible. When accessing SA attributes, entities use a pointer or identifier refered to as the Security Parameter Index (SPI). [SEC-ARCH] provides details on IP Security Associations (SA) and Security Parameter Index (SPI) definitions.

1.4.1 Security Associations and Registration

The SA attributes required and recommended for the IP Security (AH, ESP) are defined in [SEC-ARCH]. The attributes specified for an IP Security SA include, but are not limited to, authentication mechanism, cryptographic algorithm, algorithm mode, key length, and Initialization Vector (IV). Other protocols that provide algorithm and mechanism independent security MUST define their requirements for SA attributes. The separation of ISAKMP from a specific SA definition is important to ensure ISAKMP can es tablish SAs for all possible security protocols and applications.

NOTE: See [IPDOI] for a discussion of SA attributes that should be considered when defining a security protocol or application.

In order to facilitate easy identification of specific attributes (e.g. a specific encryption algorithm) among different network entites the attributes must be assigned identifiers and these identifiers must be registered by a central authority. The Internet Assigned Numbers Authority (IANA) provides this function for the Internet.

1.4.2 ISAKMP Requirements

Security Association (SA) establishment MUST be part of the key
management protocol defined for IP based networks. The SA concept is
required to support security protocols in a diverse and dynamic
networking environment. Just as authentication and key exchange must
be linked to provide assurance that the key is established with the
authenticated party [DOW92], SA establishment must be linked with the
authentication and the key exchange protocol.

ISAKMP provides the protocol exchanges to establish a security
association between negotiating entities followed by the
establishment of a security association by these negotiating entities
in behalf of some protocol (e.g. ESP/AH). First, an initial protocol
exchange allows a basic set of security attributes to be agreed upon.
This basic set provides protection for subsequent ISAKMP exchanges.
It also indicates the authentication method and key exchange that
will be performed as part of the ISAKMP protocol. If a basic set of
security attributes is already in place between the negotiating
server entities, the initial ISAKMP exchange may be skipped and the
establishment of a security association can be done directly. After
the basic set of security attributes has been agreed upon, initial
identity authenticated, and required keys generated, the established
SA can be used for subsequent communications by the entity that
invoked ISAKMP. The basic set of SA attributes that MUST be
implemented to provide ISAKMP interoperability are defined in
Appendix A.

1.5 Authentication

A very important step in establishing secure network communications
is authentication of the entity at the other end of the
communication. Many authentication mechanisms are available.
Authentication mechanisms fall into two catagories of strength - weak
and strong. Sending cleartext keys or other unprotected
authenticating information over a network is weak, due to the threat
of reading them with a network sniffer. Additionally, sending one-
way hashed poorly-chosen keys with low entropy is also weak, due to
the threat of brute-force guessing attacks on the sniffed messages.
While passwords can be used for establishing identity, they are not
considered in this context because of recent statements from the
Internet Architecture Board [IAB]. Digital signatures, such as the
Digital Signature Standard (DSS) and the Rivest-Shamir-Adleman (RSA)
signature, are public key based strong authentication mechanisms.
When using public key digital signatures each entity requires a
public key and a private key. Certificates are an essential part of
a digital signature authentication mechanism. Certificates bind a
specific entity's identity (be it host, network, user, or

application) to its public keys and possibly other security-related
information such as privileges, clearances, and compartments.
Authentication based on digital signatures requires a trusted third
party or certificate authority to create, sign and properly
distribute certificates. For more detailed information on digital
signatures, such as DSS and RSA, and certificates see [Schneier].

1.5.1 Certificate Authorities

Certificates require an infrastructure for generation, verification,
revocation, management and distribution. The Internet Policy
Registration Authority (IPRA) [RFC-1422] has been established to
direct this infrastructure for the IETF. The IPRA certifies Policy
Certification Authorities (PCA). PCAs control Certificate Authorities
(CA) which certify users and subordinate entities. Current
certificate related work includes the Domain Name System (DNS)
Security Extensions [DNSSEC] which will provide signed entity keys in
the DNS. The Public Key Infrastucture (PKIX) working group is
specifying an Internet profile for X.509 certificates. There is also
work going on in industry to develop X.500 Directory Services which
would provide X.509 certificates to users. The U.S. Post Office is
developing a (CA) hierarchy. The NIST Public Key Infrastructure
Working Group has also been doing work in this area. The DOD Multi
Level Information System Security Initiative (MISSI) program has
begun deploying a certificate infrastructure for the U.S. Government.
Alternatively, if no infrastructure exists, the PGP Web of Trust
certificates can be used to provide user authentication and privacy
in a community of users who know and trust each other.

1.5.2 Entity Naming

An entity's name is its identity and is bound to its public keys in
certificates. The CA MUST define the naming semantics for the
certificates it issues. See the UNINETT PCA Policy Statements
[Berge] for an example of how a CA defines its naming policy. When
the certificate is verified, the name is verified and that name will
have meaning within the realm of that CA. An example is the DNS
security extensions which make DNS servers CAs for the zones and
nodes they serve. Resource records are provided for public keys and
signatures on those keys. The names associated with the keys are IP
addresses and domain names which have meaning to entities accessing
the DNS for this information. A Web of Trust is another example.
When webs of trust are set up, names are bound with the public keys.
In PGP the name is usually the entity's e-mail address which has
meaning to those, and only those, who understand e-mail. Another web
of trust could use an entirely different naming scheme.

1.5.3 ISAKMP Requirements

Strong authentication MUST be provided on ISAKMP exchanges. Without being able to authenticate the entity at the other end, the Security Association (SA) and session key established are suspect. Without authentication you are unable to trust an entity's identification, which makes access control questionable. While encryption (e.g. ESP) and integrity (e.g. AH) will protect subsequent communications from passive eavesdroppers, without authentication it is possible that the SA and key may have been established with an adversary who performed an active man-in-the-middle attack and is now stealing all your personal data.

A digital signature algorithm MUST be used within ISAKMP's authentication component. However, ISAKMP does not mandate a specific signature algorithm or certificate authority (CA). ISAKMP allows an entity initiating communications to indicate which CAs it supports. After selection of a CA, the protocol provides the messages required to support the actual authentication exchange. The protocol provides a facility for identification of different certificate authorities, certificate types (e.g. X.509, PKCS #7, PGP, DNS SIG and KEY records), and the exchange of the certificates identified.

ISAKMP utilizes digital signatures, based on public key cryptography, for authentication. There are other strong authentication systems available, which could be specified as additional optional authentication mechanisms for ISAKMP. Some of these authentication systems rely on a trusted third party called a key distribution center (KDC) to distribute secret session keys. An example is Kerberos, where the trusted third party is the Kerberos server, which holds secret keys for all clients and servers within its network domain. A client's proof that it holds its secret key provides authenticaton to a server.

The ISAKMP specification does not specify the protocol for communicating with the trusted third parties (TTP) or certificate directory services. These protocols are defined by the TTP and directory service themselves and are outside the scope of this specification. The use of these additional services and protocols will be described in a Key Exchange specific document.

1.6 Public Key Cryptography

Public key cryptography is the most flexible, scalable, and efficient way for users to obtain the shared secrets and session keys needed to support the large number of ways Internet users will interoperate. Many key generation algorithms, that have different properties, are

available to users (see [DOW92], [ANSI], and [Oakley]). Properties
of key exchange protocols include the key establishment method,
authentication, symmetry, perfect forward secrecy, and back traffic
protection.

NOTE: Cryptographic keys can protect information for a considerable
length of time. However, this is based on the assumption that keys
used for protection of communications are destroyed after use and not
kept for any reason.

1.6.1 Key Exchange Properties

Key Establishment (Key Generation / Key Transport): The two common
methods of using public key cryptography for key establishment are
key transport and key generation. An example of key transport is the
use of the RSA algorithm to encrypt a randomly generated session key
(for encrypting subsequent communications) with the recipient's
public key. The encrypted random key is then sent to the recipient,
who decrypts it using his private key. At this point both sides have
the same session key, however it was created based on input from only
one side of the communications. The benefit of the key transport
method is that it has less computational overhead than the following
method. The Diffie-Hellman (D-H) algorithm illustrates key
generation using public key cryptography. The D-H algorithm is begun
by two users exchanging public information. Each user then
mathematically combines the other's public information along with
their own secret information to compute a shared secret value. This
secret value can be used as a session key or as a key encryption key
for encrypting a randomly generated session key. This method
generates a session key based on public and secret information held
by both users. The benefit of the D-H algorithm is that the key used
for encrypting messages is based on information held by both users
and the independence of keys from one key exchange to another
provides perfect forward secrecy. Detailed descriptions of these
algorithms can be found in [Schneier]. There are a number of
variations on these two key generation schemes and these variations
do not necessarily interoperate.

Key Exchange Authentication: Key exchanges may be authenticated
during the protocol or after protocol completion. Authentication of
the key exchange during the protocol is provided when each party
provides proof it has the secret session key before the end of the
protocol. Proof can be provided by encrypting known data in the
secret session key during the protocol echange. Authentication after
the protocol must occur in subsequent commu nications.
Authentication during the protocol is preferred so subsequent
communications are not initiated if the secret session key is not
established with the desired party.

Key Exchange Symmetry: A key exchange provides symmetry if either party can initiate the exchange and exchanged messages can cross in transit without affecting the key that is generated. This is desirable so that computation of the keys does not require either party to know who initated the exchange. While key exchange symmetry is desirable, symmetry in the entire key management protocol may provide a vulnerablity to reflection attacks.

Perfect Forward Secrecy: As described in [DOW92], an authenticated key exchange protocol provides perfect forward secrecy if disclosure of longterm secret keying material does not compromise the secrecy of the exchanged keys from previous communications. The property of perfect forward secrecy does not apply to key exchange without authentication.

1.6.2 ISAKMP Requirements

An authenticated key exchange MUST be supported by ISAKMP. Users SHOULD choose additional key establishment algorithms based on their requirements. ISAKMP does not specify a specific key exchange. However, [IKE] describes a proposal for using the Oakley key exchange [Oakley] in conjunction with ISAKMP. Requirements that should be evaluated when choosing a key establishment algorithm include establishment method (generation vs. transport), perfect forward secrecy, computational overhead, key escrow, and key strength. Based on user requirements, ISAKMP allows an entity initiating communications to indicate which key exchanges it supports. After selection of a key exchange, the protocol provides the messages required to support the actual key establishment.

1.7 ISAKMP Protection

1.7.1 Anti-Clogging (Denial of Service)

Of the numerous security services available, protection against denial of service always seems to be one of the most difficult to address. A "cookie" or anti-clogging token (ACT) is aimed at protecting the computing resources from attack without spending excessive CPU resources to determine its authenticity. An exchange prior to CPU-intensive public key operations can thwart some denial of service attempts (e.g. simple flooding with bogus IP source addresses). Absolute protection against denial of service is impossible, but this anti-clogging token provides a technique for making it easier to handle. The use of an anti-clogging token was introduced by Karn and Simpson in [Karn].

It should be noted that in the exchanges shown in section 4, the anticlogging mechanism should be used in conjuction with a garbage-state collection mechanism; an attacker can still flood a server using packets with bogus IP addresses and cause state to be created. Such aggressive memory management techniques SHOULD be employed by protocols using ISAKMP that do not go through an initial, anti-clogging only phase, as was done in [Karn].

1.7.2 Connection Hijacking

ISAKMP prevents connection hijacking by linking the authentication, key exchange and security association exchanges. This linking prevents an attacker from allowing the authentication to complete and then jumping in and impersonating one entity to the other during the key and security association exchanges.

1.7.3 Man-in-the-Middle Attacks

Man-in-the-Middle attacks include interception, insertion, deletion, and modification of messages, reflecting messages back at the sender, replaying old messages and redirecting messages. ISAKMP features prevent these types of attacks from being successful. The linking of the ISAKMP exchanges prevents the insertion of messages in the protocol exchange. The ISAKMP protocol state machine is defined so deleted messages will not cause a partial SA to be created, the state machine will clear all state and return to idle. The state machine also prevents reflection of a message from causing harm. The requirement for a new cookie with time variant material for each new SA establishment prevents attacks that involve replaying old messages. The ISAKMP strong authentication requirement prevents an SA from being established with anyone other than the intended party. Messages may be redirected to a different destination or modified but this will be detected and an SA will not be established. The ISAKMP specification defines where abnormal processing has occurred and recommends notifying the appropriate party of this abnormality.

1.8 Multicast Communications

It is expected that multicast communications will require the same security services as unicast communications and may introduce the need for additional security services. The issues of distributing SPIs for multicast traffic are presented in [SEC-ARCH]. Multicast security issues are also discussed in [RFC-1949] and [BC]. A future extension to ISAKMP will support multicast key distribution. For an introduction to the issues related to multicast security, consult the Internet Drafts, [RFC-2094] and [RFC-2093], describing Sparta's research in this area.

2 Terminology and Concepts

2.1 ISAKMP Terminology

   Security Protocol: A Security Protocol consists of an entity at a
   single point in the network stack, performing a security service for
   network communication. For example, IPSEC ESP and IPSEC AH are two
   different security protocols. TLS is another example. Security
   Protocols may perform more than one service, for example providing
   integrity and confidentiality in one module.

   Protection Suite: A protection suite is a list of the security
   services that must be applied by various security protocols. For
   example, a protection suite may consist of DES encryption in IP ESP,
   and keyed MD5 in IP AH. All of the protections in a suite must be
   treated as a single unit. This is necessary because security
   services in different security protocols can have subtle
   interactions, and the effects of a suite must be analyzed and
   verified as a whole.

   Security Association (SA): A Security Association is a security-
   protocol- specific set of parameters that completely defines the
   services and mechanisms necessary to protect traffic at that security
   protocol location. These parameters can include algorithm
   identifiers, modes, cryptographic keys, etc. The SA is referred to
   by its associated security protocol (for example, "ISAKMP SA", "ESP
   SA", "TLS SA").

   ISAKMP SA: An SA used by the ISAKMP servers to protect their own
   traffic. Sections 2.3 and 2.4 provide more details about ISAKMP SAs.

   Security Parameter Index (SPI): An identifier for a Security
   Assocation, relative to some security protocol. Each security
   protocol has its own "SPI-space". A (security protocol, SPI) pair
   may uniquely identify an SA. The uniqueness of the SPI is
   implementation dependent, but could be based per system, per
   protocol, or other options. Depending on the DOI, additional
   information (e.g. host address) may be necessary to identify an SA.
   The DOI will also determine which SPIs (i.e. initiator's or
   responder's) are sent during communication.

   Domain of Interpretation: A Domain of Interpretation (DOI) defines
   payload formats, exchange types, and conventions for naming
   security-relevant information such as security policies or
   cryptographic algorithms and modes. A Domain of Interpretation (DOI)
   identifier is used to interpret the payloads of ISAKMP payloads. A
   system SHOULD support multiple Domains of Interpretation
   simultaneously. The concept of a DOI is based on previous work by

the TSIG CIPSO Working Group, but extends beyond security label
interpretation to include naming and interpretation of security
services. A DOI defines:

o A "situation": the set of information that will be used to
   determine the required security services.

o The set of security policies that must, and may, be supported.

o A syntax for the specification of proposed security services.

o A scheme for naming security-relevant information, including
   encryption algorithms, key exchange algorithms, security policy
   attributes, and certificate authorities.

o The specific formats of the various payload contents.

o Additional exchange types, if required.

The rules for the IETF IP Security DOI are presented in [IPDOI].
Specifications of the rules for customized DOIs will be presented in
separate documents.

Situation: A situation contains all of the security-relevant
information that a system considers necessary to decide the security
services required to protect the session being negotiated. The
situation may include addresses, security classifications, modes of
operation (normal vs. emergency), etc.

Proposal: A proposal is a list, in decreasing order of preference, of
the protection suites that a system considers acceptable to protect
traffic under a given situation.

Payload: ISAKMP defines several types of payloads, which are used to
transfer information such as security association data, or key
exchange data, in DOI-defined formats. A payload consists of a
generic payload header and a string of octets that is opaque to
ISAKMP. ISAKMP uses DOI- specific functionality to synthesize and
interpret these payloads. Multiple payloads can be sent in a single
ISAKMP message. See section 3 for more details on the payload types,
and [IPDOI] for the formats of the IETF IP Security DOI payloads.

Exchange Type: An exchange type is a specification of the number of
messages in an ISAKMP exchange, and the payload types that are
contained in each of those messages. Each exchange type is designed
to provide a particular set of security services, such as anonymity
of the participants, perfect forward secrecy of the keying material,
authentication of the participants, etc. Section 4.1 defines the

default set of ISAKMP exchange types. Other exchange types can be
added to support additional key exchanges, if required.

2.2 ISAKMP Placement

Figure 1 is a high level view of the placement of ISAKMP within a
system context in a network architecture. An important part of
negotiating security services is to consider the entire "stack" of
individual SAs as a unit. This is referred to as a "protection
suite".

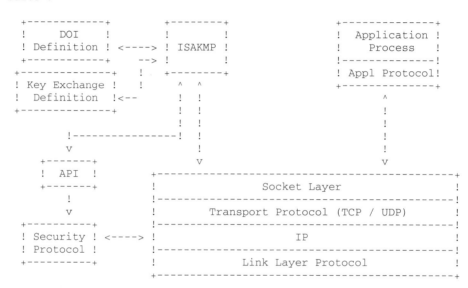

Figure 1: ISAKMP Relationships

2.3 Negotiation Phases

ISAKMP offers two "phases" of negotiation. In the first phase, two
entities (e.g. ISAKMP servers) agree on how to protect further
negotiation traffic between themselves, establishing an ISAKMP SA.
This ISAKMP SA is then used to protect the negotiations for the
Protocol SA being requested. Two entities (e.g. ISAKMP servers) can
negotiate (and have active) multiple ISAKMP SAs.

The second phase of negotiation is used to establish security
associations for other security protocols. This second phase can be
used to establish many security associations. The security
associations established by ISAKMP during this phase can be used by a
security protocol to protect many message/data exchanges.

While the two-phased approach has a higher start-up cost for most
simple scenarios, there are several reasons that it is beneficial for
most cases.

First, entities (e.g. ISAKMP servers) can amortize the cost of the
first phase across several second phase negotiations. This allows
multiple SAs to be established between peers over time without having
to start over for each communication.

Second, security services negotiated during the first phase provide
security properties for the second phase. For example, after the
first phase of negotiation, the encryption provided by the ISAKMP SA
can provide identity protection, potentially allowing the use of
simpler second-phase exchanges. On the other hand, if the channel
established during the first phase is not adequate to protect
identities, then the second phase must negotiate adequate security
mechanisms.

Third, having an ISAKMP SA in place considerably reduces the cost of
ISAKMP management activity - without the "trusted path" that an
ISAKMP SA gives you, the entities (e.g. ISAKMP servers) would have
to go through a complete re-authentication for each error
notification or deletion of an SA.

Negotiation during each phase is accomplished using ISAKMP-defined
exchanges (see section 4) or exchanges defined for a key exchange
within a DOI.

Note that security services may be applied differently in each
negotiation phase. For example, different parties are being
authenticated during each of the phases of negotiation. During the
first phase, the parties being authenticated may be the ISAKMP
servers/hosts, while during the second phase, users or application
level programs are being authenticated.

2.4 Identifying Security Associations

While bootstrapping secure channels between systems, ISAKMP cannot
assume the existence of security services, and must provide some
protections for itself. Therefore, ISAKMP considers an ISAKMP
Security Association to be different than other types, and manages
ISAKMP SAs itself, in their own name space. ISAKMP uses the two

cookie fields in the ISAKMP header to identify ISAKMP SAs. The
Message ID in the ISAKMP Header and the SPI field in the Proposal
payload are used during SA establishment to identify the SA for other
security protocols. The interpretation of these four fields is
dependent on the operation taking place.

The following table shows the presence or absence of several fields
during SA establishment. The following fields are necessary for
various operations associated with SA establishment: cookies in the
ISAKMP header, the ISAKMP Header Message ID field, and the SPI field
in the Proposal payload. An 'X' in the column means the value MUST
be present. An 'NA' in the column means a value in the column is Not
Applicable to the operation.

```
 #              Operation           I-Cookie  R-Cookie  Message ID  SPI
(1)  Start ISAKMP SA negotiation    X         0         0           0
(2)  Respond ISAKMP SA negotiation  X         X         0           0
(3)  Init other SA negotiation      X         X         X           X
(4)  Respond other SA negotiation   X         X         X           X
(5)  Other (KE, ID, etc.)           X         X         X/0         NA
(6)  Security Protocol (ESP, AH)    NA        NA        NA          X
```

In the first line (1) of the table, the initiator includes the
Initiator Cookie field in the ISAKMP Header, using the procedures
outlined in sections 2.5.3 and 3.1.

In the second line (2) of the table, the responder includes the
Initiator and Responder Cookie fields in the ISAKMP Header, using the
procedures outlined in sections 2.5.3 and 3.1. Additional messages
may be exchanged between ISAKMP peers, depending on the ISAKMP
exchange type used during the phase 1 negotiation. Once the phase 1
exchange is completed, the Initiator and Responder cookies are
included in the ISAKMP Header of all subsequent communications
between the ISAKMP peers.

During phase 1 negotiations, the initiator and responder cookies
determine the ISAKMP SA. Therefore, the SPI field in the Proposal
payload is redundant and MAY be set to 0 or it MAY contain the
transmitting entity's cookie.

In the third line (3) of the table, the initiator associates a
Message ID with the Protocols contained in the SA Proposal. This
Message ID and the initiator's SPI(s) to be associated with each
protocol in the Proposal are sent to the responder. The SPI(s) will
be used by the security protocols once the phase 2 negotiation is
completed.

In the fourth line (4) of the table, the responder includes the same
Message ID and the responder's SPI(s) to be associated with each
protocol in the accepted Proposal. This information is returned to
the initiator.

In the fifth line (5) of the table, the initiator and responder use
the Message ID field in the ISAKMP Header to keep track of the in-
progress protocol negotiation. This is only applicable for a phase 2
exchange and the value MUST be 0 for a phase 1 exchange because the
combined cookies identify the ISAKMP SA. The SPI field in the
Proposal payload is not applicable because the Proposal payload is
only used during the SA negotiation message exchange (steps 3 and 4).

In the sixth line (6) of the table, the phase 2 negotiation is
complete. The security protocols use the SPI(s) to determine which
security services and mechanisms to apply to the communication
between them. The SPI value shown in the sixth line (6) is not the
SPI field in the Proposal payload, but the SPI field contained within
the security protocol header.

During the SA establishment, a SPI MUST be generated. ISAKMP is
designed to handle variable sized SPIs. This is accomplished by
using the SPI Size field within the Proposal payload during SA
establishment. Handling of SPIs will be outlined by the DOI
specification (e.g. [IPDOI]).

When a security association (SA) is initially established, one side
assumes the role of initiator and the other the role of responder.
Once the SA is established, both the original initiator and responder
can initiate a phase 2 negotiation with the peer entity. Thus,
ISAKMP SAs are bidirectional in nature.

Additionally, ISAKMP allows both initiator and responder to have some
control during the negotiation process. While ISAKMP is designed to
allow an SA negotiation that includes multiple proposals, the
initiator can maintain some control by only making one proposal in
accordance with the initiator's local security policy. Once the
initiator sends a proposal containing more than one proposal (which
are sent in decreasing preference order), the initiator relinquishes
control to the responder. Once the responder is controlling the SA
establishment, the responder can make its policy take precedence over
the initiator within the context of the multiple options offered by
the initiator. This is accomplished by selecting the proposal best
suited for the responder's local security policy and returning this
selection to the initiator.

2.5 Miscellaneous

2.5.1 Transport Protocol

   ISAKMP can be implemented over any transport protocol or over IP
   itself. Implementations MUST include send and receive capability for
   ISAKMP using the User Datagram Protocol (UDP) on port 500. UDP Port
   500 has been assigned to ISAKMP by the Internet Assigned Numbers
   Authority (IANA). Implementations MAY additionally support ISAKMP
   over other transport protocols or over IP itself.

2.5.2 RESERVED Fields

   The existence of RESERVED fields within ISAKMP payloads are used
   strictly to preserve byte alignment. All RESERVED fields in the
   ISAKMP protocol MUST be set to zero (0) when a packet is issued. The
   receiver SHOULD check the RESERVED fields for a zero (0) value and
   discard the packet if other values are found.

2.5.3 Anti-Clogging Token ("Cookie") Creation

   The details of cookie generation are implementation dependent, but
   MUST satisfy these basic requirements (originally stated by Phil Karn
   in [Karn]):

      1.   The cookie must depend on the specific parties. This
            prevents an attacker from obtaining a cookie using a real IP
            address and UDP port, and then using it to swamp the victim
            with Diffie-Hellman requests from randomly chosen IP
            addresses or ports.

      2.   It must not be possible for anyone other than the issuing
            entity to generate cookies that will be accepted by that
            entity. This implies that the issuing entity must use local
            secret information in the generation and subsequent
            verification of a cookie. It must not be possible to deduce
            this secret information from any particular cookie.

      3.   The cookie generation function must be fast to thwart
            attacks intended to sabotage CPU resources.

   Karn's suggested method for creating the cookie is to perform a fast
   hash (e.g. MD5) over the IP Source and Destination Address, the UDP
   Source and Destination Ports and a locally generated secret random
   value. ISAKMP requires that the cookie be unique for each SA
   establishment to help prevent replay attacks, therefore, the date and
   time MUST be added to the information hashed. The generated cookies
   are placed in the ISAKMP Header (described in section 3.1) Initiator

and Responder cookie fields. These fields are 8 octets in length,
thus, requiring a generated cookie to be 8 octets. Notify and Delete
messages (see sections 3.14, 3.15, and 4.8) are uni-directional
transmissions and are done under the protection of an existing ISAKMP
SA, thus, not requiring the generation of a new cookie. One
exception to this is the transmission of a Notify message during a
Phase 1 exchange, prior to completing the establishment of an SA.
Sections 3.14 and 4.8 provide additional details.

3 ISAKMP Payloads

ISAKMP payloads provide modular building blocks for constructing
ISAKMP messages. The presence and ordering of payloads in ISAKMP is
defined by and dependent upon the Exchange Type Field located in the
ISAKMP Header (see Figure 2). The ISAKMP payload types are discussed
in sections 3.4 through 3.15. The descriptions of the ISAKMP
payloads, messages, and exchanges (see Section 4) are shown using
network octet ordering.

3.1 ISAKMP Header Format

An ISAKMP message has a fixed header format, shown in Figure 2,
followed by a variable number of payloads. A fixed header simplifies
parsing, providing the benefit of protocol parsing software that is
less complex and easier to implement. The fixed header contains the
information required by the protocol to maintain state, process
payloads and possibly prevent denial of service or replay attacks.

The ISAKMP Header fields are defined as follows:

  o Initiator Cookie (8 octets) - Cookie of entity that initiated SA
     establishment, SA notification, or SA deletion.

  o Responder Cookie (8 octets) - Cookie of entity that is responding
     to an SA establishment request, SA notification, or SA deletion.

```
                         1                   2                   3
     0 1 2 3 4 5 6 7 8 9 0 1 2 3 4 5 6 7 8 9 0 1 2 3 4 5 6 7 8 9 0 1
    +-+-+-+-+-+-+-+-+-+-+-+-+-+-+-+-+-+-+-+-+-+-+-+-+-+-+-+-+-+-+-+-+
    !                          Initiator                           !
    !                           Cookie                             !
    +-+-+-+-+-+-+-+-+-+-+-+-+-+-+-+-+-+-+-+-+-+-+-+-+-+-+-+-+-+-+-+-+
    !                          Responder                           !
    !                           Cookie                             !
    +-+-+-+-+-+-+-+-+-+-+-+-+-+-+-+-+-+-+-+-+-+-+-+-+-+-+-+-+-+-+-+-+
    ! Next Payload ! MjVer ! MnVer ! Exchange Type !     Flags     !
    +-+-+-+-+-+-+-+-+-+-+-+-+-+-+-+-+-+-+-+-+-+-+-+-+-+-+-+-+-+-+-+-+
    !                          Message ID                          !
    +-+-+-+-+-+-+-+-+-+-+-+-+-+-+-+-+-+-+-+-+-+-+-+-+-+-+-+-+-+-+-+-+
    !                           Length                             !
    +-+-+-+-+-+-+-+-+-+-+-+-+-+-+-+-+-+-+-+-+-+-+-+-+-+-+-+-+-+-+-+-+
```

Figure 2: ISAKMP Header Format

o Next Payload (1 octet) - Indicates the type of the first payload
   in the message. The format for each payload is defined in
   sections 3.4 through 3.16. The processing for the payloads is
   defined in section 5.

```
          Next Payload Type          Value
          NONE                         0
          Security Association (SA)    1
          Proposal (P)                 2
          Transform (T)                3
          Key Exchange (KE)            4
          Identification (ID)          5
          Certificate (CERT)           6
          Certificate Request (CR)     7
          Hash (HASH)                  8
          Signature (SIG)              9
          Nonce (NONCE)               10
          Notification (N)            11
          Delete (D)                  12
          Vendor ID (VID)             13
          RESERVED                14 - 127
          Private USE            128 - 255
```

o Major Version (4 bits) - indicates the major version of the ISAKMP
   protocol in use. Implementations based on this version of the
   ISAKMP Internet-Draft MUST set the Major Version to 1.
   Implementations based on previous versions of ISAKMP Internet-
   Drafts MUST set the Major Version to 0. Implementations SHOULD

never accept packets with a major version number larger than its own.

o Minor Version (4 bits) - indicates the minor version of the
   ISAKMP protocol in use. Implementations based on this version of
   the ISAKMP Internet-Draft MUST set the Minor Version to 0.
   Implementations based on previous versions of ISAKMP Internet-
   Drafts MUST set the Minor Version to 1. Implementations SHOULD
   never accept packets with a minor version number larger than its
   own, given the major version numbers are identical.

o Exchange Type (1 octet) - indicates the type of exchange being
   used. This dictates the message and payload orderings in the
   ISAKMP exchanges.

```
              Exchange Type        Value
          NONE                       0
          Base                       1
          Identity Protection        2
          Authentication Only        3
          Aggressive                 4
          Informational             5
          ISAKMP Future Use       6 - 31
          DOI Specific Use       32 - 239
          Private Use           240 - 255
```

o Flags (1 octet) - indicates specific options that are set for the
   ISAKMP exchange. The flags listed below are specified in the
   Flags field beginning with the least significant bit, i.e the
   Encryption bit is bit 0 of the Flags field, the Commit bit is bit
   1 of the Flags field, and the Authentication Only bit is bit 2 of
   the Flags field. The remaining bits of the Flags field MUST be
   set to 0 prior to transmission.

   - E(ncryption Bit) (1 bit) - If set (1), all payloads following
      the header are encrypted using the encryption algorithm
      identified in the ISAKMP SA. The ISAKMP SA Identifier is the
      combination of the initiator and responder cookie. It is
      RECOMMENDED that encryption of communications be done as soon
      as possible between the peers. For all ISAKMP exchanges
      described in section 4.1, the encryption SHOULD begin after
      both parties have exchanged Key Exchange payloads. If the
      E(ncryption Bit) is not set (0), the payloads are not
      encrypted.

-- C(ommit Bit) (1 bit) - This bit is used to signal key exchange
   synchronization. It is used to ensure that encrypted material
   is not received prior to completion of the SA establishment.
   The Commit Bit can be set (at anytime) by either party
   participating in the SA establishment, and can be used during
   both phases of an ISAKMP SA establishment. However, the value
   MUST be reset after the Phase 1 negotiation. If set(1), the
   entity which did not set the Commit Bit MUST wait for an
   Informational Exchange containing a Notify payload (with the
   CONNECTED Notify Message) from the entity which set the Commit
   Bit. In this instance, the Message ID field of the
   Informational Exchange MUST contain the Message ID of the
   original ISAKMP Phase 2 SA negotiation. This is done to
   ensure that the Informational Exchange with the CONNECTED
   Notify Message can be associated with the correct Phase 2 SA.
   The receipt and processing of the Informational Exchange
   indicates that the SA establishment was successful and either
   entity can now proceed with encrypted traffic communication.
   In addition to synchronizing key exchange, the Commit Bit can
   be used to protect against loss of transmissions over
   unreliable networks and guard against the need for multiple
   re-transmissions.

   NOTE: It is always possible that the final message of an
   exchange can be lost. In this case, the entity expecting to
   receive the final message of an exchange would receive the
   Phase 2 SA negotiation message following a Phase 1 exchange or
   encrypted traffic following a Phase 2 exchange. Handling of
   this situation is not standardized, but we propose the
   following possibilities. If the entity awaiting the
   Informational Exchange can verify the received message (i.e.
   Phase 2 SA negotiation message or encrypted traffic), then
   they MAY consider the SA was established and continue
   processing. The other option is to retransmit the last ISAKMP
   message to force the other entity to retransmit the final
   message. This suggests that implementations may consider
   retaining the last message (locally) until they are sure the
   SA is established.

-- A(uthentication Only Bit) (1 bit) - This bit is intended for
   use with the Informational Exchange with a Notify payload and
   will allow the transmission of information with integrity
   checking, but no encryption (e.g. "emergency mode"). Section
   4.8 states that a Phase 2 Informational Exchange MUST be sent
   under the protection of an ISAKMP SA. This is the only
   exception to that policy. If the Authentication Only bit is
   set (1), only authentication security services will be applied
   to the entire Notify payload of the Informational Exchange and

the payload will not be encrypted.

o Message ID (4 octets) - Unique Message Identifier used to
   identify protocol state during Phase 2 negotiations. This value
   is randomly generated by the initiator of the Phase 2
   negotiation. In the event of simultaneous SA establishments
   (i.e. collisions), the value of this field will likely be
   different because they are independently generated and, thus, two
   security associations will progress toward establishment.
   However, it is unlikely there will be absolute simultaneous
   establishments. During Phase 1 negotiations, the value MUST be
   set to 0.

o Length (4 octets) - Length of total message (header + payloads)
   in octets. Encryption can expand the size of an ISAKMP message.

3.2 Generic Payload Header

Each ISAKMP payload defined in sections 3.4 through 3.16 begins with
a generic header, shown in Figure 3, which provides a payload
"chaining" capability and clearly defines the boundaries of a
payload.

```
                      1                   2                   3
  0 1 2 3 4 5 6 7 8 9 0 1 2 3 4 5 6 7 8 9 0 1 2 3 4 5 6 7 8 9 0 1
 +-+-+-+-+-+-+-+-+-+-+-+-+-+-+-+-+-+-+-+-+-+-+-+-+-+-+-+-+-+-+-+-+
 ! Next Payload  !   RESERVED    !          Payload Length       !
 +-+-+-+-+-+-+-+-+-+-+-+-+-+-+-+-+-+-+-+-+-+-+-+-+-+-+-+-+-+-+-+-+
```

Figure 3: Generic Payload Header

The Generic Payload Header fields are defined as follows:

o Next Payload (1 octet) - Identifier for the payload type of the
   next payload in the message. If the current payload is the last
   in the message, then this field will be 0. This field provides
   the "chaining" capability.

o RESERVED (1 octet) - Unused, set to 0.

o Payload Length (2 octets) - Length in octets of the current
   payload, including the generic payload header.

3.3 Data Attributes

There are several instances within ISAKMP where it is necessary to
represent Data Attributes. An example of this is the Security
Association (SA) Attributes contained in the Transform payload

(described in section 3.6). These Data Attributes are not an ISAKMP
payload, but are contained within ISAKMP payloads. The format of the
Data Attributes provides the flexibility for representation of many
different types of information. There can be multiple Data
Attributes within a payload. The length of the Data Attributes will
either be 4 octets or defined by the Attribute Length field. This is
done using the Attribute Format bit described below. Specific
information about the attributes for each domain will be described in
a DOI document, e.g. IPSEC DOI [IPDOI].

```
                    1                   2                   3
0 1 2 3 4 5 6 7 8 9 0 1 2 3 4 5 6 7 8 9 0 1 2 3 4 5 6 7 8 9 0 1
+-+-+-+-+-+-+-+-+-+-+-+-+-+-+-+-+-+-+-+-+-+-+-+-+-+-+-+-+-+-+-+-+
!A!      Attribute Type       !   AF=0  Attribute Length     !
!F!                           !   AF=1  Attribute Value      !
+-+-+-+-+-+-+-+-+-+-+-+-+-+-+-+-+-+-+-+-+-+-+-+-+-+-+-+-+-+-+-+-+
.                   AF=0  Attribute Value                   .
.                   AF=1  Not Transmitted                   .
+-+-+-+-+-+-+-+-+-+-+-+-+-+-+-+-+-+-+-+-+-+-+-+-+-+-+-+-+-+-+-+-+
```

                        Figure 4: Data Attributes

The Data Attributes fields are defined as follows:

o Attribute Type (2 octets) - Unique identifier for each type of
   attribute. These attributes are defined as part of the DOI-
   specific information.

   The most significant bit, or Attribute Format (AF), indicates
   whether the data attributes follow the Type/Length/Value (TLV)
   format or a shortened Type/Value (TV) format. If the AF bit is a
   zero (0), then the Data Attributes are of the Type/Length/Value
   (TLV) form. If the AF bit is a one (1), then the Data Attributes
   are of the Type/Value form.

o Attribute Length (2 octets) - Length in octets of the Attribute
   Value. When the AF bit is a one (1), the Attribute Value is only
   2 octets and the Attribute Length field is not present.

o Attribute Value (variable length) - Value of the attribute
   associated with the DOI-specific Attribute Type. If the AF bit
   is a zero (0), this field has a variable length defined by the
   Attribute Length field. If the AF bit is a one (1), the
   Attribute Value has a length of 2 octets.

3.4 Security Association Payload

   The Security Association Payload is used to negotiate security
   attributes and to indicate the Domain of Interpretation (DOI) and
   Situation under which the negotiation is taking place. Figure 5
   shows the format of the Security Association payload.

```
                     1                   2                   3
 0 1 2 3 4 5 6 7 8 9 0 1 2 3 4 5 6 7 8 9 0 1 2 3 4 5 6 7 8 9 0 1
+-+-+-+-+-+-+-+-+-+-+-+-+-+-+-+-+-+-+-+-+-+-+-+-+-+-+-+-+-+-+-+-+
! Next Payload  !   RESERVED    !          Payload Length       !
+-+-+-+-+-+-+-+-+-+-+-+-+-+-+-+-+-+-+-+-+-+-+-+-+-+-+-+-+-+-+-+-+
!               Domain of Interpretation  (DOI)                 !
+-+-+-+-+-+-+-+-+-+-+-+-+-+-+-+-+-+-+-+-+-+-+-+-+-+-+-+-+-+-+-+-+
!                                                               !
~                            Situation                          ~
!                                                               !
+-+-+-+-+-+-+-+-+-+-+-+-+-+-+-+-+-+-+-+-+-+-+-+-+-+-+-+-+-+-+-+-+
```

                 Figure 5: Security Association Payload

   o Next Payload (1 octet) - Identifier for the payload type of the
      next payload in the message. If the current payload is the last
      in the message, then this field will be 0. This field MUST NOT
      contain the values for the Proposal or Transform payloads as they
      are considered part of the security association negotiation. For
      example, this field would contain the value "10" (Nonce payload)
      in the first message of a Base Exchange (see Section 4.4) and the
      value "0" in the first message of an Identity Protect Exchange
      (see Section 4.5).

   o RESERVED (1 octet) - Unused, set to 0.

   o Payload Length (2 octets) - Length in octets of the entire
      Security Association payload, including the SA payload, all
      Proposal payloads, and all Transform payloads associated with the
      proposed Security Association.

   o Domain of Interpretation (4 octets) - Identifies the DOI (as
      described in Section 2.1) under which this negotiation is taking
      place. The DOI is a 32-bit unsigned integer. A DOI value of 0
      during a Phase 1 exchange specifies a Generic ISAKMP SA which can
      be used for any protocol during the Phase 2 exchange. The
      necessary SA Attributes are defined in A.4. A DOI value of 1 is
      assigned to the IPsec DOI [IPDOI]. All other DOI values are
      reserved to IANA for future use. IANA will not normally assign a
      DOI value without referencing some public specification, such as

an Internet RFC. Other DOI's can be defined using the description
in appendix B. This field MUST be present within the Security
Association payload.

o   Situation (variable length) - A DOI-specific field that
    identifies the situation under which this negotiation is taking
    place. The Situation is used to make policy decisions regarding
    the security attributes being negotiated. Specifics for the IETF
    IP Security DOI Situation are detailed in [IPDOI]. This field
    MUST be present within the Security Association payload.

3.5 Proposal Payload

The Proposal Payload contains information used during Security
Association negotiation. The proposal consists of security
mechanisms, or transforms, to be used to secure the communications
channel. Figure 6 shows the format of the Proposal Payload. A
description of its use can be found in section 4.2.

```
                    1                   2                   3
0 1 2 3 4 5 6 7 8 9 0 1 2 3 4 5 6 7 8 9 0 1 2 3 4 5 6 7 8 9 0 1
+-+-+-+-+-+-+-+-+-+-+-+-+-+-+-+-+-+-+-+-+-+-+-+-+-+-+-+-+-+-+-+-+
! Next Payload  !   RESERVED    !         Payload Length        !
+-+-+-+-+-+-+-+-+-+-+-+-+-+-+-+-+-+-+-+-+-+-+-+-+-+-+-+-+-+-+-+-+
!  Proposal #   !  Protocol-Id  !    SPI Size   !# of Transforms!
+-+-+-+-+-+-+-+-+-+-+-+-+-+-+-+-+-+-+-+-+-+-+-+-+-+-+-+-+-+-+-+-+
!                        SPI (variable)                         !
+-+-+-+-+-+-+-+-+-+-+-+-+-+-+-+-+-+-+-+-+-+-+-+-+-+-+-+-+-+-+-+-+
```

Figure 6: Proposal Payload Format

The Proposal Payload fields are defined as follows:

o   Next Payload (1 octet) - Identifier for the payload type of the
    next payload in the message. This field MUST only contain the
    value "2" or "0". If there are additional Proposal payloads in
    the message, then this field will be 2. If the current Proposal
    payload is the last within the security association proposal,
    then this field will be 0.

o   RESERVED (1 octet) - Unused, set to 0.

o   Payload Length (2 octets) - Length in octets of the entire
    Proposal payload, including generic payload header, the Proposal
    payload, and all Transform payloads associated with this
    proposal. In the event there are multiple proposals with the
    same proposal number (see section 4.2), the Payload Length field

only applies to the current Proposal payload and not to all
Proposal payloads.

o Proposal # (1 octet) - Identifies the Proposal number for the
   current payload. A description of the use of this field is found
   in section 4.2.

o Protocol-Id (1 octet) - Specifies the protocol identifier for the
   current negotiation. Examples might include IPSEC ESP, IPSEC AH,
   OSPF, TLS, etc.

o SPI Size (1 octet) - Length in octets of the SPI as defined by
   the Protocol-Id. In the case of ISAKMP, the Initiator and
   Responder cookie pair from the ISAKMP Header is the ISAKMP SPI,
   therefore, the SPI Size is irrelevant and MAY be from zero (0) to
   sixteen (16). If the SPI Size is non-zero, the content of the
   SPI field MUST be ignored. If the SPI Size is not a multiple of
   4 octets it will have some impact on the SPI field and the
   alignment of all payloads in the message. The Domain of
   Interpretation (DOI) will dictate the SPI Size for other
   protocols.

o # of Transforms (1 octet) - Specifies the number of transforms
   for the Proposal. Each of these is contained in a Transform
   payload.

o SPI (variable) - The sending entity's SPI. In the event the SPI
   Size is not a multiple of 4 octets, there is no padding applied
   to the payload, however, it can be applied at the end of the
   message.

The payload type for the Proposal Payload is two (2).

3.6 Transform Payload

The Transform Payload contains information used during Security
Association negotiation. The Transform payload consists of a
specific security mechanism, or transforms, to be used to secure the
communications channel. The Transform payload also contains the
security association attributes associated with the specific
transform. These SA attributes are DOI-specific. Figure 7 shows the
format of the Transform Payload. A description of its use can be
found in section 4.2.

```
                    1                   2                   3
0 1 2 3 4 5 6 7 8 9 0 1 2 3 4 5 6 7 8 9 0 1 2 3 4 5 6 7 8 9 0 1
+-+-+-+-+-+-+-+-+-+-+-+-+-+-+-+-+-+-+-+-+-+-+-+-+-+-+-+-+-+-+-+-+
! Next Payload  !   RESERVED    !         Payload Length        !
+-+-+-+-+-+-+-+-+-+-+-+-+-+-+-+-+-+-+-+-+-+-+-+-+-+-+-+-+-+-+-+-+
!  Transform #  !  Transform-Id !            RESERVED2          !
+-+-+-+-+-+-+-+-+-+-+-+-+-+-+-+-+-+-+-+-+-+-+-+-+-+-+-+-+-+-+-+-+
!                                                               !
~                         SA Attributes                         ~
!                                                               !
+-+-+-+-+-+-+-+-+-+-+-+-+-+-+-+-+-+-+-+-+-+-+-+-+-+-+-+-+-+-+-+-+
```

Figure 7: Transform Payload Format

The Transform Payload fields are defined as follows:

o   Next Payload (1 octet) - Identifier for the payload type of the
    next payload in the message. This field MUST only contain the
    value "3" or "0". If there are additional Transform payloads in
    the proposal, then this field will be 3. If the current
    Transform payload is the last within the proposal, then this
    field will be 0.

o   RESERVED (1 octet) - Unused, set to 0.

o   Payload Length (2 octets) - Length in octets of the current
    payload, including the generic payload header, Transform values,
    and all SA Attributes.

o   Transform # (1 octet) - Identifies the Transform number for the
    current payload. If there is more than one transform proposed
    for a specific protocol within the Proposal payload, then each
    Transform payload has a unique Transform number. A description
    of the use of this field is found in section 4.2.

o   Transform-Id (1 octet) - Specifies the Transform identifier for
    the protocol within the current proposal. These transforms are
    defined by the DOI and are dependent on the protocol being
    negotiated.

o   RESERVED2 (2 octets) - Unused, set to 0.

o   SA Attributes (variable length) - This field contains the
    security association attributes as defined for the transform
    given in the Transform-Id field. The SA Attributes SHOULD be
    represented using the Data Attributes format described in section
    3.3. If the SA Attributes are not aligned on 4-byte boundaries,

then subsequent payloads will not be aligned and any padding will
be added at the end of the message to make the message 4-octet
aligned.

The payload type for the Transform Payload is three (3).

3.7 Key Exchange Payload

The Key Exchange Payload supports a variety of key exchange
techniques. Example key exchanges are Oakley [Oakley], Diffie-
Hellman, the enhanced Diffie-Hellman key exchange described in X9.42
[ANSI], and the RSA-based key exchange used by PGP. Figure 8 shows
the format of the Key Exchange payload.

The Key Exchange Payload fields are defined as follows:

o Next Payload (1 octet) - Identifier for the payload type of the
   nextpayload in the message. If the current payload is the last
   in the message, then this field will be 0.

```
                        1                   2                   3
    0 1 2 3 4 5 6 7 8 9 0 1 2 3 4 5 6 7 8 9 0 1 2 3 4 5 6 7 8 9 0 1
   +-+-+-+-+-+-+-+-+-+-+-+-+-+-+-+-+-+-+-+-+-+-+-+-+-+-+-+-+-+-+-+-+
   ! Next Payload  !   RESERVED    !         Payload Length        !
   +-+-+-+-+-+-+-+-+-+-+-+-+-+-+-+-+-+-+-+-+-+-+-+-+-+-+-+-+-+-+-+-+
   !                                                               !
   ~                       Key Exchange Data                       ~
   !                                                               !
   +-+-+-+-+-+-+-+-+-+-+-+-+-+-+-+-+-+-+-+-+-+-+-+-+-+-+-+-+-+-+-+-+
```

                 Figure 8: Key Exchange Payload Format

o RESERVED (1 octet) - Unused, set to 0.

o Payload Length (2 octets) - Length in octets of the current
   payload, including the generic payload header.

o Key Exchange Data (variable length) - Data required to generate a
   session key. The interpretation of this data is specified by the
   DOI and the associated Key Exchange algorithm. This field may
   also contain pre-placed key indicators.

The payload type for the Key Exchange Payload is four (4).

3.8 Identification Payload

The Identification Payload contains DOI-specific data used to
exchange identification information. This information is used for
determining the identities of communicating peers and may be used for
determining authenticity of information. Figure 9 shows the format
of the Identification Payload.

The Identification Payload fields are defined as follows:

  o Next Payload (1 octet) - Identifier for the payload type of the
     next payload in the message. If the current payload is the last
     in the message, then this field will be 0.

  o RESERVED (1 octet) - Unused, set to 0.

  o Payload Length (2 octets) - Length in octets of the current
     payload, including the generic payload header.

  o ID Type (1 octet) - Specifies the type of Identification being
     used.

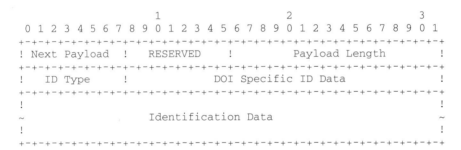

```
                    1                   2                   3
0 1 2 3 4 5 6 7 8 9 0 1 2 3 4 5 6 7 8 9 0 1 2 3 4 5 6 7 8 9 0 1
+-+-+-+-+-+-+-+-+-+-+-+-+-+-+-+-+-+-+-+-+-+-+-+-+-+-+-+-+-+-+-+-+
! Next Payload  !   RESERVED    !         Payload Length        !
+-+-+-+-+-+-+-+-+-+-+-+-+-+-+-+-+-+-+-+-+-+-+-+-+-+-+-+-+-+-+-+-+
!   ID Type     !              DOI Specific ID Data             !
+-+-+-+-+-+-+-+-+-+-+-+-+-+-+-+-+-+-+-+-+-+-+-+-+-+-+-+-+-+-+-+-+
!                                                               !
~                    Identification Data                        ~
!                                                               !
+-+-+-+-+-+-+-+-+-+-+-+-+-+-+-+-+-+-+-+-+-+-+-+-+-+-+-+-+-+-+-+-+
```

            Figure 9: Identification Payload Format

     This field is DOI-dependent.

  o DOI Specific ID Data (3 octets) - Contains DOI specific
     Identification data. If unused, then this field MUST be set to
     0.

  o Identification Data (variable length) - Contains identity
     information. The values for this field are DOI-specific and the
     format is specified by the ID Type field. Specific details for
     the IETF IP Security DOI Identification Data are detailed in
     [IPDOI].

The payload type for the Identification Payload is five (5).

3.9 Certificate Payload

The Certificate Payload provides a means to transport certificates or
other certificate-related information via ISAKMP and can appear in
any ISAKMP message. Certificate payloads SHOULD be included in an
exchange whenever an appropriate directory service (e.g. Secure DNS
[DNSSEC]) is not available to distribute certificates. The
Certificate payload MUST be accepted at any point during an exchange.
Figure 10 shows the format of the Certificate Payload.

NOTE: Certificate types and formats are not generally bound to a DOI
- it is expected that there will only be a few certificate types, and
that most DOIs will accept all of these types.

The Certificate Payload fields are defined as follows:

o Next Payload (1 octet) - Identifier for the payload type of the
   next payload in the message. If the current payload is the last
   in the message, then this field will be 0.

```
                    1                   2                   3
0 1 2 3 4 5 6 7 8 9 0 1 2 3 4 5 6 7 8 9 0 1 2 3 4 5 6 7 8 9 0 1
+-+-+-+-+-+-+-+-+-+-+-+-+-+-+-+-+-+-+-+-+-+-+-+-+-+-+-+-+-+-+-+-+
! Next Payload  !   RESERVED    !           Payload Length      !
+-+-+-+-+-+-+-+-+-+-+-+-+-+-+-+-+-+-+-+-+-+-+-+-+-+-+-+-+-+-+-+-+
! Cert Encoding !                                              !
+-+-+-+-+-+-+-+-+-+                                            !
~                         Certificate Data                     ~
!                                                              !
+-+-+-+-+-+-+-+-+-+-+-+-+-+-+-+-+-+-+-+-+-+-+-+-+-+-+-+-+-+-+-+-+
```

Figure 10: Certificate Payload Format

o RESERVED (1 octet) - Unused, set to 0.

o Payload Length (2 octets) - Length in octets of the current
   payload, including the generic payload header.

o Certificate Encoding (1 octet) - This field indicates the type of
   certificate or certificate-related information contained in the
   Certificate Data field.

```
                  Certificate Type            Value
          NONE                                  0
          PKCS #7 wrapped X.509 certificate     1
          PGP Certificate                       2
          DNS Signed Key                        3
          X.509 Certificate - Signature         4
          X.509 Certificate - Key Exchange      5
          Kerberos Tokens                       6
          Certificate Revocation List (CRL)     7
          Authority Revocation List (ARL)       8
          SPKI Certificate                      9
          X.509 Certificate - Attribute         10
          RESERVED                              11 - 255
```

   o Certificate Data (variable length) - Actual encoding of
      certificate data. The type of certificate is indicated by the
      Certificate Encoding field.

   The payload type for the Certificate Payload is six (6).

3.10 Certificate Request Payload

   The Certificate Request Payload provides a means to request
   certificates via ISAKMP and can appear in any message. Certificate
   Request payloads SHOULD be included in an exchange whenever an
   appropriate directory service (e.g. Secure DNS [DNSSEC]) is not
   available to distribute certificates. The Certificate Request
   payload MUST be accepted at any point during the exchange. The
   responder to the Certificate Request payload MUST send its
   certificate, if certificates are supported, based on the values
   contained in the payload. If multiple certificates are required,
   then multiple Certificate Request payloads SHOULD be transmitted.
   Figure 11 shows the format of the Certificate Request Payload.

```
                     1                   2                   3
 0 1 2 3 4 5 6 7 8 9 0 1 2 3 4 5 6 7 8 9 0 1 2 3 4 5 6 7 8 9 0 1
+-+-+-+-+-+-+-+-+-+-+-+-+-+-+-+-+-+-+-+-+-+-+-+-+-+-+-+-+-+-+-+-+
! Next Payload  !   RESERVED    !         Payload Length        !
+-+-+-+-+-+-+-+-+-+-+-+-+-+-+-+-+-+-+-+-+-+-+-+-+-+-+-+-+-+-+-+-+
! Cert. Type    !                                               !
+-+-+-+-+-+-+-+-+                                               !
~                      Certificate Authority                    ~
!                                                               !
+-+-+-+-+-+-+-+-+-+-+-+-+-+-+-+-+-+-+-+-+-+-+-+-+-+-+-+-+-+-+-+-+
```

         Figure 11: Certificate Request Payload Format

The Certificate Payload fields are defined as follows:

o Next Payload (1 octet) - Identifier for the payload type of the
   next payload in the message. If the current payload is the last
   in the message, then this field will be 0.

o RESERVED (1 octet) - Unused, set to 0.

o Payload Length (2 octets) - Length in octets of the current
   payload, including the generic payload header.

o Certificate Type (1 octet) - Contains an encoding of the type of
   certificate requested. Acceptable values are listed in section
   3.9.

o Certificate Authority (variable length) - Contains an encoding of
   an acceptable certificate authority for the type of certificate
   requested. As an example, for an X.509 certificate this field
   would contain the Distinguished Name encoding of the Issuer Name
   of an X.509 certificate authority acceptable to the sender of
   this payload. This would be included to assist the responder in
   determining how much of the certificate chain would need to be
   sent in response to this request. If there is no specific
   certificate authority requested, this field SHOULD not be
   included.

The payload type for the Certificate Request Payload is seven (7).

3.11 Hash Payload

   The Hash Payload contains data generated by the hash function
   (selected during the SA establishment exchange), over some part of
   the message and/or ISAKMP state. This payload may be used to verify
   the integrity of the data in an ISAKMP message or for authentication
   of the negotiating entities. Figure 12 shows the format of the Hash
   Payload.

```
                      1                   2                   3
  0 1 2 3 4 5 6 7 8 9 0 1 2 3 4 5 6 7 8 9 0 1 2 3 4 5 6 7 8 9 0 1
 +-+-+-+-+-+-+-+-+-+-+-+-+-+-+-+-+-+-+-+-+-+-+-+-+-+-+-+-+-+-+-+-+
 ! Next Payload  !   RESERVED    !         Payload Length        !
 +-+-+-+-+-+-+-+-+-+-+-+-+-+-+-+-+-+-+-+-+-+-+-+-+-+-+-+-+-+-+-+-+
 !                                                               !
 ~                           Hash Data                           ~
 !                                                               !
 +-+-+-+-+-+-+-+-+-+-+-+-+-+-+-+-+-+-+-+-+-+-+-+-+-+-+-+-+-+-+-+-+
```

                   Figure 12: Hash Payload Format

   The Hash Payload fields are defined as follows:

   o Next Payload (1 octet) - Identifier for the payload type of the
      next payload in the message. If the current payload is the last
      in the message, then this field will be 0.

   o RESERVED (1 octet) - Unused, set to 0.

   o Payload Length (2 octets) - Length in octets of the current
      payload, including the generic payload header.

   o Hash Data (variable length) - Data that results from applying the
      hash routine to the ISAKMP message and/or state.

3.12 Signature Payload

The Signature Payload contains data generated by the digital
signature function (selected during the SA establishment exchange),
over some part of the message and/or ISAKMP state. This payload is
used to verify the integrity of the data in the ISAKMP message, and
may be of use for non-repudiation services. Figure 13 shows the
format of the Signature Payload.

```
                    1                   2                   3
 0 1 2 3 4 5 6 7 8 9 0 1 2 3 4 5 6 7 8 9 0 1 2 3 4 5 6 7 8 9 0 1
+-+-+-+-+-+-+-+-+-+-+-+-+-+-+-+-+-+-+-+-+-+-+-+-+-+-+-+-+-+-+-+-+
! Next Payload  !   RESERVED    !         Payload Length        !
+-+-+-+-+-+-+-+-+-+-+-+-+-+-+-+-+-+-+-+-+-+-+-+-+-+-+-+-+-+-+-+-+
!                                                               !
~                      Signature Data                           ~
!                                                               !
+-+-+-+-+-+-+-+-+-+-+-+-+-+-+-+-+-+-+-+-+-+-+-+-+-+-+-+-+-+-+-+-+
```

Figure 13: Signature Payload Format

The Signature Payload fields are defined as follows:

o Next Payload (1 octet) - Identifier for the payload type of the
   next payload in the message. If the current payload is the last
   in the message, then this field will be 0.

o RESERVED (1 octet) - Unused, set to 0.

o Payload Length (2 octets) - Length in octets of the current
   payload, including the generic payload header.

o Signature Data (variable length) - Data that results from
   applying the digital signature function to the ISAKMP message
   and/or state.

The payload type for the Signature Payload is nine (9).

3.13 Nonce Payload

The Nonce Payload contains random data used to guarantee liveness
during an exchange and protect against replay attacks. Figure 14
shows the format of the Nonce Payload. If nonces are used by a
particular key exchange, the use of the Nonce payload will be
dictated by the key exchange. The nonces may be transmitted as part
of the key exchange data, or as a separate payload. However, this is
defined by the key exchange, not by ISAKMP.

```
                     1                   2                   3
 0 1 2 3 4 5 6 7 8 9 0 1 2 3 4 5 6 7 8 9 0 1 2 3 4 5 6 7 8 9 0 1
+-+-+-+-+-+-+-+-+-+-+-+-+-+-+-+-+-+-+-+-+-+-+-+-+-+-+-+-+-+-+-+-+
! Next Payload  !   RESERVED    !         Payload Length        !
+-+-+-+-+-+-+-+-+-+-+-+-+-+-+-+-+-+-+-+-+-+-+-+-+-+-+-+-+-+-+-+-+
!                                                               !
~                         Nonce Data                            ~
!                                                               !
+-+-+-+-+-+-+-+-+-+-+-+-+-+-+-+-+-+-+-+-+-+-+-+-+-+-+-+-+-+-+-+-+
```

Figure 14: Nonce Payload Format

The Nonce Payload fields are defined as follows:

o Next Payload (1 octet) - Identifier for the payload type of the
   next payload in the message. If the current payload is the last
   in the message, then this field will be 0.

o RESERVED (1 octet) - Unused, set to 0.

o Payload Length (2 octets) - Length in octets of the current
   payload, including the generic payload header.

o Nonce Data (variable length) - Contains the random data generated
   by the transmitting entity.

The payload type for the Nonce Payload is ten (10).

3.14 Notification Payload

The Notification Payload can contain both ISAKMP and DOI-specific
data and is used to transmit informational data, such as error
conditions, to an ISAKMP peer. It is possible to send multiple
Notification payloads in a single ISAKMP message. Figure 15 shows
the format of the Notification Payload.

Notification which occurs during, or is concerned with, a Phase 1
negotiation is identified by the Initiator and Responder cookie pair
in the ISAKMP Header. The Protocol Identifier, in this case, is
ISAKMP and the SPI value is 0 because the cookie pair in the ISAKMP
Header identifies the ISAKMP SA. If the notification takes place
prior to the completed exchange of keying information, then the
notification will be unprotected.

Notification which occurs during, or is concerned with, a Phase 2
negotiation is identified by the Initiator and Responder cookie pair
in the ISAKMP Header and the Message ID and SPI associated with the
current negotiation. One example for this type of notification is to
indicate why a proposal was rejected.

```
                      1                   2                   3
  0 1 2 3 4 5 6 7 8 9 0 1 2 3 4 5 6 7 8 9 0 1 2 3 4 5 6 7 8 9 0 1
 +-+-+-+-+-+-+-+-+-+-+-+-+-+-+-+-+-+-+-+-+-+-+-+-+-+-+-+-+-+-+-+-+
 ! Next Payload  !   RESERVED    !         Payload Length        !
 +-+-+-+-+-+-+-+-+-+-+-+-+-+-+-+-+-+-+-+-+-+-+-+-+-+-+-+-+-+-+-+-+
 !              Domain of Interpretation  (DOI)                  !
 +-+-+-+-+-+-+-+-+-+-+-+-+-+-+-+-+-+-+-+-+-+-+-+-+-+-+-+-+-+-+-+-+
 ! Protocol-ID  !   SPI Size    !      Notify Message Type       !
 +-+-+-+-+-+-+-+-+-+-+-+-+-+-+-+-+-+-+-+-+-+-+-+-+-+-+-+-+-+-+-+-+
 !                                                               !
 ~                Security Parameter Index (SPI)                 ~
 !                                                               !
 +-+-+-+-+-+-+-+-+-+-+-+-+-+-+-+-+-+-+-+-+-+-+-+-+-+-+-+-+-+-+-+-+
 !                                                               !
 ~                      Notification Data                        ~
 !                                                               !
 +-+-+-+-+-+-+-+-+-+-+-+-+-+-+-+-+-+-+-+-+-+-+-+-+-+-+-+-+-+-+-+-+
```

Figure 15: Notification Payload Format

The Notification Payload fields are defined as follows:

o Next Payload (1 octet) - Identifier for the payload type of the
   next payload in the message. If the current payload is the last
   in the message, then this field will be 0.

o RESERVED (1 octet) - Unused, set to 0.

o Payload Length (2 octets) - Length in octets of the current
   payload, including the generic payload header.

o Domain of Interpretation (4 octets) - Identifies the DOI (as
   described in Section 2.1) under which this notification is taking
   place. For ISAKMP this value is zero (0) and for the IPSEC DOI
   it is one (1). Other DOI's can be defined using the description
   in appendix B.

o Protocol-Id (1 octet) - Specifies the protocol identifier for the
   current notification. Examples might include ISAKMP, IPSEC ESP,
   IPSEC AH, OSPF, TLS, etc.

o   SPI Size (1 octet) - Length in octets of the SPI as defined by
    the Protocol-Id. In the case of ISAKMP, the Initiator and
    Responder cookie pair from the ISAKMP Header is the ISAKMP SPI,
    therefore, the SPI Size is irrelevant and MAY be from zero (0) to
    sixteen (16). If the SPI Size is non-zero, the content of the
    SPI field MUST be ignored. The Domain of Interpretation (DOI)
    will dictate the SPI Size for other protocols.

o   Notify Message Type (2 octets) - Specifies the type of
    notification message (see section 3.14.1). Additional text, if
    specified by the DOI, is placed in the Notification Data field.

o   SPI (variable length) - Security Parameter Index. The receiving
    entity's SPI. The use of the SPI field is described in section
    2.4. The length of this field is determined by the SPI Size
    field and is not necessarily aligned to a 4 octet boundary.

o   Notification Data (variable length) - Informational or error data
    transmitted in addition to the Notify Message Type. Values for
    this field are DOI-specific.

The payload type for the Notification Payload is eleven (11).

3.14.1 Notify Message Types

Notification information can be error messages specifying why an SA
could not be established. It can also be status data that a process
managing an SA database wishes to communicate with a peer process.
For example, a secure front end or security gateway may use the
Notify message to synchronize SA communication. The table below
lists the Nofitication messages and their corresponding values.
Values in the Private Use range are expected to be DOI-specific
values.

                    NOTIFY MESSAGES - ERROR TYPES

Errors	Value
INVALID-PAYLOAD-TYPE	1
DOI-NOT-SUPPORTED	2
SITUATION-NOT-SUPPORTED	3
INVALID-COOKIE	4
INVALID-MAJOR-VERSION	5
INVALID-MINOR-VERSION	6
INVALID-EXCHANGE-TYPE	7
INVALID-FLAGS	8
INVALID-MESSAGE-ID	9
INVALID-PROTOCOL-ID	10
INVALID-SPI	11

```
            INVALID-TRANSFORM-ID              12
            ATTRIBUTES-NOT-SUPPORTED          13
            NO-PROPOSAL-CHOSEN                14
            BAD-PROPOSAL-SYNTAX               15
            PAYLOAD-MALFORMED                 16
            INVALID-KEY-INFORMATION           17
            INVALID-ID-INFORMATION            18
            INVALID-CERT-ENCODING             19
            INVALID-CERTIFICATE               20
            CERT-TYPE-UNSUPPORTED             21
            INVALID-CERT-AUTHORITY            22
            INVALID-HASH-INFORMATION          23
            AUTHENTICATION-FAILED             24
            INVALID-SIGNATURE                 25
            ADDRESS-NOTIFICATION              26
            NOTIFY-SA-LIFETIME                27
            CERTIFICATE-UNAVAILABLE           28
            UNSUPPORTED-EXCHANGE-TYPE         29
            UNEQUAL-PAYLOAD-LENGTHS           30
            RESERVED (Future Use)        31 - 8191
            Private Use                8192 - 16383


              NOTIFY MESSAGES - STATUS TYPES
                    Status           Value
            CONNECTED                  16384
             RESERVED (Future Use)   16385 - 24575
            DOI-specific codes       24576 - 32767
            Private Use              32768 - 40959
            RESERVED (Future Use)    40960 - 65535
```

3.15 Delete Payload

   The Delete Payload contains a protocol-specific security association
   identifier that the sender has removed from its security association
   database and is, therefore, no longer valid. Figure 16 shows the
   format of the Delete Payload. It is possible to send multiple SPIs
   in a Delete payload, however, each SPI MUST be for the same protocol.
   Mixing of Protocol Identifiers MUST NOT be performed with the Delete
   payload.

   Deletion which is concerned with an ISAKMP SA will contain a
   Protocol-Id of ISAKMP and the SPIs are the initiator and responder
   cookies from the ISAKMP Header. Deletion which is concerned with a
   Protocol SA, such as ESP or AH, will contain the Protocol-Id of that
   protocol (e.g. ESP, AH) and the SPI is the sending entity's SPI(s).

NOTE: The Delete Payload is not a request for the responder to delete
an SA, but an advisory from the initiator to the responder. If the
responder chooses to ignore the message, the next communication from
the responder to the initiator, using that security association, will
fail. A responder is not expected to acknowledge receipt of a Delete
payload.

```
                     1                   2                   3
 0 1 2 3 4 5 6 7 8 9 0 1 2 3 4 5 6 7 8 9 0 1 2 3 4 5 6 7 8 9 0 1
+-+-+-+-+-+-+-+-+-+-+-+-+-+-+-+-+-+-+-+-+-+-+-+-+-+-+-+-+-+-+-+-+
! Next Payload  !   RESERVED    !         Payload Length        !
+-+-+-+-+-+-+-+-+-+-+-+-+-+-+-+-+-+-+-+-+-+-+-+-+-+-+-+-+-+-+-+-+
!                 Domain of Interpretation  (DOI)               !
+-+-+-+-+-+-+-+-+-+-+-+-+-+-+-+-+-+-+-+-+-+-+-+-+-+-+-+-+-+-+-+-+
! Protocol-Id  !   SPI Size    !           # of SPIs            !
+-+-+-+-+-+-+-+-+-+-+-+-+-+-+-+-+-+-+-+-+-+-+-+-+-+-+-+-+-+-+-+-+
!                                                               !
~                 Security Parameter Index(es) (SPI)            ~
!                                                               !
+-+-+-+-+-+-+-+-+-+-+-+-+-+-+-+-+-+-+-+-+-+-+-+-+-+-+-+-+-+-+-+-+
```

Figure 16: Delete Payload Format

The Delete Payload fields are defined as follows:

o Next Payload (1 octet) - Identifier for the payload type of the
   next payload in the message. If the current payload is the last
   in the message, then this field will be 0.

o RESERVED (1 octet) - Unused, set to 0.

o Payload Length (2 octets) - Length in octets of the current
   payload, including the generic payload header.

o Domain of Interpretation (4 octets) - Identifies the DOI (as
   described in Section 2.1) under which this deletion is taking
   place. For ISAKMP this value is zero (0) and for the IPSEC DOI
   it is one (1). Other DOI's can be defined using the description
   in appendix B.

o Protocol-Id (1 octet) - ISAKMP can establish security
   associations for various protocols, including ISAKMP and IPSEC.
   This field identifies which security association database to
   apply the delete request.

o SPI Size (1 octet) - Length in octets of the SPI as defined by
   the Protocol-Id. In the case of ISAKMP, the Initiator and
   Responder cookie pair is the ISAKMP SPI. In this case, the SPI
   Size would be 16 octets for each SPI being deleted.

o # of SPIs (2 octets) - The number of SPIs contained in the Delete
   payload. The size of each SPI is defined by the SPI Size field.

o Security Parameter Index(es) (variable length) - Identifies the
   specific security association(s) to delete. Values for this
   field are DOI and protocol specific. The length of this field is
   determined by the SPI Size and # of SPIs fields.

The payload type for the Delete Payload is twelve (12).

3.16 Vendor ID Payload

The Vendor ID Payload contains a vendor defined constant. The
constant is used by vendors to identify and recognize remote
instances of their implementations. This mechanism allows a vendor
to experiment with new features while maintaining backwards
compatibility. This is not a general extension facility of ISAKMP.
Figure 17 shows the format of the Vendor ID Payload.

The Vendor ID payload is not an announcement from the sender that it
will send private payload types. A vendor sending the Vendor ID MUST
not make any assumptions about private payloads that it may send
unless a Vendor ID is received as well. Multiple Vendor ID payloads
MAY be sent. An implementation is NOT REQUIRED to understand any
Vendor ID payloads. An implementation is NOT REQUIRED to send any
Vendor ID payload at all. If a private payload was sent without
prior agreement to send it, a compliant implementation may reject a
proposal with a notify message of type INVALID-PAYLOAD-TYPE.

If a Vendor ID payload is sent, it MUST be sent during the Phase 1
negotiation. Reception of a familiar Vendor ID payload in the Phase
1 negotiation allows an implementation to make use of Private USE
payload numbers (128-255), described in section 3.1 for vendor
specific extensions during Phase 2 negotiations. The definition of
"familiar" is left to implementations to determine. Some vendors may
wish to implement another vendor's extension prior to
standardization. However, this practice SHOULD not be widespread and
vendors should work towards standardization instead.

The vendor defined constant MUST be unique. The choice of hash and
text to hash is left to the vendor to decide. As an example, vendors
could generate their vendor id by taking a plain (non-keyed) hash of
a string containing the product name, and the version of the product.

A hash is used instead of a vendor registry to avoid local
cryptographic policy problems with having a list of "approved"
products, to keep away from maintaining a list of vendors, and to
allow classified products to avoid having to appear on any list. For
instance:

"Example Company IPsec. Version 97.1"

(not including the quotes) has MD5 hash:
48544f9b1fe662af98b9b39e50c01a5a, when using MD5file. Vendors may
include all of the hash, or just a portion of it, as the payload
length will bound the data. There are no security implications of
this hash, so its choice is arbitrary.

```
                    1                   2                   3
0 1 2 3 4 5 6 7 8 9 0 1 2 3 4 5 6 7 8 9 0 1 2 3 4 5 6 7 8 9 0 1
+-+-+-+-+-+-+-+-+-+-+-+-+-+-+-+-+-+-+-+-+-+-+-+-+-+-+-+-+-+-+-+-+
! Next Payload  !   RESERVED    !         Payload Length        !
+-+-+-+-+-+-+-+-+-+-+-+-+-+-+-+-+-+-+-+-+-+-+-+-+-+-+-+-+-+-+-+-+
!                                                               !
~                       Vendor ID (VID)                         ~
!                                                               !
+-+-+-+-+-+-+-+-+-+-+-+-+-+-+-+-+-+-+-+-+-+-+-+-+-+-+-+-+-+-+-+-+
```

Figure 17: Vendor ID Payload Format

The Vendor ID Payload fields are defined as follows:

o Next Payload (1 octet) - Identifier for the payload type of the
   next payload in the message. If the current payload is the last
   in the message, then this field will be 0.

o RESERVED (1 octet) - Unused, set to 0.

o Payload Length (2 octets) - Length in octets of the current
   payload, including the generic payload header.

o Vendor ID (variable length) - Hash of the vendor string plus
   version (as described above).

The payload type for the Vendor ID Payload is thirteen (13).

4 ISAKMP Exchanges

ISAKMP supplies the basic syntax of a message exchange. The basic
building blocks for ISAKMP messages are the payload types described
in section 3. This section describes the procedures for SA

establishment and SA modification, followed by a default set of
exchanges that MAY be used for initial interoperability. Other
exchanges will be defined depending on the DOI and key exchange.
[IPDOI] and [IKE] are examples of how this is achieved. Appendix B
explains the procedures for accomplishing these additions.

4.1 ISAKMP Exchange Types

ISAKMP allows the creation of exchanges for the establishment of
Security Associations and keying material. There are currently five
default Exchange Types defined for ISAKMP. Sections 4.4 through 4.8
describe these exchanges. Exchanges define the content and ordering
of ISAKMP messages during communications between peers. Most
exchanges will include all the basic payload types - SA, KE, ID, SIG
- and may include others. The primary difference between exchange
types is the ordering of the messages and the payload ordering within
each message. While the ordering of payloads within messages is not
mandated, for processing efficiency it is RECOMMENDED that the
Security Association payload be the first payload within an exchange.
Processing of each payload within an exchange is described in section
5.

Sections 4.4 through 4.8 provide a default set of ISAKMP exchanges.
These exchanges provide different security protection for the
exchange itself and information exchanged. The diagrams in each of
the following sections show the message ordering for each exchange
type as well as the payloads included in each message, and provide
basic notes describing what has happened after each message exchange.
None of the examples include any "optional payloads", like
certificate and certificate request. Additionally, none of the
examples include an initial exchange of ISAKMP Headers (containing
initiator and responder cookies) which would provide protection
against clogging (see section 2.5.3).

The defined exchanges are not meant to satisfy all DOI and key
exchange protocol requirements. If the defined exchanges meet the
DOI requirements, then they can be used as outlined. If the defined
exchanges do not meet the security requirements defined by the DOI,
then the DOI MUST specify new exchange type(s) and the valid
sequences of payloads that make up a successful exchange, and how to
build and interpret those payloads. All ISAKMP implementations MUST
implement the Informational Exchange and SHOULD implement the other
four exchanges. However, this is dependent on the definition of the
DOI and associated key exchange protocols.

As discussed above, these exchange types can be used in either phase
of negotiation. However, they may provide different security
properties in each of the phases. With each of these exchanges, the
combination of cookies and SPI fields identifies whether this
exchange is being used in the first or second phase of a negotiation.

4.1.1 Notation

The following notation is used to describe the ISAKMP exchange types,
shown in the next section, with the message formats and associated
payloads:

   HDR is an ISAKMP header whose exchange type defines the payload
       orderings
   SA is an SA negotiation payload with one or more Proposal and
       Transform payloads. An initiator MAY provide multiple proposals
       for negotiation; a responder MUST reply with only one.
   KE is the key exchange payload.
   IDx is the identity payload for "x". x can be: "ii" or "ir"
       for the ISAKMP initiator and responder, respectively, or x can
       be: "ui", "ur" (when the ISAKMP daemon is a proxy negotiator),
       for the user initiator and responder, respectively.
   HASH is the hash payload.
   SIG is the signature payload. The data to sign is exchange-specific.
   AUTH is a generic authentication mechanism, such as HASH or SIG.
   NONCE is the nonce payload.
   '*' signifies payload encryption after the ISAKMP header. This
       encryption MUST begin immediately after the ISAKMP header and
       all payloads following the ISAKMP header MUST be encrypted.

   => signifies "initiator to responder" communication
   <= signifies "responder to initiator" communication

4.2 Security Association Establishment

The Security Association, Proposal, and Transform payloads are used
to build ISAKMP messages for the negotiation and establishment of
SAs. An SA establishment message consists of a single SA payload
followed by at least one, and possibly many, Proposal payloads and at
least one, and possibly many, Transform payloads associated with each
Proposal payload. Because these payloads are considered together,
the SA payload will point to any following payloads and not to the
Proposal payload included with the SA payload. The SA Payload
contains the DOI and Situation for the proposed SA. Each Proposal
payload contains a Security Parameter Index (SPI) and ensures that
the SPI is associated with the Protocol-Id in accordance with the
Internet Security Architecture [SEC-ARCH]. Proposal payloads may or
may not have the same SPI, as this is implementation dependent. Each

Transform Payload contains the specific security mechanisms to be
used for the designated protocol. It is expected that the Proposal
and Transform payloads will be used only during SA establishment
negotiation. The creation of payloads for security association
negotiation and establishment described here in this section are
applicable for all ISAKMP exchanges described later in sections 4.4
through 4.8. The examples shown in 4.2.1 contain only the SA,
Proposal, and Transform payloads and do not contain other payloads
that might exist for a given ISAKMP exchange.

The Proposal payload provides the initiating entity with the
capability to present to the responding entity the security protocols
and associated security mechanisms for use with the security
association being negotiated. If the SA establishment negotiation is
for a combined protection suite consisting of multiple protocols,
then there MUST be multiple Proposal payloads each with the same
Proposal number. These proposals MUST be considered as a unit and
MUST NOT be separated by a proposal with a different proposal number.
The use of the same Proposal number in multiple Proposal payloads
provides a logical AND operation, i.e. Protocol 1 AND Protocol 2.
The first example below shows an ESP AND AH protection suite. If the
SA establishment negotiation is for different protection suites, then
there MUST be multiple Proposal payloads each with a monotonically
increasing Proposal number. The different proposals MUST be
presented in the initiator's preference order. The use of different
Proposal numbers in multiple Proposal payloads provides a logical OR
operation, i.e. Proposal 1 OR Proposal 2, where each proposal may
have more than one protocol. The second example below shows either
an AH AND ESP protection suite OR just an ESP protection suite. Note
that the Next Payload field of the Proposal payload points to another
Proposal payload (if it exists). The existence of a Proposal payload
implies the existence of one or more Transform payloads.

The Transform payload provides the initiating entity with the
capability to present to the responding entity multiple mechanisms,
or transforms, for a given protocol. The Proposal payload identifies
a Protocol for which services and mechanisms are being negotiated.
The Transform payload allows the initiating entity to present several
possible supported transforms for that proposed protocol. There may
be several transforms associated with a specific Proposal payload
each identified in a separate Transform payload. The multiple
transforms MUST be presented with monotonically increasing numbers in
the initiator's preference order. The receiving entity MUST select a
single transform for each protocol in a proposal or reject the entire
proposal. The use of the Transform number in multiple Transform
payloads provides a second level OR operation, i.e. Transform 1 OR
Transform 2 OR Transform 3. Example 1 below shows two possible
transforms for ESP and a single transform for AH. Example 2 below

shows one transform for AH AND one transform for ESP OR two
transforms for ESP alone. Note that the Next Payload field of the
Transform payload points to another Transform payload or 0. The
Proposal payload delineates the different proposals.

When responding to a Security Association payload, the responder MUST
send a Security Association payload with the selected proposal, which
may consist of multiple Proposal payloads and their associated
Transform payloads. Each of the Proposal payloads MUST contain a
single Transform payload associated with the Protocol. The responder
SHOULD retain the Proposal # field in the Proposal payload and the
Transform # field in each Transform payload of the selected Proposal.
Retention of Proposal and Transform numbers should speed the
initiator's protocol processing by negating the need to compare the
respondor's selection with every offered option. These values enable
the initiator to perform the comparison directly and quickly. The
initiator MUST verify that the Security Association payload received
from the responder matches one of the proposals sent initially.

4.2.1 Security Association Establishment Examples

This example shows a Proposal for a combined protection suite with
two different protocols. The first protocol is presented with two
transforms supported by the proposer. The second protocol is
presented with a single transform. An example for this proposal
might be: Protocol 1 is ESP with Transform 1 as 3DES and Transform 2
as DES AND Protocol 2 is AH with Transform 1 as SHA. The responder
MUST select from the two transforms proposed for ESP. The resulting
protection suite will be either (1) 3DES AND SHA OR (2) DES AND SHA,
depending on which ESP transform was selected by the responder. Note
this example is shown using the Base Exchange.

```
                              1                   2                   3
            0 1 2 3 4 5 6 7 8 9 0 1 2 3 4 5 6 7 8 9 0 1 2 3 4 5 6 7 8 9 0 1
        /+-+-+-+-+-+-+-+-+-+-+-+-+-+-+-+-+-+-+-+-+-+-+-+-+-+-+-+-+-+-+-+-+
       / ! NP = Nonce   ! RESERVED     !         Payload Length          !
      /   +-+-+-+-+-+-+-+-+-+-+-+-+-+-+-+-+-+-+-+-+-+-+-+-+-+-+-+-+-+-+-+-+
 SA Pay !              Domain of Interpretation (DOI)                    !
      \   +-+-+-+-+-+-+-+-+-+-+-+-+-+-+-+-+-+-+-+-+-+-+-+-+-+-+-+-+-+-+-+-+
       \ !                        Situation                             !
        >+-+-+-+-+-+-+-+-+-+-+-+-+-+-+-+-+-+-+-+-+-+-+-+-+-+-+-+-+-+-+-+-+
       / ! NP = Proposal ! RESERVED     !         Payload Length         !
      /   +-+-+-+-+-+-+-+-+-+-+-+-+-+-+-+-+-+-+-+-+-+-+-+-+-+-+-+-+-+-+-+-+
 Prop 1 ! Proposal # = 1! Protocol-Id  !   SPI Size    !# of Trans. = 2!
 Prot 1 +-+-+-+-+-+-+-+-+-+-+-+-+-+-+-+-+-+-+-+-+-+-+-+-+-+-+-+-+-+-+-+-+
       \ !                        SPI (variable)                        !
        >+-+-+-+-+-+-+-+-+-+-+-+-+-+-+-+-+-+-+-+-+-+-+-+-+-+-+-+-+-+-+-+-+
       / ! NP = Transform! RESERVED     !         Payload Length         !
```

```
     /  +-+-+-+-+-+-+-+-+-+-+-+-+-+-+-+-+-+-+-+-+-+-+-+-+-+-+-+-+-+-+-+-+
Tran 1 ! Transform # 1 ! Transform ID  !             RESERVED2          !
     \  +-+-+-+-+-+-+-+-+-+-+-+-+-+-+-+-+-+-+-+-+-+-+-+-+-+-+-+-+-+-+-+-+
      \ !                        SA Attributes                          !
       >+-+-+-+-+-+-+-+-+-+-+-+-+-+-+-+-+-+-+-+-+-+-+-+-+-+-+-+-+-+-+-+-+
      / ! NP = 0        !    RESERVED   !          Payload Length        !
     /  +-+-+-+-+-+-+-+-+-+-+-+-+-+-+-+-+-+-+-+-+-+-+-+-+-+-+-+-+-+-+-+-+
Tran 2 ! Transform # 2 ! Transform ID  !             RESERVED2          !
     \  +-+-+-+-+-+-+-+-+-+-+-+-+-+-+-+-+-+-+-+-+-+-+-+-+-+-+-+-+-+-+-+-+
      \ !                        SA Attributes                          !
       >+-+-+-+-+-+-+-+-+-+-+-+-+-+-+-+-+-+-+-+-+-+-+-+-+-+-+-+-+-+-+-+-+
      / ! NP = 0        !    RESERVED   !          Payload Length        !
     /  +-+-+-+-+-+-+-+-+-+-+-+-+-+-+-+-+-+-+-+-+-+-+-+-+-+-+-+-+-+-+-+-+
Prop 1 ! Proposal # = 1! Protocol ID  !   SPI Size   !# of Trans. = 1!
Prot 2 +-+-+-+-+-+-+-+-+-+-+-+-+-+-+-+-+-+-+-+-+-+-+-+-+-+-+-+-+-+-+-+-+
      \ !                        SPI (variable)                         !
       >+-+-+-+-+-+-+-+-+-+-+-+-+-+-+-+-+-+-+-+-+-+-+-+-+-+-+-+-+-+-+-+-+
      / ! NP = 0        !    RESERVED   !          Payload Length        !
     /  +-+-+-+-+-+-+-+-+-+-+-+-+-+-+-+-+-+-+-+-+-+-+-+-+-+-+-+-+-+-+-+-+
Tran 1 ! Transform # 1 ! Transform ID  !             RESERVED2          !
     \  +-+-+-+-+-+-+-+-+-+-+-+-+-+-+-+-+-+-+-+-+-+-+-+-+-+-+-+-+-+-+-+-+
      \ !                        SA Attributes                          !
       \+-+-+-+-+-+-+-+-+-+-+-+-+-+-+-+-+-+-+-+-+-+-+-+-+-+-+-+-+-+-+-+-+
```

This second example shows a Proposal for two different protection
suites. The SA Payload was omitted for space reasons. The first
protection suite is presented with one transform for the first
protocol and one transform for the second protocol. The second
protection suite is presented with two transforms for a single
protocol. An example for this proposal might be: Proposal 1 with
Protocol 1 as AH with Transform 1 as MD5 AND Protocol 2 as ESP with
Transform 1 as 3DES. This is followed by Proposal 2 with Protocol 1
as ESP with Transform 1 as DES and Transform 2 as 3DES. The responder
MUST select from the two different proposals. If the second Proposal
is selected, the responder MUST select from the two transforms for
ESP. The resulting protection suite will be either (1) MD5 AND 3DES
OR the selection between (2) DES OR (3) 3DES.

```
                       1                   2                   3
       0 1 2 3 4 5 6 7 8 9 0 1 2 3 4 5 6 7 8 9 0 1 2 3 4 5 6 7 8 9 0 1
     /+-+-+-+-+-+-+-+-+-+-+-+-+-+-+-+-+-+-+-+-+-+-+-+-+-+-+-+-+-+-+-+-+
     / ! NP = Proposal !    RESERVED   !          Payload Length        !
    /  +-+-+-+-+-+-+-+-+-+-+-+-+-+-+-+-+-+-+-+-+-+-+-+-+-+-+-+-+-+-+-+-+
Prop 1 ! Proposal # = 1! Protocol ID  !   SPI Size   !# of Trans. = 1!
Prot 1 +-+-+-+-+-+-+-+-+-+-+-+-+-+-+-+-+-+-+-+-+-+-+-+-+-+-+-+-+-+-+-+-+
      \ !                        SPI (variable)                         !
       >+-+-+-+-+-+-+-+-+-+-+-+-+-+-+-+-+-+-+-+-+-+-+-+-+-+-+-+-+-+-+-+-+
      / ! NP = 0        !    RESERVED   !          Payload Length        !
```

```
    /   +-+-+-+-+-+-+-+-+-+-+-+-+-+-+-+-+-+-+-+-+-+-+-+-+-+-+-+-+-+-+-+-+
Tran 1 ! Transform # 1 ! Transform ID !            RESERVED2            !
    \   +-+-+-+-+-+-+-+-+-+-+-+-+-+-+-+-+-+-+-+-+-+-+-+-+-+-+-+-+-+-+-+-+
     \  !                        SA Attributes                          !
     >+-+-+-+-+-+-+-+-+-+-+-+-+-+-+-+-+-+-+-+-+-+-+-+-+-+-+-+-+-+-+-+-+-+
    /  ! NP = Proposal !   RESERVED   !          Payload Length         !
    /   +-+-+-+-+-+-+-+-+-+-+-+-+-+-+-+-+-+-+-+-+-+-+-+-+-+-+-+-+-+-+-+-+
Prop 1 ! Proposal # = 1! Protocol ID  !   SPI Size   !# of Trans. = 1!
Prot 2 +-+-+-+-+-+-+-+-+-+-+-+-+-+-+-+-+-+-+-+-+-+-+-+-+-+-+-+-+-+-+-+-+
    \  !                        SPI (variable)                         !
     >+-+-+-+-+-+-+-+-+-+-+-+-+-+-+-+-+-+-+-+-+-+-+-+-+-+-+-+-+-+-+-+-+-+
    /  ! NP = 0        !   RESERVED   !          Payload Length         !
    /   +-+-+-+-+-+-+-+-+-+-+-+-+-+-+-+-+-+-+-+-+-+-+-+-+-+-+-+-+-+-+-+-+
Tran 1 ! Transform # 1 ! Transform ID !            RESERVED2            !
    \   +-+-+-+-+-+-+-+-+-+-+-+-+-+-+-+-+-+-+-+-+-+-+-+-+-+-+-+-+-+-+-+-+
     \  !                        SA Attributes                          !
     >+-+-+-+-+-+-+-+-+-+-+-+-+-+-+-+-+-+-+-+-+-+-+-+-+-+-+-+-+-+-+-+-+-+
    /  ! NP = 0        !   RESERVED   !          Payload Length         !
    /   +-+-+-+-+-+-+-+-+-+-+-+-+-+-+-+-+-+-+-+-+-+-+-+-+-+-+-+-+-+-+-+-+
Prop 2 ! Proposal # = 2! Protocol ID  !   SPI Size   !# of Trans. = 2!
Prot 1 +-+-+-+-+-+-+-+-+-+-+-+-+-+-+-+-+-+-+-+-+-+-+-+-+-+-+-+-+-+-+-+-+
     \  !                        SPI (variable)                        !
     >+-+-+-+-+-+-+-+-+-+-+-+-+-+-+-+-+-+-+-+-+-+-+-+-+-+-+-+-+-+-+-+-+-+
    /  ! NP = Transform!   RESERVED   !          Payload Length         !
    /   +-+-+-+-+-+-+-+-+-+-+-+-+-+-+-+-+-+-+-+-+-+-+-+-+-+-+-+-+-+-+-+-+
Tran 1 ! Transform # 1 ! Transform ID !            RESERVED2            !
    \   +-+-+-+-+-+-+-+-+-+-+-+-+-+-+-+-+-+-+-+-+-+-+-+-+-+-+-+-+-+-+-+-+
     \  !                        SA Attributes                          !
     >+-+-+-+-+-+-+-+-+-+-+-+-+-+-+-+-+-+-+-+-+-+-+-+-+-+-+-+-+-+-+-+-+-+
    /  ! NP = 0        !   RESERVED   !          Payload Length         !
    /   +-+-+-+-+-+-+-+-+-+-+-+-+-+-+-+-+-+-+-+-+-+-+-+-+-+-+-+-+-+-+-+-+
Tran 2 ! Transform # 2 ! Transform ID !            RESERVED2            !
    \   +-+-+-+-+-+-+-+-+-+-+-+-+-+-+-+-+-+-+-+-+-+-+-+-+-+-+-+-+-+-+-+-+
     \  !                        SA Attributes                          !
     \+-+-+-+-+-+-+-+-+-+-+-+-+-+-+-+-+-+-+-+-+-+-+-+-+-+-+-+-+-+-+-+-+-+
```

4.3 Security Association Modification

Security Association modification within ISAKMP is accomplished by
creating a new SA and initiating communications using that new SA.
Deletion of the old SA can be done anytime after the new SA is
established. Deletion of the old SA is dependent on local security
policy. Modification of SAs by using a "Create New SA followed by
Delete Old SA" method is done to avoid potential vulnerabilities in
synchronizing modification of existing SA attributes. The procedure
for creating new SAs is outlined in section 4.2. The procedure for
deleting SAs is outlined in section 5.15.

Modification of an ISAKMP SA (phase 1 negotiation) follows the same procedure as creation of an ISAKMP SA. There is no relationship between the two SAs and the initiator and responder cookie pairs SHOULD be different, as outlined in section 2.5.3.

Modification of a Protocol SA (phase 2 negotiation) follows the same procedure as creation of a Protocol SA. The creation of a new SA is protected by the existing ISAKMP SA. There is no relationship between the two Protocol SAs. A protocol implementation SHOULD begin using the newly created SA for outbound traffic and SHOULD continue to support incoming traffic on the old SA until it is deleted or until traffic is received under the protection of the newly created SA. As stated previously in this section, deletion of an old SA is then dependent on local security policy.

4.4 Base Exchange

The Base Exchange is designed to allow the Key Exchange and Authentication related information to be transmitted together. Combining the Key Exchange and Authentication-related information into one message reduces the number of round-trips at the expense of not providing identity protection. Identity protection is not provided because identities are exchanged before a common shared secret has been established and, therefore, encryption of the identities is not possible. The following diagram shows the messages with the possible payloads sent in each message and notes for an example of the Base Exchange.

                         BASE EXCHANGE

```
 #  Initiator Direction  Responder              NOTE
(1)  HDR; SA; NONCE  =>              Begin ISAKMP-SA or Proxy negotiation

(2)                     <=  HDR; SA; NONCE
                            Basic SA agreed upon
(3)  HDR; KE;          =>
     IDii; AUTH                     Key Generated (by responder)
                                    Initiator Identity Verified by
                                    Responder
(4)                     <=  HDR; KE;
                            IDir; AUTH
                                    Responder Identity Verified by
                                    Initiator Key Generated (by
                                    initiator) SA established
```

In the first message (1), the initiator generates a proposal it considers adequate to protect traffic for the given situation. The Security Association, Proposal, and Transform payloads are included in the Security Association payload (for notation purposes). Random information which is used to guarantee liveness and protect against replay attacks is also transmitted. Random information provided by both parties SHOULD be used by the authentication mechanism to provide shared proof of participation in the exchange.

In the second message (2), the responder indicates the protection suite it has accepted with the Security Association, Proposal, and Transform payloads. Again, random information which is used to guarantee liveness and protect against replay attacks is also transmitted. Random information provided by both parties SHOULD be used by the authentication mechanism to provide shared proof of participation in the exchange. Local security policy dictates the action of the responder if no proposed protection suite is accepted. One possible action is the transmission of a Notify payload as part of an Informational Exchange.

In the third (3) and fourth (4) messages, the initiator and responder, respectively, exchange keying material used to arrive at a common shared secret and identification information. This information is transmitted under the protection of the agreed upon authentication function. Local security policy dictates the action if an error occurs during these messages. One possible action is the transmission of a Notify payload as part of an Informational Exchange.

4.5 Identity Protection Exchange

The Identity Protection Exchange is designed to separate the Key Exchange information from the Identity and Authentication related information. Separating the Key Exchange from the Identity and Authentication related information provides protection of the communicating identities at the expense of two additional messages. Identities are exchanged under the protection of a previously established common shared secret. The following diagram shows the messages with the possible payloads sent in each message and notes for an example of the Identity Protection Exchange.

IDENTITY PROTECTION EXCHANGE

```
 #      Initiator       Direction     Responder       NOTE
(1)  HDR; SA                =>                         Begin ISAKMP-SA or
                                                       Proxy negotiation

(2)                         <=       HDR; SA
                                                       Basic SA agreed upon

(3)  HDR; KE; NONCE         =>
(4)                         <=       HDR; KE; NONCE
                                                       Key Generated (by
                                                       Initiator and
                                                       Responder)

(5)  HDR*; IDii; AUTH       =>
                                                       Initiator Identity
                                                       Verified by
                                                       Responder
(6)                         <=       HDR*; IDir; AUTH
                                                       Responder Identity
                                                       Verified by
                                                       Initiator
                                                       SA established
```

   In the first message (1), the initiator generates a proposal it
   considers adequate to protect traffic for the given situation. The
   Security Association, Proposal, and Transform payloads are included
   in the Security Association payload (for notation purposes).

   In the second message (2), the responder indicates the protection
   suite it has accepted with the Security Association, Proposal, and
   Transform payloads. Local security policy dictates the action of the
   responder if no proposed protection suite is accepted. One possible
   action is the transmission of a Notify payload as part of an
   Informational Exchange.

   In the third (3) and fourth (4) messages, the initiator and
   responder, respectively, exchange keying material used to arrive at a
   common shared secret and random information which is used to
   guarantee liveness and protect against replay attacks. Random
   information provided by both parties SHOULD be used by the
   authentication mechanism to provide shared proof of participation in
   the exchange. Local security policy dictates the action if an error
   occurs during these messages. One possible action is the
   transmission of a Notify payload as part of an Informational
   Exchange.

   In the fifth (5) and sixth (6) messages, the initiator and responder,
   respectively, exchange identification information and the results of
   the agreed upon authentication function. This information is

transmitted under the protection of the common shared secret. Local
security policy dictates the action if an error occurs during these
messages. One possible action is the transmission of a Notify
payload as part of an Informational Exchange.

4.6 Authentication Only Exchange

The Authentication Only Exchange is designed to allow only
Authentication related information to be transmitted. The benefit of
this exchange is the ability to perform only authentication without
the computational expense of computing keys. Using this exchange
during negotiation, none of the transmitted information will be
encrypted. However, the information may be encrypted in other
places. For example, if encryption is negotiated during the first
phase of a negotiation and the authentication only exchange is used
in the second phase of a negotiation, then the authentication only
exchange will be encrypted by the ISAKMP SAs negotiated in the first
phase. The following diagram shows the messages with possible
payloads sent in each message and notes for an example of the
Authentication Only Exchange.

                    AUTHENTICATION ONLY EXCHANGE

```
 #      Initiator       Direction      Responder       NOTE
(1)  HDR; SA; NONCE       =>                            Begin ISAKMP-SA or
                                                        Proxy negotiation
(2)                       <=       HDR; SA; NONCE;
                                   IDir; AUTH
                                                        Basic SA agreed upon
                                                        Responder Identity
                                                        Verified by Initiator
(3)  HDR; IDii; AUTH      =>
                                                        Initiator Identity
                                                        Verified by Responder
                                                        SA established
```

In the first message (1), the initiator generates a proposal it
considers adequate to protect traffic for the given situation. The
Security Association, Proposal, and Transform payloads are included
in the Security Association payload (for notation purposes). Random
information which is used to guarantee liveness and protect against
replay attacks is also transmitted. Random information provided by
both parties SHOULD be used by the authentication mechanism to
provide shared proof of participation in the exchange.

In the second message (2), the responder indicates the protection
suite it has accepted with the Security Association, Proposal, and
Transform payloads. Again, random information which is used to

guarantee liveness and protect against replay attacks is also
transmitted. Random information provided by both parties SHOULD be
used by the authentication mechanism to provide shared proof of
participation in the exchange. Additionally, the responder transmits
identification information. All of this information is transmitted
under the protection of the agreed upon authentication function.
Local security policy dictates the action of the responder if no
proposed protection suite is accepted. One possible action is the
transmission of a Notify payload as part of an Informational
Exchange.

In the third message (3), the initiator transmits identification
information. This information is transmitted under the protection of
the agreed upon authentication function. Local security policy
dictates the action if an error occurs during these messages. One
possible action is the transmission of a Notify payload as part of an
Informational Exchange.

4.7 Aggressive Exchange

The Aggressive Exchange is designed to allow the Security
Association, Key Exchange and Authentication related payloads to be
transmitted together. Combining the Security Association, Key
Exchange, and Authentication-related information into one message
reduces the number of round-trips at the expense of not providing
identity protection. Identity protection is not provided because
identities are exchanged before a common shared secret has been
established and, therefore, encryption of the identities is not
possible. Additionally, the Aggressive Exchange is attempting to
establish all security relevant information in a single exchange.
The following diagram shows the messages with possible payloads sent
in each message and notes for an example of the Aggressive Exchange.

AGGRESSIVE EXCHANGE

```
 #    Initiator   Direction    Responder     NOTE
(1)  HDR; SA; KE;    =>                       Begin ISAKMP-SA or
                                              Proxy negotiation
     NONCE; IDii                              and Key Exchange

(2)                  <=       HDR; SA; KE;
                              NONCE; IDir; AUTH
                                              Initiator Identity
                                              Verified by Responder
                                              Key Generated
                                              Basic SA agreed upon
(3)  HDR*; AUTH      =>
                                              Responder Identity
                                              Verified by Initiator
                                              SA established
```

In the first message (1), the initiator generates a proposal it
considers adequate to protect traffic for the given situation. The
Security Association, Proposal, and Transform payloads are included
in the Security Association payload (for notation purposes). There
can be only one Proposal and one Transform offered (i.e. no choices)
in order for the aggressive exchange to work. Keying material used
to arrive at a common shared secret and random information which is
used to guarantee liveness and protect against replay attacks are
also transmitted. Random information provided by both parties SHOULD
be used by the authentication mechanism to provide shared proof of
participation in the exchange. Additionally, the initiator transmits
identification information.

In the second message (2), the responder indicates the protection
suite it has accepted with the Security Association, Proposal, and
Transform payloads. Keying material used to arrive at a common
shared secret and random information which is used to guarantee
liveness and protect against replay attacks is also transmitted.
Random information provided by both parties SHOULD be used by the
authentication mechanism to provide shared proof of participation in
the exchange. Additionally, the responder transmits identification
information. All of this information is transmitted under the
protection of the agreed upon authentication function. Local
security policy dictates the action of the responder if no proposed
protection suite is accepted. One possible action is the
transmission of a Notify payload as part of an Informational
Exchange.

In the third (3) message, the initiator transmits the results of the
agreed upon authentication function. This information is transmitted
under the protection of the common shared secret. Local security
policy dictates the action if an error occurs during these messages.
One possible action is the transmission of a Notify payload as part
of an Informational Exchange.

4.8 Informational Exchange

The Informational Exchange is designed as a one-way transmittal of
information that can be used for security association management.
The following diagram shows the messages with possible payloads sent
in each message and notes for an example of the Informational
Exchange.

```
                 INFORMATIONAL EXCHANGE

    #   Initiator  Direction Responder  NOTE
   (1)  HDR*; N/D     =>                 Error Notification or Deletion
```

In the first message (1), the initiator or responder transmits an
ISAKMP Notify or Delete payload.

If the Informational Exchange occurs prior to the exchange of keying
meterial during an ISAKMP Phase 1 negotiation, there will be no
protection provided for the Informational Exchange. Once keying
material has been exchanged or an ISAKMP SA has been established, the
Informational Exchange MUST be transmitted under the protection
provided by the keying material or the ISAKMP SA.

All exchanges are similar in that with the beginning of any exchange,
cryptographic synchronization MUST occur. The Informational Exchange
is an exchange and not an ISAKMP message. Thus, the generation of an
Message ID (MID) for an Informational Exchange SHOULD be independent
of IVs of other on-going communication. This will ensure
cryptographic synchronization is maintained for existing
communications and the Informational Exchange will be processed
correctly. The only exception to this is when the Commit Bit of the
ISAKMP Header is set. When the Commit Bit is set, the Message ID
field of the Informational Exchange MUST contain the Message ID of
the original ISAKMP Phase 2 SA negotiation, rather than a new Message
ID (MID). This is done to ensure that the Informational Exchange with
the CONNECTED Notify Message can be associated with the correct Phase
2 SA. For a description of the Commit Bit, see section 3.1.

5 ISAKMP Payload Processing

Section 3 describes the ISAKMP payloads. These payloads are used in
the exchanges described in section 4 and can be used in exchanges
defined for a specific DOI. This section describes the processing for
each of the payloads. This section suggests the logging of events to
a system audit file. This action is controlled by a system security
policy and is, therefore, only a suggested action.

5.1 General Message Processing

Every ISAKMP message has basic processing applied to insure protocol
reliability, and to minimize threats, such as denial of service and
replay attacks. All processing SHOULD include packet length checks
to insure the packet received is at least as long as the length given
in the ISAKMP Header. If the ISAKMP message length and the value in
the Payload Length field of the ISAKMP Header are not the same, then
the ISAKMP message MUST be rejected. The receiving entity (initiator
or responder) MUST do the following:

1. The event, UNEQUAL PAYLOAD LENGTHS, MAY be logged in the
    appropriate system audit file.

2. An Informational Exchange with a Notification payload containing
    the UNEQUAL-PAYLOAD-LENGTHS message type MAY be sent to the
    transmitting entity. This action is dictated by a system
    security policy.

When transmitting an ISAKMP message, the transmitting entity
(initiator or responder) MUST do the following:

1. Set a timer and initialize a retry counter.

    NOTE: Implementations MUST NOT use a fixed timer. Instead,
    transmission timer values should be adjusted dynamically based on
    measured round trip times. In addition, successive
    retransmissions of the same packet should be separated by
    increasingly longer time intervals (e.g., exponential backoff).

2. If the timer expires, the ISAKMP message is resent and the retry
    counter is decremented.

3. If the retry counter reaches zero (0), the event, RETRY LIMIT
    REACHED, MAY be logged in the appropriate system audit file.

4. The ISAKMP protocol machine clears all states and returns to
    IDLE.

5.2 ISAKMP Header Processing

When creating an ISAKMP message, the transmitting entity (initiator or responder) MUST do the following:

1. Create the respective cookie. See section 2.5.3 for details.

2. Determine the relevant security characteristics of the session (i.e. DOI and situation).

3. Construct an ISAKMP Header with fields as described in section 3.1.

4. Construct other ISAKMP payloads, depending on the exchange type.

5. Transmit the message to the destination host as described in section5.1.

When an ISAKMP message is received, the receiving entity (initiator or responder) MUST do the following:

1. Verify the Initiator and Responder "cookies". If the cookie validation fails, the message is discarded and the following actions are taken:

    (a) The event, INVALID COOKIE, MAY be logged in the appropriate system audit file.

    (b) An Informational Exchange with a Notification payload containing the INVALID-COOKIE message type MAY be sent to the transmitting entity. This action is dictated by a system security policy.

2. Check the Next Payload field to confirm it is valid. If the Next Payload field validation fails, the message is discarded and the following actions are taken:

    (a) The event, INVALID NEXT PAYLOAD, MAY be logged in the appropriate system audit file.

    (b) An Informational Exchange with a Notification payload containing the INVALID-PAYLOAD-TYPE message type MAY be sent to the transmitting entity. This action is dictated by a system security policy.

3. Check the Major and Minor Version fields to confirm they are correct (see section 3.1). If the Version field validation fails, the message is discarded and the following actions are

taken:

(a) The event, INVALID ISAKMP VERSION, MAY be logged in the
     appropriate system audit file.

(b) An Informational Exchange with a Notification payload
     containing the INVALID-MAJOR-VERSION or INVALID-MINOR-
     VERSION message type MAY be sent to the transmitting entity.
     This action is dictated by a system security policy.

4. Check the Exchange Type field to confirm it is valid. If the
   Exchange Type field validation fails, the message is discarded
   and the following actions are taken:

(a) The event, INVALID EXCHANGE TYPE, MAY be logged in the
     appropriate system audit file.

(b) An Informational Exchange with a Notification payload
     containing the INVALID-EXCHANGE-TYPE message type MAY be
     sent to the transmitting entity. This action is dictated by
     a system security policy.

5. Check the Flags field to ensure it contains correct values. If
   the Flags field validation fails, the message is discarded and
   the following actions are taken:

(a) The event, INVALID FLAGS, MAY be logged in the appropriate
     systemaudit file.

(b) An Informational Exchange with a Notification payload
     containing the INVALID-FLAGS message type MAY be sent to the
     transmitting entity. This action is dictated by a system
     security policy.

6. Check the Message ID field to ensure it contains correct values.
   If the Message ID validation fails, the message is discarded and
   the following actions are taken:

(a) The event, INVALID MESSAGE ID, MAY be logged in the
     appropriate system audit file.

(b) An Informational Exchange with a Notification payload
     containing the INVALID-MESSAGE-ID message type MAY be sent
     to the transmitting entity. This action is dictated by a
     system security policy.

7. Processing of the ISAKMP message continues using the value in the
   Next Payload field.

5.3 Generic Payload Header Processing

When creating any of the ISAKMP Payloads described in sections 3.4 through 3.15 a Generic Payload Header is placed at the beginning of these payloads. When creating the Generic Payload Header, the transmitting entity (initiator or responder) MUST do the following:

1. Place the value of the Next Payload in the Next Payload field. These values are described in section 3.1.

2. Place the value zero (0) in the RESERVED field.

3. Place the length (in octets) of the payload in the Payload Length field.

4. Construct the payloads as defined in the remainder of this section.

When any of the ISAKMP Payloads are received, the receiving entity (initiator or responder) MUST do the following:

1. Check the Next Payload field to confirm it is valid. If the Next Payload field validation fails, the message is discarded and the following actions are taken:

    (a) The event, INVALID NEXT PAYLOAD, MAY be logged in the appropriate system audit file.

    (b) An Informational Exchange with a Notification payload containing the INVALID-PAYLOAD-TYPE message type MAY be sent to the transmitting entity. This action is dictated by a system security policy.

2. Verify the RESERVED field contains the value zero. If the value in the RESERVED field is not zero, the message is discarded and the following actions are taken:

    (a) The event, INVALID RESERVED FIELD, MAY be logged in the appropriate system audit file.

    (b) An Informational Exchange with a Notification payload containing the BAD-PROPOSAL-SYNTAX or PAYLOAD-MALFORMED message type MAY be sent to the transmitting entity. This action is dictated by a system security policy.

3. Process the remaining payloads as defined by the Next Payload field.

5.4 Security Association Payload Processing

When creating a Security Association Payload, the transmitting entity
(initiator or responder) MUST do the following:

1. Determine the Domain of Interpretation for which this negotiation
    is being performed.

2. Determine the situation within the determined DOI for which this
    negotiation is being performed.

3. Determine the proposal(s) and transform(s) within the situation.
    These are described, respectively, in sections 3.5 and 3.6.

4. Construct a Security Association payload.

5. Transmit the message to the receiving entity as described in
    section 5.1.

When a Security Association payload is received, the receiving entity
(initiator or responder) MUST do the following:

1. Determine if the Domain of Interpretation (DOI) is supported. If
    the DOI determination fails, the message is discarded and the
    following actions are taken:

    (a) The event, INVALID DOI, MAY be logged in the appropriate
         system audit file.

    (b) An Informational Exchange with a Notification payload
         containing the DOI-NOT-SUPPORTED message type MAY be sent to
         the transmitting entity. This action is dictated by a
         system security policy.

2. Determine if the given situation can be protected. If the
    Situation determination fails, the message is discarded and the
    following actions are taken:

    (a) The event, INVALID SITUATION, MAY be logged in the
         appropriate system audit file.

    (b) An Informational Exchange with a Notification payload
         containing the SITUATION-NOT-SUPPORTED message type MAY be
         sent to the transmitting entity. This action is dictated by
         a system security policy.

3. Process the remaining payloads (i.e. Proposal, Transform) of the
    Security Association Payload. If the Security Association

Proposal (as described in sections 5.5 and 5.6) is not accepted,
then the following actions are taken:

(a) The event, INVALID PROPOSAL, MAY be logged in the
     appropriate system audit file.

(b) An Informational Exchange with a Notification payload
     containing the NO-PROPOSAL-CHOSEN message type MAY be sent
     to the transmitting entity. This action is dictated by a
     system security policy.

5.5 Proposal Payload Processing

When creating a Proposal Payload, the transmitting entity (initiator
or responder) MUST do the following:

1. Determine the Protocol for this proposal.

2. Determine the number of proposals to be offered for this protocol
    and the number of transforms for each proposal. Transforms are
    described in section 3.6.

3. Generate a unique pseudo-random SPI.

4. Construct a Proposal payload.

When a Proposal payload is received, the receiving entity (initiator
or responder) MUST do the following:

1. Determine if the Protocol is supported. If the Protocol-ID field
    is invalid, the payload is discarded and the following actions
    are taken:

    (a) The event, INVALID PROTOCOL, MAY be logged in the
         appropriate system audit file.

    (b) An Informational Exchange with a Notification payload
         containing the INVALID-PROTOCOL-ID message type MAY be sent
         to the transmitting entity. This action is dictated by a
         system security policy.

2. Determine if the SPI is valid. If the SPI is invalid, the
    payload is discarded and the following actions are taken:

    (a) The event, INVALID SPI, MAY be logged in the appropriate
         system audit file.

> (b) An Informational Exchange with a Notification payload
> containing the INVALID-SPI message type MAY be sent to the
> transmitting entity. This action is dictated by a system
> security policy.

3. Ensure the Proposals are presented according to the details given
   in section 3.5 and 4.2. If the proposals are not formed
   correctly, the following actions are taken:

   (a) Possible events, BAD PROPOSAL SYNTAX, INVALID PROPOSAL, are
   logged in the appropriate system audit file.

   (b) An Informational Exchange with a Notification payload
   containing the BAD-PROPOSAL-SYNTAX or PAYLOAD-MALFORMED
   message type MAY be sent to the transmitting entity. This
   action is dictated by a system security policy.

4. Process the Proposal and Transform payloads as defined by the
   Next Payload field. Examples of processing these payloads are
   given in section 4.2.1.

5.6 Transform Payload Processing

When creating a Transform Payload, the transmitting entity (initiator
or responder) MUST do the following:

1. Determine the Transform # for this transform.

2. Determine the number of transforms to be offered for this
   proposal. Transforms are described in sections 3.6.

3. Construct a Transform payload.

When a Transform payload is received, the receiving entity (initiator
or responder) MUST do the following:

1. Determine if the Transform is supported. If the Transform-ID
   field contains an unknown or unsupported value, then that
   Transform payload MUST be ignored and MUST NOT cause the
   generation of an INVALID TRANSFORM event. If the Transform-ID
   field is invalid, the payload is discarded and the following
   actions are taken:

   (a) The event, INVALID TRANSFORM, MAY be logged in the
   appropriate system audit file.

   (b) An Informational Exchange with a Notification payload
   containing the INVALID-TRANSFORM-ID message type MAY be sent

to the transmitting entity. This action is dictated by a
system security policy.

2. Ensure the Transforms are presented according to the details
    given in section 3.6 and 4.2. If the transforms are not formed
    correctly, the following actions are taken:

    (a) Possible events, BAD PROPOSAL SYNTAX, INVALID TRANSFORM,
         INVALID ATTRIBUTES, are logged in the appropriate system
         audit file.

    (b) An Informational Exchange with a Notification payload
         containing the BAD-PROPOSAL-SYNTAX, PAYLOAD-MALFORMED or
         ATTRIBUTES-NOT-SUPPORTED message type MAY be sent to the
         transmitting entity. This action is dictated by a system
         security policy.

3. Process the subsequent Transform and Proposal payloads as defined
    by the Next Payload field. Examples of processing these payloads
    are given in section 4.2.1.

5.7 Key Exchange Payload Processing

   When creating a Key Exchange Payload, the transmitting entity
   (initiator or responder) MUST do the following:

   1. Determine the Key Exchange to be used as defined by the DOI.

   2. Determine the usage of the Key Exchange Data field as defined by
       the DOI.

   3. Construct a Key Exchange payload.

   4. Transmit the message to the receiving entity as described in
       section 5.1.

   When a Key Exchange payload is received, the receiving entity
   (initiator or responder) MUST do the following:

   1. Determine if the Key Exchange is supported. If the Key Exchange
       determination fails, the message is discarded and the following
       actions are taken:

       (a) The event, INVALID KEY INFORMATION, MAY be logged in the
            appropriate system audit file.

       (b) An Informational Exchange with a Notification payload
            containing the INVALID-KEY-INFORMATION message type MAY be

sent to the transmitting entity. This action is dictated by
a system security policy.

5.8 Identification Payload Processing

When creating an Identification Payload, the transmitting entity
(initiator or responder) MUST do the following:

1. Determine the Identification information to be used as defined by
    the DOI (and possibly the situation).

2. Determine the usage of the Identification Data field as defined
    by the DOI.

3. Construct an Identification payload.

4. Transmit the message to the receiving entity as described in
    section 5.1.

When an Identification payload is received, the receiving entity
(initiator or responder) MUST do the following:

1. Determine if the Identification Type is supported. This may be
    based on the DOI and Situation. If the Identification
    determination fails, the message is discarded and the following
    actions are taken:

    (a) The event, INVALID ID INFORMATION, MAY be logged in the
         appropriate system audit file.

    (b) An Informational Exchange with a Notification payload
         containing the INVALID-ID-INFORMATION message type MAY be
         sent to the transmitting entity. This action is dictated by
         a system security policy.

5.9 Certificate Payload Processing

When creating a Certificate Payload, the transmitting entity
(initiator or responder) MUST do the following:

1. Determine the Certificate Encoding to be used. This may be
    specified by the DOI.

2. Ensure the existence of a certificate formatted as defined by the
    Certificate Encoding.

3. Construct a Certificate payload.

4. Transmit the message to the receiving entity as described in
    section 5.1.

When a Certificate payload is received, the receiving entity
(initiator or responder) MUST do the following:

1. Determine if the Certificate Encoding is supported. If the
    Certificate Encoding is not supported, the payload is discarded
    and the following actions are taken:

    (a) The event, INVALID CERTIFICATE TYPE, MAY be logged in the
         appropriate system audit file.

    (b) An Informational Exchange with a Notification payload
         containing the INVALID-CERT-ENCODING message type MAY be
         sent to the transmitting entity. This action is dictated by
         a system security policy.

2. Process the Certificate Data field. If the Certificate Data is
    invalid or improperly formatted, the payload is discarded and the
    following actions are taken:

    (a) The event, INVALID CERTIFICATE, MAY be logged in the
         appropriate system audit file.

    (b) An Informational Exchange with a Notification payload
         containing the INVALID-CERTIFICATE message type MAY be sent
         to the transmitting entity. This action is dictated by a
         system security policy.

5.10 Certificate Request Payload Processing

When creating a Certificate Request Payload, the transmitting entity
(initiator or responder) MUST do the following:

1. Determine the type of Certificate Encoding to be requested. This
    may be specified by the DOI.

2. Determine the name of an acceptable Certificate Authority which
    is to be requested (if applicable).

3. Construct a Certificate Request payload.

4. Transmit the message to the receiving entity as described in
    section 5.1.

When a Certificate Request payload is received, the receiving entity
(initiator or responder) MUST do the following:

1. Determine if the Certificate Encoding is supported. If the
    Certificate Encoding is invalid, the payload is discarded and the
    following actions are taken:

    (a) The event, INVALID CERTIFICATE TYPE, MAY be logged in
         the appropriate system audit file.

    (b) An Informational Exchange with a Notification payload
         containing the INVALID-CERT-ENCODING message type MAY be
         sent to the transmitting entity. This action is dictated by
         a system security policy.

    If the Certificate Encoding is not supported, the payload is
    discarded and the following actions are taken:

    (a) The event, CERTIFICATE TYPE UNSUPPORTED, MAY be logged in
         the appropriate system audit file.

    (b) An Informational Exchange with a Notification payload
         containing the CERT-TYPE-UNSUPPORTED message type MAY be
         sent to the transmitting entity. This action is dictated by
         a system security policy.

2. Determine if the Certificate Authority is supported for the
    specified Certificate Encoding. If the Certificate Authority is
    invalid or improperly formatted, the payload is discarded and the
    following actions are taken:

    (a) The event, INVALID CERTIFICATE AUTHORITY, MAY be logged in
         the appropriate system audit file.

    (b) An Informational Exchange with a Notification payload
         containing the INVALID-CERT-AUTHORITY message type MAY be
         sent to the transmitting entity. This action is dictated by
         a system security policy.

3. Process the Certificate Request. If a requested Certificate Type
    with the specified Certificate Authority is not available, then
    the payload is discarded and the following actions are taken:

    (a) The event, CERTIFICATE-UNAVAILABLE, MAY be logged in the
         appropriate system audit file.

    (b) An Informational Exchange with a Notification payload
         containing the CERTIFICATE-UNAVAILABLE message type MAY be
         sent to the transmitting entity. This action is dictated by
         a system security policy.

5.11 Hash Payload Processing

When creating a Hash Payload, the transmitting entity (initiator or responder) MUST do the following:

1. Determine the Hash function to be used as defined by the SA negotiation.

2. Determine the usage of the Hash Data field as defined by the DOI.

3. Construct a Hash payload.

4. Transmit the message to the receiving entity as described in section 5.1.

When a Hash payload is received, the receiving entity (initiator or responder) MUST do the following:

1. Determine if the Hash is supported. If the Hash determination fails, the message is discarded and the following actions are taken:

    (a) The event, INVALID HASH INFORMATION, MAY be logged in the appropriate system audit file.

    (b) An Informational Exchange with a Notification payload containing the INVALID-HASH-INFORMATION message type MAY be sent to the transmitting entity. This action is dictated by a system security policy.

2. Perform the Hash function as outlined in the DOI and/or Key Exchange protocol documents. If the Hash function fails, the message is discarded and the following actions are taken:

    (a) The event, INVALID HASH VALUE, MAY be logged in the appropriate system audit file.

    (b) An Informational Exchange with a Notification payload containing the AUTHENTICATION-FAILED message type MAY be sent to the transmitting entity. This action is dictated by a system security policy.

5.12 Signature Payload Processing

When creating a Signature Payload, the transmitting entity (initiator or responder) MUST do the following:

1. Determine the Signature function to be used as defined by the SA
    negotiation.

2. Determine the usage of the Signature Data field as defined by the
    DOI.

3. Construct a Signature payload.

4. Transmit the message to the receiving entity as described in
    section 5.1.

When a Signature payload is received, the receiving entity (initiator
or responder) MUST do the following:

1. Determine if the Signature is supported. If the Signature
    determination fails, the message is discarded and the following
    actions are taken:

    (a) The event, INVALID SIGNATURE INFORMATION, MAY be logged in
         the appropriate system audit file.

    (b) An Informational Exchange with a Notification payload
         containing the INVALID-SIGNATURE message type MAY be sent to
         the transmitting entity. This action is dictated by a
         system security policy.

2. Perform the Signature function as outlined in the DOI and/or Key
    Exchange protocol documents. If the Signature function fails,
    the message is discarded and the following actions are taken:

    (a) The event, INVALID SIGNATURE VALUE, MAY be logged in the
         appropriate system audit file.

    (b) An Informational Exchange with a Notification payload
         containing the AUTHENTICATION-FAILED message type MAY be
         sent to the transmitting entity. This action is dictated by
         a system security policy.

5.13 Nonce Payload Processing

When creating a Nonce Payload, the transmitting entity (initiator or
responder) MUST do the following:

1. Create a unique random value to be used as a nonce.

2. Construct a Nonce payload.

3. Transmit the message to the receiving entity as described in
    section 5.1.

When a Nonce payload is received, the receiving entity (initiator or
responder) MUST do the following:

1. There are no specific procedures for handling Nonce payloads.
    The procedures are defined by the exchange types (and possibly
    the DOI and Key Exchange descriptions).

5.14 Notification Payload Processing

During communications it is possible that errors may occur. The
Informational Exchange with a Notify Payload provides a controlled
method of informing a peer entity that errors have occurred during
protocol processing. It is RECOMMENDED that Notify Payloads be sent
in a separate Informational Exchange rather than appending a Notify
Payload to an existing exchange.

When creating a Notification Payload, the transmitting entity
(initiator or responder) MUST do the following:

1. Determine the DOI for this Notification.

2. Determine the Protocol-ID for this Notification.

3. Determine the SPI size based on the Protocol-ID field. This
    field is necessary because different security protocols have
    different SPI sizes. For example, ISAKMP combines the Initiator
    and Responder cookie pair (16 octets) as a SPI, while ESP and AH
    have 4 octet SPIs.

4. Determine the Notify Message Type based on the error or status
    message desired.

5. Determine the SPI which is associated with this notification.

6. Determine if additional Notification Data is to be included.
    This is additional information specified by the DOI.

7. Construct a Notification payload.

8. Transmit the message to the receiving entity as described in
    section 5.1.

Because the Informational Exchange with a Notification payload is a
unidirectional message a retransmission will not be performed. The
local security policy will dictate the procedures for continuing.

However, we RECOMMEND that a NOTIFICATION PAYLOAD ERROR event be
logged in the appropriate system audit file by the receiving entity.

If the Informational Exchange occurs prior to the exchange of keying
material during an ISAKMP Phase 1 negotiation there will be no
protection provided for the Informational Exchange. Once the keying
material has been exchanged or the ISAKMP SA has been established,
the Informational Exchange MUST be transmitted under the protection
provided by the keying material or the ISAKMP SA.

When a Notification payload is received, the receiving entity
(initiator or responder) MUST do the following:

1. Determine if the Informational Exchange has any protection
    applied to it by checking the Encryption Bit and the
    Authentication Only Bit in the ISAKMP Header. If the Encryption
    Bit is set, i.e. the Informational Exchange is encrypted, then
    the message MUST be decrypted using the (in-progress or
    completed) ISAKMP SA. Once the decryption is complete the
    processing can continue as described below. If the
    Authentication Only Bit is set, then the message MUST be
    authenticated using the (in-progress or completed) ISAKMP SA.
    Once the authentication is completed, the processing can continue
    as described below. If the Informational Exchange is not
    encrypted or authentication, the payload processing can continue
    as described below.

2. Determine if the Domain of Interpretation (DOI) is supported. If
    the DOI determination fails, the payload is discarded and the
    following action is taken:

    (a) The event, INVALID DOI, MAY be logged in the appropriate
         system audit file.

3. Determine if the Protocol-Id is supported. If the Protocol-Id
    determination fails, the payload is discarded and the following
    action is taken:

    (a) The event, INVALID PROTOCOL-ID, MAY be logged in the
         appropriate system audit file.

4. Determine if the SPI is valid. If the SPI is invalid, the
    payload is discarded and the following action is taken:

    (a) The event, INVALID SPI, MAY be logged in the appropriate
         system audit file.

5. Determine if the Notify Message Type is valid. If the Notify
    Message Type is invalid, the payload is discarded and the
    following action is taken:

    (a) The event, INVALID MESSAGE TYPE, MAY be logged in the
         appropriate system audit file.

6. Process the Notification payload, including additional
    Notification Data, and take appropriate action, according to
    local security policy.

5.15 Delete Payload Processing

During communications it is possible that hosts may be compromised or
that information may be intercepted during transmission. Determining
whether this has occurred is not an easy task and is outside the
scope of this memo. However, if it is discovered that transmissions
are being compromised, then it is necessary to establish a new SA and
delete the current SA.

The Informational Exchange with a Delete Payload provides a
controlled method of informing a peer entity that the transmitting
entity has deleted the SA(s). Deletion of Security Associations MUST
always be performed under the protection of an ISAKMP SA. The
receiving entity SHOULD clean up its local SA database. However,
upon receipt of a Delete message the SAs listed in the Security
Parameter Index (SPI) field of the Delete payload cannot be used with
the transmitting entity. The SA Establishment procedure must be
invoked to re-establish secure communications.

When creating a Delete Payload, the transmitting entity (initiator or
responder) MUST do the following:

1. Determine the DOI for this Deletion.

2. Determine the Protocol-ID for this Deletion.

3. Determine the SPI size based on the Protocol-ID field. This
    field is necessary because different security protocols have
    different SPI sizes. For example, ISAKMP combines the Initiator
    and Responder cookie pair (16 octets) as a SPI, while ESP and AH
    have 4 octet SPIs.

4. Determine the # of SPIs to be deleted for this protocol.

5. Determine the SPI(s) which is (are) associated with this
    deletion.

6. Construct a Delete payload.

7. Transmit the message to the receiving entity as described in section 5.1.

Because the Informational Exchange with a Delete payload is a unidirectional message a retransmission will not be performed. The local security policy will dictate the procedures for continuing. However, we RECOMMEND that a DELETE PAYLOAD ERROR event be logged in the appropriate system audit file by the receiving entity.

As described above, the Informational Exchange with a Delete payload MUST be transmitted under the protection provided by an ISAKMP SA.

When a Delete payload is received, the receiving entity (initiator or responder) MUST do the following:

1. Because the Informational Exchange is protected by some security service (e.g. authentication for an Auth-Only SA, encryption for other exchanges), the message MUST have these security services applied using the ISAKMP SA. Once the security service processing is complete the processing can continue as described below. Any errors that occur during the security service processing will be evident when checking information in the Delete payload. The local security policy SHOULD dictate any action to be taken as a result of security service processing errors.

2. Determine if the Domain of Interpretation (DOI) is supported. If the DOI determination fails, the payload is discarded and the following action is taken:

    (a) The event, INVALID DOI, MAY be logged in the appropriate system audit file.

3. Determine if the Protocol-Id is supported. If the Protocol-Id determination fails, the payload is discarded and the following action is taken:

    (a) The event, INVALID PROTOCOL-ID, MAY be logged in the appropriate system audit file.

4. Determine if the SPI is valid for each SPI included in the Delete payload. For each SPI that is invalid, the following action is taken:

    (a) The event, INVALID SPI, MAY be logged in the appropriate system audit file.

   5. Process the Delete payload and take appropriate action, according
       to local security policy. As described above, one appropriate
       action SHOULD include cleaning up the local SA database.

6 Conclusions

   The Internet Security Association and Key Management Protocol
   (ISAKMP) is a well designed protocol aimed at the Internet of the
   future. The massive growth of the Internet will lead to great
   diversity in network utilization, communications, security
   requirements, and security mechanisms. ISAKMP contains all the
   features that will be needed for this dynamic and expanding
   communications environment.

   ISAKMP's Security Association (SA) feature coupled with
   authentication and key establishment provides the security and
   flexibility that will be needed for future growth and diversity.
   This security diversity of multiple key exchange techniques,
   encryption algorithms, authentication mechanisms, security services,
   and security attributes will allow users to select the appropriate
   security for their network, communications, and security needs. The
   SA feature allows users to specify and negotiate security
   requirements with other users. An additional benefit of supporting
   multiple techniques in a single protocol is that as new techniques
   are developed they can easily be added to the protocol. This
   provides a path for the growth of Internet security services. ISAKMP
   supports both publicly or privately defined SAs, making it ideal for
   government, commercial, and private communications.

   ISAKMP provides the ability to establish SAs for multiple security
   protocols and applications. These protocols and applications may be
   session-oriented or sessionless. Having one SA establishment
   protocol that supports multiple security protocols eliminates the
   need for multiple, nearly identical authentication, key exchange and
   SA establishment protocols when more than one security protocol is in
   use or desired. Just as IP has provided the common networking layer
   for the Internet, a common security establishment protocol is needed
   if security is to become a reality on the Internet. ISAKMP provides
   the common base that allows all other security protocols to
   interoperate.

   ISAKMP follows good security design principles. It is not coupled to
   other insecure transport protocols, therefore it is not vulnerable or
   weakened by attacks on other protocols. Also, when more secure
   transport protocols are developed, ISAKMP can be easily migrated to
   them. ISAKMP also provides protection against protocol related
   attacks. This protection provides the assurance that the SAs and
   keys established are with the desired party and not with an attacker.

ISAKMP also follows good protocol design principles. Protocol
specific information only is in the protocol header, following the
design principles of IPv6. The data transported by the protocol is
separated into functional payloads. As the Internet grows and
evolves, new payloads to support new security functionality can be
added without modifying the entire protocol.

A ISAKMP Security Association Attributes

A.1 Background/Rationale

   As detailed in previous sections, ISAKMP is designed to provide a
   flexible and extensible framework for establishing and managing
   Security Associations and cryptographic keys. The framework provided
   by ISAKMP consists of header and payload definitions, exchange types
   for guiding message and payload exchanges, and general processing
   guidelines. ISAKMP does not define the mechanisms that will be used
   to establish and manage Security Associations and cryptographic keys
   in an authenticated and confidential manner. The definition of
   mechanisms and their application is the purview of individual Domains
   of Interpretation (DOIs).

   This section describes the ISAKMP values for the Internet IP Security
   DOI, supported security protocols, and identification values for
   ISAKMP Phase 1 negotiations. The Internet IP Security DOI is
   MANDATORY to implement for IP Security. [Oakley] and [IKE] describe,
   in detail, the mechanisms and their application for establishing and
   managing Security Associations and cryptographic keys for IP
   Security.

A.2 Internet IP Security DOI Assigned Value

   As described in [IPDOI], the Internet IP Security DOI Assigned Number
   is one (1).

A.3 Supported Security Protocols

   Values for supported security protocols are specified in the most
   recent "Assigned Numbers" RFC [STD-2]. Presented in the following
   table are the values for the security protocols supported by ISAKMP
   for the Internet IP Security DOI.

                     Protocol Assigned Value
                     RESERVED   0
                     ISAKMP   1

   All DOIs MUST reserve ISAKMP with a Protocol-ID of 1. All other
   security protocols within that DOI will be numbered accordingly.

   Security protocol values 2-15359 are reserved to IANA for future use.
   Values 15360-16383 are permanently reserved for private use amongst
   mutually consenting implementations. Such private use values are
   unlikely to be interoperable across different implementations.

A.4 ISAKMP Identification Type Values

   The following table lists the assigned values for the Identification
   Type field found in the Identification payload during a generic Phase
   1 exchange, which is not for a specific protocol.

                          ID Type   Value
                   ID_IPV4_ADDR   0
                   ID_IPV4_ADDR_SUBNET   1
                   ID_IPV6_ADDR   2
                   ID_IPV6_ADDR_SUBNET   3

A.4.1 ID_IPV4_ADDR

   The ID_IPV4_ADDR type specifies a single four (4) octet IPv4 address.

A.4.2 ID_IPV4_ADDR_SUBNET

   The ID_IPV4_ADDR_SUBNET type specifies a range of IPv4 addresses,
   represented by two four (4) octet values. The first value is an IPv4
   address. The second is an IPv4 network mask. Note that ones (1s) in
   the network mask indicate that the corresponding bit in the address
   is fixed, while zeros (0s) indicate a "wildcard" bit.

A.4.3 ID_IPV6_ADDR

   The ID_IPV6_ADDR type specifies a single sixteen (16) octet IPv6
   address.

A.4.4 ID_IPV6_ADDR_SUBNET

   The ID_IPV6_ADDR_SUBNET type specifies a range of IPv6 addresses,
   represented by two sixteen (16) octet values. The first value is an
   IPv6 address. The second is an IPv6 network mask. Note that ones
   (1s) in the network mask indicate that the corresponding bit in the
   address is fixed, while zeros (0s) indicate a "wildcard" bit.

B Defining a new Domain of Interpretation

The Internet DOI may be sufficient to meet the security requirements
of a large portion of the internet community. However, some groups
may have a need to customize some aspect of a DOI, perhaps to add a
different set of cryptographic algorithms, or perhaps because they
want to make their security-relevant decisions based on something
other than a host id or user id. Also, a particular group may have a
need for a new exchange type, for example to support key management
for multicast groups.

This section discusses guidelines for defining a new DOI. The full
specification for the Internet DOI can be found in [IPDOI].

Defining a new DOI is likely to be a time-consuming process. If at
all possible, it is recommended that the designer begin with an
existing DOI and customize only the parts that are unacceptable.

If a designer chooses to start from scratch, the following MUST be
defined:

   o A "situation": the set of information that will be used to
      determine the required security services.

   o The set of security policies that must be supported.

   o A scheme for naming security-relevant information, including
      encryption algorithms, key exchange algorithms, etc.

   o A syntax for the specification of proposed security services,
      attributes, and certificate authorities.

   o The specific formats of the various payload contents.

   o Additional exchange types, if required.

B.1 Situation

The situation is the basis for deciding how to protect a
communications channel. It must contain all of the data that will be
used to determine the types and strengths of protections applied in
an SA. For example, a US Department of Defense DOI would probably use
unpublished algorithms and have additional special attributes to
negotiate. These additional security attributes would be included in
the situation.

B.2 Security Policies

   Security policies define how various types of information must be
   categorized and protected. The DOI must define the set of security
   policies supported, because both parties in a negotiation must trust
   that the other party understands a situation, and will protect
   information appropriately, both in transit and in storage. In a
   corporate setting, for example, both parties in a negotiation must
   agree to the meaning of the term "proprietary information" before
   they can negotiate how to protect it.

   Note that including the required security policies in the DOI only
   specifies that the participating hosts understand and implement those
   policies in a full system context.

B.3 Naming Schemes

   Any DOI must define a consistent way to name cryptographic
   algorithms, certificate authorities, etc. This can usually be done
   by using IANA naming conventions, perhaps with some private
   extensions.

B.4 Syntax for Specifying Security Services

   In addition to simply specifying how to name entities, the DOI must
   also specify the format for complete proposals of how to protect
   traffic under a given situation.

B.5 Payload Specification

   The DOI must specify the format of each of the payload types. For
   several of the payload types, ISAKMP has included fields that would
   have to be present across all DOI (such as a certificate authority in
   the certificate payload, or a key exchange identifier in the key
   exchange payload).

B.6 Defining new Exchange Types

   If the basic exchange types are inadequate to meet the requirements
   within a DOI, a designer can define up to thirteen extra exchange
   types per DOI. The designer creates a new exchange type by choosing
   an unused exchange type value, and defining a sequence of messages
   composed of strings of the ISAKMP payload types.

   Note that any new exchange types must be rigorously analyzed for
   vulnerabilities. Since this is an expensive and imprecise
   undertaking, a new exchange type should only be created when
   absolutely necessary.

Security Considerations

   Cryptographic analysis techniques are improving at a steady pace.
   The continuing improvement in processing power makes once
   computationally prohibitive cryptographic attacks more realistic.
   New cryptographic algorithms and public key generation techniques are
   also being developed at a steady pace. New security services and
   mechanisms are being developed at an accelerated pace. A consistent
   method of choosing from a variety of security services and mechanisms
   and to exchange attributes required by the mechanisms is important to
   security in the complex structure of the Internet. However, a system
   that locks itself into a single cryptographic algorithm, key exchange
   technique, or security mechanism will become increasingly vulnerable
   as time passes.

   UDP is an unreliable datagram protocol and therefore its use in
   ISAKMP introduces a number of security considerations. Since UDP is
   unreliable, but a key management protocol must be reliable, the
   reliability is built into ISAKMP. While ISAKMP utilizes UDP as its
   transport mechanism, it doesn't rely on any UDP information (e.g.
   checksum, length) for its processing.

   Another issue that must be considered in the development of ISAKMP is
   the effect of firewalls on the protocol. Many firewalls filter out
   all UDP packets, making reliance on UDP questionable in certain
   environments.

   A number of very important security considerations are presented in
   [SEC-ARCH]. One bears repeating. Once a private session key is
   created, it must be safely stored. Failure to properly protect the
   private key from access both internal and external to the system
   completely nullifies any protection provided by the IP Security
   services.

IANA Considerations

   This document contains many "magic" numbers to be maintained by the
   IANA. This section explains the criteria to be used by the IANA to
   assign additional numbers in each of these lists.

Domain of Interpretation

   The Domain of Interpretation (DOI) is a 32-bit field which identifies
   the domain under which the security association negotiation is taking
   place. Requests for assignments of new DOIs must be accompanied by a
   standards-track RFC which describes the specific domain.

Supported Security Protocols

   ISAKMP is designed to provide security association negotiation and
   key management for many security protocols. Requests for identifiers
   for additional security protocols must be accompanied by a
   standards-track RFC which describes the security protocol and its
   relationship to ISAKMP.

Acknowledgements

   Dan Harkins, Dave Carrel, and Derrell Piper of Cisco Systems provided
   design assistance with the protocol and coordination for the [IKE]
   and [IPDOI] documents.

   Hilarie Orman, via the Oakley key exchange protocol, has
   significantly influenced the design of ISAKMP.

   Marsha Gross, Bill Kutz, Mike Oehler, Pete Sell, and Ruth Taylor
   provided significant input and review to this document.

   Scott Carlson ported the TIS DNSSEC prototype to FreeBSD for use with
   the ISAKMP prototype.

   Jeff Turner and Steve Smalley contributed to the prototype
   development and integration with ESP and AH.

   Mike Oehler and Pete Sell performed interoperability testing with
   other ISAKMP implementors.

   Thanks to Carl Muckenhirn of SPARTA, Inc. for his assistance with
   LaTeX.

References

   [ANSI]   ANSI, X9.42: Public Key Cryptography for the Financial
              Services Industry - Establishment of Symmetric Algorithm
              Keys Using Diffie-Hellman, Working Draft, April 19, 1996.

   [BC]   Ballardie, A., and J. Crowcroft, Multicast-specific
              Security Threats and Countermeasures, Proceedings of 1995
              ISOC Symposium on Networks & Distributed Systems Security,
              pp. 17-30, Internet Society, San Diego, CA, February 1995.

   [Berge]   Berge, N., "UNINETT PCA Policy Statements", RFC 1875,
              December 1995.

[CW87]   Clark, D.D. and D.R. Wilson, A Comparison of Commercial
           and Military Computer Security Policies, Proceedings of
           the IEEE Symposium on Security & Privacy, Oakland, CA,
           1987, pp. 184-193.

[DNSSEC]   D. Eastlake III, Domain Name System Protocol Security
           Extensions, Work in Progress.

[DOW92]   Diffie, W., M.Wiener, P. Van Oorschot, Authentication and
           Authenticated Key Exchanges, Designs, Codes, and
           Cryptography, 2, 107-125, Kluwer Academic Publishers,
           1992.

[IAB]   Bellovin, S., "Report of the IAB Security Architecture
           Workshop", RFC 2316, April 1998.

[IKE]   Harkins, D., and D. Carrel, "The Internet Key Exchange
           (IKE)", RFC 2409, November 1998.

[IPDOI]   Piper, D., "The Internet IP Security Domain of
           Interpretation for ISAKMP", RFC 2407, November 1998.

[Karn]   Karn, P., and B. Simpson, Photuris: Session Key
           Management Protocol, Work in Progress.

[Kent94]   Steve Kent, IPSEC SMIB, e-mail to ipsec@ans.net, August
           10, 1994.

[Oakley]   Orman, H., "The Oakley Key Determination Protocol", RFC
           2412, November 1998.

[RFC-1422] Kent, S., "Privacy Enhancement for Internet Electronic
           Mail: Part II: Certificate-Based Key Management", RFC
           1422, February 1993.

[RFC-1949] Ballardie, A., "Scalable Multicast Key Distribution", RFC
           1949, May 1996.

[RFC-2093] Harney, H., and C. Muckenhirn, "Group Key Management
           Protocol (GKMP) Specification", RFC 2093, July 1997.

[RFC-2094] Harney, H., and C. Muckenhirn, "Group Key Management
           Protocol (GKMP) Architecture", RFC 2094, July 1997.

[RFC-2119] Bradner, S., "Key Words for use in RFCs to Indicate
           Requirement Levels", BCP 14, RFC 2119, March 1997.

[Schneier] Bruce Schneier, Applied Cryptography - Protocols,
            Algorithms, and Source Code in C (Second Edition), John
            Wiley & Sons, Inc., 1996.

[SEC-ARCH] Atkinson, R., and S. Kent, "Security Architecture for the
            Internet Protocol", RFC 2401, November 1998.

[STD-2]   Reynolds, J., and J. Postel, "Assigned Numbers", STD 2, RFC
            1700, October 1994. See also:
            http://www.iana.org/numbers.html

Authors' Addresses

Douglas Maughan
National Security Agency
ATTN: R23
9800 Savage Road
Ft. Meade, MD. 20755-6000

Phone: 301-688-0847
EMail:wdm@tycho.ncsc.mil

Mark Schneider
National Security Agency
ATTN: R23
9800 Savage Road
Ft. Meade, MD. 20755-6000

Phone: 301-688-0851
EMail:mss@tycho.ncsc.mil

Mark Schertler
Securify, Inc.
2415-B Charleston Road
Mountain View, CA 94043

Phone: 650-934-9303
EMail:mjs@securify.com

Jeff Turner
RABA Technologies, Inc.
10500 Little Patuxent Parkway
Columbia, MD. 21044

Phone: 410-715-9399
EMail:jeff.turner@raba.com

Full Copyright Statement

   Copyright (C) The Internet Society (1998). All Rights Reserved.

   This document and translations of it may be copied and furnished to
   others, and derivative works that comment on or otherwise explain it
   or assist in its implementation may be prepared, copied, published
   and distributed, in whole or in part, without restriction of any
   kind, provided that the above copyright notice and this paragraph are
   included on all such copies and derivative works. However, this
   document itself may not be modified in any way, such as by removing
   the copyright notice or references to the Internet Society or other
   Internet organizations, except as needed for the purpose of
   developing Internet standards in which case the procedures for
   copyrights defined in the Internet Standards process must be
   followed, or as required to translate it into languages other than
   English.

   The limited permissions granted above are perpetual and will not be
   revoked by the Internet Society or its successors or assigns.

   This document and the information contained herein is provided on an
   "AS IS" basis and THE INTERNET SOCIETY AND THE INTERNET ENGINEERING
   TASK FORCE DISCLAIMS ALL WARRANTIES, EXPRESS OR IMPLIED, INCLUDING
   BUT NOT LIMITED TO ANY WARRANTY THAT THE USE OF THE INFORMATION
   HEREIN WILL NOT INFRINGE ANY RIGHTS OR ANY IMPLIED WARRANTIES OF
   MERCHANTABILITY OR FITNESS FOR A PARTICULAR PURPOSE.

Network Working Group   D. Harkins
Request for Comments: 2409   D. Carrel
Category: Standards Track   cisco Systems
                                                         November 1998

The Internet Key Exchange (IKE)

Status of this Memo

   This document specifies an Internet standards track protocol for the
   Internet community, and requests discussion and suggestions for
   improvements. Please refer to the current edition of the "Internet
   Official Protocol Standards" (STD 1) for the standardization state
   and status of this protocol. Distribution of this memo is unlimited.

Copyright Notice

Table Of Contents

1. Abstract

   ISAKMP ([MSST98]) provides a framework for authentication and key
   exchange but does not define them. ISAKMP is designed to be key
   exchange independant; that is, it is designed to support many
   different key exchanges.

   Oakley ([Orm96]) describes a series of key exchanges- called
   "modes"- and details the services provided by each (e.g. perfect
   forward secrecy for keys, identity protection, and authentication).

   SKEME ([SKEME]) describes a versatile key exchange technique which
   provides anonymity, repudiability, and quick key refreshment.

   This document describes a protocol using part of Oakley and part of
   SKEME in conjunction with ISAKMP to obtain authenticated keying
   material for use with ISAKMP, and for other security associations
   such as AH and ESP for the IETF IPsec DOI.

2. Discussion

   This memo describes a hybrid protocol. The purpose is to negotiate,
   and provide authenticated keying material for, security associations
   in a protected manner.

   Processes which implement this memo can be used for negotiating
   virtual private networks (VPNs) and also for providing a remote user
   from a remote site (whose IP address need not be known beforehand)
   access to a secure host or network.

   Client negotiation is supported. Client mode is where the
   negotiating parties are not the endpoints for which security
   association negotiation is taking place. When used in client mode,
   the identities of the end parties remain hidden.

This does not implement the entire Oakley protocol, but only a subset necessary to satisfy its goals. It does not claim conformance or compliance with the entire Oakley protocol nor is it dependant in any way on the Oakley protocol.

Likewise, this does not implement the entire SKEME protocol, but only the method of public key encryption for authentication and its concept of fast re-keying using an exchange of nonces. This protocol is not dependant in any way on the SKEME protocol.

3. Terms and Definitions

3.1 Requirements Terminology

Keywords "MUST", "MUST NOT", "REQUIRED", "SHOULD", "SHOULD NOT" and "MAY" that appear in this document are to be interpreted as described in [Bra97].

3.2 Notation

The following notation is used throughout this memo.

HDR is an ISAKMP header whose exchange type is the mode. When writen as HDR* it indicates payload encryption.

SA is an SA negotiation payload with one or more proposals. An initiator MAY provide multiple proposals for negotiation; a responder MUST reply with only one.

<P>_b indicates the body of payload <P>- the ISAKMP generic vpayload is not included.

SAi_b is the entire body of the SA payload (minus the ISAKMP generic header)- i.e. the DOI, situation, all proposals and all transforms offered by the Initiator.

CKY-I and CKY-R are the Initiator's cookie and the Responder's cookie, respectively, from the ISAKMP header.

g^xi and g^xr are the Diffie-Hellman ([DH]) public values of the initiator and responder respectively.

g^xy is the Diffie-Hellman shared secret.

KE is the key exchange payload which contains the public information exchanged in a Diffie-Hellman exchange. There is no particular encoding (e.g. a TLV) used for the data of a KE payload.

Nx is the nonce payload; x can be: i or r for the ISAKMP initiator and responder respectively.

IDx is the identification payload for "x". x can be: "ii" or "ir" for the ISAKMP initiator and responder respectively during phase one negotiation; or "ui" or "ur" for the user initiator and responder respectively during phase two. The ID payload format for the Internet DOI is defined in [Pip97].

SIG is the signature payload. The data to sign is exchange-specific.

CERT is the certificate payload.

HASH (and any derivitive such as HASH(2) or HASH_I) is the hash payload. The contents of the hash are specific to the authentication method.

prf(key, msg) is the keyed pseudo-random function-- often a keyed hash function-- used to generate a deterministic output that appears pseudo-random. prf's are used both for key derivations and for authentication (i.e. as a keyed MAC). (See [KBC96]).

SKEYID is a string derived from secret material known only to the active players in the exchange.

SKEYID_e is the keying material used by the ISAKMP SA to protect the confidentiality of its messages.

SKEYID_a is the keying material used by the ISAKMP SA to authenticate its messages.

SKEYID_d is the keying material used to derive keys for non-ISAKMP security associations.

<x>y indicates that "x" is encrypted with the key "y".

--> signifies "initiator to responder" communication (requests).

<-- signifies "responder to initiator" communication (replies).

 | signifies concatenation of information-- e.g. X | Y is the concatentation of X with Y.

[x] indicates that x is optional.

Message encryption (when noted by a '*' after the ISAKMP header) MUST begin immediately after the ISAKMP header. When communication is protected, all payloads following the ISAKMP header MUST be encrypted. Encryption keys are generated from SKEYID_e in a manner that is defined for each algorithm.

3.3 Perfect Forward Secrecy

When used in the memo Perfect Forward Secrecy (PFS) refers to the notion that compromise of a single key will permit access to only data protected by a single key. For PFS to exist the key used to protect transmission of data MUST NOT be used to derive any additional keys, and if the key used to protect transmission of data was derived from some other keying material, that material MUST NOT be used to derive any more keys.

Perfect Forward Secrecy for both keys and identities is provided in this protocol. (Sections 5.5 and 8).

3.4 Security Association

A security association (SA) is a set of policy and key(s) used to protect information. The ISAKMP SA is the shared policy and key(s) used by the negotiating peers in this protocol to protect their communication.

4. Introduction

Oakley and SKEME each define a method to establish an authenticated key exchange. This includes payloads construction, the information payloads carry, the order in which they are processed and how they are used.

While Oakley defines "modes", ISAKMP defines "phases". The relationship between the two is very straightforward and IKE presents different exchanges as modes which operate in one of two phases.

Phase 1 is where the two ISAKMP peers establish a secure, authenticated channel with which to communicate. This is called the ISAKMP Security Association (SA). "Main Mode" and "Aggressive Mode" each accomplish a phase 1 exchange. "Main Mode" and "Aggressive Mode" MUST ONLY be used in phase 1.

Phase 2 is where Security Associations are negotiated on behalf of services such as IPsec or any other service which needs key material and/or parameter negotiation. "Quick Mode" accomplishes a phase 2 exchange. "Quick Mode" MUST ONLY be used in phase 2.

"New Group Mode" is not really a phase 1 or phase 2. It follows
phase 1, but serves to establish a new group which can be used in
future negotiations. "New Group Mode" MUST ONLY be used after phase
1.

The ISAKMP SA is bi-directional. That is, once established, either
party may initiate Quick Mode, Informational, and New Group Mode
Exchanges. Per the base ISAKMP document, the ISAKMP SA is identified
by the Initiator's cookie followed by the Responder's cookie- the
role of each party in the phase 1 exchange dictates which cookie is
the Initiator's. The cookie order established by the phase 1 exchange
continues to identify the ISAKMP SA regardless of the direction the
Quick Mode, Informational, or New Group exchange. In other words, the
cookies MUST NOT swap places when the direction of the ISAKMP SA
changes.

With the use of ISAKMP phases, an implementation can accomplish very
fast keying when necessary. A single phase 1 negotiation may be used
for more than one phase 2 negotiation. Additionally a single phase 2
negotiation can request multiple Security Associations. With these
optimizations, an implementation can see less than one round trip per
SA as well as less than one DH exponentiation per SA. "Main Mode"
for phase 1 provides identity protection. When identity protection
is not needed, "Aggressive Mode" can be used to reduce round trips
even further. Developer hints for doing these optimizations are
included below. It should also be noted that using public key
encryption to authenticate an Aggressive Mode exchange will still
provide identity protection.

This protocol does not define its own DOI per se. The ISAKMP SA,
established in phase 1, MAY use the DOI and situation from a non-
ISAKMP service (such as the IETF IPSec DOI [Pip97]). In this case an
implementation MAY choose to restrict use of the ISAKMP SA for
establishment of SAs for services of the same DOI. Alternately, an
ISAKMP SA MAY be established with the value zero in both the DOI and
situation (see [MSST98] for a description of these fields) and in
this case implementations will be free to establish security services
for any defined DOI using this ISAKMP SA. If a DOI of zero is used
for establishment of a phase 1 SA, the syntax of the identity
payloads used in phase 1 is that defined in [MSST98] and not from any
DOI- e.g. [Pip97]- which may further expand the syntax and
semantics of identities.

The following attributes are used by IKE and are negotiated as part
of the ISAKMP Security Association. (These attributes pertain only
to the ISAKMP Security Association and not to any Security
Associations that ISAKMP may be negotiating on behalf of other
services.)

- encryption algorithm

- hash algorithm

- authentication method

- information about a group over which to do Diffie-Hellman.

All of these attributes are mandatory and MUST be negotiated. In addition, it is possible to optionally negotiate a psuedo-random function ("prf"). (There are currently no negotiable pseudo-random functions defined in this document. Private use attribute values can be used for prf negotiation between consenting parties). If a "prf" is not negotiation, the HMAC (see [KBC96]) version of the negotiated hash algorithm is used as a pseudo-random function. Other non-mandatory attributes are described in Appendix A. The selected hash algorithm MUST support both native and HMAC modes.·

The Diffie-Hellman group MUST be either specified using a defined group description (section 6) or by defining all attributes of a group (section 5.6). Group attributes (such as group type or prime-see Appendix A) MUST NOT be offered in conjunction with a previously defined group (either a reserved group description or a private use description that is established after conclusion of a New Group Mode exchange).

IKE implementations MUST support the following attribute values:

- DES [DES] in CBC mode with a weak, and semi-weak, key check (weak and semi-weak keys are referenced in [Sch96] and listed in Appendix A). The key is derived according to Appendix B.

- MD5 [MD5] and SHA [SHA}.

- Authentication via pre-shared keys.

- MODP over default group number one (see below).

In addition, IKE implementations SHOULD support: 3DES for encryption; Tiger ([TIGER]) for hash; the Digital Signature Standard, RSA [RSA] signatures and authentication with RSA public key encryption; and MODP group number 2. IKE implementations MAY support any additional encryption algorithms defined in Appendix A and MAY support ECP and EC2N groups.

The IKE modes described here MUST be implemented whenever the IETF IPsec DOI [Pip97] is implemented. Other DOIs MAY use the modes described here.

5. Exchanges

   There are two basic methods used to establish an authenticated key
   exchange: Main Mode and Aggressive Mode. Each generates authenticated
   keying material from an ephemeral Diffie-Hellman exchange. Main Mode
   MUST be implemented; Aggressive Mode SHOULD be implemented. In
   addition, Quick Mode MUST be implemented as a mechanism to generate
   fresh keying material and negotiate non-ISAKMP security services. In
   addition, New Group Mode SHOULD be implemented as a mechanism to
   define private groups for Diffie-Hellman exchanges. Implementations
   MUST NOT switch exchange types in the middle of an exchange.

   Exchanges conform to standard ISAKMP payload syntax, attribute
   encoding, timeouts and retransmits of messages, and informational
   messages-- e.g a notify response is sent when, for example, a
   proposal is unacceptable, or a signature verification or decryption
   was unsuccessful, etc.

   The SA payload MUST precede all other payloads in a phase 1 exchange.
   Except where otherwise noted, there are no requirements for ISAKMP
   payloads in any message to be in any particular order.

   The Diffie-Hellman public value passed in a KE payload, in either a
   phase 1 or phase 2 exchange, MUST be the length of the negotiated
   Diffie-Hellman group enforced, if necessary, by pre-pending the value
   with zeros.

   The length of nonce payload MUST be between 8 and 256 bytes
   inclusive.

   Main Mode is an instantiation of the ISAKMP Identity Protect
   Exchange: The first two messages negotiate policy; the next two
   exchange Diffie-Hellman public values and ancillary data (e.g.
   nonces) necessary for the exchange; and the last two messages
   authenticate the Diffie-Hellman Exchange. The authentication method
   negotiated as part of the initial ISAKMP exchange influences the
   composition of the payloads but not their purpose. The XCHG for Main
   Mode is ISAKMP Identity Protect.

   Similarly, Aggressive Mode is an instantiation of the ISAKMP
   Aggressive Exchange. The first two messages negotiate policy,
   exchange Diffie-Hellman public values and ancillary data necessary
   for the exchange, and identities. In addition the second message
   authenticates the responder. The third message authenticates the
   initiator and provides a proof of participation in the exchange. The
   XCHG for Aggressive Mode is ISAKMP Aggressive. The final message MAY
   NOT be sent under protection of the ISAKMP SA allowing each party to

postpone exponentiation, if desired, until negotiation of this
exchange is complete. The graphic depictions of Aggressive Mode show
the final payload in the clear; it need not be.

Exchanges in IKE are not open ended and have a fixed number of
messages. Receipt of a Certificate Request payload MUST NOT extend
the number of messages transmitted or expected.

Security Association negotiation is limited with Aggressive Mode. Due
to message construction requirements the group in which the Diffie-
Hellman exchange is performed cannot be negotiated. In addition,
different authentication methods may further constrain attribute
negotiation. For example, authentication with public key encryption
cannot be negotiated and when using the revised method of public key
encryption for authentication the cipher and hash cannot be
negotiated. For situations where the rich attribute negotiation
capabilities of IKE are required Main Mode may be required.

Quick Mode and New Group Mode have no analog in ISAKMP. The XCHG
values for Quick Mode and New Group Mode are defined in Appendix A.

Main Mode, Aggressive Mode, and Quick Mode do security association
negotiation. Security Association offers take the form of Tranform
Payload(s) encapsulated in Proposal Payload(s) encapsulated in
Security Association (SA) payload(s). If multiple offers are being
made for phase 1 exchanges (Main Mode and Aggressive Mode) they MUST
take the form of multiple Transform Payloads for a single Proposal
Payload in a single SA payload. To put it another way, for phase 1
exchanges there MUST NOT be multiple Proposal Payloads for a single
SA payload and there MUST NOT be multiple SA payloads. This document
does not proscribe such behavior on offers in phase 2 exchanges.

There is no limit on the number of offers the initiator may send to
the responder but conformant implementations MAY choose to limit the
number of offers it will inspect for performance reasons.

During security association negotiation, initiators present offers
for potential security associations to responders. Responders MUST
NOT modify attributes of any offer, attribute encoding excepted (see
Appendix A). If the initiator of an exchange notices that attribute
values have changed or attributes have been added or deleted from an
offer made, that response MUST be rejected.

Four different authentication methods are allowed with either Main
Mode or Aggressive Mode- digital signature, two forms of
authentication with public key encryption, or pre-shared key. The
value SKEYID is computed seperately for each authentication method.

```
   For signatures:              SKEYID = prf(Ni_b | Nr_b, g^xy)
   For public key encryption: SKEYID = prf(hash(Ni_b | Nr_b), CKY-I |
CKY-R)
   For pre-shared keys:         SKEYID = prf(pre-shared-key, Ni_b |
Nr_b)
```

The result of either Main Mode or Aggressive Mode is three groups of
authenticated keying material:

```
   SKEYID_d = prf(SKEYID, g^xy | CKY-I | CKY-R | 0)
   SKEYID_a = prf(SKEYID, SKEYID_d | g^xy | CKY-I | CKY-R | 1)
   SKEYID_e = prf(SKEYID, SKEYID_a | g^xy | CKY-I | CKY-R | 2)
```

and agreed upon policy to protect further communications. The values
of 0, 1, and 2 above are represented by a single octet. The key used
for encryption is derived from SKEYID_e in an algorithm-specific
manner (see appendix B).

To authenticate either exchange the initiator of the protocol
generates HASH_I and the responder generates HASH_R where:

```
 HASH_I = prf(SKEYID, g^xi | g^xr | CKY-I | CKY-R | SAi_b | IDii_b )
 HASH_R = prf(SKEYID, g^xr | g^xi | CKY-R | CKY-I | SAi_b | IDir_b )
```

For authentication with digital signatures, HASH_I and HASH_R are
signed and verified; for authentication with either public key
encryption or pre-shared keys, HASH_I and HASH_R directly
authenticate the exchange. The entire ID payload (including ID type,
port, and protocol but excluding the generic header) is hashed into
both HASH_I and HASH_R.

As mentioned above, the negotiated authentication method influences
the content and use of messages for Phase 1 Modes, but not their
intent. When using public keys for authentication, the Phase 1
exchange can be accomplished either by using signatures or by using
public key encryption (if the algorithm supports it). Following are
Phase 1 exchanges with different authentication options.

5.1 IKE Phase 1 Authenticated With Signatures

Using signatures, the ancillary information exchanged during the
second roundtrip are nonces; the exchange is authenticated by signing
a mutually obtainable hash. Main Mode with signature authentication
is described as follows:

```
    Initiator                           Responder
    -----------                         ----------
    HDR, SA                      -->
                                 <--     HDR, SA
    HDR, KE, Ni                  -->
                                 <--     HDR, KE, Nr
    HDR*, IDii, [ CERT, ] SIG_I  -->
                                 <--     HDR*, IDir, [ CERT, ] SIG_R
```

Aggressive mode with signatures in conjunction with ISAKMP is
described as follows:

```
    Initiator                           Responder
    -----------                         ----------
    HDR, SA, KE, Ni, IDii        -->
                                 <--     HDR, SA, KE, Nr, IDir,
                                           [ CERT, ] SIG_R
    HDR, [ CERT, ] SIG_I         -->
```

In both modes, the signed data, SIG_I or SIG_R, is the result of the
negotiated digital signature algorithm applied to HASH_I or HASH_R
respectively.

In general the signature will be over HASH_I and HASH_R as above
using the negotiated prf, or the HMAC version of the negotiated hash
function (if no prf is negotiated). However, this can be overridden
for construction of the signature if the signature algorithm is tied
to a particular hash algorithm (e.g. DSS is only defined with SHA's
160 bit output). In this case, the signature will be over HASH_I and
HASH_R as above, except using the HMAC version of the hash algorithm
associated with the signature method. The negotiated prf and hash
function would continue to be used for all other prescribed pseudo-
random functions.

Since the hash algorithm used is already known there is no need to
encode its OID into the signature. In addition, there is no binding
between the OIDs used for RSA signatures in PKCS #1 and those used in
this document. Therefore, RSA signatures MUST be encoded as a private
key encryption in PKCS #1 format and not as a signature in PKCS #1
format (which includes the OID of the hash algorithm). DSS signatures
MUST be encoded as r followed by s.

One or more certificate payloads MAY be optionally passed.

5.2 Phase 1 Authenticated With Public Key Encryption

   Using public key encryption to authenticate the exchange, the
   ancillary information exchanged is encrypted nonces. Each party's
   ability to reconstruct a hash (proving that the other party decrypted
   the nonce) authenticates the exchange.

   In order to perform the public key encryption, the initiator must
   already have the responder's public key. In the case where the
   responder has multiple public keys, a hash of the certificate the
   initiator is using to encrypt the ancillary information is passed as
   part of the third message. In this way the responder can determine
   which corresponding private key to use to decrypt the encrypted
   payloads and identity protection is retained.

   In addition to the nonce, the identities of the parties (IDii and
   IDir) are also encrypted with the other party's public key. If the
   authentication method is public key encryption, the nonce and
   identity payloads MUST be encrypted with the public key of the other
   party. Only the body of the payloads are encrypted, the payload
   headers are left in the clear.

   When using encryption for authentication, Main Mode is defined as
   follows.

```
         Initiator                        Responder
         -----------                      ----------
         HDR, SA                  -->
                                  <--     HDR, SA
         HDR, KE, [ HASH(1), ]
           <IDii_b>PubKey_r,
             <Ni_b>PubKey_r       -->
                                          HDR, KE, <IDir_b>PubKey_i,
                                  <--            <Nr_b>PubKey_i
         HDR*, HASH_I             -->
                                  <--     HDR*, HASH_R
```

   Aggressive Mode authenticated with encryption is described as
   follows:

```
         Initiator                        Responder
         -----------                      ----------
         HDR, SA, [ HASH(1),] KE,
           <IDii_b>Pubkey_r,
             <Ni_b>Pubkey_r       -->
                                          HDR, SA, KE, <IDir_b>PubKey_i,
                                  <--            <Nr_b>PubKey_i, HASH_R
         HDR, HASH_I              -->
```

Where HASH(1) is a hash (using the negotiated hash function) of the
certificate which the initiator is using to encrypt the nonce and
identity.

RSA encryption MUST be encoded in PKCS #1 format. While only the body
of the ID and nonce payloads is encrypted, the encrypted data must be
preceded by a valid ISAKMP generic header. The payload length is the
length of the entire encrypted payload plus header. The PKCS #1
encoding allows for determination of the actual length of the
cleartext payload upon decryption.

Using encryption for authentication provides for a plausably deniable
exchange. There is no proof (as with a digital signature) that the
conversation ever took place since each party can completely
reconstruct both sides of the exchange. In addition, security is
added to secret generation since an attacker would have to
successfully break not only the Diffie-Hellman exchange but also both
RSA encryptions. This exchange was motivated by [SKEME].

Note that, unlike other authentication methods, authentication with
public key encryption allows for identity protection with Aggressive
Mode.

5.3 Phase 1 Authenticated With a Revised Mode of Public Key Encryption

Authentication with Public Key Encryption has significant advantages
over authentication with signatures (see section 5.2 above).
Unfortunately, this is at the cost of 4 public key operations- two
public key encryptions and two private key decryptions. This
authentication mode retains the advantages of authentication using
public key encryption but does so with half the public key
operations.

In this mode, the nonce is still encrypted using the public key of
the peer, however the peer's identity (and the certificate if it is
sent) is encrypted using the negotiated symmetric encryption
algorithm (from the SA payload) with a key derived from the nonce.
This solution adds minimal complexity and state yet saves two costly
public key operations on each side. In addition, the Key Exchange
payload is also encrypted using the same derived key. This provides
additional protection against cryptanalysis of the Diffie-Hellman
exchange.

As with the public key encryption method of authentication (section
5.2), a HASH payload may be sent to identify a certificate if the
responder has multiple certificates which contain useable public keys
(e.g. if the certificate is not for signatures only, either due to
certificate restrictions or algorithmic restrictions). If the HASH

payload is sent it MUST be the first payload of the second message
exchange and MUST be followed by the encrypted nonce. If the HASH
payload is not sent, the first payload of the second message exchange
MUST be the encrypted nonce. In addition, the initiator my optionally
send a certificate payload to provide the responder with a public key
with which to respond.

When using the revised encryption mode for authentication, Main Mode
is defined as follows.

```
     Initiator                          Responder
     -----------                        -----------
     HDR, SA                     -->
                                 <--    HDR, SA
     HDR, [ HASH(1), ]
       <Ni_b>Pubkey_r,
       <KE_b>Ke_i,
       <IDii_b>Ke_i,
       [<<Cert-I_b>Ke_i]         -->
                                        HDR, <Nr_b>PubKey_i,
                                           <KE_b>Ke_r,
                                 <--       <IDir_b>Ke_r,
     HDR*, HASH_I                -->
                                 <--    HDR*, HASH_R
```

Aggressive Mode authenticated with the revised encryption method is
described as follows:

```
     Initiator                          Responder
     -----------                        -----------
     HDR, SA, [ HASH(1),]
       <Ni_b>Pubkey_r,
       <KE_b>Ke_i, <IDii_b>Ke_i
       [, <Cert-I_b>Ke_i ]       -->
                                        HDR, SA, <Nr_b>PubKey_i,
                                           <KE_b>Ke_r, <IDir_b>Ke_r,
                                 <--       HASH_R
     HDR, HASH_I                 -->
```

where HASH(1) is identical to section 5.2. Ke_i and Ke_r are keys to
the symmetric encryption algorithm negotiated in the SA payload
exchange. Only the body of the payloads are encrypted (in both public
key and symmetric operations), the generic payload headers are left
in the clear. The payload length includes that added to perform
encryption.

The symmetric cipher keys are derived from the decrypted nonces as
follows. First the values Ne_i and Ne_r are computed:

```
Ne_i = prf(Ni_b, CKY-I)
Ne_r = prf(Nr_b, CKY-R)
```

The keys Ke_i and Ke_r are then taken from Ne_i and Ne_r respectively
in the manner described in Appendix B used to derive symmetric keys
for use with the negotiated encryption algorithm. If the length of
the output of the negotiated prf is greater than or equal to the key
length requirements of the cipher, Ke_i and Ke_r are derived from the
most significant bits of Ne_i and Ne_r respectively. If the desired
length of Ke_i and Ke_r exceed the length of the output of the prf
the necessary number of bits is obtained by repeatedly feeding the
results of the prf back into itself and concatenating the result
until the necessary number has been achieved. For example, if the
negotiated encryption algorithm requires 320 bits of key and the
output of the prf is only 128 bits, Ke_i is the most significant 320
bits of K, where

```
K = K1 | K2 | K3 and
K1 = prf(Ne_i, 0)
K2 = prf(Ne_i, K1)
K3 = prf(Ne_i, K2)
```

For brevity, only derivation of Ke_i is shown; Ke_r is identical. The
length of the value 0 in the computation of K1 is a single octet.
Note that Ne_i, Ne_r, Ke_i, and Ke_r are all ephemeral and MUST be
discarded after use.

Save the requirements on the location of the optional HASH payload
and the mandatory nonce payload there are no further payload
requirements. All payloads-- in whatever order-- following the
encrypted nonce MUST be encrypted with Ke_i or Ke_r depending on the
direction.

If CBC mode is used for the symmetric encryption then the
initialization vectors (IVs) are set as follows. The IV for
encrypting the first payload following the nonce is set to 0 (zero).
The IV for subsequent payloads encrypted with the ephemeral symmetric
cipher key, Ke_i, is the last ciphertext block of the previous
payload. Encrypted payloads are padded up to the nearest block size.
All padding bytes, except for the last one, contain 0x00. The last
byte of the padding contains the number of the padding bytes used,
excluding the last one. Note that this means there will always be
padding.

5.4 Phase 1 Authenticated With a Pre-Shared Key

    A key derived by some out-of-band mechanism may also be used to
    authenticate the exchange. The actual establishment of this key is
    out of the scope of this document.

    When doing a pre-shared key authentication, Main Mode is defined as
    follows:

```
                Initiator                        Responder
                ----------                       ----------
                HDR, SA                -->
                                       <--      HDR, SA
                HDR, KE, Ni            -->
                                       <--      HDR, KE, Nr
                HDR*, IDii, HASH_I     -->
                                       <--      HDR*, IDir, HASH_R
```

    Aggressive mode with a pre-shared key is described as follows:

```
                Initiator                        Responder
                ----------                       ----------
                HDR, SA, KE, Ni, IDii -->
                                       <--      HDR, SA, KE, Nr, IDir, HASH_R
                HDR, HASH_I            -->
```

    When using pre-shared key authentication with Main Mode the key can
    only be identified by the IP address of the peers since HASH_I must
    be computed before the initiator has processed IDir. Aggressive Mode
    allows for a wider range of identifiers of the pre-shared secret to
    be used. In addition, Aggressive Mode allows two parties to maintain
    multiple, different pre-shared keys and identify the correct one for
    a particular exchange.

5.5 Phase 2 - Quick Mode

    Quick Mode is not a complete exchange itself (in that it is bound to
    a phase 1 exchange), but is used as part of the SA negotiation
    process (phase 2) to derive keying material and negotiate shared
    policy for non-ISAKMP SAs. The information exchanged along with Quick
    Mode MUST be protected by the ISAKMP SA-- i.e. all payloads except
    the ISAKMP header are encrypted. In Quick Mode, a HASH payload MUST
    immediately follow the ISAKMP header and a SA payload MUST
    immediately follow the HASH. This HASH authenticates the message and
    also provides liveliness proofs.

The message ID in the ISAKMP header identifies a Quick Mode in progress for a particular ISAKMP SA which itself is identified by the cookies in the ISAKMP header. Since each instance of a Quick Mode uses a unique initialization vector (see Appendix B) it is possible to have multiple simultaneous Quick Modes, based off a single ISAKMP SA, in progress at any one time.

Quick Mode is essentially a SA negotiation and an exchange of nonces that provides replay protection. The nonces are used to generate fresh key material and prevent replay attacks from generating bogus security associations. An optional Key Exchange payload can be exchanged to allow for an additional Diffie-Hellman exchange and exponentiation per Quick Mode. While use of the key exchange payload with Quick Mode is optional it MUST be supported.

Base Quick Mode (without the KE payload) refreshes the keying material derived from the exponentiation in phase 1. This does not provide PFS. Using the optional KE payload, an additional exponentiation is performed and PFS is provided for the keying material.

The identities of the SAs negotiated in Quick Mode are implicitly assumed to be the IP addresses of the ISAKMP peers, without any implied constraints on the protocol or port numbers allowed, unless client identifiers are specified in Quick Mode. If ISAKMP is acting as a client negotiator on behalf of another party, the identities of the parties MUST be passed as IDci and then IDcr. Local policy will dictate whether the proposals are acceptable for the identities specified. If the client identities are not acceptable to the Quick Mode responder (due to policy or other reasons), a Notify payload with Notify Message Type INVALID-ID-INFORMATION (18) SHOULD be sent.

The client identities are used to identify and direct traffic to the appropriate tunnel in cases where multiple tunnels exist between two peers and also to allow for unique and shared SAs with different granularities.

All offers made during a Quick Mode are logically related and must be consistant. For example, if a KE payload is sent, the attribute describing the Diffie-Hellman group (see section 6.1 and [Pip97]) MUST be included in every transform of every proposal of every SA being negotiated. Similarly, if client identities are used, they MUST apply to every SA in the negotiation.

Quick Mode is defined as follows:

```
        Initiator                        Responder
        -----------                      -----------
        HDR*, HASH(1), SA, Ni
          [, KE ] [, IDci, IDcr ] -->
                                    <--   HDR*, HASH(2), SA, Nr
                                                [, KE ] [, IDci, IDcr ]
        HDR*, HASH(3)               -->
```

Where:
HASH(1) is the prf over the message id (M-ID) from the ISAKMP header
concatenated with the entire message that follows the hash including
all payload headers, but excluding any padding added for encryption.
HASH(2) is identical to HASH(1) except the initiator's nonce-- Ni,
minus the payload header-- is added after M-ID but before the
complete message. The addition of the nonce to HASH(2) is for a
liveliness proof. HASH(3)-- for liveliness-- is the prf over the
value zero represented as a single octet, followed by a concatenation
of the message id and the two nonces-- the initiator's followed by
the responder's-- minus the payload header. In other words, the
hashes for the above exchange are:

```
HASH(1) = prf(SKEYID_a, M-ID | SA | Ni [ | KE ] [ | IDci | IDcr )
HASH(2) = prf(SKEYID_a, M-ID | Ni_b | SA | Nr [ | KE ] [ | IDci |
IDcr )
HASH(3) = prf(SKEYID_a, 0 | M-ID | Ni_b | Nr_b)
```

With the exception of the HASH, SA, and the optional ID payloads,
there are no payload ordering restrictions on Quick Mode. HASH(1) and
HASH(2) may differ from the illustration above if the order of
payloads in the message differs from the illustrative example or if
any optional payloads, for example a notify payload, have been
chained to the message.

If PFS is not needed, and KE payloads are not exchanged, the new
keying material is defined as

    KEYMAT = prf(SKEYID_d, protocol | SPI | Ni_b | Nr_b).

If PFS is desired and KE payloads were exchanged, the new keying
material is defined as

    KEYMAT = prf(SKEYID_d, g(qm)^xy | protocol | SPI | Ni_b | Nr_b)

where g(qm)^xy is the shared secret from the ephemeral Diffie-Hellman
exchange of this Quick Mode.

In either case, "protocol" and "SPI" are from the ISAKMP Proposal
Payload that contained the negotiated Transform.

A single SA negotiation results in two security assocations-- one
inbound and one outbound. Different SPIs for each SA (one chosen by
the initiator, the other by the responder) guarantee a different key
for each direction. The SPI chosen by the destination of the SA is
used to derive KEYMAT for that SA.

For situations where the amount of keying material desired is greater
than that supplied by the prf, KEYMAT is expanded by feeding the
results of the prf back into itself and concatenating results until
the required keying material has been reached. In other words,

```
KEYMAT = K1 | K2 | K3 | ...
where
  K1 = prf(SKEYID_d, [ g(qm)^xy | ] protocol | SPI | Ni_b | Nr_b)
  K2 = prf(SKEYID_d, K1 | [ g(qm)^xy | ] protocol | SPI | Ni_b |
  Nr_b)
  K3 = prf(SKEYID_d, K2 | [ g(qm)^xy | ] protocol | SPI | Ni_b |
  Nr_b)
  etc.
```

This keying material (whether with PFS or without, and whether
derived directly or through concatenation) MUST be used with the
negotiated SA. It is up to the service to define how keys are derived
from the keying material.

In the case of an ephemeral Diffie-Hellman exchange in Quick Mode,
the exponential (g(qm)^xy) is irretrievably removed from the current
state and SKEYID_e and SKEYID_a (derived from phase 1 negotiation)
continue to protect and authenticate the ISAKMP SA and SKEYID_d
continues to be used to derive keys.

Using Quick Mode, multiple SA's and keys can be negotiated with one
exchange as follows:

```
    Initiator                       Responder
    -----------                     -----------
    HDR*, HASH(1), SA0, SA1, Ni,
      [, KE ] [, IDci, IDcr ] -->
                                <--  HDR*, HASH(2), SA0, SA1, Nr,
                                       [, KE ] [, IDci, IDcr ]
    HDR*, HASH(3)              -->
```

The keying material is derived identically as in the case of a single
SA. In this case (negotiation of two SA payloads) the result would be
four security associations-- two each way for both SAs.

5.6 New Group Mode

New Group Mode MUST NOT be used prior to establishment of an ISAKMP
SA. The description of a new group MUST only follow phase 1
negotiation. (It is not a phase 2 exchange, though).

```
    Initiator                        Responder
    -----------                      -----------
    HDR*, HASH(1), SA        -->
                             <--      HDR*, HASH(2), SA
```

where HASH(1) is the prf output, using SKEYID_a as the key, and the
message-ID from the ISAKMP header concatenated with the entire SA
proposal, body and header, as the data; HASH(2) is the prf output,
using SKEYID_a as the key, and the message-ID from the ISAKMP header
concatenated with the reply as the data. In other words the hashes
for the above exchange are:

```
    HASH(1) = prf(SKEYID_a, M-ID | SA)
    HASH(2) = prf(SKEYID_a, M-ID | SA)
```

The proposal will specify the characteristics of the group (see
appendix A, "Attribute Assigned Numbers"). Group descriptions for
private Groups MUST be greater than or equal to 2^{15}. If the group
is not acceptable, the responder MUST reply with a Notify payload
with the message type set to ATTRIBUTES-NOT-SUPPORTED (13).

ISAKMP implementations MAY require private groups to expire with the
SA under which they were established.

Groups may be directly negotiated in the SA proposal with Main Mode.
To do this the component parts-- for a MODP group, the type, prime
and generator; for a EC2N group the type, the Irreducible Polynomial,
Group Generator One, Group Generator Two, Group Curve A, Group Curve
B and Group Order-- are passed as SA attributes (see Appendix A).
Alternately, the nature of the group can be hidden using New Group
Mode and only the group identifier is passed in the clear during
phase 1 negotiation.

5.7 ISAKMP Informational Exchanges

This protocol protects ISAKMP Informational Exchanges when possible.
Once the ISAKMP security association has been established (and
SKEYID_e and SKEYID_a have been generated) ISAKMP Information
Exchanges, when used with this protocol, are as follows:

```
   Initiator                          Responder
   -----------                        -----------
   HDR*, HASH(1), N/D        -->
```

where N/D is either an ISAKMP Notify Payload or an ISAKMP Delete
Payload and HASH(1) is the prf output, using SKEYID_a as the key, and
a M-ID unique to this exchange concatenated with the entire
informational payload (either a Notify or Delete) as the data. In
other words, the hash for the above exchange is:

    HASH(1) = prf(SKEYID_a, M-ID | N/D)

As noted the message ID in the ISAKMP header-- and used in the prf
computation-- is unique to this exchange and MUST NOT be the same as
the message ID of another phase 2 exchange which generated this
informational exchange. The derivation of the initialization vector,
used with SKEYID_e to encrypt this message, is described in Appendix
B.

If the ISAKMP security association has not yet been established at
the time of the Informational Exchange, the exchange is done in the
clear without an accompanying HASH payload.

6 Oakley Groups

With IKE, the group in which to do the Diffie-Hellman exchange is
negotiated. Four groups-- values 1 through 4-- are defined below.
These groups originated with the Oakley protocol and are therefore
called "Oakley Groups". The attribute class for "Group" is defined in
Appendix A. All values 2^{15} and higher are used for private group
identifiers. For a discussion on the strength of the default Oakley
groups please see the Security Considerations section below.

These groups were all generated by Richard Schroeppel at the
University of Arizona. Properties of these groups are described in
[Orm96].

6.1 First Oakley Default Group

Oakley implementations MUST support a MODP group with the following
prime and generator. This group is assigned id 1 (one).

    The prime is: $2^{768} - 2^{704} - 1 + 2^{64} * \{ [2^{638} pi] + 149686 \}$
    Its hexadecimal value is

```
        FFFFFFFF FFFFFFFF C90FDAA2 2168C234 C4C6628B 80DC1CD1
        29024E08 8A67CC74 020BBEA6 3B139B22 514A0879 8E3404DD
        EF9519B3 CD3A431B 302B0A6D F25F1437 4FE1356D 6D51C245
        E485B576 625E7EC6 F44C42E9 A63A3620 FFFFFFFF FFFFFFFF
```

    The generator is: 2.

6.2 Second Oakley Group

   IKE implementations SHOULD support a MODP group with the following
   prime and generator. This group is assigned id 2 (two).

   The prime is 2^1024 - 2^960 - 1 + 2^64 * { [2^894 pi] + 129093 }.
   Its hexadecimal value is

```
        FFFFFFFF FFFFFFFF C90FDAA2 2168C234 C4C6628B 80DC1CD1
        29024E08 8A67CC74 020BBEA6 3B139B22 514A0879 8E3404DD
        EF9519B3 CD3A431B 302B0A6D F25F1437 4FE1356D 6D51C245
        E485B576 625E7EC6 F44C42E9 A637ED6B 0BFF5CB6 F406B7ED
        EE386BFB 5A899FA5 AE9F2411 7C4B1FE6 49286651 ECE65381
        FFFFFFFF FFFFFFFF
```

   The generator is 2 (decimal)

6.3 Third Oakley Group

   IKE implementations SHOULD support a EC2N group with the following
   characteristics. This group is assigned id 3 (three). The curve is
   based on the Galois Field GF[2^155]. The field size is 155. The
   irreducible polynomial for the field is:
        u^155 + u^62 + 1.
   The equation for the elliptic curve is:
        y^2 + xy = x^3 + ax^2 + b.

   Field Size: 155
   Group Prime/Irreducible Polynomial:
                  0x0800000000000000000000004000000000000001
   Group Generator One: 0x7b
   Group Curve A: 0x0
   Group Curve B: 0x07338f

   Group Order: 0X080000000000000000000057db5698537193aef944

   The data in the KE payload when using this group is the value x from
   the solution (x,y), the point on the curve chosen by taking the
   randomly chosen secret Ka and computing Ka*P, where * is the
   repetition of the group addition and double operations, P is the
   curve point with x coordinate equal to generator 1 and the y

coordinate determined from the defining equation. The equation of
curve is implicitly known by the Group Type and the A and B
coefficients. There are two possible values for the y coordinate;
either one can be used successfully (the two parties need not agree
on the selection).

6.4 Fourth Oakley Group

IKE implementations SHOULD support a EC2N group with the following
characteristics. This group is assigned id 4 (four). The curve is
based on the Galois Field GF[2^185]. The field size is 185. The
irreducible polynomial for the field is:
        u^185 + u^69 + 1. The
equation for the elliptic curve is:
        y^2 + xy = x^3 + ax^2 + b.

Field Size: 185
Group Prime/Irreducible Polynomial:
                0x020000000000000000000000000000000200000000000000001
Group Generator One: 0x18
Group Curve A: 0x0
Group Curve B: 0x1ee9

Group Order: 0X01ffffffffffffffffffffffffdbf2f889b73e484175f94ebc

The data in the KE payload when using this group will be identical to
that as when using Oakley Group 3 (three).

Other groups can be defined using New Group Mode. These default
groups were generated by Richard Schroeppel at the University of
Arizona. Properties of these primes are described in [Orm96].

7. Payload Explosion for a Complete IKE Exchange

This section illustrates how the IKE protocol is used to:

   - establish a secure and authenticated channel between ISAKMP
   processes (phase 1); and

   - generate key material for, and negotiate, an IPsec SA (phase 2).

7.1 Phase 1 using Main Mode

The following diagram illustrates the payloads exchanged between the
two parties in the first round trip exchange. The initiator MAY
propose several proposals; the responder MUST reply with one.

```
 0 1 2 3 4 5 6 7 8 9 0 1 2 3 4 5 6 7 8 9 0 1 2 3 4 5 6 7 8 9 0 1
+-+-+-+-+-+-+-+-+-+-+-+-+-+-+-+-+-+-+-+-+-+-+-+-+-+-+-+-+-+-+-+-+
~           ISAKMP Header with XCHG of Main Mode,              ~
~               and Next Payload of ISA_SA                     ~
+-+-+-+-+-+-+-+-+-+-+-+-+-+-+-+-+-+-+-+-+-+-+-+-+-+-+-+-+-+-+-+-+
!     0       !    RESERVED    !        Payload Length          !
+-+-+-+-+-+-+-+-+-+-+-+-+-+-+-+-+-+-+-+-+-+-+-+-+-+-+-+-+-+-+-+-+
!                   Domain of Interpretation                   !
+-+-+-+-+-+-+-+-+-+-+-+-+-+-+-+-+-+-+-+-+-+-+-+-+-+-+-+-+-+-+-+-+
!                          Situation                           !
+-+-+-+-+-+-+-+-+-+-+-+-+-+-+-+-+-+-+-+-+-+-+-+-+-+-+-+-+-+-+-+-+
!     0       !    RESERVED    !        Payload Length          !
+-+-+-+-+-+-+-+-+-+-+-+-+-+-+-+-+-+-+-+-+-+-+-+-+-+-+-+-+-+-+-+-+
! Proposal #1 !  PROTO_ISAKMP  ! SPI size = 0  | # Transforms   !
+-+-+-+-+-+-+-+-+-+-+-+-+-+-+-+-+-+-+-+-+-+-+-+-+-+-+-+-+-+-+-+-+
!   ISA_TRANS !    RESERVED    !        Payload Length          !
+-+-+-+-+-+-+-+-+-+-+-+-+-+-+-+-+-+-+-+-+-+-+-+-+-+-+-+-+-+-+-+-+
! Transform #1 !  KEY_OAKLEY   |            RESERVED2           !
+-+-+-+-+-+-+-+-+-+-+-+-+-+-+-+-+-+-+-+-+-+-+-+-+-+-+-+-+-+-+-+-+
~                    prefered SA attributes                    ~
+-+-+-+-+-+-+-+-+-+-+-+-+-+-+-+-+-+-+-+-+-+-+-+-+-+-+-+-+-+-+-+-+
!     0       !    RESERVED    !        Payload Length          !
+-+-+-+-+-+-+-+-+-+-+-+-+-+-+-+-+-+-+-+-+-+-+-+-+-+-+-+-+-+-+-+-+
! Transform #2 !  KEY_OAKLEY   |            RESERVED2           !
+-+-+-+-+-+-+-+-+-+-+-+-+-+-+-+-+-+-+-+-+-+-+-+-+-+-+-+-+-+-+-+-+
~                   alternate SA attributes                    ~
+-+-+-+-+-+-+-+-+-+-+-+-+-+-+-+-+-+-+-+-+-+-+-+-+-+-+-+-+-+-+-+-+
```

The responder replies in kind but selects, and returns, one transform
proposal (the ISAKMP SA attributes).

The second exchange consists of the following payloads:

```
 0 1 2 3 4 5 6 7 8 9 0 1 2 3 4 5 6 7 8 9 0 1 2 3 4 5 6 7 8 9 0 1
+-+-+-+-+-+-+-+-+-+-+-+-+-+-+-+-+-+-+-+-+-+-+-+-+-+-+-+-+-+-+-+-+
~           ISAKMP Header with XCHG of Main Mode,              ~
~               and Next Payload of ISA_KE                     ~
+-+-+-+-+-+-+-+-+-+-+-+-+-+-+-+-+-+-+-+-+-+-+-+-+-+-+-+-+-+-+-+-+
!   ISA_NONCE !    RESERVED    !        Payload Length          !
+-+-+-+-+-+-+-+-+-+-+-+-+-+-+-+-+-+-+-+-+-+-+-+-+-+-+-+-+-+-+-+-+
~   D-H Public Value (g^xi from initiator g^xr from responder) ~
+-+-+-+-+-+-+-+-+-+-+-+-+-+-+-+-+-+-+-+-+-+-+-+-+-+-+-+-+-+-+-+-+
!     0       !    RESERVED    !        Payload Length          !
+-+-+-+-+-+-+-+-+-+-+-+-+-+-+-+-+-+-+-+-+-+-+-+-+-+-+-+-+-+-+-+-+
~          Ni (from initiator) or  Nr (from responder)         ~
+-+-+-+-+-+-+-+-+-+-+-+-+-+-+-+-+-+-+-+-+-+-+-+-+-+-+-+-+-+-+-+-+
```

The shared keys, SKEYID_e and SKEYID_a, are now used to protect and
authenticate all further communication. Note that both SKEYID_e and
SKEYID_a are unauthenticated.

```
 0 1 2 3 4 5 6 7 8 9 0 1 2 3 4 5 6 7 8 9 0 1 2 3 4 5 6 7 8 9 0 1
+-+-+-+-+-+-+-+-+-+-+-+-+-+-+-+-+-+-+-+-+-+-+-+-+-+-+-+-+-+-+-+-+
~             ISAKMP Header with XCHG of Main Mode,             ~
~     and Next Payload of ISA_ID and the encryption bit set    ~
+-+-+-+-+-+-+-+-+-+-+-+-+-+-+-+-+-+-+-+-+-+-+-+-+-+-+-+-+-+-+-+-+
!    ISA_SIG   !   RESERVED   !          Payload Length         !
+-+-+-+-+-+-+-+-+-+-+-+-+-+-+-+-+-+-+-+-+-+-+-+-+-+-+-+-+-+-+-+-+
~         Identification Data of the ISAKMP negotiator         ~
+-+-+-+-+-+-+-+-+-+-+-+-+-+-+-+-+-+-+-+-+-+-+-+-+-+-+-+-+-+-+-+-+
!      0      !   RESERVED   !          Payload Length          !
+-+-+-+-+-+-+-+-+-+-+-+-+-+-+-+-+-+-+-+-+-+-+-+-+-+-+-+-+-+-+-+-+
~       signature verified by the public key of the ID above   ~
+-+-+-+-+-+-+-+-+-+-+-+-+-+-+-+-+-+-+-+-+-+-+-+-+-+-+-+-+-+-+-+-+
```

The key exchange is authenticated over a signed hash as described in
section 5.1. Once the signature has been verified using the
authentication algorithm negotiated as part of the ISAKMP SA, the
shared keys, SKEYID_e and SKEYID_a can be marked as authenticated.
(For brevity, certificate payloads were not exchanged).

7.2 Phase 2 using Quick Mode

The following payloads are exchanged in the first round of Quick Mode
with ISAKMP SA negotiation. In this hypothetical exchange, the ISAKMP
negotiators are proxies for other parties which have requested
authentication.

```
 0 1 2 3 4 5 6 7 8 9 0 1 2 3 4 5 6 7 8 9 0 1 2 3 4 5 6 7 8 9 0 1
+-+-+-+-+-+-+-+-+-+-+-+-+-+-+-+-+-+-+-+-+-+-+-+-+-+-+-+-+-+-+-+-+
~            ISAKMP Header with XCHG of Quick Mode,            ~
~    Next Payload of ISA_HASH and the encryption bit set       ~
+-+-+-+-+-+-+-+-+-+-+-+-+-+-+-+-+-+-+-+-+-+-+-+-+-+-+-+-+-+-+-+-+
!     ISA_SA   !   RESERVED   !          Payload Length         !
+-+-+-+-+-+-+-+-+-+-+-+-+-+-+-+-+-+-+-+-+-+-+-+-+-+-+-+-+-+-+-+-+
~                    keyed hash of message                     ~
+-+-+-+-+-+-+-+-+-+-+-+-+-+-+-+-+-+-+-+-+-+-+-+-+-+-+-+-+-+-+-+-+
!  ISA_NONCE   !   RESERVED   !          Payload Length         !
+-+-+-+-+-+-+-+-+-+-+-+-+-+-+-+-+-+-+-+-+-+-+-+-+-+-+-+-+-+-+-+-+
!                    Domain Of Interpretation                  !
+-+-+-+-+-+-+-+-+-+-+-+-+-+-+-+-+-+-+-+-+-+-+-+-+-+-+-+-+-+-+-+-+
!                           Situation                          !
+-+-+-+-+-+-+-+-+-+-+-+-+-+-+-+-+-+-+-+-+-+-+-+-+-+-+-+-+-+-+-+-+
!      0      !   RESERVED   !          Payload Length          !
+-+-+-+-+-+-+-+-+-+-+-+-+-+-+-+-+-+-+-+-+-+-+-+-+-+-+-+-+-+-+-+-+
```

```
        !  Proposal #1  ! PROTO_IPSEC_AH! SPI size = 4  | # Transforms  !
        +-+-+-+-+-+-+-+-+-+-+-+-+-+-+-+-+-+-+-+-+-+-+-+-+-+-+-+-+-+-+-+-+
        ~                     SPI (4 octets)                            ~
        +-+-+-+-+-+-+-+-+-+-+-+-+-+-+-+-+-+-+-+-+-+-+-+-+-+-+-+-+-+-+-+-+
        !  ISA_TRANS  !   RESERVED   !        Payload Length           !
        +-+-+-+-+-+-+-+-+-+-+-+-+-+-+-+-+-+-+-+-+-+-+-+-+-+-+-+-+-+-+-+-+
        ! Transform #1 !    AH_SHA    |            RESERVED2            !
        +-+-+-+-+-+-+-+-+-+-+-+-+-+-+-+-+-+-+-+-+-+-+-+-+-+-+-+-+-+-+-+-+
        !                    other SA attributes                       !
        +-+-+-+-+-+-+-+-+-+-+-+-+-+-+-+-+-+-+-+-+-+-+-+-+-+-+-+-+-+-+-+-+
        !     0     !    RESERVED    !        Payload Length           !
        +-+-+-+-+-+-+-+-+-+-+-+-+-+-+-+-+-+-+-+-+-+-+-+-+-+-+-+-+-+-+-+-+
        ! Transform #2 !    AH_MD5    |            RESERVED2            !
        +-+-+-+-+-+-+-+-+-+-+-+-+-+-+-+-+-+-+-+-+-+-+-+-+-+-+-+-+-+-+-+-+
        !                    other SA attributes                       !
        +-+-+-+-+-+-+-+-+-+-+-+-+-+-+-+-+-+-+-+-+-+-+-+-+-+-+-+-+-+-+-+-+
        !  ISA_ID   !    RESERVED   !        Payload Length            !
        +-+-+-+-+-+-+-+-+-+-+-+-+-+-+-+-+-+-+-+-+-+-+-+-+-+-+-+-+-+-+-+-+
        ~                         nonce                                ~
        +-+-+-+-+-+-+-+-+-+-+-+-+-+-+-+-+-+-+-+-+-+-+-+-+-+-+-+-+-+-+-+-+
        !  ISA_ID   !    RESERVED   !        Payload Length            !
        +-+-+-+-+-+-+-+-+-+-+-+-+-+-+-+-+-+-+-+-+-+-+-+-+-+-+-+-+-+-+-+-+
        ~           ID of source for which ISAKMP is a client          ~
        +-+-+-+-+-+-+-+-+-+-+-+-+-+-+-+-+-+-+-+-+-+-+-+-+-+-+-+-+-+-+-+-+
        !     0     !    RESERVED   !        Payload Length            !
        +-+-+-+-+-+-+-+-+-+-+-+-+-+-+-+-+-+-+-+-+-+-+-+-+-+-+-+-+-+-+-+-+
        ~        ID of destination for which ISAKMP is a client        ~
        +-+-+-+-+-+-+-+-+-+-+-+-+-+-+-+-+-+-+-+-+-+-+-+-+-+-+-+-+-+-+-+-+
```

where the contents of the hash are described in 5.5 above. The
responder replies with a similar message which only contains one
transform- the selected AH transform. Upon receipt, the initiator
can provide the key engine with the negotiated security association
and the keying material. As a check against replay attacks, the
responder waits until receipt of the next message.

```
         0 1 2 3 4 5 6 7 8 9 0 1 2 3 4 5 6 7 8 9 0 1 2 3 4 5 6 7 8 9 0 1
        +-+-+-+-+-+-+-+-+-+-+-+-+-+-+-+-+-+-+-+-+-+-+-+-+-+-+-+-+-+-+-+-+
        ~           ISAKMP Header with XCHG of Quick Mode,             ~
        ~    Next Payload of ISA_HASH and the encryption bit set       ~
        +-+-+-+-+-+-+-+-+-+-+-+-+-+-+-+-+-+-+-+-+-+-+-+-+-+-+-+-+-+-+-+-+
        !     0     !    RESERVED    !        Payload Length           !
        +-+-+-+-+-+-+-+-+-+-+-+-+-+-+-+-+-+-+-+-+-+-+-+-+-+-+-+-+-+-+-+-+
        ~                         hash data                            ~
        +-+-+-+-+-+-+-+-+-+-+-+-+-+-+-+-+-+-+-+-+-+-+-+-+-+-+-+-+-+-+-+-+
```

where the contents of the hash are described in 5.5 above.

8. Perfect Forward Secrecy Example

   This protocol can provide PFS of both keys and identities. The
   identies of both the ISAKMP negotiating peer and, if applicable, the
   identies for whom the peers are negotiating can be protected with
   PFS.

   To provide Perfect Forward Secrecy of both keys and all identities,
   two parties would perform the following:

        o A Main Mode Exchange to protect the identities of the ISAKMP
          peers.
          This establishes an ISAKMP SA.
        o A Quick Mode Exchange to negotiate other security protocol
          protection.
          This establishes a SA on each end for this protocol.
        o Delete the ISAKMP SA and its associated state.

   Since the key for use in the non-ISAKMP SA was derived from the
   single ephemeral Diffie-Hellman exchange PFS is preserved.

   To provide Perfect Forward Secrecy of merely the keys of a non-ISAKMP
   security association, it in not necessary to do a phase 1 exchange if
   an ISAKMP SA exists between the two peers. A single Quick Mode in
   which the optional KE payload is passed, and an additional Diffie-
   Hellman exchange is performed, is all that is required. At this point
   the state derived from this Quick Mode must be deleted from the
   ISAKMP SA as described in section 5.5.

9. Implementation Hints

   Using a single ISAKMP Phase 1 negotiation makes subsequent Phase 2
   negotiations extremely quick. As long as the Phase 1 state remains
   cached, and PFS is not needed, Phase 2 can proceed without any
   exponentiation. How many Phase 2 negotiations can be performed for a
   single Phase 1 is a local policy issue. The decision will depend on
   the strength of the algorithms being used and level of trust in the
   peer system.

   An implementation may wish to negotiate a range of SAs when
   performing Quick Mode. By doing this they can speed up the "re-
   keying". Quick Mode defines how KEYMAT is defined for a range of SAs.
   When one peer feels it is time to change SAs they simply use the next
   one within the stated range. A range of SAs can be established by
   negotiating multiple SAs (identical attributes, different SPIs) with
   one Quick Mode.

An optimization that is often useful is to establish Security Associations with peers before they are needed so that when they become needed they are already in place. This ensures there would be no delays due to key management before initial data transmission. This optimization is easily implemented by setting up more than one Security Association with a peer for each requested Security Association and caching those not immediately used.

Also, if an ISAKMP implementation is alerted that a SA will soon be needed (e.g. to replace an existing SA that will expire in the near future), then it can establish the new SA before that new SA is needed.

The base ISAKMP specification describes conditions in which one party of the protocol may inform the other party of some activity- either deletion of a security association or in response to some error in the protocol such as a signature verification failed or a payload failed to decrypt. It is strongly suggested that these Informational exchanges not be responded to under any circumstances. Such a condition may result in a "notify war" in which failure to understand a message results in a notify to the peer who cannot understand it and sends his own notify back which is also not understood.

10. Security Considerations

This entire memo discusses a hybrid protocol, combining parts of Oakley and parts of SKEME with ISAKMP, to negotiate, and derive keying material for, security associations in a secure and authenticated manner.

Confidentiality is assured by the use of a negotiated encryption algorithm. Authentication is assured by the use of a negotiated method: a digital signature algorithm; a public key algorithm which supports encryption; or, a pre-shared key. The confidentiality and authentication of this exchange is only as good as the attributes negotiated as part of the ISAKMP security association.

Repeated re-keying using Quick Mode can consume the entropy of the Diffie-Hellman shared secret. Implementors should take note of this fact and set a limit on Quick Mode Exchanges between exponentiations. This memo does not prescribe such a limit.

Perfect Forward Secrecy (PFS) of both keying material and identities is possible with this protocol. By specifying a Diffie-Hellman group, and passing public values in KE payloads, ISAKMP peers can establish PFS of keys- the identities would be protected by SKEYID_e from the ISAKMP SA and would therefore not be protected by PFS. If PFS of both keying material and identities is desired, an ISAKMP peer MUST

establish only one non-ISAKMP security association (e.g. IPsec
Security Association) per ISAKMP SA. PFS for keys and identities is
accomplished by deleting the ISAKMP SA (and optionally issuing a
DELETE message) upon establishment of the single non-ISAKMP SA. In
this way a phase one negotiation is uniquely tied to a single phase
two negotiation, and the ISAKMP SA established during phase one
negotiation is never used again.

The strength of a key derived from a Diffie-Hellman exchange using
any of the groups defined here depends on the inherent strength of
the group, the size of the exponent used, and the entropy provided by
the random number generator used. Due to these inputs it is difficult
to determine the strength of a key for any of the defined groups. The
default Diffie-Hellman group (number one) when used with a strong
random number generator and an exponent no less than 160 bits is
sufficient to use for DES. Groups two through four provide greater
security. Implementations should make note of these conservative
estimates when establishing policy and negotiating security
parameters.

Note that these limitations are on the Diffie-Hellman groups
themselves. There is nothing in IKE which prohibits using stronger
groups nor is there anything which will dilute the strength obtained
from stronger groups. In fact, the extensible framework of IKE
encourages the definition of more groups; use of elliptical curve
groups will greatly increase strength using much smaller numbers.

For situations where defined groups provide insufficient strength New
Group Mode can be used to exchange a Diffie-Hellman group which
provides the necessary strength. In is incumbent upon implementations
to check the primality in groups being offered and independently
arrive at strength estimates.

It is assumed that the Diffie-Hellman exponents in this exchange are
erased from memory after use. In particular, these exponents must not
be derived from long-lived secrets like the seed to a pseudo-random
generator.

IKE exchanges maintain running initialization vectors (IV) where the
last ciphertext block of the last message is the IV for the next
message. To prevent retransmissions (or forged messages with valid
cookies) from causing exchanges to get out of sync IKE
implementations SHOULD NOT update their running IV until the
decrypted message has passed a basic sanity check and has been
determined to actually advance the IKE state machine-- i.e. it is not
a retransmission.

While the last roundtrip of Main Mode (and optionally the last
message of Aggressive Mode) is encrypted it is not, strictly
speaking, authenticated. An active substitution attack on the
ciphertext could result in payload corruption. If such an attack
corrupts mandatory payloads it would be detected by an authentication
failure, but if it corrupts any optional payloads (e.g. notify
payloads chained onto the last message of a Main Mode exchange) it
might not be detectable.

11. IANA Considerations

This document contains many "magic numbers" to be maintained by the
IANA. This section explains the criteria to be used by the IANA to
assign additional numbers in each of these lists.

11.1 Attribute Classes

Attributes negotiated in this protocol are identified by their class.
Requests for assignment of new classes must be accompanied by a
standards-track RFC which describes the use of this attribute.

11.2 Encryption Algorithm Class

Values of the Encryption Algorithm Class define an encryption
algorithm to use when called for in this document. Requests for
assignment of new encryption algorithm values must be accompanied by
a reference to a standards-track or Informational RFC or a reference
to published cryptographic literature which describes this algorithm.

11.3 Hash Algorithm

Values of the Hash Algorithm Class define a hash algorithm to use
when called for in this document. Requests for assignment of new hash
algorithm values must be accompanied by a reference to a standards-
track or Informational RFC or a reference to published cryptographic
literature which describes this algorithm. Due to the key derivation
and key expansion uses of HMAC forms of hash algorithms in IKE,
requests for assignment of new hash algorithm values must take into
account the cryptographic properties-- e.g it's resistance to
collision- of the hash algorithm itself.

11.4 Group Description and Group Type

Values of the Group Description Class identify a group to use in a
Diffie-Hellman exchange. Values of the Group Type Class define the
type of group. Requests for assignment of new groups must be
accompanied by a reference to a standards-track or Informational RFC
which describes this group. Requests for assignment of new group

types must be accompanied by a reference to a standards-track or
Informational RFC or by a reference to published cryptographic or
mathmatical literature which describes the new type.

11.5 Life Type

Values of the Life Type Class define a type of lifetime to which the
ISAKMP Security Association applies. Requests for assignment of new
life types must be accompanied by a detailed description of the units
of this type and its expiry.

12. Acknowledgements

This document is the result of close consultation with Hugo Krawczyk,
Douglas Maughan, Hilarie Orman, Mark Schertler, Mark Schneider, and
Jeff Turner. It relies on protocols which were written by them.
Without their interest and dedication, this would not have been
written.

Special thanks Rob Adams, Cheryl Madson, Derrell Piper, Harry Varnis,
and Elfed Weaver for technical input, encouragement, and various
sanity checks along the way.

We would also like to thank the many members of the IPSec working
group that contributed to the development of this protocol over the
past year.

13. References

[CAST]   Adams, C., "The CAST-128 Encryption Algorithm", RFC 2144,
          May 1997.

[BLOW]   Schneier, B., "The Blowfish Encryption Algorithm", Dr.
          Dobb's Journal, v. 19, n. 4, April 1994.

[Bra97]   Bradner, S., "Key Words for use in RFCs to indicate
          Requirement Levels", BCP 14, RFC 2119, March 1997.

[DES]   ANSI X3.106, "American National Standard for Information
          Systems-Data Link Encryption", American National Standards
          Institute, 1983.

[DH]   Diffie, W., and Hellman M., "New Directions in
          Cryptography", IEEE Transactions on Information Theory, V.
          IT-22, n. 6, June 1977.

[DSS]   NIST, "Digital Signature Standard", FIPS 186, National
           Institute of Standards and Technology, U.S. Department of
           Commerce, May, 1994.

[IDEA]   Lai, X., "On the Design and Security of Block Ciphers," ETH
           Series in Information Processing, v. 1, Konstanz: Hartung-
           Gorre Verlag, 1992

[KBC96]   Krawczyk, H., Bellare, M., and R. Canetti, "HMAC: Keyed-
           Hashing for Message Authentication", RFC 2104, February
           1997.

[SKEME]   Krawczyk, H., "SKEME: A Versatile Secure Key Exchange
           Mechanism for Internet", from IEEE Proceedings of the 1996
           Symposium on Network and Distributed Systems Security.

[MD5]   Rivest, R., "The MD5 Message Digest Algorithm", RFC 1321,
           April 1992.

[MSST98]   Maughhan, D., Schertler, M., Schneider, M., and J. Turner,
           "Internet Security Association and Key Management Protocol
           (ISAKMP)", RFC 2408, November 1998.

[Orm96]   Orman, H., "The Oakley Key Determination Protocol", RFC
           2412, November 1998.

[PKCS1]   RSA Laboratories, "PKCS #1: RSA Encryption Standard",
           November 1993.

[Pip98]   Piper, D., "The Internet IP Security Domain Of
           Interpretation for ISAKMP", RFC 2407, November 1998.

[RC5]   Rivest, R., "The RC5 Encryption Algorithm", Dr. Dobb's
           Journal, v. 20, n. 1, January 1995.

[RSA]   Rivest, R., Shamir, A., and Adleman, L., "A Method for
           Obtaining Digital Signatures and Public-Key Cryptosystems",
           Communications of the ACM, v. 21, n. 2, February 1978.

[Sch96]   Schneier, B., "Applied Cryptography, Protocols, Algorithms,
           and Source Code in C", 2nd edition.

[SHA]   NIST, "Secure Hash Standard", FIPS 180-1, National Institue
           of Standards and Technology, U.S. Department of Commerce,
           May 1994.

[TIGER]   Anderson, R., and Biham, E., "Fast Software Encryption",
           Springer LNCS v. 1039, 1996.

Appendix A

   This is a list of DES Weak and Semi-Weak keys.   The keys come from
   [Sch96]. All keys are listed in hexidecimal.

        DES Weak Keys
        0101 0101 0101 0101
        1F1F 1F1F E0E0 E0E0
        E0E0 E0E0 1F1F 1F1F
        FEFE FEFE FEFE FEFE

        DES Semi-Weak Keys
        01FE 01FE 01FE 01FE
        1FE0 1FE0 0EF1 0EF1
        01E0 01E0 01F1 01F1
        1FFE 1FFE 0EFE 0EFE
        011F 011F 010E 010E
        E0FE E0FE F1FE F1FE

        FE01 FE01 FE01 FE01
        E01F E01F F10E F10E
        E001 E001 F101 F101
        FE1F FE1F FE0E FE0E
        1F01 1F01 0E01 0E01
        FEE0 FEE0 FEF1 FEF1

   Attribute Assigned Numbers

   Attributes negotiated during phase one use the following definitions.
   Phase two attributes are defined in the applicable DOI specification
   (for example, IPsec attributes are defined in the IPsec DOI), with
   the exception of a group description when Quick Mode includes an
   ephemeral Diffie-Hellman exchange. Attribute types can be either
   Basic (B) or Variable-length (V). Encoding of these attributes is
   defined in the base ISAKMP specification as Type/Value (Basic) and
   Type/Length/Value (Variable).

   Attributes described as basic MUST NOT be encoded as variable.
   Variable length attributes MAY be encoded as basic attributes if
   their value can fit into two octets. If this is the case, an
   attribute offered as variable (or basic) by the initiator of this
   protocol MAY be returned to the initiator as a basic (or variable).

Attribute Classes

```
        class                          value           type
        ----------------------------------------------------------------
        Encryption Algorithm            1               B
        Hash Algorithm                  2               B
        Authentication Method           3               B
        Group Description               4               B
        Group Type                      5               B
        Group Prime/Irreducible Polynomial  6           V
        Group Generator One             7               V
        Group Generator Two             8               V
        Group Curve A                   9               V
        Group Curve B                   10              V
        Life Type                       11              B
        Life Duration                   12              V
        PRF                             13              B
        Key Length                      14              B
        Field Size                      15              B
        Group Order                     16              V
```

values 17-16383 are reserved to IANA. Values 16384-32767 are for private use among mutually consenting parties.

Class Values

```
- Encryption Algorithm                          Defined In
    DES-CBC                 1               RFC 2405
    IDEA-CBC                2
    Blowfish-CBC            3
    RC5-R16-B64-CBC         4
    3DES-CBC                5
    CAST-CBC                6
```

values 7-65000 are reserved to IANA. Values 65001-65535 are for private use among mutually consenting parties.

```
- Hash Algorithm                                Defined In
    MD5                     1               RFC 1321
    SHA                     2               FIPS 180-1
    Tiger                   3               See Reference [TIGER]
```

values 4-65000 are reserved to IANA. Values 65001-65535 are for private use among mutually consenting parties.

    - Authentication Method
       pre-shared key   1
       DSS signatures   2
       RSA signatures   3
       Encryption with RSA   4
       Revised encryption with RSA   5

    values 6-65000 are reserved to IANA. Values 65001-65535 are for
    private use among mutually consenting parties.

    - Group Description
       default 768-bit MODP group (section 6.1)   1

       alternate 1024-bit MODP group (section 6.2)   2

       EC2N group on GP[2^155] (section 6.3)   3

       EC2N group on GP[2^185] (section 6.4)   4

    values 5-32767 are reserved to IANA. Values 32768-65535 are for
    private use among mutually consenting parties.

    - Group Type
       MODP (modular exponentiation group)   1
       ECP (elliptic curve group over GF[P])   2
       EC2N (elliptic curve group over GF[2^N]) 3

    values 4-65000 are reserved to IANA. Values 65001-65535 are for
    private use among mutually consenting parties.

    - Life Type
       seconds   1
       kilobytes   2

    values 3-65000 are reserved to IANA. Values 65001-65535 are for
    private use among mutually consenting parties. For a given "Life
    Type" the value of the "Life Duration" attribute defines the actual
    length of the SA life-- either a number of seconds, or a number of
    kbytes protected.

    - PRF
    There are currently no pseudo-random functions defined.

    values 1-65000 are reserved to IANA. Values 65001-65535 are for
    private use among mutually consenting parties.

- Key Length

    When using an Encryption Algorithm that has a variable length key,
    this attribute specifies the key length in bits. (MUST use network
    byte order). This attribute MUST NOT be used when the specified
    Encryption Algorithm uses a fixed length key.

- Field Size

    The field size, in bits, of a Diffie-Hellman group.

- Group Order

    The group order of an elliptical curve group. Note the length of
    this attribute depends on the field size.

```
Additional Exchanges Defined-- XCHG values
   Quick Mode                       32
   New Group Mode                   33
```

Appendix B

   This appendix describes encryption details to be used ONLY when
   encrypting ISAKMP messages. When a service (such as an IPSEC
   transform) utilizes ISAKMP to generate keying material, all
   encryption algorithm specific details (such as key and IV generation,
   padding, etc...) MUST be defined by that service. ISAKMP does not
   purport to ever produce keys that are suitable for any encryption
   algorithm. ISAKMP produces the requested amount of keying material
   from which the service MUST generate a suitable key. Details, such
   as weak key checks, are the responsibility of the service.

   Use of negotiated PRFs may require the PRF output to be expanded due
   to the PRF feedback mechanism employed by this document. For example,
   if the (ficticious) DOORAK-MAC requires 24 bytes of key but produces
   only 8 bytes of output, the output must be expanded three times
   before being used as the key for another instance of itself. The
   output of a PRF is expanded by feeding back the results of the PRF
   into itself to generate successive blocks. These blocks are
   concatenated until the requisite number of bytes has been acheived.
   For example, for pre-shared key authentication with DOORAK-MAC as the
   negotiated PRF:

     BLOCK1-8 = prf(pre-shared-key, Ni_b | Nr_b)
     BLOCK9-16 = prf(pre-shared-key, BLOCK1-8 | Ni_b | Nr_b)
     BLOCK17-24 = prf(pre-shared-key, BLOCK9-16 | Ni_b | Nr_b)
   and
     SKEYID = BLOCK1-8 | BLOCK9-16 | BLOCK17-24

   so therefore to derive SKEYID_d:

     BLOCK1-8 = prf(SKEYID, g^xy | CKY-I | CKY-R | 0)
     BLOCK9-16 = prf(SKEYID, BLOCK1-8 | g^xy | CKY-I | CKY-R | 0)
     BLOCK17-24 = prf(SKEYID, BLOCK9-16 | g^xy | CKY-I | CKY-R | 0)
   and
     SKEYID_d = BLOCK1-8 | BLOCK9-16 | BLOCK17-24

   Subsequent PRF derivations are done similarly.

   Encryption keys used to protect the ISAKMP SA are derived from
   SKEYID_e in an algorithm-specific manner. When SKEYID_e is not long
   enough to supply all the necessary keying material an algorithm
   requires, the key is derived from feeding the results of a pseudo-
   random function into itself, concatenating the results, and taking
   the highest necessary bits.

For example, if (ficticious) algorithm AKULA requires 320-bits of key
(and has no weak key check) and the prf used to generate SKEYID_e
only generates 120 bits of material, the key for AKULA, would be the
first 320-bits of Ka, where:

```
    Ka = K1 | K2 | K3
and
    K1 = prf(SKEYID_e, 0)
    K2 = prf(SKEYID_e, K1)
    K3 = prf(SKEYID_e, K2)
```

where prf is the negotiated prf or the HMAC version of the negotiated
hash function (if no prf was negotiated) and 0 is represented by a
single octet. Each result of the prf provides 120 bits of material
for a total of 360 bits. AKULA would use the first 320 bits of that
360 bit string.

In phase 1, material for the initialization vector (IV material) for
CBC mode encryption algorithms is derived from a hash of a
concatenation of the initiator's public Diffie-Hellman value and the
responder's public Diffie-Hellman value using the negotiated hash
algorithm. This is used for the first message only. Each message
should be padded up to the nearest block size using bytes containing
0x00. The message length in the header MUST include the length of the
pad since this reflects the size of the ciphertext. Subsequent
messages MUST use the last CBC encryption block from the previous
message as their initialization vector.

In phase 2, material for the initialization vector for CBC mode
encryption of the first message of a Quick Mode exchange is derived
from a hash of a concatenation of the last phase 1 CBC output block
and the phase 2 message id using the negotiated hash algorithm. The
IV for subsequent messages within a Quick Mode exchange is the CBC
output block from the previous message. Padding and IVs for
subsequent messages are done as in phase 1.

After the ISAKMP SA has been authenticated all Informational
Exchanges are encrypted using SKEYID_e. The initiaization vector for
these exchanges is derived in exactly the same fashion as that for a
Quick Mode-- i.e. it is derived from a hash of a concatenation of the
last phase 1 CBC output block and the message id from the ISAKMP
header of the Informational Exchange (not the message id from the
message that may have prompted the Informational Exchange).

Note that the final phase 1 CBC output block, the result of
encryption/decryption of the last phase 1 message, must be retained
in the ISAKMP SA state to allow for generation of unique IVs for each
Quick Mode. Each post- phase 1 exchange (Quick Modes and

Informational Exchanges) generates IVs independantly to prevent IVs
from getting out of sync when two different exchanges are started
simultaneously.

In all cases, there is a single bidirectional cipher/IV context.
Having each Quick Mode and Informational Exchange maintain a unique
context prevents IVs from getting out of sync.

The key for DES-CBC is derived from the first eight (8) non-weak and
non-semi-weak (see Appendix A) bytes of SKEYID_e. The IV is the first
8 bytes of the IV material derived above.

The key for IDEA-CBC is derived from the first sixteen (16) bytes of
SKEYID_e. The IV is the first eight (8) bytes of the IV material
derived above.

The key for Blowfish-CBC is either the negotiated key size, or the
first fifty-six (56) bytes of a key (if no key size is negotiated)
derived in the aforementioned pseudo-random function feedback method.
The IV is the first eight (8) bytes of the IV material derived above.

The key for RC5-R16-B64-CBC is the negotiated key size, or the first
sixteen (16) bytes of a key (if no key size is negotiated) derived
from the aforementioned pseudo-random function feedback method if
necessary. The IV is the first eight (8) bytes of the IV material
derived above. The number of rounds MUST be 16 and the block size
MUST be 64.

The key for 3DES-CBC is the first twenty-four (24) bytes of a key
derived in the aforementioned pseudo-random function feedback method.
3DES-CBC is an encrypt-decrypt-encrypt operation using the first,
middle, and last eight (8) bytes of the entire 3DES-CBC key. The IV
is the first eight (8) bytes of the IV material derived above.

The key for CAST-CBC is either the negotiated key size, or the first
sixteen (16) bytes of a key derived in the aforementioned pseudo-
random function feedback method. The IV is the first eight (8) bytes
of the IV material derived above.

Support for algorithms other than DES-CBC is purely optional. Some
optional algorithms may be subject to intellectual property claims.

Authors' Addresses

    Dan Harkins
    cisco Systems
    170 W. Tasman Dr.
    San Jose, California, 95134-1706
    United States of America

    Phone: +1 408 526 4000
    EMail: dharkins@cisco.com

    Dave Carrel
    76 Lippard Ave.
    San Francisco, CA 94131-2947
    United States of America

    Phone: +1 415 337 8469
    EMail: carrel@ipsec.org

Authors' Note

    The authors encourage independent implementation, and
    interoperability testing, of this hybrid protocol.

Full Copyright Statement

Network Working Group   R. Glenn
Request for Comments: 2410   NIST
Category: Standards Track   S. Kent
                                                         BBN Corp
                                                    November 1998

             The NULL Encryption Algorithm and Its Use With IPsec

Status of this Memo

Copyright Notice

Abstract

   This memo defines the NULL encryption algorithm and its use with the
   IPsec Encapsulating Security Payload (ESP). NULL does nothing to
   alter plaintext data. In fact, NULL, by itself, does nothing. NULL
   provides the means for ESP to provide authentication and integrity
   without confidentiality.

   Further information on the other components necessary for ESP
   implementations is provided by [ESP] and [ROAD].

1. Introduction

   This memo defines the NULL encryption algorithm and its use with the
   IPsec Encapsulating Security Payload [ESP] to provide authentication
   and integrity without confidentiality.

   NULL is a block cipher the origins of which appear to be lost in
   antiquity. Despite rumors that the National Security Agency
   suppressed publication of this algorithm, there is no evidence of
   such action on their part. Rather, recent archaeological evidence
   suggests that the NULL algorithm was developed in Roman times, as an
   exportable alternative to Ceaser ciphers. However, because Roman
   numerals lack a symbol for zero, written records of the algorithm's
   development were lost to historians for over two millennia.

[ESP] specifies the use of an optional encryption algorithm to
provide confidentiality and the use of an optional authentication
algorithm to provide authentication and integrity. The NULL
encryption algorithm is a convenient way to represent the option of
not applying encryption. This is referred to as ESP_NULL in [DOI].

The IPsec Authentication Header [AH] specification provides a similar
service, by computing authentication data which covers the data
portion of a packet as well as the immutable in transit portions of
the IP header. ESP_NULL does not include the IP header in
calculating the authentication data. This can be useful in providing
IPsec services through non-IP network devices. The discussion on how
ESP_NULL might be used with non-IP network devices is outside the
scope of this document.

In this memo, NULL is used within the context of ESP. For further
information on how the various pieces of ESP fit together to provide
security services, refer to [ESP] and [ROAD].

The key words "MUST", "MUST NOT", "REQUIRED", "SHALL", "SHALL NOT",
"SHOULD", "SHOULD NOT", "RECOMMENDED", "MAY", and "OPTIONAL" in this
document are to be interpreted as described in [RFC 2119].

2. Algorithm Definition

NULL is defined mathematically by the use of the Identity function I
applied to a block of data b such that:

   NULL(b) = I(b) = b

2.1 Keying Material

Like other modern ciphers, e.g., RC5 [RFC-2040], the NULL encryption
algorithm can make use of keys of varying lengths. However, no
measurable increase in security is afforded by the use of longer key
lengths.

2.2 Cryptographic Synchronization

Because of the stateless nature of the NULL encryption algorithm, it
is not necessary to transmit an IV or similar cryptographic
synchronization data on a per packet (or even a per SA) basis. The
NULL encryption algorithm combines many of the best features of both
block and stream ciphers, while still not requiring the transmission
of an IV or analogous cryptographic synchronization data.

2.3 Padding

    NULL has a block size of 1 byte, thus padding is not necessary.

2.4. Performance

    The NULL encryption algorithm is significantly faster than other
    commonly used symmetric encryption algorithms and implementations of
    the base algorithm are available for all commonly used hardware and
    OS platforms.

2.5 Test Vectors

    The following is a set of test vectors to facilitate in the
    development of interoperable NULL implementations.

```
test_case =       1
data =            0x123456789abcdef
data_len =        8
NULL_data =       0x123456789abcdef

test_case =       2
data =            "Network Security People Have A Strange Sense Of Humor"
data_len =        53
NULL_data =       "Network Security People Have A Strange Sense Of Humor"
```

3. ESP_NULL Operational Requirements

    ESP_NULL is defined by using NULL within the context of ESP. This
    section further defines ESP_NULL by pointing out particular
    operational parameter requirements.

    For purposes of IKE [IKE] key extraction, the key size for this
    algorithm MUST be zero (0) bits, to facilitate interoperability and
    to avoid any potential export control problems.

    To facilitate interoperability, the IV size for this algorithm MUST
    be zero (0) bits.

    Padding MAY be included on outgoing packets as specified in [ESP].

4. Security Considerations

    The NULL encryption algorithm offers no confidentiality nor does it
    offer any other security service. It is simply a convenient way to
    represent the optional use of applying encryption within ESP. ESP
    can then be used to provide authentication and integrity without
    confidentiality. Unlike AH these services are not applied to any

part of the IP header. At the time of this writing there is no
evidence to support that ESP_NULL is any less secure than AH when
using the same authentication algorithm (i.e. a packet secured using
ESP_NULL with some authentication algorithm is as cryptographically
secure as a packet secured using AH with the same authentication
algorithm).

As stated in [ESP], while the use of encryption algorithms and
authentication algorithms are optional in ESP, it is imperative that
an ESP SA specifies the use of at least one cryptographically strong
encryption algorithm or one cryptographically strong authentication
algorithm or one of each.

At the time of this writing there are no known laws preventing the
exportation of NULL with a zero (0) bit key length.

5. Intellectual Property Rights

   Pursuant to the provisions of [RFC-2026], the authors represent that
   they have disclosed the existence of any proprietary or intellectual
   property rights in the contribution that are reasonably and
   personally known to the authors. The authors do not represent that
   they personally know of all potentially pertinent proprietary and
   intellectual property rights owned or claimed by the organizations
   they represent or third parties.

6. Acknowledgments

   Steve Bellovin suggested and provided the text for the Intellectual
   Property Rights section.

   Credit also needs to be given to the participants of the Cisco/ICSA
   IPsec & IKE March 1998 Interoperability Workshop since it was there
   that the need for this document became apparent.

7. References

   [ESP]   Kent, S., and R. Atkinson, "IP Encapsulating Security
                Payload", RFC 2406, November 1998.

   [AH]   Kent, S., and R. Atkinson, "IP Authentication Header",
                RFC 2402, November 1998.

   [ROAD]   Thayer, R., Doraswamy, N., and R. Glenn, "IP Security
                Document Roadmap", RFC 2411, November 1998.

   [DOI]   Piper, D., "The Internet IP Security Domain of
                Interpretation for ISAKMP", RFC 2408, November 1998.

[IKE]   Harkins, D., and D. Carrel, "The Internet Key Exchange
               (IKE)", RFC 2409, November 1998.

[RFC-2026]   Bradner, S., "The Internet Standards Process — Revision
               3", BCP 9, RFC 2026, October 1996.

[RFC-2040]   Baldwin, R., and R. Rivest, "The RC5, RC5-CBC, RC5-CBC-
               Pad, and RC5-CTS Algorithms", RFC 2040, October 1996

[RFC-2119]   Bradner, S., "Key words for use in RFCs to Indicate
               Requirement Levels", BCP 14, RFC 2119, March 1997.

6. Editors' Addresses

Rob Glenn
NIST

EMail: rob.glenn@nist.gov

Stephen Kent
BBN Corporation

EMail: kent@bbn.com

The IPsec working group can be contacted through the chairs:

Robert Moskowitz
ICSA

EMail: rgm@icsa.net

Ted T'so
Massachusetts Institute of Technology

EMail: tytso@mit.edu

7. Full Copyright Statement

Network Working Group   R. Thayer
Request for Comments: 2411   Sable Technology Corporation
Category: Informational   N. Doraswamy
                                                    Bay Networks
                                                       R. Glenn
                                                           NIST
                                                  November 1998

RFC 2411   1

                          IP Security
                       Document Roadmap

Status of this Memo

Copyright Notice

Abstract

   The IPsec protocol suite is used to provide privacy and
   authentication services at the IP layer. Several documents are used
   to describe this protocol suite. The interrelationship and
   organization of the various documents covering the IPsec protocol are
   discussed here. An explanation of what to find in which document,
   and what to include in new Encryption Algorithm and Authentication
   Algorithm documents are described.

Table of Contents

1. Introduction

   This document is intended to provide guidelines for the development
   of collateral specifications describing the use of new encryption and
   authentication algorithms with the ESP protocol, described in [ESP]
   and new authentication algorithms used with the AH protocol,
   described in [AH]. ESP and AH are part of the IP Security
   architecture described in [Arch]. There is a requirement for a
   well-known procedure that can be used to add new encryption
   algorithms or authentication algorithms to ESP and AH, not only while
   the initial document set is undergoing development but after the base
   documents have achieved RFC status. Following the guidelines
   discussed below simplifies adding new algorithms and reduces that
   amount of redundant documentation.

   The goal in writing a new Encryption Algorithm or Authentication
   Algorithm document is to concentrate on the application of the
   specific algorithm within ESP and AH. General ESP and AH concepts,
   definitions, and issues are covered in the ESP and AH documents. The
   algorithms themselves are not described in these documents. This
   gives us the capability to add new algorithms and also specify how
   any given algorithm might interact with other algorithms. The intent
   is to achieve the goal of avoiding duplication of information and
   excessive numbers of documents, the so-called "draft explosion"
   effect.

2. Interrelationship of IPsec Documents

   The documents describing the set of IPsec protocols are divided into
   seven groups. This is illustrated in Figure 1. There is a main
   Architecture document which broadly covers the general concepts,
   security requirements, definitions, and mechanisms defining IPsec
   technology.

   There is an ESP Protocol document and an AH Protocol document which
   covers the packet format and general issues regarding the respective
   protocols. These protocol documents also contain default values if
   appropriate, such as the default padding contents, and mandatory to
   implement algorithms. These documents dictate some of the values in
   the Domain Of Interpretation document [DOI]. Note the DOI document
   is itself part of the IANA Assigned Numbers mechanism and so the
   values described in the DOI are well-known. See [DOI] for more
   information on the mechanism.

   The "Encryption Algorithm" document set, shown on the left, is the
   set of documents describing how various encryption algorithms are
   used for ESP. These documents are intended to fit in this roadmap,
   and should avoid overlap with the ESP protocol document and with the

Authentication Algorithm documents. Examples of this document are
the [DES-Detroit] and [CBC] documents. When these or other
encryption algorithms are used for ESP, the DOI document has to
indicate certain values, such as an encryption algorithm identifier,
so these documents provide input to the DOI.

The "Authentication Algorithm" document set, shown on the right, is
the set of documents describing how various authentication algorithms
are used for both ESP and AH. These documents are intended to fit in
this roadmap, and should avoid overlap with the AH protocol document
and with the Encryption Algorithm documents. Examples of this
document are the [HMAC-MD5], and [HMAC-SHA-1] documents. When these
or other algorithms are used for either ESP or AH, the DOI document
has to indicate certain values, such as algorithm type, so these
documents provide input to the DOI.

The "Key Management Documents", shown at the bottom, are the
documents describing the IETF standards-track key management schemes.
These documents provide certain values for the DOI also. Note that
issues of key management should be indicated here and not in, for
example, the ESP and AH protocol documents. Currently this box
represents [ISAKMP], [Oakley], and [Resolution].

The DOI document, shown in the middle, contains values needed for the
other documents to relate to each other. This includes for example
encryption algorithms, authentication algorithms, and operational
parameters such as key lifetimes.

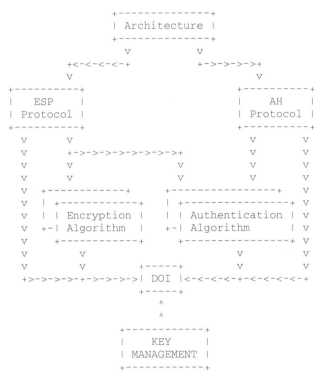

Figure 1. IPsec Document Roadmap.

3. Keying Material

   Describing the encryption and authentication algorithms in different
   documents raises the issue of how the key management protocols knows
   the required keying material length for the desired algorithms when
   used together with ESP. It also raises the issue of how to divide
   the keying material. This is known as the "slicing and dicing"
   information.

   Each Encryption Algorithm and Authentication Algorithm document
   should specify their respective key attributes (e.g. how to pad,
   location of parity bits, key order for multi-keyed algorithms, and
   length). The key management protocols should use the length of the
   keys specified in the respective Algorithm documents to generate the
   keying material of required length.

The key management protocol generates keying material with enough
strength and size to generate keys for individual algorithms. The
IPsec Architecture document specifies how keys are extracted from a
single block of keying material when multiple keys are required (e.g.
ESP with authentication). The Encryption Algorithm and

Authentication Algorithm documents are responsible for specifying the
key sizes and strengths for each algorithm. However, whether the
entire keying material is passed down to the kernel to perform
slicing and dicing or if the keys are sliced and diced by key
management protocol is an implementation issue. The AH protocol
document has no such requirement.

4. Recommended Content of Algorithm Documents

The document describing how a specific encryption or authentication
algorithm is used should contain information appropriate to that
encryption or authentication algorithm. This section enumerates what
information should be provided. It is the intention of the document
roadmap that:

  . General protocol information goes in the respective ESP or AH
    protocol documents.
  . Key management information goes in the key management documents.
  . Assigned values and constants of negotiable items go in the DOI
    document.

Encryption and authentication algorithms require some set of optional
parameters or have optional modes of operation (e.g. IVs,
authentication data lengths, and key lengths). To help eliminate
some complexity involved with key management having to negotiate
large numbers of algorithm-specific parameters, encryption and
authentication algorithm documents will select fixed values for these
parameters when it is deemed technically reasonable and feasible.

Note, the following information is intended as a general guideline
only.

4.1 Encryption and Authentication Algorithms

This section describes the information that should be included in
both Encryption Algorithm and Authentication Algorithm documents.

Keying Material

  . Size of keys, including minimum, maximum, recommended and/or
    required sizes. Note: the security considerations section should
    address any weakness in specific sizes.

. Recommended or required pseudo-random number generator techniques
  and attributes to provide sufficiently strong keys. [RANDOM]
  provides recommendations on generating strong randomness for use
  with security.
. Format of keying material.
. Known weak keys or references to documentation on known weak keys.
. Recommended or required processing of input keying material such
  as parity generation or checking.
. Requirements and/or recommendations on how often the keying
  material should be refreshed.

Performance Considerations
. Any available estimates on performance of this algorithm.
. Any available comparison data (e.g., compared against DES or
  MD5).
. Input size or other considerations that could improve or degrade
  performance.

ESP Environmental Considerations
. Any known issues regarding interactions between this algorithm and
  other aspects of ESP, such as use of certain authentication
  schemes. Note: As new encryption and authentication algorithms
  are applied to ESP, the later documents will be required to
  address interactions with previously specified algorithms.

Payload Content and Format Description
. Specification of size, placement, and content of algorithm-
  specific fields not defined in the ESP or AH protocol documents
  (e.g., IV).

Security Considerations
. Discuss any known attacks.
. Discuss any known common implementation pitfalls, such as use of
  weak random number generators.
. Discuss any relevant validation procedures, such as test vectors.
  [RFC-2202] is an example document containing test vectors for
  a set of authentication algorithms.

4.2 Encryption Algorithms

  This section describes the information that should be included in the
  Encryption Algorithm documents.

  Encryption Algorithm Description
. General information how this encryption algorithm is to be used in
  ESP.
. Description of background material and formal algorithm
  description.

. Features of this encryption algorithm to be used by ESP, including
   encryption and/or authentication.
. Mention of any availability issues such as Intellectual Property
   considerations.
. References, in IETF style, to background material such as FIPS
   documents.

Algorithm Modes of Operation
. Description of how the algorithm is operated, whether it is block
   mode or streaming mode or other.
. Requirements for input or output block format.
. Padding requirements of this algorithm. Note: there is a default
   for padding, specified in the base ESP document, so this is only
   needed if the default cannot be used.
. Any algorithm-specific operating parameters, such as number of
   rounds.
. Identify optional parameters and optional methods of operation and
   pick reasonable fixed values and methods with explicit technical
   explanations.
. Identify those optional parameters in which values and methods
   should remain optional with explicit technical explanations on why
   fixed values and methods should not be used.
. Defaults and mandatory ranges on algorithm-specific optional
   parameters that could not be fixed.

4.3 Authentication Algorithms

   This section describes the information that should be included in the
   Authentication Algorithm documents. In most cases, an authentication
   algorithm will operate the same whether it is used for ESP or AH.
   This should be represented in a single Authentication Algorithm
   document.

   Authentication Algorithm Description
   . General information on how this authentication algorithm is to be
      used with ESP and AH.
   . Description of background material and formal algorithm
      description.
   . Features of this authentication algorithm.
   . Mention of any availability issues such as Intellectual Property
      considerations.
   . References, in IETF style, to background material such as
      FIPS documents and definitive descriptions of underlying
      algorithms.

   Algorithm Modes of Operation
   . Description of how the algorithm is operated.

- Algorithm-specific operating parameters, such as number of rounds, and input or output block format.
- Implicit and explicit padding requirements of this algorithm. Note: There is a default method for padding of the authentication data field specified in the AH protocol document. This is only needed if the default cannot be used.
- Identify optional parameters and optional methods of operation and pick reasonable fixed values and methods with explicit technical explanations.
- Identify those optional parameters in which values and methods should remain optional with explicit technical explanations on why fixed values and methods should not be used.
- Defaults and mandatory ranges on algorithm-specific optional parameters that could not be fixed.
- Authentication data comparison criteria for this algorithm. Note: There is a default method for verifying the authentication data specified in the AH protocol document. This is only needed if the default cannot be used (e.g. when using a signed hash).

5. Security Considerations

   This document provides a roadmap and guidelines for writing
   Encryption and Authentication Algorithm documents. The reader should
   follow all the security procedures and guidelines described in the
   IPsec Architecture, ESP Protocol, AH Protocol, Encryption Algorithm,
   and Authentication Algorithm documents. Note that many encryption
   algorithms are not considered secure if they are not used with some
   sort of authentication mechanism.

6. Acknowledgments

   Several Internet drafts were referenced in writing this document.
   Depending on where the documents are on (or off) the IETF standards
   track these may not be available through the IETF RFC repositories.
   In certain cases the reader may want to know what version of these
   documents were referenced. These documents are:

   - DES-Detroit: this is the ANX Workshop style of ESP, based on the Hughes draft as modified by Cheryl Madson and published on the ANX mailing list.
   - DOI: draft-ietf-ipsec-ipsec-doi-02.txt.
   - 3DES: this is <the Triple-DES shim document>.
   - CAST: this is draft-ietf-ipsec-esp-cast-128-cbc-00.txt, as revised to relate to this document.
   - ESP: draft-ietf-ipsec-esp-04.txt, mailed to the IETF mailing list in May/June 1997.
   - AH: draft-ietf-ipsec-auth-05.txt, mailed to the IETF mailing list in May/June 1997.

. HUGHES: this is draft-ietf-ipsec-esp-des-md5-03.txt
. ISAKMP: There are three documents describing ISAKMP. These are
   draft-ietf-ipsec-isakmp-07.txt, draft-ietf-ipsec-isakmp-oakley-
   03.txt, and draft-ietf-ipsec-ipsec-doi-02.txt.

7. References

[CBC]   Periera, R., and R. Adams, "The ESP CBC-Mode Cipher
                 Algorithms", RFC 2451, November 1998.

[Arch]   Kent, S., and R. Atkinson, "Security Architecture for
                 the Internet Protocol", RFC 2401, November 1998.

[DES-Detroit]   Madson, C., and N. Doraswamy, "The ESP DES-CBC Cipher
                 Algorithm With Explicit IV", RFC 2405, November 1998.

[DOI]   Piper, D., "The Internet IP Security Domain of
                 Interpretation for ISAKMP", RFC 2407, November 1998.

[AH]   Kent, S., and R. Atkinson, "IP Authentication Header",
                 RFC 2402, November 1998.

[ESP]   Kent, S., and R. Atkinson, "IP Encapsulating Security
                 Payload (ESP)", RFC 2406, November 1998.

[HMAC]   Krawczyk, K., Bellare, M., and R. Canetti, "HMAC:
                 Keyed-Hashing for Message Authentication", RFC 2104,
                 February 1997.

[HMAC-MD5]   Madson, C., and R. Glenn, "The Use of HMAC-MD5 within
                 ESP and AH", RFC 2403, November 1998.

[HMAC-SHA-1]   Madson, C., and R. Glenn, "The Use of HMAC-SHA-1 within
                 ESP and AH", RFC 2404, November 1998.

[RANDOM]   Eastlake, D., Crocker, S., and J. Schiller, "Randomness
                 Recommendations for Security", RFC 1750, December 1994.

[RFC-2202]   Cheng, P., and R. Glenn, "Test Cases for HMAC-MD5 and
                 HMAC-SHA-1", RFC 2202, March 1997.

8. Authors' Addresses

Rodney Thayer
Sable Technology Corporation
246 Walnut Street
Newton, Massachusetts 02160

EMail: mailto:rodney@sabletech.com

Naganand Doraswamy
Bay Networks

EMail: naganand@baynetworks.com

Rob Glenn
NIST

EMail: rob.glenn@nist.gov

9. Full Copyright Statement

   Copyright (C) The Internet Society (1998). All Rights Reserved.

Network Working Group   H. Orman
Request for Comments: 2412   Department of Computer Science
Category: Informational   University of Arizona
                                                   November 1998

                 The OAKLEY Key Determination Protocol

Status of this Memo

   This memo provides information for the Internet community. It does
   not specify an Internet standard of any kind. Distribution of this
   memo is unlimited.

Abstract

   This document describes a protocol, named OAKLEY, by which two
   authenticated parties can agree on secure and secret keying material.
   The basic mechanism is the Diffie-Hellman key exchange algorithm.

   The OAKLEY protocol supports Perfect Forward Secrecy, compatibility
   with the ISAKMP protocol for managing security associations, user-
   defined abstract group structures for use with the Diffie-Hellman
   algorithm, key updates, and incorporation of keys distributed via
   out-of-band mechanisms.

1. INTRODUCTION

   Key establishment is the heart of data protection that relies on
   cryptography, and it is an essential component of the packet
   protection mechanisms described in [RFC2401], for example. A
   scalable and secure key distribution mechanism for the Internet is a
   necessity. The goal of this protocol is to provide that mechanism,
   coupled with a great deal of cryptographic strength.

   The Diffie-Hellman key exchange algorithm provides such a mechanism.
   It allows two parties to agree on a shared value without requiring
   encryption. The shared value is immediately available for use in
   encrypting subsequent conversation, e.g. data transmission and/or
   authentication. The STS protocol [STS] provides a demonstration of
   how to embed the algorithm in a secure protocol, one that ensures
   that in addition to securely sharing a secret, the two parties can be
   sure of each other's identities, even when an active attacker exists.

Because OAKLEY is a generic key exchange protocol, and because the keys that it generates might be used for encrypting data with a long privacy lifetime, 20 years or more, it is important that the algorithms underlying the protocol be able to ensure the security of the keys for that period of time, based on the best prediction capabilities available for seeing into the mathematical future. The protocol therefore has two options for adding to the difficulties faced by an attacker who has a large amount of recorded key exchange traffic at his disposal (a passive attacker). These options are useful for deriving keys which will be used for encryption.

The OAKLEY protocol is related to STS, sharing the similarity of authenticating the Diffie-Hellman exponentials and using them for determining a shared key, and also of achieving Perfect Forward Secrecy for the shared key, but it differs from the STS protocol in several ways.

   The first is the addition of a weak address validation mechanism
   ("cookies", described by Phil Karn in the Photuris key exchange
   protocol work in progress) to help avoid denial of service
   attacks.

   The second extension is to allow the two parties to select
   mutually agreeable supporting algorithms for the protocol: the
   encryption method, the key derivation method, and the
   authentication method.

   Thirdly, the authentication does not depend on encryption using
   the Diffie-Hellman exponentials; instead, the authentication
   validates the binding of the exponentials to the identities of the
   parties.

   The protocol does not require the two parties compute the shared
   exponentials prior to authentication.

   This protocol adds additional security to the derivation of keys
   meant for use with encryption (as opposed to authentication) by
   including a dependence on an additional algorithm. The derivation
   of keys for encryption is made to depend not only on the Diffie-
   Hellman algorithm, but also on the cryptographic method used to
   securely authenticate the communicating parties to each other.

   Finally, this protocol explicitly defines how the two parties can
   select the mathematical structures (group representation and
   operation) for performing the Diffie-Hellman algorithm; they can
   use standard groups or define their own. User-defined groups
   provide an additional degree of long-term security.

OAKLEY has several options for distributing keys. In addition to the classic Diffie-Hellman exchange, this protocol can be used to derive a new key from an existing key and to distribute an externally derived key by encrypting it.

The protocol allows two parties to use all or some of the anti-clogging and perfect forward secrecy features. It also permits the use of authentication based on symmetric encryption or non-encryption algorithms. This flexibility is included in order to allow the parties to use the features that are best suited to their security and performance requirements.

This document draws extensively in spirit and approach from the Photuris work in progress by Karn and Simpson (and from discussions with the authors), specifics of the ISAKMP document by Schertler et al. the ISAKMP protocol document, and it was also influenced by papers by Paul van Oorschot and Hugo Krawcyzk.

2. The Protocol Outline

2.1 General Remarks

The OAKLEY protocol is used to establish a shared key with an assigned identifier and associated authenticated identities for the two parties. The name of the key can be used later to derive security associations for the RFC 2402 and RFC 2406 protocols (AH and ESP) or to achieve other network security goals.

Each key is associated with algorithms that are used for authentication, privacy, and one-way functions. These are ancillary algorithms for OAKLEY; their appearance in subsequent security association definitions derived with other protocols is neither required nor prohibited.

The specification of the details of how to apply an algorithm to data is called a transform. This document does not supply the transform definitions; they will be in separate RFC's.

The anti-clogging tokens, or "cookies", provide a weak form of source address identification for both parties; the cookie exchange can be completed before they perform the computationally expensive part of the protocol (large integer exponentiations).

It is important to note that OAKLEY uses the cookies for two purposes: anti-clogging and key naming. The two parties to the protocol each contribute one cookie at the initiation of key establishment; the pair of cookies becomes the key identifier (KEYID), a reusable name for the keying material. Because of this

dual role, we will use the notation for the concatenation of the
cookies ("COOKIE-I, COOKIE-R") interchangeably with the symbol
"KEYID".

OAKLEY is designed to be a compatible component of the ISAKMP
protocol [ISAKMP], which runs over the UDP protocol using a well-
known port (see the RFC on port assignments, STD02-RFC-1700). The
only technical requirement for the protocol environment is that the
underlying protocol stack must be able to supply the Internet address
of the remote party for each message. Thus, OAKLEY could, in theory,
be used directly over the IP protocol or over UDP, if suitable
protocol or port number assignments were available.

The machine running OAKLEY must provide a good random number
generator, as described in [RANDOM], as the source of random numbers
required in this protocol description. Any mention of a "nonce"
implies that the nonce value is generated by such a generator. The
same is true for "pseudorandom" values.

2.2 Notation

The section describes the notation used in this document for message
sequences and content.

2.2.1 Message descriptions

The protocol exchanges below are written in an abbreviated notation
that is intended to convey the essential elements of the exchange in
a clear manner. A brief guide to the notation follows. The detailed
formats and assigned values are given in the appendices.

In order to represent message exchanges succinctly, this document
uses an abbreviated notation that describes each message in terms of
its source and destination and relevant fields.

Arrows ("->") indicate whether the message is sent from the initiator
to the responder, or vice versa ("<-").

The fields in the message are named and comma separated. The
protocol uses the convention that the first several fields constitute
a fixed header format for all messages.

For example, consider a HYPOTHETICAL exchange of messages involving a
fixed format message, the four fixed fields being two "cookies", the
third field being a message type name, the fourth field being a
multi-precision integer representing a power of a number:

```
      Initiator                                          Responder
         ->    Cookie-I, 0, OK_KEYX, g^x                      ->
         <-    Cookie-R, Cookie-I, OK_KEYX, g^y               <-
```

The notation describes a two message sequence. The initiator begins
by sending a message with 4 fields to the responder; the first field
has the unspecified value "Cookie-I", second field has the numeric
value 0, the third field indicates the message type is OK_KEYX, the
fourth value is an abstract group element g to the x'th power.

The second line indicates that the responder replies with value
"Cookie-R" in the first field, a copy of the "Cookie-I" value in the
second field, message type OK_KEYX, and the number g raised to the
y'th power.

The value OK_KEYX is in capitals to indicate that it is a unique
constant (constants are defined in the appendices).

Variable precision integers with length zero are null values for the
protocol.

Sometimes the protocol will indicate that an entire payload (usually
the Key Exchange Payload) has null values. The payload is still
present in the message, for the purpose of simplifying parsing.

2.2.2 Guide to symbols

Cookie-I and Cookie-R (or CKY-I and CKY-R) are 64-bit pseudo-random
numbers. The generation method must ensure with high probability
that the numbers used for each IP remote address are unique over some
time period, such as one hour.

KEYID is the concatenation of the initiator and responder cookies and
the domain of interpretation; it is the name of keying material.

sKEYID is used to denote the keying material named by the KEYID. It
is never transmitted, but it is used in various calculations
performed by the two parties.

OK_KEYX and OK_NEWGRP are distinct message types.

IDP is a bit indicating whether or not material after the encryption
boundary (see appendix B), is encrypted. NIDP means not encrypted.

g^x and g^y are encodings of group elements, where g is a special
group element indicated in the group description (see Appendix A) and
g^x indicates that element raised to the x'th power. The type of the
encoding is either a variable precision integer or a pair of such

integers, as indicated in the group operation in the group description. Note that we will write g^xy as a short-hand for g^(xy). See Appendix F for references that describe implementing large integer computations and the relationship between various group definitions and basic arithmetic operations.

EHAO is a list of encryption/hash/authentication choices. Each item is a pair of values: a class name and an algorithm name.

EHAS is a set of three items selected from the EHAO list, one from each of the classes for encryption, hash, authentication.

GRP is a name (32-bit value) for the group and its relevant parameters: the size of the integers, the arithmetic operation, and the generator element. There are a few pre-defined GRP's (for 768 bit modular exponentiation groups, 1024 bit modexp, 2048 bit modexp, 155-bit and 210-bit elliptic curves, see Appendix E), but participants can share other group descriptions in a later protocol stage (see the section NEW GROUP). It is important to separate notion of the GRP from the group descriptor (Appendix A); the former is a name for the latter.

The symbol vertical bar "|" is used to denote concatenation of bit strings. Fields are concatenated using their encoded form as they appear in their payload.

Ni and Nr are nonces selected by the initiator and responder, respectively.

ID(I) and ID(R) are the identities to be used in authenticating the initiator and responder respectively.

E{x}Ki indicates the encryption of x using the public key of the initiator. Encryption is done using the algorithm associated with the authentication method; usually this will be RSA.

S{x}Ki indicates the signature over x using the private key (signing key) of the initiator. Signing is done using the algorithm associated with the authentication method; usually this will be RSA or DSS.

prf(a, b) denotes the result of applying pseudo-random function "a" to data "b". One may think of "a" as a key or as a value that characterizes the function prf; in the latter case it is the index into a family of functions. Each function in the family provides a "hash" or one-way mixing of the input.

prf(0, b) denotes the application of a one-way function to data "b".

The similarity with the previous notation is deliberate and indicates
that a single algorithm, e.g. MD5, might will used for both purposes.
In the first case a "keyed" MD5 transform would be used with key "a";
in the second case the transform would have the fixed key value zero,
resulting in a one-way function.

The term "transform" is used to refer to functions defined in
auxiliary RFC's. The transform RFC's will be drawn from those
defined for IPSEC AH and ESP (see RFC 2401 for the overall
architecture encompassing these protocols).

2.3 The Key Exchange Message Overview

The goal of key exchange processing is the secure establishment of
common keying information state in the two parties. This state
information is a key name, secret keying material, the identification
of the two parties, and three algorithms for use during
authentication: encryption (for privacy of the identities of the two
parties), hashing (a pseudorandom function for protecting the
integrity of the messages and for authenticating message fields), and
authentication (the algorithm on which the mutual authentication of
the two parties is based). The encodings and meanings for these
choices are presented in Appendix B.

The main mode exchange has five optional features: stateless cookie
exchange, perfect forward secrecy for the keying material, secrecy
for the identities, perfect forward secrecy for identity secrecy, use
of signatures (for non-repudiation). The two parties can use any
combination of these features.

The general outline of processing is that the Initiator of the
exchange begins by specifying as much information as he wishes in his
first message. The Responder replies, supplying as much information
as he wishes. The two sides exchange messages, supplying more
information each time, until their requirements are satisfied.

The choice of how much information to include in each message depends
on which options are desirable. For example, if stateless cookies
are not a requirement, and identity secrecy and perfect forward
secrecy for the keying material are not requirements, and if non-
repudiatable signatures are acceptable, then the exchange can be
completed in three messages.

Additional features may increase the number of roundtrips needed for
the keying material determination.

ISAKMP provides fields for specifying the security association
parameters for use with the AH and ESP protocols. These security

association payload types are specified in the ISAKMP memo; the
payload types can be protected with OAKLEY keying material and
algorithms, but this document does not discuss their use.

2.3.1 The Essential Key Exchange Message Fields

There are 12 fields in an OAKLEY key exchange message. Not all the
fields are relevant in every message; if a field is not relevant it
can have a null value or not be present (no payload).

```
     CKY-I            originator cookie.
     CKY-R            responder cookie.
     MSGTYPE          for key exchange, will be ISA_KE&AUTH_REQ or
                      ISA_KE&AUTH_REP; for new group definitions,
                      will be ISA_NEW_GROUP_REQ or ISA_NEW_GROUP_REP
     GRP              the name of the Diffie-Hellman group used for
                      the exchange
     g^x (or g^y)     variable length integer representing a power of
                      group generator
     EHAO or EHAS     encryption, hash, authentication functions,
                      offered and selectedj, respectively
     IDP              an indicator as to whether or not encryption with
                      g^xy follows (perfect forward secrecy for ID's)
     ID(I)            the identity for the Initiator
     ID(R)            the identity for the Responder
     Ni               nonce supplied by the Initiator
     Nr               nonce supplied by the Responder
```

The construction of the cookies is implementation dependent. Phil
Karn has recommended making them the result of a one-way function
applied to a secret value (changed periodically), the local and
remote IP address, and the local and remote UDP port. In this way,
the cookies remain stateless and expire periodically. Note that with
OAKLEY, this would cause the KEYID's derived from the secret value to
also expire, necessitating the removal of any state information
associated with it.

In order to support pre-distributed keys, we recommend that
implementations reserve some portion of their cookie space to
permanent keys. The encoding of these depends only on the local
implementation.

The encryption functions used with OAKLEY must be cryptographic
transforms which guarantee privacy and integrity for the message
data. Merely using DES in CBC mode is not permissible. The
MANDATORY and OPTIONAL transforms will include any that satisfy this
criteria and are defined for use with RFC 2406 (ESP).

The one-way (hash) functions used with OAKLEY must be cryptographic
transforms which can be used as either keyed hash (pseudo-random) or
non-keyed transforms. The MANDATORY and OPTIONAL transforms will
include any that are defined for use with RFC 2406 (AH).

Where nonces are indicated, they will be variable precision integers
with an entropy value that matches the "strength" attribute of the
GRP used with the exchange. If no GRP is indicated, the nonces must
be at least 90 bits long. The pseudo-random generator for the nonce
material should start with initial data that has at least 90 bits of
entropy; see RFC 1750.

2.3.1.1 Exponent Advice

Ideally, the exponents will have at least 180 bits of entropy for
every key exchange. This ensures complete independence of keying
material between two exchanges (note that this applies if only one of
the parties chooses a random exponent). In practice, implementors
may wish to base several key exchanges on a single base value with
180 bits of entropy and use one-way hash functions to guarantee that
exposure of one key will not compromise others. In this case, a good
recommendation is to keep the base values for nonces and cookies
separate from the base value for exponents, and to replace the base
value with a full 180 bits of entropy as frequently as possible.

The values 0 and p-1 should not be used as exponent values;
implementors should be sure to check for these values, and they
should also refuse to accept the values 1 and p-1 from remote parties
(where p is the prime used to define a modular exponentiation group).

2.3.2 Mapping to ISAKMP Message Structures

All the OAKLEY message fields correspond to ISAKMP message payloads
or payload components. The relevant payload fields are the SA
payload, the AUTH payload, the Certificate Payload, the Key Exchange
Payload. The ISAKMP protocol framwork is a work in progress at this
time, and the exact mapping of Oakley message fields to ISAKMP
payloads is also in progress (to be known as the Resolution
document).

Some of the ISAKMP header and payload fields will have constant
values when used with OAKLEY. The exact values to be used will be
published in a Domain of Interpretation document accompanying the
Resolution document.

In the following we indicate where each OAKLEY field appears in the
ISAKMP message structure. These are recommended only; the Resolution
document will be the final authority on this mapping.

```
CKY-I             ISAKMP header
CKY-R             ISAKMP header
MSGTYPE           Message Type in ISAKMP header
GRP               SA payload, Proposal section
g^x (or g^y)      Key Exchange Payload, encoded as a variable
                  precision integer
EHAO and EHAS     SA payload, Proposal section
IDP               A bit in the RESERVED field in the AUTH header
ID(I)             AUTH payload, Identity field
ID(R)             AUTH payload, Identity field
Ni                AUTH payload, Nonce Field
Nr                AUTH payload, Nonce Field
S{...}Kx          AUTH payload, Data Field
prf{K,...}        AUTH payload, Data Field
```

2.4 The Key Exchange Protocol

The exact number and content of messages exchanged during an OAKLEY
key exchange depends on which options the Initiator and Responder
want to use. A key exchange can be completed with three or more
messages, depending on those options.

The three components of the key determination protocol are the

1. cookie exchange (optionally stateless)
2. Diffie-Hellman half-key exchange (optional, but essential for
   perfect forward secrecy)
3. authentication (options: privacy for ID's, privacy for ID's
   with PFS, non-repudiable)

The initiator can supply as little information as a bare exchange
request, carrying no additional information. On the other hand the
initiator can begin by supplying all of the information necessary for
the responder to authenticate the request and complete the key
determination quickly, if the responder chooses to accept this
method. If not, the responder can reply with a minimal amount of
information (at the minimum, a cookie).

The method of authentication can be digital signatures, public key
encryption, or an out-of-band symmetric key. The three different
methods lead to slight variations in the messages, and the variations
are illustrated by examples in this section.

The Initiator is responsible for retransmitting messages if the
protocol does not terminate in a timely fashion. The Responder must
therefore avoid discarding reply information until it is acknowledged
by Initiator in the course of continuing the protocol.

The remainder of this section contains examples demonstrating how to use OAKLEY options.

2.4.1 An Aggressive Example

The following example indicates how two parties can complete a key exchange in three messages. The identities are not secret, the derived keying material is protected by PFS.

By using digital signatures, the two parties will have a proof of communication that can be recorded and presented later to a third party.

The keying material implied by the group exponentials is not needed for completing the exchange. If it is desirable to defer the computation, the implementation can save the "x" and "g^y" values and mark the keying material as "uncomputed". It can be computed from this information later.

```
Initiator                                                   Responder
---------                                                   ---------
 -> CKY-I, 0,     OK_KEYX, GRP, g^x, EHAO, NIDP,                  ->
    ID(I), ID(R), Ni, 0,
    S{ID(I) | ID(R) | Ni | 0 | GRP | g^x | 0 | EHAO}Ki
 <- CKY-R, CKY-I, OK_KEYX, GRP, g^y, EHAS, NIDP,
    ID(R), ID(I), Nr, Ni,
    S{ID(R) | ID(I) | Nr | Ni | GRP | g^y | g^x | EHAS}Kr      <-
 -> CKY-I, CKY-R, OK_KEYX, GRP, g^x, EHAS, NIDP,                  ->
    ID(I), ID(R), Ni, Nr,
    S{ID(I) | ID(R) | Ni | Nr | GRP | g^x | g^y | EHAS}Ki
```

NB "NIDP" means that the PFS option for hiding identities is not used.
   i.e., the identities are not encrypted using a key based on g^xy

NB Fields are shown separated by commas in this document; they are concatenated in the actual protocol messages using their encoded forms as specified in the ISAKMP/Oakley Resolution document.

The result of this exchange is a key with KEYID = CKY-I|CKY-R and value

sKEYID = prf(Ni | Nr, g^xy | CKY-I | CKY-R).

The processing outline for this exchange is as follows:

Initiation

>   The Initiator generates a unique cookie and associates it with the
>   expected IP address of the responder, and its chosen state
>   information: GRP (the group identifier), a pseudo-randomly
>   selected exponent x, g^x, EHAO list, nonce, identities. The first
>   authentication choice in the EHAO list is an algorithm that
>   supports digital signatures, and this is used to sign the ID's and
>   the nonce and group id. The Initiator further

>   notes that the key is in the initial state of "unauthenticated",
>   and

>   sets a timer for possible retransmission and/or termination of the
>   request.

When the Responder receives the message, he may choose to ignore all
the information and treat it as merely a request for a cookie,
creating no state. If CKY-I is not already in use by the source
address in the IP header, the responder generates a unique cookie,
CKY-R. The next steps depend on the Responder's preferences. The
minimal required response is to reply with the first cookie field set
to zero and CKY-R in the second field. For this example we will
assume that the responder is more aggressive (for the alternatives,
see section 6) and accepts the following:

>   group with identifier GRP,
>   first authentication choice (which must be the digital signature
>   method used to sign the Initiator message),
>   lack of perfect forward secrecy for protecting the identities,
>   identity ID(I) and identity ID(R)

In this example the Responder decides to accept all the information
offered by the initiator. It validates the signature over the signed
portion of the message, and associate the pair (CKY-I, CKY-R) with
the following state information:

>   the source and destination network addresses of the message

>   key state of "unauthenticated"

>   the first algorithm from the authentication offer

>   group GRP, a "y" exponent value in group GRP, and g^x from the
>   message

>   the nonce Ni and a pseudorandomly selected value Nr

a timer for possible destruction of the state.

The Responder computes g^y, forms the reply message, and then signs the ID and nonce information with the private key of ID(R) and sends it to the Initiator. In all exchanges, each party should make sure that he neither offers nor accepts 1 or g^(p-1) as an exponential.

In this example, to expedite the protocol, the Responder implicitly accepts the first algorithm in the Authentication class of the EHAO list. This because he cannot validate the Initiator signature without accepting the algorithm for doing the signature. The Responder's EHAS list will also reflect his acceptance.

The Initiator receives the reply message and
   validates that CKY-I is a valid association for the network
   address of the incoming message,

   adds the CKY-R value to the state for the pair (CKY-I, network
   address), and associates all state information with the pair
   (CKY-I, CKY-R),

   validates the signature of the responder over the state
   information (should validation fail, the message is discarded)

   adds g^y to its state information,

   saves the EHA selections in the state,

   optionally computes (g^y)^x (= g^xy) (this can be deferred until
   after sending the reply message),

   sends the reply message, signed with the public key of ID(I),

   marks the KEYID (CKY-I|CKY-R) as authenticated,

   and composes the reply message and signature.

When the Responder receives the Initiator message, and if the signature is valid, it marks the key as being in the authenticated state. It should compute g^xy and associate it with the KEYID.

Note that although PFS for identity protection is not used, PFS for the derived keying material is still present because the Diffie-Hellman half-keys g^x and g^y are exchanged.

Even if the Responder only accepts some of the Initiator information, the Initiator will consider the protocol to be progressing. The Initiator should assume that fields that were not accepted by the

Responder were not recorded by the Responder.

If the Responder does not accept the aggressive exchange and selects another algorithm for the A function, then the protocol will not continue using the signature algorithm or the signature value from the first message.

2.4.1.1 Fields Not Present

If the Responder does not accept all the fields offered by the Initiator, he should include null values for those fields in his response. Section 6 has guidelines on how to select fields in a "left-to-right" manner. If a field is not accepted, then it and all following fields must have null values.

The Responder should not record any information that it does not accept. If the ID's and nonces have null values, there will not be a signature over these null values.

2.4.1.2 Signature via Pseudo-Random Functions

The aggressive example is written to suggest that public key technology is used for the signatures. However, a pseudorandom function can be used, if the parties have previously agreed to such a scheme and have a shared key.

If the first proposal in the EHAO list is an "existing key" method, then the KEYID named in that proposal will supply the keying material for the "signature" which is computed using the "H" algorithm associated with the KEYID.

Suppose the first proposal in EHAO is
    EXISTING-KEY, 32
and the "H" algorithm for KEYID 32 is MD5-HMAC, by prior negotiation. The keying material is some string of bits, call it sK32. Then in the first message in the aggressive exchange, where the signature

        S{ID(I), ID(R), Ni, 0, GRP, g^x, EHAO}Ki

is indicated, the signature computation would be performed by
    MD5-HMAC_func(KEY=sK32, DATA = ID(I) | ID(R) | Ni | 0 | GRP | g^x | g^y | EHAO) (The exact definition of the algorithm corresponding to "MD5-HMAC- func" will appear in the RFC defining that transform).

The result of this computation appears in the Authentication payload.

2.4.2 An Aggressive Example With Hidden Identities

   The following example indicates how two parties can complete a key
   exchange without using digital signatures. Public key cryptography
   hides the identities during authentication. The group exponentials
   are exchanged and authenticated, but the implied keying material
   (g^xy) is not needed during the exchange.

   This exchange has an important difference from the previous signature
   scheme -- in the first message, an identity for the responder is
   indicated as cleartext: ID(R'). However, the identity hidden with
   the public key cryptography is different: ID(R). This happens
   because the Initiator must somehow tell the Responder which
   public/private key pair to use for the decryption, but at the same
   time, the identity is hidden by encryption with that public key.

   The Initiator might elect to forgo secrecy of the Responder identity,
   but this is undesirable. Instead, if there is a well-known identity
   for the Responder node, the public key for that identity can be used
   to encrypt the actual Responder identity.

```
   Initiator                                                 Responder
   ---------                                                 ---------
     -> CKY-I, 0,      OK_KEYX, GRP, g^x, EHAO, NIDP,              ->
        ID(R'), E{ID(I), ID(R), E{Ni}Kr}Kr'
   <-  CKY-R, CKY-I, OK_KEYX, GRP, g^y, EHAS, NIDP,
       E{ID(R), ID(I), Nr}Ki,
       prf(Kir, ID(R) | ID(I) | GRP | g^y | g^x | EHAS) <-
     -> CKY-I, CKY-R, OK_KEYX, GRP, 0, 0, NIDP,
        prf(Kir, ID(I) | ID(R) | GRP | g^x | g^y | EHAS)    ->
```

   Kir = prf(0, Ni | Nr)

   NB "NIDP" means that the PFS option for hiding identities is not used.

   NB The ID(R') value is included in the Authentication payload as
       described in Appendix B.

   The result of this exchange is a key with KEYID = CKY-I|CKY-R and
   value sKEYID = prf(Ni | Nr, g^xy | CKY-I | CKY-R).

   The processing outline for this exchange is as follows:

   Initiation
      The Initiator generates a unique cookie and associates it with the
      expected IP address of the responder, and its chosen state
      information: GRP, g^x, EHAO list. The first authentication choice
      in the EHAO list is an algorithm that supports public key

encryption. The Initiator also names the two identities to be
used for the connection and enters these into the state. A well-
known identity for the responder machine is also chosen, and the
public key for this identity is used to encrypt the nonce Ni and
the two connection identities. The Initiator further

notes that the key is in the initial state of "unauthenticated",
and

sets a timer for possible retransmission and/or termination of the
request.

When the Responder receives the message, he may choose to ignore all
the information and treat it as merely a request for a cookie,
creating no state.

If CKY-I is not already in use by the source address in the IP
header, the Responder generates a unique cookie, CKY-R. As before,
the next steps depend on the responder's preferences. The minimal
required response is a message with the first cookie field set to
zero and CKY-R in the second field. For this example we will assume
that responder is more aggressive and accepts the following:

group GRP, first authentication choice (which must be the public
key encryption algorithm used to encrypt the payload), lack of
perfect forward secrecy for protecting the identities, identity
ID(I), identity ID(R)

The Responder must decrypt the ID and nonce information, using the
private key for the R' ID. After this, the private key for the R ID
will be used to decrypt the nonce field.

The Responder now associates the pair (CKY-I, CKY-R) with the
following state information:

the source and destination network addresses of the message

key state of "unauthenticated"

the first algorithm from each class in the EHAO (encryption-hash-
authentication algorithm offers) list

group GRP and a y and g^y value in group GRP

the nonce Ni and a pseudorandomly selected value Nr

a timer for possible destruction of the state.

The Responder then encrypts the state information with the public key
of ID(I), forms the prf value, and sends it to the Initiator.

The Initiator receives the reply message and
    validates that CKY-I is a valid association for the network
    address of the incoming message,

    adds the CKY-R value to the state for the pair (CKY-I, network
    address), and associates all state information with the pair
    (CKY-I, CKY-R),

    decrypts the ID and nonce information

    checks the prf calculation (should this fail, the message is
    discarded)

    adds g^y to its state information,

    saves the EHA selections in the state,

    optionally computes (g^x)^y (= g^xy) (this may be deferred), and

    sends the reply message, encrypted with the public key of ID(R),

    and marks the KEYID (CKY-I|CKY-R) as authenticated.

When the Responder receives this message, it marks the key as being
in the authenticated state. If it has not already done so, it should
compute g^xy and associate it with the KEYID.

The secret keying material sKEYID = prf(Ni | Nr, g^xy | CKY-I |
CKY-R)

Note that although PFS for identity protection is not used, PFS for
the derived keying material is still present because the Diffie-
Hellman half-keys g^x and g^y are exchanged.

2.4.3 An Aggressive Example With Private Identities and Without Diffie-
    Hellman

Considerable computational expense can be avoided if perfect forward
secrecy is not a requirement for the session key derivation. The two
parties can exchange nonces and secret key parts to achieve the
authentication and derive keying material. The long-term privacy of
data protected with derived keying material is dependent on the
private keys of each of the parties.

In this exchange, the GRP has the value 0 and the field for the group
exponential is used to hold a nonce value instead.

As in the previous section, the first proposed algorithm must be a
public key encryption system; by responding with a cookie and a non-
zero exponential field, the Responder implicitly accepts the first
proposal and the lack of perfect forward secrecy for the identities
and derived keying material.

```
 Initiator                                                   Responder
 ---------                                                   ---------
   -> CKY-I, 0,      OK_KEYX, 0, 0, EHAO, NIDP,                  ->
      ID(R'), E{ID(I), ID(R), sKi}Kr', Ni
   <- CKY-R, CKY-I, OK_KEYX, 0, 0, EHAS, NIDP,
      E{ID(R), ID(I), sKr}Ki, Nr,
      prf(Kir, ID(R) | ID(I) | Nr | Ni | EHAS)                  <-
   -> CKY-I, CKY-R, OK_KEYX, EHAS, NIDP,
      prf(Kir, ID(I) | ID(R) | Ni | Nr | EHAS)                  ->
```

Kir = prf(0, sKi | sKr)

NB The sKi and sKr values go into the nonce fields. The change in
notation is meant to emphasize that their entropy is critical to
setting the keying material.

NB "NIDP" means that the PFS option for hiding identities is not
used.

The result of this exchange is a key with KEYID = CKY-I|CKY-R and
value sKEYID = prf(Kir, CKY-I | CKY-R).

2.4.3 A Conservative Example

In this example the two parties are minimally aggressive; they use
the cookie exchange to delay creation of state, and they use perfect
forward secrecy to protect the identities. For this example, they
use public key encryption for authentication; digital signatures or
pre-shared keys can also be used, as illustrated previously. The
conservative example here does not change the use of nonces, prf's,
etc., but it does change how much information is transmitted in each
message.

The responder considers the ability of the initiator to repeat CKY-R
as weak evidence that the message originates from a "live"
correspondent on the network and the correspondent is associated with
the initiator's network address. The initiator makes similar
assumptions when CKY-I is repeated to the initiator.

All messages must have either valid cookies or at least one zero
cookie. If both cookies are zero, this indicates a request for a
cookie; if only the initiator cookie is zero, it is a response to a
cookie request.

Information in messages violating the cookie rules cannot be used for
any OAKLEY operations.

Note that the Initiator and Responder must agree on one set of EHA
algorithms; there is not one set for the Responder and one for the
Initiator. The Initiator must include at least MD5 and DES in the
initial offer.

Fields not indicated have null values.

```
Initiator                                              Responder
---------                                              ---------
 ->     0, 0, OK_KEYX                                       ->
 <-     0, CKY-R, OK_KEYX                                   <-
 ->     CKY-I, CKY-R, OK_KEYX, GRP, g^x, EHAO               ->
 <-     CKY-R, CKY-I, OK_KEYX, GRP, g^y, EHAS               <-
 ->     CKY-I, CKY-R, OK_KEYX, GRP, g^x, IDP*,
        ID(I), ID(R), E{Ni}Kr,                             ->
 <-     CKY-R, CKY-I, OK_KEYX, GRP, 0  , 0, IDP,            <-
        E{Nr, Ni}Ki, ID(R), ID(I),
        prf(Kir, ID(R) | ID(I) | GRP | g^y | g^x | EHAS )
 ->     CKY-I, CKY-R, OK_KEYX, GRP, 0  , 0, IDP,
        prf(Kir, ID(I) | ID(R) | GRP | g^x | g^y | EHAS ) ->
```

Kir = prf(0, Ni | Nr)

* when IDP is in effect, authentication payloads are encrypted with
  the selected encryption algorithm using the keying material prf(0,
  g^xy). (The transform defining the encryption algorithm will
  define how to select key bits from the keying material.) This
  encryption is in addition to and after any public key encryption.
  See Appendix B.

  Note that in the first messages, several fields are omitted from
  the description. These fields are present as null values.

The first exchange allows the Responder to use stateless cookies; if
the responder generates cookies in a manner that allows him to
validate them without saving them, as in Photuris, then this is
possible. Even if the Initiator includes a cookie in his initial
request, the responder can still use stateless cookies by merely
omitting the CKY-I from his reply and by declining to record the
Initiator cookie until it appears in a later message.

After the exchange is complete, both parties compute the shared key material sKEYID as prf(Ni | Nr, g^xy | CKY-I | CKY-R) where "prf" is the pseudo-random function in class "hash" selected in the EHA list.

As with the cookies, each party considers the ability of the remote side to repeat the Ni or Nr value as a proof that Ka, the public key of party a, speaks for the remote party and establishes its identity.

In analyzing this exchange, it is important to note that although the IDP option ensures that the identities are protected with an ephemeral key g^xy, the authentication itself does not depend on g^xy. It is essential that the authentication steps validate the g^x and g^y values, and it is thus imperative that the authentication not involve a circular dependency on them. A third party could intervene with a "man-in-middle" scheme to convince the initiator and responder to use different g^xy values; although such an attack might result in revealing the identities to the eavesdropper, the authentication would fail.

2.4.4 Extra Strength for Protection of Encryption Keys

The nonces Ni and Nr are used to provide an extra dimension of secrecy in deriving session keys. This makes the secrecy of the key depend on two different problems: the discrete logarithm problem in the group G, and the problem of breaking the nonce encryption scheme. If RSA encryption is used, then this second problem is roughly equivalent to factoring the RSA public keys of both the initiator and responder.

For authentication, the key type, the validation method, and the certification requirement must be indicated.

2.5 Identity and Authentication

2.5.1 Identity

In OAKLEY exchanges the Initiator offers Initiator and Responder ID's -- the former is the claimed identity for the Initiator, and the latter is the requested ID for the Responder.

If neither ID is specified, the ID's are taken from the IP header source and destination addresses.

If the Initiator doesn't supply a responder ID, the Responder can reply by naming any identity that the local policy allows. The Initiator can refuse acceptance by terminating the exchange.

The Responder can also reply with a different ID than the Initiator
suggested; the Initiator can accept this implicitly by continuing the
exchange or refuse it by terminating (not replying).

2.5.2 Authentication

The authentication of principals to one another is at the heart of
any key exchange scheme. The Internet community must decide on a
scalable standard for solving this problem, and OAKLEY must make use
of that standard. At the time of this writing, there is no such
standard, though several are emerging. This document attempts to
describe how a handful of standards could be incorporated into
OAKLEY, without attempting to pick and choose among them.

The following methods can appear in OAKLEY offers:

a. Pre-shared Keys
   When two parties have arranged for a trusted method of
   distributing secret keys for their mutual authentication, they can
   be used for authentication. This has obvious scaling problems for
   large systems, but it is an acceptable interim solution for some
   situations. Support for pre-shared keys is REQUIRED.

   The encryption, hash, and authentication algorithm for use with a
   pre-shared key must be part of the state information distributed
   with the key itself.

   The pre-shared keys have a KEYID and keying material sKEYID; the
   KEYID is used in a pre-shared key authentication option offer.
   There can be more than one pre-shared key offer in a list.

   Because the KEYID persists over different invocations of OAKLEY
   (after a crash, etc.), it must occupy a reserved part of the KEYID
   space for the two parties. A few bits can be set aside in each
   party's "cookie space" to accommodate this.

   There is no certification authority for pre-shared keys. When a
   pre-shared key is used to generate an authentication payload, the
   certification authority is "None", the Authentication Type is
   "Preshared", and the payload contains

       the KEYID, encoded as two 64-bit quantities, and the result of
       applying the pseudorandom hash function to the message body
       with the sKEYID forming the key for the function

b. DNS public keys
   Security extensions to the DNS protocol [DNSSEC] provide a
   convenient way to access public key information, especially for
   public keys associated with hosts. RSA keys are a requirement for
   secure DNS implementations; extensions to allow optional DSS keys
   are a near-term possibility.

   DNS KEY records have associated SIG records that are signed by a
   zone authority, and a hierarchy of signatures back to the root
   server establishes a foundation for trust. The SIG records
   indicate the algorithm used for forming the signature.

   OAKLEY implementations must support the use of DNS KEY and SIG
   records for authenticating with respect to IPv4 and IPv6 addresses
   and fully qualified domain names. However, implementations are
   not required to support any particular algorithm (RSA, DSS, etc.).

c. RSA public keys w/o certification authority signature PGP
   [Zimmerman] uses public keys with an informal method for
   establishing trust. The format of PGP public keys and naming
   methods will be described in a separate RFC. The RSA algorithm
   can be used with PGP keys for either signing or encryption; the
   authentication option should indicate either RSA-SIG or RSA-ENC,
   respectively. Support for this is OPTIONAL.

d.1 RSA public keys w/ certificates There are various formats and
   naming conventions for public keys that are signed by one or more
   certification authorities. The Public Key Interchange Protocol
   discusses X.509 encodings and validation. Support for this is
   OPTIONAL.

d.2 DSS keys w/ certificates Encoding for the Digital Signature
   Standard with X.509 is described in draft-ietf-ipsec-dss-cert-
   00.txt. Support for this is OPTIONAL; an ISAKMP Authentication
   Type will be assigned.

2.5.3 Validating Authentication Keys

   The combination of the Authentication algorithm, the Authentication
   Authority, the Authentication Type, and a key (usually public) define
   how to validate the messages with respect to the claimed identity.
   The key information will be available either from a pre-shared key,
   or from some kind of certification authority.

   Generally the certification authority produces a certificate binding
   the entity name to a public key. OAKLEY implementations must be
   prepared to fetch and validate certificates before using the public
   key for OAKLEY authentication purposes.

The ISAKMP Authentication Payload defines the Authentication
Authority field for specifying the authority that must be apparent in
the trust hierarchy for authentication.

Once an appropriate certificate is obtained (see 2.4.3), the
validation method will depend on the Authentication Type; if it is
PGP then the PGP signature validation routines can be called to
satisfy the local web-of-trust predicates; if it is RSA with X.509
certificates, the certificate must be examined to see if the
certification authority signature can be validated, and if the
hierarchy is recognized by the local policy.

2.5.4 Fetching Identity Objects

In addition to interpreting the certificate or other data structure
that contains an identity, users of OAKLEY must face the task of
retrieving certificates that bind a public key to an identifier and
also retrieving auxiliary certificates for certifying authorities or
co-signers (as in the PGP web of trust).

The ISAKMP Credentials Payload can be used to attach useful
certificates to OAKLEY messages. The Credentials Payload is defined
in Appendix B.

Support for accessing and revoking public key certificates via the
Secure DNS protocol [SECDNS] is MANDATORY for OAKLEY implementations.
Other retrieval methods can be used when the AUTH class indicates a
preference.

The Public Key Interchange Protocol discusses a full protocol that
might be used with X.509 encoded certificates.

2.6 Interface to Cryptographic Transforms

The keying material computed by the key exchange should have at least
90 bits of entropy, which means that it must be at least 90 bits in
length. This may be more or less than is required for keying the
encryption and/or pseudorandom function transforms.

The transforms used with OAKLEY should have auxiliary algorithms
which take a variable precision integer and turn it into keying
material of the appropriate length. For example, a DES algorithm
could take the low order 56 bits, a triple DES algorithm might use
the following:

                K1 = low 56 bits of md5(0|sKEYID)
                K2 = low 56 bits of md5(1|sKEYID)
                K3 = low 56 bits of md5(2|sKEYID)

The transforms will be called with the keying material encoded as a
variable precision integer, the length of the data, and the block of
memory with the data. Conversion of the keying material to a
transform key is the responsibility of the transform.

2.7 Retransmission, Timeouts, and Error Messages

If a response from the Responder is not elicited in an appropriate
amount of time, the message should be retransmitted by the Initiator.
These retransmissions must be handled gracefully by both parties; the
Responder must retain information for retransmitting until the
Initiator moves to the next message in the protocol or completes the
exchange.

Informational error messages present a problem because they cannot be
authenticated using only the information present in an incomplete
exchange; for this reason, the parties may wish to establish a
default key for OAKLEY error messages. A possible method for
establishing such a key is described in Appendix B, under the use of
ISA_INIT message types.

In the following the message type is OAKLEY Error, the KEYID supplies
the H algorithm and key for authenticating the message contents; this
value is carried in the Sig/Prf payload.

The Error payload contains the error code and the contents of the
rejected message.

```
                              1                   2                   3
         0 1 2 3 4 5 6 7 8 9 0 1 2 3 4 5 6 7 8 9 0 1 2 3 4 5 6 7 8 9 0 1
         +-+-+-+-+-+-+-+-+-+-+-+-+-+-+-+-+-+-+-+-+-+-+-+-+-+-+-+-+-+-+-+-+
         !                                                               !
         ~                      Initiator-Cookie                        ~
      /  !                                                               !
KEYID    +-+-+-+-+-+-+-+-+-+-+-+-+-+-+-+-+-+-+-+-+-+-+-+-+-+-+-+-+-+-+-+-+
      \  !                                                               !
         ~                      Responder-Cookie                        ~
         !                                                               !
         +-+-+-+-+-+-+-+-+-+-+-+-+-+-+-+-+-+-+-+-+-+-+-+-+-+-+-+-+-+-+-+-+
         !                   Domain of Interpretation                   !
         +-+-+-+-+-+-+-+-+-+-+-+-+-+-+-+-+-+-+-+-+-+-+-+-+-+-+-+-+-+-+-+-+
         ! Message Type  ! Exch  ! Vers  !            Length            !
         +-+-+-+-+-+-+-+-+-+-+-+-+-+-+-+-+-+-+-+-+-+-+-+-+-+-+-+-+-+-+-+-+
         !                        SPI (unused)                          !
         +-+-+-+-+-+-+-+-+-+-+-+-+-+-+-+-+-+-+-+-+-+-+-+-+-+-+-+-+-+-+-+-+
         !                        SPI (unused)                          !
         +-+-+-+-+-+-+-+-+-+-+-+-+-+-+-+-+-+-+-+-+-+-+-+-+-+-+-+-+-+-+-+-+
         !                        Error Payload                         !
         ~                                                               ~
         +-+-+-+-+-+-+-+-+-+-+-+-+-+-+-+-+-+-+-+-+-+-+-+-+-+-+-+-+-+-+-+-+
         !                        Sig/prf Payload                       !
         ~                                                               ~
         +-+-+-+-+-+-+-+-+-+-+-+-+-+-+-+-+-+-+-+-+-+-+-+-+-+-+-+-+-+-+-+-+
```

The error message will contain the cookies as presented in the
offending message, the message type OAKLEY_ERROR, and the reason for
the error, followed by the rejected message.

Error messages are informational only, and the correctness of the
protocol does not depend on them.

Error reasons:

```
TIMEOUT                    exchange has taken too long, state destroyed
AEH_ERROR                  an unknown algorithm appears in an offer
GROUP_NOT_SUPPORTED        GRP named is not supported
EXPONENTIAL_UNACCEPTABLE   exponential too large/small or is +-1
SELECTION_NOT_OFFERED      selection does not occur in offer
NO_ACCEPTABLE_OFFERS       no offer meets host requirements
AUTHENTICATION_FAILURE     signature or hash function fails
RESOURCE_EXCEEDED          too many exchanges or too much state info
NO_EXCHANGE_IN_PROGRESS    a reply received with no request in progress
```

2.8 Additional Security for Privacy Keys: Private Groups

   If the two parties have need to use a Diffie-Hellman key
   determination scheme that does not depend on the standard group
   definitions, they have the option of establishing a private group.
   The authentication need not be repeated, because this stage of the
   protocol will be protected by a pre-existing authentication key. As
   an extra security measure, the two parties will establish a private
   name for the shared keying material, so even if they use exactly the
   same group to communicate with other parties, the re-use will not be
   apparent to passive attackers.

   Private groups have the advantage of making a widespread passive
   attack much harder by increasing the number of groups that would have
   to be exhaustively analyzed in order to recover a large number of
   session keys. This contrasts with the case when only one or two
   groups are ever used; in that case, one would expect that years and
   years of session keys would be compromised.

   There are two technical challenges to face: how can a particular user
   create a unique and appropriate group, and how can a second party
   assure himself that the proposed group is reasonably secure?

   The security of a modular exponentiation group depends on the largest
   prime factor of the group size. In order to maximize this, one can
   choose "strong" or Sophie Germaine primes, $P = 2Q + 1$, where P and Q
   are prime. However, if $P = kQ + 1$, where k is small, then the
   strength of the group is still considerable. These groups are known
   as Schnorr subgroups, and they can be found with much less
   computational effort than Sophie-Germaine primes.

   Schnorr subgroups can also be validated efficiently by using probable
   prime tests.

   It is also fairly easy to find P, k, and Q such that the largest
   prime factor can be easily proven to be Q.

   We estimate that it would take about 10 minutes to find a new group
   of about 2^{1024} elements, and this could be done once a day by a
   scheduled process; validating a group proposed by a remote party
   would take perhaps a minute on a 25 MHz RISC machine or a 66 MHz CISC
   machine.

   We note that validation is done only between previously mutually
   authenticated parties, and that a new group definition always follows
   and is protected by a key established using a well-known group.
   There are five points to keep in mind:

a. The description and public identifier for the new group are protected by the well-known group.

b. The responder can reject the attempt to establish the new group, either because he is too busy or because he cannot validate the largest prime factor as being sufficiently large.

c. The new modulus and generator can be cached for long periods of time; they are not security critical and need not be associated with ongoing activity.

d. Generating a new g^x value periodically will be more expensive if there are many groups cached; however, the importance of frequently generating new g^x values is reduced, so the time period can be lengthened correspondingly.

e. All modular exponentiation groups have subgroups that are weaker than the main group. For Sophie Germain primes, if the generator is a square, then there are only two elements in the subgroup: 1 and g^(-1) (same as g^(p-1)) which we have already recommended avoiding. For Schnorr subgroups with k not equal to 2, the subgroup can be avoided by checking that the exponential is not a kth root of 1 (e^k != 1 mod p).

2.8.1 Defining a New Group

This section describes how to define a new group. The description of the group is hidden from eavesdroppers, and the identifier assigned to the group is unique to the two parties. Use of the new group for Diffie-Hellman key exchanges is described in the next section.

The secrecy of the description and the identifier increases the difficulty of a passive attack, because if the group descriptor is not known to the attacker, there is no straightforward and efficient way to gain information about keys calculated using the group.

Only the description of the new group need be encrypted in this exchange. The hash algorithm is implied by the OAKLEY session named by the group. The encryption is the encryption function of the OAKLEY session.

The descriptor of the new group is encoded in the new group payload. The nonces are encoded in the Authentication Payload.

Data beyond the encryption boundary is encrypted using the transform named by the KEYID.

The following messages use the ISAKMP Key Exchange Identifier OAKLEY
New Group.

To define a new modular exponentiation group:

```
   Initiator                                        Responder
   -----                                            -----
   ->   KEYID,                                         ->
        INEWGRP,
        Desc(New Group), Na
        prf(sKEYID, Desc(New Group) | Na)

   <-   KEYID,
        INEWGRPRS,
        Na, Nb
        prf(sKEYID, Na | Nb | Desc(New Group))        <-

    ->  KEYID,
        INEWGRPACK
        prf(sKEYID, Nb | Na | Desc(New Group))         ->
```

These messages are encrypted at the encryption boundary using the key
indicated. The hash value is placed in the "digital signature" field
(see Appendix B).

New GRP identifier = trunc16(Na) | trunc16(Nb)

(trunc16 indicates truncation to 16 bits; the initiator and
responder must use nonces that have distinct upper bits from any
used for current GRPID's)

Desc(G) is the encoding of the descriptor for the group descriptor
(see Appendix A for the format of a group descriptor)

The two parties must store the mapping between the new group
identifier GRP and the group descriptor Desc(New Group). They must
also note the identities used for the KEYID and copy these to the
state for the new group.

Note that one could have the same group descriptor associated with
several KEYID's. Pre-calculation of g^x values may be done based
only on the group descriptor, not the private group name.

2.8.2 Deriving a Key Using a Private Group

Once a private group has been established, its group id can be used
in the key exchange messages in the GRP position. No changes to the
protocol are required.

2.9 Quick Mode: New Keys From Old,

When an authenticated KEYID and associated keying material sKEYID already exist, it is easy to derive additional KEYID's and keys sharing similar attributes (GRP, EHA, etc.) using only hashing functions. The KEYID might be one that was derived in Main Mode, for example.

On the other hand, the authenticated key may be a manually distributed key, one that is shared by the initiator and responder via some means external to OAKLEY. If the distribution method has formed the KEYID using appropriately unique values for the two halves (CKY-I and CKY-R), then this method is applicable.

In the following, the Key Exchange Identifier is OAKLEY Quick Mode. The nonces are carried in the Authentication Payload, and the prf value is carried in the Authentication Payload; the Authentication Authority is "None" and the type is "Pre-Shared".

The protocol is:

```
  Initiator                                          Responder
  ---------                                          ---------
  -> KEYID, INEWKRQ, Ni, prf(sKEYID, Ni)                ->
 <-  KEYID, INEWKRS, Nr, prf(sKEYID, 1 | Nr | Ni)      <-
  -> KEYID, INEWKRP, 0, prf(sKEYID,  0 | Ni | Nr)       ->
```

The New KEYID, NKEYID, is Ni | Nr

sNKEYID = prf(sKEYID, Ni | Nr)

The identities and EHA values associated with NKEYID are the same as those associated with KEYID.

Each party must validate the hash values before using the new key for any purpose.

2.10 Defining and Using Pre-Distributed Keys

If a key and an associated key identifier and state information have been distributed manually, then the key can be used for any OAKLEY purpose. The key must be associated with the usual state information: ID's and EHA algorithms.

Local policy dictates when a manual key can be included in the OAKLEY database. For example, only privileged users would be permitted to introduce keys associated with privileged ID's, an unprivileged user could only introduce keys associated with her own ID.

2.11 Distribution of an External Key

   Once an OAKLEY session key and ancillary algorithms are established,
   the keying material and the "H" algorithm can be used to distribute
   an externally generated key and to assign a KEYID to it.

   In the following, KEYID represents an existing, authenticated OAKLEY
   session key, and sNEWKEYID represents the externally generated keying
   material.

   In the following, the Key Exchange Identifier is OAKLEY External
   Mode. The Key Exchange Payload contains the new key, which is
   protected

   Initiator   Responder
   ---------   ---------
   -> KEYID, IEXTKEY, Ni, prf(sKEYID, Ni)   ->
   <- KEYID, IEXTKEY, Nr, prf(sKEYID, 1 | Nr | Ni)   <-
   -> KEYID, IEXTKEY, Kir xor sNEWKEYID*, prf(Kir, sNEWKEYID | Ni | Nr) ->

   Kir = prf(sKEYID, Ni | Nr)

   * this field is carried in the Key Exchange Payload.

   Each party must validate the hash values using the "H" function in
   the KEYID state before changing any key state information.

   The new key is recovered by the Responder by calculating the xor of
   the field in the Authentication Payload with the Kir value.

   The new key identifier, naming the keying material sNEWKEYID, is
   prf(sKEYID, 1 | Ni | Nr).

   Note that this exchange does not require encryption. Hugo Krawcyzk
   suggested the method and noted its advantage.

2.11.1 Cryptographic Strength Considerations

   The strength of the key used to distribute the external key must be
   at least equal to the strength of the external key. Generally, this
   means that the length of the sKEYID material must be greater than or
   equal to the length of the sNEWKEYID material.

   The derivation of the external key, its strength or intended use are
   not addressed by this protocol; the parties using the key must have
   some other method for determining these properties.

As of early 1996, it appears that for 90 bits of cryptographic
strength, one should use a modular exponentiation group modulus of
2000 bits. For 128 bits of strength, a 3000 bit modulus is required.

3. Specifying and Deriving Security Associations

When a security association is defined, only the KEYID need be given.
The responder should be able to look up the state associated with the
KEYID value and find the appropriate keying material, sKEYID.

Deriving keys for use with IPSEC protocols such as ESP or AH is a
subject covered in the ISAKMP/Oakley Resolution document. That
document also describes how to negotiate acceptable parameter sets
and identifiers for ESP and AH, and how to exactly calculate the
keying material for each instance of the protocols. Because the
basic keying material defined here (g^xy) may be used to derive keys
for several instances of ESP and AH, the exact mechanics of using
one-way functions to turn g^xy into several unique keys is essential
to correct usage.

4. ISAKMP Compatibility

OAKLEY uses ISAKMP header and payload formats, as described in the
text and in Appendix B. There are particular noteworthy extensions
beyond the version 4 draft.

4.1 Authentication with Existing Keys

In the case that two parties do not have suitable public key
mechanisms in place for authenticating each other, they can use keys
that were distributed manually. After establishment of these keys
and their associated state in OAKLEY, they can be used for
authentication modes that depend on signatures, e.g. Aggressive Mode.

When an existing key is to appear in an offer list, it should be
indicated with an Authentication Algorithm of ISAKMP_EXISTING. This
value will be assigned in the ISAKMP RFC.

When the authentication method is ISAKMP_EXISTING, the authentication
authority will have the value ISAKMP_AUTH_EXISTING; the value for
this field must not conflict with any authentication authority
registered with IANA and is defined in the ISAKMP RFC.

The authentication payload will have two parts:

   the KEYID for the pre-existing key

   the identifier for the party to be authenticated by the pre-
   existing key.

The pseudo-random function "H" in the state information for that
KEYID will be the signature algorithm, and it will use the keying
material for that key (sKEYID) when generating or checking the
validity of message data.

E.g. if the existing key has an KEYID denoted by KID and 128 bits of
keying material denoted by sKID and "H" algorithm a transform named
HMAC, then to generate a "signature" for a data block, the output of
HMAC(sKID, data) will be the corresponding signature payload.

The KEYID state will have the identities of the local and remote
parties for which the KEYID was assigned; it is up to the local
policy implementation to decide when it is appropriate to use such a
key for authenticating other parties. For example, a key distributed
for use between two Internet hosts A and B may be suitable for
authenticating all identities of the form "alice@A" and "bob@B".

4.2 Third Party Authentication

A local security policy might restrict key negotiation to trusted
parties. For example, two OAKLEY daemons running with equal
sensitivity labels on two machines might wish to be the sole arbiters
of key exchanges between users with that same sensitivity label. In
this case, some way of authenticating the provenance of key exchange
requests is needed. I.e., the identities of the two daemons should
be bound to a key, and that key will be used to form a "signature"
for the key exchange messages.

The Signature Payload, in Appendix B, is for this purpose. This
payload names a KEYID that is in existence before the start of the
current exchange. The "H" transform for that KEYID is used to
calculate an integrity/authentication value for all payloads
preceding the signature.

Local policy can dictate which KEYID's are appropriate for signing
further exchanges.

4.3 New Group Mode

   OAKLEY uses a new KEI for the exchange that defines a new group.

5. Security Implementation Notes

   Timing attacks that are capable of recovering the exponent value used
   in Diffie-Hellman calculations have been described by Paul Kocher
   [Kocher]. In order to nullify the attack, implementors must take
   pains to obscure the sequence of operations involved in carrying out
   modular exponentiations.

   A "blinding factor" can accomplish this goal. A group element, r, is
   chosen at random. When an exponent x is chosen, the value $r^{(-x)}$ is
   also calculated. Then, when calculating $(g^y)^x$, the implementation
   will calculate this sequence:

              A = (rg^y)
              B = A^x = (rg^y)^x = (r^x)(g^(xy))
              C = B*r^(-x) = (r^x)(r^-(x))(g^(xy)) = g^(xy)

   The blinding factor is only necessary if the exponent x is used more
   than 100 times (estimate by Richard Schroeppel).

6. OAKLEY Parsing and State Machine

   There are many pathways through OAKLEY, but they follow a left-to-
   right parsing pattern of the message fields.

   The initiator decides on an initial message in the following order:

      1. Offer a cookie. This is not necessary but it helps with
      aggressive exchanges.

      2. Pick a group. The choices are the well-known groups or any
      private groups that may have been negotiated. The very first
      exchange between two Oakley daemons with no common state must
      involve a well-known group (0, meaning no group, is a well-known
      group). Note that the group identifier, not the group descriptor,
      is used in the message.

      If a non-null group will be used, it must be included with the
      first message specifying EHAO. It need not be specified until
      then.

      3. If PFS will be used, pick an exponent x and present g^x.

      4. Offer Encryption, Hash, and Authentication lists.

5. Use PFS for hiding the identities

If identity hiding is not used, then the initiator has this option:

6. Name the identities and include authentication information

The information in the authentication section depends on the first authentication offer. In this aggressive exchange, the Initiator hopes that the Responder will accept all the offered information and the first authentication method. The authentication method determines the authentication payload as follows:

1. Signing method. The signature will be applied to all the offered information.

2. A public key encryption method. The algorithm will be used to encrypt a nonce in the public key of the requested Responder identity. There are two cases possible, depending on whether or not identity hiding is used:

   a. No identity hiding. The ID's will appear as plaintext.
   b. Identity hiding. A well-known ID, call it R', will appear as plaintext in the authentication payload. It will be followed by two ID's and a nonce; these will be encrypted using the public key for R'.

3. A pre-existing key method. The pre-existing key will be used to encrypt a nonce. If identity hiding is used, the ID's will be encrypted in place in the payload, using the "E" algorithm associated with the pre-existing key.

The Responder can accept all, part or none of the initial message.

The Responder accepts as many of the fields as he wishes, using the same decision order as the initiator. At any step he can stop, implicitly rejecting further fields (which will have null values in his response message). The minimum response is a cookie and the GRP.

1. Accept cookie. The Responder may elect to record no state information until the Initiator successfully replies with a cookie chosen by the responder. If so, the Responder replies with a cookie, the GRP, and no other information.

2. Accept GRP. If the group is not acceptable, the Responder will not reply. The Responder may send an error message indicating the the group is not acceptable (modulus too small, unknown identifier, etc.) Note that "no group" has two meanings during

the protocol: it may mean the group is not yet specified, or it
may mean that no group will be used (and thus PFS is not
possible).

3. Accept the g^x value. The Responder indicates his acceptance
of the g^x value by including his own g^y value in his reply. He
can postpone this by ignoring g^x and putting a zero length g^y
value in his reply. He can also reject the g^x value with an
error message.

4. Accept one element from each of the EHA lists. The acceptance
is indicated by a non-zero proposal.

5. If PFS for identity hiding is requested, then no further data
will follow.

6. If the authentication payload is present, and if the first item
in the offered authentication class is acceptable, then the
Responder must validate/decrypt the information in the
authentication payload and signature payload, if present. The
Responder should choose a nonce and reply using the same
authentication/hash algorithm as the Initiator used.

The Initiator notes which information the Responder has accepted,
validates/decrypts any signed, hashed, or encrypted fields, and if
the data is acceptable, replies in accordance to the EHA methods
selected by the Responder. The Initiator replies are distinguished
from his initial message by the presence of the non-zero value for
the Responder cookie.

The output of the signature or prf function will be encoded as a
variable precision integer as described in Appendix C. The KEYID
will indicate KEYID that names keying material and the Hash or
Signature function.

7. The Credential Payload

Useful certificates with public key information can be attached to
OAKLEY messages using Credential Payloads as defined in the ISAKMP
document. It should be noted that the identity protection option
applies to the credentials as well as the identities.

Security Considerations

The focus of this document is security; hence security considerations
permeate this memo.

Author's Address

    Hilarie K. Orman
    Department of Computer Science
    University of Arizona

    EMail: ho@darpa.mil

APPENDIX A Group Descriptors

Three distinct group representations can be used with OAKLEY. Each
group is defined by its group operation and the kind of underlying
field used to represent group elements. The three types are modular
exponentiation groups (named MODP herein), elliptic curve groups over
the field GF[2^N] (named EC2N herein), and elliptic curve groups over
GF[P] (named ECP herein) For each representation, many distinct
realizations are possible, depending on parameter selection.

With a few exceptions, all the parameters are transmitted as if they
were non-negative multi-precision integers, using the format defined
in this appendix (note, this is distinct from the encoding in
Appendix C). Every multi-precision integer has a prefixed length
field, even where this information is redundant.

For the group type EC2N, the parameters are more properly thought of
as very long bit fields, but they are represented as multi-precision
integers, (with length fields, and right-justified). This is the
natural encoding.

MODP means the classical modular exponentiation group, where the
operation is to calculate G^X (mod P). The group is defined by the
numeric parameters P and G. P must be a prime. G is often 2, but
may be a larger number. 2 <= G <= P-2.

ECP is an elliptic curve group, modulo a prime number P. The
defining equation for this kind of group is
 $Y^2 = X^3 + AX + B$ The group operation is taking a multiple of an
elliptic-curve point. The group is defined by 5 numeric parameters:
The prime P, two curve parameters A and B, and a generator (X,Y).
A,B,X,Y are all interpreted mod P, and must be (non-negative)
integers less than P. They must satisfy the defining equation,
modulo P.

EC2N is an elliptic curve group, over the finite field F[2^N]. The
defining equation for this kind of group is
 $Y^2 + XY = X^3 + AX^2 + B$ (This equation differs slightly from the
mod P case: it has an XY term, and an AX^2 term instead of an AX
term.)

We must specify the field representation, and then the elliptic
curve. The field is specified by giving an irreducible polynomial
(mod 2) of degree N. This polynomial is represented as an integer of
size between 2^N and $2^{(N+1)}$, as if the defining polynomial were
evaluated at the value U=2.

For example, the field defined by the polynomial U^155 + U^62 + 1 is
represented by the integer 2^155 + 2^62 + 1. The group is defined by
4 more parameters, A,B,X,Y. These parameters are elements of the
field GF[2^N], and can be thought of as polynomials of degree < N,
with (mod 2) coefficients. They fit in N-bit fields, and are
represented as integers < 2^N, as if the polynomial were evaluated at
U=2. For example, the field element U^2 + 1 would be represented by
the integer 2^2+1, which is 5. The two parameters A and B define the
curve. A is frequently 0. B must not be 0. The parameters X and Y
select a point on the curve. The parameters A,B,X,Y must satisfy the
defining equation, modulo the defining polynomial, and mod 2.

Group descriptor formats:

Type of group: A two-byte field,
        assigned values for the types "MODP", "ECP", "EC2N"
        will be defined (see ISAKMP-04).
Size of a field element, in bits. This is either Ceiling(log2 P)
   or the degree of the irreducible polynomial: a 32-bit integer.
The prime P or the irreducible field polynomial: a multi-precision
   integer.
The generator: 1 or 2 values, multi-precision integers.
EC only: The parameters of the curve: 2 values, multi-precision
   integers.

The following parameters are Optional (each of these may appear
independently):
   a value of 0 may be used as a place-holder to represent an unspecified
   parameter; any number of the parameters may be sent, from 0 to 3.

The largest prime factor: the encoded value that is the LPF of the
   group size, a multi-precision integer.

EC only: The order of the group: multi-precision integer.
   (The group size for MODP is always P-1.)

Strength of group: 32-bit integer.
   The strength of the group is approximately the number of key-bits
   protected.
      It is determined by the log2 of the effort to attack the group.
      It may change as we learn more about cryptography.

This is a generic example for a "classic" modular exponentiation group:
   Group type: "MODP"
   Size of a field element in bits: Log2 (P) rounded *up*. A 32bit
      integer.
   Defining prime P: a multi-precision integer.
   Generator G: a multi-precision integer. 2 <= G <= P-2.

    <optional>
    Largest prime factor of P-1: the multi-precision integer Q
    Strength of group: a 32-bit integer. We will specify a formula
      for calculating this number (TBD).

This is a generic example for an elliptic curve group, mod P:
    Group type: "ECP"
    Size of a field element in bits: Log2 (P) rounded *up*,
      a 32 bit integer.
    Defining prime P: a multi-precision integer.
    Generator (X,Y): 2 multi-precision integers, each < P.
    Parameters of the curve A,B: 2 multi-precision integers, each < P.
    <optional>
    Largest prime factor of the group order: a multi-precision integer.
    Order of the group: a multi-precision integer.
    Strength of group: a 32-bit integer. Formula TBD.

This is a specific example for an elliptic curve group:
    Group type: "EC2N"
    Degree of the irreducible polynomial: 155
    Irreducible polynomial: $U^{155} + U^{62} + 1$, represented as the
      multi-precision integer $2^{155} + 2^{62} + 1$.
    Generator (X,Y) : represented as 2 multi-precision integers, each
      $< 2^{155}$.
    For our present curve, these are (decimal) 123 and 456. Each is
      represented as a multi-precision integer.
    Parameters of the curve A,B: represented as 2 multi-precision
      integers, each $< 2^{155}$.
    For our present curve these are 0 and (decimal) 471951, represented
      as two multi-precision integers.

    <optional>
    Largest prime factor of the group order:

     3805993847215893016155463826195386266397436443,

    represented as a multi-precision integer.
    The order of the group:

     45671926166590716193865565914344635196769237316

    represented as a multi-precision integer.

    Strength of group: 76, represented as a 32-bit integer.

The variable precision integer encoding for group descriptor fields
is the following. This is a slight variation on the format defined
in Appendix C in that a fixed 16-bit value is used first, and the

length is limited to 16 bits. However, the interpretation is
otherwise identical.

```
                      1                   2                   3
  0 1 2 3 4 5 6 7 8 9 0 1 2 3 4 5 6 7 8 9 0 1 2 3 4 5 6 7 8 9 0 1
 +-+-+-+-+-+-+-+-+-+-+-+-+-+-+-+-+-+-+-+-+-+-+-+-+-+-+-+-+-+-+-+-+
 !   Fixed value (TBD)           !            Length             !
 +-+-+-+-+-+-+-+-+-+-+-+-+-+-+-+-+-+-+-+-+-+-+-+-+-+-+-+-+-+-+-+-+
 .                                                               .
 .                       Integer                                 .
 .                                                               .
 +-+-+-+-+-+-+-+-+-+-+-+-+-+-+-+-+-+-+-+-+-+-+-+-+-+-+-+-+-+-+-+-+
```

The format of a group descriptor is:
```
                      1                   2                   3
  0 1 2 3 4 5 6 7 8 9 0 1 2 3 4 5 6 7 8 9 0 1 2 3 4 5 6 7 8 9 0 1
 +-+-+-+-+-+-+-+-+-+-+-+-+-+-+-+-+-+-+-+-+-+-+-+-+-+-+-+-+-+-+-+-+
 !1!1!   Group Description       !            MODP               !
 +-+-+-+-+-+-+-+-+-+-+-+-+-+-+-+-+-+-+-+-+-+-+-+-+-+-+-+-+-+-+-+-+
 !1!0!      Field Size           !            Length             !
 +-+-+-+-+-+-+-+-+-+-+-+-+-+-+-+-+-+-+-+-+-+-+-+-+-+-+-+-+-+-+-+-+
 !                              MPI                              !
 +-+-+-+-+-+-+-+-+-+-+-+-+-+-+-+-+-+-+-+-+-+-+-+-+-+-+-+-+-+-+-+-+
 !1!0!        Prime             !            Length             !
 +-+-+-+-+-+-+-+-+-+-+-+-+-+-+-+-+-+-+-+-+-+-+-+-+-+-+-+-+-+-+-+-+
 !                              MPI                              !
 +-+-+-+-+-+-+-+-+-+-+-+-+-+-+-+-+-+-+-+-+-+-+-+-+-+-+-+-+-+-+-+-+
 !1!0!      Generator1          !            Length             !
 +-+-+-+-+-+-+-+-+-+-+-+-+-+-+-+-+-+-+-+-+-+-+-+-+-+-+-+-+-+-+-+-+
 !                              MPI                              !
 +-+-+-+-+-+-+-+-+-+-+-+-+-+-+-+-+-+-+-+-+-+-+-+-+-+-+-+-+-+-+-+-+
 !1!0!      Generator2          !            Length             !
 +-+-+-+-+-+-+-+-+-+-+-+-+-+-+-+-+-+-+-+-+-+-+-+-+-+-+-+-+-+-+-+-+
 !                              MPI                              !
 +-+-+-+-+-+-+-+-+-+-+-+-+-+-+-+-+-+-+-+-+-+-+-+-+-+-+-+-+-+-+-+-+
 !1!0!      Curve-p1            !            Length             !
 +-+-+-+-+-+-+-+-+-+-+-+-+-+-+-+-+-+-+-+-+-+-+-+-+-+-+-+-+-+-+-+-+
 !                              MPI                              !
 +-+-+-+-+-+-+-+-+-+-+-+-+-+-+-+-+-+-+-+-+-+-+-+-+-+-+-+-+-+-+-+-+
 !1!0!      Curve-p2            !            Length             !
 +-+-+-+-+-+-+-+-+-+-+-+-+-+-+-+-+-+-+-+-+-+-+-+-+-+-+-+-+-+-+-+-+
 !                              MPI                              !
 +-+-+-+-+-+-+-+-+-+-+-+-+-+-+-+-+-+-+-+-+-+-+-+-+-+-+-+-+-+-+-+-+
 !1!0! Largest Prime Factor     !            Length             !
 +-+-+-+-+-+-+-+-+-+-+-+-+-+-+-+-+-+-+-+-+-+-+-+-+-+-+-+-+-+-+-+-+
 !                              MPI                              !
 +-+-+-+-+-+-+-+-+-+-+-+-+-+-+-+-+-+-+-+-+-+-+-+-+-+-+-+-+-+-+-+-+
```

```
 !1!0!      Order of Group         !            Length           !
 +-+-+-+-+-+-+-+-+-+-+-+-+-+-+-+-+-+-+-+-+-+-+-+-+-+-+-+-+-+-+-+
 !                              MPI                             !
 +-+-+-+-+-+-+-+-+-+-+-+-+-+-+-+-+-+-+-+-+-+-+-+-+-+-+-+-+-+-+-+
 !0!0!      Strength of Group      !            Length           !
 +-+-+-+-+-+-+-+-+-+-+-+-+-+-+-+-+-+-+-+-+-+-+-+-+-+-+-+-+-+-+-+
 !                              MPI                             !
 +-+-+-+-+-+-+-+-+-+-+-+-+-+-+-+-+-+-+-+-+-+-+-+-+-+-+-+-+-+-+-+
```

APPENDIX B Message formats

The encodings of Oakley messages into ISAKMP payloads is deferred to
the ISAKMP/Oakley Resolution document.

APPENDIX C Encoding a variable precision integer.

   Variable precision integers will be encoded as a 32-bit length field
   followed by one or more 32-bit quantities containing the
   representation of the integer, aligned with the most significant bit
   in the first 32-bit item.

```
                        1                   2                   3
     0 1 2 3 4 5 6 7 8 9 0 1 2 3 4 5 6 7 8 9 0 1 2 3 4 5 6 7 8 9 0 1
    +-+-+-+-+-+-+-+-+-+-+-+-+-+-+-+-+-+-+-+-+-+-+-+-+-+-+-+-+-+-+-+-+
    !    length                                                    !
    +-+-+-+-+-+-+-+-+-+-+-+-+-+-+-+-+-+-+-+-+-+-+-+-+-+-+-+-+-+-+-+-+
    !    first value word (most significant bits)                  !
    +-+-+-+-+-+-+-+-+-+-+-+-+-+-+-+-+-+-+-+-+-+-+-+-+-+-+-+-+-+-+-+-+
    !                                                              !
    ~        additional value words                               ~
    !                                                              !
    +-+-+-+-+-+-+-+-+-+-+-+-+-+-+-+-+-+-+-+-+-+-+-+-+-+-+-+-+-+-+-+-+
```

An example of such an encoding is given below, for a number with 51
bits of significance. The length field indicates that 2 32-bit
quantities follow. The most significant non-zero bit of the number
is in bit 13 of the first 32-bit quantity, the low order bits are in
the second 32-bit quantity.

```
                        1                   2                   3
     0 1 2 3 4 5 6 7 8 9 0 1 2 3 4 5 6 7 8 9 0 1 2 3 4 5 6 7 8 9 0 1
    +-+-+-+-+-+-+-+-+-+-+-+-+-+-+-+-+-+-+-+-+-+-+-+-+-+-+-+-+-+-+-+-+
    !                                                          1 0!
    +-+-+-+-+-+-+-+-+-+-+-+-+-+-+-+-+-+-+-+-+-+-+-+-+-+-+-+-+-+-+-+-+
    !0 0 0 0 0 0 0 0 0 0 0 0 0 1 x x x x x x x x x x x x x x x x x x!
    +-+-+-+-+-+-+-+-+-+-+-+-+-+-+-+-+-+-+-+-+-+-+-+-+-+-+-+-+-+-+-+-+
    !x x x x x x x x x x x x x x x x x x x x x x x x x x x x x x x x!
    +-+-+-+-+-+-+-+-+-+-+-+-+-+-+-+-+-+-+-+-+-+-+-+-+-+-+-+-+-+-+-+-+
```

APPENDIX D Cryptographic strengths

The Diffie-Hellman algorithm is used to compute keys that will be used with symmetric algorithms. It should be no easier to break the Diffie-Hellman computation than it is to do an exhaustive search over the symmetric key space. A recent recommendation by an group of cryptographers [Blaze] has recommended a symmetric key size of 75 bits for a practical level of security. For 20 year security, they recommend 90 bits.

Based on that report, a conservative strategy for OAKLEY users would be to ensure that their Diffie-Hellman computations were as secure as at least a 90-bit key space. In order to accomplish this for modular exponentiation groups, the size of the largest prime factor of the modulus should be at least 180 bits, and the size of the modulus should be at least 1400 bits. For elliptic curve groups, the LPF should be at least 180 bits.

If long-term secrecy of the encryption key is not an issue, then the following parameters may be used for the modular exponentiation group: 150 bits for the LPF, 980 bits for the modulus size.

The modulus size alone does not determine the strength of the Diffie-Hellman calculation; the size of the exponent used in computing powers within the group is also important. The size of the exponent in bits should be at least twice the size of any symmetric key that will be derived from it. We recommend that ISAKMP implementors use at least 180 bits of exponent (twice the size of a 20-year symmetric key).

The mathematical justification for these estimates can be found in texts that estimate the effort for solving the discrete log problem, a task that is strongly related to the efficiency of using the Number Field Sieve for factoring large integers. Readers are referred to [Stinson] and [Schneier].

APPENDIX E The Well-Known Groups

The group identifiers:

    0   No group (used as a placeholder and for non-DH exchanges)
    1   A modular exponentiation group with a 768 bit modulus
    2   A modular exponentiation group with a 1024 bit modulus
    3   A modular exponentiation group with a 1536 bit modulus (TBD)
    4   An elliptic curve group over GF[2^155]
    5   An elliptic curve group over GF[2^185]

    values 2^31 and higher are used for private group identifiers

Richard Schroeppel performed all the mathematical and computational
work for this appendix.

Classical Diffie-Hellman Modular Exponentiation Groups

The primes for groups 1 and 2 were selected to have certain
properties. The high order 64 bits are forced to 1. This helps the
classical remainder algorithm, because the trial quotient digit can
always be taken as the high order word of the dividend, possibly +1.
The low order 64 bits are forced to 1. This helps the Montgomery-
style remainder algorithms, because the multiplier digit can always
be taken to be the low order word of the dividend. The middle bits
are taken from the binary expansion of pi. This guarantees that they
are effectively random, while avoiding any suspicion that the primes
have secretly been selected to be weak.

Because both primes are based on pi, there is a large section of
overlap in the hexadecimal representations of the two primes. The
primes are chosen to be Sophie Germain primes (i.e., (P-1)/2 is also
prime), to have the maximum strength against the square-root attack
on the discrete logarithm problem.

The starting trial numbers were repeatedly incremented by 2^64 until
suitable primes were located.

Because these two primes are congruent to 7 (mod 8), 2 is a quadratic
residue of each prime. All powers of 2 will also be quadratic
residues. This prevents an opponent from learning the low order bit
of the Diffie-Hellman exponent (AKA the subgroup confinement
problem). Using 2 as a generator is efficient for some modular
exponentiation algorithms. [Note that 2 is technically not a
generator in the number theory sense, because it omits half of the
possible residues mod P. From a cryptographic viewpoint, this is a
virtue.]

E.1. Well-Known Group 1:   A 768 bit prime

The prime is 2^768 - 2^704 - 1 + 2^64 * { [2^638 pi] + 149686 }.   Its
decimal value is
          155251809230070893513091813125848175563133404943451431320235
          119490029662399491021072586694538765916424429100076802888642 2
          915080371891804634263272761303128298374438082089019628850917
          069131659317536746955176311984337163722100721057 7919

This has been rigorously verified as a prime.

The representation of the group in OAKLEY is

          Type of group: "MODP"
          Size of field element (bits):   768
          Prime modulus: 21 (decimal)
             Length (32 bit words):   24
             Data (hex):
                FFFFFFFF FFFFFFFF C90FDAA2 2168C234 C4C6628B 80DC1CD1
                29024E08 8A67CC74 020BBEA6 3B139B22 514A0879 8E3404DD
                EF9519B3 CD3A431B 302B0A6D F25F1437 4FE1356D 6D51C245
                E485B576 625E7EC6 F44C42E9 A63A3620 FFFFFFFF FFFFFFFF
          Generator: 22 (decimal)
             Length (32 bit words):   1
             Data (hex):   2

          Optional Parameters:
          Group order largest prime factor: 24 (decimal)
             Length (32 bit words):   24
             Data (hex):
                7FFFFFFF FFFFFFFF E487ED51 10B4611A 62633145 C06E0E68
                94812704 4533E63A 0105DF53 1D89CD91 28A5043C C71A026E
                F7CA8CD9 E69D218D 98158536 F92F8A1B A7F09AB6 B6A8E122
                F242DABB 312F3F63 7A262174 D31D1B10 7FFFFFFF FFFFFFFF
          Strength of group: 26 (decimal)
             Length (32 bit words)   1
             Data (hex):
                00000042

E.2. Well-Known Group 2:   A 1024 bit prime

The prime is 2^1024 - 2^960 - 1 + 2^64 * { [2^894 pi] + 129093 }.
Its decimal value is
          179769313486231590770839156793787453197860296048756011706444
          423684197180216158519369894783379586492554150218056548598050 3
          646440548199239100050792877003355816639229553136239076508735
          759914822574862575007425302077447712589550957937778424442426
          617334727629299387668709205606050270810842907692932019128194

467627007

The primality of the number has been rigorously proven.

The representation of the group in OAKLEY is
    Type of group: "MODP"
    Size of field element (bits):   1024
    Prime modulus: 21 (decimal)
      Length (32 bit words):   32
      Data (hex):
        FFFFFFFF FFFFFFFF C90FDAA2 2168C234 C4C6628B 80DC1CD1
        29024E08 8A67CC74 020BBEA6 3B139B22 514A0879 8E3404DD
        EF9519B3 CD3A431B 302B0A6D F25F1437 4FE1356D 6D51C245
        E485B576 625E7EC6 F44C42E9 A637ED6B 0BFF5CB6 F406B7ED
        EE386BFB 5A899FA5 AE9F2411 7C4B1FE6 49286651 ECE65381
        FFFFFFFF FFFFFFFF
    Generator: 22 (decimal)
      Length (32 bit words):   1
      Data (hex):   2

    Optional Parameters:
    Group order largest prime factor: 24 (decimal)
      Length (32 bit words):   32
      Data (hex):
        7FFFFFFF FFFFFFFF E487ED51 10B4611A 62633145 C06E0E68
        94812704 4533E63A 0105DF53 1D89CD91 28A5043C C71A026E
        F7CA8CD9 E69D218D 98158536 F92F8A1B A7F09AB6 B6A8E122
        F242DABB 312F3F63 7A262174 D31BF6B5 85FFAE5B 7A035BF6
        F71C35FD AD44CFD2 D74F9208 BE258FF3 24943328 F67329C0
        FFFFFFFF FFFFFFFF
    Strength of group: 26 (decimal)
      Length (32 bit words)   1
      Data (hex):
        0000004D

E.3. Well-Known Group 3: An Elliptic Curve Group Definition

The curve is based on the Galois field GF[2^{155}] with 2^{155} field
elements. The irreducible polynomial for the field is $u^{155} + u^{62} +$
1. The equation for the elliptic curve is

$$Y^2 + X Y = X^3 + A X + B$$

X, Y, A, B are elements of the field.

For the curve specified, A = 0 and

  B = u^{18} + u^{17} + u^{16} + u^{13} + u^{12} + u^9 + u^8 + u^7 + u^3 + u^2 +

u + 1.

B is represented in binary as the bit string 1110011001110001111; in decimal this is 471951, and in hex 7338F.

The generator is a point (X,Y) on the curve (satisfying the curve equation, mod 2 and modulo the field polynomial).

X = u^6 + u^5 + u^4 + u^3 + u + 1

and

Y = u^8 + u^7 + u^6 + u^3.

The binary bit strings for X and Y are 1111011 and 111001000; in decimal they are 123 and 456.

The group order (the number of curve points) is
     45671926166590716193865565914344635196769237316
which is 12 times the prime

     3805993847215893016155463826195386266397436443.
(This prime has been rigorously proven.) The generating point (X,Y) has order 4 times the prime; the generator is the triple of some curve point.

```
OAKLEY representation of this group:
     Type of group:                    "EC2N"
     Size of field element (bits):      155
     Irreducible field polynomial:      21 (decimal)
        Length (32 bit words):          5
        Data (hex):
           08000000 00000000 00000000 40000000 00000001
     Generator:
        X coordinate:                   22 (decimal)
           Length (32 bit words):       1
           Data (hex):                  7B
        Y coordinate:                   22 (decimal)
           Length (32 bit words):       1
           Data (hex):                  1C8
     Elliptic curve parameters:
        A parameter:                    23 (decimal)
           Length (32 bit words):       1
           Data (hex):                  0
        B parameter:                    23 (decimal)
           Length (32 bit words):       1
           Data (hex):                  7338F
```

        Optional Parameters:
        Group order largest prime factor: 24 (decimal)
           Length (32 bit words):   5
           Data (hex):
              00AAAAAA AAAAAAAA AAAAB1FC F1E206F4 21A3EA1B
        Group order: 25 (decimal)
           Length (32 bit words):   5
           Data (hex):
              08000000 00000000 000057DB 56985371 93AEF944
        Strength of group: 26 (decimal)
           Length (32 bit words)   1
           Data (hex):
              0000004C

E.4. Well-Known Group 4: A Large Elliptic Curve Group Definition

   This curve is based on the Galois field GF[2^185] with 2^185 field
   elements. The irreducible polynomial for the field is

   u^185 + u^69 + 1.

   The equation for the elliptic curve is

   Y^2 + X Y = X^3 + A X + B.

   X, Y, A, B are elements of the field. For the curve specified, A = 0
   and

   B = u^12 + u^11 + u^10 + u^9 + u^7 + u^6 + u^5 + u^3 + 1.

   B is represented in binary as the bit string 1111011101001; in
   decimal this is 7913, and in hex 1EE9.

   The generator is a point (X,Y) on the curve (satisfying the curve
   equation, mod 2 and modulo the field polynomial);

   X = u^4 + u^3 and Y = u^3 + u^2 + 1.

   The binary bit strings for X and Y are 11000 and 1101; in decimal
   they are 24 and 13. The group order (the number of curve points) is

        4903985730770844346746710485765268224805238500104505311ω

   which is 4 times the prime

        12259964326927110866866776214413170562013096250261263279.

   (This prime has been rigorously proven.)

The generating point (X,Y) has order 2 times the prime; the generator is the double of some curve point.

OAKLEY representation of this group:

```
    Type of group:                  "EC2N"
    Size of field element (bits):   185
    Irreducible field polynomial:   21 (decimal)
       Length (32 bit words):       6
       Data (hex):
           02000000 00000000 00000000 00000020 00000000 00000001
    Generator:
       X coordinate:                22 (decimal)
          Length (32 bit words):    1
          Data (hex):               18
       Y coordinate:                22 (decimal)
          Length (32 bit words):    1
          Data (hex):               D
    Elliptic curve parameters:
       A parameter:                 23 (decimal)
          Length (32 bit words):    1
          Data (hex):               0
       B parameter:                 23 (decimal)
          Length (32 bit words):    1
          Data (hex):               1EE9

    Optional parameters:
    Group order largest prime factor: 24 (decimal)
       Length (32 bit words):       6
       Data (hex):
           007FFFFF FFFFFFFF FFFFFFFF F6FCBE22 6DCF9210 5D7E53AF
    Group order:                    25 (decimal)
       Length (32 bit words):       6
       Data (hex):
           01FFFFFF FFFFFFFF FFFFFFFF DBF2F889 B73E4841 75F94EBC
    Strength of group:              26 (decimal)
       Length (32 bit words)        1
       Data (hex):
           0000005B
```

E.5. Well-Known Group 5: A 1536 bit prime

The prime is 2^1536 - 2^1472 - 1 + 2^64 * { [2^1406 pi] +   741804 }.

Its decimal value is

```
        2410312426921032588552076022197566074856950548502459942654 11
        6941958108831682612228890093858261341614673227141477904012 19
        6503648957050582631942730706805009223062734745341073406696 24
```

```
6014589361659774041027169249453200378729434170325843778659198
1437631937768598695240889401955773461198435453015470437472077
4996976375008430892633929555996888245787241299381012913029459
2999947926365264059284647209730384947211681434464714438485209
40127459844288859336526896320919633919
```

The primality of the number has been rigorously proven.

The representation of the group in OAKLEY is
```
    Type of group:                       "MODP"
    Size of field element (bits):        1536
    Prime modulus:                       21 (decimal)
        Length (32 bit words):           48
        Data (hex):
            FFFFFFFF FFFFFFFF C90FDAA2 2168C234 C4C6628B 80DC1CD1
            29024E08 8A67CC74 020BBEA6 3B139B22 514A0879 8E3404DD
            EF9519B3 CD3A431B 302B0A6D F25F1437 4FE1356D 6D51C245
            E485B576 625E7EC6 F44C42E9 A637ED6B 0BFF5CB6 F406B7ED
            EE386BFB 5A899FA5 AE9F2411 7C4B1FE6 49286651 ECE45B3D
            C2007CB8 A163BF05 98DA4836 1C55D39A 69163FA8 FD24CF5F
            83655D23 DCA3AD96 1C62F356 208552BB 9ED52907 7096966D
            670C354E 4ABC9804 F1746C08 CA237327 FFFFFFFF FFFFFFFF
    Generator:                           22 (decimal)
        Length (32 bit words):           1
        Data (hex):                      2
```

```
    Optional Parameters:
    Group order largest prime factor:    24 (decimal)
        Length (32 bit words):           48
        Data (hex):
            7FFFFFFF FFFFFFFF E487ED51 10B4611A 62633145 C06E0E68
            94812704 4533E63A 0105DF53 1D89CD91 28A5043C C71A026E
            F7CA8CD9 E69D218D 98158536 F92F8A1B A7F09AB6 B6A8E122
            F242DABB 312F3F63 7A262174 D31BF6B5 85FFAE5B 7A035BF6
            F71C35FD AD44CFD2 D74F9208 BE258FF3 24943328 F6722D9E
            E1003E5C 50B1DF82 CC6D241B 0E2AE9CD 348B1FD4 7E9267AF
            C1B2AE91 EE51D6CB 0E3179AB 1042A95D CF6A9483 B84B4B36
            B3861AA7 255E4C02 78BA3604 6511B993 FFFFFFFF FFFFFFFF
    Strength of group:                   26 (decimal)
        Length (32 bit words)            1
        Data (hex):
            0000005B
```

Appendix F   Implementing Group Operations

   The group operation must be implemented as a sequence of arithmetic
   operations; the exact operations depend on the type of group. For
   modular exponentiation groups, the operation is multi-precision
   integer multiplication and remainders by the group modulus. See
   Knuth Vol. 2 [Knuth] for a discussion of how to implement these for
   large integers. Implementation recommendations for elliptic curve
   group operations over GF[2^N] are described in [Schroeppel].

BIBLIOGRAPHY

    [RFC2401]   Atkinson, R., "Security Architecture for the
                      Internet Protocol", RFC 2401, November 1998.

    [RFC2406]   Atkinson, R., "IP Encapsulating Security Payload (ESP)",
                      RFC 2406, November 1998.

    [RFC2402]   Atkinson, R., "IP Authentication Header", RFC 2402,
                      November 1998.

    [Blaze]   Blaze, Matt et al., MINIMAL KEY LENGTHS FOR SYMMETRIC
                      CIPHERS TO PROVIDE ADEQUATE COMMERCIAL SECURITY. A
                      REPORT BY AN AD HOC GROUP OF CRYPTOGRAPHERS AND COMPUTER
                      SCIENTISTS... -
                      http://www.bsa.org/policy/encryption/cryptographers.html

    [STS]   W. Diffie, P.C. Van Oorschot, and M.J. Wiener,
                      "Authentication and Authenticated Key Exchanges," in
                      Designs, Codes and Cryptography, Kluwer Academic
                      Publishers, 1992, pp. 107

    [SECDNS]   Eastlake, D. and C. Kaufman, "Domain Name System
                      Security Extensions", RFC 2065, January 1997.

    [Random]   Eastlake, D., Crocker, S. and J. Schiller, "Randomness
                      Recommendations for Security", RFC 1750, December 1994.

    [Kocher]   Kocher, Paul, Timing Attack,

http://www.cryptography.com/timingattack.old/timingattack.html

    [Knuth]   Knuth, Donald E., The Art of Computer Programming, Vol.
                      2, Seminumerical Algorithms, Addison Wesley, 1969.

    [Krawcyzk]   Krawcyzk, Hugo, SKEME: A Versatile Secure Key Exchange
                      Mechanism for Internet, ISOC Secure Networks and
                      Distributed Systems Symposium, San Diego, 1996

    [Schneier]   Schneier, Bruce, Applied cryptography: protocols,
                      algorithms, and source code in C, Second edition, John
                      Wiley & Sons, Inc. 1995, ISBN 0-471-12845-7, hardcover.
                      ISBN 0-471-11709-9, softcover.

    [Schroeppel] Schroeppel, Richard, et al.; Fast Key Exchange with
                      Elliptic Curve Systems, Crypto '95, Santa Barbara, 1995.
                      Available on-line as
                      ftp://ftp.cs.arizona.edu/reports/1995/TR95-03.ps (and
                      .Z).

[Stinson]   Stinson, Douglas, Cryptography Theory and Practice. CRC
               Press, Inc., 2000, Corporate Blvd., Boca Raton, FL,
               33431-9868, ISBN 0-8493-8521-0, 1995

[Zimmerman]   Philip Zimmermann, The Official Pgp User's Guide,
               Published by MIT Press Trade, Publication date: June
               1995, ISBN: 0262740176

Full Copyright Statement

Network Working Group   R. Pereira
Request for Comments: 2451   TimeStep Corporation
Category: Standards Track   R. Adams
                                                Cisco Systems Inc.
                                                   November 1998

The ESP CBC-Mode Cipher Algorithms

Status of this Memo

Copyright Notice

Abstract

   This document describes how to use CBC-mode cipher algorithms with
   the IPSec ESP (Encapsulating Security Payload) Protocol. It not only
   clearly states how to use certain cipher algorithms, but also how to
   use all CBC-mode cipher algorithms.

Table of Contents

1. Introduction

   The Encapsulating Security Payload (ESP) [Kent98] provides
   confidentiality for IP datagrams by encrypting the payload data to be
   protected. This specification describes the ESP use of CBC-mode
   cipher algorithms.

   While this document does not describe the use of the default cipher
   algorithm DES, the reader should be familiar with that document.
   [Madson98]

   It is assumed that the reader is familiar with the terms and concepts
   described in the "Security Architecture for the Internet Protocol"
   [Atkinson95], "IP Security Document Roadmap" [Thayer97], and "IP
   Encapsulating Security Payload (ESP)" [Kent98] documents.

   Furthermore, this document is a companion to [Kent98] and MUST be
   read in its context.

1.1 Specification of Requirements

   The keywords "MUST", "MUST NOT", "REQUIRED", "SHOULD", "SHOULD NOT",
   and "MAY" that appear in this document are to be interpreted as
   described in [Bradner97].

1.2 Intellectual Property Rights Statement

   The IETF takes no position regarding the validity or scope of any
   intellectual property or other rights that might be claimed to
   pertain to the implementation or use of the technology described in
   this document or the extent to which any license under such rights
   might or might not be available; neither does it represent that it
   has made any effort to identify any such rights. Information on the
   IETF's procedures with respect to rights in standards-track and
   standards-related documentation can be found in BCP-11. Copies of
   claims of rights made available for publication and any assurances of
   licenses to be made available, or the result of an attempt made to
   obtain a general license or permission for the use of such
   proprietary rights by implementers or users of this specification can
   be obtained from the IETF Secretariat.

2. Cipher Algorithms

   All symmetric block cipher algorithms share common characteristics
   and variables. These include mode, key size, weak keys, block size,
   and rounds. All of which will be explained below.

While this document illustrates certain cipher algorithms such as
Blowfish [Schneier93], CAST-128 [Adams97], 3DES, IDEA [Lai] [MOV],
and RC5 [Baldwin96], any other block cipher algorithm may be used
with ESP if all of the variables described within this document are
clearly defined.

2.1 Mode

All symmetric block cipher algorithms described or insinuated within
this document use Cipher Block Chaining (CBC) mode. This mode
requires an Initialization Vector (IV) that is the same size as the
block size. Use of a randomly generated IV prevents generation of
identical ciphertext from packets which have identical data that
spans the first block of the cipher algorithm's blocksize.

The IV is XOR'd with the first plaintext block, before it is
encrypted. Then for successive blocks, the previous ciphertext block
is XOR'd with the current plaintext, before it is encrypted.

More information on CBC mode can be obtained in [Schneier95].

2.2 Key Size

Some cipher algorithms allow for variable sized keys, while others
only allow a specific key size. The length of the key correlates
with the strength of that algorithm, thus larger keys are always
harder to break than shorter ones.

This document stipulates that all key sizes MUST be a multiple of 8
bits.

This document does specify the default key size for each cipher
algorithm. This size was chosen by consulting experts on the
algorithm and by balancing strength of the algorithm with
performance.

Algorithm	Key Sizes (bits)	Popular Sizes	Default
CAST-128 [1]	40 to 128	40, 64, 80, 128	128
RC5	40 to 2040	40, 128, 160	128
IDEA	128	128	128
Blowfish	40 to 448	128	128
3DES [2]	192	192	192

Notes:

[1] With CAST-128, keys less than 128 bits MUST be padded with zeros
in the rightmost, or least significant, positions out to 128 bits
since the CAST-128 key schedule assumes an input key of 128 bits.
Thus if you had a key with a size of 80 bits '3B5D831CFE', it would
be padded to produce a key with a size of 128 bits
'3B5D831CFE000000'.

[2] The first 3DES key is taken from the first 64 bits, the second
from the next 64 bits, and the third from the last 64 bits.
Implementations MUST take into consideration the parity bits when
initially accepting a new set of keys. Each of the three keys is
really 56 bits in length with the extra 8 bits used for parity.

The reader should note that the minimum key size for all of the above
cipher algorithms is 40 bits, and that the authors strongly advise
that implementations do NOT use key sizes smaller than 40 bits.

2.3 Weak Keys

Weak key checks SHOULD be performed. If such a key is found, the key
SHOULD be rejected and a new SA requested. Some cipher algorithms
have weak keys or keys that MUST not be used due to their weak
nature.

New weak keys might be discovered, so this document does not in any
way contain all possible weak keys for these ciphers. Please check
with other sources of cryptography such as [MOV] and [Schneier] for
further weak keys.

CAST-128:

No known weak keys.

RC5:

No known weak keys when used with 16 rounds.

IDEA:

IDEA has been found to have weak keys. Please check with [MOV] and [Schneier] for more information.

Blowfish:

Weak keys for Blowfish have been discovered. Weak keys are keys that produce the identical entries in a given S-box. Unfortunately, there is no way to test for weak keys before the S- box values are generated. However, the chances of randomly generating such a key are small.

3DES:

DES has 64 known weak keys, including so-called semi-weak keys and possibly-weak keys [Schneier95, pp 280-282]. The likelihood of picking one at random is negligible.

For DES-EDE3, there is no known need to reject weak or complementation keys. Any weakness is obviated by the use of multiple keys.

However, if the first two or last two independent 64-bit keys are equal (k1 == k2 or k2 == k3), then the 3DES operation is simply the same as DES. Implementers MUST reject keys that exhibit this property.

2.4 Block Size and Padding

All of the algorithms described in this document use a block size of eight octets (64 bits).

Padding is used to align the payload type and pad length octets as specified in [Kent98]. Padding must be sufficient to align the data to be encrypted to an eight octet (64 bit) boundary.

2.5 Rounds

This variable determines how many times a block is encrypted. While
this variable MAY be negotiated, a default value MUST always exist
when it is not negotiated.

```
+====================+============+======================+
| Algorithm          | Negotiable | Default Rounds       |
+====================+============+======================+
| CAST-128           | No         | key<=80 bits, 12     |
|                    |            | key>80 bits, 16      |
+--------------------+------------+----------------------+
| RC5                | No         | 16                   |
+--------------------+------------+----------------------+
| IDEA               | No         | 8                    |
+--------------------+------------+----------------------+
| Blowfish           | No         | 16                   |
+--------------------+------------+----------------------+
| 3DES               | No         | 48 (16x3)            |
+--------------------+------------+----------------------+
```

2.6 Backgrounds

CAST-128:

The CAST design procedure was originally developed by Carlisle Adams
and Stafford Tavares at Queen's University, Kingston, Ontario,
Canada. Subsequent enhancements have been made over the years by
Carlisle Adams and Michael Wiener of Entrust Technologies. CAST-128
is the result of applying the CAST Design Procedure as outlined in
[Adams97].

RC5:

The RC5 encryption algorithm was developed by Ron Rivest for RSA Data
Security Inc. in order to address the need for a high- performance
software and hardware ciphering alternative to DES. It is patented
(pat.no. 5,724,428). A description of RC5 may be found in [MOV] and
[Schneier].

IDEA:

Xuejia Lai and James Massey developed the IDEA (International Data
Encryption Algorithm) algorithm. The algorithm is described in
detail in [Lai], [Schneier] and [MOV].

The IDEA algorithm is patented in Europe and in the United States with patent application pending in Japan. Licenses are required for commercial uses of IDEA.

For patent and licensing information, contact:

        Ascom Systec AG, Dept. CMVV
        Gewerbepark, CH-5506
        Magenwil, Switzerland
        Phone: +41 64 56 59 83
        Fax: +41 64 56 59 90
        idea@ascom.ch
        http://www.ascom.ch/Web/systec/policy/normal/exhibit1.html

Blowfish:

Bruce Schneier of Counterpane Systems developed the Blowfish block cipher algorithm. The algorithm is described in detail in [Schneier93], [Schneier95] and [Schneier].

3DES:

This DES variant, colloquially known as "Triple DES" or as DES-EDE3, processes each block three times, each time with a different key. This technique of using more than one DES operation was proposed in [Tuchman79].

```
              P1                 P2                 Pi
              |                  |                  |
      IV->->(X)      +>->->->(X)      +>->->->(X)
              v      ^           v      ^           v
          +-----+    ^       +-----+    ^       +-----+
      k1->|  E  |    ^ k1->|  E  |    ^ k1->|  E  |
          +-----+    ^       +-----+    ^       +-----+
              |      ^           |      ^           |
              v      ^           v      ^           v
          +-----+    ^       +-----+    ^       +-----+
      k2->|  D  |    ^ k2->|  D  |    ^ k2->|  D  |
          +-----+    ^       +-----+    ^       +-----+
              |      ^           |      ^           |
              v      ^           v      ^           v
          +-----+    ^       +-----+    ^       +-----+
      k3->|  E  |    ^ k3->|  E  |    ^ k3->|  E  |
          +-----+    ^       +-----+    ^       +-----+
              |      ^           |      ^           |
          +>->->+          +>->->+          +>->->
              |                  |                  |
              C1                 C2                 Ci
```

The DES-EDE3-CBC algorithm is a simple variant of the DES-CBC algorithm [FIPS-46]. The "outer" chaining technique is used.

In DES-EDE3-CBC, an Initialization Vector (IV) is XOR'd with the first 64-bit (8 byte) plaintext block (P1). The keyed DES function is iterated three times, an encryption (Ek1) followed by a decryption (Dk2) followed by an encryption (Ek3), and generates the ciphertext (C1) for the block. Each iteration uses an independent key: k1, k2 and k3.

For successive blocks, the previous ciphertext block is XOR'd with the current plaintext (Pi). The keyed DES-EDE3 encryption function generates the ciphertext (Ci) for that block.

To decrypt, the order of the functions is reversed: decrypt with k3, encrypt with k2, decrypt with k1, and XOR the previous ciphertext block.

Note that when all three keys (k1, k2 and k3) are the same, DES-EDE3-CBC is equivalent to DES-CBC. This property allows the DES-EDE3 hardware implementations to operate in DES mode without modification.

For more explanation and implementation information for Triple DES, see [Schneier95].

2.7 Performance

For a comparison table of the estimated speed of any of these and other cipher algorithms, please see [Schneier97] or for an up-to-date performance comparison, please see [Bosseleaers].

3. ESP Payload

The ESP payload is made up of the IV followed by raw cipher-text. Thus the payload field, as defined in [Kent98], is broken down according to the following diagram:

```
+---------------+---------------+---------------+---------------+
|                                                               |
+               Initialization Vector (8 octets)                +
|                                                               |
+---------------+---------------+---------------+---------------+
|                                                               |
~               Encrypted Payload (variable length)             ~
|                                                               |
+---------------------------------------------------------------+
 1 2 3 4 5 6 7 8 1 2 3 4 5 6 7 8 1 2 3 4 5 6 7 8 1 2 3 4 5 6 7 8
```

The IV field MUST be same size as the block size of the cipher
algorithm being used. The IV MUST be chosen at random. Common
practice is to use random data for the first IV and the last block of
encrypted data from an encryption process as the IV for the next
encryption process.

Including the IV in each datagram ensures that decryption of each
received datagram can be performed, even when some datagrams are
dropped, or datagrams are re-ordered in transit.

To avoid ECB encryption of very similar plaintext blocks in different
packets, implementations MUST NOT use a counter or other low-Hamming
distance source for IVs.

3.1 ESP Environmental Considerations

Currently, there are no known issues regarding interactions between
these algorithms and other aspects of ESP, such as use of certain
authentication schemes.

3.2 Keying Material

The minimum number of bits sent from the key exchange protocol to
this ESP algorithm must be greater or equal to the key size.

The cipher's encryption and decryption key is taken from the first
<x> bits of the keying material, where <x> represents the required
key size.

4. Security Considerations

Implementations are encouraged to use the largest key sizes they can
when taking into account performance considerations for their
particular hardware and software configuration. Note that encryption
necessarily impacts both sides of a secure channel, so such
consideration must take into account not only the client side, but
the server as well.

For information on the case for using random values please see
[Bell97].

For further security considerations, the reader is encouraged to read
the documents that describe the actual cipher algorithms.

5. References

[Adams97]   Adams, C, "The CAST-128 Encryption Algorithm",
             RFC2144, 1997.

[Atkinson98]Kent, S. and R. Atkinson, "Security Architecture for the
             Internet Protocol", RFC 2401, November 1998.

[Baldwin96] Baldwin, R. and R. Rivest, "The RC5, RC5-CBC, RC5-CBC-
             Pad, and RC5-CTS Algorithms", RFC 2040, October 1996.

[Bell97]   S. Bellovin, "Probable Plaintext Cryptanalysis of the IP
             Security Protocols", Proceedings of the Symposium on
             Network and Distributed System Security, San Diego, CA,
             pp. 155-160, February 1997 (also
             http://www.research.att.com/~smb/probtxt.{ps, pdf}).

[Bosselaers]A. Bosselaers, "Performance of Pentium implementations",
             http://www.esat.kuleuven.ac.be/~bosselae/

[Bradner97] Bradner, S., "Key words for use in RFCs to indicate
             Requirement Levels", BCP 14, RFC 2119, March 1997.

[Crypto93] J. Daemen, R. Govaerts, J. Vandewalle, "Weak Keys for
             IDEA", Advances in Cryptology, CRYPTO 93 Proceedings,
             Springer-Verlag, pp. 224-230.

[FIPS-46]   US National Bureau of Standards, "Data Encryption
             Standard", Federal Information Processing Standard (FIPS)
             Publication 46, January 1977.

[Kent98]   Kent, S. and R. Atkinson, "IP Encapsulating Security
             Payload (ESP)", RFC 2406, November 1998.

[Lai]   X. Lai, "On the Design and Security of Block Ciphers",
             ETH Series in Information Processing, v. 1, Konstanz:
             Hartung-Gorre Verlag, 1992.

[Madson98] Madson, C. and N. Dorswamy, "The ESP DES-CBC Cipher
             Algorithm With Explicit IV", RFC 2405, November 1998.

[MOV]   A. Menezes, P. Van Oorschot, S. Vanstone, "Handbook of
             Applied Cryptography", CRC Press, 1997. ISBN 0-8493-
             8523-7

[Schneier] B. Schneier, "Applied Cryptography Second Edition", John
             Wiley & Sons, New York, NY, 1995. ISBN 0-471-12845-7

[Schneier93]B. Schneier, "Description of a New Variable-Length Key,
          64-Bit Block Cipher", from "Fast Software Encryption,
          Cambridge Security Workshop Proceedings", Springer-
          Verlag, 1994, pp. 191-204.
          http://www.counterpane.com/bfsverlag.html

[Schneier95]B. Schneier, "The Blowfish Encryption Algorithm - One
          Year Later", Dr. Dobb's Journal, September 1995,
          http://www.counterpane.com/bfdobsoyl.html

[Schneier97]B. Scheier, "Speed Comparisons of Block Ciphers on a
          Pentium." February 1997,
          http://www.counterpane.com/speed.html

[Thayer97] Thayer, R., Doraswamy, N. and R. Glenn, "IP Security
          Document Roadmap", RFC 2411, November 1998.

[Tuchman79] Tuchman, W, "Hellman Presents No Shortcut Solutions to
          DES", IEEE Spectrum, v. 16 n. 7, July 1979, pp. 40-41.

6. Acknowledgments

   This document is a merger of most of the ESP cipher algorithm
   documents. This merger was done to facilitate greater understanding
   of the commonality of all of the ESP algorithms and to further the
   development of these algorithm within ESP.

   The content of this document is based on suggestions originally from
   Stephen Kent and subsequent discussions from the IPSec mailing list
   as well as other IPSec documents.

   Special thanks to Carlisle Adams and Paul Van Oorschot both of
   Entrust Technologies who provided input and review of CAST.

   Thanks to all of the editors of the previous ESP 3DES documents; W.
   Simpson, N. Doraswamy, P. Metzger, and P. Karn.

   Thanks to Brett Howard from TimeStep for his original work of ESP-
   RC5.

   Thanks to Markku-Juhani Saarinen, Helger Lipmaa and Bart Preneel for
   their input on IDEA and other ciphers.

7. Editors' Addresses

   Roy Pereira
   TimeStep Corporation

   Phone: +1 (613) 599-3610 x 4808
   EMail: rpereira@timestep.com

   Rob Adams
   Cisco Systems Inc.

   Phone: +1 (408) 457-5397
   EMail: adams@cisco.com

   Contributors:

   Robert W. Baldwin
   RSA Data Security, Inc.

   Phone: +1 (415) 595-8782
   EMail: baldwin@rsa.com or baldwin@lcs.mit.edu

   Greg Carter
   Entrust Technologies

   Phone: +1 (613) 763-1358
   EMail: carterg@entrust.com

   Rodney Thayer
   Sable Technology Corporation

   Phone: +1 (617) 332-7292
   EMail: rodney@sabletech.com

The IPSec working group can be contacted via the IPSec working group's mailing list (ipsec@tis.com) or through its chairs:

Robert Moskowitz
International Computer Security Association

EMail: rgm@icsa.net

Theodore Y. Ts'o
Massachusetts Institute of Technology

EMail: tytso@MIT.EDU

8. Full Copyright Statement

Network Working Group   E. Rescorla
Request for Comments: 2631   RTFM Inc.
Category: Standards Track   June 1999

Diffie-Hellman Key Agreement Method

Status of this Memo

Copyright Notice

Abstract

   This document standardizes one particular Diffie-Hellman variant,
   based on the ANSI X9.42 draft, developed by the ANSI X9F1 working
   group. Diffie-Hellman is a key agreement algorithm used by two
   parties to agree on a shared secret. An algorithm for converting the
   shared secret into an arbitrary amount of keying material is
   provided. The resulting keying material is used as a symmetric
   encryption key. The Diffie-Hellman variant described requires the
   recipient to have a certificate, but the originator may have a static
   key pair (with the public key placed in a certificate) or an
   ephemeral key pair.

Table of Contents

1. Introduction

   In [DH76] Diffie and Hellman describe a means for two parties to
   agree upon a shared secret in such a way that the secret will be
   unavailable to eavesdroppers. This secret may then be converted into
   cryptographic keying material for other (symmetric) algorithms. A
   large number of minor variants of this process exist. This document
   describes one such variant, based on the ANSI X9.42 specification.

1.1. Requirements Terminology

   Keywords "MUST", "MUST NOT", "REQUIRED", "SHOULD", "SHOULD NOT" and
   "MAY" that appear in this document are to be interpreted as described
   in [RFC2119].

2. Overview Of Method

   Diffie-Hellman key agreement requires that both the sender and
   recipient of a message have key pairs. By combining one's private key
   and the other party's public key, both parties can compute the same
   shared secret number. This number can then be converted into
   cryptographic keying material. That keying material is typically
   used as a key-encryption key (KEK) to encrypt (wrap) a content-
   encryption key (CEK) which is in turn used to encrypt the message
   data.

2.1. Key Agreement

   The first stage of the key agreement process is to compute a shared
   secret number, called ZZ. When the same originator and recipient
   public/private key pairs are used, the same ZZ value will result.
   The ZZ value is then converted into a shared symmetric cryptographic
   key. When the originator employs a static private/public key pair,
   the introduction of a public random value ensures that the resulting
   symmetric key will be different for each key agreement.

2.1.1. Generation of ZZ

   X9.42 defines that the shared secret ZZ is generated as follows:

      ZZ = g ^ (xb * xa) mod p

   Note that the individual parties actually perform the computations:

      ZZ = (yb ^ xa) mod p = (ya ^ xb) mod p

   where ^ denotes exponentiation

         ya is party a's public key; ya = g ^ xa mod p
         yb is party b's public key; yb = g ^ xb mod p
         xa is party a's private key
         xb is party b's private key
         p is a large prime
         q is a large prime
         g = h^{(p-1)/q} mod p, where
         h is any integer with 1 < h < p-1 such that h{(p-1)/q} mod p > 1
           (g has order q mod p; i.e. g^q mod p = 1 if g!=1)
         j a large integer such that p=qj + 1
         (See Section 2.2 for criteria for keys and parameters)

   In [CMS], the recipient's key is identified by the CMS
   RecipientIdentifier, which points to the recipient's certificate.
   The sender's public key is identified using the
   OriginatorIdentifierOrKey field, either by reference to the sender's
   certificate or by inline inclusion of a public key.

2.1.2. Generation of Keying Material

   X9.42 provides an algorithm for generating an essentially arbitrary
   amount of keying material from ZZ. Our algorithm is derived from that
   algorithm by mandating some optional fields and omitting others.

      KM = H (ZZ || OtherInfo)

   H is the message digest function SHA-1 [FIPS-180] ZZ is the shared
   secret value computed in Section 2.1.1. Leading zeros MUST be
   preserved, so that ZZ occupies as many octets as p. For instance, if
   p is 1024 bits, ZZ should be 128 bytes long. OtherInfo is the DER
   encoding of the following structure:

      OtherInfo ::= SEQUENCE {
        keyInfo KeySpecificInfo,
        partyAInfo [0] OCTET STRING OPTIONAL,
        suppPubInfo [2] OCTET STRING

```
  }

  KeySpecificInfo ::= SEQUENCE {
    algorithm OBJECT IDENTIFIER,
    counter OCTET STRING SIZE (4..4) }
```

Note that these ASN.1 definitions use EXPLICIT tagging. (In ASN.1,
EXPLICIT tagging is implicit unless IMPLICIT is explicitly
specified.)

algorithm is the ASN.1 algorithm OID of the CEK wrapping algorithm
  with which this KEK will be used. Note that this is NOT an
  AlgorithmIdentifier, but simply the OBJECT IDENTIFIER. No
  parameters are used.

counter is a 32 bit number, represented in network byte order. Its
  initial value is 1 for any ZZ, i.e. the byte sequence 00 00 00 01
  (hex), and it is incremented by one every time the above key
  generation function is run for a given KEK.

partyAInfo is a random string provided by the sender. In CMS, it is
  provided as a parameter in the UserKeyingMaterial field (encoded as
  an OCTET STRING). If provided, partyAInfo MUST contain 512 bits.

suppPubInfo is the length of the generated KEK, in bits, represented
  as a 32 bit number in network byte order. E.g. for 3DES it would be
  the byte sequence 00 00 00 C0.

To generate a KEK, one generates one or more KM blocks (incrementing
counter appropriately) until enough material has been generated. The
KM blocks are concatenated left to right I.e. KM(counter=1) ||
KM(counter=2)...

Note that the only source of secret entropy in this computation is
ZZ. Even if a string longer than ZZ is generated, the effective key
space of the KEK is limited by the size of ZZ, in addition to any
security level considerations imposed by the parameters p and q.
However, if partyAInfo is different for each message, a different KEK
will be generated for each message. Note that partyAInfo MUST be used
in Static-Static mode, but MAY appear in Ephemeral-Static mode.

2.1.3. KEK Computation

Each key encryption algorithm requires a specific size key (n). The
KEK is generated by mapping the left n-most bytes of KM onto the key.
For 3DES, which requires 192 bits of keying material, the algorithm
must be run twice, once with a counter value of 1 (to generate K1',
K2', and the first 32 bits of K3') and once with a counter value of 2

(to generate the last 32 bits of K3). K1',K2' and K3' are then parity
adjusted to generate the 3 DES keys K1,K2 and K3. For RC2-128, which
requires 128 bits of keying material, the algorithm is run once, with
a counter value of 1, and the left-most 128 bits are directly
converted to an RC2 key. Similarly, for RC2-40, which requires 40
bits of keying material, the algorithm is run once, with a counter
value of 1, and the leftmost 40 bits are used as the key.

2.1.4. Keylengths for common algorithms

Some common key encryption algorithms have KEKs of the following
lengths.

    3-key 3DES   192 bits
    RC2-128   128 bits
    RC2-40   40 bits

RC2 effective key lengths are equal to RC2 real key lengths.

2.1.5. Public Key Validation

The following algorithm MAY be used to validate a received public key
y.

    1. Verify that y lies within the interval [2,p-1]. If it does not,
       the key is invalid.
    2. Compute y^q mod p. If the result == 1, the key is valid.
       Otherwise the key is invalid.

The primary purpose of public key validation is to prevent a small
subgroup attack [LAW98] on the sender's key pair. If Ephemeral-Static
mode is used, this check may not be necessary. See also [P1363] for
more information on Public Key validation.

Note that this procedure may be subject to pending patents.

2.1.6. Example 1

ZZ is the 20 bytes 00 01 02 03 04 05 06 07 08 09
                   0a 0b 0c 0d 0e 0f 10 11 12 13

The key wrap algorithm is 3DES-EDE wrap.

No partyAInfo is used.

Consequently, the input to the first invocation of SHA-1 is:

00 01 02 03 04 05 06 07 08 09 0a 0b 0c 0d 0e 0f 10 11 12 13 ; ZZ

```
30 1d
   30 13
      06 0b 2a 86 48 86 f7 0d 01 09 10 03 06        ; 3DES wrap OID
      04 04
         00 00 00 01                                ; Counter
   a2 06
      04 04
      00 00 00 c0                                   ; key length
```

And the output is the 20 bytes:

a0 96 61 39 23 76 f7 04 4d 90 52 a3 97 88 32 46 b6 7f 5f 1e

The input to the second invocation of SHA-1 is:

```
00 01 02 03 04 05 06 07 08 09 0a 0b 0c 0d 0e 0f 10 11 12 13 ; ZZ
30 1d
   30 13
      06 0b 2a 86 48 86 f7 0d 01 09 10 03 06        ; 3DES wrap OID
      04 04
         00 00 00 02                                ; Counter
   a2 06
      04 04
      00 00 00 c0                                   ; key length
```

And the output is the 20 bytes:

f6 3e b5 fb 5f 56 d9 b6 a8 34 03 91 c2 d3 45 34 93 2e 11 30

```
Consequently,
K1'=a0 96 61 39 23 76 f7 04
K2'=4d 90 52 a3 97 88 32 46
K3'=b6 7f 5f 1e f6 3e b5 fb
```

Note: These keys are not parity adjusted

2.1.7. Example 2

ZZ is the 20 bytes 00 01 02 03 04 05 06 07 08 09
                   0a 0b 0c 0d 0e 0f 10 11 12 13

The key wrap algorithm is RC2-128 key wrap, so we need 128 bits (16 bytes) of keying material.

The partyAInfo used is the 64 bytes

01 23 45 67 89 ab cd ef fe dc ba 98 76 54 32 01
01 23 45 67 89 ab cd ef fe dc ba 98 76 54 32 01

```
01 23 45 67 89 ab cd ef fe dc ba 98 76 54 32 01
01 23 45 67 89 ab cd ef fe dc ba 98 76 54 32 01
```

Consequently, the input to SHA-1 is:

```
00 01 02 03 04 05 06 07 08 09 0a 0b 0c 0d 0e 0f 10 11 12 13 ; ZZ
30 61
   30 13
      06 0b 2a 86 48 86 f7 0d 01 09 10 03 07            ; RC2 wrap OID
      04 04
         00 00 00 01                                    ; Counter
   a0 42
      04 40
         01 23 45 67 89 ab cd ef fe dc ba 98 76 54 32 01 ; partyAInfo
         01 23 45 67 89 ab cd ef fe dc ba 98 76 54 32 01
         01 23 45 67 89 ab cd ef fe dc ba 98 76 54 32 01
         01 23 45 67 89 ab cd ef fe dc ba 98 76 54 32 01
   a2 06
      04 04
         00 00 00 80                                    ; key length
```

And the output is the 20 bytes:

```
48 95 0c 46 e0 53 00 75 40 3c ce 72 88 96 04 e0 3e 7b 5d e9
```

Consequently,
K=48 95 0c 46 e0 53 00 75 40 3c ce 72 88 96 04 e0

2.2. Key and Parameter Requirements

X9.42 requires that the group parameters be of the form p=jq + 1
where q is a large prime of length m and j>=2. An algorithm for
generating primes of this form (derived from the algorithms in FIPS
PUB 186-1[FIPS-186] and [X942]can be found in appendix A.

X9.42 requires that the private key x be in the interval [2, (q -
2)]. x should be randomly generated in this interval. y is then
computed by calculating g^x mod p. To comply with this memo, m MUST
be >=160 bits in length, (consequently, q MUST be at least 160 bits
long). When symmetric ciphers stronger than DES are to be used, a
larger m may be advisable. p must be a minimum of 512 bits long.

2.2.1. Group Parameter Generation

Agents SHOULD generate domain parameters (g,p,q) using the following
algorithm, derived from [FIPS-186] and [X942]. When this algorithm is
used, the correctness of the generation procedure can be verified by
a third party by the algorithm of 2.2.2.

2.2.1.1. Generation of p, q

   This algorithm generates a p, q pair where q is of length m and p is
   of length L.

   1. Set m' = m/160 where / represents integer division with rounding
      upwards. I.e. 200/160 = 2.

   2. Set L'= L/160

   3. Set N'= L/1024

   4. Select an arbitrary bit string SEED such that the length of SEED
      >= m

   5. Set U = 0

   6. For i = 0 to m' - 1

         U = U + (SHA1[SEED + i] XOR SHA1[(SEED + m' + i)) * 2^(160 * i)

   Note that for m=160, this reduces to the algorithm of [FIPS-186]

         U = SHA1[SEED] XOR SHA1[(SEED+1) mod 2^160].

   5. Form q from U by computing U mod (2^m) and setting the most
      significant bit (the 2^(m-1) bit) and the least significant bit to
      1. In terms of boolean operations, q = U OR 2^(m-1) OR 1. Note
      that 2^(m-1) < q < 2^m

   6. Use a robust primality algorithm to test whether q is prime.

   7. If q is not prime then go to 4.

   8. Let counter = 0

   9. Set R = seed + 2*m' + (L' * counter)

   10. Set V = 0

   12. For i = 0 to L'-1 do

         V = V + SHA1(R + i) * 2^(160 * i)

   13. Set W = V mod 2^L

   14. Set X = W OR 2^(L-1)

Note that 0 <= W < 2^(L-1) and hence X >= 2^(L-1)

15. Set p = X - (X mod (2*q)) + 1

6. If p > 2^(L-1) use a robust primality test to test whether p is
    prime. Else go to 18.

17. If p is prime output p, q, seed, counter and stop.

18. Set counter = counter + 1

19. If counter < (4096 * N) then go to 8.

20. Output "failure"

Note: A robust primality test is one where the probability of a non-
prime number passing the test is at most 2^-80. [FIPS-186] provides a
suitable algorithm, as does [X942].

2.2.1.2. Generation of g

This section gives an algorithm (derived from [FIPS-186]) for
generating g.

1. Let j = (p - 1)/q.

2. Set h = any integer, where 1 < h < p - 1 and h differs
   from any value previously tried.

3. Set g = h^j mod p

4. If g = 1 go to step 2

2.2.2. Group Parameter Validation

The ASN.1 for DH keys in [PKIX] includes elements j and validation-
Parms which MAY be used by recipients of a key to verify that the
group parameters were correctly generated. Two checks are possible:

   1. Verify that p=qj + 1. This demonstrates that the parameters meet
      the X9.42 parameter criteria.
   2. Verify that when the p,q generation procedure of [FIPS-186]
      Appendix 2 is followed with seed 'seed', that p is found when
      'counter' = pgenCounter.

This demonstrates that the parameters were randomly chosen and
do not have a special form.

Whether agents provide validation information in their certificates is a local matter between the agents and their CA.

2.3. Ephemeral-Static Mode

In Ephemeral-Static mode, the recipient has a static (and certified) key pair, but the sender generates a new key pair for each message and sends it using the originatorKey production. If the sender's key is freshly generated for each message, the shared secret ZZ will be similarly different for each message and partyAInfo MAY be omitted, since it serves merely to decouple multiple KEKs generated by the same set of pairwise keys. If, however, the same ephemeral sender key is used for multiple messages (e.g. it is cached as a performance optimization) then a separate partyAInfo MUST be used for each message. All implementations of this standard MUST implement Ephemeral-Static mode.

In order to resist small subgroup attacks, the recipient SHOULD perform the check described in 2.1.5. If an opponent cannot determine success or failure of a decryption operation by the recipient, the recipient MAY choose to omit this check. See also [LL97] for a method of generating keys which are not subject to small subgroup attack.

2.4. Static-Static Mode

In Static-Static mode, both the sender and the recipient have a static (and certified) key pair. Since the sender's and recipient's keys are therefore the same for each message, ZZ will be the same for each message. Thus, partyAInfo MUST be used (and different for each message) in order to ensure that different messages use different KEKs. Implementations MAY implement Static-Static mode.

In order to prevent small subgroup attacks, both originator and recipient SHOULD either perform the validation step described in Section 2.1.5 or verify that the CA has properly verified the validity of the key. See also [LL97] for a method of generating keys which are not subject to small subgroup attack.

Acknowledgements

The Key Agreement method described in this document is based on work done by the ANSI X9F1 working group. The author wishes to extend his thanks for their assistance.

The author also wishes to thank Stephen Henson, Paul Hoffman, Russ Housley, Burt Kaliski, Brian Korver, John Linn, Jim Schaad, Mark Schertler, Peter Yee, and Robert Zuccherato for their expert advice and review.

References

    [CMS]   Housley, R., "Cryptographic Message Syntax", RFC 2630,
               June 1999.

    [FIPS-46-1] Federal Information Processing Standards Publication
               (FIPS PUB) 46-1, Data Encryption Standard, Reaffirmed
               1988 January 22 (supersedes FIPS PUB 46, 1977 January
               15).

    [FIPS-81]   Federal Information Processing Standards Publication
               (FIPS PUB) 81, DES Modes of Operation, 1980 December 2.

    [FIPS-180] Federal Information Processing Standards Publication
               (FIPS PUB) 180-1, "Secure Hash Standard", 1995 April 17.

    [FIPS-186] Federal Information Processing Standards Publication
               (FIPS PUB) 186, "Digital Signature Standard", 1994 May
               19.

    [P1363]   "Standard Specifications for Public Key Cryptography",
               IEEE P1363 working group draft, 1998, Annex D.

    [PKIX]   Housley, R., Ford, W., Polk, W. and D. Solo, "Internet
               X.509 Public Key Infrastructure Certificate and CRL
               Profile", RFC 2459, January 1999.

    [LAW98]   L. Law, A. Menezes, M. Qu, J. Solinas and S. Vanstone,
               "An efficient protocol for authenticated key agreement",
               Technical report CORR 98-05, University of Waterloo,
               1998.

    [LL97]   C.H. Lim and P.J. Lee, "A key recovery attack on discrete
               log-based schemes using a prime order subgroup", B.S.
               Kaliski, Jr., editor, Advances in Cryptology - Crypto
               '97, Lecture Notes in Computer Science, vol. 1295, 1997,
               Springer-Verlag, pp. 249-263.

    [RFC2119]   Bradner, S., "Key words for use in RFCs to Indicate
               Requirement Levels", BCP 14, RFC 2119, March 1997.

    [X942]   "Agreement Of Symmetric Keys Using Diffie-Hellman and MQV
               Algorithms", ANSI draft, 1998.

11

RFC 2631

Security Considerations

All the security in this system is provided by the secrecy of the private keying material. If either sender or recipient private keys are disclosed, all messages sent or received using that key are compromised. Similarly, loss of the private key results in an inability to read messages sent using that key.

Static Diffie-Hellman keys are vulnerable to a small subgroup attack [LAW98]. In practice, this issue arises for both sides in Static-Static mode and for the receiver during Ephemeral-Static mode. Sections 2.3 and 2.4 describe appropriate practices to protect against this attack. Alternatively, it is possible to generate keys in such a fashion that they are resistant to this attack. See [LL97]

The security level provided by these methods depends on several factors. It depends on the length of the symmetric key (typically, a 2^l security level if the length is l bits); the size of the prime q (a $2^{m/2}$ security level); and the size of the prime p (where the security level grows as a subexponential function of the size in bits). A good design principle is to have a balanced system, where all three security levels are approximately the same. If many keys are derived from a given pair of primes p and q, it may be prudent to have higher levels for the primes. In any case, the overall security is limited by the lowest of the three levels.

Author's Address

Eric Rescorla
RTFM Inc.
30 Newell Road, #16
East Palo Alto, CA 94303

EMail: ekr@rtfm.com

Full Copyright Statement

Acknowledgement

   Funding for the RFC Editor function is currently provided by the
   Internet Society.

Index

Related Titles
from
Morgan Kaufmann

Morgan Kaufmann

http://www.mkp.com

- **TCP / IP ADDRESSING**
  Buck Graham
  November 1996; 0-12-294630-8
  Academic Press Professional

- **PERSONAL ENCRYPTION CLEARLY EXPLAINED**
  Pete Loshin
  May 1998; 0-12-455837-2
  Academic Press Professional

- **TCP / IP CLEARLY EXPLAINED**
  Pete Loshin
  July 1999; 0-12-455826-7
  Morgan Kaufmann Publishers

- **IPv6 CLEARLY EXPLAINED**
  Pete Loshin
  January 1999; 0-12-455838-0
  Morgan Kaufmann Publishers

- **ADDRESS UNKNOWN: A GUIDE TO IPv6**
  Peter H. Salus
  June 2000; 0-12-616770-2
  Morgan Kaufmann Publishers

Coming Soon
from
Morgan Kaufmann

Morgan
Kaufmann

http://www.mkp.com

- BIG BOOK OF BORDER GATEWAY PROTOCOL (BGP) RFCs

- BIG BOOK OF INTERNET FILE TRANSFER RFCs

- BIG BOOK OF INTERNET HOST STANDARDS

- BIG BOOK OF LIGHTWEIGHT DIRECTORY ACCESS PROTOCOL (LDAP) RFCs

- BIG BOOK OF TERMINAL EMULATION RFCs

- BIG BOOK OF WORLD WIDE WEB RFCs